The Origins of International Investment Law

International investment law is a complex and dynamic field. Yet, the implications of its history are under-explored. Kate Miles examines the historical evolution of international investment law, assessing its origins in the commercial and political expansionism of dominant states during the seventeenth to early twentieth centuries and the continued resonance of those origins within modern foreign investment protection law. In particular, her exploration of the activities of the Dutch East India Company, Grotius' treatises, and pre-World War II international investment disputes provides insight into current controversies surrounding the interplay of public and private interests, the systemic design of investor–state arbitration, the substantive focus of principles, and the treatment of environmental issues within international investment law. In adopting such an approach, this book provides a fresh conceptual framework through which contemporary issues can be examined and creates new understandings of those controversies.

Kate Miles is a Fellow and College Lecturer in Law at Gonville and Caius College, Cambridge. She currently serves on the International Law Association's New Study Group on the Role of Soft Law Instruments in International Investment Law. She is also a Research Fellow of the Centre for International Sustainable Development Law, Montreal, and co-ordinates the International Investment Law Network for the Society of International Economic Law.

CAMBRIDGE STUDIES IN INTERNATIONAL AND COMPARATIVE LAW

Established in 1946, this series produces high-quality scholarship in the fields of public and private international law and comparative law. Although these are distinct legal sub-disciplines, developments since 1946 confirm their interrelations.

Comparative law is increasingly used as a tool in the making of law at national, regional and international levels. Private international law is now often affected by international conventions, and the issues faced by classical conflicts rules are frequently dealt with by substantive harmonisation of law under international auspices. Mixed international arbitrations, especially those involving state economic activity, raise mixed questions of public and private international law, while in many fields (such as the protection of human rights and democratic standards, investment guarantees and international criminal law) international and national systems interact. National constitutional arrangements relating to 'foreign affairs', and to the implementation of international norms, are a focus of attention.

The series welcomes works of a theoretical or interdisciplinary character, and those focusing on the new approaches to international or comparative law or conflicts of law. Studies of particular institutions or problems are equally welcome, as are translations of the best work published in other languages.

A list of books in the series can be found at the end of this volume.

The Origins of International Investment Law

Empire, Environment and the Safeguarding of Capital

Kate Miles

CAMBRIDGE
UNIVERSITY PRESS

University Printing House, Cambridge CB2 8BS, United Kingdom

Published in the United States of America by Cambridge University Press, New York

Cambridge University Press is part of the University of Cambridge.

It furthers the University's mission by disseminating knowledge in the pursuit of education, learning, and research at the highest international levels of excellence.

www.cambridge.org
Information on this title: www.cambridge.org/9781107039391

First published 2013

Printed in the United Kingdom by CPI Group Ltd, Croydon CR0 4YY

A catalogue record for this publication is available from the British Library

Library of Congress Cataloguing in Publication data
Miles, Kate, 1971–
The origins of international investment law: empire, environment, and the safeguarding of capital / Kate Miles.
pages cm. – (Cambridge studies in international and comparative law)
Includes bibliographical references and index.
ISBN 978-1-107-03939-1
1. Investments, Foreign (International law) – History. 2. Investments, Foreign – Law and legislation. I. Title.
K3830.M55 2013
346′.092–dc23

2013013105

ISBN 978-1-107-03939-1 Hardback

For Sam

Contents

Acknowledgements

For a number of years, my studies focused on public international law, while, in private practice, I worked in commercial litigation. During this time, these different spheres did not cross paths in my work. In 2002, however, I was directed towards a field of international law that seemed to grapple with issues of fundamental importance concerning how to reconcile 'the public' and 'the private' within its own substance, structure, and institutions. It was in that year that Professor Philippe Sands QC, University College London, handed me an investor–state arbitral award, *Metalclad Corporation* v. *United States of Mexico*, and suggested I investigate the treatment of environmental issues within international investment law. Exposure to this award was the trigger for the subject of this book, as well as for my now deeply held fascination with international investment law and its interaction with other fields of law and policy. I am indebted to Professor Sands for introducing me to this area of law and for his ongoing support in my academic endeavours.

This book originated as a doctoral thesis and I am grateful for the extraordinary guidance, patience, and attention to detail of my supervisors, Emeritus Professor Ben Boer and Associate Professor Tim Stephens, both of the Faculty of Law, University of Sydney. Their advice and support throughout the writing of my thesis was invaluable. Furthermore, I am particularly appreciative of the generosity of spirit and friendship extended to me by Professor Boer. This book also benefited greatly from the detailed comments provided by the examiners of my thesis, Professors Tony Anghie, Peter Muchlinski, and Benjamin J. Richardson. I am very appreciative of the assistance provided by Kieran Kelly and Emanuel Blum in the final preparations of the book manuscript. I would like to thank Finola O'Sullivan, Nienke van Schaverbeke, Elisabeth Spicer, and Helen Francis at Cambridge

University Press. In particular, I owe an additional debt of gratitude to Finola O'Sullivan for her patience. I would also like to acknowledge the long-term support and encouragement of Dr Julie Maxton, formerly Professor of Law and Dean, Faculty of Law, at the University of Auckland, and now of the Royal Society, London.

In developing my research and thinking on international investment law, parts of this book have been presented in seminars and have been previously published in somewhat different form in the following works: 'Transforming Foreign Investment: Globalisation, the Environment, and a Climate of Controversy' (2007) 7 *Macquarie Law Journal* 81; 'Targeting Financiers: Can Voluntary Codes of Conduct for the Investment and Financing Sectors Achieve Environmental and Sustainability Objectives?', in Kurt Deketelaere et al. (eds.), *Critical Issues in Environmental Taxation – vol. V* (Oxford University Press, 2008); 'International Investment Law: Origins, Imperialism and Conceptualizing the Environment' (2010) 21 *Colorado Journal of International Environmental Law and Policy* 1; 'Arbitrating Climate Change: Regulatory Regimes and Investor-State Disputes' (2010) 1 *Climate Law* 63; 'Reconceptualising International Investment Law: Bringing the Public Interest into Private Business', in Meredith Kolsky-Lewis and Susy Frankel (eds.), *International Economic Law and National Autonomy: Convergence or Divergence?* (Cambridge University Press, 2010); 'Sustainable Development, National Treatment and Like Circumstances in Investment Law' in Marie-Claire Cordonier Segger, Andrew Newcombe and Markus Gehring (eds.), *Sustainable Development in World Investment Law* (Kluwer, 2011); 'Soft Law Instruments in Environmental Law: Models for International Investment Law?' in Andrea K. Bjorklund and August Reinisch (eds.), *International Investment Law and Soft Law* (Cheltenham: Edward Elgar, 2012).

At a fundamental level, I would like to thank my father, Julian Miles QC, for instilling in me a passion for the law, and my mother, Sue Miles, for inspiring me by example, herself a journalist and author, so that, throughout my childhood, it never occurred to me that I would not pursue a similarly challenging career. Above all, I wish to thank my son, Sam, for his patience and sense of humour throughout the many years of research and writing involved in the completion of both my thesis and this book, for which I am immensely grateful.

List of abbreviations

BHP	Broken Hill Proprietary Co.
BIAC	Business and Industry Advisory Committee
BIT	Bilateral investment treaty
CDSE	Compañía del Desarrollo de Santa Elena
CERDS	Charter of Economic Rights and Duties of States
CERES	Coalition for Environmentally Responsible Economies
CISDL	Centre for International Sustainable Development Law
CITES	Convention on International Trade in Endangered Species of Wild Fauna and Flora
CSR	Corporate social responsibility
ECHR	European Court of Human Rights
ECJ	European Court of Justice
EHRR	European Human Rights Reports
EPFIs	Equator Principles Financial Institutions
FIELD	Foundation for International Environmental Law and Development
FOE	Friends of the Earth
GA	United Nations General Assembly
GAOR	United Nations General Assembly Official Records
GATT	General Agreement on Tariffs and Trade
ICC	International Chamber of Commerce
ICJ	International Court of Justice
ICJ Rep.	International Court of Justice Reports
ICSID	International Centre for the Settlement of Investment Disputes
ICSID Rep.	International Centre for the Settlement of Investment Disputes Reports

IFC	International Finance Corporation
IISD	International Institute for Sustainable Development
ILM	International Legal Materials
ILR	International Law Reports
IMF	International Monetary Fund
MAI	Draft Multilateral Agreement on Investment
MMT	Methylcyclopentadienyl manganese tricarbonyl
MTBE	Methyl tertiary butyl ether
NAFTA	North American Free Trade Agreement
NGOs	Non-governmental organisations
NIEO	New International Economic Order
NIEO Declaration	Declaration of the Establishment of a New International Economic Order
OECD	Organisation for Economic Cooperation and Development
PCBs	Polychlorinated biphenyl
RIAA	Reports of International Arbitral Awards
SEA	Social and Environmental Assessment
SEIC	Sakhalin Energy Investment Company
SRII	Socially responsible institutional investment
UN	United Nations
UNCED	United Nations Conference on Environment and Development
UNCITRAL	United Nations Commission on International Trade Law
UNCLOS	United Nations Convention on the Law of the Sea
UNCTAD	United Nations Conference on Trade and Development
UNEP	United Nations Environment Programme
UNFCCC	United Nations Framework Convention on Climate Change
UN Norms	United Nations Norms on the Responsibilities of Transnational Corporations and Other Business Enterprises with Regard to Human Rights
UNPRI	United Nations Principles for Responsible Investment
UNTS	United Nations Treaty Series
VOC	Verenigde Oostindische Compagnie; Dutch East India Company
WTO	World Trade Organisation

Table of international and domestic cases

Agua del Tunari SA v. *The Republic of Bolivia* (ICSID Case No. ARB/03/02, Award of 21 October 2005).

Aguas Argentinas, S.A. and Vivendi Universal, S.A. v. *Argentine Republic* (ICSID Case No. ARB/03/19, Award of 19 May 2005).

Aguas Provinciales de Santa Fe, S.A., Suez, Sociedad General de Aguas de Barcelona, S.A. and Intergua Servicios Integrales de Agua, S.A. v. *Argentine Republic* (ICSID Case No. ARB/03/18, Award of May 12 2005).

Aguinda v. *Texaco, Inc*, 945 F. Supp. 625 (S.D.N.Y. 1996).

Al-Adsani v. *United Kingdom* (2002) 34 EHRR 11 (ECHR).

Anglo-Iranian Oil Co. Case (UK v. *Iran)* (1952) ICJ Rep 93.

Arcelor S.A. v. *European Parliament and Council* (2004) Case T-16/04.

Ashanga v. *Texaco*, S.D.N.Y. Dkt. No.94 Civ. 9266 (Aug. 13, 1997).

Asian Agricultural Products Ltd v. *Republic of Sri Lanka* (1990) 4 ICSID Rep 245.

Azurix Corp. v. *Republic of Argentina* (ICSID Case No. ARB/01/12, Award of July 14, 2006).

Biwater Gauff Limited v. *United Republic of Tanzania*, Procedural Order No. 5 (2 February 2007).

Britain (Finlay) v. *Greece* (1846) 39 *British and Foreign State Papers* 410.

Britain v. *The Kingdom of the Two Sicilies* (1839–1840) 28 *British and Foreign State Papers* 1163–1242.

Broken Hill Proprietary Company Ltd v. *Dagi and Others* [1996] 2 VR 117.

Case Concerning Oil Platforms (Iran v. *United States of America)* (2003) 42 *International Legal Materials* 1334.

Case Concerning the Gabčikovo-Nagymaros Project (Hungary/Slovakia) (1997) ICJ Rep 7.

Clayton and Bilcon of Delaware v. *Government of Canada*, Notice of Intent to Submit a Claim to Arbitration under Section B of Chapter 11 of NAFTA, February 2008.

CME Czech Republic B.V. (the Netherlands) v. *Czech Republic*, Partial Award, 13 September 2001, Final Award, 14 March 2003.

CME Czech Republic BV v. *Czech Republic* (Damages) (2003) 15(4) *World Trade and Arbitration Materials* 83.

CMS Gas Transmission Co v. *Argentine Republic* (2005) 44 *International Legal Materials* 1205.

CMS Gas Transmission Company v. *Argentine Republic* (Decision on Annulment) (2007) (ICSID Case No. ARB/01/8).

Compañía de Aguas del Aconquija S.A. and Vivendi Universal v. *Republic of Argentina* (ICSID Case No. ARB/97/3, Award of 20 August 2007).

Compañía del Desarrollo de Santa Elena, S A v. *The Republic of Costa Rica* (2000) 39 *International Legal Materials* 1317.

Continental Casualty Company v. *Argentine Republic* (ICSID Case No. ARB/03/9, Award of 5 September 2008).

Dagi and Others v. *The Broken Hill Proprietary Company Ltd and Another (No. 2)* [1997] 1 VR 428.

Delagoa Bay Railroad Arbitration, JB Moore, *A History and Digest of the International Arbitrations to which the United States has been a Party* (1898) vol. II, 1865.

Dow AgroSciences LLC v. *Government of Canada*, Notice of Arbitration, 31 March 2009.

Enron Corp. & Ponderosa Assets LP v. *Argentina* (ICSID Case No ARB/01/3, Award of 7 October 2007).

Ethyl Corporation v. *Canada*, Jurisdiction Phase, (1999) 38 *International Legal Materials* 708.

European Communities-Measures Affecting the Approval and Marketing of Biotech Products, WT/DS291, WT/DS292, WT/DS293 (29 September 2006).

Final Award in an Arbitration Procedure under the UNCITRAL Arbitration Rules between Karaha Bodas Company and Perusahaan Pertambangan Minyak dan Gas Bumi Negara and Pt PLN, 18 December 2000.

Fogarty v. *United Kingdom* (2001) 123 ILR 54.

Gippsland Coastal Board v. *South Gippsland Shire Council (No 2)* [2008] VCAT 1545.

Glamis Gold Ltd v. *United States of America*, Award, 8 June 2009.

Gray v. *Minister for Planning* (2006) 152 LGERA 258.

In Re Union Carbide Corporation Gas Plant Disaster, 634 F. Supp. 842 (S.D.N.Y. 1986).

In the Matter of a NAFTA Arbitration under UNCITRAL Arbitration Rules between International Thunderbird Gaming Corp. v. *United Mexican States*, Award, 26 January 2006.

In the Matter of an Arbitration under the Rules of the United Nations Commission on International Trade Law, Chevron Corporation and Texaco Petroleum Company v. *Republic of Ecuador*, Notice of Arbitration, 23 September 2009.

In the Matter of a UNCITRAL Arbitration between Ronald S Lauder v. *the Czech Republic*, Final Award, 3 September 2001.

Inceysa Vallisoletana S.L. v. *Republic of El Salvador* (ICSID Case No. ARB/03/26, Award of 2 August 2006).

Kasky v. *Nike, Inc.*, 45 P 3d 243 (Cal. 2002).

LG&E Energy Corp. v. *Argentina* (ICSID Case No. ARB/02/1, Award of 25 July 2007).

Lubbe v. *Cape Plc* [2000] 4 All ER 268.

Marion Unglaube v. *Republic of Costa Rica* (ICSID Case No. ARB/08/01, Notice of Intent registered 25 January 2008).

Marvin Roy Feldman Karpa v. *United Mexican States* (2001) 40 *International Legal Materials* 615.

Metalclad Corporation v. *The United States of Mexico*, Award, 25 August 2000, (2001) 40 *International Legal Materials* 35.

Methanex Corporation v. *United States of America*, (2005) 44 *International Legal Materials* 1345.

MTD Equity Sdn Bhd & anor v. *Republic of Chile* (Award) (2005) 44 *International Legal Materials* 91.

The Neer Claim (United States v. *Mexico)* (1926) 4 *Reports of International Arbitral Awards* 60.

Noble Ventures Inc v. *Romania*, ICSID Case No ARB/01/11, Award, 12 October 2005.

Northcape Properties Pty Ltd v. *District Council of Yorke Peninsula* [2008] SASC 57.

Occidental Exploration and Production Co v. *Republic of Ecuador* (Award) Case No UN3467 (UNCITRAL, 2004).

The Oscar Chinn Case (1934) *Permanent Court of International Justice Series A/B*, No. 63.

Owusu v. *Jackson*, ECJ C-281/02, Judgment 1 March 2005.

Parkerings-Compagniet AS v. *Republic of Lithuania* (ICSID Arbitration Case No. ARB/05/8, Award of 11 September 2007).

Petroleum Development Ltd v. *The Sheikh of Abu Dhabi* (1951) 18 *International Law Reports* 144.

Pope & Talbot v. *Canada*, Award on the Merits of Phase II, 10 April 2001.

Pope & Talbot Inc v. *Canada*, Award on Damages, (2002) 41 *International Legal Materials* 1347.

Portuguese Religious Properties Case (1920) I RIAA 7.

Ruler of Qatar v. *International Marine Oil Co* (1953) 20 *International Law Reports* 534.

Saluka Investments BV (The Netherlands) v. *Czech Republic* (Partial Award) (UNCITRAL, 2006).

S.D. Myers, Inc v. *Canada*, Partial Award (Decision on the Merits), November 2000.

Sempra Energy International v. *Argentina* (ICSID Case No. ARB/02/16, Award of 28 September 2007).

Sequihua v. *Texaco, Inc*, 847 F. Supp. 61 (S.D. Tex. 1994).

Société Arcelor Atlantique et Lorraine v. *Premier Ministre, Ministre de l'Économie, des Finances et de l'Industrie, Ministre de l'Écologie et du Développement Durable*, Case C-127/07; *Official Journal of the European Union*, 26/5/2007, C117/8.

Tecnicas Medioambientales Tecmed, SA v. *United Mexican States* (2004) 43 *International Legal Materials* 133.

Texaco Overseas Petroleum Co. & California Asiatic Oil Co v. *The Government of the Libyan Arab Republic* (1975) 53 *International Law Reports* 389.

The United States and Paraguay Navigation Company Claim, JB Moore, *A History and Digest of the International Arbitrations to which the United States has been a Party* (1898) vol. II, 1485.

Tza Yap Shum v. *Republic of Peru*, (filed 2007) ICSID Case No. 6/07.

Union of India v. *Union Carbide Corporation*, Bhopal Gas Claim Case No. 113 of 1986.

United States–Import Prohibition of Certain Shrimp and Shrimp Products, Report of the Panel, WT/DS58/R (15 May 1998).

United States–Import Prohibition of Certain Shrimp and Shrimp Products, Report of the Appellate Body (1999) 38 ILM 118.

United States–Standards for Reformulated and Conventional Gasoline, Report of the Appellate Body, WT/DS52/AB/R (20 May 1996).

Uruguayan Insurance Monopoly Case (1911), G Hackworth, *Digest of International Law* (1940) vol. V, 588.

USA (Savage) v. *Salvador* (1852), JB Moore, *A History and Digest of the International Arbitrations to which the United States has been a Party* (1898) vol. II, 1855.

Vattenfall AB v. *Federal Republic of Germany*, Request for Arbitration, 30 March 2009.

Venezuelan Arbitrations, Jackson H. Ralston, *Venezuelan Arbitrations of 1903* (1904).
Voth v. *Manildra Flour Mills Pty Ltd* (1990) 171 CLR 538.
Waste Management v. *Mexico* (2004) 43 *International Legal Materials* 967.
World Duty Free Company v. *The Republic of Kenya* (ICSID Case No. ARB/00/7, Award of 4 October 2006).

Table of treaties and other international instruments

Accord entre la Confédération Suisse et la République Orientale de l'Uruguay Concernant la Promotion et la Protection Réciproques des Investissements (entered into force 7 October 1988).

Accord entre le Gouvernement de la République du Cameroun et le Gouvernement de la République Populaire de Chine pour la Promotion et la Protection Réciproques des Investissements (signed on 10 May 1997).

Acuerdo para la Promoción y Protección Reciproca de Inversiones entre el Reino de España y los Estados Unidos Mexicanos (signed 22 June 1995, entered into force 18 December 1996).

African Charter on Human and Peoples' Rights (opened for signature 21 June 1981, 21 ILM 58, entered into force 21 October 1986).

Agenda 21, Report of the UNCED, UN Doc. A/CONF.151/26/Rev.1 (vol. I), (1992) 31 ILM 874.

Agreement Among the Azerbaijan Republic, Georgia and the Republic of Turkey, 18 November 1999, available at http://subsites.bp.com/caspian/BTC/Eng/agmt4/agmt4.PDF (last accessed 15 December 2011).

Agreement between Canada and the Republic of Peru for the Promotion and Protection of Investments (2006).

Agreement between the Government of Hong Kong and the Government of Australia for the Promotion and Protection of Investments (signed on 15 September 1993).

Agreement between the Government of the People's Republic of China and the Government of the Republic of Bolivia Concerning the Encouragement and Reciprocal Protection of Investments (signed on 8 May 1992, entered into force 1 September 1996).

Agreement between the Government of the Republic of Peru and the Government of the People's Republic of China Concerning the

Encouragement and Reciprocal Protection of Investments (signed on 9 June 1994, entered into force 1 February 1995).

American Convention on Human Rights (opened for signature 22 November 1969, 9 ILM 673, entered into force 18 July 1978).

Charter of Economic Rights and Duties of States, GA Res 3281 (XXIX), UN Doc A/RES/3281 (XXIX) (1974).

Comprehensive Economic Cooperation Agreement between the Republic of India and the Republic of Singapore (signed on 29 June 2005).

Conference on the World Financial and Economic Crisis, Report of the Secretary-General, UN Doc. A/CONF.214/4 (2009).

Convention for the Protection of Human Rights and Fundamental Freedoms, opened for signature 4 November 1950, 213 UNTS 222 (entered into force 3 September 1953).

Convention for the Protection of the World Cultural and Natural Heritage, opened for signature 16 November 1972, (1972) 11 ILM 1358 (entered into force 17 December 1975).

Convention on the Control of Transboundary Movement of Hazardous Wastes and their Disposal (opened for signature 22 March 1989, (1989) 28 ILM 657, entered into force 1992).

Convention on International Trade in Endangered Species of Wild Fauna and Flora (opened for signature 3 March 1973, 993 UNTS 243, entered into force 1 July 1975).

Convention on the Settlement of Investment Disputes between States and Nationals of Other States (signed 18 March 1965, (1966) 575 UNTS 159, entered into force 14 October 1966).

Copenhagen Accord, Decision 2/CP.15, Taking Note of the Copenhagen Accord (18 December 2009), Report of the Conference of the Parties on its Fifteenth Session, held in Copenhagen from 7 to 19 December 2009, FCCC/CP/2009/11/Add.1, 30 March 2010.

Declaration on Permanent Sovereignty over Natural Resources, GA Res 1803 (XVII), 17 GAOR, Supp. 17, UN Doc A/5217, 15 (1962).

Declaration on the Establishment of a New International Economic Order, GA Res 3201 (S-VI), UN Doc A/Res/S-6/3201 (1974)

Declaration of the Fourth Ministerial Conference, Doha, Qatar, WT/MIN (01)/DEC/1, 20 November 2001.

European Convention for the Protection of Human Rights and Fundamental Freedoms (opened for signature 4 November 1950, 213 UNTS 221, entered into force 3 September 1953).

Energy Charter Treaty, Annex I, Final Act of the European Energy Charter Conference, 17 December 1994, 34 ILM 373.

First Additional Protocol to the Convention for the Protection of Human Rights and Fundamental Freedoms (opened for signature 20 March 1952).

General Agreement on Tariffs and Trade, Annex 1A, Agreement Establishing the World Trade Organization (opened for signature 15 April 1994, (1994) 33 ILM 28, entered into force 1 January 1995).

Havana Charter for an International Trade Organization (1948) UN Conference on Trade and Employment, UN Doc. E/CONF.2/78, Sales no. 1948.II.D.4.

Hungary–Czechoslovakia Treaty Providing for the Construction and Joint Operation of the Gabčikovo-Nagymaros Barrage System (entered into force 16 September 1977, 1109 UNTS 236).

International Covenant on Civil and Political Rights, opened for signature 16 December 1966, 999 UNTS 171 (entered into force 23 March 1976).

International Covenant on Economic, Social and Cultural Rights, opened for signature 16 December 1966, 993 UNTS 3 (entered into force 3 January 1976).

Johannesburg Declaration on Sustainable Development, Report of the United Nations World Summit on Sustainable Development, UN Doc. A/CONF. 199/20 (2002).

Johannesburg Plan of Implementation, Report of the World Summit on Sustainable Development, UN Doc A/CONF.199/20 (2002).

Kyoto Protocol to the United Nations Framework Convention on Climate Change (opened for signature 11 December 1997, (1998) 37 ILM 22, entered into force 16 February 2005).

Monterrey Consensus of the International Conference on Financing for Development, UN Doc. A/AC.257/32 (2002).

North American Free Trade Agreement (NAFTA) (adopted 17 December 1992, (1992) 32 ILM 612, entered into force 1 January 1994).

North American Agreement on Environmental Cooperation (signed 14 September 1993, entered into force 1 January 1994).

North American Agreement on Labor Cooperation (signed 14 September 1993, entered into force 1 January 1994).

Permanent Sovereignty over Natural Resources, GA Res 1720 (XVI), 19 December 1961.

Permanent Sovereignty over Natural Resources, GA Res 2158 (XXI), 25 November 1966.

Ramsar Convention on Wetlands of International Importance especially as Waterfowl Habitat (opened for signature 2 February 1971, 996 UNTS 245, entered into force 21 December 1975).

Regional Convention for the Management and Conservation of Natural Forest Ecosystems and the Development of Forest Plantations (signed 29 October 1993).

Rio Declaration on Environment and Development, Report of the UNCED, UN Doc. A/CONF.151/6/Rev.1 (1992), (1992) 31 ILM 874.

Rome Statute for the International Criminal Court (opened for signature 17 July 1998, UN Doc. A/CONF.183/9, 37 ILM 999, entered into force 1 July 2002).

Statute of the International Criminal Tribunal for the Former Yugoslavia, UN Doc. S/RES/827, (1993) 32 ILM 1203.

Statute of the International Criminal Tribunal for Rwanda UN Doc. SC Res 955 (1994) 33 ILM 1600.

Treaty between the Federal Republic of Germany and Pakistan for the Promotion and Protection of Investments (signed 25 November 1959, (1963) 457 UNTS 23, entered into force 28 April 1962).

Treaty between the United States of America and the Argentine Republic Concerning the Reciprocal Encouragement and Protection of Investment (signed 14 November 1991, entered into force 20 October 1994).

Treaty between the United States of America and the Oriental Republic of Uruguay Concerning the Encouragement and Reciprocal Protection of Investment (2005).

Treaty between the United States of America and the Republic of Ecuador concerning the Encouragement and Reciprocal Protection of Investment (signed on 27 August 1993, entered into force 11 May 1997).

Treaty of Amity, Economic Relations and Consular Rights between Iran and the United States of America (1955) (signed on 15 August 1955, entered into force 16 June 1957).

Treaty of Friendship and Commerce between Her Majesty and the Kings of Siam, 18 April 1855 (the Bowring Treaty).

Treaty of Nanking (Britain–China) (1842) 93 Consolidated Treaty Series 465.

Treaty of Peking (Austria-Hungary–China) (1869) 139 Consolidated Treaty Series 477.

Treaty of Tientsin (Russia–China) (1858) 119 Consolidated Treaty Series 113.

Treaty of Tientsin (German States–China) (1861) 124 Consolidated Treaty Series 299.

Treaty of Wang Hiya (USA–China) (1844) 97 Consolidated Treaty Series 105.

Treaty of Whampoa (France–China) (1844) 97 Consolidated Treaty Series 375.

Understanding on Rules and Procedures Governing the Settlement of Disputes, art. 3.2, Annex 2, Agreement Establishing the World Trade Organization (opened for signature 15 April 1994, (1994) 33 ILM 28, entered into force 1 January 1995).

United Nations Convention on Biological Diversity, opened for signature 5 June 1992, (1992) 31 ILM 822 (entered into force 29 December 1993).

United Nations Convention on the Law of the Sea, opened for signature 10 December 1982, (1982) 21 ILM 1261 (entered into force 16 November 1994).

United Nations Millennium Declaration, UNGA Res. A/55/2 (2000); United Nations Development Goals, available at www.un.org/millenniumgoals/ (last accessed 17 July 2009).

United States–Paraguay Treaty of Friendship, Commerce and Navigation (1859) in W. M. Malloy, *Treaties, Conventions, International Acts, Protocols and Agreements between the United States and other Powers 1776–1909* (1910) Vol. II 1364.

United Nations Convention on the Law of the Sea, opened for signature 10 December 1982, (1982) 21 ILM 1261 (entered into force 16 November 1994).

United Nations Framework Convention on Climate Change, opened for signature 9 May 1992, 31 ILM 849 (entered into force 24 March 1994).

Universal Declaration on Human Rights, GA Resolution 217A (III), UNGAOR, 3rd Sess, 183rd plen mtg, UN Doc A/RES/217A.

Vienna Convention on the Law of Treaties (opened for signature 23 May 1969, 1155 UNTS 331, entered into force 27 January 1980).

Introduction

The questions that occupy this book concern the evolution of international investment law and the notion that the circumstances of its original emergence continue to have resonance in its modern manifestation. Several years ago, I was struck by what appeared to be the inseparability of international investment law from its socio-political environment and I sought to explore the implications of such a proposition. Indeed, throughout the investigation of these issues, I came to the view that politics and commerce are not only important to the substance of international investment law, but that the social, commercial, and political context in which its rules emerged, in fact, determined its core character.

As the origins and historical evolution of international rules on foreign investment protection are analysed, it is ever more apparent that this character has confronting implications for the current form of international investment law. If its substantive principles and institutional frameworks are, in essence, drawn from centuries-old conceptualisations, and continue to this day to reflect those origins, then a re-evaluation of the modern manifestation of international investment law and its contemporary tensions will be needed. Engagement with theories of international law-making, political narratives, histories of colonialism, and questions on the relationship between host states, capital-exporting states, investors, and the use of legal doctrine would be central to such a re-articulation of the present system of investment protection. Ultimately, an historical account of international investment law would also provide insight into current controversies surrounding the interplay of public and private interests within investment law, the systemic design of international investment dispute resolution, the substantive focus of investment law principles, and the treatment of non-investment issues within international investment law. In this way, a complex story can begin to emerge of intertwined actors and interests, constructed doctrines of international law, and recurring dynamics.

The origins of international investment law are located well before the modern network of bilateral investment treaties was established in the latter half of the twentieth century. They are, in fact, deeply embedded within the global expansion of European trading and investment activities that occurred during the seventeenth to early twentieth centuries.[1] Although international rules on the protection of foreign-owned property initially emerged from legal arrangements amongst European nations,[2] it was the transformation from a regional system into international investment law that fundamentally changed its character. In broadening their application to non-European nations, foreign investment and trade protection rules became part of an array of tools used to further the political and commercial aspirations of European states, and, in so doing, became rooted within the processes of colonialism and oppressive protection of commercial interests.[3]

While considering the more enduring impact of these historical circumstances, a picture emerged of international investment law as having been shaped at a fundamental level through this 'colonial encounter'[4] into a mechanism that protected only the interests of capital-exporting states, excluding the host state from the protective sphere of investment rules.[5] It appeared that, as a result of this early moulding, the host state was unable to call upon the rules of international investment law to address damage suffered at the hands of foreign investors. Furthermore, by the mid-nineteenth century, in a seeming continuation of this initial mode of exclusion, international investment principles had been constructed, using the language of universality and neutrality, to create an ostensibly objective and apolitical regime, but, in fact, one that largely consisted of protection for investors and obligations for capital-importing states to facilitate trade

[1] Lipson, *Standing Guard*, pp. 11–12.

[2] Lipson, *Standing Guard*, pp. 11–12; see also Neufeld, *The International Protection of Private Creditors*, p. 6; Dawson and Head, *International Law*, pp. 4–5.

[3] Lipson, *Standing Guard*, pp. 11–12; Dawson and Head, *International Law*, p. 5.

[4] Anghie, *Imperialism*, pp. 6–7. Anghie conceptualises the doctrines, principles, and institutions of international law as products of the interaction between coloniser and colonised, that is, the legal resolution to problems arising within the colonial context. He coins the phrase 'colonial encounter' to encapsulate this process.

[5] Lipson, *Standing Guard*, pp. 4, 8, 37–8; Schrijver, *Sovereignty*, pp. 173–4; Malanczuk, *Akehurst's Modern International Law*, pp. 9–10.

and investment.[6] This generated a permanent condition of 'otherness' in the host state within international investment law, one that seemed to me to still inform its modern context.[7] What, then, did all this mean for the twenty-first century? For the current raft of investor–state disputes, the thousands of bilateral investment treaties now in existence, and the states in negotiations for new investment agreements?

These were the questions that carried me into this book to explore the origins of international investment law and their implications for foreign investment protection law and policy in the twenty-first century. In essence, my argument is that the political context in which the rules emerged shaped international investment law in fundamental ways, and that these origins still resonate within its modern principles, structures, agreements, and dispute resolution systems. I seek to show how this is illustrated in its sole focus on investor protection,[8] its lack of responsiveness to the impact of investor activity on the local communities and environment of the host state,[9] the alignment of home state interests with those of the investor,[10] the categorisation of public welfare regulation as a treaty violation,[11] and the commodification of the environment in host states for the use of foreign entities. I put forward the argument that these factors are not isolated occurrences

[6] Lipson, *Standing Guard*, pp. 37–8; Anghie, *Imperialism*, pp. 224, 238–9.

[7] For a discussion of the concept of 'otherness' in international law and colonialism, see Anghie, *Imperialism*, pp. 3–12; Koskenniemi, *The Gentle Civilizer of Nations*, pp. 126–30; Anghie, 'Finding the Peripheries'; Weeramantry and Berman, 'The Grotius Lecture Series', 1555–69; Fitzpatrick, 'Terminal Legality', 9; Gathii 'Imperialism, Colonialism, and International Law'.

[8] See the discussion in Mann et al., *IISD Model International Agreement*; Sornarajah, 'The Clash of Globalizations'.

[9] For a discussion of this issue, see Bernasconi-Osterwalder and Brown Weiss, 'International Investment Rules and Water', 263; Cosbey et al., *Investment and Sustainable Development*.

[10] See the discussion on 'commercial diplomacy' in Sands, 'Turtles and Torturers', 541–3; Lee, 'The Growing Influence of Business in UK Diplomacy'; Sherman and Eliasson, 'Trade Disputes and Non-State Actors'.

[11] See, e.g., *Methanex Corporation* v. *United States of America*, (2005) 44 *International Legal Materials* 1345; *S.D. Myers, Inc.* v. *Canada*, Partial Award (Decision on the Merits), November 2000; *Ethyl Corporation* v. *Canada*, Jurisdiction Phase, (1999) 38 *International Legal Materials* 708; *Metalclad Corporation* v. *The United States of Mexico*, Award, 25 August 2000, (2001) 40 *International Legal Materials* 35; *Clayton and Bilcon of Delaware* v. *Government of Canada*, Notice of Intent to Submit a Claim to Arbitration under Section B of Chapter 11 of NAFTA, February 2008, Appleton & Associates, available at www.appletonlaw.com/Media/2008/Bilcon%20NAFTA%20Notice%20of%20Intent.pdf (last accessed 13 March 2008); *Marion Unglaube* v. *Republic of Costa Rica*, (ICSID Case No. ARB/08/01, Notice of Intent registered 25 January 2008).

or approaches, but are, instead, linked and part of a more homogenous web of law, politics, culture, and commerce. In exploring these connections that reach across centuries, this book examines the historical context within which core principles of this area of law were developed, the methodologies of imposition, and modern manifestations of the historical relationship between foreign investors, the host state, and international law. In particular, this research examines recent factors contributing to current pressure to reform international investment law, such as environmentalism, emerging principles of corporate social responsibility (CSR), and the sustainable finance movement.

Notions of empire, colonialism, and imperialism have been afforded a range of meanings within different analytical frameworks and disciplines.[12] Throughout this book, however, I use the term 'colonialism' as a reference to explicit policies of formal territory acquisition and establishment of colonies. 'Imperialism' has more informal implications, referring to policies that were not limited to formal colonialism, but rather those that continued to employ the practices of dominance, pursued commercial and political expansionism, and involved the economic exploitation of target territories in circumstances beyond actual annexation.[13] The term 'empire' is used here to refer to the continuation of these imperialist practices, as well as to refer to the colonial empires created by Britain, France, Germany, the Netherlands, Spain, and Portugal, from the seventeenth to early twentieth centuries.[14] For Doyle, 'empire' constitutes:[15]

> a relationship, formal or informal, in which one state controls the effective political sovereignty of another society. It can be achieved by force, by political collaboration, by economic, social or cultural dependence. Imperialism is simply the process or policy of maintaining an empire.

[12] See the discussion in Alvarez, 'Contemporary Foreign Investment Law'. Alvarez traverses a number of approaches, including that of limiting the term 'empire' to only those classical empires of Ancient Greece and Rome, examining the characteristics of empire, such as the pursuit of universality and control, and considering the application of the term 'imperialism' by political scientists to contemporary hegemonic international relations.

[13] Anghie, *Imperialism*, pp. 11–12; Said, *Culture and Imperialism*, p. 8; Craven, *The Decolonization of International Law*, pp. 19–21; see also the description of 'empire' in Doyle, *Empires*, pp. 19–20, 45–6.

[14] Anghie, *Imperialism*, pp. 11–12; Said, *Culture*, p. 8; Craven, *The Decolonization*, pp. 19–21; Doyle, *Empires*, pp. 45–6.

[15] Doyle, *Empires*, p. 45.

Although Anghie states that '[c]olonialism refers, generally to the practice of settling territories, while "imperialism" refers to the practices of an empire', he also explains that he tends to use the terms interchangeably because of their close relationship with each other.[16] He goes on to describe 'imperialism' as:

> a broader and more accurate term with which to describe the practices of powerful Western states in the period following the establishment of the United Nations. This period witnessed the end of formal colonialism, but the continuation, consolidations and elaboration of imperialism.[17]

For Hopkins, the operation of 'informal empire' or 'imperialism' entails the 'diminution of sovereignty through the exercise of power', a state of affairs which itself constitutes a complex set of relations and processes taking many forms.[18] In particular, Hopkins refers to the theories of Strange to explore the power dynamics of informal empire, applying her concepts of 'structural power' and 'relational power' to imperialism.[19] Structural power is described by Strange as entailing control over credit, production, security, knowledge, beliefs, and ideas. A consideration of the interrelated concept of relational power examines the outcomes within contested spaces of authority.[20] Encompassing such spheres of influence clearly takes the examination of empire beyond the limited acts of formal annexation of territory. These approaches, then, of Anghie, Craven, Doyle, and Hopkins, are essentially the understandings and conceptualisations of colonialism, imperialism, and empire that are also employed throughout this book.

I. Patterns, challenge, and reconceptualisation

At the outset of this research, I was very much of the view that through an historical analysis of its evolution, new light could be shed on the

16 Anghie, *Imperialism*, p. 11. 17 Ibid., pp. 11–12.

18 Hopkins, 'Informal Empire', 476–7; see further Cain and Hopkins, *British Imperialism*; see also the discussion in Akita, *Gentlemanly Capitalism*, pp. 1–5; see further the definition of 'imperialism' in the seminal article of Gallagher and Robinson, 'The Imperialism of Free Trade', 5–6:

> Imperialism, perhaps, may be defined as a sufficient political function of this process of integrating new regions into the expanding economy; its character is largely decided by the various and changing relationships between the political and economic elements of expansion in any particular region and time.

19 Hopkins, 'Informal Empire', 477–8; Strange, *States*, pp. 24–8.

20 Strange, *States*, pp. 24–8; Hopkins, 'Informal Empire', 477–8.

current form of foreign investment protection law. I was, of course, at that stage, unsure as to quite what would emerge through such an investigation. However, by adopting an historical perspective, patterns of 'assertion of power and responses to power'[21] in the evolution of international investment law began to take shape. And those conceptualisations and dynamics derived from its origins in imperialism appeared to have remained imbued within modern international investment law. Deliberating further on whether this was the case, I also asked the question: can those patterns be broken, and, if so, what form would a reconceptualised international investment law take?

A. *Structure*

Approaching these questions through a prism of historical evaluation, this book is divided into three components that mirror significant periods in the development of international investment law: emergence and early events, contemporary interaction, and future trajectories.

1. Origins of international investment law

Part I of the book contains two chapters examining the origins of foreign investment protection law through to the changing dynamic generated by the process of decolonisation in the mid-twentieth century. This section serves as the foundation for key arguments developed throughout the book, establishing the historical links between investor and state, the political circumstances surrounding the emergence of international rules on foreign investment protection, the interplay of power and responses to power, and the deeply intertwined processes of assertion and creation of international investment law.

To this end, Chapter 1 explores the trading and investment arrangements of seventeenth- to early twentieth-century Western states with non-European nations. It examines the close alignment of state interests with those of their trading and investing nationals, with a particular focus on the Dutch East India Company,[22] and the way in which these

[21] The power relations involved in processes of emergence of legal rules and regimes are explored in Benton, *Law and Colonial Cultures*. Her framing of the emergence of international law as a process of 'repetitive assertions of power and responses to power' and its implications for the emergence of international rules on foreign investment protection are explained further in this chapter and explored in depth below in Chapter 1.

[22] This book concentrates on the Dutch East India Company as illustrative of the relationship between states and the large trading companies, such as the English East

entwined relationships influenced the development of international legal doctrine to protect foreign-owned property.[23] It examines the legal tools that were used at the time to legitimise the commercial and political aspirations of capital-exporting states and their nationals, together with the influence of these approaches on the emergence of international rules of foreign investment protection.[24]

Chapter 1 also applies Benton's theories on the power relations involved in the emergence of international law to the evolution of international investment law.[25] Benton identifies the creation of legal institutions and international rules during this era with social, political, and economic control, asserting that international law emerged through a process of 'repetitive assertions of power and responses to power'.[26] This insight is equally applicable to the development of the legal rules that formed the basis of the modern system of international investment law. Viewing early forms of interaction in this field through an understanding of Benton's theories reveals that the emergence of these rules involved a dual process of assertion and creation. Through the assertion of foreign investment protection rules as existing international law, together with the use of force, capital-exporting states directed the evolution of the substance of international investment law solely into that of investor protection. It was a process by which one perspective became entrenched as law and the methods used to enforce that perspective were legitimised by the conferring of legal justification. And by the nineteenth century, capital-exporting states were regularly asserting their viewpoint on foreign investment protection as representing international law and they enforced it as such.[27] These assertions by

India Company, Dutch West India Company, and French East India Company. It is beyond the scope of this book to analyse all international trading companies of the sixteenth to nineteenth centuries. For information on the trading companies and the sovereign powers they exercised, see Steensgaard, 'The Dutch East India Company', 235, 237, 244–6, 251; Vos, *Gentle Janus*, p. 1; Philips, *The East India Company*, p. 23; Keay, *The Honourable Company*, pp. 9, 39, 363; Sutherland, *The East India Company*, pp. 3–5.

[23] Anghie, *Imperialism*, p. 224; Sornarajah, *The International Law on Foreign Investment*, p. 38.

[24] See, e.g., the use of the doctrine of diplomatic protection of alien property, concession contracts, capitulation treaties, diplomatic pressure, extraterritorial jurisdiction, military intervention, colonial annexation of territory, and friendship, commerce, and navigation treaties. See the discussion in Lipson, *Standing Guard*, pp. 12–21; Sornarajah, *Foreign Investment*, pp. 19–20; Schrijver, *Sovereignty*, pp. 173–5; see also Porras, 'Constructing International Law', 744–7, 802–4.

[25] Benton, *Law and Colonial Cultures*, pp. 10–11. [26] Ibid., p. 11.

[27] See, e.g., the disputes surrounding *The United States and Paraguay Navigation Company Claim* (Moore, *A History and Digest*, pp. 1485, 1865); *Britain (Finlay)* v. *Greece* (1846) 39 *British*

capital-exporting states, however, did not go uncontested by capital-importing states.[28] Chapter 1 explores the outcomes of that contest.

Chapter 1 also considers the relationship of early traders, investors, and colonisers with the environment of host states and argues that this historical mode of interaction has shaped the modern relationship between foreign investors and the environment and the narrow conceptualisation of the environment reflected in modern international investment law – essentially that of a commodity for exploitation – and that the contentious nature of current interaction between the investment sector and environmental protection advocates may be related to this core form of perception.

The approach to the environment of the host state in the era of empire was largely one of possession and control. Its manifestation ranged from indiscriminate destruction, such as the devastation of St Helena[29] and Mauritius,[30] to controlled regimes, such as imperial forestry conservation programmes in India,[31] and to the indirect consequences of colonial activities.[32] Despite individual variants, colonial encounters with the environment of host states were experienced by foreign traders, investors, and settlers through the lenses of their own European culture.[33] Although they adapted to the local context, their fundamental understanding of the land and its inhabitants was created through Western expansionist eyes.[34] It was that vision that shaped imperial natural resource extraction, local environmental management practices, regulatory regimes, and the displacement of indigenous communities from their land.[35] The effects of this imperial perspective are still felt in the

and Foreign State Papers 410; *Delagoa Bay Railroad Arbitration*; *Britain* v. *The Kingdom of the Two Sicilies* (1839–1840) 28 *British and Foreign State Papers*, pp. 1163–1242; and the *Venezuelan Arbitrations* (Ralston, *Venezuelan Arbitrations*).

28 Schrijver, *Sovereignty*, pp. 177–8; Shea, *The Calvo Clause*, pp. 21–30.

29 Grove, *Green Imperialism*, pp. 98–9.

30 Ibid., pp. 150–1.

31 Ibid., pp. 6–12; Barton, *Empire Forestry*, pp. 163–6.

32 See, e.g., the treatment of the island of St Helena. Accounts are given of ships' crews in the early seventeenth century destroying trees on the island for the sole purpose of preventing rival nations from benefiting from the fruit. Following the 1658 acquisition of St Helena by the English East India Company, the activities of the Company and the settlers caused the once lush tropical island to suffer droughts, deforestation, soil erosion, species loss, and multiple effects from the introduction of foreign species: see the discussion in Grove, *Green Imperialism*, pp. 98–9, 103–25.

33 Richardson, Mgbeoji, and Botchway, 'Environmental Law', 413, 415–16; Dunlap, 'Ecology', 76, 76.

34 Dunlap, 'Ecology', 76.

35 Gathii, 'Imperialism'; Kameri-Mbote and Cullet, 'Law, Colonialism'.

land management regulations of postcolonial societies[36] – and I sought to explore whether a comparable process had occurred with respect to modern international investment rules.

2. Foreign investment protection in a changing political environment

Politics were central to the formation of international rules on foreign investment protection, and, in multiple ways, they continued to play a fundamental role in the development of this field. Significantly, as global political conditions shifted during the twentieth century, challenges were made to the form and substance of foreign investment protection law.[37] Chapter 2 of this book examines those challenges. It analyses key events and the emergence of social movements that embodied host state resistance to the international system of foreign investment protection asserted by capital-exporting states. It examines the agrarian reforms of the Soviet Union and Mexico in the early part of the twentieth century.[38] It considers the postcolonial nationalisations and the promotion of the New International Economic Order (NIEO) in the mid-twentieth century as attempts by postcolonial states to play an active role in the development of international investment law and to reshape the rules to take account of their needs.[39]

While the decolonisation period initially held the promise of economic autonomy and prosperity for postcolonial states, it also posed a significant challenge to the structural hegemony of capital-exporting states within foreign investment protection law.[40] It brought uncertainty and political risk to investments secured under colonial regimes.[41] I argue in Chapter 2 that this era of postcolonial nationalisations and calls for reform to international economic structures embodied an assertion of

[36] Kameri-Mbote and Cullet, 'Law, Colonialism'; Richardson, Mgbeoji, and Botchway, 'Environmental Law', 415–21; for a discussion on the connections between the impacts of 'empire-building' on indigenous peoples and the continuing effects of those policies, see Richardson, Imai, and McNeil, 'Indigenous Peoples', 3, 4–5.

[37] Anghie, *Imperialism*, pp. 10–11, 196–9, 211–20; Lipson, *Standing Guard*, pp. 65–70, 77; Odumosu, 'Law and Politics'.

[38] Lipson, *Standing Guard*, pp. 65–70, 77; Kunz, 'The Mexican Expropriations', 25–7; Gathii, 'Third World Approaches', 255, 257; see also the discussion in Newcombe and Paradell, *Law and Practice*, p. 18.

[39] Anghie, *Imperialism*, pp. 10–11, 211–20; see the discussion in Newcombe and Paradell, *Law and Practice*, pp. 18–19; Subedi, *International Investment Law*, p. 21.

[40] Anghie, *Imperialism*, pp. 196–9, 212–15; Odumosu, 'Law and Politics', 255; Mickelson, 'Rhetoric and Rage', 362; Richardson, 'Environmental Law', 2.

[41] Odumosu, 'Law and Politics', 255; Anghie, *Imperialism*, pp. 196–9, 212–15.

host state interests within international investment rules – and that this generated responses from the investment sector and capital-exporting states designed to constrain those attempts and maintain a similar *de facto* level of control as had been enjoyed under colonial systems. It is argued that capital-exporting states and investor interests framed host state attempts to ameliorate the often harsh effects of the investor-focused international rules on foreign investment as 'politicising' investment disputes. This chapter examines the response to this need for 'depoliticisation'.

In considering the role of social movements in bringing pressure to reform international investment law,[42] Chapter 2 also examines the NIEO as a movement developed within a wider context of protest. It continues to develop the idea of international investment law evolving through a complex process of 'ebb and flow', 'challenge and response', but, in Chapter 2, these themes are unpacked within the context of social movements and investment sector responses to those challenges. I argue that this particular form of engagement has been instrumental in the construction of new rules, mechanisms, and institutions designed to maintain high levels of foreign investment protection as close as possible to that created under the era of empire. Adding a further layer to this picture, I also explore the proposition that while social movements of various kinds have agitated for reform of international investment law since the mid-twentieth century, ironically they have also provided fuel for the investment sector to legitimise the means taken to preserve the prevailing conceptualisations of investor protection regimes.[43] Again, in this milieu, the spectre of the 'political' is often raised to support investor perspectives and the consequential need to remove it from investment disputes.[44]

To animate these arguments, Chapter 2 focuses on two forms of social movement that have been particularly potent in the foreign investment discourse – grassroots activism and environmentalism. It explores

[42] See, e.g., the discussion on the New International Economic Order in Anghie, *Imperialism*, pp. 10–11, 211–20; see Odumosu, 'Law and Politics'; see also for a discussion on the role of social movements in the development of international institutions, Rajagopal, 'From Resistance to Renewal'.

[43] For examples of recent arguments warning of the need to protect against the influence of pressure groups on investment issues, see Wälde and Kolo, 'Environmental Regulation'; Wälde and Ndi, 'Stabilizing', 230–1.

[44] Wälde and Kolo, 'Environmental Regulation'; see also Wälde and Ndi, 'Stabilizing'; see also, e.g., the comments in Weiler, 'Good Faith', 701.

the nature of these movements that emerged in the latter part of the twentieth century, considering resistance movements within developing states,[45] global forms of environmentalism, non-governmental organisations (NGOs), the cultural infusion of international environmentalism, and the potential impact of these movements on international investment law.

3. Contemporary interaction

Contemporary attempts to reshape international investment law are addressed in Part II of this book. Multi-layered and interrelated, a complex range of factors are involved in recent pressures to reform the foreign investment sector.[46] The particular focus in this section, however, is on the relationship between investment, environmental concerns, and sustainable development objectives as this form of interaction has evolved into a primary source of current tensions surrounding international investment law.[47] It is in Chapter 3 that I consider the polarisation of positions that continues to inform the relationship between the investment sector and those supporting the need for host state environmental policy space within international investment regimes. And, within that context, I explore the theory that investment regimes are reproducing conceptualisations derived from the era of empire. In the course of this

45 The problematic nature of the terms 'developing state' and 'developed state' is acknowledged. In particular, as Anghie makes clear, it can be seen as a continuation of the colonial framing of states as 'civilised' or 'uncivilised'. There is no entirely satisfactory answer to the issue of terminology as all potential descriptions, to a certain extent, have negative connotations, are misleading, or do not encompass the complexities of the relations involved. In this sense, there are unsatisfactory aspects to the use of any of the 'North–South' terminology, the 'Third World' grouping, and the 'developing–developed state' distinction. Nevertheless, as some form of categorisation is necessary in this analysis, I have reluctantly adopted the terms 'developing state' and 'developed state' for ease of recognition within the current vocabulary of the majority of contemporary international legal discourse. This book is, of course, profoundly indebted to the work of those scholars identified with the Third World Approaches to International Law network.

46 See, e.g., the range of issues discussed in Subedi, *International Investment Law*; Sornarajah, 'Globalizations'; Mann et al., *IISD Model International Agreement*; see the discussion on consequences of unmanaged investment and capital markets liberalisation in Stiglitz, *Making Globalization Work*, pp. 33–46; see also the issues discussed in Udobong, 'Multinational Corporations'; Stephens, 'The Amorality of Profit'; Kimerling, 'Indigenous Peoples'; see further Neumayer and Spess, 'Bilateral Investment Treaties' 7.

47 For examples of this type of critique, see Cosbey et al., *Investment*; Brown Weiss, Boisson de Chazournes, and Bernasconi-Osterwalder, *Fresh Water*; Tienhaara, 'What You Don't Know'; de Waart, 'Sustainable Development', 273; Mabey and McNally, *Foreign Direct Investment*, pp. 3, 13–17; Zarsky, *International Investment*.

enquiry, I examine several notable cases of misconduct by foreign-owned corporations and the use of legal doctrine to avoid responsibility for the environmental damage caused.[48] Increasingly, international investment agreements are also being invoked to challenge environmental and health regulation enacted by the host state.[49] This chapter examines a selection of these cases in detail and explores their implications for the relationship between investment protection and environmental concerns.

Chapter 4 then takes the discussion in a slightly different direction. Although the approach to the consideration of environmental issues within international investment law is one traditionally characterised by hostility, recent shifts in corporate behaviour also point to the possibility of more harmonious forms of interaction. Chapter 4 examines these new trends and their implications for the development of socially and environmentally responsible principles of international investment law.

As the wider effects of corporate practices have been increasingly publicised over the last two decades, companies have had to respond to pressure from consumers, NGOs, shareholders, and other stakeholders to improve their social and environmental performance.[50] The development of voluntary codes of environmental corporate conduct,

[48] E.g., *Dagi and Others* v. *The Broken Hill Proprietary Company Ltd and Another (No. 2)* [1997] 1 VR 428; *Sequihua* v. *Texaco, Inc*, 847 F. Supp. 61 (S.D. Tex. 1994); *Aguinda* v. *Texaco, Inc*, 945 F. Supp. 625 (S.D.N.Y. 1996); *Ashanga* v. *Texaco*, S.D.N.Y. Dkt. No.94 Civ. 9266 (Aug. 13, 1997); *Re Union Carbide Corporation Gas Plant Disaster*, 634 F. Supp. 842 (S.D.N.Y. 1986); see also the discussion in Chesterman, 'Oil and Water'; Chopra, 'Multinational Corporations'.

[49] See, e.g., *Methanex Corporation* v. *United States of America*, (2005) 44 *International Legal Materials* 1345; *S.D. Myers, Inc* v. *Canada*, Partial Award (Decision on the Merits), November 2000; *Ethyl Corporation* v. *Canada*, Jurisdiction Phase, (1999) 38 *International Legal Materials* 708; *Metalclad Corporation* v. *The United States of Mexico*, Award, 25 August 2000, (2001) 40 *International Legal Materials* 35; *Clayton and Bilcon of Delaware* v. *Government of Canada*, Notice of Intent to Submit a Claim to Arbitration under Section B of Chapter 11 of NAFTA, February 2008, Appleton & Associates, available at www.appletonlaw.com/Media/2008/Bilcon%20NAFTA%20Notice%20of%20Intent.pdf (last accessed 13 February 2009); *Marion Unglaube* v. *Republic of Costa Rica*, (ICSID Case No. ARB/08/01, Notice of Intent registered 25 January 2008); *Dow AgroSciences LLC* v. *Government of Canada*, Notice of Arbitration, 31 March 2009, available at www.nafta claims.com/Disputes/Canada/Dow/Dow-Canada-NOA.pdf (last accessed 4 May 2009); see also the discussion in Schneiderman, *Constitutionalizing Economic Globalization*; see further Tienhaara, *Expropriation*.

[50] OECD, *Foreign Direct Investment*, pp. 14–15; Gunningham and Sinclair, *Voluntary Approaches*; Cernea, 'Ripple Effect' 65, 67–8.

the adoption of CSR programmes, and the emergence of sustainable financing practices have certainly been strategic responses to these pressures.[51] However, they have also generated cultural shifts within business sectors.[52] For example, there is a growing appreciation amongst company representatives that operating as a 'good global corporate citizen' can improve financial performance.[53] The adoption of social and environmental voluntary initiatives is viewed as an opportunity to enhance the reputation of the corporation and avoid negative publicity, which can, in turn, translate into lowering the costs of doing business.[54] It is widely acknowledged that a corporate culture of responsible environmental management can reduce commercial risks in foreign investment activities,[55] and that voluntary codes, initially developed to ensure environmental credibility and maintain the so-called 'social licence to operate',[56] are increasingly forming the expected standards of environmental corporate behaviour generally.[57]

It seemed to me that these developments have implications for international investment law and Chapter 4 provides the vehicle for an exploration of those possibilities. Not only do the CSR and sustainable finance movements provide a central platform from which to bring about reform in the foreign investment sector, but when such initiatives are viewed through a constructivist prism,[58] they already

[51] Gunningham and Sinclair, *Voluntary Approaches*, p. 2; OECD, *Foreign Direct*, pp. 14–15; Assadourian, 'Transforming Corporations', 171–89; OECD, *Corporate Responsibility*.

[52] Gill, 'Corporate Governance'.

[53] Assadourian, 'Transforming Corporations', 172–3; Guzy, 'Reconciling Environmentalist and Industry Differences', 414; Forster, 'Environmental Responsibilities', 68, 71–3.

[54] Gunningham and Sinclair, *Voluntary Approaches*, pp. 2–7.

[55] Forster, 'Environmental Responsibilities', 69–71, 73–4.

[56] The importance of maintaining environmental credibility and the 'social license to operate' is discussed in detail in Gunningham and Sinclair, *Voluntary Approaches*, pp. 2–7.

[57] See Cernea, 'Ripple Effect', for a discussion on the evolution of World Bank initiatives on socially and environmentally responsible codes of practice into expected standards or norms of corporate behaviour; see also Rock and Angel, *Industrial Transformation*, pp. 151, 170–6 for a discussion of firm-based adoption by multinational corporations of global environmental standards; see also the advice given by Australian commercial law firm Allens Arthur Robinson to its clients as an example of the commercial response:

> Having now been adopted by lenders who provide the bulk of project finance around the globe, the Equator Principles are close to becoming an industry standard so it is important that borrowers and lenders understand their potential impact on project financing transactions.
>
> Allens Arthur Robinson, 'The Equator Principles'.

[58] See Brunnée and Toope, 'International Law'.

indicate pre-normative activity in international investment law. The analysis here adopts an interdisciplinary approach to the examination of patterns in the evolution of foreign investment law-making, much in line with an interactional legal theory and constructivist international relations view of norm-creation.[59] A useful account of the constructivist international law/international relations position is set out by Abbott:

IR [international relations] helps us describe legal institutions richly, incorporating the political factors that shape the law: the interests, power, and governance structures of states and other actors; the information, ideas and understandings on which they operate; the institutions within which they interact. . . .

In terms of legal doctrine, for constructivists all is subjective and perpetually 'in play.' Constructivists would look to a variety of normative expressions, including practice, to define the subjective element of custom or the meaning of treaty commitments. In addition, normative understandings vary with historical and political context. . . .

Constructivists see numerous engines of change: historical events . . . political activity by human rights groups and TANs [transnational advocacy networks], governmental actions . . . judicial decisions . . . All of these provide cognitive and moral focal points for social consensus and action. Political activists are expert at framing issues in ways that mobilize political support, resonating with broadly held cognitive and ideological principles. The key for constructivists is the transformative impact such actions have on subjective understandings of interest, appropriate behavior and identity.[60]

Brunnée and Toope propose an interactional theory of international law that draws on constructivist international relations theory.[61] Focusing on the assertion that legal rules evolve out of a continuing and organic process of interaction amongst the participants, Brunnée and Toope argue that the process of international norm-creation is bound in with social practice and structures, identity and interaction, shared understandings and shifting perspectives.[62] They draw attention to the crucial role played by numerous actors in the 'pre-legal norm' stage of rule evolution in international law:

Pre-legal normativity is valuable in itself, and is not purely a set of instruments on the road to law. But looking back from the perspective of a legal norm or

[59] Ibid., See also Brunnée and Toope, *Legitimacy and Legality*; see further the discussion in Finnemore and Sikkink, 'International Norm Dynamics'.

[60] Abbott, 'International Relations Theory', 362–77.

[61] Brunnée and Toope, 'International Law'. [62] Ibid., 30–1, 68–71.

system, one can see that the actors involved in pre-legal norm creation and elaboration serve also as builders of the legal system ... NGOs, corporations, informal intergovernmental expert networks, and a variety of other groups are actively engaged in the creation of shared understandings and the promotion of learning amongst states.[63]

Chapter 4 argues that Brunnée and Toope's theory can be applied to new trends in CSR and international investment law. From a constructivist perspective, 'soft law' CSR and sustainable finance initiatives are creating pre-normative 'noise'.[64] The array of instruments, codes, standards, policies, and domestic regulation related to CSR specifications are part of a process of exploring the most effective mechanisms to bring about more socially and environmentally responsible corporate conduct. Not only is this process leading to the normalisation of CSR within the private sector,[65] it is also influencing state behaviour – and this, arguably, points to the future emergence of international customary rules on CSR.[66] Chapter 4 then engages with the idea that international CSR principles are, perhaps, in the process of emerging and considers the implications of such a possibility for international investment law.

4. Foreign investment law, practices, and policy: future trends

Part III of this book explores future trajectories for foreign investment law, practices, and policy. To this end, Chapter 5 examines transformations that have been occurring in the international legal system over several decades and considers their application to international investment law. It points to the increasing presence of non-state actors and transnational networks on the international plane, the emergence of what has been termed 'global public law', and the transfer of concepts and principles between discrete areas of international law.[67] It is argued that these recent developments are contributing to current pressure to reform international investment law, but that they also simultaneously provide channels through which reorientation of this field could occur. Accordingly, Chapter 6 examines how these possible paths towards a

[63] Ibid., 70.

[64] See the discussion in Zerk, *Multinationals*, pp. 101–2; see also Brunnée and Toope, 'International Law'.

[65] Gill, 'Corporate Governance', 461–2.

[66] Zerk, *Multinationals*, pp. 262–3; Moore Dickerson, 'Norms and Empathy'.

[67] See, e.g., the discussion in Sands, 'Turtles and Torturers'; Slaughter, *A New World Order*; Krisch and Kingsbury, 'Introduction'; Garcia, 'Globalization'; Crawford, *International Law*, p. 17; Triggs, *International Law*, pp. 17–20.

reconceptualised international investment law could manifest, such as through modification of its substantive principles,[68] reform of the dispute settlement system,[69] the potential for new international regulatory frameworks,[70] and the infusion of a cognitive and cultural shift amongst decision-makers in the investment sector through the influence of epistemic communities and transnational networks.[71]

Ultimately, of course, fundamental questions run through this book from first reflections to fully formed viewpoints: how were the complexities of law and variegated legal spaces encompassed in the imperial context? What factors shaped the formation of the international rules on foreign investment protection? What evolutionary course did the law take? How have assertions of power and challenges to power in foreign investment protection been played out? What of these contested areas of shifting authority? Can the conceptualisations of empire still be imbued within modern international investment law, policy, and practices? If so, how has this manifested and what forms of re-articulation could be entertained? Could a cultural transformation of such magnitude occur? Can ingrained patterns be disrupted? Whose narratives, whose histories, will be legitimised? Whatever the outcomes, it is certainly the case that an appreciation of the history of this field will lead to a more profound understanding of both the current framework and future paths for this area of international law. And, perhaps, after all, the 'ebb and flow' will, indeed, edge us a little closer to a reoriented form of international investment law.

[68] See the suggestions in Mann et al., *IISD Model International Agreement*; Cosbey et al., *Investment*.

[69] Van Harten, *Investment Treaty Arbitration*; Brower, Brower II and Sharpe, 'The Coming Crisis'; Tienhaara, 'Third Party Participation'; see also the discussion in Choudhury, 'Recapturing Public Power'.

[70] Zerk, *Multinationals*; see also Friends of the Earth, 'Binding Corporate Accountability'.

[71] See the discussion in Haas, 'Epistemic Communities', 791; see also for the categorisation of arbitrators as an 'epistemic community', Dezalay and Garth, *Dealing in Virtue*, p. 16.

PART I

Historical evolution of foreign investment protection law

1 Origins of international investment law

Delving into current debates surrounding foreign investment protection tends to leave an impression that the law in this field is a relatively recent treaty-based phenomenon. In much of the discourse, little mention is made of the law prior to the advent of the modern network of bilateral investment treaties. The frequent, but fleeting, references to the signing of the first such treaty in 1959 between Germany and Pakistan only serve to compound the sense that this is the 'starting point' of the law.[1] An historical exploration of international investment law, however, reveals a far more complex picture.

Reaching back beyond the 1959 marker, the origins of the law in this field can be found in the expansion of European trade and investment activity from the seventeenth to early twentieth centuries. Emerging from an international legal system established amongst European nations, the rules on foreign investment protection evolved throughout the 'colonial encounter'[2] as a tool to protect the interests of capital-exporting states and their nationals.[3] International investment principles materialised, claiming universality and impartiality, but essentially comprised protection for investors and obligations for capital-importing states to facilitate trade and investment.[4] This book is about the

[1] Treaty between the Federal Republic of Germany and Pakistan for the Promotion and Protection of Investments, signed 25 November 1959, (1963) 457 UNTS 23 (entered into force 28 April 1962).

[2] Anghie, *Imperialism*, pp. 6–7. See the introduction for a discussion on Anghie's conceptualisation of the interaction between coloniser and colonised and his use of the phrase 'colonial encounter'.

[3] Lipson, *Standing Guard*, pp. 4, 8, 37–8; Schrijver, *Sovereignty*, pp. 173–4; Malanczuk, *Akehurst's*, pp. 9–10.

[4] Lipson, *Standing Guard*, pp. 37–8; Anghie, *Imperialism*, pp. 224, 238–9.

significance of those origins for the substance of international investment law in the twentieth and twenty-first centuries. In this chapter, then, I examine those origins and consider the multi-layered commercial, political, and legal circumstances that were responsible for the formation of those rules.

My argument derives from the idea that the content and form of foreign investment protection law cannot be separated from its socio-political context. In exploring this proposition, I begin, in section I of this chapter, by examining the era in which core elements of international investment law emerged and argue that the political and commercial aspirations of European trading nations had a profound effect on the character of investment law. I offer an account of this period that considers the links between imperialism, the pursuit of trade and investment, and the development of international law. As an important component of this account, I explore the traditional alignment of states' interests with those of their nationals engaging in foreign investment, with a particular focus on the Dutch East India Company (Verenigde Oostindische Compagnie (VOC)).[5]

This section also reflects on the environmental practices of these early traders, investors, and colonisers, arguing that this relationship was characterised by environmental degradation and control. Exploitation and the commodification of natural resources for consumption in European markets is closely linked with the environmental damage that occurred during this period in capital-importing states, colonised nations, and non-European trading partners.[6] Conversely, the development of aspects of conservationism within the imperial framework exemplifies the complexity of that relationship. Not all environmental transformation as a result of colonial and commercial encounters was negative and conservationism did introduce more sustainable use practices to colonial resource extraction and enterprise.[7] However, conservationism was undoubtedly a control mechanism, regulating the use of natural resources to ensure continued supply lines for European markets.[8] Furthermore, it was also a colonial tool for political subjugation of indigenous communities, imposing control structures

[5] As referred to in the Introduction, this book analyses the activities of the Dutch East India Company as illustrative of the relationship between states and the large trading companies, such as the English East India Company, the Dutch West India Company, and the French East India Company.

[6] Beinart and Hughes, *Environment and Empire*, pp. 1–21.

[7] Ibid., pp. 1–3, 14.

[8] Ibid., pp. 1–3; Richardson, Mgbeoji, and Botchway, 'Environmental Law', 413, 415–16.

through land use regulation.[9] As such, early foreign investors, traders, and colonising states tended to view the environment as a resource for exploitation, a commodity to be conserved to ensure longevity of supply, or a means for maintaining power imbalances. Section I of this chapter proposes that these social, political, and economic conditions were key factors in the narrative of international investment law, contributing significantly to the character of foreign investment protection rules developed in this era.

Elaborating on these propositions, section II of this chapter sets out the substance of international investment law prior to World War I. It examines treatises, diplomatic pronouncements, state practice, and early disputes. It argues that the focus on investor protection, the entwining of state and investor interests, and the methods of enforcement adopted by Western investor states, all reflected the political and commercial interests of investor states from the seventeenth to the nineteenth centuries.

I. Commerce, politics, and imperialism: the framework for the emergence of international investment law

It is a matter of historical fact that the international rules on the protection of foreign-owned property originated in the reciprocal arrangements of European nations.[10] These states possessed relatively equal bargaining power and sought to secure minimum standards of treatment for their citizens engaging in investment activity within the region.[11] The transformation into international investment law, however, changed the character of these rules fundamentally. It was this process of applying these standards to non-European states that became inextricably linked with colonialism, oppressive protection of commercial interests, and military intervention.[12] And as a result of this shift in practice, foreign investment protection law moved from a base of reciprocity, to one of imposition.

On a separate point, it should be noted that the focus in this chapter on seventeenth- to nineteenth-century European trading and

[9] Beinart and Hughes, *Environment and Empire*, pp. 269–71; Ngugi, 'Decolonization-Modernization'.

[10] Lipson, *Standing Guard*, 11–12; see also Neufeld, *International Protection*, p. 6; Dawson and Head, *International Law*, pp. 4–5.

[11] Lipson, *Standing Guard*, pp. 11–12.

[12] Ibid.; Dawson and Head, *International Law*, p. 5.

investment arrangements is due to the sourcing of modern international law from within European legal interaction during this period.[13] Over the course of history, many groups of nations or peoples have developed international legal regimes to govern their interactions.[14] Indeed, the scope of the foreign trade and investment systems that evolved through Western expansionism during the seventeenth to early nineteenth centuries could not have been contemplated if indigenous trading networks had not already been in place.[15] The significance of this for the evolution of modern international law is that Europeans were not creating legal regimes on a blank canvas. Rather, there were political and jurisdictional contests at work and existing legal systems vying for supremacy.[16] Ultimately, it was the European form and content of international law, along with its particular conceptions of property, private wealth, economy, and regulation, that emerged out of this contest as the foundation for the modern international legal system.[17]

Benton argues that the emergence of international law from European legal regimes was intimately bound up with power relations.[18] She identifies the creation and control of legal bodies and laws with social, political, and economic control, stating that 'legal institutions emerged with capitalist relations of production through repetitive assertions of power and responses to power.'[19] Benton's insight is also critical in understanding the interplay of power and the development of the legal rules that formed the basis of the modern system of international law on foreign investment protection. Her suggestion that disputes over property in a colonial context were also about the imposition of power, jurisdictional primacy, and the creation of legal regimes

[13] Malanczuk, *Akehurst's*, p. 9.

[14] Ibid., See generally, Benton, *Colonial Cultures*; see also Sornarajah, *Foreign Investment*, p. 19; Alexandrowicz, *History in the East Indies*, pp. 97–9; Prakash, 'Trade', 117.

[15] Alexandrowicz, *History in the East Indies*, pp. 97–9; see also the discussion in Melville, 'Global Developments', 185 on the extensive inter-regional commercial arrangements in the pre-Hispanic era of Central and South America. Spanish colonisers and merchants used these existing systems to establish themselves politically and economically. It is, however, outside the scope of this book to conduct a comparative analysis of pre-eighteenth-century non-European legal regimes and inter-nation trading systems.

[16] Benton, *Colonial Cultures*, pp. 10–11.

[17] Anghie, *Imperialism*, pp. 32–3, 115; Lipson, *Standing Guard*, pp. 16, 20–1.

[18] Benton, *Colonial Cultures*, pp. 10–11; see also the theories on power and the creation of rules of international law in Byers, *Custom, Power*, pp. 35–40.

[19] Benton, *Colonial Cultures*, p. 11.

rather than just the minutiae of the particular property rights involved,[20] provides an important perspective on the dynamics of the era and an understanding of the origins of international investment law – the emergence of these rules involved a dual process of assertion and creation. Through the assertion of foreign investment protection rules as existing international law, together with the use of force, capital-exporting states directed the evolution of international investment law into a mechanism that protected only the investor.

A. Commercial expansion, colonialism, and the law: origins in imposition

Non-European inter-nation legal regimes and trading and investment arrangements were ultimately replaced with a universal system of international law based on European conceptions of property – and it is clear that power struggles, military force, and the use of legal doctrine were deeply involved in that process of replacement. The development of international rules on the protection of foreign investment was also closely tied to the methods of commercial expansion adopted by European and North American powers in the eighteenth and nineteenth centuries.[21] The strategies included the securing of 'friendship, commerce and navigation' treaties, the acquiring of concessions, diplomatic pressure, capitulation treaties, extraterritorial jurisdiction, military intervention, and colonial annexation of territory.[22] Significantly, this process of Western commercial and political expansionism was facilitated by international law.

What is particularly interesting is that capital-exporting states asserted the legitimacy of these strategies within international law and that the impact of their reiterated assertions was so profound. In sharing a political and economic base in liberalism, powerful Western nations had a common understanding of the principles of international law pertaining to foreign investment.[23] It is not surprising that this understanding reflected their interests, and accentuated the obligations of nations to

[20] Ibid.

[21] Lipson, *Standing Guard*, pp. 16, 20–1; Sornarajah, *Foreign Investment*, pp. 19–21; Schrijver, *Sovereignty*, pp. 173–5; Anghie, *Imperialism*, pp. 67–71, 224, 239.

[22] Sornarajah, *Foreign Investment*, pp. 19–21, pp. 180–1; Lipson, *Standing Guard*, pp. 12–21; Schrijver, *Sovereignty*, pp. 173–5; Herrick, 'The Merger of Two Systems', 686–8.

[23] Lipson, *Standing Guard*, p. 24; Foighel, *Nationalization*, p. 12; Fry, *International Investment*, pp. 29–30; Weston, 'International Law', 1080–1.

facilitate trade and investment.[24] It was, however, the repeated assertion of those obligations, and appeals to the legitimacy of actions taken to enforce them, that contributed so significantly to the solidifying of assertions as rules of international law. Furthermore, such processes also had indirect, yet fundamentally important, cultural implications. The techniques adopted to protect foreign-owned assets also served to disseminate Western notions of property, transplant the European view of international law within other territories, and develop international legal doctrine to assist with the securing of Western political and commercial hegemony in the nineteenth century.[25]

1. Friendship, commerce, and navigation treaties

In exploring these strategies in more detail, it is, perhaps, the friendship, commerce and navigation treaty that is most familiar to the modern investment lawyer. Indeed, such instruments have been described as a forerunner of modern bilateral investment treaties.[26] These agreements involved the granting of reciprocal commercial privileges, but also addressed a wide range of subjects relating to the treatment of nationals of the state parties.[27] They focused on protecting individuals and their property, ensuring freedom of movement and worship, assuring rights to trade and engage in commercial enterprise, granting national treatment and most-favoured-nation status, allowing for access to ports, and granting navigation rights through territorial waters.[28] These agreements created a network of reciprocal trade

[24] Lipson, *Standing Guard*, pp. 37–8; Anghie, *Imperialism*, pp. 67–71; Herrick, 'The Merger of Two Systems', 686–7.

[25] Anghie, *Imperialism*, pp. 6–8, 32–3, 67–71, 141–2; Lipson, *Standing Guard*, pp. 16–18, 20–1, 37–8; Sornarajah, *Foreign Investment*, p. 19; see, e.g., the use of the doctrine of diplomatic protection of alien property and the development of the international minimum standard to legitimise military intervention in the host state by the home state of the investor. This doctrine is discussed in detail below in section II of this chapter.

[26] Sornarajah, *Foreign Investment*, p. 180; see also the discussion in Vandevalde, *Bilateral Investment Treaties*, pp. 21–2.

[27] Lipson, *Standing Guard*, p. 96; Sornarajah, *Foreign Investment*, pp. 180–1; Schrijver, *Sovereignty*, p. 190; Blumenwitz, 'Treaties of Friendship', 484–8; Walker, 'Modern Treaties of Friendship', 805.

[28] Sornarajah, *Foreign Investment*, pp. 180–1; Schrijver, *Sovereignty*, p. 190; Blumenwitz, 'Treaties of Friendship'; see for examples of friendship, commerce and navigation treaties: United States–Paraguay Treaty of Friendship, Commerce and Navigation (1859) in W. M. Malloy, *Treaties, Conventions, International Acts, Protocols and Agreements between the United States and other Powers 1776–1909* (Washington, 1910) Vol. II 1364. Most-favoured-nation status refers to a guarantee by one state to confer on another any benefits enjoyed by third states in their relationship with the first state.

protection measures and formed a framework for international protection of foreign capital.[29]

Extending the principles embodied in these agreements beyond Europe, however, altered their character from one of reciprocity to enforced compliance.[30] Although initially concluded on equal terms, these agreements were also often the first stepping stone to establishing a more intrusive presence within non-European nations.[31] As the political strength of the non-European partner waned, overly favourable investor interpretations of these treaties were imposed on the host state[32] and incursions into their sovereignty systematically increased in scale and scope, so as to further trade and investment activity.[33] This gradual cementing of Western economic and political control of non-European territories was a complex and multi-layered process facilitated through the granting of far-reaching concessions to foreigners, the extraterritorial application of laws from European states and the United States of America to their nationals, and the imposition of 'unequal treaties'.[34]

2. Unequal treaties

Unequal, or capitulation, treaties conferred one-sided rights and were the product of actual or threatened use of force by the dominant Western commercial powers of the day.[35] They addressed a number of issues, but were designed to prise open reluctant non-European territories to Western trade and investment.[36] Ostensibly, they were treaties of cession entered into voluntarily between states, but the neutrality of the language disguised the imposed nature of the agreement and the violence inflicted to secure financial benefits for European states,

29 Lipson, *Standing Guard*, p. 9. 30 Ibid., pp. 12–14.

31 Anghie, *Imperialism*, pp. 85–6. In this context, Anghie refers to capitulation treaties entered into voluntarily and cites the *Treaty of Friendship and Commerce between Her Majesty and the Kings of Siam*, 18 April 1855 (the Bowring Treaty), pp. 172–3.

32 Lipson, *Standing Guard*, pp. 13–14. Lipson discusses this process using the example of increasingly assertive European investors in Ottoman territories and the imposition of their interpretation of commercial treaties during the decline of the Ottoman Empire.

33 Anghie, *Imperialism*, pp. 84–6.

34 Ibid., pp. 67–74, 84–6; Lipson, *Standing Guard*, pp. 12–14, 16. The extraterritorial application of national laws was most commonly adopted by the Dutch, English, Spanish, Portuguese, and French administrations.

35 Sornarajah, *Foreign Investment*, p. 20; Lipson, *Standing Guard*, pp. 13–14; Schrijver, *Sovereignty*, p. 174; Morvay, 'Unequal Treaties', 514–17.

36 Lipson, *Standing Guard*, pp. 13–14; see also the discussion in Detter, 'Unequal Treaties', 1073–5.

traders, and investors.[37] The use of these treaties fitted within the European framing of freedom of commerce as a 'right', the protection of which justified the use of force.[38] Regarding a non-European nation's refusal to trade or to allow foreign nationals to engage in commercial activity within its territory as a 'hostile act', Western states constructed a legal entitlement to military redress.[39] As a result, conflict followed by the imposition of unequal treaties was a key legal strategy in the realisation of European territorial and commercial aspirations.[40]

Quintessential examples of unequal treaties were those concluded between China and foreign powers from the 1840s to the 1860s following military conflict.[41] These agreements granted a series of non-reciprocal rights and established areas of extraterritorial jurisdiction.[42] In this way, regimes of exclusive consular rule were created within the territory of the host state, under which foreign nationals and their property were not subject to local laws, but remained within the jurisdiction of their home state.[43] This mode of governance was humiliating for host nations, effectively setting up what Schrijver describes as 'quasi-colonies of Western powers, companies or even individuals.'[44] Unsurprisingly, imposed systems of this nature were a source of great resentment amongst the local citizens of states subjected to unequal treaties.[45]

Unequal treaties also represent the complexities of law in the imperial context, in which 'legal variations' and parallel legal orders co-existed within the same territory.[46] In this context, they were

[37] Anghie, *Imperialism*, pp. 71–4. [38] Ibid., pp. 20–2, 67–74, 270–1. [39] Ibid.

[40] Ibid., pp. 72–4.

[41] Lipson, *Standing Guard*, p. 14; Detter, 'Unequal Treaties', 1073–5; see also the discussion in Herrick, 'The Merger of Two Systems', 686–8; see, e.g., the following treaties referred to in Morvay, 'Unequal Treaties', p. 515: Treaty of Nanking with Britain (1842) 93 *Consolidated Treaty Series* 465; Treaty of Wang Hiya with the USA (1844) 97 *Consolidated Treaty Series* 105; Treaty of Whampoa with France (1844) 97 *Consolidated Treaty Series* 375; Treaty of Tientsin with Russia (1858) 119 *Consolidated Treaty Series* 113; Treaty of Tientsin with the German States (1861) 124 *Consolidated Treaty Series* 299; Treaty of Peking with Austria-Hungary (1869) 139 *Consolidated Treaty Series* 477.

[42] Lipson, *Standing Guard*, p. 14; Detter, 'Unequal Treaties', 1078–81.

[43] Schrijver, *Sovereignty*, p. 174; Lipson, *Standing Guard*, p. 14; Detter, 'Unequal Treaties', 1078–81; Alvarez, 'Contemporary Foreign Investment Law', 959–60; Chen, 'Law, Empire, and Historiography', 1–4.

[44] Schrijver, *Sovereignty*, p. 174.

[45] Ibid., pp. 174–5; Sornarajah, *Foreign Investment*, p. 20.

[46] Benton, *Search for Sovereignty*, pp. 2–8. Benton adopts the term 'legal variations' to describe the differentiated legal zones that simultaneously existed within colonial regimes.

demonstrations of political dominance of wide-ranging scope, ensuring social and political conditions that would provide an enhanced level of security for, amongst other objectives, pursuing foreign trade and investment.[47] Unequal treaties addressed issues such as the travel prerogatives of foreign traders, the securing of extensive trading and investment rights, non-discriminatory commercial access to the host state, the granting of concessions to foreign companies, the protection of Christian missionaries, the leasing or ceding of territory to foreign states, and governance powers.[48] The acquired powers of governance were extensive, often entailing both civil and criminal jurisdiction, the result of which was that foreign officials could determine matters implicating local citizens if a foreign national was involved.[49] As an observable display of political control, such incursions into the spatial realm of jurisdiction played an essential role in the displacement of local authority and were very much a manifestation of the entwining of law, power, and politics within imperial projects.[50]

Establishing direct consular control in this way also proved an effective method of ensuring the security of foreign-owned property and the continued expansion of foreign business interests.[51] Extraterritoriality virtually guaranteed the application of a European conceptualisation of the international law on foreign investment protection.[52] And direct consular rule enabled the level of control necessary to enforce that conceptualisation of property rights.[53] Not only were diplomatic avenues explored when circumstances arose that might threaten foreign trade and investment interests, but coercion and 'gunboat diplomacy' were also employed.[54] European powers, particularly Britain due to its naval prowess, were well placed to enforce their view of the legal rights of their nationals and did so

[47] Lipson, *Standing Guard*, pp. 14–15; Fidler, 'A Kinder, Gentler System', 390–1.

[48] Schrijver, *Sovereignty*, p. 174; Lipson, *Standing Guard*, p. 14; Morvay, 'Unequal Treaties', 515.

[49] Lipson, *Standing Guard*, p. 14.

[50] Benton, *Search for Sovereignty*, pp. 2–8; Maier, *Among Empires*, p. 101.

[51] Lipson, *Standing Guard*, p. 14. Fidler, 'A Kinder, Gentler System', 390–1; Fidler, 'International Human Rights Law', 142–4.

[52] Fidler, 'International Human Rights Law', 142–4; Lipson, *Standing Guard*, p. 14.

[53] Lipson, *Standing Guard*, p. 14.

[54] Ibid., pp. 14–15; see also Herrick, 'The Merger of Two Systems', 686–8. The term 'gunboat diplomacy' is used to describe the European practice of coercion via a show of military force to obtain commercial or political advantages.

when they deemed it necessary to protect their nationals and their interests.[55]

3. Concessions

Key tools through which the historical narrative of empire and international investment law intersected also included 'concessions'. Concession agreements were generally concluded between a host state and an individual or company and allowed that individual to engage in an activity that had previously been the sole realm of the state.[56] This ordinarily entailed the extraction of natural resources or the construction and operation of public utilities such as postal systems and the railways.[57] The rights obtained by concessionaires were often extensive, involving jurisdictional control of substantial areas of land and significant natural resources for lengthy terms in return for payment of royalties.[58] The scope of individual agreements varied, and, although this type of arrangement often concerned only an isolated enterprise, it still effectively involved the transfer of sovereign rights held by the state to the holder of the concession.[59] These agreements were often exploitative, occurring pursuant to unequal treaties or within protectorates, and frequently involved the exertion of pressure from Western states to grant favourable concessions to their nationals.[60]

Once obtained, concessions were protected by the military strength of the home state and any coercive action taken was legitimised by international rules on investment protection.[61] Despite their blanket

[55] Lipson, *Standing Guard*, pp. 14, 40, 53–4, 187. Lipson refers to 40 incidents involving British armed intervention in Latin America between 1820 and 1914 to protect its citizens against injury and seizure of property, in addition to numerous examples of threatened use of force. See also Wortley, *Expropriation*, p. 58; Lillich, 'Current Status of the Law', 1, 3.

[56] Fischer, 'Historic Aspects', 222, 224–5; see also Carlston, 'Concession Agreements', 260.

[57] Fischer, 'Historic Aspects', 224; Carlston, 'Concession Agreements', 260.

[58] Sornarajah, *Foreign Investment*, pp. 38–41.

[59] Ibid., pp. 40–2, 405–6; Schrijver, *Sovereignty*, pp. 174–5.

[60] Sornarajah, *Foreign Investment*, pp. 38–41, 280; Schrijver, *Sovereignty*, pp. 174–5; Anghie, 'The Heart of My Home', 472–3. A protectorate was a regime under which a non-European state was under the protection of a European power. Technically, the protectorate retained control of its internal affairs, while the European state spoke for it on the international stage and took control of any external matters relating to the protectorate: Anghie, *Imperialism*, pp. 87–8.

[61] Sornarajah, *Foreign Investment*, p. 38; Schrijver, *Sovereignty*, pp. 174–6; Lipson, *Standing Guard*, pp. 53–7; see, e.g., the doctrine of diplomatic protection of alien property, a

invocation by capital-exporting states, however, these rules were, of course, still in the process of emerging. The legal principles became part of the process of building and maintaining Western economic and political dominance and evolved into imposed assertions of universally applicable international law as the colonial encounter unfolded.[62] In this way, the invocation of international property rights by concessionaires and their reiteration by the home state were at once assertions of the existent law, but also part of the creation of its principles.

Securing particular concessions was often a component of investor states' wider aims of commercial and political influence, even where the general policy was to leave matters to market forces.[63] For example, for most of the nineteenth century, a *laissez-faire* approach was the dominant economic theory driving British foreign policy on international trade and investment.[64] Ordinarily, the British government saw its role in the acquisition of concessions as one limited to ensuring the general security of trading and investment environments and the furthering of Britain's general interests, but not the promoting of individual investors.[65] As a consequence, while Britain's commanding position in the world of international trade and investment was unthreatened, it generally recoiled from lending support to the actual negotiation of investors' contracts with foreign governments and the granting of concessions.[66] However, this policy shifted in the face of increasingly fierce competition from other states, particularly from the 1880s onwards.[67] Diplomatic pressure was being employed by several European states to secure concessions and, in these circumstances, Britain authorised its diplomats to assist British applicants so as to ensure 'fair treatment' for British investors.[68]

Britain made a distinction between what it termed 'commercial' concessions and 'political' or 'strategic' concessions.[69] Non-interventionist, *laissez-faire* policies applied to the obtaining of commercial concessions;

breach of which enlivened a right of intervention by the home state of the investor. The substance of foreign investment protection law in the nineteenth century is set out below in section II of this chapter.

62 Anghie, *Imperialism*, pp. 4–10, 67–9, 211–16.

63 Fischer, 'Historic Aspects', 254–6; Platt, *Finance*, pp. 63–6.

64 Platt, *Finance*, pp. xix, xxxiii–xxxiv; Lipson, *Standing Guard*, pp. 39–42; Pitruzzello, 'Trade Globalization', 717; see also the discussion in Davis and Huttenback, *Mammon*, p. 263.

65 Lipson, *Standing Guard*, pp. 39–42; Platt, *Finance*, pp. xxxiii–xxxiv.

66 Platt, *Finance*, pp. 54–7.

67 Lipson, *Standing Guard*, pp. 42–3; McGowan and Kordan, 'Imperialism', 55–6.

68 Platt, *Finance*, pp. 57–9; Platt, 'Economic Factors', 123–6.

69 Platt, *Finance*, p. 63.

quite the opposite applied to political concessions. If the government considered it was in Britain's political interests to obtain particular concessions, pressure would be applied to the host state, including the use of force.[70] Selectivity of this nature illustrates the way in which variations were accommodated within the same legal space, a characteristic of irregularity readily discernible in the context of law and empire.[71]

Obtaining strategic concession agreements that locked out the influence of other states had become another aspect of the political and commercial rivalries played out amongst the European capital-exporting states.[72] Obvious examples of earlier state and private investor collaboration in the pursuit of concession agreements as part of wider commercial and political objectives were those effected by the English East India Company and the VOC in the seventeenth and eighteenth centuries.[73] These companies were granted exceptional powers by their home states to enter into treaties, to annex territory, and to obtain commercial concession agreements, through which they acquired wide-ranging trading, investment, and jurisdictional rights within host territories.[74] The resulting concession agreements and capitulation treaties ensured the creation of a network of European political and commercial influence across the targeted regions.

The agreements concluded by these trading companies were not concerned solely with the operation of singular business entities, but often entailed the establishment of settlements administered according to British or Dutch law.[75] Through these agreements, the trading companies secured both civil and criminal jurisdictional rights over British or Dutch nationals[76] and, in certain circumstances, even over local citizens.[77] Adopting Benton's view of the implications of the creation

[70] Ibid., pp. 63–5. [71] Benton, *Search for Sovereignty*, pp. 2–8, 28–30.

[72] Platt, *Finance*, pp. 64–5; for a discussion on the pressure placed on host states and the unequal context in which the provision of foreign capital occurred and trade and investment negotiations conducted, see Hopkins, 'Informal Empire', 478–80.

[73] Fischer, 'Historic Aspects', 254–6; Schrijver, *Sovereignty*, pp. 174–5.

[74] Schrijver, *Sovereignty*, pp. 174–5; Fischer, 'Historic Aspects', 254–6; Anghie, *Imperialism*, pp. 68–9, 224; Neal, 'Dutch and English', 196.

[75] Anghie, *Imperialism*, pp. 68–9, 224; Schrijver, *Sovereignty*, p. 174.

[76] See, e.g., the concession from the Ruler of Achen obtained by the English East India Company in 1602; Treaty between the Ruler of Achen and the Dutch East India Company in 1607, referred to in Alexandrowicz, *History in the East Indies*, pp. 104–5.

[77] See, e.g., the concession granted by the Bringab Raja to the English East India Company in 1758, referred to in Alexandrowicz, *History in the East Indies*, p. 108. Circumstances in which local citizens could find themselves under foreign jurisdiction included, for instance, when the Company alleged breach of contract.

and control of legal rules, this type of interaction would inevitably lead to shifts in the regional power balance. In this way, the transfer of economic and jurisdictional control that often accompanied the granting of concessions also contributed to the process of infusing European-based notions of property rights and the creation of replacement legal regimes.

4. International law, foreign investment, and the 'other'

European imperialism, trade, and foreign investment were entwined throughout the seventeenth to the twentieth centuries in a myriad of ways.[78] But it is clear that international law was an important tool in facilitating the objectives of Western commercial and political hegemony, in particular, in the eighteenth and nineteenth centuries. Scholars argue that international legal doctrines were developed and moulded to legitimise the use of oppressive techniques by European powers throughout the colonial encounter.[79] The formulation of categories such as 'civilised' and 'uncivilised' nations enabled the application of a different conceptualisation of international law to non-European territories; one that applied a concept of 'otherness' to non-European communities and enabled their exclusion.[80] Anghie argues that concepts such as sovereignty, statehood, territory acquisition, and treaty-making acquired new meanings and evolved so as to further European expansionist objectives in engaging with non-European nations.[81] He argues further that these origins are not simply historical, but continue to inform the modern conceptualisation of sovereignty doctrine.[82]

Anghie's theories also implicate the development of international investment law. The translation of European trading and investment

[78] Anghie, *Imperialism*, pp. 67–74, 84–6; Lipson, *Standing Guard*, pp. 12–14, 16; Frieden, 'International Investment', 574, 575, 580, 593.

[79] Anghie, *Imperialism*, pp. 3–12; Koskenniemi, *Gentle Civilizer*, pp. 126–30; Anghie, 'Finding the Peripheries'; Weeramantry and Berman, 'The Grotius Lecture Series', 1555–69; Fitzpatrick, 'Terminal Legality', 9; Gathii 'Imperialism'.

[80] Anghie, *Imperialism*, pp. 3–12; Koskenniemi, *Gentle Civilizer*, pp. 126–30; Fitzpatrick, 'Terminal Legality'; Anghie, *Imperialism*, p. 447; Anghie, 'Finding the Peripheries'. The concept of 'otherness' is also referred to in Kirkby and Coleborne, 'Introduction', 1, 4.

[81] Anghie, *Imperialism*, pp. 3–12, 65–114; Anghie, 'Heart of My Home', 448; Anghie, 'Finding the Peripheries'.

[82] Anghie, *Imperialism*, pp. 3–12; Anghie, 'Heart of My Home', 447–9; 505–6; Anghie, 'Finding the Peripheries'; for a discussion on the complexities of the relationship between, and perceptions of, nineteenth-and twentieth-century international legal doctrine, see also Kennedy, 'International Law', 127–38.

principles into universal rules of international law on foreign investment protection is bound up with this history of colonialism, the calculated, often brutal, use of force, and the manipulation of legal doctrines to acquire commercial benefits.[83] These historical circumstances drove the construction of international investment law. Legal principles were developed and used by capital-exporting states to legitimise their often repressive actions in acquiring commercial advantages and protecting property.[84] Of course, examples of capricious behaviour by host states can be found and there were individual circumstances in which the property of foreign investors needed protection.[85] The key point, however, is more generalised and conceptual than any one property dispute – it is of fundamental importance to the shape and character of international investment law that the context in which its principles were developed was one of exploitation and imperialism. The rules evolved so as to advance the interests of Western capital-exporting states in engaging with the non-European world, and, as such, they protected only the investor.[86] The colonial encounter created 'otherness' in the concept of the host state, excluding it from the protective principles of international investment law. Thus, the host state was, and remains, unable to call upon the rules of international investment law to address damage suffered at the hands of foreign investors.[87]

It is important to appreciate that the principles of foreign investment protection law formed an integral part of European commercial and political expansionism in the eighteenth and nineteenth centuries, and they validated the use of force to achieve those wider objectives.[88] Referring to this role, Lipson states:

83 Lipson, *Standing Guard*, pp. 12–16; Anghie, *Imperialism*, pp. 211–16; Sornarajah, *Foreign Investment*, pp. 20, 38.

84 Schrijver, *Sovereignty*, pp. 173–6; Anghie, *Imperialism*, pp. 3–10, 67–74; Sornarajah, *Foreign Investment*, pp. 19–20.

85 Sornarajah, *Foreign Investment*, pp. 21, 448. Sornarajah cites as an example the expropriation of the railway by the Portuguese government in the *Delagoa Bay Railroad Arbitration*: Moore, *International Arbitrations*, p. 1865.

86 Lipson, *Standing Guard*, pp. 12–16; Schrijver, *Sovereignty*, pp. 173–6; Anghie, *Imperialism*, pp. 3–10, 67–74; Sornarajah, *Foreign Investment*, pp. 19–20.

87 Sornarajah, *Foreign Investment*, pp. 145–6. Recent scholarship has turned attention to the mechanisms through which home state obligations for the activities of corporate nationals can be created: see, e.g., Sornarajah, *Foreign Investment*, pp. 155–71; see also Zerk, *Multinationals*; McCorquodale and Simons, 'Responsibility beyond Borders'.

88 Schrijver, *Sovereignty*, pp. 173–6; Lipson, *Standing Guard*, pp. 16, 53–7; Anghie, *Imperialism*, pp. 3–10, 67–74; Sornarajah, *Foreign Investment*, pp. 19–20, 36.

nineteenth-century international property law, developed in Europe and enforced elsewhere mainly by the British, was undeniably successful in its central task. It legitimated, regulated, and obscured well enough to permit the internationalization of capital.[89]

At the time, the content of these rules of international property law, as well as their application, were also often chaotic and complex spaces of legal contestation. In law and empire, inconsistencies were accommodated, violence justified, parallel jurisdictions co-existed, control unevenly experienced, and variegated layers of law created; this was not a smooth, bloodless, or wholly intact emergence of an international legal order. And it was that era, with the ideas, conceptualisations, practices, rules, and principles developed within it, that formed the basis of modern international investment law.

B. *Alignment of state interests with investor interests*

Aligning the interests of private investors with those of their home state is a practice with a long history. During European expansionism, this association went well beyond invoking rules on diplomatic protection,[90] and gave rise to a relationship of interdependency and an intermingling of the functions of state and investor.[91] Not only was there a merging of imperialist and commercial objectives in this relationship, but the major European trading companies also played an active role in the development of international legal doctrine favourable to their needs.[92] The clearest historical example of this type of relationship is that between the state and entities such as the VOC, the English East India Company, and the French East India Company.

1. Trading companies and the development of international law

In the seventeenth century, an innovative technique was adopted to pursue state interests through the activities of a select group of trading companies – the granting of sovereign rights and privileges to the English East India Company, the VOC, the French East India Company, and the

[89] Lipson, *Standing Guard*, p. 57.

[90] The substance of these rules is addressed in Part II of this chapter.

[91] With respect to the relationship between state and the Dutch East India Company, Dutch West India Company, and English East India Company, see Schnurmann, 'Profit Leads Us', 477–80.

[92] Sornarajah, *Foreign Investment*, p. 38; Anghie, *Imperialism*, pp. 68–9.

Dutch West India Company.[93] This approach effectively created new international legal doctrine to enable non-sovereign actors to operate in the international sphere.[94] In possessing delegated sovereign powers, these companies were entitled to enter into treaties, found and administer settlements, engage in military conquest, and build forts.[95] However, they were also expected to reflect and advance their home states' political positions in their overseas operations, as well as in their own dealings with trading companies from other European states.[96]

Initially, the East India Companies followed different policies in their approach to obtaining commercial advantages in new territories. At the outset, the English East India Company sought out trading rights without incurring the associated administrative and political burdens of formal annexation of territory.[97] However, this changed in the face of, amongst other things, Britain's trading and political rivalries with other European states.[98] By the late eighteenth century, the Company's primary objective had shifted away from commercial enterprise and had instead turned to imperial acquisition and management.[99] As such, the activities of the Company reflected its relationship with the government, manifesting in a blurring of its commercial interests with the political objectives of the state. Certainly, in the case of the VOC and English East India Company, the entwining of state and Company interests significantly influenced the actions of both parties.

It also influenced the development of international investment law. Not only were international rules on foreign investment protection developed to protect the imperialist and commercial interests of

93 Schnurmann, 'Profit Leads Us', 477–80; Anghie, *Imperialism*, p. 68; Neal, 'Dutch and English', 196; Anghie, 'Finding the Peripheries', 36–8; see also the description in Lindley, *Acquisition and Government*, pp. 91, 94.

94 Anghie, *Imperialism*, p. 68.

95 Lindley, *Acquisition and Government*, p. 94; Schnurmann, 'Profit Leads Us', 477–80; see also the discussion on dual commercial and governmental role of the trading companies in McLean, 'Transnational Corporation', 368–9.

96 Schnurmann, 'Profit Leads Us', 476–80, 482; Sutherland, *East India*, pp. 4–5; see the discussion on the enmeshed commercial and military roles of the English East India Company in Peers, 'Mars and Mammon'.

97 Lindley, *Acquisition and Government*, pp. 91, 94; Sutherland, *East India*, pp. 2–3; Reid, *Commerce and Conquest*, pp. 34–43.

98 Sutherland, *East India*, pp. 2–5; Reid, *Commerce and Conquest*, pp. 34–43; see, e.g., the discussion on the two-year war in the 1820s between the English East India Company and the Kingdom of Burma before the Company secured the territories of Assam, Arakan, and Tenasserim, in Headick, *The Tools of Empire*, pp. 20–1.

99 Lindley, *Acquisition and Government*; Philips, *East India Company*, p. 23; Fieldhouse, *Colonial Empires*, pp. 149–52, 161–73; Bowen, 'Investment and Empire', 187.

European capital-exporting states and their nationals, but trading companies were also actively involved in the development of relevant international legal doctrines.[100] Indeed, Grotius, described as 'the father of international law', was engaged as a legal advisor to the VOC.[101] Far from embodying a disinterested representation of the law, several of his most significant theories were actually designed to provide a legal basis for the activities of the VOC.[102] For example, *De Iure Praede* (the law of prize and booty) and *De Mare Liberum* (freedom of the high seas) were devised by Grotius to legitimise the capture of a Portuguese ship, the *Santa Catarina*, and the confiscation of its valuable cargo by a Dutch merchant fleet belonging to the VOC.[103]

The historical alignment of state interests with those of foreign investors, and in particular with those of the trading companies, together with their influence over the development of international property rules, meant that those laws represented the interests of capital-exporting states and their nationals. The extent of their association and the implications of this for the substance of international investment law are considered in the next section through a more detailed examination of the activities of one of the most influential trading companies at the time – the VOC.

(a) Verenigde Oostindishe Compagnie

The VOC was formed in 1602 by the Dutch governing body, the States General. Not only did the state grant the Company the exclusive trading rights for Asia, but it also conferred powers to enter into treaties, acquire territory, keep armed soldiers, and build fortifications to protect its business enterprises.[104] In empowering the VOC in this way, the government was interested in the potential utility of the Company's activities for its own political objectives.[105] In particular, it was envisaged that the VOC would take an active role in the war with Portugal, eliminating Portuguese trading posts on the East African coast and in the Goa region

[100] Sornarajah, *Foreign Investment*, pp. 38; Anghie, *Imperialism*, pp. 68, 224.

[101] Anghie, *Imperialism*, p. 224; Sornarajah, *Foreign Investment*, p. 38; Porras, 'Constructing International Law', 742–3, 744–7.

[102] Porras, 'Constructing International Law', 744–7; Sornarajah, *Foreign Investment*, p. 38; Anghie, *Imperialism*, p. 224; van Ittersum, 'Hugo Grotius'.

[103] Porras, 'Constructing International Law', 744–7; van Ittersum, 'Hugo Grotius'; Sornarajah, *Foreign Investment*, p. 38; Borschberg, 'Seizure of the *Sta. Catarina*', 32, 57.

[104] Schnurmann, 'Profit Leads Us', 477–80; Anghie, 'Finding the Peripheries', 36–8; de Vries and van der Woude, *First Modern Economy*, p. 385; Irwin, 'Mercantilism', 1300.

[105] De Vries and van der Woude, *First Modern Economy*, p. 384.

of India.[106] And, indeed, the VOC fulfilled these expectations, targeting and destroying Portuguese outposts along those coastlines, and replaced them with Dutch-controlled trade centres and factories.[107]

The States General's charter set out the organisational structure for the capitalisation and management of the VOC.[108] Individuals who invested in the Company were categorised into one of two groups – either *participanten* (shareholders) or *bewindhebbers* (managers). *Participanten* simply provided capital, while the *bewindhebbers*, of which there were seventy-six, were responsible for the business management of the Company.[109] There was also a further level in the hierarchy, with seventeen directors being drawn from the ranks of the *bewindhebbers*. This panel of directors, the *Heren XVII* (literally, 'the Seventeen Gentlemen'), was responsible for the central administration of the Company.[110] The *Heren XVII* had close ties with the government, and, as the Company itself depended on the government for its existence and monopoly privileges, the political objectives of the States General regarding Spain and Portugal impacted on the character and activities of the Company.[111] From the outset, the VOC adopted aggressive tactics designed to eliminate commercial rivals and to ensure the political dominance of the Dutch. It combined military activities with the extraction of exclusive trading rights from local rulers, actively seeking to lock out both the Portuguese and the English.[112]

It was also this process of welding warfare and commerce that produced new international legal doctrine and embedded private commercial interests deep within the notion of the national interest.[113] Porras argues that these militarised encounters between private trading companies initiated the creation of new international law to justify the

[106] Borschberg, 'Seizure of the *Sta. Catarina*', 33–4, 55–6; Schnurmann, 'Profit Leads Us', 481–2.

[107] Schnurmann, 'Profit Leads Us', 481–2.

[108] De Vries and van der Woude, *First Modern Economy*, pp. 384–5; Prakash, *Commercial Enterprise*, pp. 72–5.

[109] Schnurmann, 'Profit Leads Us', 479; De Vries and van der Woude, *First Modern Economy*, pp. 384–5; Prakash, *Commercial Enterprise*, pp. 72–5.

[110] Prakash, *Commercial Enterprise*, pp. 74–5; de Vries and van der Woude, *First Modern Economy*, pp. 384–5; Braudel, *Wheels of Commerce*, pp. 446–7.

[111] Schnurmann, 'Profit Leads Us', 476–80, 482; Steensgaard, 'Dutch East India', 235, 240, 243–6.

[112] Steensgaard, 'Dutch East India', 243–6; see also the discussion in van Ittersum, 'Hugo Grotius', 511–20; Borschberg, 'Seizure of the *Sta. Catarina*', 33–4; Schnurmann, 'Profit Leads Us', 476–80, 482.

[113] Porras, 'Constructing International Law', 802–4.

state's protection of private commercial interests.[114] She argues that Grotius' treatise, *De Iure Praedae*, elevated the protection of commerce to a level commensurate with the national identity, stating that 'commerce inhabits every inflection of the text'.[115] Grotius framed his arguments for the VOC in such a way that a threat to private commercial interests became a legitimate legal basis for the state to go to war – and, in so doing, ensured that the historical trajectories of warfare, commerce, and the development of international law would be inextricably intertwined.[116]

The creation of rules in international investment law employed a similar level of self-justification and reiteration of the enmeshed interests of state and private commerce. This was effected through the development of the doctrine of diplomatic protection of alien property in the nineteenth century, requiring a minimum standard of treatment for foreign nationals, breach of which permitted home state intervention.[117] Once again, international legal doctrine was utilised to serve the interests of capital-exporting states. In essence, the development of these rules in the nineteenth century was a continuation of the path set by the VOC, its rival trading companies, and their home states.

The VOC considered itself primarily a commercial enterprise, but readily annexed territory as a way to secure and preserve trading and investment opportunities.[118] Ball describes the VOC approach to ensuring their pre-eminence in the East India trade:

> Territorial rights were seen as subservient to its mercantile system. To secure a monopoly of the spice trade, the VOC had to conquer the Spice Islands. To secure the Spice Islands, it had to establish a base for its shipping. To secure the base, it had to annex and rule the surrounding territory with sovereign powers.[119]

This desire for commercial dominance saw the VOC employing imperialistic practices in the East Asia region from very early on in its existence, merging its role as merchant with that of sovereign entity and administrator.[120] It established a Government for Jakarta, or as it was renamed, Batavia, appointed a Governor-General, and assumed

[114] Ibid. See also the discussion in Anghie, 'Finding the Peripheries'; see further the discussion in Loth, 'Armed Incidents', 718–20.

[115] Porras, 'Constructing International Law', 803.

[116] Ibid., 802–4; see also the discussion in Roelofsen, 'Grotius' 5, 49–54.

[117] The substance of the rules on the diplomatic protection of alien property is discussed below in section II of this chapter.

[118] Ball, *Indonesian Legal History*, p. 5. [119] Ibid.

[120] Schnurmann, 'Profit Leads Us', 484–5; Arasaratnam, 'Monopoly and Free Trade', 3–5.

responsibility for enacting regulations, the policing of VOC territories, and the establishment of courts and a civil and criminal justice system that applied Dutch law.[121] From there, this VOC-ruled town grew into a busy trading centre which by 1673 counted 27,000 residents of many nationalities and ethnic groups, including indigenous peoples, Dutch, Chinese, and slaves brought in from the surrounding regions.[122]

In 1620, the VOC established what became known as the Council of Justice to hear both civil and criminal matters involving VOC personnel.[123] Its jurisdiction encompassed disputes between VOC servants, and disputes between a VOC servant and a non-VOC citizen or foreigner.[124] It also created the Court of Aldermen, the jurisdiction of which covered both civil and criminal matters and applied to all those who were not VOC servants.[125] The maintenance of law and order was the responsibility of the VOC-appointed Bailiff for the Jakarta region and he was authorised to bring Dutch nationals, indigenous residents, foreigners, and slaves before the Court of Aldermen.[126]

This VOC justice system was an unforgiving one. Reports of the harshness of punishments meted out by the regime were common, as were assertions of the torture of prisoners.[127] Furthermore, conflict

[121] Ball, *Indonesian Legal History*, pp. 9–10. [122] Winchester, *Krakatoa*, pp. 44–5.

[123] Ball, *Indonesian Legal History*, pp. 17–19; see also the discussion on the VOC political control, governance structures, and legal system in the province of Amboina in Knaap, 'City of Migrants', 106–7, 110–11, 113–15, 125–6.

[124] Ball, *Indonesian Legal History*, pp. 17–19; Gall, 'Indonesian Legal History', 117.

[125] Gall, 'Indonesian Legal History', 117; Ball, *Indonesian Legal History*, pp. 21–2.

[126] Ball, *Indonesian Legal History*, pp. 22–3; see also the discussion on the 'power over life and death' of both Dutch and indigenous populations exercised by VOC officials in van Der Kroef, 'Indonesia' 1, 152; see also the discussion on VOC extraterritoriality and judicial systems within the Kingdom of Siam in Ruangsilp, *Dutch Perceptions*, pp. 31–41.

[127] Winchester, *Krakatoa*, pp. 46–7. Winchester reproduces the following description of retribution under the VOC justice system recorded by a visiting soldier in 1676:

> The 29th. Four Seamen were publicly Beheaded at Batavia (which is here the common Death of Criminals) for having killed a Chinese. At the same time, six slaves that had Murthered their master in the night were broke upon the Wheel. A Mulatto (as they call those that are betwixt a Black-a-Moor and a White) was Hang'd for Theft. Eight other Seamen were Whipt for Stealing, and running away, and were besides this Burnt on the Shoulder with the Arms of the East India Company. Two Dutch Soldiers that had absented themselves from the Guard two days, ran the Gauntlet. A Dutch Schoolmaster's Wife that was caught in Bed with another Man (it being her frequent Practice) was put in the Pillory, and Condemn'd to 12 years Imprisonment in the Spinhuys, the women's prison.

Account of Christopher Schweitzer on the sentencing practice in Batavia in 1676, reproduced in Winchester.

of interest was a significant problem in the administration of justice in Batavia. The judiciary were entirely dependent on the VOC Batavian government and, if the results were not in line with the expectations of the VOC Administration, the offending judge was subject to dismissal and relocation to the Netherlands.[128] In other words, the VOC was not simply a commercial entity amongst others doing business in Batavia – it was effectively the government, the police, the army, the judge, the prosecutor, the gaoler, and the executioner. This level of control over the legal system enabled the VOC to govern the settlement according to the European worldview and Dutch conceptions of trading and property rights. Jurisdictional control meant the settlement could be run in the way that was most commercially and politically advantageous for the VOC.[129]

The VOC also attempted to extend the jurisdiction of its courts to encompass the indigenous inhabitants throughout the Jakarta region. While this was achievable in Batavia, in reality, the Company was not able to exercise effective control over the indigenous population in the areas much beyond Batavia and its immediate surroundings.[130] Indeed, the relationships between the Dutch, the indigenous populations, and the migrant Asian groups within VOC settlements other than Batavia were of a significantly more complex and interactive nature, in which the VOC often had to absorb and work with the existing networks and customs of the territory.[131] As such, in the outlying areas, the administration of justice in matters concerning indigenous residents was largely left to the indigenous legal systems and courts.[132] Reflecting the complexity of colonial rule, issues of jurisdictional control, and methods of maintaining social order, the VOC did allow indigenous communities in Batavia to practise their own local customs, as long as they did not interfere with the VOC's commercial interests. As a consequence of this approach, indigenous leaders were authorised to resolve small legal matters according to indigenous law.[133] More

[128] Ball, *Indonesian Legal History*, p. 36.

[129] Anghie, *Imperialism*, pp. 68–9, 224; Lev, 'Colonial Law', 58–9, 65; see further, e.g., the discussion on VOC requirements of compulsory labour from indigenous populations in Henley, 'Conflict, Justice', 132.

[130] Ball, *Indonesian Legal History*, pp. 50–1.

[131] See, e.g., the discussion in Andrade, 'Pirates, Pelts, and Promises'.

[132] Lev, 'Colonial Law', 58–9, 65; Ball, *Indonesian Legal History*, pp. 50–1; see also the discussion on the role of the VOC as a mediator between warring factions in remote areas of Indonesia in Henley, 'Conflict, Justice'.

[133] Ball, *Indonesian Legal History*, p. 52; Lev, 'Colonial Law', 58–9, 65.

complicated civil and criminal matters, however, went to the Court of Aldermen.[134]

The existence of such variegated legal zones in the VOC's operations corresponds with what Benton terms 'layered sovereignties'.[135] She describes the unevenness and multiplicity of jurisdiction as 'one of the defining characteristics of empire. ... The layers of authority thickened and thinned as one traveled between enclaves and through the territories at their margins.'[136] International law was, of course, one such layer within this milieu of legal spheres. And, despite the repeated assertions as to the substance of particular rules of international law, its authority also waxed and waned amongst and within territories in line with Benton's description of jurisdiction in empire. What is evident is that although imperial legal positions were often presented in terms of absolutes, the reality was rather one of grey areas. These were rarely spaces of lawlessness, even if framed as such in colonial accounts, but, rather, were more often contested areas of shifting authority. For this reason, assertions of jurisdiction were not solely about the interaction between colonised and coloniser, but were also designed to send implicit messages of possession to other rival European states.[137]

From 1630 onwards, the VOC experienced a period of extraordinary growth and profit and, via its multilateral operations throughout Asia, became what the twenty-first century would have recognised as a global corporation. No longer simply an import business with one-way traffic from Asia to Europe, the VOC had built up a vast network of inter-Asian trade.[138] This structural shift in its trading policy was a revolutionary concept. It was a modern way of doing business and distinguished the VOC significantly from the English East India Company.[139] While the seat of control of the VOC ultimately remained with the *Heren XVII* in Amsterdam, Batavia was the hub of this Asian business.[140] In many ways, it was run as if it were independent from the Company's European head office.[141]

[134] Ball, *Indonesian Legal History*, p. 52. [135] Benton, *Search for Sovereignty*, p. 30.

[136] Ibid., pp. 31–2. [137] Ibid., pp. 55–9.

[138] De Vries and van der Woude, *First Modern Economy*, pp. 389–96; Schnurmann, 'Profit Leads Us', 484–5; Prakash, *Commercial Enterprise*, pp. 89–92; Blussé, 'No Boat to China', 62–6, 68, 75; de Bruyn Kops, 'Unpromising Beginning', 537; Gaastra, 'Competition', pp. 189–90.

[139] De Vries and van der Woude, *First Modern Economy*, pp. 389–96; Steensgaard, 'Dutch East India', 238; Gaastra, 'Competition', 189.

[140] Steensgaard, 'Dutch East India'.

[141] De Vries and van der Woude, *First Modern Economy*, pp. 389–92.

Towards the end of the eighteenth century, however, this vast conglomerate was in decline.[142] A variety of reasons have been cited for the demise of the VOC – problems with its inter-Asian trade, corruption and mismanagement, the high mortality rate of its personnel, the high cost of maintaining military operations, the expense of managing settlements, increasing competition, the high dividends the Company continued to declare even as profits were shrinking, and the Anglo-Dutch Wars.[143] The close relationship between the VOC and the Dutch government saw the state pour immense sums of money into the Company to prop it up.[144] However, even these state funds did not ultimately help the Company and in 1795 its assets were seized by the newly formed Dutch state, the Batavian Republic.[145]

2. Implications for International Investment Law

Inarguably, the VOC was a fusion of sovereign power and commercial entity. Although its *raison d'être* was the generation of profit, the Company was imbued with a variety of governmental powers and carried out militaristic functions more usually associated with state bodies.[146] The alignment of Company interests with those of the Dutch state was explicit and extensive, and their activities were deeply entwined. This relationship shaped the character of the VOC's trade and investment activities.[147] It also shaped the law. In the midst of the overlapping, contested, and, at times, tenuous nature of legal spaces within the imperial context, the VOC and the Dutch state used international legal doctrine and jurisdictional control over their trading posts and settlements to cement their conceptualisation of international commercial rights, international property rights, and territorial rights.[148] This type of

142 Ibid., pp. 454–5; Blussé, 'No Boat to China', 75–6; Adams, 'Principals and Agents'.

143 Schnurmann, 'Profit Leads Us', 485–6; De Vries and van der Woude, *First Modern Economy*, pp. 449–55; Adams, 'Principals and Agents'; Prakash, *Commercial Enterprise*, pp. 268–9, 273; Ormrod, *Commercial Empires*, p. 197.

144 De Vries and van der Woude, *First Modern Economy*, p. 456. The government provided the Company with over 100 million guilders between 1784 and 1795.

145 Ibid., The Republic of the Seven United Netherlands was proclaimed in 1581 and collapsed in 1795, at which point the Batavian Republic was formed.

146 Steensgaard, 'Dutch East India Company', 237, 244–6, 251; Blussé, 'No Boat to China', 61; Ruangsilp, 'Dutch Perceptions', 7; Ormrod, *Commercial Empires*, p. 203; Vos, *Gentle Janus*, p. 1.

147 Schnurmann, 'Profit Leads Us', 476–80; Steensgaard, 'Dutch East India Company', 237, 244–6, 251.

148 Sornarajah, *Foreign Investment*, p. 38; Anghie, *Imperialism*, p. 224.

alignment of state interests with those of private investors at the inception of international rules on foreign investment protection moving into the nineteenth century established a close association between state and investor within the very nature of the law. Inevitably, such conditions contributed to the creation of 'otherness' within the international investment law that emerged, manifesting most visibly in the exclusion of the host state from the protection of its principles.

This close association also set the tone for a predisposition towards cooperation between state and investor in the twentieth and twenty-first centuries. For this reason, the historical linkages raise questions about the apparent neutrality of modern international investment law and the extent of any current influence of business interests in the development of its principles. Has that early 'otherness' remained? Is there any modern-day alignment of the interests of the state with those of its foreign investors, and, if so, does it influence international investment law and foreign investment practices? Is this at the expense of the public interest?[149] Does this relationship undermine democracy?[150] Is the imperialism of early investment law reproducing itself today?[151] But these are questions to be explored in later chapters. For now, a further set of formative relationships and interactions in the evolution of international investment law also needs to be excavated.

C. *Imperialism, investment, and the environment*

In this section of the book, I consider the relationship of early traders, investors, and colonisers with the environment of host states and explore the idea that this historical mode of interaction has shaped both the modern relationship between foreign investors and the environment and the narrow conceptualisation of the environment reflected in modern international investment law – essentially, that of a commodity for exploitation.

The ecological conditions within host states and colonised territories were obviously very different as between the many settlements and trading posts across non-European nations.[152] As such, individual interactive experiences of those environments varied, were to a certain extent driven by location-specific factors, and also often involved

[149] Cutler, Haufler, and Porter, *Private Authority*, pp. 333, 369–70; see generally for a discussion on the replacement of the power of states by the power of world markets and private commercial interests, Strange, *Retreat of the State*.

[150] Cutler, Haufler, and Porter, *Private Authority*.

[151] Anghie, 'Heart of My Home', 505–6.

[152] Flannery, 'Fate of Empire', p. 46.

different forms of imperialist control.[153] However, these diverse colonial encounters with the environment shared the common element that they were experienced by the traders, investors, and settlers through the lenses of their own European culture and their own imaginings of the 'non-European environment'.[154] Therefore, although the Europeans involved adapted to the local context, their fundamental understanding of the land and its inhabitants was coloured by Western expansionism.[155] It was also profoundly influenced by what Price terms 'colonial knowledge systems', being the cultural legitimising of the roles of 'coloniser' and 'colonised' within the narrative of empire.[156] This, again, was a condition constructed out of the colonial encounter itself, evolving through the interaction between the settlers, traders, investors, and administrators and their experiences within indigenous cultures, and it was used to justify methods of control adopted by colonial administrations.[157] It was that European expansionist vision that shaped imperial natural resource extraction, environmental management practices, governance approaches, legal regimes, and the displacement of indigenous communities from their land.[158] The effects of this imperial era have proven pervasive and can still be seen in, amongst other manifestations, the land management regulations of postcolonial societies.[159]

European expansionism from the seventeenth to the nineteenth centuries sought to use the land of non-European territories and extract their raw materials, in a process described by Williams as 'commodifying nature', for the benefit of Europe.[160] In engaging with the environment of non-European nations, colonial administrators, trading companies, and foreign investors had a targeted focus – the efficient exploitation of natural resources for European purposes, the subjugation of nature to enable commercial enterprise, and the management of

[153] MacKenzie, 'Ecological Apocalypse', 222; Lowenthal, 'Empires and Ecologies', 229.
[154] Richardson, Mgbeoji, and Botchway, 'Environmental Law', 415–16; Dunlap, 'Ecology', 76.
[155] Dunlap, 'Ecology', 76. [156] Price, *Making Empire*, pp. 154–6. [157] Ibid.
[158] Gathii, 'Imperialism, Colonialism'; Kameri-Mbote and Cullet, 'Environmental Management'.
[159] Kameri-Mbote and Cullet, 'Management in Africa'; Richardson, Mgbeoji, and Botchway, 'Environmental Law', 415–21; see also the discussion in Richardson, Imai, and McNeil, 'Indigenous Peoples', 3, 4–5.
[160] Williams, 'World-System Integration', 101, 109.

supply lines of raw materials to Europe.[161] Lowenthal encapsulates the general imperial approach to the environment and local communities in which European business operations were established:

> Local livelihood and ecology, indigenous or settler, were of no moment in themselves; all that mattered was producing as much as possible as cheaply as possible for the home market.[162]

There were exceptions to the prevailing viewpoint. A number of individuals, including governmental officials, who were appalled at the activities in the settlements and trading posts, spoke out against the treatment of indigenous communities and the environmental degradation resulting from imperial control.[163] These expressions of dissent within colonial administrations tended to be quashed, and, in at least one high-profile case, resulted in the dismissal of a critic from his official position.[164] Such observations did, however, spark scientific investigation into the connections between colonial activities and ecological change, and ultimately led to conservationist lines of thinking.[165]

Although the environmental impacts of this period of Western commercial and political expansionism were by no means homogenous, they were, in aggregate, immense.[166] Extensive deforestation, salinisation, and the loss of biodiversity, together with indigenous alienation from land and the destruction of traditional resource use patterns of the local communities, tended to accompany European commercial enterprise in non-European territories.[167] Vast resources

[161] Anghie, 'Heart of My Home', 472–3; Richardson, Mgbeoji, and Botchway, 'Environmental Law', 415–16; Kameri-Mbote and Cullet, 'Management in Africa', 23, 25–7; Lowenthal, 'Empires and Ecologies', 230, 232–3; Murali, 'Whose Trees?', 86, 96–104, 121–2.

[162] Lowenthal, 'Empires and Ecologies', 230.

[163] See, e.g., Multatuli, *Max Havelaar* (1860) discussed in Beekman, *Troubled Pleasures*; for further examples see also Beinart and Hughes, *Environment and Empire*, pp. 120–1; Murali, 'Whose Trees?', 100; Grove, 'Scotland in South Africa', 139.

[164] Grove, 'Scotland in South Africa', 140. Reverend John Croumbie Brown was engaged by the Cape Colony government in 1862. He became a strident critic of the ecological impacts of the colonial regime, but was ultimately removed from his position in 1866 because of his outspoken views. See also Beinart and Hughes, *Environment and Empire*, pp. 120–1; Murali, 'Whose Trees?', 100.

[165] Grove, 'Conserving Eden', 320.

[166] Lowenthal, 'Empires and Ecologies', 232; Grove, 'Conserving Eden', 320; Williams, 'Ecology, Imperialism', 170, 176–7.

[167] Williams, 'Deforestation', 170, 175–8, 181; Kameri-Mbote and Cullet, 'Management in Africa'; Lowenthal, 'Empires and Ecologies', 232.

were used and ecologies dramatically altered in the construction of railways, the establishment of large-scale, cash-crop plantations, the founding of factories, the process of mining, and, significantly, in the transfer to systems of individual land ownership.[168] As the ecological impacts of colonial operations began to damage supply lines and resources came under pressure, authorities responded with a number of mechanisms, some of the most invasive being imperial forestry management and the conservationist policies of setting aside land as national parks.[169]

Conservationism embodies a complex range of approaches to the environment. Grove argues that characterisations of colonial forestry regulation as a form of 'resource exploitation and land seizures by the state ... overlook the remarkably innovative nature of early colonial conservationism.'[170] There were undoubtedly revolutionary techniques employed in imperial forestry management, and significant preservation projects initiated,[171] but Grove seems to downplay the cost to others for the knowledge gained by the colonial authorities.[172] Observing the environmental degradation that followed imperial activity resulted in a more sophisticated European understanding of ecological processes.[173] Conservationism and imperial forestry instigated new colonial resource management techniques.[174] The origins of environmentalism are linked in with the forestry use systems devised under colonial control.[175] But these elements do not negate the fact that the primary objective of the system was to ensure continued resource exploitation for Europe.[176]

[168] Williams, 'Deforestation', 175–8; Kameri-Mbote and Cullet, 'Management in Africa'; see also Anghie, 'Heart of My Home', 483–7 for a discussion on the impacts of phosphate mining on Nauru from 1900 by the British Pacific Phosphate Company, and the British, Australian, and New Zealand authorities.

[169] Beinart and Hughes, *Environment and Empire*, pp. 269–71; Williams, 'Deforestation', 178; Kameri-Mbote and Cullet, 'Management in Africa'.

[170] Grove, 'Conserving Eden', 321. [171] See also Barton, *Empire Forestry*, p. 164.

[172] See, e.g., Grove 'Conserving Eden', 325, where he states: 'Thus on the earliest European island colonies the destructive effects of capital-intensive economic activity first became fully apparent and elicited an environmental critique.'

[173] Grove, 'Conserving Eden', 320; Grove, *Green Imperialism: Colonial Expansion*, pp. 2–3, 7.

[174] Ibid., p. 321; ibid., p. 7.

[175] Barton, *Empire Forestry*, pp. 164–6; Grove, 'Conserving Eden', 320; Grove, '*Green Imperialism*', pp. 2–3.

[176] Williams, 'World-System Integration', 109; Williams, 'Deforestation', 178; Lowenthal, 'Empires and Ecologies', 230, 232; Richardson, Mgbeoji, and Botchway, 'Environmental Law', 415–16.

Conservationism in the nineteenth century can certainly be regarded as an imposed Western perspective on land management.[177] It brought more sophisticated management practices to colonial resource use systems. However, the ideology did not, on the whole, engage with indigenous perspectives on sustainability and it perpetuated indigenous displacement from the communal land holdings that had been central to their resource management systems.[178] In fact, colonial land use regimes were very much political control mechanisms as well as revenue-raising tools effected through the imposition of taxes and fines.[179] They set in motion inappropriate regulatory patterns that continued into the postcolonial setting.[180] They have irrevocably broken local communities.[181] The experiences and observations of scientists accompanying the traders and settlers may well have generated the emergence of ecological ideas in Europe and injected new perspectives into Western conceptualisations of nature.[182] It seems a high price, however, for the non-European world to have to pay for European environmental enlightenment – particularly so, when it is recalled that the prevailing view of imperial commercial operators remained stolidly one of exploitation of the resources of non-European nations.[183]

It would also appear that this commercial culture in the imperial era, which viewed the natural resources of colonised nations or the host state as commodities for the use of Western interests, shaped the core relationship between the international investor and the environment of the host state. It was an instrumentalist view of the environment, conceptualising it as an object to be controlled and used by the foreign entity. Unsurprisingly, perhaps, this form of engagement with the environment was also reflected in the investment protection rules that developed at the time. Conceptually, the law did not take account of the complexities of the environment as a dynamic, multi-layered

177 Kameri-Mbote and Cullet, 'Management in Africa', 24.

178 Ibid., 26–9; Beinart and Hughes, *Environment and Empire*, pp. 269–71; Murali, 'Whose Trees?'; Williams, 'Deforestation', 178.

179 Beinart and Hughes, *Environment and Empire*, pp. 119–21, 269–71; Williams, 'World-System Integration', 178; Murali, 'Whose Trees?'.

180 Richardson, Mgbeoji, and Botchway, 'Environmental Law', 415–21; Kameri-Mbote and Cullet, 'Management in Africa'.

181 Kameri-Mbote and Cullet, 'Management in Africa'.

182 Grove, 'Conserving Eden', 321–2; Grove, *Green Imperialism*, pp. 2–3, 7.

183 Lowenthal, 'Empires and Ecologies', 230, 232.

system with local and global dimensions and multiple stakeholders. Of course, the environment constitutes, to use Beinart and Hughes' words, a series of 'contested social spaces'.[184] It is not a neutral entity. But, rather, one over which power relations and uneven legal spaces are constructed. It would seem that foreign investors created a dominant position for themselves in that contest in the nineteenth century. What of the substance, then, of those nineteenth-century rules?

II. The law of diplomatic protection of alien property in the nineteenth and early twentieth centuries

A. State responsibility for the treatment of aliens: expropriation

Foreign investment protection law in the nineteenth century developed within a branch of international law known as the diplomatic protection of aliens.[185] It established an international minimum standard for the treatment of foreigners, including foreign companies, and addressed the protection of their person and property while abroad.[186] A breach of those rules entailed international state responsibility and enlivened a right of intervention by the home state.[187]

The locating of foreign investment protection within this doctrine necessarily linked the activities of state and investor within the very nature and operation of the law. The doctrine was premised on the theory that an injury done to a foreigner was an injury to their state, and, as such, enabled the home state to take action on their nationals' behalf.[188] The response elicited from the home state varied, as the options open to an injured state ranged from diplomatic protest to military intervention.[189] However, the ultimate method of enforcement chosen by a government depended on the political and economic

[184] Beinart and Hughes, *Environment and Empire*, p. 119.

[185] Brownlie, *Principles*, p. 522.

[186] Dawson and Head, *International Law*, p. 10; Sornarajah, *Foreign Investment*, p. 18; Borchard, *Diplomatic Protection*, pp. 25–9, 39–42; Amerasinghe, *State Responsibility*, pp. 38, 56; Eagleton, *Responsibility of States*, pp. 3, 6, 22.

[187] Borchard, *Diplomatic Protection*, pp. 25–9, 39; Sornarajah, *Foreign Investment*, p. 18; Amerasinghe, *State Responsibility*, p. 56; Eagleton, *Responsibility of States*, pp. 3, 6, 22.

[188] Sornarajah, *Foreign Investment*, pp. 18, 121. It was a notion articulated in the eighteenth century by E de Vattel, *The Law of Nations*, Book II, ch. VI (1758) (translation) 136: '[w]hoever ill-treats a citizen injures the State, which must protect that citizen.'

[189] Borchard, *Diplomatic Protection*, pp. 439–56; Lipson, *Standing Guard*, p. 53; Dawson and Head, *International Law*, pp. 10–11; Wortley, *Expropriation*, p. 58.

issues involved in the matter.[190] If the home state decided to take no action, the investor was left with no avenue for recovery of any losses.[191]

International law on the treatment of alien property started from the position that on entering and carrying on business in the host state, the alien had submitted to the application of local jurisdiction.[192] This presumption was then tempered by rights held under the principles of diplomatic protection, which included the protection of international minimum standards of treatment for aliens.[193] Uncompensated expropriation of the property of aliens fell within this category and triggered a right of intervention.[194] International law in the nineteenth century allowed the expropriation of alien property only if the following conditions were met:[195]

a) the expropriation was carried out for a public purpose;
b) it was not arbitrary or discriminatory; and
c) prompt, adequate, and effective compensation was paid.[196]

These international rules on investment protection were heavily weighted towards the interests of the investor and capital-exporting states. There was no scope to take into account the social, economic, or developmental needs of the host state, or to consider the capacity of the state to pay the full amount of compensation. Investor conduct was not relevant. And as a breach of the international minimum standard enlivened a right of intervention, this rule was used, at times, as a premise for political interference within the host state.[197] With the

[190] Lipson, *Standing Guard*, p. 53; Borchard, *Diplomatic Protection*, pp. 439–56; Wortley, *Expropriation*, p. 58; Dawson and Head, *International Law*, pp. 10–11; Sands, *Lawless World*, pp. 123–4.

[191] Sands, *Lawless World*, p. 124.

[192] Brownlie, *Principles*, p. 524; Borchard, *Diplomatic Protection*, p. 28.

[193] Borchard, *Diplomatic Protection*, pp. 25–7, 39; Dawson and Head, *International Law*, p. 10; Amerasinghe, *State Responsibility*, pp. 38, 56; Sornarajah, *Foreign Investment*, p. 120–1; Oppenheim, *International Law*, p. 374.

[194] Wortley, *Expropriation*, pp. 33–5; Foighel, *Nationalization*, p. 76.

[195] Borchard, *Diplomatic Protection*, pp. 439–56; Wortley, *Expropriation*, pp. 33–5; Foighel, *Nationalization*, p. 76; Malanczuk, *Akehurst's*; Lipson, *Standing Guard*, p. 53; Cheng, *Principles of Law*, pp. 47–9;Kunz, 'Mexican Expropriations', 31.

[196] Although the phrase 'prompt, adequate and effective' was coined in 1940 by United States Secretary of State Hull in diplomatic correspondence with Mexico, and became known as the 'Hull Formula', its essence had been practised by capital-exporting states since the nineteenth century: see Note of Secretary Hull, in Hackworth, p. 662; Lipson, *Standing Guard*, pp. 37–8, 80; Kronfol, *Protection*, p. 28.

[197] Sornarajah, *Foreign Investment*, pp. 36–9, 120–3; Schrijver, *Sovereignty*, pp. 177–8.

enmeshing of state and investor interests in the principles of diplomatic protection, capital-exporting states were able to exert control over the investment protection process and ensure their wider commercial and political objectives were also met. This level of control over the shape of the law was not, however, universally accepted. Although the application of an international minimum standard was strongly asserted, and enforced, by capital-exporting states, it was not uncontested.[198]

1. National treatment vs international minimum standard

An attempt by host states to ameliorate the unbalanced nature of international property rules manifested in the assertion of the national treatment standard. Advocates of this rule argued that it was an infringement of territorial sovereignty to cloak an alien with rights and privileges that placed them in a better position than citizens of the host state.[199] In other words, aliens should be afforded no more than equal treatment with local citizens. Those promoting the international minimum standard argued that national treatment did not provide sufficient protection for foreign investors and that international legal obligations were not to be determined by reference to the domestic laws of individual states.[200] It was considered an inadequate response to allegations of violations of the international minimum standard to argue that the host state treats its own citizens in like fashion.[201] The dominant nineteenth-century view favoured the international minimum standard, as Borchard explained:

> The establishment of the limit of rights which the state must grant the alien is the result of the operation of custom and treaty, and is supported by

[198] Brownlie, *Principles*, pp. 524–6; Schrijver, *Sovereignty*, pp. 177–8; Vandevelde, 'International Investment Agreements', 159–60.

[199] Brownlie, *Principles*, pp. 524–6.

[200] See, e.g., Secretary of State Baynard to Mr Connery, 1 November 1887, *Compilation of Reports of Committee on Foreign Relations, U.S. Senate*, 1887, 751, 753, reproduced in Fachiri, 'Expropriation', 163:

> If a Government could set up its own municipal laws as the final test of its international rights and obligations, then the rules of international law would be but the shadow of a name, and would afford no protection either to states or to individuals. It has been constantly maintained and also admitted by the Government of the United States that a Government cannot appeal to its municipal regulations as an answer to demands for the fulfilment of international duties.

[201] Borchard, *Diplomatic Protection*, pp. 37–9; Brownlie, *Principles*, pp. 527–9; Oppenheim, *International Law*, pp. 495–6.

the right of protection of the alien's national state. This limit has been fixed along certain broad lines by treaties and international practice. It has secured to the alien a certain minimum of rights necessary to the enjoyment of life, liberty and property, and has so controlled the arbitrary action of the state. ....

International law is concerned not with the specific provisions of the municipal legislation of states in the matter of aliens, but with the establishment of a somewhat indefinite standard of treatment which the state cannot violate without incurring international responsibility. The state's liberty of action, therefore, is limited by the right of other states to be assured that a certain minimum in this respect will not be overstepped. A stipulation in treaties or municipal statutes to the effect that the state is not responsible to aliens to any greater extent to nationals has never prevented international claims where the minimum has been considered as violated, nor can the state's international obligations be avoided or reduced by provisions of municipal law, or by the fact that it violates the rights of its own citizens.[202]

From the 1860s, however, Latin American host states were persistent advocates of the national treatment rule. Registering their dissatisfaction with the imposed international rules protecting alien property and with the abuse of the diplomatic protection system by capital-exporting states, they adopted a position that came to be called the Calvo Doctrine.[203]

(a) Latin American dissent: the Calvo Doctrine

The Calvo Doctrine questioned the legality of the invocation of diplomatic protection and involved two main propositions:

a) The doctrine of state sovereignty precludes states from intervening in the affairs of another, both diplomatically and by force.
b) Aliens should be afforded no more than the same treatment as nationals and must limit themselves to filing claims in the local judicial system.[204]

[202] Borchard, *Diplomatic Protection*, p. 39.

[203] Schrijver, *Sovereignty*, pp. 177–8; Lipson, *Standing Guard*, pp. 76–7; Sornarajah, *Foreign Investment*, pp. 36–7, 120–3; Shea, *Calvo Clause*, pp. 5, 12–13. One of the most prominent advocates of this position was the Argentinean lawyer and legal scholar, Carlos Calvo, after whom the doctrine is named. He completed a six-volume treatise, *Le Droit International Théorique et Pratique*, first published in 1868, and then, five editions later, in its final form in 1896.

[204] Dawson and Head, *International Law*, p. 15; Shea, *Calvo Clause*, p. 19; Schrijver, *Sovereignty*, p. 178; Shan, 'Revival', 632.

In essence, the goal of the Calvo Doctrine was to eradicate the ever-present threat of foreign state intervention triggered by investor, trader, or settler disputes.[205] Manifesting in the insertion of provisions in treaties, national constitutions, municipal legislation, and private contracts with foreigners, this was an attempt by host states to shape international legal doctrine so as to protect their interests. It was not successful.[206] As the propositions did not find favour with the international legal community in Europe and the United States, the Latin American attempt to propel the Calvo Doctrine into an accepted rule of international law was dismissed.[207] The legitimising authority of international legal status was withheld by capital-exporting states from a rule that did not serve their commercial or political interests.

The Calvo Doctrine did, however, carry some impact through the adoption of the 'Calvo Clause'. This was a provision in a contract under which foreigners agreed to waive their rights to claim diplomatic protection and to restrict themselves to the local judicial system should a dispute arise.[208] This had the obvious difficulty in that it was not the individual's right to waive; the state itself is injured if its citizen is harmed while abroad and it possesses the right of redress.[209] Britain and the United States took the view that a Calvo Clause did not in any way affect their rights and duties under international law, but that it might be a factor taken into account when considering whether or not to intervene on behalf of their national.[210] Needless to say, despite support from capital-importing states beyond Latin America, the Calvo Doctrine did

[205] Shea, *Calvo Clause*, p. 30; see also Inter-American Bar Association, 'Third Conference', 57–8.

[206] Shea, *Calvo Clause*, pp. 21–7.

[207] Ibid., p. 20; see also the commentary in Borchard, 'Minimum Standard'; see, e.g., the following resolution of the Institute of International Law which typified the general response to the Calvo Doctrine:

> The Institute of International Law recommends that states should refrain from inserting in treaties clauses of reciprocal irresponsibility. It thinks that such clauses are wrong in excusing states from the performance of their duty to protect their nationals abroad and their duty to protect foreigners within their own territory.

Moore, *International Law*, vol. VI, pp. 323–4.

[208] Shea, *Calvo Clause*; Schrijver, *Sovereignty*, pp. 178–9; Dawson and Head, *International Law*, p. 18; Vicuña, 'Carlos Calvo', 20; see also for a discussion on the application of the Calvo Clause, Feller, 'Observations'.

[209] Shea, *Calvo Clause*, p. 45; Borchard, *Diplomatic Protection*, p. 799; Schrijver, *Sovereignty*, p. 179; see also the discussion in Hornsey, 'Foreign Investment', 558–9.

[210] Borchard, *Diplomatic Protection*, pp. 796–7; Shea, *Calvo Clause*, pp. 44–5, 49–50.

not make a serious impact on the prevailing system of international law.[211] Decades later, however, similar sentiments were again asserted in the League of Nations,[212] and later still in the United Nations.[213]

2. Expropriation in the nineteenth century

How did these international rules on expropriation operate in practice? What did the nineteenth-century investor and capital-exporting state consider to be 'expropriation'? The political conditions at the time ensured that large-scale expropriation was an infrequent event.[214] Minor skirmishes and isolated incidents of seizure of property, however, were more common.[215] By the mid-nineteenth century, capital-exporting states were regularly asserting the existence of legal rights under international law as a basis for compensation claims arising out of such altercations.[216] Fischer Williams pointed out that these assertions of principles in diplomatic correspondence and in the course of proceedings did not in themselves constitute authority for the existence of the legal rules.[217] Such statements from capital-exporting states, and the military action taken by them, do, however, provide evidence of their views on the law and the lengths to which they would go to enforce those views.[218] Significantly for the arguments put forward in this book, it was this process of assertion and enforcement that, in fact, also constituted an important part of the very creation of the international rules on foreign investment protection.

The nineteenth-century response to an interference with foreign-owned property varied. Tortious acts endangering person or property were differentiated from breach of contract claims, which were often in

[211] Shan, *Calvo Clause*, p. 632; for an example of hostile responses to capital-importing states' attempts to reshape the law on investment through the promotion of the Calvo Doctrine, describing their proposal as 'so sinister and so deplorable', see Freeman, 'Recent Aspects', 125.

[212] League of Nations, Committee of Experts, 182.

[213] Schrijver, *Sovereignty*, p. 180; see, e.g., Declaration on Permanent Sovereignty Over Natural Resources, GA Res 1803 (XVII), 17 GAOR, Supp. 17, UN Doc. A/5217, 15 (1962); Charter of Economic Rights and Duties of States, GA Res 3281 (XXIX), UN Doc. A/RES/3281 (XXIX) (1974); Declaration on the Establishment of a New International Economic Order, GA Res 3201 (S-VI), UN Doc. A/Res/S-6/3201 (1974). These instruments are discussed in detail in Chapter 3.

[214] Foighel, *Nationalization*, p. 64; Lipson, *Standing Guard*, pp. 31, 81; Platt, *Finance*, p. 70.

[215] Lipson, *Standing Guard*, pp. 31, 81; Platt, *Finance*, p. 70; Weston, 'Deprivation of Foreign Wealth', 1080–1.

[216] Dawson and Head, *International Law*, pp. 9–10.

[217] Williams, 'International Law', 6. [218] Ibid.

turn treated differently from foreign bond default claims.[219] Furthermore, the response of the home state not only depended on the circumstances of the alleged expropriation, but also on the identity of the investor's state.[220] The United States and Britain tended to be more hesitant when the expropriation involved a breach of contract or unpaid bonds, usually waiting until the investor had exhausted local remedies or until they could point to a 'denial of justice' by the host state as a basis for intervention.[221]

This policy of non-intervention for contract disputes was not universal. Borchard suggests that other capital-exporting states, such as Germany, France and Italy, were less reticent in defending their nationals' contract claims and were not so ready to make exclusionary distinctions between types of expropriatory acts.[222] A very different view was also taken by the United States and Britain when the contract claim constituted an 'arbitrary act or confiscatory breach of contract'. Such circumstances took the claim out of the ordinary realm of breach of contract case and generated a right of intervention on the part of the home state.[223] This policy was not only applied to the annulment of concessions, but was also extended to the devaluing of foreign-owned bonds.[224]

The appropriate response to the non-payment of bonds was problematic. As a class of contract claim, it was the most tenuous on which to base armed intervention.[225] Stated policy of European governments was generally one of non-intervention; however, state practice was not consistent.[226] Borchard sets out the contrasting views – on the one hand, the use of military force to collect debts owed to bondholders was

219 Borchard, *Diplomatic Protection*, pp. 281–2; Dawson and Head, *International Law*, pp. 11–12; Borchard, 'Contractual Claims', 457.

220 Dawson and Head, *International Law*, pp. 11–12; Borchard, *Diplomatic Protection*, pp. 281–2, 284–7.

221 Eagleton, *Responsibility of States*, pp. 178–9; Borchard, *Diplomatic Protection*, pp. 284–7. An exception to the exhaustion of local remedies rule exists when the home state considers it so unlikely that the investor would receive any justice through the local court system that the requirement is waived.

222 Borchard, *Diplomatic Protection*, pp. 286–7.

223 Ibid., p. 291; see also the discussion regarding the differences between bondholders' claims, breach of contract claims, claims involving expropriation of concessions in Borchard, *Diplomatic Protection*.

224 Neufeld, *Protection of Private Creditors*, pp. 107, 109; Borchard, *Diplomatic Protection*, pp. 293, 295.

225 Borchard, *Diplomatic Protection*, p. 282.

226 Ibid., p. 313; Borchard, *Diplomatic Protection*; Fishlow, 'Lessons from the Past', 398; Waibel, *Sovereign Defaults*, pp. 22–5.

considered to be unwarranted; on the other, it could be considered a legitimate course of action if bad faith on the part of the defaulting state was involved.[227] Borchard notes that while Britain had always professed a policy of non-intervention with respect to the interests of bondholders, it had also always reserved its right to intervene should it wish to do so.[228] He does comment, however, that the decision whether or not to use force tended to be one based on 'power and politics rather than a rule of law'.[229]

Under the direction of Lord Salisbury in the 1880s and 1890s, the approach of the British Foreign Office appeared to soften and to cultivate an atmosphere more receptive to bondholder claims.[230] Lord Salisbury commented that he did not:

> quite understand the principle of absolute abstinence from interference in such cases. We always interfered when a foreign Government committed a wrong towards a single British subject; why should we not interfere when that wrong was done to hundreds?[231]

Despite this partial shift in attitude, bondholders were officially viewed in a different light, seen as private speculators taking high risks in the hope of substantial profits without advancing Britain's national interest.[232] Generally, some additional act amounting to a denial of justice was required before the government would intervene on their behalf.[233] The implementation of the policy, however, was a great deal murkier than the clear-cut official position might indicate.[234] 'Good offices' from British Consulates within host states were often

227 Borchard, *Diplomatic Protection*, pp. 312–13.

228 Ibid., pp. 314–15; Eagleton, *Responsibility of States*, pp. 178–9; see also the discussion in Mathew, 'Imperialism of Free Trade'; see also the discussion on instances where states did intervene militarily on behalf of bondholders in Suter and Stamm, 'Global Debt Crises', 655–6.

229 Borchard, *Diplomatic Protection*, p. 314; Fishlow, 'Lessons from the Past', 398; Suter and Stamm, 'Global Debt Crises', 655–6; see also the discussion in Strange, 'Debts, Defaulters and Development', 527–8.

230 Platt, *Finance*, pp. 39–41.

231 Annexure to a Foreign Office Minute, 1 October 1878, Public Record Office, London, *Foreign Office Papers* 61/323, reproduced in Platt, *Finance*, p. 39.

232 Platt, *Finance*, p. 41.

233 Ibid., pp. 39–40.

234 Ibid., pp. 41–4; Fishlow, 'Lessons from the Past', 398; Borchard, *Diplomatic Protection*; Eichengreen, 'Historical Research', 163–4. The lack of an official policy of assistance led to the establishment in Britain in 1868 of the Council of the Corporation of Foreign Bondholders to negotiate with debtor states on behalf of bondholders as a form of 'self-help'. For a discussion on the Council of the Corporation of Foreign Bondholders, see also Strange, 'Defaulters', 527.

made available to bondholders and in practice the lines between unofficial assistance and official diplomatic intervention could become blurred.[235] Furthermore, there were a limited number of additional circumstances in which the Foreign Office was prepared to intervene, both diplomatically and militarily, namely when physical assets assigned to bondholders as securities came under threat, or when the rights of convention bondholders were infringed.[236]

Generally, capital-exporting states adopted practices on intervention that suited their political and commercial interests, tailored to the individual circumstances of particular incidents – and international law on expropriation in the nineteenth century legitimised these practices. Indeed, it proved to be a particularly useful tool in entrenching the perspectives of capital-exporting states as law and in providing a mechanism through which to enforce that viewpoint. Disputes from the pre-World War I era, and the diplomatic correspondence they generated, demonstrate the way in which the international rules on foreign investment protection were utilised to this effect.

B. *Pre-World War I disputes*

Property disputes within colonial territories tended to be dealt with by the colonial authorities and their court systems.[237] This continuous form of legal engagement was an ongoing process of asserting, creating, and reinforcing the dominance of imperial state law and its conceptualisation of property rights.[238] This also means, however, that nineteenth-century case law on international expropriation is largely located outside the formal colonial context.[239] As such, significant expropriation cases arose out of the relationship of informal imperialism between Latin American states and the United States and Europe.[240]

235 Borchard, *Diplomatic Protection*, pp. 463–4; Platt, *Finance*, pp. 41–4.

236 Platt, *Finance*, pp. 47, 52. The Foreign Office made a distinction between convention bondholders and ordinary bondholders. Convention bondholders were those who had accepted bonds as part of a settlement for other claims under international law and the settlement had been memorialised in a diplomatic convention between states. Britain considered that a breach of such an agreement gave rise to a right of intervention on behalf of the bondholders.

237 Sornarajah, *Foreign Investment*, pp. 19–20; see also the discussion in Benton, *Colonial Cultures*, pp. 134, 161–6 on the authority of English East India Company officials to preside over revenue and property disputes in India and on the role of imperial law in redefining property in India and French West Africa; see also the discussion in Weaver, 'The Construction of Property Rights', 221.

238 Benton, *Colonial Cultures*, pp. 161–6; see also Weaver, 'Property Rights', 221.

239 Sornarajah, *Foreign Investment*, pp. 19–20. 240 Ibid., pp. 20–1.

Several inter-European disputes in this period are also useful in demonstrating the way in which the principles were framed. The following discussion illustrates the application of the law, the use of armed enforcement, and the way in which assertions of international legal doctrine were used by capital-exporting states to create principles in this formative period of international investment law.

1. *The United States and Paraguay Navigation Company Claim*[241]

This case involved the alleged confiscation by Paraguayan authorities in 1854 of land, factories, machinery, and steamboats belonging to a United States' company, the United States and Paraguay Navigation Company.[242] The claim for $1,000,000 in compensation also included damages for losses resulting from the sale of bonds, the revocation of patents, the loss of profits, and the loss of the value of its initial capital expenditure in 'intelligence, investigation, time, enterprise, risk, and anxiety'.[243]

Edward Hopkins was both the company agent in Paraguay and the United States Consul to Paraguay, and he was responsible for establishing the planned agricultural and manufacturing operations of the company.[244] Substantial assistance was extended to the company by the Paraguayan government through the selection of appropriate sites for the operations, the organisation of labourers, the provision of government barracks for the company's use, and the grant of a loan of $10,000.[245]

A series of incidents involving Hopkins led to a deterioration in his relationship with the President of Paraguay and generated a great deal of ill-will amongst the local residents of Asunción.[246] Formal complaints were made to the United States about Hopkins' conduct.[247] Ultimately, a dispute arose over the land occupied by the company, property was repossessed pursuant to the mortgage granted as security for the loan, and a failure to comply with licensing regulations resulted in the closure of the company's cigar factory and saw mill.[248] Hopkins left Paraguay, alleging that he had been expelled and that the business

[241] Moore, *Digest*, vol. II, p. 1485. [242] Ibid., p. 1508; Whiteman, *Damages*, p. 1405.
[243] Moore, *Digest*, pp. 1498–9. [244] Ibid., p. 1486; Whiteman, *Damages*, p. 1406.
[245] Moore, *Digest*, pp. 1486, 1503.
[246] Ibid., pp. 1486–7; Ynsfran, 'Sam Ward's Bargain', 317–19; Peterson, 'Pioneer Promoter', 257.
[247] Moore, *Digest*, p. 1487. [248] Ibid., pp. 1523–7.

operations of the company had been broken up and its property seized.[249]

Hopkins requested the intervention of the United States to recover compensation for the losses suffered by the company.[250] Following unsatisfactory diplomatic exchanges between the United States and Paraguay, Congress authorised the United States' President to 'use such force as in his judgment may be necessary' to obtain 'just satisfaction' from Paraguay for several matters including the Hopkins incident.[251] Accordingly, the United States sent a fully armed naval fleet of nineteen ships along the Parana River to where the Argentinian and Paraguayan territorial waters meet, to 'adjust the differences between the United States and the Republic of Paraguay'.[252] This display of naval force caused considerable alarm throughout South America and great consternation as to the wider intentions of the United States.[253] Shortly after the arrival of the fleet, a treaty was signed by the Paraguayan President agreeing to submit the claim by the United States and Paraguay Navigation Company to a tribunal for settlement. Having effectively forced the capitulation of the Paraguayan government through the use of armed intervention, the special commissioner of the United States also had further instructions that if a damages figure could not be agreed upon, a treaty agreeing to refer that specific question to a commission would suffice, 'it being an indispensable preliminary that the Paraguayan Government should acknowledge its liability to the company.'[254] In other words, the treaty was conditional on the Paraguayan government admitting liability for the losses incurred by the company, an admission that had been secured solely through the unreasonable threat of force.

The international commission established pursuant to that treaty found that the evidence presented did not support any right to damages on the part of the company.[255] No internationally compensable acts had occurred – the property had not been seized, the business had not been

[249] Ibid., p. 1487.

[250] Ibid., p. 1491; Ynsfran, 'Sam Ward's Bargain', 319–20; Peterson, 'Pioneer Promoter', 258.

[251] Moore, *Digest*, p. 1493; see also the report in Ynsfran, 'Sam Ward's Bargain', 320.

[252] Moore, *Digest*, pp. 1490–4. [253] Ynsfan, 'Sam Ward's Bargain', 322.

[254] Moore, *Digest*, p. 1494.

[255] Ibid., p. 1501; the award and reasons for the award are reproduced on pp. 1501, 1502–28; see also the discussion on Ynsfan, 'Sam Ward's Bargain', 330; Flickema, 'Sam Ward's Bargain', 538; see also the criticism of this decision in Clarke, 'Permanent Tribunal', 369–70.

rendered worthless by the actions of the Paraguayan government, and Hopkins had not been expelled from the country.[256] Rather, Hopkins had induced ill-feeling in the local community through his own arrogant conduct and offensive language, the land had been legitimately repossessed as it had been mortgaged for a sum greatly exceeding its worth and the debt remained unpaid, the machinery had been abandoned by Hopkins, the factories could have remained open if Hopkins had submitted a licence application in compliance with state regulations, and Hopkins was not compelled to leave Paraguay by the authorities, but left of his own accord.[257]

The President of the United States considered the commission exceeded its jurisdiction in deciding that the company had no claim. He asserted that the commission had been limited to determining the amount of damages suffered by the company as liability had already been admitted by Paraguay.[258] Again, a 'man-of-war' was dispatched to Paraguay with instructions to secure a settlement of the company's claim by negotiation.[259] The President of Paraguay refused to reopen the claim.[260] The matter languished for a number of years while the United States was embroiled in civil war, before being reignited again by the United States in 1885.[261] This renewed diplomatic activity ultimately resulted in Paraguay signing a protocol in 1887 to pay US $90,000. However, the protocol was not ratified by the Paraguayan upper house. The claim does not appear to have been pursued beyond this point.[262]

This case is particularly interesting for its illustration of the interplay of politics and commercial interests in issues implicating foreign investment. It demonstrates the willingness of capital-exporting states to validate the grievances of their investor nationals and to use armed intervention to force the results desired by the investor. Indeed, it is of particular note that, despite the commission's findings, the United States chose to override that decision and continued to pursue Paraguay for the sums claimed by the company through diplomatic channels and a show of naval force.

256 Moore, *Digest*, pp. 1508, 1514–28.

257 Ibid., pp. 1514–28; see also the discussion in Peterson, 'Paraguay', 257; Flickema, 'A Reappraisal', 52.

258 Whiteman, *Damages*, p. 1407; Moore, *Digest*, pp. 1538–9; see also the critique of the commission's decision on this same basis in Clarke, 'Permanent Tribunal', 369–70.

259 Moore, *Digest*, p. 1542. 260 Ibid. 261 Ibid., 1542–3.

262 Ibid., 1544–5; see also the discussion in Clarke, 'Permanent Tribunal', 370.

2. *Britain (Finlay)* v. *Greece*[263]

Seizure of land owned by a British citizen, George Finlay, by King Otho of Greece in 1836 gave rise to the following correspondence setting out the British view of the law on the matter:

> Now in all countries it is understood that when land belonging to a private individual is required for purposes of great public utility or of national defence, private right must so far yield to public interest, that the individual is compelled by law to give up his land to the public, provided always that he shall receive for it from the public its full and fair value ...
>
> M. Coletti [the Greek Minister for Foreign Affairs], indeed, has tendered to Mr. Finlay an entirely inadequate compensation, alleging that it is calculated at the same rate as that which has been offered to and accepted by other persons, both Greeks and foreigners, who were deprived of their land at the same time and under the same circumstances as Mr. Finlay. ... and when the question is whether a British subject in a foreign country shall or shall not be compelled to accept an inadequate compensation for an act of injustice by which he has suffered, the British Government can pay no attention to the argument, that compensations equally inadequate have been accepted by natives or by subjects of other States, for similar injuries sustained by them.[264]

The letter makes it clear that in 1846, Britain considered the provision of full compensation for expropriated property to be a well-settled proposition and asserted it as such. It also expressly refuted the applicability of the national treatment standard. Having agreed to arbitration of the dispute, the Greek government maintained that as the legal principles involved were not contested, the only matter for determination was the amount of compensation to be paid.[265] The matter was ultimately resolved in 1850 when the British government accepted the sum of £1,066 17s from the Greek government.[266]

3. *The Delagoa Bay Railroad Arbitration*[267]

This case entailed the cancellation of a concession and the seizure of the Delagoa Bay Railway. It involved the investment of an American citizen

263 (1849–1850) 39 *British and State Papers* 410.

264 Lord Palmerston to British Envoy at Athens, 7 August 1846, 39 *British and Foreign State Papers* 431–2, reproduced in Whiteman, *Damages*, vol. 2, pp. 1386–7; see also the references to the dispute in Miller, 'Finlay Papers', 390.

265 Whiteman, *Damages*, p. 1387. 266 Ibid. 267 Moore, *Digest*, p. 1865.

and a British-registered company within Portuguese-controlled territory in East Africa. Accordingly, as well as illustrating the approach taken by capital-exporting states to a cancellation of a concession, the dispute between the United States and Britain and Portugal also exemplified the complexities of colonial rivalries between Western powers and the way in which they were played out within non-European territories.

In 1883, an American citizen, Colonel MacMurdo, was granted a concession by the Portuguese government for 99 years to construct and operate a railway across East Africa from Portuguese-controlled territory at Lourenço Marques to the Transvaal.[268] MacMurdo's operating rights included the ability to determine the freight rates along the line running down to the port at Lourenço Marques.[269] MacMurdo formed a Portuguese-registered company to carry out the works and later set up a London-registered company, the Delagoa Bay and East African Railway Company, to provide further capital for the project.[270] The railway line was completed to the original prescription although a number of time extensions had been granted by the Portuguese government. A dispute arose, however, over the Portuguese requirement for the construction of a further nine kilometres of railway line within an allegedly impossible timeframe.[271] As a result of MacMurdo's inability to meet this demand, the Portuguese government cancelled the concession and seized all the related business operations and the virtually completed railroad.[272]

The seizure of the railway alarmed the British, for reasons that went well beyond the immediate dispute.[273] Portuguese control of the railway had the potential to threaten Britain's economic interests,

[268] Ibid., pp. 1865–6, 1880; Fachiri, 'Expropriation', 165. [269] Moore, *Digest*, p. 1880.

[270] Ibid., p. 1867.

[271] Ibid., pp. 1868, 1880–1. The issues were complicated and involved a dispute with the Transvaal government over boundary lines and MacMurdo's ability to fix the rates for carriage for freight, as it had been unable to reach an agreement with MacMurdo on appropriate charges. There were also allegations that the Portuguese government had engaged in secret negotiations with Transvaal and had granted a concession to a Dutch company on terms that conflicted with MacMurdo's and had thereby devalued his investment.

[272] Ibid., p. 1868; Fachiri, 'Expropriation', 165; Hammond, 'Economic Imperialism', 589–90.

[273] Henshaw, 'Key to South Africa', 531–5; see also the discussion of the role power politics played in Portugal's seizure of the railway in Weston, 'Deprivation of Foreign Wealth', 1091.

including the restriction of access to crucial trade routes, preference given to Portuguese, French, or German traders, and the flow-on effects for extensive British investments in the gold mines of Africa.[274] As such, the expropriation made headlines in London as well as in the United States.[275] On the cancellation of the concession, the British Consul in Delagoa Bay sought the intervention of the British government, requesting a 'man-of-war' be sent to Delagoa Bay to protect the interests of British nationals.[276] *The New York Times* reported that Germany had also become involved in the dispute and was backing Portugal in an attempt to counteract British influence in East Africa.[277] Further altercations occurred between the Portuguese authorities and British residents, prompting the British government to send additional naval war ships to Delagoa Bay.[278]

The United States and Britain protested on behalf of MacMurdo and the British company. Britain asserted in correspondence with Portugal that:[279]

> The question at issue is not the motive but the justice of the seizure. Her Majesty's Government are of the opinion that the Portuguese Government had no right to cancel the concession, nor to forfeit the line already constructed. ... In their judgment, the British investors have suffered a grievous wrong in consequence of the possible confiscation by the Portuguese Government of the line and the materials belonging to the

274 Ibid., See the discussion in Penner, 'Germany and the Transvaal', 36–8.

275 See, e.g., *The Illustrated London News*, 25 January 1890, 'The Dispute with Portugal: Seizure of the Delagoa Bay Railway by the Portuguese June 26 1889'; *New York Times*, 27 June 1889, 'Portugal Gives Offense: Delagoa Bay Railroad Cancelled. England Much Affronted and Claiming that Germany is Backing the Lisbon Authorities', New York Times Archives, available at http://query.nytimes.com/mem/archive-free/pdf?res=9B07E6DB133AE033A25754C2A9609C94689FD7CF (last accessed 19 November 2011).

276 *New York Times*, 'Dispute with Portugal'; *New York Times*, 1 July 1889, 'Going to Delagoa Bay: British Gunboats Ordered There to Protect British Interests', New York Times Archives, available at http://query.nytimes.com/mem/archive-free/pdf?res=9A0CE0DF143AEF33A25751C0A9619C94689FD7CF (last accessed 19 November 2011).

277 *New York Times*, 'Dispute with Portugal'.

278 *New York Times*, 29 July 1889, 'Disorder at Delagoa Bay', New York Times Archives, available at http://query.nytimes.com/mem/archive-free/pdf?_r=1&res=9803E3DB133AE033A25753C3A9609C94689FD7CF (last accessed 19 November 2011).

279 See Lord Salisbury's correspondence to the Portuguese government, 10 September 1889, (1888–1889) 81 *British and Foreign State Papers* 691, reproduced in Fachiri, 'Expropriation', 165–6.

British Company . . . and for that wrong Her Majesty's Government are bound to ask for compensation from the Government of Portugal. . . . If the Portuguese Government admit their liability to compensate the British Company for an injury to which their interests or property have been subjected by the confiscation of the line and the seizure of the materials upon it, Her Majesty's Government will admit that the amount of that compensation is a proper matter for arbitration.

The United States made the following statement in correspondence with Portugal:[280]

Upon full consideration of the circumstances of the case, this government is forced to the conclusion that the violent seizure of the railway by the Portuguese Government was an act of confiscation which renders it the duty of the Government of the United States to ask that compensation should be made to such citizens of this country as may be involved.

Following diplomatic exchanges with the United States and Britain, Portugal admitted the fact of cancellation of the concession and agreed to refer the question of quantum to arbitration.[281] As a consequence, the issues addressed during the arbitration focused on the appropriate classification of the Portuguese actions, whether the factual circumstances generated a right of rescission of the concession, and the calculation of damages.[282] The tribunal reasoned that:[283]

the effect [of the government's action] was to dispossess private persons from their rights and privileges of a private nature conferred upon them by the concession, and that in the absence of legal provisions to the contrary – none of which has been alleged to exist in this case – the State, which is the author of such dispossession, is bound to make full reparation for injuries done by it.

[280] Moore, *Digest*, p. 1869.

[281] Fachiri, 'Expropriation', 166; Carlston, 'Concession Agreements', 261; Wilson, 'Property Protection', 88; Art. I of the Protocol between Britain, the United States and Portugal, 13 June 1891, reproduced in Moore, *Digest*, 1874, stated:

> The mandate which the three governments have agreed to refer to the arbitration tribunal is, to fix, as it shall deem most just, the amount of the compensation due by the Portuguese Government to the claimants of the other two countries, in consequence of the rescission of the concession of the Lourenço Marques Railroad, and the taking possession of that railroad by the Portuguese Government, and thereby to settle the controversy existing between the three governments on the subject.

[282] Moore, *Digest*, pp. 1878–99; Whiteman, *Damages*, pp. 1697–1703.

[283] Whiteman, *Damages*, p. 1698.

The tribunal awarded the claimants a sum of 15,314,000 francs, or £950,821.13, in damages.[284]

The *Delagoa Bay Railroad Arbitration* exemplifies the process of creation and consolidation of international rules on foreign investment protection through the assertion of rules as settled law. There was no dispute between the states (all traditionally capital-exporting states) as to the existence or content of the rules, only their applicability on the facts. It is also an interesting case for its illustration of the role international politics played in the protection of foreign investors in the nineteenth century. The politically strategic nature of European commercial activity in the area, the resort to naval intervention to protect the interests of investors and traders, and the altercations that surrounded the dispute, all demonstrate the entwined nature of the interests of capital-exporting states with those of their nationals engaged in international commercial enterprise.

4. *Britain* v. *The Kingdom of the Two Sicilies* (*Sicilian Sulphur Monopoly Case*)[285]

This case involved a more subtle form of interference with an investment, one in which the incidental effects of government action were characterised by the investor's state as expropriation. In 1838, the Kingdom of the Two Sicilies negotiated a contract granting exclusive sulphur mining and export rights to a French company.[286] It was clear that the French monopoly would have a major impact on the interests of non-French foreign-owned commercial entities involved in the Sicilian sulphur mining industry and, as such, the British made a formal complaint on behalf of its affected traders and investors.[287]

[284] Ibid., p. 1703; See also the report in the *New York Times*, 21 July 1900, 'Delagoa Bay Award Paid', New York Times Archives, available at http://query.nytimes.com/mem/archive-free/pdf?res=9803E4D9113BEE33A25751C2A9619C946197D6CF (last accessed 19 November 2011). *The New York Times* reported on Portugal's announcement that a sum of 'about $3,500,000' had been deposited with a Parisian bank in payment of the award. In fact, after application of the exchange rate, the sum was closer to $4,500,000: Whiteman, *Damages*, p. 1703.

[285] Correspondence concerning the dispute can be found at (1839–1840) 28 *British & Foreign State Papers* 1163–1242. See also the discussion of this case in Fachiri, 'Expropriation', 163–4; Christie, 'Taking of Property', 320–1.

[286] Fachiri, 'Expropriation', 163. [287] Christie, 'Taking of Property', 320.

Britain considered the Sicilian action to be an appropriation of commercial investments owned by its nationals.[288] Not content with diplomatic protest alone, Britain resorted to the threat of military force, preparing to send its naval ships into the Kingdom's waters to hammer home its position on the issue.[289] Following these events, the French monopoly was suspended, British sulphur-mining operations in Sicily were resumed, and the Kingdom acknowledged its obligation to recompense British owners and lessees of Sicilian sulphur mines for losses suffered as a result of its exclusive contract with the French company.[290] A commission was established to hear the claims and, in addition to the mine-owners and lessees, claims for compensation were also accepted from British nationals who had been unable to fulfil their contracts for the supply of sulphur and those who had bought sulphur and were then unable to export it.[291]

The British complaint was largely, although not solely, based on the monopoly's alleged violation of a treaty between Britain and the Kingdom of the Two Sicilies, to the effect that:

> British commerce in general, and the British subjects who carry that commerce on, shall be treated throughout the dominions of the King of the Two Sicilies upon the same footing as the commerce and subjects of the most favoured nations, not only with respect to the persons and property of such British subjects, but also with regard to every species of article in which they may traffic.[292]

[288] (1839–1840) 28 *British & Foreign State Papers* 1173; see in particular the comments of Mr Temple in correspondence to Prince Cassaro, 8 February 1838:

> . . . the grant of this monopoly must necessarily destroy all confidence in commercial transactions with Sicily, for there can be no security that similar monopolies would not be granted, and who then will invest capital in a country in which he incurs the risk of being arbitrarily and suddenly deprived of the free disposal of his property?

[289] Fachiri, 'Expropriation', 163–4; Christie, 'Taking of Property', 320; see also the discussion in Wortley, *Expropriation*, p. 113.

[290] (1840–1841) 29 *British and Foreign State Papers* 1225–6; see also the discussion in Christie, 320; Fachiri, 'Expropriation', 164; see also the discussion of this case in Herz, 'Expropriation', 257–8.

[291] (1841–1842) 30 *British and Foreign State Papers* 111–120; Fachiri, 'Expropriation', 164; Christie, 'Taking of Property', 320–1.

[292] Viscount Palmerston to Mr Temple, 27 October 1837, (1839–1840) 28 *British and Foreign State Papers* 1165; see also the discussion in Wilson, 'Property Protection', 88.

The *Sicilian Sulphur Monopoly Case* exemplifies the attitude of capital-exporting states towards any encroachment on their nationals' trading and investment activities, the ferocity with which they were prepared to protect them, and state practice of the day in using a range of techniques to enforce international rules on foreign investment protection, including diplomatic protest, military intervention, and arbitral proceedings. Christie argues that this case also demonstrates that in the nineteenth century something less than an outright taking of physical assets could amount to an act of international expropriation.[293] Signing the contract with the French company and creating a monopoly constituted a taking of both the British-owned property used in the industry and their sulphur-mining business as a whole, including the profits due under the stymied British contracts of supply.[294] There are a number of other similar reported instances of alleged expropriation through the creation of monopolies in the nineteenth and early twentieth centuries. And the consistent response of investor states, being diplomatic protest or threatened use of force, indicates that this more indirect form of taking was also considered a breach of host state obligations.[295]

293 Christie, 'Taking of Property', 320–1.

294 Ibid., The Permanent Court of International Justice later dealt with this issue in *The Oscar Chinn* case, (1934) *Permanent Court of International Justice Series A/B*, No. 63, finding that the creation of a *de facto* monopoly did not constitute a taking for which compensation was due.

295 Christie, 'Taking of Property'; Fachiri, 'Expropriation'; see, e.g., the following instances of alleged expropriation via the granting of monopolies:

USA (Savage) v. *Salvador* (1852), Moore, *Digest*, p. 1855. In this case, Salvador set up a gunpowder monopoly to the detriment of a US citizen, Savage, who was awarded damages by an arbitration panel following protests by the USA.

Uruguayan Insurance Monopoly Case (1911), Hackworth, *Digest* Vol. V, p. 588. An insurance monopoly proposed by the Uruguayan government met with protests from Britain and France, which succeeded in bringing about its cancellation.

Italian Life Insurance Monopoly (1911), Fachiri, 'Expropriation', 166–7. Protests were made to Italy by Austria-Hungary, France, Germany, Britain, and the United States of America at the proposed creation of a state monopoly on life insurance, forcing all other business entities in the industry to cease trading. The protests were largely directed to the losses that would be sustained by their nationals on the forced sale of their assets. Italian legislation was altered, allowing foreign investors to continue in business for ten years, during which they were permitted to dispose of their assets for value.

5. *Portuguese Religious Properties Case*[296]

In 1910, the Portuguese government enacted legislation by which it confiscated property held by certain religious entities, without providing any form of compensation to the owners. Formal protests were issued by the Spanish, British, and French governments, and the matter eventually went to arbitration.[297] Submissions from the British maintained that the Portuguese confiscations violated the general 'principles of the law of nations', stating that:

> Respect of property, respect of acquired rights ... are the legal principles of all civilized countries. It is upon the security which they assure and the confidence they inspire that the relations entertained by nations with each other are based. It cannot be objected here that it is ill founded for a foreigner to complain of the measures applied to him when those measures are equally applicable to the nationals of the state on the territory of which he finds himself; the position in the two cases is not the same. Foreigners neither have nor had in Portugal the enjoyment of political rights; they neither have nor had any part in the public affairs of the country. When the nation demands, or lets its Government take, such and such a political measure, it has no right to complain.[298]

As Fachiri noted, the importance of this case lies in the submissions presented by Britain and the Portuguese reply.[299] The Portuguese government accepted the British description of the applicable rules of international law, stating that 'far from contesting the legal principles upon which the three Governments base these arguments, they approve them without reserve, respectful of law and equity.'[300] The Portuguese, in fact, based their defence on the assertion that the property was not owned by the individual nationals, but rather it belonged to their religious organisations.[301]

The case demonstrates that capital-exporting states in the pre-World War I period considered legislative action capable of

[296] *Portuguese Religious Properties Case* (1920) I RIAA 7.

[297] Fachiri, 'Expropriation', 167–9; Foighel, *Nationalization*, pp. 69, 70–1.

[298] *Observations Génerales*, H.M. Government, translation in Fachiri, 'Expropriation', 168.

[299] Fachiri, 'Expropriation', 168–9. France and Spain presented submissions in a similar vein.

[300] Ibid., 169.

[301] Ibid., See the reference to religious motives for the deprivation of foreign-owned Jesuit property in this case in Weston, 'Deprivation of Foreign Wealth', 1097.

constituting expropriation. It is a further illustration of the readiness with which states would draw upon international law to defend the property of their nationals. The exchange in the *Observations Génerales* on the applicable legal principles also evidences the way in which capital-exporting states would frame their invocation of international legal principles - property rights were paramount.

6. *Venezuelan Arbitrations*[302]

Mixed claims commissions were employed on a number of occasions in the nineteenth and early twentieth centuries when the circumstances surrounding the alleged expropriation of alien property produced a multitude of claims.[303] The *Venezuelan Arbitrations* of 1903 are a particularly well-known example of this approach to settling investment disputes. The grievances giving rise to the *Venezuelan Arbitrations* occurred during periods of civil war in Venezuela from 1898 to 1902. The allegations made by foreign nationals ranged from personal injury and unlawful imprisonment to seizure of property and cancellation of contracts and concessions.[304] There were also claims made by German and British bondholders of default on loans on the part of the Venezuelan government.[305] Diplomatic intervention on the part of Germany, Britain, and Italy did not, from their point of view, produce a satisfactory result.[306] Venezuela continued to insist on the exclusive jurisdiction of its local courts, arguing for the application of the national standard rule, and refused to consent to international arbitration to settle the claims.[307]

302 Ralston, *Venezuelan Arbitrations*.

303 Brownlie, *Principles*, p. 522; Newcombe and Paradell, *Investment Treaties*, pp. 7–8. Mixed claims commissions are ad hoc tribunals established by agreement between states to address multiple claims regarding the treatment of foreign nationals. Such commissions hear individual complaints filed by foreign nationals and assess the losses incurred as a result of actions attributable to the host state.

304 Ralston, *Venezuelan Arbitrations*; see also Clarke, 'Permanent Tribunal', 365–6.

305 Ralston, *Venezuelan Arbitrations*; see the discussion in Scott, 'Causes of Conflict', 77–9.

306 See the diplomatic correspondence between the Imperial Legation of Germany in Venezuela and the Ministry of Foreign Relations of the United States of Venezuela, 1900–1902, *Venezuelan Yellow Book*, reproduced in Ralston, *Venezuelan Arbitration*, pp. 957–73; see also the diplomatic correspondence between the British Legation and the Department of Foreign Relations of Venezuela, 1900–1902, *Venezuelan Yellow Book*, reproduced in Ralston, *Venezuelan Arbitration*, pp. 973–88.

307 Ibid.

Accordingly, in December 1902, Britain and Germany bombarded Caracas and blockaded the surrounding coastline.[308] Venezuela then agreed to the setting up of a series of mixed claims commissions to adjudicate on the claims made by foreign nationals.[309] Throughout the proceedings of the mixed claims commissions, however, it was never in dispute that, in principle, Venezuela would be liable to compensate those foreign nationals who had had their property expropriated or damaged by the state or its agents. Indeed, Article III of the British-Venezuelan Mixed Claims Commission Protocol of February 13, 1903, said as much:

> The Venezuelan Government admit their liability in cases where the claim is for injury to, or wrongful seizure of property, and consequently the questions which the Mixed Commission will have to decide in such cases will only be:
>
> (a) Whether the injury took place and whether the seizure was wrongful, and
>
> (b) If so, what amounts of compensation is due.
>
> In other cases the claims shall be referred to the Mixed Commission without reservation.[310]

The diplomatic correspondence prior to the 1902 bombardment of Caracas illustrates the polarised positions of the capital-exporting and host states in the nineteenth century. Venezuela strenuously argued for non-intervention on the basis of the national standard rule;[311] Britain and Germany reiterated their right under international law to protect their nationals and their assets.[312] It was, however, the military strength of Britain and Germany that ultimately decided the matter, enabling them to enforce their viewpoint of their rights under international law and impose an agreement to arbitrate the disputes. As such, the mixed claims commissions applied the international

[308] Platt, *Finance*, p. 340; See references to this incident in Borchard, *Diplomatic Protection*, pp. 482–3, 486–7; see also Suter and Stamm, 'Global Debt Crises', 655–6; see also the references in Newcombe and Paradell, *Law and Practice*, pp. 9–10; see the discussion in Hershey, 'Venezuelan Affair'; see also Hood, *Gunboat Diplomacy*, pp. 163–88.

[309] Ten mixed claims commissions were established in February, March, and April 1903: American-Venezuelan; Belgian-Venezuelan; British-Venezuelan; French-Venezuelan; German-Venezuelan; Italian-Venezuelan; Mexican-Venezuelan; Netherlands-Venezuelan; Spanish-Venezuelan; Swedish and Norwegian-Venezuelan.

[310] Art. III, British-Venezuelan Mixed Claims Commission: Protocol of February 13 (1903) reproduced in Ralston, *Arbitration*, p. 292.

[311] Ralston, *Venezuelan Arbitrations*; See also the discussion in Hershey, 'Doctrines'.

[312] Ibid., See also Hershey, 'Venezuelan Affair'.

minimum standard and operated according to the prescription of the enforced Protocols signed in 1903.[313] Again, this episode served to reinforce the crystallising, although still contested, rules of international law on the treatment of foreign nationals and to continue to legitimise the use of military force to preserve commercial interests.[314]

III. Conclusion

It can be seen from the historical explorations in this chapter that international law on foreign investment protection was developed in the nineteenth century as a mechanism to protect the interests of capital-exporting states.[315] That evolutionary process involved repetitive assertions by capital-exporting states of their viewpoint as representing international law. Significantly for powerful Western states, they were also in a political position to enforce their perspective as law. It was the political and commercial circumstances of the era that enabled capital-exporting states to exert control over the content of the rules, the framing of foreign investment protection within the doctrine of state responsibility, and methods of implementation. Accordingly, the rules reflected their interests.[316] The law focused on the protection of the investor, enmeshed the interests of state and investor within the operation of diplomatic protection, and legitimised military intervention against host states.[317]

Key cases on international expropriation in the pre-World War I era exemplify that dual process of assertion and creation. They illustrate the one-sided nature of the rules, the attempts to counteract that

[313] Additional requirements of the commissions also needed to be met, such as jurisdictional requirements. The mixed claims commissions could only hear claims from foreign nationals of specified nations, that is, claimants before the American-Venezuelan Mixed Claims Commission were required to be American citizens. There were requirements regarding the losses claimed, that is, those that were too speculative and uncertain were not compensable.

[314] Hood, *Gunboat Diplomacy*, pp. 189–92.

[315] Lipson, *Standing Guard*, pp. 4, 8, 37–8; Schrijver, *Sovereignty*, pp. 173–4; Malanczuk, *Akehurst's*, pp. 9–10.

[316] Sornarajah, *Foreign Investment*, pp. 19–20; Lipson, *Standing Guard*, pp. 12–21, 24, 37–8; Schrijver, *Sovereignty*, pp. 173–5; Anghie, *Imperialism*, pp. 67–71.

[317] Borchard, *Diplomatic Protection*, pp. 25–7, 39, 439–56; Wortley, *Expropriation*, pp. 33–5, 58; Foighel, *Nationalization*, p. 76; Dawson and Head, *International Law*, pp. 10–11; Malanczuk, *Akehurst's*, pp. 9–10; Lipson, *Standing Guard*, p. 53.

imbalance through the Calvo Doctrine, and the quashing of those challenges by capital-exporting states through legal discourse, arbitration, and use of force. International investment law emerged as the product of that contest between the interests of investor and host state. Accordingly, its legal doctrines were not neutral in the nineteenth century. Having established the purpose and nature of the law at origin, the question then becomes: well, what of it? What ripple effects have there been for the law as it continued to evolve? What are the implications of this?

Challenges to the nineteenth-century rules were, of course, made throughout the twentieth century. As global social and political conditions changed, so too did the ability of host states to challenge the substance of the international rules on foreign investment protection. These twentieth-century challenges, their implications, the responses from capital-exporting states, and the enduring effect of the origins of international investment law are explored next in Chapter 2 of this book.

2 'The dynamic of a politically oriented law':[1] foreign investment protection in a changing political environment

International investment law is innately 'political', in the sense of it having evolved out of the political and commercial aspirations of Western capital-exporting nations and with its core purpose designed to further those interests.[2] This basic feature certainly continued to find form into the twentieth century, with international investment law remaining entrenched in the investor protection tradition that had governed its emergence. This state of affairs, however, did not go uncontested. Indeed, as global political conditions shifted, significant challenges were made to the international rules on foreign investment protection.[3] This chapter examines those challenges. In particular, my interest lies in the patterns of interaction that unfolded in the early twentieth century and their significance for the law we have in the twenty-first. From an historical perspective, it seemed to me that political attempts to generate an active role for the host state under international investment law were continually met with reassertions of the protected position of the foreign investor. I wanted to explore the idea that it was in this way that a pattern emerged of reproducing the imperialist origins of international investment law.

Engaging in such an exploration requires the analysing of key events and movements throughout the twentieth century that embodied host state resistance to the prevailing system of foreign investment protection. To this end, section I of this chapter examines the agrarian reforms of the Soviet Union and Mexico (1915–38) and the use of the term

[1] Koskenniemi, *Gentle Civilizer*, p. 488.

[2] Lipson, *Standing Guard*, pp. 4, 8, 37–8; Schrijver, *Sovereignty*, pp. 173–4; Malanczuk, *Akehurst's*, pp. 9–10.

[3] Lipson, *Standing Guard*, pp. 65–70, 77.

'nationalisation' by those host states to denote a separate category of property-taking, one in which no compensation would be due to the foreign investor if the taking was part of a widespread programme of land reform.[4] Section II of this chapter considers postcolonial nationalisations and the assertion of the New International Economic Order (NIEO) as an attempt by postcolonial states to participate in the development of global economic structures and to shape international legal doctrine.[5] These challenges to investor protection were met with hostility from capital-exporting states similar to that seen in response to the Calvo Doctrine proposals of the nineteenth century.[6] Although mechanisms of the NIEO, such as the doctrine of permanent sovereignty over natural resources,[7] fared somewhat better than the Calvo Doctrine in making inroads into the international legal order, capital-exporting states sought to counteract host state assertions with further international legal tools – the doctrine of acquired rights, 'internationalised' contracts, and the modern bilateral investment treaty.[8] Accordingly, section II of this chapter examines whether the proliferation of bilateral investment treaties and the emergence of new doctrine were essentially novel means by which investor access to the host state could be maintained in much the same form as in the era of empire.

Section III of this chapter analyses a further area of significant resistance to imperialist conceptualisations of the host state–foreign investor relationship – the emergence of social movements in both developed and developing states as an essential element in current pressure to reform international investment law.[9] Ironically, at the same time as

[4] See the discussion of Mexico's arguments in Kunz, 'Mexican Expropriations', 26–7.

[5] Anghie, *Imperialism*, pp. 10–11, 211–20.

[6] See the discussion of the Calvo Doctrine above in Chapter 1; for a comprehensive treatment of the Calvo Doctrine, see Shea, *Calvo Clause*; see also for more recent commentary, Shan, 'Revival of the Calvo Doctrine'.

[7] See the General Resolution, Permanent Sovereignty Over Natural Resources, G.A. Res. 1803, 17 GAOR, Supp. 17, U.N. Doc. A/5217.

[8] See the discussion in Anghie, *Imperialism*, pp. 212–13, 235–44.

[9] Subedi, *International Investment Law*, pp. 3–4; see also for a discussion on the role of social movements in the development of international institutions, Rajagopal, 'Resistance to Renewal', 529; see for a discussion on the increasing role of NGOs in international law and policy, Raustiala, 'Participatory Revolution'; see also the discussion on the development of environmentalism as a global political force in Eckersley, *Environmentalism*, pp. 7–21; see more specifically for examples of NGO work directed towards foreign investors, International Institute for Sustainable Development, *Foreign Investment For Sustainable Development* available at www.iisd.org/investment/ (last

seeking change, the efforts of non-governmental organisations (NGOs) and grassroots activists also provide fuel for the investment sector to justify maintaining the status quo.[10] Domestic opposition or civil unrest provide a basis for asserting the need for more stringent investor protections, rather than greater policy space for governments.[11] Such arguments are often framed in terms of needing to protect the investor from pressure groups and the need for a neutral dispute resolution forum removed from domestic political influences.[12]

Section III of this chapter argues that the establishment of the International Centre for the Settlement of Investment Disputes (ICSID)[13] and the development of bilateral investment treaties were responses to the challenges posed to investor protection rules by social movements, as well as by postcolonial nationalisations and the NIEO. In particular, capital-exporting states reacted strongly to environmentalism.[14] Environmentalism and grassroots activism interfered directly with the traditional approach of foreign investors to the environment of the host state as an entity for their unimpeded use. Accordingly, forms of environmentalism in developed and developing states posed a significant form of resistance to investor activity, and have, in turn, generated strong responses from the investment sector.[15] My argument

accessed 6 December 2011); Centre for International Environmental Law, *Trade and Investment* available at http://ciel.org/Tae/Trade_Investment.html (last accessed 6 December 2011); Amazon Defense Coalition, 'ChevronToxico', available at www.chevrontoxico.com/article.php?list=type&type=3 (last accessed 5 December 2011); see the commentary on investor conduct in Indonesia at WALHI-Indonesian Forum for Environment, 'Conflict and Militarism', December 2004, available at www.eng.walhi.or.id/kampanye/psda/konflikmil/conflict_info/ (last accessed 6 December 2011).

10 See the discussion on environmental movements and the World Bank in Rajagopal, 'Resistance to Renewal', 555–7.

11 See for a discussion on the concept of reduction of policy space, Cho and Dubash, *Investment Rules*, available at www.iisd.org/pdf/2003/trade_investment_rules.pdf (last accessed 6 December 2011).

12 See, e.g., the comments in Wälde and Kolo, 'Environmental Regulation'; Wälde and Ndi, 'Stabilizing', 230–1; see also claims that the 'neutral' forum provided by investor–state arbitration is contributing to the establishment of principles of global administrative law in Weiler and Wälde, 'Investment Arbitration'.

13 Convention on the Settlement of Investment Disputes between States and Nationals of Other States, signed 18 March 1965, (1966) 575 UNTS 159 (entered into force 14 October 1966).

14 Rajagopal points to the potency of grassroots environmental movements in developing state resistance to World Bank policies in Rajagopal, 'Resistance to Renewal', 555–7.

15 For examples of investment sector responses, see Wälde and Kolo, 'Environmental Regulation'; see also Wälde and Ndi, 'Stabilizing'; for a discussion on the growth of environmental consciousness as a social movement in developing and developed states, see Rajagopal, 'Resistance to Renewal', 556–7; see also the discussion of the

is that this combative mode of interaction has continued into the twenty-first century, dominating the relationship between investment liberalisation and environmental activism, and that it remains a primary source of current tensions to reform international investment law.[16]

What became clear in analysing this period was that significant attempts had been made throughout the twentieth century to challenge capital-exporting state assertions that the international rules on foreign investment protection were well settled. The legitimising authority of international legal status, however, had been withheld from those alternative rules promoted by capital-importing states and, indeed, reassertion of investor rights was a recurring response. In the face of increasing postcolonial host state resistance to high-level investment protection, new doctrines were developed, new institutions established, and new mechanisms utilised by capital-exporting states to maintain the traditional approaches of international investment law. In other words, imperialism continued to manifest itself even as postcolonial societies were establishing their own separate identities as new states.[17]

I. Agrarian reform: a challenge to investor protection

In the early twentieth century, challenges by Mexico, the Soviet Union, and other Eastern European states to investor protection rules took the form of widespread and uncompensated land seizures.[18] It was asserted that the specific purpose of the seizures, and the context in which they were carried out, transported them into a different category, being

emergence of a 'global environmental consciousness' in Jamison, *Green Knowledge*, pp. 16–17.

[16] Current manifestations of the interaction between environmental protection objectives and international investment law are examined in Chapter 4; see also Soloway, 'Environmental Regulation'; Sands, 'Searching for Balance'; Bernasconi-Osterwalder and Brown Weiss, 'International Investment Rules', 263; Cosbey et al., *Investment*, available at www.iisd.org/pdf/2004/investment_invest_and_sd.pdf (last accessed 6 December 2011).

[17] Anghie, *Imperialism*, pp. 197–9; see also the discussion in Pahuja, 'Comparative Visions', 463–5.

[18] Lipson, *Standing Guard*, pp. 65–70, 77; Kunz, 'Mexican Expropriations', 25–7; Herz, 'Expropriation', 252, 258–9; Gathii, 'Third World Approaches', 255, 257. Agrarian reform in which foreign-owned property was confiscated occurred in a number of Eastern European states following World War I, including the Soviet Union, Hungary, Poland, Romania, Czechoslovakia and Yugoslavia.

'nationalisation' rather than confiscation or expropriation.[19] As they occurred within a general programme of land reform directed at both citizens and foreign investors, it was argued that this social objective changed the character of the seizures, relieving the host state of any obligation to pay compensation.[20] At a broader level, it was also an attempt to reshape the international rules on investment protection to take better account of the social and political needs of the host state.

Foreign investors and their home states objected strongly to these assertions.[21] Lodging protests on behalf of their affected citizens, home states reiterated that international rules on the treatment of foreigners were clear and that compensation was required.[22] Such protests also served an additional purpose in contributing to the entrenchment of capital-exporting states' views as principles of international law. One set of correspondence, in particular, acquired long-standing significance, its phrases evolving into a prevailing, if controversial, compensation standard. The Mexican–United States disputes over land holdings and oil operations gave rise to what became known as the 'Hull Formula', a term derived from a communiqué sent by the American Secretary of State, Cordell Hull.[23] Hull maintained the American position that 'adequate, effective and prompt payment' for seizure of foreign-owned property was required under international law.[24] In responding to Mexico's 'social purpose' justification, the United States encapsulated the viewpoint of capital-exporting states in providing:

[19] Kunz, 'Mexican Expropriations', 2, 26–7; see the discussion in White, *Nationalization*, pp. 3–18; Doman, 'Postwar Nationalization'. The Mexican land reforms were also followed by nationalisation of the oil industry in 1938 as part of a programme of 'Mexicanisation of industry'.

[20] Kunz, 'Mexican Expropriations', 26–7; Newcombe and Paradell, *Investment Treaties*, p. 18; Foighel, *Nationalization*, pp. 14–23.

[21] See the discussion in Kunz, 'Mexican Expropriations', 9–16; see also, e.g., the arguments put forward in Borchard, 'The Minimum Standard'.

[22] Newcombe and Paradell, *Law and Practice*, p. 18; Kunz, 'Mexican Expropriations', 9; see also the discussion in Wortley, 'The Mexican Oil Dispute'.

[23] US Secretary of State to Mexican Ambassador (1 September 1938), reproduced in 'Mexico-United States: Expropriation by Mexico of Agrarian Properties Owned by American Citizens' (1938) 33 *American Journal of International Law Supplement*, 181; see also the discussion in Newcombe and Paradell, *Law and Practice*, p. 18; see also the discussion on further correspondence from Secretary Hull in Kunz, 'Mexican Expropriations', 53–4.

[24] US Secretary of State, above n. 23; Newcombe and Paradell, *Law and Practice*, p. 18; see further the discussion on the American position in Kunz, 'Mexican Expropriations', 53–54.

The purpose of this program, however desirable, is entirely unrelated to and apart from the real issue. The issue is not whether Mexico should pursue social and economic policies designed to improve the standard of living of its people. The issue is whether in pursuing them the property of American nationals may be taken without making prompt payment of just compensation under international law.[25]

Kunz declared in 1940 that the pre-war rules were reaffirmed by home state responses, the commentary of entities such as the International Law Association, the writings of experts, and the decisions from arbitral tribunals and mixed claims commissions.[26] He concluded by stating:

It has been reaffirmed and upheld by the practice of states against Soviet Russia, against the Eastern European agrarian reforms, at the League of Nations by the majority of states, in all the many post-war negotiations of the United States with Mexico. . . .

As a rule of international law cannot be changed or abolished by the action of one or a few governments, a study of the problem reveals that the rule of international law, forbidding the expropriation without just compensation of the private property of aliens, continues to be the positive international law. This rule, it is true, has been attacked, and may be, from a sociological point of view, in a state of transition. But the jurist has to state what the law at a given moment is. And as the actions of certain states have not been recognized, have been protested against, and certainly have failed, up to now, to win the consent of the majority of states, the pre-war rule has legally lost nothing of its validity and is, and would be today, the law governing the decision of international courts.[27]

In this way, and with relative ease, the validity of an exemption for social need was dismissed by those states with a vested interest in its rejection. Indeed, the actions of the host states were not considered law-making 'practice of states', unlike the protests of the home states. It provides an illuminating perspective to view these events in the context of Benton's description of the emergence of international law in general as a process of assertions, responses, and reassertions of power and the

[25] Statement of Hughes (7 June 1921), 'The U.S. and Mexico, International Conciliation' (1923) as cited in Kunz, 'Mexican Expropriations', 27.

[26] Kunz, 'Mexican Expropriations', 13–16; see, for examples of authorities cited by Kunz: International Law Association, *Report of the Protection of Private Property Committee* (1926); Harvard Research in International Law, 'Responsibility of States' (1929) *American Journal of International Law Supplement XXIII* 133, Art. 2; the decisions of the United States of America–Mexican Mixed Claims Commission; see also *USA (de Sabla)* v. *Panama* (1934) 28 *American Journal of International Law* 602.

[27] Kunz, 'Mexican Expropriations', 13, 15–16.

playing out of legal contests to represent the interests of the successful power base.[28] Applying Benton's theories to the specific evolution of international investment law, these early challenges can be seen as part of a dynamic process of engagement, constituting attempts by host states to participate in the development of international rules on foreign investment protection and to create regimes that had space for their social requirements. They also form part of an historical pattern of seeking to participate in international investment law and meeting with capital-exporting state hostility – a pattern that has, in my view, continued into the modern context. With this in mind, it is interesting to note the similarity of language in the American response set out above to Mexico's appeal to the social purpose of its actions[29] and the arbitral tribunal's statements in the 2000 award of *Compania del Desarrollo de Santa Elena, SA* v. *The Republic of Costa Rica* (*Santa Elena*):

> While an expropriation or taking for environmental reasons may be classified as a taking for a public purpose, and thus may be legitimate, the fact that the Property was taken for this reason does not affect either the nature or the measure of the compensation to be paid for the taking. That is, the purpose of protecting the environment for which the Property was taken does not alter the legal character of the taking for which adequate compensation must be paid. The international source of the obligation to protect the environment makes no difference.
>
> Expropriatory environmental measures – no matter how laudable and beneficial to society as a whole – are, in this respect, similar to any other expropriatory measures that a state may take in order to implement its policies: where property is expropriated, even for environmental purposes, whether domestic or international, the state's obligation to pay compensation remains.[30]

The responses to the agrarian reforms in the early twentieth century and the decision in *Santa Elena*[31] at the start of the twenty-first reveal the way in which traditional reasoning continues to manifest well beyond the colonial era and to operate so as to exclude the host state perspective from international investment law. It is the intervening period, however, to which I now turn.

[28] Benton, *Law and Colonial Cultures*, pp. 10–11. Benton's theories are discussed above in the Introduction and Chapter 1.

[29] Statement of Hughes, above n. 25.

[30] *Compañía del Desarrollo de Santa Elena SA* v. *Republic of Costa Rica* (ICSID Case No. ARB(AF)/00/01, Final Award of 17 February 2000). This case is discussed in detail below in Chapter 3.

[31] Ibid.

II. Shifting political threats: postcolonial states and the New International Economic Order

The decolonisation process led to shifts in the global political landscape. From the perspective of postcolonial states, it was an era initially characterised by optimism, heralding prosperity and autonomy as their emergence from colonial control formally enabled equal participation on the international plane as independent states.[32] For capital-exporting states, it represented a period of new political risk to investments made under colonial regimes.[33]

A. *Postcolonial states and nationalisation*

The assumption of formal sovereignty promised postcolonial states the capacity to implement social, political, and economic policies furthering their own interests. A high priority in this regard was regaining control over natural resources, many of which had been subject to foreign-owned concessions.[34] As such, newly independent states sought to revisit these contracts and nationalise essential operations in a series of widespread social and economic reforms.[35] The resulting investor claims led to the development of arbitral jurisprudence that reaffirmed the traditional position of capital-exporting states and left postcolonial nations with few practical avenues to benefit from concession-controlled natural resources and rebuild their economies.[36] The central doctrines through which investors and their home states sought to submit these disputes to international arbitration were those of the

[32] Mickelson, 'Rhetoric and Rage', 362; Richardson, 'Environmental Law', 2.

[33] See the discussion Anghie, *Imperialism*, pp. 196–9, 212–15; Odumosu, 'Law and Politics', 255.

[34] Anghie, *Imperialism*, pp. 211–15; Subedi, *International Investment Law*, p. 21. The conditions under which concessions were granted in the colonial context and their implications for the development for international rules on foreign investment protection are explored above in Chapter 1.

[35] See the discussion in Newcombe and Paradell, *Law and Practice*, pp. 18–19; Anghie, *Imperialism*, pp. 211–15; Rubin 'Nationalization and Private Foreign Investment'; Foighel, *Nationalization*, pp. 11–12.

[36] See the discussion in Anghie, *Imperialism*, pp. 211–15; see, e.g., the following notable disputes: *Petroleum Development Ltd* v. *The Sheikh of Abu Dhabi* (1951) 18 *International Law Reports* 144; *Anglo-Iranian Oil Co. Case (UK* v. *Iran)* (1952) ICJ Rep. 93; *Ruler of Qatar* v. *International Marine Oil Co* (1953) 20 *International Law Reports* 534; *Texaco Overseas Petroleum Co. & California Asiatic Oil Co* v. *The Government of the Libyan Arab Republic* (1975) 53 *International Law Reports* 389.

'internationalised contract' and acquired rights.[37] However, in the face of increasing postcolonial nationalisations and calls for reforms to international economic frameworks, a more systematic approach to ensuring investor protection was developed – bilateral investment treaties and ICSID.[38] In this way, the modern architecture for international investment law was constructed through politico-legal processes of assertion and response as between capital-importing and investor home states. And at each crucial juncture, in which space could have been made for the host state within international investment law, its core imperialist approach was instead preserved.

1. Responding through legal doctrine

A key issue in the postcolonial nationalisation disputes was whether these new states were bound by the acquired rights of foreign investors under concessions granted during colonial administration.[39] Newly independent states argued that they were free to conduct a reappraisal of such concessions on the basis that the contract ceased at the extinction of the colonial territory.[40] Furthermore, as concessions had frequently been obtained through coercion, postcolonial states argued that all contracts needed to be reviewed for their legality and the level of profits generated through the concession.[41] In a further attempt to reshape international investment law, postcolonial host states asserted that compensation rules governing nationalisations of concessions were to be derived from domestic law, rather than international standards.[42]

[37] Anghie, *Imperialism*, pp. 214–16, 223–44; see also the discussion in Shalakany, 'Arbitration and the Third World', 444, 454–7.

[38] Convention on the Settlement of Investment Disputes between States and Nationals of Other States, signed 18 March 1965, (1966) 575 UNTS 159 (entered into force 14 October 1966); see the discussion in Odumosu, 'Law and Politics', 255; Anghie, *Imperialism*, pp. 236–7.

[39] Newcombe and Paradell, *Law and Practice*, p. 19; Anghie, *Imperialism*, pp. 214–16, 223–44; see generally the discussion in Fatouros, 'International Law'.

[40] Anghie, *Imperialism*, pp. 212–13; Anand, *New States*, pp. 38–43; Bedjaoui, *First Report*, Add. 1, 115.

[41] Anghie, *Imperialism*, p. 213; see also the discussion on the frequently exploitative nature of concessions contracts obtained pursuant to unequal treaties, under colonial regimes, or within protectorates, in Anghie, 'Heart of My Home', 472–3.

[42] Bedjaoui, *First Report*, p. 116; Anghie, *Imperialism*, p. 213; van Harten, *Investment Treaty Arbitration*, pp. 16–17.

(a) Acquired rights, state succession, and the international law of contracts

It is unsurprising that capital-exporting states and their concession-owning nationals took a very different view of the rights and obligations of newly independent host states. In essence, it was argued that well-established rules of international law required postcolonial states to honour the concessions or pay full compensation for any nationalisation of foreign-owned assets.[43] New states were bound by existing rules of international law and there was no opportunity, on attaining independence, to object to particular rules or to preclude their application to the new state.[44] It was also argued that international rules on state succession required a new state to assume the obligations and duties, as well as the rights and privileges, of the former state.[45] It followed from this that postcolonial host states were required to fulfil the contract terms of concessions that had been agreed under colonial authority.[46]

Capital-exporting states also objected to the proposition that concession contracts were governed by domestic law, arguing, rather, that disputes arising out of concessions should be determined by international arbitration and that a novel form of international law, the 'international law of contracts', was the applicable law.[47] A series of arbitral awards adopted this line of reasoning and 'internationalised' concession contracts through a number of mechanisms.[48] For example, it was held that the governing law of the contract could not be host state law, as this was inadequate to address the complexities of 'modern commercial contracts'.[49] Creating a novel international legal instrument was

[43] Anghie, *Imperialism*, pp. 213–14; see the views expressed in Lillich, 'Diplomatic Protection'; Francioni, 'Compensation', 260–2.

[44] Anghie, *Imperialism*, pp. 213–14; see also the discussion in Craven, *Decolonisation*, pp. 84–6; see also, e.g., the views expressed in Jessup, 'Non-Universal International Law'.

[45] Craven, *Decolonisation*, pp. 84–6; Anghie, *Imperialism*, p. 213.

[46] Anghie, *Imperialism*, pp. 211–16; Craven, *Decolonisation*, pp. 84–6; see also the discussion in Weeramantry, *Nauru*, pp. 307–12.

[47] Shalakany, 'Arbitration', 444, 454–7; Anghie, *Imperialism*, pp. 225–32; Sornarajah, 'International Arbitration'; Bowett, 'State Contracts'; Fatouros, 'International Law'.

[48] See, e.g., *Petroleum Development Ltd* v. *The Sheikh of Abu Dhabi* (1951) 18 *International Law Reports* 144; *Ruler of Qatar* v. *International Marine Oil Co* (1953) 20 *International Law Reports* 534; *Texaco Overseas Petroleum Co. & California Asiatic Oil Co* v. *The Government of the Libyan Arab Republic* (1975) 53 *International Law Reports* 389; see the discussion in Bowett, 'State Contracts'; see also Shalakany, 'Arbitration', 444, 454–7; see also Anghie, *Imperialism*, pp. 230–5.

[49] For a contemporary discussion of the rationale for the doctrine of the 'internationalised contract', see McNair, 'Civilised Nations', 4; see, for a critique of this approach, Anghie, *Imperialism*, pp. 226–35; see also Bowett, 'State Contracts'; see, e.g., the reasoning in

also an adopted technique, through which concession contracts were framed as forming a distinctive category of economic development agreement or 'quasi-treaty'.[50] References in the concession agreement to dispute resolution through 'international arbitration' were taken to import the new international law of contracts as the substantive law governing the contract.[51] Sources of public international law, such as 'general principles of law', were considered applicable to the contract and arbitral awards identified key principles for this new field of law.[52] Significantly, however, the general principles regarded as relevant in the context of such disputes consisted of respect for private property, respect for acquired rights, and compensation for unjust enrichment on denial of a concessionaire's rights.[53]

It is my argument here that these developments in the law did not occur in isolation or by chance. Rather, they were in response to the attempts of postcolonial states to reshape international investment law and to redress systemic impacts of colonialism.[54] It could quite clearly be seen that newly independent states, and their approach to foreign investment, threatened the hegemony held by capital-exporting states over the development of investor protection rules. In answering that threat, legal doctrine was manipulated and used so as to maintain a level of investor protection essentially commensurate to that experienced in the colonial era.[55]

Petroleum Development Ltd v. *The Sheikh of Abu Dhabi* (1951) 18 *International Law Reports* 144, 149; see also *Ruler of Qatar* v. *International Marine Oil Co* (1953) 20 *International Law Reports* 534, 545.

50 Anghie, *Imperialism*, pp. 229–35; Friedmann, 'Changing Dimensions', 1158; see also the discussion in Huang, 'International and Legal Aspects'.

51 See, e.g., *Texaco Overseas Petroleum Co. & California Asiatic Oil Co* v. *The Government of the Libyan Arab Republic* (1975) 53 *International Law Reports* 389, 455; see the discussion in Anghie, *Imperialism*, p. 231; see also White, 'Expropriation'.

52 See the discussion in Anghie, *Imperialism*, pp. 228–32; see also White, 'Expropriation'; Norton, 'Law of the Future', 477; 'general principles of law' is listed as a source of law in Art. 38(1)(c) of the Statute of the International Court of Justice; see for examples of awards taking this approach, *Petroleum Development Ltd* v. *The Sheikh of Abu Dhabi* (1951) 18 *International Law Reports* 144; *Ruler of Qatar* v. *International Marine Oil Co* (1953) 20 *International Law Reports* 534; *Texaco Overseas Petroleum Co. & California Asiatic Oil Co* v. *The Government of the Libyan Arab Republic* (1975) 53 *International Law Reports* 389.

53 Anghie, *Imperialism*, pp. 228–31; see for a contemporary discussion of the rationale for the doctrine of the 'internationalised contract' McNair, 'Civilised Nations'.

54 Anghie, *Imperialism*, pp. 235–6.

55 Ibid., pp. 235–44; see the related discussion on the perpetuation of colonial economic relations despite the attaining of political independence by postcolonial states in Thomas, 'Causes of Inequality', 4.

In addition to the construction of a new field of international law of contracts, the doctrine of acquired rights was also applied in an inconsistent manner. In the context of postcolonial nationalisation disputes, the rights of concession-holders granted under colonial administrations were considered to have priority over the sovereign rights of the new state to revisit those acquired rights.[56] In effect, this conceptualisation of the concession-holders' acquired rights precluded any reconsideration of the contract. However, as Brownlie points out, acquired rights held by foreign nationals are, in fact, able to be withdrawn at the discretion of the state.[57] Specifically referring to rights of citizenship, residency, and permission to work, Brownlie argues that as it is clear that acquired rights in certain circumstances can be revoked, the rationale for non-retractable concession rights is 'unsatisfactory'.[58] Ultimately, the manifestation of the acquired rights doctrine in the context of concession-holders had a particularly constraining impact on postcolonial governments, precluding access to the full economic benefit of their natural resources, and was clearly used to support the interests of capital-exporting states and their investor nationals.[59]

(b) Doctrinal patterns: past and present

When viewed as part of an historical continuum rather than as isolated incidents, the creation of the doctrine of the internationalised contract and the use of acquired rights and state succession can be seen as examples of a practice that extends back into the nineteenth century and continues into the twenty-first – 'arbitral law-making' that advances the interests of foreign investors.[60] Such approaches in the nineteenth century were discussed in the previous chapter; more modern examples include recent interpretations of the fair and equitable treatment standard, focusing on the legitimate expectations of the investor, and requirements to maintain a stable business and legal framework.[61] Although ostensibly reasonable obligations, they have been interpreted

[56] Anghie, *Imperialism*, pp. 211–16; see also the discussion in Weeramantry, *Nauru*, pp. 307–12.

[57] Brownlie, *Principles*, p. 549; see also Sornarajah, *International Law*, pp. 445–6.

[58] Brownlie, *Principles*, p. 549.

[59] Anghie, *Imperialism*, pp. 211–16; see also the discussion on the gradual cementing of economic patterns that reinforce Western hegemony despite the formal political independence of decolonisation in Thomas, 'Causes of Inequality', 14.

[60] Sornarajah, 'Whose Fairness?', 165, 174, 176.

[61] See, e.g., *Occidental Petroleum Corporation and Occidental Exploration and Production Company* v. *Ecuador* (ICSID Case No. ARB/06/11 Award of 1 July 2004); *Técnicas Medioambientales*

expansively, extending protection well beyond the international minimum standard's original scope of bad faith and outrageous or egregious conduct.[62] For Sornarajah, this expression of the fair and equitable treatment standard is a reflection of the innate bias of investment treaty arbitration towards the interests of foreign investors.[63] For my argument, what I am seeking to explore is the dominant historical narrative of this field, its myth-making and self-justification, and, within that, the patterns of manipulation of legal doctrine that have furthered, and continue to further, the interests of capital-exporting states and their nationals.

In this regard, it is interesting to note one of the latest manifestations of doctrinal manipulation by foreign investors. Increasingly, investors are framing their complaints in the language of human rights jurisprudence,[64] a recent form of which is in relation to the global financial crisis that engulfed financial markets in 2008 and 2009. Government action taken in many states in response to this crisis has involved extensive new regulation of the financial sector and increased state ownership of individual private banks.[65] Many investors have objected, arguing that this governmental action constitutes nationalisation of their investments.[66] Not only are investors claiming that standard

Tecmed, SA v. *United Mexican States* (ICSID Case No. ARB(AF)/00/02, Award of 29 May 2003); *MTD Equity Sdn. Bhd. & MTD Chile SA* v. *Chile* (ICSID Case No. ARB/01/7, Award of 25 May 2004); *CMS Gas Transmission Company* v. *Argentine Republic* (ICSID Case No. ARB/01/8, Award of 12 May 2005); *Azurix Corp.* v. *Argentina* (ICSID Case No. ARB/01/12, Award of 14 July 2006), paras 360–1, 372, 392, 408. The fair and equitable treatment standard is discussed in detail below in Chapter 3.

62 Sornarajah, 'Whose Fairness?', 174, 176; Van Harten, *Investment Treaty Arbitration*, pp. 88–90; Marshall, *Fair and Equitable Treatment* available at www.iisd.org/pdf/2007/inv_fair_treatment.pdf (last accessed 6 December 2011); see also the discussion in Miles, 'Sustainable Development'. The original scope of the international minimum standard was articulated in *LFH Neer & Pauline Neer* v. *United Mexico States*, 4 UNRIAA 60 (15 October 1926).

63 Sornarajah, 'Whose Fairness?', 176–80; Sornarajah, 'Clash of Globalizations', 13–17; see also the discussion in Tienhaara, 'Third Party Participation', 230–1.

64 Peterson, *Human Rights*, available at www.dd-rd.ca/site/_PDF/publications/globalization/HIRA-volume3-ENG.pdf (last accessed 6 December 2011).

65 See, e.g., the majority stakeholding taken by the British government in the Royal Bank of Scotland in 2008 and discussions in 2009 as to the percentage-holding to be taken by the United States government in Citibank.

66 Hirsch, 'Hedge Funds', available at www.guardian.co.uk/commentisfree/libertycentral/2009/jan/28/hedge-fund-human-rights (last accessed 6 December 2011); the British Institute of International and Comparative Law considered this issue in an *Open Roundtable of the Investment Treaty Forum, Global Financial Crisis: Implications for Investment Arbitration*, 18 February 2009, available at www.biicl.org/events/view/-/id/365/ (last accessed 6 December 2011).

investor protections are engaged by these actions, but more innovative arguments are also being developed. Corporate investors are now adopting rights-oriented terminology and have described government financial rescue packages as a breach of their human right to 'peaceful enjoyment of possessions'.[67]

Such an approach can certainly be framed as another illustration of the way in which imperialism reproduces itself. This particular conceptualisation of human rights recently advocated by these investors actually reflects the 'right to trade' approach of the Dutch East India Company and the development of rights-based international legal doctrine to justify the activities of commerce and military incursions into non-European territories.[68] Once an historical perspective is taken, it becomes clear that parallel methodologies were employed in the emergence of rules of foreign investment protection in the nineteenth century, the development of the doctrine of internationalised contracts in the twentieth, the recent manifestation of the fair and equitable treatment standard, and the current utilisation of human rights language to create investor claims – that is, the construction of rules, asserted as international law, and ultimately applied by arbitral tribunals as established rules of international investment law. In this way, the origins of imposition continued to manifest throughout the twentieth century and into the twenty-first.

2. Responding through regime creation

The nature and implications of Western responses to the period of change brought by decolonisation were complex and multilayered.[69] However, one particularly significant reaction to the postcolonial nationalisations was an increased focus on developing a systematic approach to investor protection through the creation of treaty regimes.[70]

[67] Hirsch, 'Hedge Funds'.

[68] Anghie, *Imperialism*, pp. 270–1; see also the discussion in Porras, 'Constructing International Law', 802–4.

[69] The issue of Western response to decolonisation is, of course, multifarious. It is outside the scope of this book to examine all facets of this interaction and it focuses instead on key aspects of the relationship for the development of international investment law.

[70] Newcombe and Paradell, *Law and Practice*, pp. 19–22, 41–4; see also the discussion in Van Harten, *Investment Treaty Arbitration*, pp. 19–28; see also the discussion on the establishment of ICSID in Odumosu, 'Law and Politics', 255.

(a) Investment treaty regimes

Several attempts at establishing a multilateral framework for foreign investment protection were made in the decolonisation era by capital-exporting states and investor organisations such as the International Chamber of Commerce (ICC).[71] These initiatives included the suggestion of investor protector provisions within the proposed International Trade Organization in 1948,[72] the 1949 International Code of Fair Treatment for Foreign Investment drafted by the ICC,[73] the International Law Association's Draft Statute of the Arbitral Tribunal for Foreign Investment and the Foreign Investment Court,[74] the 1959 investor-led Abs-Shawcross Draft Convention on Investments Abroad,[75] the 1961 Draft Convention on the International Responsibility of States for Injuries to Aliens,[76] and the 1967 Draft Convention on the Protection of Foreign Property put forward by the Organization for Economic Cooperation and Development (OECD).[77]

These proposals did not result in a multilateral investment agreement, largely due to the differing viewpoints of capital-exporting and host states on the appropriate standards for investor protection.[78] The objectives of capital-exporting states, however, remained centred on establishing a comprehensive international regime for high-level foreign investment protection, and, as a result, they turned to the pursuit of bilateral investment treaties, engaging in one-on-one negotiations.[79] The first such treaty was concluded between Germany and Pakistan in

71 Van Harten, *Investment Treaty Arbitration*, pp. 19–23; Newcombe and Paradell, *Investment Treaties*, pp. 19–22.

72 Havana Charter for an International Trade Organization (1948) UN Conference on Trade and Employment, UN Doc. E/CONF.2/78, Sales no. 1948.II.D.4.

73 International Chamber of Commerce, International Code of Fair Treatment of Foreign Investment (1948), reprinted in UNCTAD, *International Code*, p. 273.

74 International Law Association, Draft Statute of the Arbitral Tribunal for Foreign Investment and the Foreign Investment Court (1948), reprinted in UNCTAD, *International Code*, p. 259.

75 Draft Convention on Investments Abroad (1959) reprinted in Abs and Shawcross, 'Proposed Convention'.

76 Sohn and Baxter, 'Draft Convention'.

77 OECD, *Draft Convention*, available at www.oecd.org/dataoecd/35/4/39286571.pdf (last accessed 6 December 2011).

78 Newcombe and Paradell, *Law and Practice*, pp. 19–20, 41; Van Harten, *Investment Treaty Arbitration*, pp. 19–23; Sornarajah, *Foreign Investment*, p. 212; McLachlan, Shore, and Weiniger, *International Investment Arbitration*, p. 7; Brewer and Young, *Multilateral Investment System*, pp. 66–8.

79 Newcombe and Paradell, *Law and Practice*, pp. 41–2; Van Harten, *Investment Treaty Arbitration*, pp. 40–3; Dolzer and Schreuer, *International Investment Law*, pp. 18–20.

1959.[80] From that point onwards, capital-exporting states increasingly sought to enter into bilateral investment treaties with developing states.[81]

(i) International Centre for Settlement of Investment Disputes The post-colonial nationalisations and the polarised positions on investor protection standards in multilateral negotiations between capital-exporting and importing states led to a significant development in the international architecture governing foreign investment – ICSID.[82] In a move designed to avoid the impasse created by continuing host state opposition to the high levels of protection advocated by capital-exporting states, the concept of a dispute settlement framework removed from substantive standards of investor protection was proposed by the General Counsel of the World Bank, Aron Broches.[83] The rationale for the regime was framed as the 'depoliticisation' of investment disputes.[84]

This justification was, in essence, a reiteration of the nineteenth century position that only international arbitration could guarantee a foreign investor a fair hearing in a dispute with a host state.[85] The irony is that, despite the claims of neutrality and objectivity, both the system of international investment arbitration and the substantive rules of international investment law are deeply embedded in a political framework – but one that operates to the advantage of foreign investors.[86] Framing the host state position in a derogatory way as 'political' rather

[80] Treaty between the Federal Republic of Germany and Pakistan for the Promotion and Protection of Investments, signed 25 November 1959, (1963) 457 UNTS 23 (entered into force 28 April 1962).

[81] Newcombe and Paradell, *Law and Practice*, pp. 41–3; Dolzer and Schreuer, *International Investment Law*, p. 19.

[82] Odumosu, 'Law and Politics', 255; Dolzer and Schreuer, *International Investment Law*, p. 20; Convention on the Settlement of Investment Disputes between States and Nationals of Other States, signed 18 March 1965, (1966) 575 UNTS 159 (entered into force 14 October 1966).

[83] Dolzer and Schreuer, *International Investment Law*, p. 20; Newcombe and Paradell, *Law and Practice*, p. 27; Subedi, *International Investment Law*, p. 30; Schreuer, *ICSID Convention*, p. xi.

[84] Dolzer and Schreuer, *International Investment Law*, p. 20; Newcombe and Paradell, *Law and Practice*, pp. 27–8; see also Shihata, *Greater*; Shihata, 'Settlement of Disputes', 269; for a description of international arbitration as a neutral forum for foreign investors, see Yackee, 'Pacta Sunt Servanda', 1551–2, 1570.

[85] For examples of this viewpoint, see the discussion on the Calvo Doctrine in Freeman, 'Recent Aspects'; see also the commentary in Borchard, 'Minimum Standard'.

[86] Anghie, *Imperialism*, pp. 239–41; Sornarajah, 'The Clash of Globalizations', 13–17; see the discussion on the political nature of arbitrators' decisions not to engage with

than legal, together with the unacknowledged politics in the stance of investors and capital-exporting states, obscured the unspoken political ideology imbued within the rules and institutions being constructed. Crucially, it allowed the operation of a politically based system of international investment law without the appearance of doing so. The 'delocalised' forum provided by ICSID was, therefore, regarded by capital-exporting states as one of the most important features of the system.[87] It was seen as a mechanism that would operate beyond its immediate dispute resolution function and, in fact, also promote investment flows into signatory states and progress investment liberalisation amongst developing states.[88]

ICSID established a procedural framework specifically for the arbitration of investment disputes between signatory states and investor nationals of signatory states.[89] This introduced a novel feature into investment dispute settlement - investor–state arbitration - displacing the traditional state-to-state format and removing the need for an investor to rely on the exercise of diplomatic protection to recover any losses.[90] The ICSID Convention requires the consent of both parties to submit the dispute to ICSID jurisdiction.[91] However, that consent can be located in a variety of instruments. It can be found in an ICSID arbitration clause contained in a contract between a host state and investor.[92] It is also commonly located in clauses in bilateral investment treaties providing general consent to submit disputes to ICSID arbitration. Perceived as contributing to the depoliticisation of individual disputes, this approach removes the need for any specific prior agreement to arbitration between the investor and the host state, operating instead as a standing offer from the host state of ICSID arbitration which is then accepted on the filing of a claim.[93]

principles from other areas of international law in Muchlinksi, 'Corporate Social Responsibility', 637, 683.

[87] Muchlinski, *Multinational Enterprises*, p. 718. [88] Ibid.

[89] Convention on the Settlement of Investment Disputes between States and Nationals of Other States, signed 18 March 1965, (1966) 575 UNTS 159, Art. 25(1) (entered into force 14 October 1966); see also the discussion in Newcombe and Paradell, *Law and Practice*, p. 28.

[90] The implications of the investor–state dispute settlement system are examined in detail below in Chapters 5 and 6. For an in-depth analysis of the public law concerns raised by the system of investment treaty arbitration, see Van Harten, *Investment Treaty Arbitration*.

[91] Convention on the Settlement of Investment Disputes between States and Nationals of Other States, signed 18 March 1965, (1966) 575 UNTS 159, Art. 25(1) (entered into force 14 October 1966).

[92] Muchlinski, *Multinational Enterprises*, p. 719.

[93] Ibid., p. 720; Paulsson, 'Arbitration without Privity'.

ICSID did not prescribe substantive standards of international investment law to be applied in disputes. These were left to the agreements governing the particular relationship between the host state and the investor, such as the guarantees contained in a bilateral investment treaty or provisions within a contract between the state and the investor.[94] In this way, the operation of the ICSID framework has been interwoven into the network of international investment agreements emerging over the last fifty years. And although its initial case load was small, ICSID has since developed into the primary forum for hearing investor–state disputes.[95] This dominance of ICSID dispute settlement has significant implications for host states. As the establishment of ICSID was in response to postcolonial state challenges to prevailing investor protection rules,[96] the context in which this dispute settlement forum emerged was one that sought to limit a host state's ability to implement social and economic policies that detrimentally affected the interests of foreign investors. It was essentially a mechanism through which capital-exporting states sought to maintain the level of investor protection that had been built up during the colonial era. Consequently, it was not a forum that was predisposed to allowing room for host state 'policy space'.[97]

(ii) Bilateral investment treaties Seeking to conclude bilateral investment treaties was a further response to the rejection by capital-importing states of the multilateral approach, the period of postcolonial nationalisations, and the assertion of the NIEO.[98] Bilateral investment treaties contained stringent investor protection standards and guarantees, correlating to the rules repeatedly asserted as international law by capital-exporting states. Amongst other features, they provided for national

[94] Convention on the Settlement of Investment Disputes between States and Nationals of Other States, signed 18 March 1965, (1966) 575 UNTS 15, Art. 42(1) (entered into force 14 October 1966); see also the discussion in Newcombe and Paradell, *Law and Practice*, p. 29.

[95] ICSID, *About ICSID*, available at http://icsid.worldbank.org/ICSID/FrontServlet?requestType=CasesRH&actionVal=ShowHome&pageName=AboutICSID_Home (last accessed 6 December 2011).

[96] Odumosu, 'Law and Politics', 255; Dolzer and Schreuer, *International Investment Law*, p. 20.

[97] For a discussion on the concept of reduction of 'policy space', see Cho and Dubash, *Investment Rules*. The term 'policy space' refers to the capacity of governmental bodies within host states to develop and implement policies and regulation.

[98] Newcombe and Paradell, *Law and Practice*, pp. 24, 26, 31–2, 41; Vandevelde, 'A Brief History', 168–9. The NIEO is considered in detail below in this chapter.

treatment, most-favoured-nation treatment, minimum standards of treatment, security, and compensation on expropriation.[99] And although the instruments were framed as reciprocal arrangements, they had been drafted by capital-exporting states to protect the interests of their investing nationals and were largely concluded in unequal political and economic conditions between capital-exporting states and developing states.[100] Accordingly, the expectation was, on the whole, that the capital flows would be one-way and that the obligations assumed under the treaty would also effectively only be on one side.[101] Not a great many of these investment treaties were actually concluded through the 1960s and 1970s.[102] However, a relative surge in the late 1980s and 1990s has led to a network of over 2,800 international investment agreements, creating the current international framework of high-level investor protection.[103]

a. Developing states' accession to bilateral investment treaties

Why, then, did developing states enter into bilateral investment treaties and assume obligations to which they had so strongly objected in the multilateral context? It would seem that a number of factors converged to facilitate the move towards signing bilateral investment treaties. Politically, there was a general swing in the 1980s towards economic liberalisation and institutions, such as the World Bank and the International Monetary Fund, adopted specific funding policies to promote trade and investment liberalisation programmes within developing states.[104] This coincided with constricting

[99] Vandevelde, 'A Brief History', 172–3; Newcombe and Paradell, *Law and Practice*, pp. 42–3; see, e.g., Treaty between the Federal Republic of Germany and Pakistan for the Promotion and Protection of Investments, signed 25 November 1959, (1963) 457 UNTS 23 (entered into force 28 April 1962). 'National treatment' in bilateral investment treaties is not to be confused with the national treatment propositions underpinning the Calvo Doctrine. Within bilateral investment treaties, the national treatment standard entails an obligation on the part of the host state to afford treatment to foreign investors no less favourable than that afforded to its own investors.

[100] Newcombe and Paradell, *Law and Practice*, p. 43; Van Harten, *Investment Treaty Arbitration*, pp. 40–1; Garcia, 'Dirty Little Secrets', 316.

[101] Van Harten, *Investment Treaty Arbitration*, pp. 40–1; see the discussion in Newcombe and Paradell, *Law and Practice*, p. 43; Vandevelde, 'A Brief History', 170–1.

[102] Vandevelde, 'A Brief History', 171–2; Newcombe and Paradell, *Law and Practice*, p. 46.

[103] See the discussion in Newcombe and Paradell, *Law and Practice*, pp. 46–8, 57–8; Vandevelde, 'A Brief History', 175–7, 179; see the statistics provided by UNCTAD, *International Investment Rule-Making* (2007) TD/B/COM.2/EM.21/2.

[104] Van Harten, *Investment Treaty Arbitration*, p. 41; Newcombe and Paradell, *Law and Practice*, p. 48.

credit flows to developing states, declining foreign aid, and increasing debt levels in developing states.[105] As international sources of finance faltered, developing states were increasingly faced with little option other than foreign investment to fund development programmes.[106] These conditions led to competition amongst developing states to attract foreign investment. Signing a bilateral investment treaty was a relatively straightforward way in which to gain a competitive advantage over other developing states in the pursuit of capital.[107] As a group, however, the interests of developing states converged and were best served through a collective position rejecting high protection standards for investors – hence the multilateral approach to the demands of capital-exporting states.[108] The incidental effect of individual accession to bilateral investment treaties, however, further spurred pressure on all developing states to create ever more favourable conditions for investors and to agree to high levels of protection in bilateral investment treaties.[109] Ironically, this process has resulted in a global web of investment treaties effectively creating the breadth of high-level investor protection that capital-exporting states had been seeking in their attempts to conclude a multilateral agreement.[110] Disconcertingly for developing states, there is also conflicting empirical evidence as to whether signing bilateral investment treaties actually leads to an increase in investment inflows to developing states.[111] Furthermore,

[105] Newcombe and Paradell, *Law and Practice*, pp. 48–9; Van Harten, *Investment Treaty Arbitration*, p. 42; Vandevelde, 'A Brief History', 177–9.

[106] Van Harten, *Investment Treaty Arbitration*, pp. 42–3; Newcombe and Paradell, *Law and Practice*, pp. 48–9; Vandevelde, 'A Brief History', 177–9; Sandrino, 'The NAFTA Investment Chapter', 264; see also the discussion on the reasons for capital-importing states' submission to international arbitration in Lapres, 'Principles of Compensation', 98.

[107] Newcombe and Paradell, *Law and Practice*, pp. 48–9; Van Harten, *Investment Treaty Arbitration*, p. 43; Guzman, 'Bilateral Investment Treaties', 688; Elkins, Guzman, and Simmons, 'Competing for Capital'.

[108] Guzman, 'Bilateral Investment Treaties', 642–3, 671–4, 688.

[109] Van Harten, *Investment Treaty Arbitration*, p. 43; Guzman, 'Bilateral Investment Treaties', 642–3, 671–4, 688; Been and Beauvais, 'The Global Fifth Amendment', 124.

[110] Van Harten, *Investment Treaty Arbitration*, p. 23; Bergman, 'Bilateral Investment Protection Treaties', 3–4, 8–11; Salacuse, 'BIT by BIT', 656.

[111] Van Harten, *Investment Treaty Arbitration*, p. 41–2; Newcombe and Paradell, *Law and Practice*, pp. 62–3; Hallward-Driemeier, *Do Bilateral Investment Treaties Attract FDI?*, available at www-wds.worldbank.org/external/default/WDSContentServer/IW3P/IB/2003/09/23/000094946_03091104060047/additional/105505322_20041117160010.pdf (last accessed 6 December 2011); Neumayer and Spess, 'Bilateral Investment Treaties'; Rose-Ackerman and Tobin, *When BITS Have Some Bite*, available at www.law.yale.edu/

the regulatory conditions necessary to attract investment and the negotiated concessions granted to investors, such as tax exemptions, pollution permits, or labour requirements, can exact a heavy social price from the capital-importing state and cancel out the development benefits of foreign investment. As such, the hoped-for social and economic gains have not necessarily materialised despite the price paid of increased intrusion into areas of domestic policy space.[112]

b. 'South–South' bilateral investment treaties

In recent times, a perceptible shift has been occurring and a new pattern appears to be emerging in investment treaty-making. While the majority of bilateral investment treaties are still between developed and developing countries, increasingly, developing states are concluding such agreements as amongst themselves, often termed 'South–South' bilateral investment treaties.[113] Commentators argue that this new trend refutes suggestions that international investment agreements serve the neo-liberal interests of the West.[114] This argument, however, ignores an important point - that imperialism is not solely the remit of Western states.[115] The West has, of course, been particularly adept at giving expression to imperialism over previous centuries and at using international investment law to facilitate its commercial and political aspirations. However, the interesting element to note with the advent of South–South investment treaties is not that imperialism has been overcome or that developing states now concur with Western views on investment liberalisation, but rather that international investment law actually remains a tool of imperialism, but in new hands. It continues to be an instrument used to entrench unequal power relations. Certainly, the identity of capital-exporting states is beginning to shift. However, the

documents/pdf/When_BITS_Have_Some_Bite.doc; see also the discussion in Franck, 'Foreign Direct Investment'.

112 Guzman, 'Bilateral Investment Treaties', 671–2.

113 Newcombe and Paradell, *Law and Practice*, pp. 47–8, 58; Van Harten, *Investment Treaty Arbitration*, p. 40; Poulsen, 'South–South BITs', conference paper available at www.asil.org/files/ielconferencepapers/poulsen.pdf (last accessed 6 December 2011).

The artificiality and problematic nature of describing these agreements as divided into 'North–South' and 'South–South' categories is acknowledged. The terminology is used here to reflect the differentiation made in current investment treaty discourse between the recent trend in inter-developing state bilateral investment agreements and traditional agreements between developed capital-exporting states and developing states.

114 See, e.g., Dolzer and Schreuer, *International Investment Law*, p. 21.

115 Lee, 'Empire Rising', 200–1; see also Dudden, *Japan's Colonization of Korea*.

nature of the mechanism and the way in which it is used appears to be remaining the same.[116] In this regard, South–South bilateral investment treaties still tend to involve one stronger party. For example, China has recently embarked on an aggressive programme of concluding bilateral investment treaties in Latin America and Africa to protect its increasing levels of outward foreign investment flows.[117] To this end, it has entered into bilateral investment treaties with, amongst others, Bolivia,[118] Peru,[119] and Cameroon.[120] In general, the form of treaty between developing states largely follows the templates provided by traditional 'North–South' bilateral investment treaties,[121] and such an approach has been utilised in these recent treaties between China and states in Africa and Latin America.[122] In other words, similar stringent investor protections are being imposed on capital-importing states by a politically and economically dominant party – and the first arbitration claim by a Chinese investor was recently filed with ICSID, foreshadowing many more in the future.[123]

[116] Dolzer and Schreuer, *International Investment Law*, p. 21, point to the fact that South–South bilateral investment treaties are drafted in much the same form as North–South investment agreements.

[117] Tung and Cox-Alomar, 'Arbitral and Judicial Decision', 461–3; Heyman, 'International Law'; see also the discussion in Ofodile, 'Trade, Empires and Subjects'.

[118] Agreement between the Government of the People's Republic of China and the Government of the Republic of Bolivia Concerning the Encouragement and Reciprocal Protection of Investments, signed on 8 May 1992 (entered into force 1 September 1996).

[119] Agreement between the Government of the Republic of Peru and the Government of the People's Republic of China Concerning the Encouragement and Reciprocal Protection of Investments, signed on 9 June 1994 (entered into force 1 February 1995).

[120] Accord entre le Gouvernement de la Republique du Cameroun et le Gouvernement de la Republique Populaire de Chine pour la Promotion et la Protection Reciproques des Investissements, signed on 10 May 1997.

[121] Dolzer and Schreuer, *International Investment Law*, p. 21.

[122] See, e.g., Accord entre le Gouvernement de la Republique du Cameroun et le Gouvernement de la Republique Populaire de Chine pour la Promotion et la Protection Reciproques des Investissements, signed on 10 May 1997; Agreement between the Government of the Republic of Peru and the Government of the People's Republic of China Concerning the Encouragement and Reciprocal Protection of Investments, signed on 9 June 1994 (entered into force 1 February 1995); Agreement between the Government of the People's Republic of China and the Government of the Republic of Bolivia Concerning the Encouragement and Reciprocal Protection of Investments, signed on 8 May 1992 (entered into force 1 September 1996).

[123] *Tza Yap Shum* v. *Republic of Peru* (ICSID Case No. ARB/07/6, Decision on Jurisdiction and Competence of 19 June 2009); see also the discussion in Tung and Cox-Alomar, 'Arbitral and Judicial Decision'; see also Heyman, 'Disputes relating to China'.

There are, however, also signs that carefully balanced South–South bilateral investment treaties are emerging where the negotiating position of the states is more equal.[124] For example, softer national treatment requirements, more stringent capital transfer conditions, and the omission of fair and equitable treatment provisions have been notable features.[125] Malik describes this approach as 'innovative';[126] Poulsen terms it as a 'different vision of international investment rules'.[127] These developments indicate that there are two forms of bilateral investment treaty emerging out of South–South negotiations. One follows the older style, reproducing the dynamic of economic imposition found in traditional North–South bilateral investment treaties and exposing host states to wide-ranging investor challenges. The other model embodies an approach that better reflects the needs of capital-importing states and potentially leaves significantly greater policy space for the implementation of host state social, environmental, economic, and development initiatives. If this approach were to continue and expand, it would, indeed, be likely that a more balanced form of international investment agreement would emerge, genuinely reflecting host state participation.

B. *The New International Economic Order*

Bilateral investment treaties, ICSID, and new legal doctrine were not only responses to postcolonial nationalisation and the reluctance of capital-importing states to conclude a multilateral agreement; they were also part of the response to the challenge of the NIEO.[128] For postcolonial states, the initial euphoria of decolonisation was soon replaced by frustration at the lack of change in global economic systems and in the standard of living in their own states.[129] Formal independence had not alleviated the inequities of global trading and investment systems, and postcolonial states argued strongly that developed state

[124] Poulsen, 'South–South BITs', 26; see also the discussion in Malik, *Regional and Bilateral Investment Treaties*, available at www.iisd.org/pdf/2008/dci_recent_dev_bits.pdf (last accessed 6 December 2011).

[125] Malik, *Regional and Bilateral Investment Treaties*, p. 5; Poulsen, 'South–South BITs', 26; e.g., Malik discusses the Comprehensive Economic Cooperation Agreement between the Republic of India and the Republic of Singapore, signed on 29 June 2005.

[126] Malik, *Regional and Bilateral Investment Treaties*, p. 5.

[127] Poulsen, 'South–South BITS', 26.

[128] Anghie, *Imperialism*, pp. 235–6, 313.

[129] Mickelson, 'Rhetoric and Rage', 362–3; Richardson, 'Environmental Law', 2; Carrasco and Kose, 'Income Distribution', 11.

polices were exacerbating those economic disparities.[130] This sense of injustice combined with a desire to participate in the reshaping of international law and policy led to proposals for a NIEO.[131]

1. Key NIEO proposals and initiatives

In seeking to overcome institutional and systemic obstacles to global economic justice, proponents of the NIEO considered the most receptive forum was likely to be the United Nations.[132] Such conclusions were drawn from a number of circumstances, including the fact that it had proven impossible to settle the terms of a multilateral agreement establishing an international investment regime in which postcolonial viewpoints were also reflected.[133] The international trade framework under the General Agreement on Tariffs and Trade (GATT)[134] was considered averse to developing state concerns.[135] The World Bank and the International Monetary Fund (IMF) pursued vigorous trade and investment liberalisation programmes and had weighted voting procedures based on financial contributions to the institutions, which effectively gave preference to the interests of developed states.[136] The United Nations, however, had recently established the United Nations Conference on Trade and Development (UNCTAD) specifically to advance economic development through international trade.[137] It was in this setting that a collective of developing states formed as the 'Group of 77', emphasising their shared experiences of imperialism and

[130] Richardson, 'Environmental Law', 2; Carrasco and Kose, 'Income Distribution', 10–13; Anghie, *Imperialism*, pp. 196–9; Mickelson, 'Rhetoric and Rage', 362–3; Bhagwati, 'Introduction' in Bhagwati, *The New International*.

[131] Bhagwati, *The New International*; Carrasco and Kose, 'Income Distribution', 10–13; Anghie, *Imperialism*, p. 199; Richardson, 'Environmental Law', 2; Mickelson, 'Rhetoric and Rage', 364–6; Rajagopal, *International Law from Below*, pp. 77–8.

[132] Anghie, *Imperialism*, p. 216; Carrasco and Kose, 'Income Distribution', 11–12.

[133] Newcombe and Paradell, *Law and Practice*, pp. 19–20, 41; Van Harten, *Investment Treaty Arbitration*, pp. 19–23; McLachlan, Shore and Weiniger, *International Investment Arbitration*, p. 7.

[134] General Agreement on Tariffs and Trade, Annex 1A, Agreement Establishing the World Trade Organization, opened for signature 15 April 1994, (1994) 33 ILM 28 (entered into force 1 January 1995).

[135] Carrasco and Kose, 'Income Distribution', 11; Corea, 'UNCTAD', 178–9.

[136] Anghie, *Imperialism*, pp. 259–60; Carrasco and Kose, 'Income Distribution', 11; Zamora, 'Voting', 568.

[137] United Nations Conference on Trade and Development (UNCTAD); see also the discussion in Mickelson, 'Rhetoric and Rage', 362–5; see also the discussion in Corea, 'UNCTAD', 179–80.

seeking to remould international economic law and policy.[138] The United Nations also followed a one member-one vote system, and, as such, developing states were able to take advantage of their superior numbers and ensure key resolutions reflecting an NIEO approach were passed.[139] There were a number of such instruments in the NIEO campaign, the primary ones of which were the 1962 General Assembly Resolution 1803 on the principle of permanent sovereignty over natural resources,[140] the 1974 Charter of Economic Rights and Duties of States (CERDS),[141] and the 1974 Declaration of the Establishment of a New International Economic Order (NIEO Declaration).[142]

(a) Permanent sovereignty over natural resources

Although the NIEO campaign was directed towards wider issues of economic injustice, fundamentally, postcolonial and developing states were also seeking to use the law-making mechanism of the United Nations General Assembly to reorient the international rules of foreign investment protection. A key strategy was to establish an expressly stated principle of international law that would embody the right of states to enjoy the benefits of their own resources and enable the revisiting of inequitable concessions granted by colonial authorities – the principle of permanent sovereignty over natural resources.[143] The essence of the asserted principle was contained in a combination of statements in the Declaration on Permanent Sovereignty over Natural Resources (the Declaration), such as:

> **Paragraph 1.** The right of peoples and nations to permanent sovereignty over their natural wealth and resources must be exercised in the interest of their national development and of the well-being of the people of the State concerned.

138 Mickelson, 'Rhetoric and Rage', 362–5; Carrasco and Kose, 'Income Distribution'; Gathii, 'Third World Approaches', 258.

139 Carrasco and Kose, 'Income Distribution', 11; Zamora, 'Voting', 567.

140 Declaration on Permanent Sovereignty over Natural Resources, GA Res 1803 (XVII), 17 GAOR, Supp. 17, UN Doc. A/5217, 15 (1962).

141 Charter of Economic Rights and Duties of States, GA Res 3281 (XXIX), UN Doc. A/RES/3281 (XXIX) (1974).

142 Declaration on the Establishment of a New International Economic Order, GA Res 3201 (S-VI), UN Doc. A/Res/S-6/3201 (1974).

143 Anghie, *Imperialism*, pp. 211, 216; Schrijver, *Natural Resources*, pp. 1–3, 20; Newcombe and Paradell, *Law and Practice*, pp. 26–7; see also the discussion in White, 'A New International'; see the discussion in Pahuja, *Decolonising*, p. 119.

> **Paragraph 2.** The exploration, development and disposition of such resources, as well as the import of the foreign capital required for these purposes, should be in conformity with the rules and conditions which the peoples and nations freely consider to be necessary or desirable with regard to the authorization, restriction or prohibition of such activities.[144]

Countering the 'adequate, effective and prompt payment' standard of the Hull Formula, paragraph 4 of the Declaration contained the controversial assertion of an 'appropriate' compensation standard for expropriation of foreign-owned assets.[145] Paragraph 7 explicitly framed violations of the principle of permanent sovereignty over natural resources as contrary to the 'spirit and principles' of the United Nations Charter and as hindering 'the development of international economic cooperation and the maintenance of peace'.[146] Throughout the text of the Declaration, the sovereignty of the state was emphasised, as was the crucial role played by sovereign control over natural resources in the promotion of economic development.[147] There were also overt links with the right of self-determination in the references to 'peoples and nations' and there were potential compensation implications for violations of the principle during colonial control of the newly independent states.[148] For these reasons, the Declaration proved controversial. During the negotiating process, Western states objected on a number of levels to, amongst other aspects, the association with self-determination, the minimising of host state obligations under international law, the meaning of sovereignty within the Declaration, and the framing of the compensation standard.[149] Ultimately, compromises were made and the Declaration contained references to arbitration or international adjudication of disputes and to compensation being determined in accordance with international law.[150] The final form of the

[144] Declaration on Permanent Sovereignty over Natural Resources, GA Res 1803 (XVII), 17 GAOR, Supp. 17, UN Doc A/5217, 15 (1962).

[145] Ibid., para. 4; the Hull Formula is discussed above in section I of this chapter; for further discussion on the Hull Formula, see Kunz, 'Mexican Expropriations', 9, 27; Newcombe and Paradell, *Law and Practice*, p. 18.

[146] Declaration on Permanent Sovereignty over Natural Resources, GA Res 1803 (XVII), para. 7, 17 GAOR, Supp. 17, UN Doc A/5217, 15 (1962).

[147] See the discussion in Anghie, *Imperialism*, pp. 211–20.

[148] Anghie, *Imperialism*, pp. 211–20; Schrijver, *Natural Resources*, pp. 369–71.

[149] See the detailed discussion in Schrijver, *Natural Resources*, pp. 42–76; see also Gess, 'Permanent Sovereignty'.

[150] Declaration on Permanent Sovereignty over Natural Resources, GA Res 1803 (XVII), para. 4, 17 GAOR, Supp. 17, UN Doc A/5217, 15 (1962).

Declaration was generally considered to have been a mechanism through which developing states could pursue their reform agenda, but also a reflection of the traditional position of Western states emphasising that protection for foreign investors would be in accordance with international law.[151] This willingness to compromise on the part of developing states, however, soon gave way to a more radical stance as it became increasingly apparent that international economic systems were not shifting to accommodate their position.[152] This approach culminated in the adoption of CERDS[153] and the NIEO Declaration.[154]

(b) Charter of Economic Rights and Duties of States

Despite various United Nations General Assembly Resolutions of the 1960s,[155] global economic conditions continued to disadvantage developing states through deteriorating terms of trade, tightening of Western markets, and increasing levels of developing state debt.[156] These circumstances were reflected in the approach of the NIEO Declaration[157] and CERDS,[158] which embodied the hardened position of the Group of 77 in their attempts to reshape international economic law through the United Nations. As such, the NIEO Declaration expressly addressed issues relating to the impact of colonialism, terms of trade, financial assistance for development, and reform of the international monetary system.[159] For capital-exporting states and their investor nationals, the provisions on permanent sovereignty over

151 Schrijver, *Natural Resources*, pp. 85, 180, 371–2; see also the discussion in Anghie, *Imperialism*, pp. 220–1.

152 Anghie, *Imperialism*, p. 221; Schrijver, *Natural Resources*, pp. 82–3.

153 *Charter of Economic Rights and Duties of States*, GA Res 3281 (XXIX), UN Doc A/RES/3281 (XXIX) (1974).

154 Declaration on the Establishment of a New International Economic Order, GA Res 3201 (S-VI), UN Doc A/Res/S-6/3201 (1974).

155 E.g., Permanent Sovereignty Over Natural Resources, GA Res 1720 (XVI), 19 December 1961; Declaration on Permanent Sovereignty Over Natural Resources, GA Res 1803 (XVII), 17 GAOR, Supp. 17, UN Doc A/5217, 15 (1962); Permanent Sovereignty Over Natural Resources, GA Res 2158 (XXI), 25 November 1966.

156 Richardson, 'Environmental Law', 2; Carrasco and Kose, 'Income Distribution', 10–13; Corea, 'UNCTAD', 178–80; Anghie, *Imperialism*, pp. 196–9, 221; Mickelson, 'Rhetoric and Rage', 362–5; Schrijver, *Natural Resources*, p. 93.

157 Declaration on the Establishment of a New International Economic Order, GA Res 3201 (S-VI), UN Doc. A/Res/S-6/3201 (1974).

158 Charter of Economic Rights and Duties of States, GA Res 3281 (XXIX), UN Doc. A/RES/3281 (XXIX) (1974).

159 Declaration on the Establishment of a New International Economic Order, GA Res 3201 (S-VI), UN Doc A/Res/S-6/3201 (1974).

natural resources were of particular concern as they focused on a state's right to nationalise without reference to compensation.[160] These key elements were set out as follows:

4. The new international economic order should be founded on full respect for the following principles:

...

e. Full permanent sovereignty of every State over its natural resources and all economic activities. In order to safeguard these resources, each State is entitled to exercise effective control over them and their exploitation with means suitable to its own situation, including the right to nationalization or transfer of ownership to its nationals, this right being an expression of the full permanent sovereignty of the State. No State may be subjected to economic, political or any other type of coercion to prevent the free and full exercise of this inalienable right;

...

g. Regulation and supervision of the activities of transnational corporations by taking measures in the interest of the national economies of the countries where such transnational corporations operate on the basis of the full sovereignty of those countries;
h. The right of the developing countries and the peoples of territories under colonial and racial domination and foreign occupation to achieve their liberation and to regain effective control over their natural resources and economic activities;[161]

CERDS reinforced this approach, stating that compensation would be assessed under national laws and made no mention of such determinations being 'in accordance with international law', as had been the case with the 1962 Declaration on Permanent Sovereignty over Natural Resources.[162] Article 2 of CERDS also referred to disputes over compensation being 'settled under the domestic law of the nationalising state

[160] Schrijver, *Natural Resources*, pp. 98–100; Weston, 'Charter'; Brookens, 'Diplomatic Protection'; see, e.g., the comments from the United States' delegation that the resolution did not 'represent unanimity of opinion in this Assembly . . . the steamroller is not the vehicle for solving vital, complex problems' in the Report of the Ad Hoc Committee of the Sixth Special Session, UN GAOR, 6th Spec. Sess. (2229th plen. mtg.), UN Doc. A/PV.2229 (1 May 1974) 7, para. 81.

[161] Declaration on the Establishment of a New International Economic Order, GA Res 3201 (S-VI), para. 4, UN Doc A/Res/S-6/3201 (1974).

[162] Declaration on Permanent Sovereignty over Natural Resources, GA Res 1803 (XVII), para. 4, 17 GAOR, Supp. 17, UN Doc A/5217, 15 (1962); Charter of Economic Rights and Duties of States, GA Res 3281 (XXIX), art. 2, UN Doc A/RES/3281 (XXIX) (1974).

and by its tribunals',[163] clearly invoking the approach of the Calvo Doctrine from the previous century.[164] In the ensuing debates, therefore, it was unsurprising that developed and developing states were polarised over CERDS' treatment of permanent sovereignty and issues of compensation.[165] However, despite opposition from the majority of industrialised states, the sheer numbers of developing states in the United Nations General Assembly enabled the adoption of CERDS without amendment.[166]

2. Shaping international investment law: familiar patterns

From an historical perspective, it can be seen that the NIEO was a key movement through which postcolonial states sought to reorient international investment law.[167] With echoes of nineteenth-century attempts to assert the Calvo Doctrine as a rule of international law,[168] host states endeavoured again to ameliorate the unbalanced nature of foreign investment protection law through the introduction of principles reflecting their interests. In this way, postcolonial states attempted to confront and neutralise the 'otherness' of international investment law and truly participate in its development. However, there was a familiar antagonism to host state attempts to reshape the rules of foreign investment protection.[169] In much the same way as the Calvo Doctrine had been denied the legitimacy of international legal status by

[163] Charter of Economic Rights and Duties of States, GA Res 3281 (XXIX), Art. 2, UN Doc. A/RES/3281 (XXIX) (1974).

[164] The Calvo Doctrine is discussed in detail above in Chapter 2. For an in-depth examination of the Calvo Doctrine, see Shea, *The Calvo Clause*.

[165] The objections of developing states are discussed in detail in Schrijver, *Natural Resources*, pp. 100–11; see also White, 'A New International Economic Order'; see also the discussion in Dolzer, 'New Foundations'; see for a discussion of the United States' position Ferguson, 'The Politics'.

[166] The Charter was adopted 120 votes to six, with ten abstentions. The OECD states that voted for the adoption of the Charter were Australia, Greece, Finland, New Zealand, Sweden, and Turkey. See for further detail Schrijver, *Natural Resources*, pp. 100–11; see also Newcombe and Paradell, *Law and Practice*, p. 32.

[167] Anghie, *Imperialism*, pp. 235, 312–13; Weston, 'The Charter', 437–9; Gathii, 'Third World Approaches'; see also the discussion in Rajagopal, *International Law from Below*, pp. 78–9; see also Chattergee, 'The Charter of Economic Rights and Duties'; Farer, 'The United States and the Third World', 83–84; see the discussion in Flory, 'Adapting International Law', 13.

[168] See the references to the Calvo Doctrine above in Chapter 1 and in Shea, *The Calvo Clause*.

[169] Anghie, *Imperialism*, pp. 235, 312–13; Bunn, 'The Right to Development', 1430–1.

capital-exporting states,[170] any rule-creating potential of the NIEO instruments was also dismissed. Several developed states expressly disavowed that CERDS or the NIEO Declaration reflected any unanimity amongst states.[171] Subsequent arbitral awards rejected submissions that the NIEO instruments were evidence of rules of international customary law on the grounds that developed states had not supported the resolutions.[172] A concerted effort was then made by capital-exporting states to conclude bilateral investment treaties containing provisions that directly countered NIEO measures.[173] For these reasons, the objectives of the NIEO did not make lasting impressions upon foreign investment protection law.[174] Again, the patterns of assertion and response had resurfaced.

III. Social movements, the environment, and foreign investment protection

For all the apparent failure of the NIEO to reshape the rules of foreign investment protection, social movements have remained an enduring source of pressure to reform international investment law. The push for the NIEO was a manifestation of attempts to assert a 'host state' version of international investment law, but it was also a movement embedded within a more generalised context of protest. From the late 1950s through to the 1970s, grassroots activism in developing states and protest movements within the West emerged around issues such as the reordering of social and economic class structures, anti-colonialism, anti-capitalism, environmentalism, human rights, civil rights, women's rights, and gay and lesbian rights.[175] Forms of popular mobilisation have shifted, as have the subjects of their focus, but social movements

[170] See the discussion on the Calvo Doctrine above in Chapter 1. For examples of hostile responses to capital-importing states' promotion of the Calvo Doctrine, see Freeman, 'Recent Aspects', 125; see also the commentary in Borchard, 'Minimum Standard'.

[171] See the discussion in Schrijver, *Natural Resources*, pp. 98–100; see, e.g., the comments of the United States' delegation referred to above in the United Nations Report, above n. 160.

[172] See, e.g., *Texaco Overseas Petroleum Co. & California Asiatic Oil Co* v. *The Government of the Libyan Arab Republic* (1975) 53 *International Law Reports* 389; see the discussion in Anghie, *Imperialism*, pp. 228–32.

[173] Newcombe and Paradell, *Law and Practice*, pp. 24, 26, 31–2, 41.

[174] Anghie, *Imperialism*, p. 245.

[175] B. Rajagopal, 'Social Movements', 407–8; see the discussion in Habermas, 'New Social Movements'; Boggs, *Social Movements*, pp. 38–40; Edelman, 'Social Movements', 285.

have remained intimately connected to attempts to reframe international investment law and responses to those attempts. As such, this section focuses on two forms of social movement that have been particularly influential on the issue of foreign investment - grassroots activism and environmentalism.

A. Host state grassroots activism

1. Constituting a social movement

Although NGOs provide focal points around which social movements can mobilise, such movements are not limited to this form of institutional embodiment of a cause. They have a significantly more complex and diffuse character, encompassing an array of political spaces, actors, communities, identities, processes, and interactions.[176] In general, however, social movements tend to possess the following characteristics:[177]

a) they involve networks of informal interactions between a plurality of actors;
b) they are engaged in political or cultural conflicts; and
c) they organise on the basis of shared beliefs and collective identities.

Their particular manifestation within developing states has largely revolved around issues of survival, impacts of the globalised economy, and conflict with private sector development.[178] Rajagopal refers specifically to 'Third World' resistance in the form of 'peasant rebellions, environmental movements, and human rights movements',[179] 'the urban poor, peasants, workers in the informal sector, illiterate women, and indigenous peoples whose resources are being destroyed.'[180] These grassroots resistance movements emerged out of communities directly experiencing the detrimental impact of

[176] Rajagopal, 'Social Movements', 409–18; Tarrow, *Power in Movement*; Langman, 'Virtual Public Spheres'; Dryzek et al., *Green States*, pp. 2–4; see the discussion on 'framing processes' of social movements in Benford and Snow, 'Framing Processes'.

[177] Rajagopal, 'Social Movements', 408; see also Diani, 'The Concept of Social Movement' (1992); Diani, 'The Concept of Social Movement' (2000), 155, 160; see also the discussion on social movements in Yearley, *Cultures of Environmentalism*, p. 12.

[178] Rajagopal, 'Social Movements', 409–10, 414–17; Adam, 'Post-Marxism'; see also the discussion in Yashar, 'Resistance and Identity Politics'.

[179] Rajagopal, 'Resistance to Renewal', 532; see also the discussion in Okafor, 'Poverty, Agency', 95, 104–7.

[180] Rajagopal, 'Social Movements', 406; see also Edelman, 'Social Movements', 285; see further the discussion in Gledhill, 'Agrarian Social Movements'.

development measures, multinational corporate activity, and the inequities of the globalised economy at the local level.[181]

Catalysts for the emergence of individual social movements, and indeed for the generalised trends in increasing global resistance activity, are, of course, complex, involving a raft of factors.[182] However, it can be said that resistance movements in developing states embody a decentralised form of reaction within marginalised communities and groups seeking a voice on issues that impact directly on them.[183] It is important to note that the focus for such resistance has not been limited to the private sector actors operating within the contested physical sites, but has also often involved engagement with government officials. Indeed, it is not without irony that, in many instances, resistance communities have been brought into conflict with their own governments and, in the context of foreign investment, with their own states' desire for greater foreign capital-driven development.[184]

Faced with conflict, indifference, and disempowerment, popular mobilisation seeks equity and justice through the engagement of multiple sites of resistance.[185] And, as international law has not traditionally accommodated the phenomenon of public mobilisation or extra-institutional resistance movements, these voices within social movements have also remained at the subaltern level in international law.[186]

[181] Rajagopal, 'Resistance to Renewal', 532; Rajagopal, 'Social Movements', 400–9; see also the discussion on the water protests in Cochabamba, Bolivia, arising out of the operations of a foreign investor, in Odumosu, 'Law and Politics', 258–60; for a discussion on grassroots environmental activism in India, see Guha, *The Unquiet Woods*; see also Sethi, 'Survival and Democracy', 122; see also Omvedt, *Reinventing Revolution*.

[182] Yashar, 'Resistance and Identity Politics'; see also the discussion in Yashar, *Contesting Citizenship*, pp. 3–6; see also Polletta and Jasper, 'Collective Identity'.

[183] Yasher, 'Resistance'; Rajagopal, *International Law from Below*, pp. 96–7, 295–6; see further for a discussion on theories of underlying global processes in social movements, Tsutsui, 'Global Civil Society'.

[184] See, e.g., the discussion in Beinart and Hughes, *Environment and Empire*, pp. 276–8.

[185] Rajagopal, *International Law from Below*, pp. 291–6; Rajagopal, 'Resistance to Renewal', 534–5; Rajagopal, 'Social Movements', 400–9; Yasher, 'Resistance'; see also the discussion in Otto, 'Subalternity and International Law'.

[186] Odumosu, 'Law and Politics', 258–63; Rajagopal, 'Resistance to Renewal', 534–5; Rajagopal, 'Social Movements', 400–9; Rajagopal, *International Law from Below*, pp. 291–6. The term 'subaltern' was coined by scholars working within postcolonial theory such as Spivak, 'Can the Subaltern Speak?', p. 271. The definition and scope of 'subaltern' is disputed, but generally refers to politically and socially marginalised groups within the context of postcolonialism. It has also been suggested that a wider theory of subalternity has evolved in postcolonial discourse to encompass contemporary forms of imperialism, oppressed groups, and resistance. E.g., see the discussion in Chaturvedi, *Mapping Subaltern Studies*.

In turn, this invisibility within international law reproduces the patterns of disenfranchisement and suppression of voice that also operate at the localised site of resistance. Ironically, despite this withholding of validation under international law, social movements play a fundamental role in shaping international law through their provocation of patterns of reactive power relations[187] – new international institutions, mechanisms, and legal doctrine are repeatedly created to address the challenges to the international legal order that are embodied in grassroots activism in developing states.[188]

2. International economic law and resistance

In the context of the Bretton Woods international financial institutions, Rajagopal argues that seeking to control social movements and NGOs in developing states has been fundamental to the creation of the international legal order's institutional architecture.[189] In particular, he points to the advent of grassroots environmental activism, the resistance environmentalism generated to the international economic policies of the World Bank and the IMF, the institutions' need to constrain that opposition, and the concomitant opportunity this provided to reframe their role into 'development' and reach into the domestic law and policy areas of developing states.[190]

A version of this argument can equally be applied to the creation of ICSID and the persistent promotion of bilateral investment treaties. In the face of the NIEO and increasing environmental and human rights-based activism within host states, capital-exporting states and their investing nationals were able to frame these circumstances as requiring a 'depoliticised' environment in which to resolve investment disputes.[191] Interestingly, this still remains a key investor argument in

[187] Rajagopal, 'Resistance to Renewal', 534–5; Rajagopal, *International Law from Below*, pp. 45, 96–7; see also the related discussion on global administrative law, resistance, and response in Chimni, 'Co-Option and Resistance'.

[188] Rajagopal, *International Law from Below*, pp. 45, 96–7; see the discussion in Anghie, *Imperialism*, pp. 10–11, 211–20, 235, 312–13; Rajagopal, 'Resistance to Renewal', 555–7; Rajagopal, 'Social Movements, 399–400.

[189] Rajagopal, 'Resistance to Renewal'; see also the discussion in Gathii, 'Third World Approaches'; Anghie, 'Time Present'.

[190] Rajagopal, 'Resistance to Renewal', 555–7; see also the discussion in Anghie, 'Time Present'; see also the account given in Nash, 'Interpreting Social Movements'.

[191] See, e.g., the discussion in Dolzer and Schreuer, *International Investment Law*, p. 20; Newcombe and Paradell, *Law and Practice*, p. 27; Odumosu, 'Law and Politics', 254–5.

advocating the importance of ICSID – the 'political' needs to be removed from investment disputes.[192] It also constituted a persistent devaluing of the position of the host state as merely 'political' rather than legal.[193]

It is clear that grassroots resistance to international investment law and its impacts continues to the present day – as does the attempted neutralising of those voices. Recent examples include public mobilisation at the operation of foreign-owned water utilities in Cochabamba, Bolivia,[194] protest action from indigenous peoples at oil exploration and extraction in the Amazon, Ecuador,[195] and community protests at a hazardous waste landfill in Hermosillo, Mexico.[196] However, in investor–state arbitration, social movements tend either to be depicted as the illegitimate basis for the governmental action triggering the investor's claim, or as advocates for socio-political issues irrelevant to the determination of investors' rights under international law.[197] In this way, arbitral tribunals have conceptualised host state responses to the legitimate public interest concerns of their citizens as 'political' and therefore as necessarily constituting discriminatory action and a breach of fair and equitable treatment standards.[198] However, as Odumosu explains, the fact that action

[192] See, e.g., Wälde and Kolo, 'Environmental Regulation'; see also Wälde and Ndi, 'Stabilizing'; see also Paulsson, 'Arbitration Without Privity', 256; for further examples of similar views on host state activities, see Baker, 'Denial of Justice', 187, 187–91; see also the comments in Weiler, 'Good Faith', 701; for an argument that the 'political' needs to be re-injected back into investor–state disputes, see Choudhury, 'More Politics', conference paper available at www.asil.org/files/ielconferencepapers/choudhury.pdf (last accessed 6 December 2011); see also Choudhury, 'Recapturing Public Power'.

[193] For the discussion on ICSID and depoliticisation of investment disputes, see above at section II.A.2(a)(i).

[194] Odumosu, 'Law and Politics', 259–60; see Woodhouse, 'Guerra del Agua'; see also Sanchez-Moreno and Higgins, 'No Recourse'. The dispute gave rise to the ICSID arbitration, *Agua del Tunari SA* v. *The Republic of Bolivia* (ICSID Case No. ARB/03/02, Award of 21 October 2005).

[195] See the discussion in Kimerling, 'Indigenous Peoples'; see also Lyons, 'Case Study'. The protests led to court action being brought by local indigenous groups against the United States-based multinational corporation, *Sequihua* v. *Texaco, Inc*, 847 F. Supp. 61 (S.D. Tex. 1994); *Aguinda* v. *Texaco, Inc*, 945 F. Supp. 625 (S.D.N.Y. 1996); *Ashanga* v. *Texaco*, S.D.N.Y. Dkt. No. 94 Civ. 9266 (Aug. 13, 1997).

[196] Odumosu, 'Law and Politics', 275–9. The dispute gave rise to the ICSID arbitration, *Técnicas Medioambientales Tecmed, SA* v. *United Mexican States* (ICSID Case No. ARB (AF)/00/02, Award of 29 May 2003).

[197] Odumosu, 'Law and Politics', 275–81; see, e.g., the reasoning in *Técnicas Medioambientales Tecmed, SA* v. *United Mexican States* (ICSID Case No. ARB(AF)/00/02, Award of 29 May 2003).

[198] Odumosu, 'Law and Politics', 279.

was taken in response to domestic socio-political conditions does not render the measure inherently inequitable.[199]

There are, of course, further layers to the relationship between investment and the environment, including the complex interplay of 'development' and the 'environment'. In certain contexts, environmental protection objectives can be in direct conflict with the private sector, host state development trajectories, or the economic needs of indigenous peoples and other stakeholders.[200] When the contested areas engage the development policies of the government in partnership with foreign investors on the one hand and the environmental needs of local communities on the other, the marginalisation by host states of their own communities can ensue. It is not without irony that the goals of furthering development and attracting foreign capital have been used, at times, by developing host states to justify acting in a manner adverse to the interests of certain local communities and their environments.[201]

Despite the dismissive treatment of social movements by arbitral tribunals in investment disputes, host state grassroots activism remains a source of pressure to reform the unbalanced nature of international investment law, to give a voice to those affected by the activities of foreign investors, and to reflect the role of resistance in shaping the regulatory network of investment protection. A particularly potent focus for this form of pressure has been the environmentally harmful activities of foreign-owned operations. As Rajagopal observes, to portray environmentalism as solely a Western concern, as a number of developing states have done, is to ignore 'Third World' resistance to environmental degradation resulting from private sector development.[202] Such an approach perpetuates the invisibility of developing state social movements and marginalised voices within international law. However, in finding form as a social movement in both developing

[199] Ibid.

[200] See, e.g., the conflict between conservation environmentalists and indigenous hunters in Africa discussed in Beinart and Hughes, *Environment and Empire*, pp. 278–83.

[201] See, e.g., the discussion on the Ralco dam project in Chile in Carruthers and Rodriguez, 'Mapuche Protest'.

[202] Rajagopal, *International Law from Below*, p. 20; Rajagopal, 'Resistance to Renewal', 559. Rajagopal cites as an example the comments of the Indian Prime Minister, Indira Gandhi, that poverty was the world's worst polluter; see the discussion on environmental activism and women's rights movements in India in Omvedt, *Reinventing Revolution*, pp. 199–207; see also the discussion in Mittelman, 'Globalisation'.

state grassroots activism and Western NGOs, environmentalism has considerable potential to compel reform in international investment law.

B. Environmentalism as a global political force

Although a complex interplay of factors is at work in the current pressure to reshape international investment law, environmentalism stands out as a significant challenge to the status quo. As a social movement, environmentalism is being infused throughout a multiplicity of societies and spaces, gradually being 'internalized in our cultures and our personalities'.[203] In many ways, therefore, the continued reluctance of the investment sector to engage with host state public interest issues is in conflict with the current globalising culture of environmental consciousness.

This disinclination to incorporate environmental considerations into international investment law is also a form of response to host state attempts to create space for their social requirements. Indeed, environmentalism has triggered strong reactions from the investment sector,[204] although, it is becoming increasingly difficult for investors to frame the environmental protection objectives of host states, indigenous peoples, grassroots activists, and NGOs as unreasonable. In particular, as corporate social responsibility (CSR), environmentalism, and sustainable development become part of mainstream socio-political culture, requirements for socially and environmentally responsible investor conduct no longer appear radical.[205] It is also likely that, in shaping the cultural lens through which business activities are perceived, the modern environmental movement will remain a significant source of pressure to reshape the international regulatory frameworks governing those activities.[206]

[203] Jamison, *Green Knowledge*, p. 17.

[204] See Rajagopal's discussion of responses to environmentalism within international financial institutions; see for an example of vehement anti-environmental commentary on international investment law, Wälde and Kolo, 'Environmental Regulation'; see also Wälde and Ndi, 'Stabilizing'; see further the comments in Weiler, *International Investment Law*, p. 701.

[205] The impact of the corporate social responsibility and sustainable finance movements on the investment sector is examined below in Chapter 4.

[206] Chapters 5 and 6 below examine mechanisms through which this consideration of environmental protection objectives may occur. One immediate response from the business community to this pressure has been to become increasingly involved in

1. The modern environmental movement

Although the origins of environmentalism stretch back centuries,[207] its recent emergence as a global social movement in the 1960s and 1970s ushered in a transformation of perception as to what was meant by 'concern for the environment'. Moving away from a preoccupation with conservation, it embodied a new way of thinking about the environment, professed the need for an urgent re-evaluation of the human–environment relationship, and, crucially, accessed communications and media technology that tapped into an audience on a global scale.[208] It was at this point that a set of scientific, historical, political, philosophical, cultural, and technological circumstances converged, ultimately propelling environmentalism and international environmental law onto the global politico-legal agenda.

(a) *Emerging as a global social movement*

Forms of modern environmentalism materialised as responses to localised environmental damage, increasing pollution levels, threats to indigenous communities and livelihoods, and the recognition of a global environmental crisis.[209] This occurred against a background of growing public concern at increasing rates of Western consumption, critiques of capitalism and modernism, escalating scales of environmental degradation, the occurrence of several major environmental disasters, an appreciation of the interconnectedness of nature's elements, the spectre of nuclear war, a 'counter-culture' of political activism, a dramatic increase in the number of environmental NGOs, and the development of communications technology to publicise concerns globally.[210]

The high profile of environmental causes was maintained through the media and a series of influential works, such as Rachel Carson's

shaping the environmental agenda through the creation of bodies such as the Business Council for Sustainable Development.

207 Grove, *Green Imperialism*; Barton, *Empire Forestry*; Goodin, *Green Political Theory*, p. 1.

208 Eckersley, *Environmentalism*, pp. 7–21; Jamison, *Green Knowledge*, pp. 16–17, 83; Pepper, *Modern Environmentalism*, pp. 1–10; Worster, *Nature's Economy*, pp. 340, 351–4.

209 Rajagopal, 'Resistance to Renewal', 557–8; Rajagopal, 'Social Movements', 407–8; Eckersley, *Environmentalism*, pp. 7–21; McCormick, *Global Environmental Movement*, p. 1; see also the discussion in Ignatow, *Transnational Identity Politics*, pp. 4–28.

210 Pepper, *Modern Environmentalism*, pp. 1–10; Worster, *Nature's Economy*, pp. 340, 351–4; Eckersley, *Environmentalism*, pp. 7–21; Jamison, *Green Knowledge*, pp. 16–17; see the discussion in Ignatow, *Transnational Identity Politics*, pp. 4–28; McCormick, 'Environmental NGOs', 83, 89; Brenton, *Greening of Machiavelli*, pp. 20–4; Chasek, Downie, Porter, and Brown, *Global Environmental Politics*; Pepper, *Roots*, p. 16.

Silent Spring,[211] as well as in the organisation of events such as 'Earth Day'.[212] Carson's work extended beyond a simple warning of the dangers of organophosphate pesticides. It spoke of humanity's misplaced arrogance in its perceived dominance over the environment, the threat to survival generated by the destructive impact of human activities, and the need for an appreciation of non-human entities as something other than resources and commodities for human use.[213] It introduced the science of ecology to a worldwide audience, explaining the interconnected nature of the earth's organisms and the inescapable global implications of this for transboundary pollution issues.[214] Although Carson was by no means alone in advocating a re-evaluation of the human–environment relationship, it was her writing that proved to be particularly influential in fuelling the modern environmental movement.[215]

A gradual social process of normalising the consideration of environmental impacts was experienced generally in many states through institutional, legislative, and social developments.[216] For example, new governmental departments for the protection of the environment were created, environmental legislation proliferated, universities began offering environmentally oriented courses across the humanities and sciences, and professional specialisation in environmental issues developed.[217] Policies, procedures, and structures from local government to international entities were redesigned so as to integrate environmental considerations into social, economic, and political

[211] Carson, *Silent Spring*; see also influential works such as Ehrlich, *Population Bomb*; Commoner, *Closing Circle*; Odum, *Environment, Power*; Meadows et al., *Limits to Growth*.

[212] Brenton, *Greening of Machiavelli*, p. 19:

> The climactic coming of age of the environment movement in the US took place on 'Earth Day', 22 April 1970, in which 20 million people participated and which provoked *Time* magazine to dub the environment 'issue of the year'.

[213] Carson, *Silent Spring*, p. 297; see also the commentary on the impact of Carson's work in Worster, *Nature's Economy*, pp. 347–9; see also Ignatow, *Transnational Identity Politics*, pp. 25–6; see also Goodin, *Green Political Theory*, p. 3.

[214] *Silent Spring* was translated into twenty-two languages. See the discussion in Worster, *Nature's Economy*, p. 347; Brenton, *Greening of Machiavelli*, p. 18.

[215] Worster, *Nature's Economy*, pp. 347–9; Brenton, *Greening of Machiavelli*, p. 18; Ignatow, *Transnational Identity Politics*, pp. 25–6; see also the discussion on the importance of popular science literature in the spread of environmentalism, and, in particular, the work of Carson in Yearley, *Cultures of Environmentalism*, p. 19.

[216] Jamison, *Green Knowledge*, p. 16; Yearley, *Cultures of Environmentalism*, pp. 19–25; Coglianese, 'Social Movements, Law', 87–8.

[217] Yearley, *Cultures of Environmentalism*, pp. 7–25; Jamison, *Green Knowledge*, pp. 16–17.

activities.[218] As the notion of environmentally sustainable practices for both business and personal activities became mainstream, the concept of 'green consumerism' emerged.[219] In other words, environmentalism as a social movement significantly influenced knowledge-production on the natural environment, shifting behavioural patterns within communities, and creating what Eyerman and Jamison describe as 'a new conceptual space' resulting in the modern environmental discourse.[220]

Although borne out of shared concern for the state of the environment, as a social movement, environmentalism quickly fractured into many sub-forms.[221] Ecology fragmented into a myriad of specialisations.[222] Philosophically, the term 'environmentalism' could cover a raft of positions, spanning from deep ecology to conservative resource management.[223] Substantively, the issues were diverse, encompassing a wide range of concerns such as nuclear disarmament, marine pollution, localised environmental degradation, population growth and poverty, destruction of rainforest, whaling, and degradation of territory traditionally owned by indigenous peoples. Divisions in approach and methodology polarised environmentalists into those engaged in radical forms of protest and those employing less confrontational methods of issue presentation.[224] Ironically, environmental political thought was associated with both radical and conservative political alignments.[225] It has encompassed participation issues, 'crisis of survival' phases, environmental justice concerns, 'crisis of culture' approaches focusing on humanity's value systems, ecological modernisation, and postmodernist environmentalism.[226] These philosophical, political, and scientific

[218] Jacobs, 'Sustainable Development', 21, 29.

[219] Jamison, *Green Knowledge*, pp. 16–17; Vertovec, 'Introduction', 1, 2.

[220] Eyreman and Jamison, *Social Movements*, p. 55; see also Jamison, *Green Knowledge*; see also the discussion in Yearley, *Cultures of Environmentalism*, pp. 7–25.

[221] Pepper, *Modern Environmentalism*, p. 10; Jamison, *Green Knowledge*, p. 5; Eckersley, *Environmentalism*, p. 34; Yearley, *Cultures of Environmentalism*, pp. 18–19.

[222] Worster, *Nature's Economy*, pp. 340–1.

[223] McCormick, 'Environmental NGOs', 91–3; Eckersley, *Environmentalism*, pp. 33–47; Pepper, *Modern Environmentalism*, pp. 17–40; O'Riordan, *Environmentalism*, p. 1; see the discussion on anthropocentric approaches to environmental protection and ecocentrism in Dobson, *Green Political Thought*, p. 1; Zimmerman, 'Animal Rights', pp. vi–vii; see for a deep ecology approach, the 'Land Ethic' of Leopold, *Sand County Almanac*.

[224] See the discussion in Yearley, *Cultures of Environmentalism*, pp. 16–17.

[225] Pepper, *Modern Environmentalism*, p. 10; Eckersley, *Environmentalism*, p. 21.

[226] Eckersley, *Environmentalism*, pp. 7–21; see also Dryzek et al., *Green States*; for examples of 'crisis of survival' approaches, focusing on exceeding the carrying capacity of the earth, see Meadows, *The Limits to Growth*; see also Ehrlich, *The Population Bomb*; see for

divisions led to accusations of a lack of cohesion within the environmental movement and enabled aspersions to be cast on the scientific bases for the positions adopted by environmentalists.[227]

The dominant streams of modern environmentalism, however, have largely been informed by a relatively limited number of conceptual bases, identified by Martinez-Alier as the 'cult of wilderness', eco-efficiency, and the 'environmentalism of the poor'.[228] The first two characterisations stem from Western conceptualisations of environmental protection objectives. On the one hand, a preoccupation with 'wilderness' preservation manifests in ecocentric approaches and conservationist national parks initiatives; and, on the other, there is a form of environmentalism that focuses on the efficient use of natural resources, the impact of economic growth on the urban as well as natural environments, and the promotion of sustainable development.[229] Martinez-Alier argues that the third identified stream of environmentalism is increasingly influential in the global movement, which he categorises as the 'environmentalism of the poor'. He uses interchangeably a number of terms for this manifestation of environmentalism, including environmental justice, popular environmentalism, livelihood ecology, and liberation ecology.[230] This form of environmental activism emerges as a response to the detrimental impacts of economic development experienced directly by impoverished or indigenous communities. Accordingly, it embodies an expansive approach to environmentalism, linking social justice and human rights issues to environmental degradation.[231] Despite the diversity of

examples of the 'crisis of culture' theory Bosselmann, *When Two Worlds Collide*; see also Westra, Bosselmann, and Westra, *Reconciling Human Existence*; for an example of postmodern approaches to environmentalism see the discussion in Ignatow, *Transnational Identity Politics*, pp. 113–17.

227 See, e.g., Lomborg, *The Skeptical Environmentalist*; see also the discussion in Yearley, *Cultures of Environmentalism*, pp. 18–19.

228 Martinez-Alier, *Environmentalism of the Poor*; see also Guha and Martinez-Alier, *Varieties of Environmentalism*.

229 Martinez-Alier, *Environmentalism of the Poor*, pp. 2–10; see also the discussion in Guha and Martinez-Alier, *Varieties of Environmentalism*; see also the discussion in Jamieson, 'Justice', 85, 86–8.

230 Martinez-Alier, *Environmentalism of the Poor*, pp. vii, 10; see also the discussion in Roberts, 'Globalizing Environmental Justice', 286, 291; see also Peet and Watts, *Liberation Ecologies*.

231 Peet and Watts, *Libertarian Ecologies*; Martinez-Alier, *Environmentalism of the Poor*, pp. 10–11, 80–98; Guha and Martinez-Alier, *Varieties of Environmentalism*, pp. 3 –21; Rajagopal, 'Resistance to Renewal', 532; Rajagopal, 'Social Movements', 409–10, 414–17; Okafur, 'An African Perspective', 104–7.

the groups involved, these community organisations are linked globally by a common thread – conflict surrounding ecological distribution and the centrality of localised environmental protection to their own survival, to the continuation of their livelihoods, and to the maintenance of their communities.[232] As a movement, it also translates at the global level into theories of 'ecologically unequal exchange', ecological debt, and the continued 'disproportionate occupation of environmental space' as between developing and developed states.[233]

As discussed above, in a further twist, this third form of environmentalism has also, at times, seen the interests of marginalised communities within developing countries pitched in direct opposition to the policies and objectives of their own governments. From an historical perspective, the postcolonial indifference of state authorities to the environmental protection needs of local communities is, in many respects, an adoption of the commodification of the environment experienced under colonial regimes. If such approaches have been internalised in this fashion by developing states, manifesting in the unstinting pursuit of the 'development paradigm' to the detriment of sectors of their own people, then this does, indeed, point to the paradox of imperial legacies finding form in unexpected ways.[234]

For all its controversies, manifestations, and divisions, however, environmentalism remains a hugely influential social movement that operates at local and global levels and across cultures. Perhaps, it was the 'diversity of ideas'[235] and the splintering of environmentalism into many forms that enabled it to manifest in such a meaningful way across

[232] Martinez-Alier, *Environmentalism of the Poor*, pp. 10–15, 263; see also the discussion in Bauer, 'Introduction', 15–19.

[233] Martinez-Alier, *Environmentalism of the Poor*, pp. xi, 213–14. 'Ecological debt' conceptualises the debt owed by the North to the South for the resources extracted and used to finance industrialisation, raise standards of living, and enrich their economies. 'Ecologically unequal exchange' refers to the practice of:

> exporting products from poor regions and countries, at prices which do not take into account the local externalities caused by these exports or the exhaustion of natural resources, in exchange for goods and services from richer countries. The concept focuses on the poverty and the lack of power of the exporting region, to emphasize the idea of the lack of alternative options, in terms of exporting other renewable goods with lower local impacts, or in terms of internalizing the externalities in the price of exports, or in terms of applying the precautionary principle to new export items produced with untested technologies.

[234] I am indebted to Tony Anghie for his comments on this point.

[235] Pepper, *Modern Environmentalism*, p. 10.

different societies and cultures, producing 'hybrid, transnational forms of environmental activism' in developed and developing countries alike.[236] This rise in the visibility of environmental politics on the international plane and the impact of environmentalism on local politics and social developments has also been deeply entwined with the emergence of influential environmental NGOs.

(b) Environmental non-governmental organisations

International environmental NGOs constituted a new type of actor in global environmental politics – one that was engaged in organised advocacy for environmental protection, with the ability to capture the attention of the media and empathy of the public, and one able to exert political pressure on government at local, national, and international levels.[237] In essence, NGOs carved out new political space within international environmental relations.[238] That influence has grown to such a degree that environmental NGOs are now considered significant actors in emerging forms of global governance through transnational civil society networks.[239]

The sphere of NGO influence is broad and the roles adopted by environmental NGOs are now sophisticated and varied, extending well beyond that of issue-identification.[240] They possess expert knowledge and engage in specialised research and policy development.[241] They work with governments and industry as partners in designing

236 Ignatow, *Transnational Identity Politics*, p. 6.

237 Hurrell and Kingsbury, 'International Politics', 1, 4; Stairs and Taylor, 'Non-Governmental Organizations', 110, 112–13, 131. Environmental NGOs were in existence in the late nineteenth century and early twentieth century in the form of conservation groups such as the Sierra Club and National Audubon Society. However, the influence of environmental NGOs in international politics became significant from the 1970s onwards. NGOs are defined by the United Nations as 'private, non-state, voluntary, non-profit organisations engaged in lobbying, direct action or policy work: United Nations, *Arrangements for Consultation*.

238 Princen and Finger, *Environmental NGOs*.

239 Raustiala, 'Resistance to Renewal', 571–3; Sands, 'Turtles and Torturers', 527, 530, 556–7; Hobb, 'Global Challenges', 193.

240 Princen and Finger, *Environmental NGOs*; Stairs and Taylor, 'Non-Governmental Organizations', 112–13, 131; Sands, 'Turtles and Torturers', 527, 556–7; Tarlock, 'Environmental Law', 64–5; DeSombre, *The Global Environment*, pp. 82–90; Wapner, *Environmental Activism*; Keck and Sikkink, *Activists beyond Borders*.

241 Hurrell and Kingsbury, 'The International Politics', 10, 20; Stairs and Taylor, 'Non-Governmental Organizations', 113; Peel, 'Giving the Public', 71; McCormick, 'The Role of Environmental NGOs', 83–4.

solutions to environmental problems.[242] They undertake information collation and dissemination and they play a crucial role in capacity-building in developing states. They fulfil a compliance-monitoring role and publicise breaches of international environmental obligations. They engage in lobbying governments, treaty-negotiators, institutions, and companies. They campaign for public participation in environmental decision-making and conduct 'direct action' activities. They voice unrepresented viewpoints.[243] They create connections across levels, linking local environmental degradation with the global environmental crisis.[244]

Concerns have been raised, however, at the increased role and influence of NGOs in the international community. Questions relating to motive, accountability, and transparency are common. For whom do NGOs really speak?[245] Are NGOs accountable for the consequences of their campaigns or for the dissemination of misinformation?[246] Do NGOs provide a channel for effective participation in international environmental decision-making, or merely reiterate Western values and interests?[247] Can their actions be counterproductive?[248]

Patently, there are multiple issues surrounding the emergence and operation of NGOs in the international politico-legal sphere. The key factors regarding environmental NGOs for this enquiry, however, are their significance for environmentalism as a global social movement, their implications for 'mainstreaming' environmental protection objectives at local, national, and international levels, and the impact of this cultural shift on pressure to reform international investment law. In short, the socio-political significance of environmental NGOs has been immense. As Yearley observes, these NGOs have come to embody:

242 Tarlock, 'Environmental Law', 64–5; Stairs and Taylor, 'Non-Governmental Organizations', 112–13, 131.

243 Raustiala, 'Resistance to Renewal', 538; Peel, 'Giving the Public', 72; McCormick, 'Environmental NGOs', 84; Hurrell and Kingsbury, 'The International Politics', 10, 20; Stairs and Taylor, 'Non-Governmental Organizations', 113; Sands, *Principles*, pp. 112–13.

244 Princen and Finger, *Environmental NGOs*; Rodrigues, *Global Environmentalism*, p. 3.

245 Wapner, 'Democratic Accountability', 197.

246 Simmons, 'Globalization at Work'.

247 Peel, 'Giving the Public', 72–3; see also the discussion in Pezzullo and Sandler, 'Revisiting', 1.

248 Cone, 'The Environment'.

the quintessential environmental actor. In cultural terms, environmental organizations stood for the environment in a way which the Environment Minister, the collected scientists of the Intergovernmental Panel on Climate Change or Shell simply could not.[249]

Environmental NGOs operate on multiple levels – and this has been a key factor in their success as vehicles for the infusion of an ecological value-system. They are at once a focal point around which public sentiment has found expression and an influence on that sentiment. They function locally and globally, linking communities and issues. And they fulfil a variety of roles, including those of 'watch-dog', protestor, policy-developer, negotiator, and business partner.[250] Environmental NGOs remain key components in environmentalism as a global social movement – and, as such, they will also continue to fuel pressure on the foreign investment sector to reform and reflect this culture of global environmentalism.

2. Implications for international investment law

Clearly, the emergence of modern environmentalism has substantial implications for international investment law. As a social movement, it has a character of infusion, shifting perceptions at local and global levels, finding spaces in a multiplicity of societies, and taking an array of forms.[251] As such, environmental consciousness is shaping the way in which business activities are perceived and influencing expectations of corporate behaviour. If it continues along the same trajectory, the impact of this gradual global cultural shift on the investment sector will be profound – potentially, it has the capacity to render the underlying approach of international investment law obsolete. Stemming from their opposing objectives, the traditional conceptualisation of the environment of the host state as a resource for the unimpeded use of the foreign investor, its protection of investors without imposition of corresponding responsibilities, the invisibility of affected local and indigenous communities, and the exclusion of the host state from protective engagement under international investment law all conflict

[249] Yearley, 'Social Movements', 39.
[250] For a discussion on the influence of NGOs, see Yearley, *Cultures of Environmentalism*; Jamison, *Green Knowledge*; McCormick, 'Environmental NGOs', 96–101; Coglianese, 'Social Movements'; Betsill, 'Transnational Actors', 172; Betsill and Corell, 'Introduction', 2–3.
[251] Jamison, *Green Knowledge*, pp. 16–17.

with the value systems embodied in the many manifestations of environmentalism.

International investment law is certainly out of step with these current trends in environmentalism, but that has not seen the law adjusted to reflect environmental concerns. Indeed, although the investment sector has responded to social movements, and to environmentalism in particular, such responses have largely been directed at constraining and neutralising resistance, rather than permitting modification. Regarded as a threat to the present system of international investor protection, the existence of social movements is framed as exemplifying the need for more stringent investor protections, as illegitimately politicising investor–state disputes, or even as providing the basis for investor claims themselves.[252] It can be seen that the challenges posed by social movements have in part provoked responses such as the establishment of ICSID, the pursuit of bilateral investment treaties, the continued resort to international arbitration to resolve disputes, and the advocating of expansive interpretations of existing investor protections. Additionally, this dynamic of assertion, challenge, and response also manifested directly in the 1990s in the continued alignment of capital-exporting states and their investor nationals and, in particular, in the events surrounding the Organisation for Economic Cooperation and Development (OECD)'s attempt to conclude a multilateral framework agreement on investment.[253]

(a) Aligning interests and the multilateral agreement on investment: reproducing investor protection without responsibility

Recent forms of engagement between states and their investors have manifested in a variety of ways. The escalation in state activity in securing bilateral investment treaties has been attributed to pressure from foreign investors for more secure and predictable legal regimes to protect investment.[254] Capital-exporting states actively promote the

[252] Odumosu, 'Law and Politics', 254–5; see, e.g., Wälde and Kolo, 'Environmental Regulation'; see also Wälde and Ndi, 'Stabilizing'; for a further example of a hostile framing of host state activities, see Baker, 'Denial of Justice', 187–91.

[253] See the text of the draft Multilateral Agreement on Investment (MAI) at OECD Negotiating Group on the Multilateral Agreement on Investment, Draft Consolidated Text, 22 April 1998, available at www1.oecd.org/daf/mai/pdf/ng/ng987r1e.pdf (last accessed 6 December 2011).

[254] Salacuse, 'BIT by BIT', 659, also extracted in Bishop, Crawford, and Reisman, *Foreign Investment Disputes*, p. 19.

spread of investment liberalisation policies, assisting with the growth in global capital flows.[255] Corporate representation in the negotiation of international agreements is increasing and states are facilitating this shift in practice through the restructuring of their diplomatic systems and the establishment of formal consultation mechanisms.[256]

There has been an intensification of private sector involvement in 'commercial diplomacy'.[257] Business representatives are now regularly placed within overseas missions and given formal diplomatic status.[258] States have thrown their weight behind individual investment negotiations in support of their nationals.[259] Ministries of Foreign Affairs and Ministries of Trade are increasingly conjoined.[260] It is now common for formal associations or partnerships to exist between government and business in the provision of diplomatic services.[261] In some countries, such as Austria, the role of commercial diplomats has been delegated entirely to business organisations.[262] The resultant concentration on the trading and foreign investment needs of corporations has led to an environment within many government circles in which the 'public interest is increasingly conceptualized as a collective of private business interests.'[263]

One of the clearest examples of these forms of influence in the foreign investment context was that of business organisations in the negotiating process of the Multilateral Agreement on Investment (MAI)[264] through their permanent body at the OECD, the Business and Industry

[255] Sands, *Lawless World*, p. 119; Cutler, 'Critical Reflections', 144; Scholte, 'Global Capitalism', 442.

[256] Cutler, 'Critical Reflections', 143–4; Lee, 'Growing Influence'; Sherman and Eliasson, 'Trade Disputes'.

[257] Sands, 'Turtles and Torturers', 541–3; Lee, 'Growing Influence', 51, defining 'commercial diplomacy' as follows:

> Commercial diplomacy is best defined as the work of a network of public and private actors who manage commercial relations using diplomatic channels and processes. . . . Commercial diplomacy involves the promotion of inward and outward investment and the promotion of exports in trade.

[258] Lee, 'Growing Influence'; Mercier, 'Commercial Diplomacy'.

[259] Lee, 'Growing Influence', 51; Mercier, 'Commercial Diplomacy'; Coolsaet, 'Trade and Diplomacy', 64; Peterson and Green Cowles, 'Clinton, Europe', 252.

[260] Mercier, 'Commercial Diplomacy', 4–5. See, e.g., Australia, Belgium, Canada, and Sweden.

[261] Ibid. [262] Ibid., 4. [263] Lee, 'Growing Influence', 51.

[264] See the text of the draft Multilateral Agreement on Investment (MAI) at OECD Negotiating Group on the Multilateral Agreement on Investment, Draft Consolidated Text, 22 April 1998, available at http://www1.oecd.org/daf/mai/pdf/ng/ng987rle.pdf (last accessed 19 November 2011).

Advisory Committee to the OECD (BIAC).[265] BIAC lobbies the OECD on behalf of the business community[266] and was intimately involved in the framing of the agenda for the MAI negotiations and in drafting preparatory documents.[267] BIAC's relationship with the OECD provided investors with direct access to shaping the rules of what was to be a global legal framework for international investment.

The OECD opened the negotiating process for the MAI in 1995 with the aim of furthering the liberalisation of international investment and creating a comprehensive, harmonised global framework for rules on investment liberalisation, foreign investment protection, and dispute settlement mechanisms and procedures.[268] Many of the substantive provisions of the MAI were modelled on existing regional agreements, such as the North American Free Trade Agreement (NAFTA),[269] and on the obligations contained in many bilateral investment treaties.[270] Accordingly, the OECD negotiators did not anticipate the move to a multilateral format being particularly controversial.[271] They were following an approach, however, that was disconnected from the social and political climate of the 1990s and its treatment of global issues as interrelated. Rather than taking an integrated approach and considering the environmental and social implications of the proposed investment rules, the OECD was operating on the traditional premise that international investment law and policy was a discrete area that did not involve environmental protection principles or human rights issues.[272]

The MAI negotiations took place behind closed doors, precluding public comment and the participation of non-OECD countries.[273] This necessarily meant that the draft text was exposed to only a limited range of viewpoints during its conceptualisation and drafting. However, once the draft text of the MAI was leaked and made publicly

[265] Tieleman, *The Failure of the Multilateral Agreement* available at www.gppi.net/fileadmin/gppi/Tieleman_MAI_GPP_Network.pdf (last accessed 24 November 2011).

[266] Business and Industry Advisory Committee to the OECD, *The Voice of OECD Business*, available at www.biac.org/aboutus.htm (last accessed 19 November 2011).

[267] Tieleman, *Failure of the Multilateral Agreement*, p. 9.

[268] Report by the Committee on International Investment and Multinational Enterprises, available at www1.oecd.org/daf/mai/htm/cmitcime95.htm (last accessed 6 December 2011).

[269] North American Free Trade Agreement (NAFTA), adopted 17 December 1992, 1992 32 ILM 612 (entered into force 1 January 1994).

[270] Geiger, 'Regulatory Expropriations', 96–7. [271] Ibid.

[272] See a discussion of this issue McDonald, 'The Multilateral Agreement', 621–2.

[273] Tieleman, *Failure of the Multilateral Agreement*.

available on the internet in 1997,[274] a global controversy erupted and it became clear that the OECD had miscalculated the likely public response to the substance of the MAI.[275] A network of environmental NGOs, human rights groups, and anti-globalisation organisations mounted a global internet campaign to publicise their concerns at the draft MAI.[276] It was a widespread and high-profile manifestation of the clash between foreign investment protection law and social movements, and, although the campaign was not the sole reason for the demise of the negotiations, it certainly contributed to the halting of the negotiation process in October 1998 and its eventual shelving altogether in 1999.[277] Many of the concerns voiced by NGOs and commentators revolved around the potential for loss of control over health and environmental regulation, risks of pollution havens and regulatory chill, and the wider implications of investment arbitration.[278] Key issues involved the MAI's ban on performance requirements, the implications of the prohibition on uncompensated expropriation, and the investor–state dispute settlement mechanism.[279] Protesters expressed the view that provisions in the MAI would 'elevate the rights of investors far above those of governments, local communities, citizens, workers and the environment'.[280]

At a fundamental level, the negotiations of the MAI also embodied the traditional approach of capital-exporting states to the development of international investment law. Locating the drafting and negotiating of the MAI within the OECD inherently favoured capital-exporting states and assured their control over the content.[281] Indeed, the very methodology of imperialism – exclusion from development of international investment law and imposition of legal doctrine – had been chosen for the negotiation of the MAI. As OECD Member States were the sole

274 McDonald, 'The Multilateral Agreement', 622.

275 Ibid.; for an example of NGO commentary, see Joint NGO Statement on the Multilateral Agreement on Investment, *NGO/OECD Consultation on the MAI*, 27 October 1997, available at www.protglob.hss.uts.edu.au/archive/issue1/lib7mai.htm (last accessed 6 December 2011).

276 MAI, above n. 253; Tieleman, *The Failure of the Multilateral Agreement*.

277 Sornarajah, *The International Law*, pp. 3, 80, 88, 296–7.

278 See, e.g., Joint NGO Statement on the Multilateral Agreement on Investment.

279 See McDonald, 'The Multilateral Agreement'; see also Crane, 'Corporations Swallowing Nations'.

280 See, e.g., Joint NGO Statement on the Multilateral Agreement on Investment, 1; see also Nova and Sforza-Roderick, 'Worse than NAFTA', available at www.globalpolicy.org/socecon/bwi-wto/mai2.htm (last accessed 6 December 2011).

281 Sornarajah, *Foreign Investment*, pp. 291–4.

formal participants in the negotiating process, developing states were effectively excluded from participation in the development of the rules.[282] The MAI protests represented a challenge to that approach. Responding to the substance and form of the MAI, as well as the conduct of its negotiations, global networks of social movements challenged the propriety of excluding the perspectives of non-OECD states, subaltern voices, and an array of issues, such as human rights, environmental protection, public health, and development needs, from consideration in foreign investment matters.

How did the foreign investment sector react? The immediate response in 1998–9 was the withdrawal and indefinite postponement of the MAI negotiating process. The mid-range response has been less accommodating, as evidenced by the arbitral decisions in the investor–state disputes examined below in Chapter 3. Effectively, there has been a reassertion of traditional power dynamics and patterns derived from imperialism. Seeking to constrain the impact of environmental and grassroots movements has remained a feature of current interaction between foreign investors, the host state, and the use of international investment law. The enduring response, however, may have to settle on a more balanced approach – one that reflects both the need to protect the interests of foreign investors and the need to pursue environmental protection objectives in the public interest. Environmentalism, in its many forms, continues to exert a profound cultural influence at local and global levels. As such, without an adequate long-term response to environmental and sustainable development issues through the reshaping of international investment law, this relationship will remain a continuing source of conflict.

IV. Conclusion

Changing political conditions over the last century led to multiple challenges to international rules on foreign investment protection. On each occasion, those attempts to assert a vision of international investment law that created space for the host state were met with new methods to preserve investor protection. New institutions were created,

[282] Tieleman, *The Failure of the Multilateral Agreement*; OECD Member States are: Australia, Austria, Belgium, Canada, Czech Republic, Denmark, Finland, France, Germany, Greece, Hungary, Iceland, Ireland, Italy, Japan, Korea, Luxembourg, Mexico, Netherlands, New Zealand, Norway, Poland, Portugal, Slovak Republic, Spain, Sweden, Switzerland, Turkey, United Kingdom, and the United States.

new doctrines were established, and new treaties were concluded so as to ensure the maintenance of high-level global protection for foreign investors. In so doing, a pattern of reproducing the imperialist origins of international investment law became entrenched.

In this chapter, I have examined key examples of those twentieth-century challenges to the prevailing international system for foreign investment protection. It was clear to me that the first half of the twentieth century was a particularly telling period in which there were significant host state responses to shifts in the global political landscape and attempts to establish new compensation rules accounting for widespread social reform in the form of 'nationalisation'. We have seen that the assertions of Mexico and the Soviet Union, that compensation was not required for a separate category of taking carried out as part of a general programme of land reform, met with strong objections by capital-exporting states. Crucially, their position was dismissed as not being of a norm-creating character, unlike those of capital-exporting states. In this way, host state attempts to participate in the shaping of the substantive rules of international investment law were thwarted in the early twentieth century.

What these events also indicate is that, on a fundamental level, patterns of assertion, response, and reassertion of power carried through from earlier periods also characterised host and home state interaction in the early twentieth century. It is my argument that subsequent events point to the continuation of that characterisation throughout the remainder of the twentieth century as well. In this regard, postcolonial nationalisations, the NIEO, and social movements embodied attempts by host states to address the 'other' in international investment law and to create legal regimes that had space for their socio-political requirements. I have argued that the modern international legal architecture for the protection of foreign investment was largely driven by the need to respond to those particular host state challenges. In my view, the use of doctrines of internationalised contracts and acquired rights, the establishment of ICSID, and the pursuit of bilateral investment treaties, can all be framed as responses to host state attempts to ameliorate the unbalanced nature and operation of the law. In no small way, therefore, it has been these new mechanisms that have ensured the maintenance of imperialist approaches within the substance of international investment law and the procedures for resolution of investment disputes.

This chapter also pointed to the continuation of these patterns in the late twentieth century and into the twenty-first. It has explored the interaction of resistance and response in the relationship between the emergence of social movements and the investment sector, emphasising the influential character of environmentalism within a multiplicity of societies, cultures, and discourses. In the course of examining such a complex set of relations, this chapter argued that environmentalism has triggered strong responses from the investment sector and capital-exporting states precisely because it does interfere directly with the traditional approach of foreign investors to the environment of the host state. Although there are several elements combining to create the most recent climate of pressure to reform international investment law, environmentalism and grassroots activism are central factors in current tensions. In particular, the focus of the international community on sustainable development means that foreign investment practices and international investment law are seen through the lens of environmental objectives and the concerns of local communities and indigenous peoples. Accordingly, the contemporary relationship between international investment agreements and principles of environmental protection is of particular significance for current attempts to reshape international investment law and are, therefore, examined in detail in the next part of this book.

PART II

Contemporary interaction: foreign investment, imperialism, and environmental protection

3 Polarisation of positions

The links between foreign investment and the environment are extensive, encompassing both the clash of norms and objectives as well as more recent attempts to accommodate non-investment issues within international investment law.[1] Dividing these contemporary modes of interaction, Part II of this book addresses their complexities in separate analyses: on one side, this chapter explores the polarisation of positions that continues to inform the relationship; expressing another side, Chapter 4 examines developments in corporate social responsibility, responsible institutional investment, sustainable finance, and modified approaches in recent bilateral investment treaties.

In analysing modern investor approaches to the use of the environment, challenges to that use, and responses to those attempts to create space for environmental protection, I argue that this form of interaction continues the traditional patterns of assertion of power and response to power that have characterised the evolution of international investment regimes.[2] It is proposed that international investment law still reflects imperialist conceptualisations of the environment in two fundamental ways: (i) the non-engagement of international investment law with the impact of investor activity on the local communities and the environment of the host state; and (ii) the treatment of environmental regulation as a violation of investment treaties.

[1] See, e.g., the discussion in Newcombe, 'Sustainable Development'; see also Hirsch, 'Interactions', 154.

[2] See above in the Introduction and Chapters 1 and 2 the discussion on the theories of Benton, *Law and Colonial Cultures*.

Although a complex range of factors are at play in recent pressures to reform the law on foreign investment protection,[3] the relationship between investment, environmental concerns, and the sustainable development needs of local communities has emerged as a primary source of current tensions surrounding international investment law.[4] This chapter examines those areas of contestation. It analyses the conflict arising out of the attempts by host states, civil society, and subaltern movements to reshape international investment law and the responses from the investment sector in seeking to maintain the status quo and to neutralise the impact of environmental issues on investor protection.

Section I of this chapter explores the unresponsiveness of international investment law to the impact of investor operations on the host state and argues for the introduction of international accountability measures for multinational corporations. To illustrate the effects of this gap in international investment law, a number of high-profile cases of misconduct by foreign-owned corporations are considered, together with the use of legal doctrine to avoid responsibility for the environmental damage caused. What emerges from this analysis is a sense that the approach to the law embodied in these cases has reproduced conceptualisations of the environment derived from imperialism. It also appears that the cases replicated traditional patterns in which legal doctrine is manipulated to sustain the position of foreign investors and capital-exporting states. Considered in this way, these cases can also be seen to illustrate the condition of 'otherness' of the host state that continues to exist within international investment law, the rules of which do not provide the host state with recourse at the international level for any damage caused by investor activity.[5]

[3] See, e.g., the range of issues discussed in Subedi, *International Investment Law*; Odumosu, 'Law and Politics'; Gathii, 'Third World Approaches', p. 255; Muchlinski, 'Corporate Social Responsibility', 431.

[4] See, e.g., the discussion on the impact of investor activity on host states and the treatment of environmental regulation as a treaty violation in Soloway, 'Environmental Regulation'; Sands, 'Searching for Balance'; Bernasconi-Osterwalder and Brown Weiss, 'International Investment Rules', 263; Cosbey et al., *Investment and Sustainable Development*; Friends of the Earth, 'Binding Corporate Accountability'; see also the use of the term 'global environmental consciousness' in Jamison, *Green Knowledge*, pp. 16–17; see also for a discussion on the growth of environmental consciousness as a social movement in developing and developed states in Rajagopal, 'Resistance to Renewal', 556–7.

[5] See, e.g., the discussion of the concept of 'otherness' in Anghie, 'Heart of My Home', 447.

Section II of this chapter examines the use of investment agreements to challenge environmental regulation. In recent years, investors have brought an increasing number of complaints that implicate a wide range of domestic regulatory measures, including allegations of indirect expropriation, discriminatory treatment, and breach of the fair and equitable treatment standard. These disputes have, for example, challenged regulations introduced to protect ground water from contamination with harmful chemicals,[6] measures prohibiting the export of hazardous waste in compliance with a multilateral environmental agreement,[7] the denial of a permit to operate a hazardous waste facility,[8] regulations prohibiting the use of certain pesticides,[9] and a ban on a fuel additive to protect human health and the environment.[10]

In examining a selection of these key disputes, it is suggested that the way in which international investment law is being used in recent investor–state arbitration has the *de facto* effect of constraining governments in their decision-making on complex areas of domestic policy, such as the protection of human health and the environment.[11] This chapter argues that such matters should not be determined solely according to international investment law as the rules do not presently allow for adequate consideration of factors other than investment protection.[12]

Consideration is also given to arguments that the potential threat of investor claims can have a chilling effect on the improvement of environmental standards. This is, of course, a particularly contentious issue and an assertion that is notoriously difficult to prove. In this vein, however, concerns have been raised that the costs of defending investor claims, together with the spectre of large damages awards, may inhibit

[6] *Methanex Corporation* v. *United States of America*, (2005) 44 *International Legal Materials* 1345 ('*Methanex Corporation*').

[7] *S.D. Myers Inc.* v. *Canada* (UNCITRAL, First Partial Award of 13 November 2000) ('*S.D. Myers Inc* (Partial Award of 2000)'). It was argued that the measure was made in compliance with the Convention on the Control of Transboundary Movement of Hazardous Wastes and their Disposal, opened for signature 22 March 1989, (1989) 28 ILM 657 (entered into force 1992) (Basel Convention).

[8] *Metalclad Corporation* v. *United Mexican States* (ICSID Case No. ARB(AF)/97/1, Award of 30 August 2000) ('*Metalclad Corporation* (Award of 2000)').

[9] *Dow Agro Sciences LLC* v. *Government of Canada*, Notice of Arbitration Under the UNCITRAL Rules and the North American Free Trade Agreement, 31 March 2009, available at www.international.gc.ca/trade-agreements-accords-commerciaux/assets/pdfs/DowAgroSciencesLLC-2.pdf (last accessed 10 December 2011).

[10] *Ethyl Corporation* v. *Canada* (UNCITRAL, Award on Jurisdiction of 24 June 1998) ('*Ethyl Corporation* (Award of 1998)').

[11] Soloway, 'Environmental Regulation', 119. [12] Ibid.

the tightening of environmental regulation, particularly in developing states.[13] Furthermore, these issues take on an added potency as national and international efforts to address climate change intensify and the adoption of domestic regulatory measures to reduce greenhouse gas emissions becomes inevitable. Accordingly, this chapter considers the categorisation of environmental regulation as a breach of international investment agreements with particular reference to the potential barriers this might pose to the implementation of climate change mitigation measures.

In adopting an historical framework in which to analyse contemporary interactions, I explore the idea that the two key issues examined in sections I and II of this chapter are manifestations of the traditional relationship between foreign investors and the environment of the host state that I set out in Chapters 1 and 2. In this chapter, I argue that modern forms of interaction between foreign investors, host states, affected local communities, and environmental protection advocates also continue those historical patterns of assertion, challenge, and response to power that have characterised the development of international investment law for so long.

I. Investor responsibility, corporate misconduct, and environmental damage

A. *Global environmental degradation and unsustainable growth*

'Foreign investment' encompasses both foreign direct investment and foreign portfolio investment. Foreign direct investment (FDI) is defined by the United Nations Conference on Trade and Development (UNCTAD) as:

> investment involving a long-term relationship and reflecting a lasting interest and control by a resident entity in one economy (foreign direct investor or parent enterprise) in an enterprise resident in an economy other than that of the foreign direct investor (FDI enterprise or affiliate enterprise or foreign affiliate). FDI implies that the investor exerts a significant degree of influence on the management of the enterprise resident in the other economy. Such investment involves both the initial transaction

13 Bernasconi-Osterwalder and Brown Weiss, 'International Investment Rules', p. 277; Sands, 'Searching for Balance'; Tienhaara, 'What You Don't Know', 80, 85–7; Peterson, 'All Roads Lead out of Rome', 123, 139.

between the two entities and all subsequent transactions between them and among foreign affiliates, both incorporated and unincorporated.[14]

Foreign portfolio investment (FPI) is described as including:

a variety of instruments which are traded (or tradeable) in organized and other financial markets: bonds, equities and money market instruments. The International Monetary Fund even includes derivatives or secondary instruments, such as options, in the category of FPI. The channels of cross-border investments are also varied: securities are acquired and sold by retail investors, commercial banks, investment trusts (mutual funds, country and regional funds, pension funds and hedge funds).[15]

Global flows of foreign capital continued to increase at exponential rates from 2000 through until the recent global financial crisis slowed growth.[16] UNCTAD reports indicate that global foreign direct investment reached an estimated US$897 billion in 2005, a 29 per cent increase on 2004 figures.[17] The trend remained upwards, with 2006 experiencing a 38 per cent increase overall on 2005, reaching US$1,306 billion in global foreign direct investment inflows,[18] followed by the high point of US$1,979 billion in 2007.[19] The financial crisis impacted significantly on global foreign capital inflows, rendering declines in investment for several years following 2007. However, foreign direct investment rates are again increasing, with a 17 per cent rise recorded for 2011, taking global capital inflows to US$1.5 trillion.[20]

In a general sense, it has been argued by commentators that increased global levels of trade and investment activity correlate to increasing

[14] United Nations Conference on Trade and Development (UNCTAD), *Foreign Direct Investment: Statistics*, available at www.unctad.org/Templates/WebFlyer.asp?intItemID=2190&lang=1 (last accessed 10 December 2011).

[15] UNCTAD, *Foreign Portfolio Investment*, 4, available at www.unctad.org/en/docs/c2em6d2&c1.en.pdf (last accessed 10 December 2011).

[16] UNCTAD, *World Investment Report 2009* iii, xvii, available at www.unctad.org/en/docs/wir2009_en.pdf (last accessed 10 December 2011).

[17] UNCTAD, 'Sharp Rise in FDI', available at www.unctad.org/en/docs/webiteiia20061_en.pdf (last accessed 10 December 2011); UNCTAD, 'Data Show Foreign Direct Investment Climbed Sharply in 2005' (Press Release, January 2006) UNCTAD/PRESS/PR/2006/002, available at www.unctad.org/press (last accessed 10 December 2011).

[18] UNCTAD, *World Investment Report 2007*, xv, available at www.unctad.org/en/docs/wir2007_en.pdf (last accessed 10 December 2011).

[19] UNCTAD, *World Investment Report 2009*, p. xix.

[20] UNCTAD, *Global Investment Trends Monitor*, No. 8, 24 January 2012, available at www.unctad.org/en/docs/webdiaeia2012d1_en.pdf (last accessed 10 May 2012).

global rates of environmental degradation and depletion of resources.[21] Additionally, the scale of this economic activity has also been pointed to as a significant contributor to complex international environmental problems such as climate change, deforestation, desertification, depletion of natural resources, and biodiversity loss.[22] Although foreign investment is credited with being a key factor in stimulating economic growth,[23] UNCTAD has also acknowledged the links between foreign investment and environmental degradation:

> The internationalization of production of goods and services through FDI increases the likelihood of the extension of any related environmental damage to a greater number of countries and, therefore, to a larger part of the world's environment.[24]

The link between foreign investment and environmental impacts also necessarily involves the broader debate on sustainable development. Concerns have been raised that the global intensification of foreign investment activity levels, together with commercial practices divorced from social and environmental considerations, perpetuates unsustainable growth patterns.[25] It is in this context that Mabey and McNally question the insufficient assessment of investment activity relative to the ecological carrying capacity of the environment at local, national, and global levels.[26]

Paradoxically, while the global increase in economic activity has negative impacts on the environment, foreign investment also has a role to play in the promotion of sustainable development. Although the issue of whether entering into bilateral investment agreements

[21] See, e.g., Zarsky, 'Havens, Halos and Spaghetti', 47, 55–6; Mabey and McNally, *Foreign Direct Investment*, pp. 3, 13–17; Morgera, 'The UN and Corporate Environmental Responsibility', 93.

[22] Mabey and McNally, *Foreign Direct Investment*, p. 3; Hunter, Salzman, and Zaelke, *International Environmental Law*, pp. 26–8.

[23] UNCTAD, *Foreign Direct Investment*, available at www.unctad.org/Templates/StartPage.asp?intItemID=2527&lang=1 (last accessed 10 December 2011); see the discussion in Gentry, 'Foreign Direct Investment?', 21–2.

[24] UNCTAD, *Environment*, available at www.unctad.org/en/docs/psiteiitd23.en.pdf (last accessed 10 December 2011). This UNCTAD report also goes on to state that foreign direct investment is important in improving the environment through the transference of environmentally sound technologies and management practices.

[25] See, e.g., Mabey and McNally, *Foreign Direct Investment*; Zarsky, 'Havens, Halos and Spaghetti'; Daly, 'Sustainable Growth?', 193.

[26] Mabey and McNally, *Foreign Direct Investment*, p. 15.

increases the flow of foreign investment remains contested,[27] the link between increasing foreign investment and achieving sustainable development is well-versed.[28] The key, however, is in the approach to foreign investment and the framework in which it is pursued.

Unfortunately, the fact that foreign direct investment *per se* does not necessarily result in sustainable development is, perhaps, sometimes lost in the discourse. Although such investment is, indeed, necessary for the attainment of many sustainable development goals, it is also clear that foreign capital requires actual direction into modalities of sustainability in order to do so.[29] The over-arching legal framework in which foreign investment occurs has been created through international investment agreements, many of which have the stated objective of increasing levels of foreign investment and of ensuring high protection for investments.[30] It is, of course, not problematic on the face of it. The difficulty, however, lies in the absence of correlating considerations to provide a balance to those objectives. For this reason, it is concerning that the majority of these agreements do not refer to sustainable development, promotion of public policy, or environmental protection.[31] Particularly so when it is realised that unmanaged investment and capital markets liberalisation can have

[27] Neumayer and Spess, 'Bilateral Investment Treaties'; Hallward-Driemeier, 'Bilateral Investment Treaties', available at www-wds.worldbank.org/external/default/WDSContentServer/IW3P/IB/2003/09/23/000094946_03091104060047/additional/105505322_20041117160010.pdf (last accessed 23 February 2008).

[28] *Agenda 21*, *Report of the UNCED*, UN Doc A/CONF.151/26/Rev.1 (vol. I) (1992), 31 ILM 874, ch. 2, para. 2.23; Mann et al., *IISD Model International Agreement*, pp. x–xi, available at www.iisd.org/pdf/2005/investment_model_int_handbook.pdf (last accessed 14 December 2011); Muchlinski, 'Towards a Multilateral Investment Agreement', p. 429; Nieuwenhuys, 'Global Development', 295.

[29] Mabey and McNally, *Foreign Direct Investment*, p. 4; Zarsky, 'Havens, Halos and Spaghetti', 49, 65–7.

[30] Mann et al., *IISD Model International Agreement*, pp. 2–3; UNCTAD, *World Investment Report 2007*, pp. 16–18. By the end of 2006, almost 5,500 international investment agreements were in existence. The breakdown of these comprised 2,573 bilateral investment agreements, 2,651 double taxation treaties, and 241 agreements that contained investment provisions. More recent estimates place the number of bilateral investment treaties as close to 3,000.

[31] Newcombe, 'Sustainable Development'. Several recent bilateral investment agreements to which the United States and Canada are parties have included references to sustainable development and protection of the environment. It has been suggested that these 'new generation BITs' were the result of the United States and Canada having had investor claims filed against them and experiencing investor–state arbitration as respondent states; see Newcombe and Paradell, *Law and Practice*, p. 61; Shan, 'Revival of the Calvo Doctrine', 652, 656.

undesirable effects within a host state.[32] Perhaps, however, investment embedded within a socially and environmentally responsible framework could assist in realising the theoretical benefits of foreign investment for developing states.[33] With this in mind, it would be worthwhile exploring avenues for a global regulatory framework in which the promotion of ecologically sustainable and socially responsible investment could be pursued. Without such a regime, capturing the development benefits of foreign investment for host states will largely be dependent on chance. Unchecked and undirected, foreign capital will continue to flow without reference to socially and environmentally responsible principles, reproducing poverty cycles, encouraging unsustainable growth and consumption patterns, and contributing to significant environmental degradation.[34] Directed into socially and ecologically sustainable production and processes, however, foreign investment could contribute to global social equity goals and enhance global environmental conditions rather than exacerbate them.[35]

International investment law currently does not engage with these issues. As we have seen, it is primarily concerned with investment protection. From the perspective of effective global environmental governance that seeks to halt and reverse ecological decline, it is troubling that the international investment legal framework remains disengaged from the wider social and environmental context in which it operates. As the regularly asserted benefits of foreign investment for developing host states relate to the social and environmental gains that follow from economic growth,[36] it is appropriate to link these

[32] Mabey and McNally, *Foreign Direct Investment*, p. 4; Stiglitz, *Making Globalization Work*, pp. 33–46. Stiglitz critiques the role of the World Bank and International Monetary Fund in the investment and monetary liberalisation policies of developing states in East Asia, South Asia, Latin America, Africa, and Russia. Gallagher and Zarsky, 'No Miracle Drug', pp. 13–15, 31–7. Gallagher and Zarsky point to the example of Mexico, in which a foreign direct investment-led programme of economic development was embraced in the 1990s. Although Mexico experienced significant foreign investment inflows, technology and knowledge transfer were virtually non-existent, local industry suffered, domestic investment was 'crowded out', job-creation was minimal, industrial pollution levels increased dramatically, and the environmental benefits failed to materialise to expected levels.

[33] Zarsky, 'Havens, Halos and Spaghetti', 49, 65–7; Gallagher and Zarsky, 'No Miracle Drug', 13.

[34] Mabey and McNalley, *Foreign Direct Investment*; Gallagher and Zarsky, 'No Miracle Drug', 29.

[35] Gallagher and Zarsky, 'No Miracle Drug', 29.

[36] Zarsky, 'Havens, Halos and Spaghetti', 55–6.

formally in international investment agreements. To this end, as an initial step, the promotion of foreign investment that enhances sustainable development should be included as a stated objective of bilateral investment treaties and of any future multilateral agreements.[37] This approach should also be infused throughout the text of such instruments, informed by the development of socially and environmentally responsible principles.[38] Such developments would greatly assist progress towards mutually supportive international investment and environmental protection regimes. This macro-level issue of global environmental degradation and unsustainable economic growth is, however, only one layer in the complex relationship between foreign investment and the environment; there is also a potent micro-level linking between these two fields – multinational corporations and the localised effects of their operations within host states.

B. *Multinational corporations and environmental misconduct*

Although a number of elements are involved in this discourse, pressure to reshape international investment law has undoubtedly been fuelled by high-profile examples of corporate environmental misconduct within host states. The imbalance in international investment law is starkly visible in these cases – investor protection is its focus, not the health, safety, and well-being of the citizens and environment of the host state. As a consequence, foreign investment protection law cannot be called upon to protect the host state from the detrimental effects of investor operations. On analysing key incidents of corporate misconduct, it becomes quite apparent that this traditional indifference of international investment law to the impact of investor activity on the local communities and environment of the host state leaves a gap in the reach of international regulation. The injustice that flows from this disparity has, unsurprisingly, led to calls for the development of an

[37] Mann et al., *IISD Model International Agreement*. An appropriate precedent for such an approach can be found in the context of the World Trade Organisation, where references to sustainable development have been included in the preamble of the General Agreement on Tariffs and Trade, Annex 1A, Agreement Establishing the World Trade Organization, opened for signature 15 April 1994, (1994) 33 *International Legal Materials* 28 (entered into force 1 January 1995).

[38] Zarsky, 'Havens, Halos and Spaghetti', 65–7. The proposed form of such a framework is set out in detail below in Chapter 6.

international regulatory framework to ensure corporate social and environmental accountability.[39]

This section examines a number of disputes to demonstrate the effects of an international investment legal regime that is solely concerned with investor rights and does not contain investor responsibilities. This discussion also illustrates the way in which the origins of international investment law are alive in the modern relationship between foreign investors and the environment of host states, in particular:

- the commodification of the environment of the host state for the use of the foreign investor;
- the adoption of that commodification by host state regimes complicit in foreign investor misconduct and the marginalisation of vulnerable communities within their own jurisdiction;
- the use of legal doctrine to legitimise investor activity;
- the powerful political position of multinational corporations and the close alignment of their interests with those of their home state; and
- the continued 'otherness' of the host state reflected in its exclusion from the protective principles of international investment law.

There are numerous recent examples of environmental malpractice by foreign-owned entities, particularly in developing countries. The disputes have involved allegations of environmental devastation, contaminated land and rivers, ravaged rainforest, damage to human health, deaths, birth defects, the fracturing of communities, human rights abuses, and collaboration with repressive state regimes. Notable conflicts include the controversy surrounding the operations of the Shell Oil Company in Nigeria,[40] Freeport and Rio Tinto in Indonesia,[41] ChevronTexaco Corporation in Ecuador,[42] Broken Hill Proprietary Co.

[39] See, e.g., Zerk, *Multinationals and Corporate Social Responsibility: Limitations and Opportunities in International Law* (2006); Friends of the Earth, 'Binding Corporate Accountability', available at www.foei.org/en/publications/corporates/accountability.html (last accessed 15 August 2007); Ward, 'Transnational Corporate Accountability', 472–4; Clapp, 'Global Environmental Governance'.

[40] See, e.g., the discussion in Udobong, 'Multinational Corporations'.

[41] Ibid., see also NGO commentary of WALHI-Indonesian Forum for Environment, 'Conflict and Militarism', December 2004, available at www.eng.walhi.or.id/kampanye/psda/konflikmil/conflict_info/ (last accessed 10 December 2011).

[42] See, e.g., the discussion in Chesterman, 'Oil and Water'; for a discussion on environmentally damaging oil industry and mining practices, see Herz, 'Litigating Environmental Abuses', 547–9; Perlez and Johnson, 'Behind Gold's Glitter', available at www.globalpolicy.org/socecon/tncs/2005/1024ring.htm (last accessed 18 January 2008);

(BHP) in Ok Tedi, Papua New Guinea,[43] and Union Carbide in Bhopal, India.[44]

1. Ok Tedi Mine, Papua New Guinea

The techniques used for resource extraction in open-cast mining often have a devastating effect on their local environments.[45] The physical scale of many of these mines is vast, consisting of pits sometimes a thousand feet deep and thousands of feet across.[46] Once manageable blocks of rock have been formed through blasting, cyanide or other highly toxic chemical mixes are used to extract gold or copper from the ore, a process that produces mine tailings, a water and dirt mixture contaminated with heavy metals and chemicals.[47]

The mining operation at Ok Tedi, of which BHP was the majority shareholder,[48] released 70 million tons of mine tailings and waste rock residue into the Ok Tedi and Fly Rivers every year from 1984 onwards.[49] This toxic sediment raised the river beds, causing the flooding of a 1,300 kilometre area and the smothering of rainforest in a process labelled by the United Nations Environment Programme (UNEP) as 'dieback'.[50] The heavily polluted waters poisoned vegetation, fish, and animals, and left the ecology of substantial parts of the rivers

see also NGO commentary of Amazon Defense Coalition, 'ChevronToxico', available at http://chevrontoxico.com/article.php?id=110 (last accessed 10 December 2011).

43 Chesterman, 'Oil and Water'; Connell, 'Trans-National', 61–4; see also NGO commentary on the environmental degradation from the mine tailings in Ghazi, 'Unearthing Controversy', available at http://newsroom.wri.org/wrifeatures_text.cfm?ContentID=1895 (last accessed 10 December 2011).

44 Chesterman, 'Oil and Water'; see also the discussion in Cassels, 'Outlaws'; Pillay, 'Absence of Justice'; Chopra, 'Multinational Corporations'; see also NGO commentary of Bhopal.net: International Campaign for Justice in Bhopal, available at http://bhopal.net/index1.html (last accessed 10 December 2011).

45 Thompson, 'A Multifaceted Approach', 79–80.

46 Ibid., 84.

47 Ibid., 84; White, 'Including Local Communities', 311.

48 BHP transferred its 52 per cent holding in the company, Ok Tedi Mining Ltd, to the Papua New Guinea Sustainable Development Program Company in 2002. The other original shareholders were Amoco Minerals, a consortium of German companies, and a 20 per cent stake held by the Papua New Guinean government.

49 See Figure 1, Mineral Policy Center, sourced from Ghazi, 'Unearthing Controversy', available at http://archive.wri.org/newsroom/wrifeatures_text.cfm?ContentID=1895&NewsletterID=39 (last accessed 14 December 2011); United Nations Environment Program (UNEP), 'Waste from Consumption and Production', available at www.vitalgraphics.net/waste/html_file/18-19_consumption_oktedi.html (last accessed 22 January 2008).

50 UNEP, 'Waste from Consumption'.

almost lifeless.[51] The contaminated rivers and soils affected the subsistence lifestyles of local indigenous peoples, who were reliant on the environment for survival.[52] Hunting lands, gardens, and crops were lost, fish in the rivers were destroyed, drinking water contaminated, and the numbers of birds and wildlife were reduced.[53]

The resultant loss of traditional lifestyles, together with the arrival of new business operatives attached to the mine, also led to the displacement of local communities, an influx of alcohol and consumer goods, the acceleration of disease, and an increase in poverty.[54] Furthermore, the cultural and spiritual life of the local indigenous peoples was deeply affected by the presence of the mine.[55] The sense of identity of the Min peoples of the Star Mountains was intimately entwined with the environment as a whole and, in particular, with Mount Fubilan, a traditional sacred site – and also the location of the mine.[56] Therefore, the effects of the massive environmental degradation inflicted on the mountain, the rivers, and the lands of the Min peoples went beyond the physical devastation and impacted on the psychological well-being of the local communities.[57] Reflecting the persistent destruction of the environment, collective memories and language that had been imbued with imagery and symbolism from the land have also been disappearing.[58] Once-powerful beliefs and rituals are now relegated to the status of quaint folk stories, leading to the loss of the intangible heritage of these communities.[59]

In seeking redress for the damage caused by the Ok Tedi mine, the local indigenous peoples turned to the domestic courts of the investor's home state, Australia.[60] In 1994, proceedings were issued in the Victorian Supreme Court against BHP and Ok Tedi Mining Ltd.[61] Practical reasons for filing an action in the home state of the parent company in this way include the lack of assets and funds held by the subsidiary company, the potential for higher damages awards in the home state, and structural obstacles to plaintiff claims in their own

[51] Ibid.; Ghazi, 'Unearthing Controversy'; White, 'Including Local Communities', 312.
[52] UNEP, 'Waste from Consumption'; Ghazi, 'Unearthing Controversy'; White, 'Including Local Communities', 311–18; Hilson, 'An Overview', 69.
[53] White, 'Including Local Communities', 312–21; Hilson, 'An Overview', 69–70.
[54] Hilson, 'An Overview', 69–70; White, 'Including Local Communities', 314–16.
[55] White, 'Including Local Communities', 315; Hyndman, 'Academic Responsibilities'.
[56] White, 'Including Local Communities', 315, 308. [57] Ibid., 315.
[58] Hyndman, 'Academic Responsibilities', 36. [59] Ibid.
[60] Connell, 'Trans-National', 61–4.
[61] *Dagi and Others* v. *The Broken Hill Proprietary Company Ltd and Another (No. 2)* [1997] 1 VR 428.

countries, such as the lack of legal aid facilities and host state unwillingness to regulate multinational corporations.[62] Ethical reasons include the desire to close the gap between law and ethics and ensure that corporate responsibility and accountability apply equally in transnational operations and home state activities.[63]

It is, however, difficult to obtain compensation from a parent company for environmental degradation caused by their operations in other countries. Jurisdictional issues, in particular the doctrine of *forum non conveniens*, and rules on corporate structure, separate legal personality, and limited liability, are regularly invoked to preclude the hearing of actions by foreign plaintiffs against multinational corporations in their home state.[64] The doctrine of *forum non conveniens* enables a court to decline jurisdiction to hear a matter on the basis that it is an inappropriate or inconvenient forum.[65] The original purpose of the doctrine was to shield defendants from an abuse of process, which was characterised as deliberate selection of an inconvenient forum by a plaintiff so as to harass the defendant.[66] Australia has retained a form of the doctrine that is close to its original intent, in which a stay of proceedings will only be granted if the forum is 'clearly inappropriate' in the sense of being oppressive or vexatious.[67] The United States and Britain, however, have adopted versions of the 'most appropriate forum' model, according to which the defendant needs only to show that an adequate alternative forum exists and that the private and public interests involved point to removing the case to that alternative forum.[68] Comparatively speaking, this standard is an easier threshold for the

62 Cassels, 'Outlaws'; Ward, 'Securing Transnational'; Chesterman, 'Oil and Water', 315; International Ban Asbestos Secretariat, 'UK Victory', available at www.btinternet.com/~ibas/lords_cape.htm (last accessed 10 December 2011).

63 Rogge, 'Towards Transnational', 316–17.

64 Chesterman, 'Oil and Water', 315–18; Ward, 'Securing Transnational', 460–1; Prince, 'Bhopal'; Anderson, 'Transnational Corporations', 412–14.

65 Prince, 'Bhopal', 573; Anderson, 'Transnational Corporations', 412; Chesterman, 'Oil and Water', 315–16; Ward, 'Securing Transnational', 460–1.

66 Prince, 'Bhopal', 573; Kaye, 'Transnational Environmental Litigation', 39.

67 *Voth* v. *Manildra Flour Mills Pty Ltd* (1990) 171 CLR 538; see also Kaye, 'Transnational Environmental Litigation', 43; Prince, 'Bhopal', 576; Chesterman, 'Oil and Water', 317.

68 Prince, 'Bhopal', 574–5; Anderson, 412; Kaye, 'Transnational Environmental Litigation', 39. There are indications that the British courts are moving away from the American model of *forum non conveniens* – see, e.g., the House of Lords' decision in *Lubbe* v. *Cape Plc* [2000] 4 All ER 268; see also the European Court of Justice case, *Owusu* v. *Jackson*, ECJ C-281/02, Judgment 1 March 2005, which restricts the availability of *forum non conveniens* in English law.

defendant to meet than the Australian approach and has been described as one that not only discriminates against foreign plaintiffs, but as one that is regularly invoked by multinational corporations to avoid responsibility for damage caused by their activities in host states.[69]

Forum non conveniens was not directly invoked in *Dagi and Others* v. *The Broken Hill Proprietary Co. Ltd and Another (No. 2)* (the *Ok Tedi Dispute*).[70] Given the Australian approach, there was little point in seeking to rely on this doctrine to dismiss the proceedings.[71] BHP did, however, put forward other jurisdiction-based challenges,[72] leading commentators to argue that the company was attempting to benefit from *forum non conveniens*-type arguments via other routes.[73] BHP also sought to prevent the proceedings through collusion with the government of Papua New Guinea, during which the government agreed to enact legislation criminalising the bringing of compensation claims against BHP.[74] Attempting to influence the governments of home and host states has been identified as a common strategy employed by multinational corporations in disputes over their conduct. In illustrating this tendency, Chesterman points not only to the Papua New Guinea and BHP collusion, but also refers to the example of ExxonMobil's actions when faced with allegations of misconduct in its Indonesian operations. In the ExxonMobil instance, the oil company solicited a United States State Department opinion that the law suit itself harmed American interests – discontinuance of the proceedings shortly followed.[75]

The plaintiffs in the *Ok Tedi Dispute* filed an application in the Supreme Court of Victoria requesting BHP be found in contempt of court, arguing that BHP's actions were 'designed to intimidate them and dissuade them from continuing to press their claims before the court'.[76] The court agreed and found BHP guilty of contempt.[77] However, the ruling

[69] Prince, 'Bhopal', 574; Kaye, 'Transnational Environmental Litigation', 39; Clagett, '*Forum Non Conveniens*'.

[70] [1997] 1 VR 428. For a discussion of this aspect of the case, see Kaye, 'Transnational Environmental Litigation', 43; Prince, 'Bhopal', 593–5.

[71] Kaye, 'Transnational Environmental Litigation', 43–4; Prince, 'Bhopal', 593–5.

[72] Such as the double actionability rule and the local action rule. For a discussion of these principles, see Kaye, 'Transnational Environmental Litigation'.

[73] See, e.g., Kaye, 'Transnational Environmental Litigation', 44.

[74] Chesterman, 'Oil and Water', 322–3; Connell, 'Trans-National', 62.

[75] Chesterman, 'Oil and Water', 322–3.

[76] *The Broken Hill Proprietary Company Ltd* v. *Dagi and Others* [1996] 2 VR 117, 120.

[77] Ibid., para. 120.

was overturned on appeal on an issue of standing, and, ultimately, the case settled.[78]

These circumstances, of course, have implications extending well beyond the outcome of the court proceedings. It can be seen how the flooding of forests downstream from the Ok Tedi mine with toxic mine tailings exemplifies the traditional exploitative approach of foreign investors to the environment of host states. Conceptually, the environment at Ok Tedi was valuable to the foreign investor for what was contained within it and for what was valued by global economic markets - gold and copper. The remaining elements of the environment were not valuable to the investor, and, as such, the prospect of substantial damage occurring to those aspects of the environment did not preclude the operation of the mine. At its core, these circumstances embodied a process of commodification of the environment of the host state for the use of foreign entities and legitimised the investor's indifference to the incidental environmental damage resulting from the operations. Significantly, it is a conceptualisation of the environment that harks back to the era of imperialism. Furthermore, it is, of course, also yet another troubling layer to the legacy of imperialism, that Papua New Guinea internalised such conceptualisations, harming its own marginalised citizens and their environment in collusion with foreign investors.

It is certainly problematic that a seventeenth- to nineteenth-century imperialist conceptual framework still informs the modern relationship between foreign investors and the environments within which they operate. The disconcerting nature of that relationship is further compounded by international investment law, which, as it currently stands, does very little to change that view of the environment. In fact, it reinforces it. At an elemental level, international investment law is premised on protecting the rights of foreign investors to carry out their activities within host states. Sourced from a purely instrumentalist conceptualisation of the environment, it is indifferent to the effects

[78] Ibid. On appeal, the matter turned on whether contempt proceedings could only be brought by the Attorney-General for the State of Victoria. The Court of Appeal determined that that was the case, due to the operation of s.46 of the Public Prosecutions Act. The Attorney-General, however, declined to pursue the matter on behalf of the plaintiffs. The Attorney-General had, in fact, been given leave to intervene in the contempt proceedings and, along with BHP, appealed the original finding of contempt. See also the discussion in Prince, 'Bhopal', 595. The settlement involved A$500,000 in compensation, including the building of a tailings containment.

of investor activity on the local communities and environments of host states. Although manifesting in a variety of ways, such an approach surely also underpins the lack of any incorporation of socially and environmentally responsible requirements within its principles. Indeed, this orientation within the relationship has even seen it argued that legitimate environmental measures must ensure their compliance with international investment rules, rather than the other way around.[79]

As solely an investor protection regime, international investment law in its current form is unable to alleviate the plight of local communities facing environmental degradation resulting from an investor's activities.Without a comprehensive international regulatory framework through which to govern the conduct of multinational corporations, there is no international avenue to pursue corporate accountability for their activities in host states. Seeking redress through the national courts of the home state is an option, but often a problematic one. As Ward points out, establishing parent company responsibility in the national courts of the home state is effectively a 'lottery'.[80] The implications of such legal obstacles are explored further in the following analysis of two other key instances of localised devastation by foreign-owned entities, Texaco in Ecuador and Union Carbide in Bhopal. In the course of this discussion, a picture emerges of the essential nature of the relationship between investor and the environment of the host state – it is clearly characterised by the commodification of the environment for the benefit of foreign investors and the investors' indifference to the damage caused by their activities.

2. Texaco in Ecuador

Thirty years of Texaco operations in Ecuador resulted in massive environmental degradation in the Amazonian region. In 1964, an American company, Texaco Inc, acquired rights for oil exploration and extraction in the Oriente region of Ecuador.[81] It transferred those rights to its wholly owned subsidiary, Texaco de Petròleos, known as TEXPET, and carried out drilling and extraction operations through TEXPET in conjunction with the wholly owned subsidiary of another

[79] Weiler and Wälde, 'Investment Arbitration', 26–7.

[80] Ward, 'Securing Transnational', 462.

[81] Kimerling, 'Environmental Audit', 204–5; Amazon Defense Coalition, 'ChevronToxico', available at www.chevrontoxico.com/article.php?list=type&type=3 (last accessed 5 February 2010).

multinational corporation, Gulf Oil Corporation.[82] Ecuador went on to establish a national oil company, CEPE (now Petroecuador), which acquired a 25 per cent share in Texaco's oil concession in 1974.[83] By 1977, Petroecuador had acquired Gulf Oil's entire share in the consortium.[84] Texaco, however, continued to operate the concession through TEXPET until 1990.[85] It designed and built all the facilities for oil exploration and extraction in Ecuador and was responsible for the day-to-day management of the operations.[86]

Texaco's practices over the ensuing thirty years constituted callous disregard for the environment and lives of the local indigenous peoples. Its operations utilised 'substandard and ultra-hazardous waste-disposal technology' which led to extensive contamination of the waterways and soil of the surrounding areas.[87] Texaco drilled over 300 oil wells across the Amazon region, which continuously discharged toxic waste into the environment.[88] The company dumped untreated crude oil into open and unlined pits, from which toxic chemicals then leached into water systems and through the soil of village lands.[89] This method of waste disposal did not comply with the industry standard in the United States at the time.[90] In the United States, waste from oil extraction processes was generally either shipped to specific disposal facilities or reinjected deep into the ground.[91] It is now clear that Texaco also ignored Ecuadorian environmental laws[92] and did not implement

[82] *Aguinda* Complaint against Texaco filed in Lago Agrio (2003), paras 1–5, English translation available at www.chevrontoxico.com/downloads/Complaint_Ecuador_English.pdf (last accessed 10 December 2011); Kimerling, 'Transnational Operations', 445.

[83] Kimerling, 'Environmental Audit', 204. [84] Ibid., 204.

[85] Ibid., 205; Lyons, 'A Case Study', 703–4. [86] Kimerling, 'Environmental Audit', 204.

[87] Rogge, 'Towards Transnational', 306; see also Lyons, 'A Case Study', 704–5; Kimerling, 'Transnational Operations', 451–3; Holwick, 'Transnational Corporate Behaviour', 199–201.

[88] Kimerling, 'Environmental Audit', 205; Clagett, '*Forum Non Conveniens*', 514; Kimerling, 'Transnational Operations', 457; Lyons, 'A Case Study', 704.

[89] Amazon Defense Coalition, 'ChevronToxico'; Lyons, 'A Case Study', 704–5; Holwick, 'Transnational Corporate Behaviour', 200–1.

[90] Lyons, 'A Case Study', 704–5; Holwick, 'Transnational Corporate Behaviour', 200.

[91] Lyons, 'A Case Study', 704–5; Abelowitz, 'Discrimination and Cultural Genocide', 146.

[92] Such as the Law of Hydrocarbons, Decreto Supremo No. 2967, R.O.711 (1978); Law of Waters, Decreto Supremo No. 369, R.O. No. 69 (1972); Law for the Prevention and Control of Environmental Contamination, passed 1976, R.O. No. 204 (1989).

environmental protection standards or environmental monitoring systems in those oil fields.[93]

Over the entire course of their operations, Texaco released billions of gallons of untreated waste waters and sludge directly into the rivers.[94] This toxic solution, known as 'produced water', contained a mix of crude oil and chemicals, typically benzene, dioxins, hydrocarbons, and heavy metals, such as arsenic, beryllium, cadmium, and nickel.[95] In addition to the waste produced directly from the extraction process, chemicals of all kinds are also used to perform a range of maintenance and operational functions at oil fields, including 'biocides, fungicides, coagulants, cleaners, dispersants, paraffin control agents, descalers, foam retardants and corrosion inhibitors'.[96] These chemicals are also typically found in produced water.[97] Furthermore, accidental spillages from the oil pipelines contributed a further 16.8 million gallons of crude oil into the Amazon River system.[98] As a result of these practices, the drinking and bathing water of local communities was contaminated in the areas in which Texaco operated.[99] Fish in the rivers used as a food source also contained toxic levels of chemicals.[100] Vast areas of once pristine rainforest still suffer the effects of Texaco's operations and remain damaged from the large-scale pollution.[101] Discarded Texaco oil barrels still line the rivers and tributaries, polluting the waterways.[102]

Local inhabitants have suffered an array of illnesses, including high rates of cancer, tumours, birth defects, respiratory illnesses, gastro-

[93] Kimerling, 'Indigenous Peoples', 433–43.

[94] Amazon Defense Coalition, 'Historic Trial', available at www.chevrontoxico.com/article.php?id=55 (last accessed 5 February 2008); Kimerling, 'Indigenous Peoples', 449–52.

[95] Lyons, 'A Case Study', 704–5; Kimerling, 'Indigenous Peoples', 450–3.

[96] Kimerling, 'Indigenous Peoples', 452; Lyons, 'A Case Study', 704–5;

[97] Kimerling, 'Indigenous Peoples', 450–2.

[98] Clagett, '*Forum Non Conveniens*', 514; Kimerling, 'Environmental Audit', 205; Lyons, 'A Case Study', 704; Rodgers Kalas, '*Jota* v. *Texaco*', 49.

[99] Amazon Defense Coalition, 'ChevronToxico'; Kimerling, 'Environmental Audit', 205; Clagett, '*Forum Non Conveniens*', 514; Rogge, 'Towards Transnational', 306; Lyons, 'A Case Study', 706–7.

[100] Lyons, 'A Case Study', 706–7; Kimerling, 'Environmental Audit', 205–6; Clagett, '*Forum Non Conveniens*', 514.

[101] Kimerling, 'Environmental Audit', 204–5; Kimerling, 'Indigenous Peoples', 464–8; Amazon Defense Coalition, 'ChevronToxico'.

[102] Amazon Watch, 'Crude Reflections'; photograph, Szymczak (2005), available at http://chevrontoxico.com/article.php?id=110 (last accessed 7 February 2010).

intestinal complaints, reproductive problems, rashes, and headaches.[103] In addition to the severe health problems suffered by the local indigenous communities, these peoples have also endured displacement from their lands and the loss of their territories, the devastation of their natural resources, the destruction of their subsistence lifestyles, and the dislocation of their cultural life.[104]

In the 1990s, local communities in the Ecuadorian Amazon affected by the pollution sought redress in the courts of the United States.[105] The plaintiffs argued that New York was the appropriate forum in which to hear the matter as the state was Texaco's principal place of business and the 'policies, procedures and decisions relating to oil exploration and drilling in Ecuador were set and made in New York'.[106] These cases were dismissed on grounds of *forum non conveniens* and the related doctrine of comity of nations.[107] The comity doctrine is premised on the notion that it may be demeaning of the courts of other states if claims of foreign plaintiffs are permitted in local courts.[108] It is invoked as a justification for dismissing claims brought by foreign plaintiffs against multinational corporations and is a significant undercurrent in determining *forum non conveniens* disputes.[109] Although the terminology in such judgments expresses a desire to be respectful of other nations,[110] the effect of the doctrine is so advantageous to the position of multinational corporations and so detrimental for the local communities and environments of host states, that it has been described as 'the rhetoric of comity'.[111]

103 Amazon Defense Coalition, 'ChevronToxico'; see also the *Aguinda* Complaint filed in an Ecuadorian court against Texaco in 2003, an English translation of which can be found at www.chevrontoxico.com/downloads/Complaint_Ecuador_English.pdf (last accessed 11 February 2008); Kimerling, 'Indigenous Peoples', 466; Clagett, '*Forum Non Conveniens*', 514; Kimerling, 'Environmental Audit', 206; Rodgers Kala, '*Jota* v. *Texico*', 51.

104 Kimerling, 'Indigenous Peoples', 657; Lyons, 'A Case Study', 706–7.

105 *Sequihua* v. *Texaco, Inc*, 847 F. Supp. 61 (S.D. Tex. 1994); *Aguinda* v. *Texaco, Inc.*, 945 F. Supp. 625 (S.D.N.Y. 1996); *Ashanga* v. *Texaco*, S.D.N.Y. Dkt. No.94 Civ. 9266 (Aug. 13, 1997).

106 *Aguinda* v. *Texaco, Inc*, 1994 WL 142006 (S.D.N.Y. 1994) Brief for Plaintiff, 3, cited in Rogge 'Towards Transnational', 313.

107 Rogge, 'Towards Transnational', 307; Chesterman, 'Oil and Water', 317.

108 Prince, 'Bhopal', 576

109 Ibid., 576–81; Northrop, 'Exporting Environmental Justice', 787.

110 See, e.g., the judgment of Justice Keenan in *Re Union Carbide Corporation Gas Plant Disaster*, 634 F. Supp. 842, 867 (S.D.N.Y. 1986). This aspect of Justice Keenan's judgment is discussed in further detail below.

111 Paul, 'Comity', 55; see also the discussion in Prince, 'Bhopal', 576–81.

Over a period of almost ten years, *Aguinda* v. *Texaco, Inc* passed through a series of hearings and appeals, at the conclusion of which the United States Court of Appeals held that the appropriate forum for the case was Ecuador.[112] The Court did, however, require Texaco to submit to the jurisdiction of Ecuadorian courts and to waive any limitation defences.[113] Although the case was dismissed in the Court of Appeals, this aspect of the judgment gave encouragement to the plaintiffs.[114] Their lawyers framed the proviso as a triumph, in which a powerful multinational oil company was ordered by its own courts to submit to the jurisdiction of the courts in a developing state.[115]

The legal wranglings have, however, continued. A case against ChevronTexaco was filed in Lago Agrio, Ecuador, in 2003, the result of which was a finding in February 2011 against the oil company and a damages award of US$18.2 billion, upheld on appeal in January 2012.[116] However, in September 2009, well before the determination of the Lago Agrio claim, Chevron commenced investor–state arbitral proceedings against Ecuador, alleging that the state had violated the United States–Ecuador bilateral investment treaty by colluding with the plaintiffs in the Lago Agrio litigation.[117]

In 2010, the Lago Agrio plaintiffs unsuccessfully sought a stay of the arbitration proceedings through the United States courts. Ecuador argued that in seeking to dismiss the original case in the United States on the grounds of *forum non conveniens*, Chevron had agreed to satisfy any valid Ecuadorian judgment and waived any right to object to the Ecuadorian proceedings. The rejection of the application was affirmed

[112] *Aguinda* v. *Texaco, Inc.*, 303 F. 3d 470 (2d Cir. 2002).

[113] Ibid., pp. 476–9; Kimerling, 'Indigenous Peoples', 416; Chesterman, 'Oil and Water', 317–18.

[114] Kimerling, 'Indigenous Peoples', 628. [115] Ibid., 628.

[116] *Aguinda* Complaint against Texaco filed in Lago Agrio (2003), an English translation of which can be found at www.chevrontoxico.com/downloads/Complaint_Ecuador_English.pdf (last accessed 11 February 2010); Judgment of the Appellate Division of the Provincial Court of Sucumbios of Ecuador (3 January 2012). Chevron Corporation bought Texaco in 2001 and, in so doing, acquired ownership of TEXPET.

[117] Notice of Arbitration, *In the Matter of an Arbitration under the Rules of the United Nations Commission on International Trade Law, Chevron Corporation and Texaco Petroleum Company* v. *Republic of Ecuador*, 23 September 2009, available at www.chevron.com/documents/pdf/EcuadorBITEn.pdf (last accessed 14 December 2011); Treaty between the United States of America and the Republic of Ecuador concerning the Encouragement and Reciprocal Protection of Investment, signed on 27 August 1993 (entered into force 11 May 1997).

on appeal in 2011 on the basis that the court at first instance was correct in finding that Ecuador's waiver and estoppel claims should be determined by the arbitral panel, not the courts in the United States.[118]

In February 2011, Chevron filed a lawsuit in the United States against the lawyers for the Lago Agrio plaintiffs, alleging that their pursuit of Chevron constituted fraud and a breach of the Racketeer Influenced and Corrupt Organizations Act.[119] The claim survived a strike-out application in May 2012.[120]

Also in February 2011, the arbitral panel presiding over the investor–state claim issued a procedural order requiring Ecuador to 'take all measures necessary to suspend or cause to be suspended the enforcement and recognition within and without Ecuador of any judgment against' ChevronTexaco in the Lago Agrio litigation. In February 2012, the arbitral panel determined that it had jurisdiction to hear the complaint brought by Chevron, and the matter will now proceed to a hearing on the merits.[121] In the meantime, a separate interim award of the panel affirmed the order of February 2011, requiring Ecuador:

> (whether by its judicial, legislative or executive branches) to take all measures necessary to suspend or cause to be suspended the enforcement and recognition within and without Ecuador of the judgments by the Provincial Court of Sucumbíos, Sole Division (Corte Provincial de Justicia de Sucumbíos, Sala Unica de la Corte Provincial de Justicia de Sucumbíos) of 3 January 2012 and of 13 January 2012 (and, to the extent confirmed by the said judgments, of the judgment by Judge Nicolás Zambrano Lozada of 14 February 2011) against the First Claimant in the Ecuadorian legal proceedings known as 'the Lago Agrio Case'.[122]

[118] *Republic of Ecuador* v. *Chevron Corporation*, 658 F.3d 384 (2d Cir. 2011).

[119] *Chevron Corporation* v. *Donziger*, USDC, S.D.N.Y. 11-Civ-0691, 1 February 2011.

[120] Opinion on Motion to Dismiss Amended Complaint, *Chevron Corporation* v. *Donziger*, USDC, S.D.N.Y. 11-Civ-0691, 14 May 2012.

[121] Third Interim Award on Jurisdiction and Admissibility, *In the Matter of an Arbitration under the Rules of the United Nations Commission on International Trade Law, Chevron Corporation and Texaco Petroleum Company* v. *Ecuador*, 27 February 2012, available at www.chevron.com/documents/pdf/ecuador/PCA-Jurisdiction-Decision.pdf (last accessed 18 July 2012).

[122] Second Interim Award, *In the Matter of an Arbitration under the Rules of the United Nations Commission on International Trade Law, Chevron Corporation and Texaco Petroleum Company* v. *Ecuador*, 16 February 2012, available at www.chevron.com/documents/pdf/ecuador/SecondTribunalInterimAward.pdf (last accessed 18 July 2012).

In May 2012, proceedings were issued in Canada by the plaintiffs in the original Lago Agrio case seeking to enforce the Ecuadorian judgment of US$18.2 billion against Chevron.[123] A further lawsuit was also filed in Brazil in June 2012, again seeking recognition and enforcement of the Ecuadorian judgment.[124] It would seem that a resolution to this protracted episode that could bring some recompense to those deeply affected Ecuadorian communities is still some way off.

3. Bhopal

The extent of the injustice that can result from the non-engagement of international investment law with the impact of investor activities on the local communities and environments of the host state is also illustrated in the infamous Union Carbide disaster at Bhopal, India. In 1984, a lethal gas leak from a pesticide factory sent clouds of poisonous fumes across Bhopal, a city of one million people, killing approximately 8,000 individuals in the first week following the disaster.[125] An estimated further 20,000 people have since died from illness and injury resulting from the exposure to methyl isocyanate gas.[126] Up to 150,000 residents of Bhopal suffered severe injuries.[127] Union Carbide Corporation, an American multinational corporation, operated in India through its subsidiary, Union Carbide of India Ltd. This Indian company owned the pesticide factory responsible for the disaster.[128]

The immediate injuries suffered by Bhopal residents were horrific. Survivors give accounts of the burning in their eyes and mouths, suffocation, vomiting, convulsions, loss of control of bladder and bowel, spontaneous miscarriages, and blindness, as well as witnessing others frothing at the mouth, writhing in agony, and dying on the streets.[129] The long-term effects for those who survived exposure to the gas have

[123] *Yaiguage et al.* v. *Chevron Corporation*, 30 May 2012, (Court File No. CV-12–454778).

[124] *María Aguinda Salazar* v. *Chevron Corporation*, 27 June 2012, an English translation of which can be found at http://lettersblogatory.com/wp-content/uploads/2012/06/Brazil-complaint-in-English.pdf (last accessed 18 July 2012).

[125] The Bhopal Medical Appeal and Sambhavna Trust, 'What Happened in Bhopal?', undated, available at www.bhopal.org/whathappened.html (last accessed 23 February 2008).

[126] Ibid., Broughton, 'The Bhopal Disaster', 2; Engel and Martin, 'Union Carbide', 478.

[127] Engel and Martin, 'Union Carbide', 478.

[128] Cassels, 'Outlaws', 314.

[129] See, e.g., the account of A. Sultan, International Campaign for Justice in Bhopal, available at www.bhopal.org/aziza.html (last accessed 10 December 2011); Trotter, Day, and Love, 'Bhopal, India', 441.

included blindness and damage to lungs, kidneys, liver, and reproductive systems.[130] There have also been high rates of cancer, stillbirths, and birth defects in the general population of Bhopal.[131]

Union Carbide asserted that the leak was the result of sabotage.[132] The Indian government concluded that human error and technical failure on the part of the company's operations was the more likely cause.[133] The company had engaged in a cost-cutting programme, resulting in inadequate training of staff, deterioration of the facility's safety systems, and the reduction of standard maintenance work.[134] As a consequence, when an error occurred during the cleaning of pipes, leading to water entering a tank containing methyl isocyanate, the resulting poisonous gas was not contained or neutralised by any of the six safety mechanisms designed to prevent gas leaks.[135]

Incidentally, it has recently become apparent that the contamination of Bhopal was not limited to the release of toxic gas in 1984. The conduct of Union Carbide following the disaster exacerbated the pollution, ensuring the continued discharge of hazardous material into the surrounding environment. Although the factory was closed down, the site was not cleaned up, and no decontamination programme was implemented.[136] Chemicals still remain dumped at the site to this day, poisoning the soil, groundwater acquifers, drinking-water wells, and the people of Bhopal.[137]

130 Broughton, 'The Bhopal Disaster', 2; Cassels, 'Outlaws', 315; Trotter, Day, and Love, 'Bhopal, India', 441.
131 Cassels, 'Outlaws', 315.
132 Broughton, 'The Bhopal Disaster', 3; Cassels, 'Outlaws', 315.
133 Cassels, 'Outlaws', 315–16.
134 Trotter, Day, and Love, 'Bhopal, India', 440; Broughton, 'The Bhopal Disaster', 2; Cassels, 'Outlaws', 316–17; Engel and Martin, 'Union Carbide', 479.
135 Broughton, 'The Bhopal Disaster', 2; Cassels, 'Outlaws', 316–17. Cassels describes the following series of failures:

> By way of example: the MIC tank that ruptured was overfilled with gas and a reserve tank was also full; the refrigeration system designed to stabilize the gas was not functional, the gas scrubbers had been shut off for maintenance and the flare tower was inoperative; the water sprayers were insufficiently pressurized to reach escaping gases, and warning systems were so inaccurate and unreliable that they were routinely ignored.

136 Broughton, 'The Bhopal Disaster', 3; Murru, 'Bhopal 20 Years On', 250.
137 Broughton, 'The Bhopal Disaster', 3; International Campaign for Justice in Bhopal, 'The Poisoning of Bhopal', available at www.bhopal.net/poisoning.html (last accessed 10 December 2011); Murru, 'Bhopal 20 Years On', 250; Labunska et al., *The Bhopal Legacy*, pp. 2–3, 23–4, available at http://archive.greenpeace.org/toxics/toxfreeasia/bhopal.pdf (last accessed 10 December 2011).

By early 1985, multiple proceedings had been filed in the United States against Union Carbide, seeking damages in the range of US$5 billion to US$50 billion.[138] At this point, the Indian government stepped in, consolidated these proceedings pursuant to the Bhopal Gas Leak Disaster (Processing of Claims) Act 1985, and declared itself the sole representative of the victims.[139] Union Carbide defended the proceedings, putting forward arguments based on *forum non conveniens* and separate corporate personality. The company argued that the United States was an inappropriate forum in which to hear the matter.[140] In seeking to support this argument, Union Carbide asserted that not only was it not responsible for the activities of the Indian company, but it did not have any operations in India at all and was unconnected with the events at the Bhopal pesticide factory.[141] It argued that there was no such thing as a 'multinational corporation' and that the American company, Union Carbide Corporation, was an entirely separate legal entity from the company the plaintiffs should have been pursuing, Union Carbide of India Ltd.[142]

India countered with an argument described as 'multinational enterprise liability'.[143] It was a line of reasoning based on the idea that a collective group of companies operating as a single economic body under the control of one multinational corporation should be regarded as one single legal entity.[144] It follows that as there is a direct level of control between the parent company and its subsidiaries, the parent company should be liable for the activities of its subsidiaries.[145] It is a theory that attempts to advance the law on corporate legal personality, ensuring it reflects the reality of transnational business in a globalised world.[146] As Cassels argues, it is indeed ironic to see '[a] major

[138] Abraham and Abraham, 'The Bhopal Case', 337.

[139] Ibid., 337–8; Cassels, 'Outlaws', 321; Engel and Martin, 'Union Carbide', 480.

[140] Prince, 'Bhopal', 586; Cassels, 'Outlaws', 325; Trotter, Day, and Love, 'Bhopal, India', 447.

[141] Cassels, 'Outlaws', 322; Engel and Martin, 'Union Carbide', 483–4.

[142] Engel and Martin, 'Union Carbide', 483–4; Cassels, 'Outlaws', 322. These arguments are based on fundamental principles of company law precluding a court from 'piercing the corporate veil' so as to look behind the façade of separate legal personality for companies within the same 'family'; see also the discussion in Blumberg, 'Asserting Human Rights'.

[143] Cassels, 'Outlaws', 323.

[144] Muchlinski, 'The Bhopal Case', 557; Cassels, 'Outlaws', 322–3.

[145] Muchlinski, 'The Bhopal Case', 557.

[146] Cassels, 'Outlaws', 323–5; see also the discussion on Bhopal and establishing a treaty on jurisdiction over transnational claims in an attempt to regulate the conduct of multinational corporations in Ott, 'Bhopal and the Law', 648.

multinational corporation, whose policy is to maintain centralized integrated corporate strategic planning, direction and control, argue that it had no responsibility for its subsidiary.'[147] The American company was the majority shareholder in Union Carbide of India Ltd. It appointed the board of directors, controlled the management of the company, designed the facility, transferred all the technology, provided all the information and training, and made the key policy and directional decisions for the operation of the factory.[148] Justice Keenan, however, was persuaded by Union Carbide's arguments that it adopted a 'hands-off' approach to the management of its Indian operations.[149] Ultimately, the proceedings were dismissed on grounds of *forum non conveniens* and comity.[150]

Proceedings were filed in the District Court of Bhopal in 1986.[151] Substantial delays in the progress of the matter, however, meant that the victims still had not received any financial relief by the end of 1987.[152] In an attempt to alleviate some of the hardship and suffering of the victims of the gas leak, the District Court made an Interim Order requiring the payment of US$270 million by Union Carbide.[153] This ruling was later affirmed by the Madhya Pradesh High Court, although the amount was reduced to US$195 million.[154] Union Carbide appealed to the Supreme Court of India, during the hearing of which a settlement was reached.[155] Union Carbide and India agreed on a figure of US$470 million and orders requiring Union Carbide to pay this sum were made in the Supreme Court of India in 1989.[156] It was a woefully inadequate sum, from which the families of the deceased each received on average US$2,200 and the injured much less, sums that were insufficient to provide for the ongoing medical needs of

147 Cassels, 'Outlaws', 331; see also the discussion in Prince, 'Bhopal', 586–7.

148 Prince, 'Bhopal', 586–7; Cassels, 'Outlaws', 329.

149 Cassels, 'Outlaws', 326–7, 329; Baxi, *Inconvenient Forum*, pp. 5, 52–3.

150 *Re Union Carbide Corporation Gas Plant Disaster*, 634 F. Supp. 842 (S.D.N.Y. 1986). The decision was affirmed by the United States Court of Appeals, 2nd Circuit (1987).

151 *Union of India* v. *Union Carbide Corporation*, Bhopal Gas Claim Case No. 113 of 1986.

152 Cassels, 'Outlaws', 328–9; Abraham and Abraham, 'The Bhopal Case', 342–3.

153 Abraham and Abraham, 'The Bhopal Case', 336, 343; Cassels, 'Outlaws', 328–9; Trotter, Day, and Love, 'Bhopal, India', 448.

154 Abraham and Abraham, 'The Bhopal Case', 336, 345; Trotter, Day, and Love, 'Bhopal, India', 448.

155 Cassels, 'Outlaws', 330; Abraham and Abraham, 'The Bhopal Case', 336.

156 Cassels, 'Outlaws', 330; Abraham and Abraham, 'The Bhopal Case', 336; Mathur and Morehouse, 'Twice Poisoned Bhopal', 73.

the victims.[157] It has been suggested that a factor in the Indian government's acceptance of such a small compensation sum was its desire to attract new foreign investment and that it did not wish to discourage potential investors with a large settlement or continued litigation.[158]

The failure to obtain adequate compensation for the victims of the Bhopal gas leak is a lengthy and disappointing story, reflecting the traditional relationship between foreign investors, their home states, and the local communities and environments of host nations. It illustrates the foreign investor's conceptualisation of the environment of the host state as one for its use and exploitation even to the extent of risking substantial damage to the territory and its inhabitants – in this case, in the form of a substandard, hazardous chemical manufacturing facility located within a city of one million people. The tactics used by Union Carbide to reframe its multinational operations as all entirely unconnected entities, its argument that the United States was an inappropriate forum for the litigation, its insistence on the sabotage theory as the cause of the gas leak, the insufficient financial and medical assistance for the victims, and the lack of public scientific information regarding the exact composition of the gas, all add force to Jasanoff's assessment that:

> Bhopal's tragedy was as much about the capacity of powerful institutions selectively to highlight and screen out knowledge as it was about maimed lives and justice denied or delayed.[159]

The legal doctrines of *forum non conveniens* and comity were used to avoid responsibility in the United States for the damage caused in Bhopal, and, like the cases of Texaco in Ecuador and BHP in Ok Tedi, the unresponsiveness of international investment law to the impact of Union Carbide's activity on the people and environment of Bhopal illustrates again the 'gap' in the international regulatory framework.

[157] Mathur and Morehouse, 'Twice Poisoned Bhopal', 73; Murru, 'Bhopal 20 Years On', 250; Broughton, 'The Bhopal Disaster', 1, 3; Cassels, 'Outlaws', 330–1; Fletcher, Ono, and Roy, 'Justice for Bhopal', 8.

[158] Engel and Martin, 'Union Carbide', 485; Mathur and Morehouse, 'Twice Poisoned Bhopal', 69.

[159] See the discussion in Baxi, *Inconvenient Forum*, pp. 1–34; Jasanoff, 'Bhopal's Trials', 344; see also the discussion in Engel and Martin, 'Union Carbide', 481–2.

4. Foreign investors and the use of legal doctrine: reproducing imperialism

Although there appears to be a growing awareness within the judiciary of the need to address the injustice that can occur from the misuse of jurisdictional doctrine,[160] *forum non conveniens* itself is problematic in a more fundamental way. The evolution of the United States' application of the doctrine of *forum non conveniens* is essentially a manifestation of a practice seen since the era of the Dutch East India Company – the use of legal doctrine to entrench the position of foreign investors and capital-exporting states.[161] As discussed in Chapter 1, Anghie points to the manipulation of international legal doctrine from the seventeenth to the nineteenth centuries to support the political and economic aspirations of European expansionism.[162] He explores the ways in which European control over the development of international law in this period meant that its rules evolved to benefit Western states and to exclude non-European territories from its protection.[163] Anghie also argues that when developing states sought to utilise international law in the postcolonial era, again doctrine was developed to the detriment of developing states, ensuring the protection of the interests of their former colonisers.[164]

It would seem that the use of international comity, *forum non conveniens*, and the doctrine of separate corporate legal personality to preclude foreign investor liability for environmental damage in host states also replicates this pattern. Rogge describes the character of the current legal framework as constituting the 'best of both worlds' for multinational corporations – they are permitted to operate in other states and to profit from politically oppressive regimes or environmentally lax regulation, but are shielded from liability for damage resulting from those

[160] Chesterman, 'Oil and Water', 317–18; see also, e.g., *Lubbe and ors* v. *Cape Plc* [2000] 1 WLR 1545 (HL) in which the House of Lords determined that 3,000 South African asbestos victims could bring compensation claims against a British company in the United Kingdom in relation to the activities of its South African subsidiaries.

[161] See Chapter 1 above for a discussion on the role of Hugo Grotius in the development of the law of the high seas while in the employment of the Dutch East India Company; see also Anghie, *Imperialism*, p. 224; Porras, 'Constructing International Law', 742–3, 744–7; van Ittersum, 'Hugo Grotius'.

[162] Anghie, *Imperialism*, pp. 3–12, 65–114; Anghie, 'The Heart', 448.

[163] Anghie, 'The Heart', 448; Anghie, *Imperialism* pp. 3–12, 65–114.

[164] Anghie, *Imperialism*, pp. 235–44; see Anghie for a discussion on the attaining of statehood and yet still being bound by decisions made under a colonial regime through the doctrine of acquired rights and *pacta sunt servanda*.

activities.[165] The same system that enables foreign investors to engage in transnational operations withholds protection from those they damage.[166]

It is even more troubling when the approach to standing in investor–state arbitration is considered. When companies have sought to bring investor claims against a host state, problematic aspects of their corporate structure have not been seen as a bar to bringing a claim.[167] For example, in *S.D. Myers Inc.* v. *Government of Canada* (*S.D. Myers*),[168] the American claimant company had no shareholding in the Canadian company that had suffered the alleged harm. They were both part of a corporate group and family members owned all the shares in both the companies, but the two companies were not themselves interlinked and were entirely separate corporate entities.[169] Reflecting the general approach in investment treaty arbitration, however, the *S.D. Myers* arbitral tribunal had no hesitation in piercing the corporate veil, stating:

> the Tribunal does not accept that an otherwise meritorious claim should fail solely by reason of the corporate structure adopted by a claimant in order to organise the way in which it conducts its business affairs.[170]

It is telling the ease with which the legal doctrine of separate corporate legal personality can be swept aside when the beneficiary of such a decision is the foreign investor – and how religiously it is clung to when accountability of the multinational corporation is sought.

In his work on the history of international law and imperialism, Anghie argues that colonialism reproduces itself.[171] It is a subtle and pervasive phenomenon that finds infinite manifestations in modern international law and politics.[172] Within the context of multinational corporate operations, examples of this can be found in the unresponsiveness of international investment law to damage caused by investor activity and the emergence of the 'most suitable forum' model of *forum non conveniens*, accompanied by the doctrine of separate corporate

[165] Rogge, 'Towards Transnational', 300–1; see also Stephens, 'Amorality of Profit', 48.
[166] Rogge, 'Towards Transnational', 300; Kimerling, 'Indigenous Peoples', 661.
[167] McLachlan, Shore, and Weiniger, *International Investment Arbitration*, pp. 184–92.
[168] *S.D. Myers Inc.* (Partial Award of 2000).
[169] McLachlan, Shore, and Weiniger, *International Investment Arbitration*, p. 186.
[170] Ibid., pp. 185–7; *S.D. Myers Inc.* (Partial Award of 2000), para. 229.
[171] Anghie, 'The Heart', 505–6; Anghie, 'Finding the Peripheries'.
[172] Anghie, 'The Heart'; Anghie, 'Finding the Peripheries'.

personality and judicial comity of nations. These legal mechanisms have effectively assisted capital-exporting states in washing their hands of the damage their corporations cause in their overseas operations. Furthermore, the reasoning that has at times been used in denying host state plaintiffs access to United States' courts suggests at least a subconscious affinity for the interests of the capital-exporting state and its multinational corporations. Along with the more understandable arguments on the location of witnesses and documents, there have also been unusual justifications for dismissing actions by host state plaintiffs, such as the unfairness of burdening the American taxpayer with the cost of hearing the matter, the need to avoid increasing the level of 'docket congestion' in American courts, and, ironically, the desire not to engage in neo-colonialism.[173] This last ground is illustrated in the following extract from the reasoning of Justice Keenan in his judgment dismissing the action filed in the United States on behalf of the victims of the Union Carbide disaster at Bhopal:

> In the Court's view to retain the litigation in this forum, as plaintiffs request, would be yet another example of imperialism, another situation in which an established sovereign inflicted its rules, its standards and values on a developing nation. This Court declines to play such a role. The Union of India is a world power in 1986, and its courts have the proven capacity to mete out fair and equal justice. To deprive the Indian judiciary of this opportunity to stand tall before the world and to pass judgment on behalf of its own people would be to revive a history of subservience and subjugation from which India has emerged. India and its people can and must vindicate their claims before the independent and legitimate judiciary created there since the Independence of 1947.[174]

The irony of this is, of course, that Justice Keenan's stated desire to allow India's courts the opportunity to 'stand tall' had a fundamentally imperialist result – United States-based multinational corporations do not have to operate according to their home state standards, are able to attach less value to the peoples and environments of host states than

[173] These factors were presented as bases for the decision dismissing the suit filed against Union Carbide on behalf of the victims in Bhopal *In Re Union Carbide Corporation Gas Plant Disaster*, 634 F. Supp. 842 (S.D.N.Y. 1986). The need to not burden American citizens with jury service 'in litigation which has no relation to their community' was also cited as a reason for dismissing a claim filed against Texaco for their operations in Ecuador in *Sequihua* v. *Texaco, Inc*, 847 F. Supp. 61 (S.D. Texas 1994). See, for a critique of these bases, Prince, 'Bhopal'; Rogge, 'Towards Transnational', 307.

[174] *In Re Union Carbide Corporation Gas Plant Disaster*, 634 F. Supp. 842 (S.D.N.Y. 1986), 867.

that of the United States, and are not accountable in the United States for the damage they cause in their transnational operations.

In other words, the law of capital-exporting states enables their multinational corporations to pursue economic activities globally, but disengages when called upon to protect the local communities and environments within which those companies operate. Through such channels, the modern foreign investor is again protected by the development and manipulation of legal doctrine, reproducing the links between law and the interests of capital-exporting states and their nationals that were established in the seventeenth to early twentieth centuries. Clearly then, there is a pressing need to break with this pattern and to explore possible mechanisms through which the accountability of multinational corporations could be established on the international plane.[175]

II. Environmental regulation as investment treaty violation

Recent framing of host state environmental regulation as an investment treaty violation is a particularly insidious manifestation of the traditional relationship between foreign investors and the environment. Increasingly, international investment agreements are being invoked to challenge environmental regulation enacted by the host state.[176] It is a move that allows foreign investors to encroach into the realm of domestic policy-making and regulation of the health and environment of the host state and its citizens.[177] Conceptually, it is also a route by which foreign investors can attempt to perpetuate their traditional control of the environment of host states – in resisting the strengthening of environmental protection measures, they are also seeking to maintain the unimpeded use of the environment for their activities. At a fundamental level, this is a cultural approach based on indifference to the condition of the environment in host states and to the impact of

[175] The form such mechanisms might take is considered below in Chapters 5 and 6.

[176] Examples of recent disputes include *S.D. Myers Inc* (Partial Award of 2000); *Ethyl Corporation* Award of 1998); *Metalclad Corporation* (Award of 2000); *Clayton and Bilcon of Delaware* v. *Government of Canada*, Notice of Intent to Submit a Claim to Arbitration under Section B of Chapter 11 of NAFTA, February 2008, Appleton & Associates, available at www.appletonlaw.com/Media/2008/Bilcon%20NAFTA%20 Notice%20of%20Intent.pdf (last accessed 13 March 2008); *Marion Unglaube* v. *Republic of Costa Rica* (ICSID Case No. ARB/08/01, Notice of Intent registered 25 January 2008) ('*Marion Unglaube* (Notice of Intent of 2008)').

[177] Soloway, 'Environmental Regulation', 119; Sands, 'Environmental Regulation'.

their operations within it. In exploring these ideas, this next section examines key investor–state disputes exemplifying this traditional approach and which have fuelled pressure to reshape the international investment legal regime.

A. *Environmental regulation as indirect expropriation*

Individual investment treaties import their own language and the extent of investor protection provided varies. However, core treatment guarantees are virtually universal. These include the national treatment standard, most-favoured-nation treatment, prohibitions on discrimination, guarantees of fair and equitable treatment, and prohibitions on uncompensated expropriation.[178]

International law allows the expropriation of foreign-owned property if the following conditions are met:[179]

a) it is for a public purpose;
b) it is non-discriminatory and is not of an arbitrary nature; and
c) compensation is paid.

Direct expropriation of an investment is not difficult to identify as it involves the seizure of physical assets.[180] More subtle forms of taking, however, are inherently less identifiable as compensable action.[181] The various manifestations are characterised by a diminution in property rights or interference with property interests without a formal transfer of ownership.[182] In discussing the concept of indirect expropriation, Been and Beauvais refer to the terms 'indirect expropriation', 'measures tantamount to expropriation', 'constructive takings', 'creeping expropriation', and 'disguised expropriation', and make the following comment:

> These terms collectively refer to the notion that governments, by means of regulatory or other measures, effectively can deprive an investor of the use

[178] McLachlan, Shore, and Weiniger, *International Investment Arbitration*, p. 207.

[179] Malanczuk, *Akehurst's*, pp. 235–8. The formula for determining the amount of compensation payable has remained controversial. Capital-exporting states persist with the promotion of the 'prompt, adequate and effective' standard and capital-importing states have pursued the less exacting standard of 'appropriate compensation'.

[180] Sornarajah, *Foreign Investment*, p. 367.

[181] Ibid., pp. 349–50; McLachlan, Shore and Weiniger, *International Investment Arbitration*, pp. 266–7.

[182] Sornarajah, *Foreign Investment*, pp. 367–9; Christie, 'Taking of Property', 309; Weston, 'Constructive Takings'.

and benefit of an investment without direct physical occupation or transfer of title.[183]

Traditionally, the rules on international expropriation do not classify certain kinds of governmental action that merely reduce the value of an investment as a compensable taking.[184] This includes the imposition of taxation, devaluation in currency, or changes to inheritance, health and safety, and planning regulations.[185] There is, of course, a fine line involved in the implementation of such measures and often the difficulty is in ascertaining where the legitimate exercise of state powers ends and expropriation has occurred.[186] It is in this context that environmental protection measures and international investment law have recently come into conflict – in the form of allegations that environmental regulation amounts to a breach of international rules on indirect expropriation.[187] The following awards illustrate the different approaches adopted by arbitral panels in addressing these competing concerns.

1. *Metalclad Corporation v. The United States of Mexico*

Metalclad Corporation v. *The United States of Mexico* (*Metalclad*) concerned a hazardous waste treatment site in Mexico owned by an American company, Metalclad Corp.[188] The company had the required clearances from the federal government to build and operate a hazardous waste treatment facility near Guadalcazar, in the state of San Luis Potosí.[189] Metalclad was, however, aware that it required further local government permits to enable authorised construction at the treatment facility site.[190] Although Metalclad did not obtain this local permit, an additional construction permit was issued by the federal government and Metalclad proceeded to build up the site at a cost of US$22 million.[191] The municipality, however, maintained that the federal permits did not remove the need for a local government building permit and

183 Been and Beauvais, 'Global Fifth Amendment?', 54.

184 Malanczuk, *Akehurst's*, p. 238; Brownlie, *Principles*, p. 536; Wortley, *Expropriation*, pp. 501.

185 Malanczuk, *Akehurst's*, p. 238; Brownlie, *Principles*, p. 538; Wortley, *Expropriation*, pp. 50–1.

186 Wortley, *Expropriation*, p. 51; Been and Beauvais, 'Global Fifth Amendment?', 54; Fachiri, 'Expropriation', 170.

187 See, e.g., *Methanex Corporation*; *S.D. Myers Inc.* (Partial Award of 2000); *Ethyl Corporation* (Award of 1998); *Metalclad Corporation* (Award of 2000).

188 *Metalclad Corporation* (Award of 2000). 189 Sands, *Principles*, p. 1066. 190 Ibid.

191 Ibid., pp. 1066–7; *Metalclad Corporation* (Award of 2000), paras 35, 114.

continued to refuse authorisation for the project under land use and environmental regulations.[192] An 'ecological decree' was also issued by the Governor of San Luis Potosí, declaring a large area, which encompassed Metalclad's hazardous waste facility, an ecological preserve so as to protect a rare species of cactus.[193]

The arbitral tribunal initially dealt with the threshold question of Mexico's responsibility for the actions of the municipal authority, finding that it was responsible.[194] The tribunal held that Mexico had not acted with the required levels of transparency and that this translated into a breach of fair and equitable treatment standards contained in Article 1105 of the North American Free Trade Agreement (NAFTA).[195] Mexico had not provided a transparent and predictable framework for Metalclad's investment and had breached the investor's legitimate expectation that it would be treated fairly and justly.[196] The tribunal held that the federal government had exclusive authority to determine the site and permitting of the hazardous waste facility[197] and that the municipality had jurisdiction only over the adequacy of the physical construction of the facility.[198] As such, the municipality had exceeded its authority in denying a permit on the grounds of environmental or geological considerations.[199] The tribunal also found that, in condoning the municipality's denial of a construction permit, Mexico had participated or acquiesced in preventing Metalclad from operating its landfill and that this in itself amounted to an act 'tantamount to expropriation'.[200] The tribunal also found a further act 'tantamount to expropriation' in the issuing of the ecological decree which prevented the use of the site as landfill altogether.[201] Metalclad was awarded US$16.7 million in compensation.[202] Without citing any authority, the tribunal stated that:

> expropriation under NAFTA includes not only open, deliberate and acknowledged takings of property, such as the outright seizure or formal or obligatory transfer of title in favour of the host State, but also covert or incidental interference with the use of property which has the effect of depriving the owner, in whole or in significant part, of the use or reasonably-to-be-expected

[192] Sands, *Principles*, pp. 1066–7. [193] *Metalclad Corporation* (Award of 2000), para. 59
[194] Ibid., para. 73.
[195] Ibid., paras 74–101; North American Free Trade Agreement (NAFTA), adopted 17 December 1992, 1992 32 ILM 612 (entered into force 1 January 1994).
[196] *Metalclad Corporation* (Award of 2000), para. 99. [197] Ibid., para. 105.
[198] Ibid., paras 105–6. [199] Ibid., para. 106. [200] Ibid., para. 104.
[201] Ibid., para. 109. [202] Ibid., para. 131.

economic benefit of property even if not necessarily to the obvious benefit of the host State.[203]

The decision was controversial.[204] The tribunal's 'effects-based' determination appeared to extend the meaning of expropriation well beyond its traditional scope and seemed to expose health and environmental regulations enacted for public welfare purposes to the risk of challenge from aggrieved foreign investors.[205] Commentators argued that using investor protection measures to attack public welfare regulation was a far cry from their intended purpose as a 'shield' against arbitrary governmental action and that the result of this approach was to stifle public policy development.[206] This case certainly exemplified a new manifestation of aggression on the part of investors in targeting government measures taken on grounds of health, environmental protection, or land use designations – and the tribunal's expansive interpretation seemed to validate this new investor strategy, providing supportive reasoning for further challenges to public welfare regulation.

2. *Ethyl Corporation v. Canada (Ethyl Corp.)*[207]

The Canadian government introduced legislation banning intra-provincial and international trade in the fuel additive, methylcyclopentadienyl manganese tricarbonyl (MMT), citing human health and environmental protection purposes.[208] An American company, Ethyl Corp., was the sole North American operator in this business, producing MMT in the United States and exporting the substance to its wholly owned Canadian subsidiary, Ethyl Canada Inc., which in turn distributed fuel containing MMT throughout Canada. There was significant disagreement at the time as to the health and environmental impacts of MMT.[209] Ethyl Corp. filed a claim under NAFTA's Chapter 11 provisions,[210] alleging that the MMT ban constituted an expropriation of its

203 Ibid., para. 103.

204 See, e.g., Klein, 'Fighting Free Trade Laws'; Knight, 'Mexico Ordered to Pay'; DePalma, 'Nafta's Powerful Little Secret'; Epstein, 'Fit Me For a Gas Mask'.

205 See for discussion of this issue Been and Beauvais, 'Global Fifth Amendment?', 33–7.

206 Ibid.; Soloway, 'Environmental Regulation', 107, 123–5; Mann and von Moltke, *NAFTA's* Chapter 11.

207 *Ethyl Corporation* (Award of 1998).

208 See Soloway, 'Environmental Regulation', 114–19 for a full discussion of this case.

209 Ibid., 115; see also Neumayer, *Greening Trade*, pp. 79–81.

210 NAFTA, adopted 17 December 1992, 1992 32 ILM 612 (entered into force 1 January 1994). Chapter 11 of NAFTA is a dispute resolution mechanism that allows foreign

investment in Canada, and claiming loss of profits from the date of the ban, loss of the value of its investment in Canada, and the loss of world-wide sales to other countries. Ethyl Corp. claimed US$251 million in compensation.[211] A little more than a year after the legislation was passed, Canada settled the matter with Ethyl Corp. Canada agreed to repeal the MMT ban, to pay approximately US$13 million in compensation, and to issue a statement to the effect that 'there was no evidence that MMT in low amounts was harmful to human health.'[212]

Concerns at these events revolve around the potential for inappropriate private sector interference with legitimate public welfare regulation. In this instance, the MMT legislation had been enacted as a precautionary measure in response to inconclusive scientific evidence as to the toxic effects of MMT. As Soloway argues, the ability of a government to make policy decisions such as this on the health and environment of its citizens should not be determined by investment rules, particularly when there is no room in those rules for the consideration of relevant factors other than investment objectives.[213] Soloway contends that if NAFTA Chapter 11 continues to be used in this way, governments will effectively be shackled by a one-dimensional consideration of the issues and that this does not in any way promote good governance. Rather, what is required is a sophisticated balancing of private and public interests with in-depth consideration of all the issues involved in the matter.[214] The current framework for investment rules, however, does not lend itself to this form of engagement, which is also, perhaps, a central reason for its growing popularity with investors as a mechanism to reassert their interests. Again, as with *Metalclad*,[215] the filing of an investor–state claim in the circumstances of *Ethyl Corp.* illustrates the novel investor response that has emerged to restrictive environmental regulation. It also, significantly, points to the potential for regulatory chill in public

investors from Canada, the United States, and Mexico to file claims directly against NAFTA state parties.

[211] *Ethyl Corporation* (Award of 1998). See further documents filed in the arbitration and awards made by the Tribunal on preliminary matters, sighted at the website of Ethyl Corp.'s lawyers, Appleton & Associates, available at www.appletonlaw.com/4b1ethyl.htm (last accessed 12 March 2008).

[212] Soloway, 'Environmental Regulation', 116. [213] Ibid. [214] Ibid.

[215] *Metalclad Corporation* (Award of 2000).

welfare decision-making, the implications of which are explored further below in this chapter.[216]

3. *Azurix Corp. v. Republic of Argentina*

Azurix Corp. v. *Republic of Argentina* (*Azurix*)[217] involved the privatisation of water utilities in Buenos Aires. In 1999, the American-owned company, Azurix, acquired a 30-year concession to operate the water facilities within the province.[218] The venture was, however, plagued with problems, the worst of which ultimately led the company to terminate its concession in October 2001.[219] The difficulties had evolved into a crisis by April 2000, when local water supplies became contaminated with toxic bacteria, which rendered the water undrinkable.[220] The government issued a warning, urging residents not to drink the water and to minimise exposure to it through limiting showers and baths.[221] The local authorities considered this to be a matter of protection of public health and imposed a fine on Azurix for non-compliance with its obligations regarding water quality under the concession agreement.[222] The authorities also issued regulations prohibiting Azurix from invoicing residents for water services during the contaminated water crisis, a situation that existed from 12 April 2000 through to 31 May 2000.[223]

In September 2001, Azurix filed a request for arbitration pursuant to the Treaty between the United States of America and the Argentine Republic Concerning the Reciprocal Encouragement and Protection of Investment (United States–Argentine Republic Bilateral Investment Treaty).[224] Azurix alleged, amongst other complaints, that the

[216] 'Regulatory chill' in this context refers to the theory that fear of investor–state arbitration can lead host state governments to reconsider the introduction of planned public welfare regulation. For a discussion on this concept, see Neumayer, *Greening Trade*; Bernasconi-Osterwalder and Brown Weiss, 'International Investment Rules', 277, 288; Tienhaara, 'What You Don't Know', 80, 85–7; Peterson, 'All Roads', 139.

[217] *Azurix Corp.* v. *Republic of Argentina* (ICSID Case No. ARB/01/12, Award of July 14, 2006) ('*Azurix Corp.* (Award of 2006)').

[218] Ibid., para. 41.

[219] Peterson, 'All Roads', 141; *Azurix Corp.* (Award of 2006), para. 244.

[220] *Azurix Corp.* (Award of 2006), paras 124–5.

[221] Peterson, 'All Roads', 141; *Azurix Corp.* v. *Republic of Argentina* (ICSID Case No. ARB/01/12, Award of July 14, 2006), paras 124–5.

[222] *Azurix Corp.* (Award of 2006), para. 130.

[223] Ibid., para. 126.

[224] Ibid., para. 3; Treaty between the United States of America and the Argentine Republic Concerning the Reciprocal Encouragement and Protection of Investment, signed 14 November 1991 (entered into force 20 October 1994), available at www.unctad.org/sections/dite/iia/docs/bits/argentina_us.pdf (last accessed 11 December 2011).

regulatory action taken by the local authorities amounted to expropriation and a breach of the fair and equitable treatment standard.[225] The subject of the complaints included the administration of the billing and tariffs zoning system applicable to the water services provided by Azurix and the prohibitions on charging for those water services during the algae contamination.[226] It also argued that the water quality problems were a result of failures on the part of local authorities to provide necessary infrastructure.[227] Azurix claimed in excess of US$600 million in damages.[228]

In considering the criteria for both expropriation and fair and equitable treatment, the tribunal found assistance in the approach taken in *Tecnicas Medioambientales Tecmed, S.A.* v. *United Mexican States* (*Tecmed*),[229] an award in which an expansive interpretation of investor protections was adopted.[230] The *Azurix* tribunal noted that when assessing indirect expropriation, arbitral tribunals cannot agree on whether to consider only the effects of the regulation on the investor or whether to consider both the effect and purpose of the measure.[231] The *Azurix* tribunal, however, was persuaded that assessment of the effect of the measure on the investment was the appropriate approach, stating:

> For the Tribunal, the issue is not so much whether the measure concerned is legitimate and serves a public purpose, but whether it is a measure that, being legitimate and serving a public purpose, should give rise to a compensation claim.[232]

The tribunal then proceeded to determine the expropriation allegation on the basis of whether the investor had been deprived in whole or in significant part of the use or reasonably-to-be-expected economic benefit of its investment.[233] The tribunal held that the actions of the local authorities breached their contractual obligations, but did not impact sufficiently so as to amount to an expropriation of the investment.[234] Argentina was, however, found to be in violation of the fair and

[225] *Azurix Corp.* (Award of 2006), paras 77, 81–6, 93–104, 107, 112, 122–5.
[226] Ibid., paras 77, 81–6, 93–104, 107, 112, 122–5. [227] Ibid., paras 120–4.
[228] Ibid., para. 414.
[229] *Tecnicas Medioambientales Tecmed S.A.* v. *United Mexican States* (2004) 43 *International Legal Materials* 133, 173 ('*Tecnicas Medioambientales Tecmed S.A.*'); *Azurix Corp.* (Award of 2006), paras 311–12, 316, 360–1, 372, 392, 408; see also the comments in Peterson, 'Analysis'.
[230] Van Harten, *Investment Treaty Arbitration*, p. 89.
[231] *Azurix Corp.* (Award of 2006), para. 309. [232] Ibid., para. 310.
[233] Ibid., paras 311–22. [234] Ibid., paras 319–22.

equitable treatment standard.[235] In reaching this decision, the tribunal adopted an overly expansive interpretation of fair and equitable treatment.[236] It discounted the application of the *Neer Claim*,[237] arguing that the protection afforded by the standard demands a higher level of treatment than solely avoidance of outrageous, egregious, or bad faith conduct.[238] Rather, the tribunal again endorsed the approach of *Tecmed*.[239] It referred to the legitimate expectations of the investor at the time of entering into the investment, the investor's right to know beforehand any rules and regulations that will govern the investment, and the presupposition of a favourable disposition towards foreign investment.[240] Based on these considerations, the tribunal found that the actions of the Argentine local authorities reflected a pervasive pattern of conduct in breach of the standard of fair and equitable treatment.[241] Azurix was awarded a sum in excess of US$165 million.[242]

Numerous other investor–state claims have been made involving the privatisation of water utilities and concessions granted to foreign investors.[243] This type of claim will continue to be of particular concern as, in addition to the environmental and health implications involved in water quality disputes, the provision of water necessarily implicates social justice issues and access rights to water.[244] At this stage of its evolution, international investment law does not ensure adequate consideration of the social, environmental, developmental, and human rights issues that arise in multi-layered investor–state disputes, such

235 Ibid., para. 377.

236 Van Harten, *Investment Treaty Arbitration*, p. 89; Peterson, 'Analysis'.

237 *Neer Claim (United States* v. *Mexico)* (1926) 4 *Reports of International Arbitral Awards* 60. This case established that outrageous, egregious, or bad faith conduct was necessary on the part of the host state before the international minimum standard of investor protection would be breached.

238 *Azurix Corp*. (Award of 2006), paras 365–77.

239 *Tecnicas Medioambientales Tecmed S.A.*

240 *Azurix Corp*. (Award of 2006), paras 371–3.

241 Ibid., paras 373–7.

242 Ibid., para. 442.

243 See, e.g., *Compañía de Aguas del Aconquija S.A. and Vivendi Universal* v. *Republic of Argentina* (ICSID Case No. ARB/97/3, Award of 20 August 2007); *Aguas del Tunari* v. *Bolivia* (ICSID Case No. ARB/02/3, Award 8 September 2003); *Aguas Provinciales de Santa Fe, S.A., Suez, Sociedad General de Aguas de Barcelona, S.A. and Intergua Servicios Integrales de Agua, S.A.* v. *Argentine Republic* (ICSID Case No. ARB/03/18, Award of May 12 2005); *Aguas Argentinas, S.A. and Vivendi Universal, S.A.* v. *Argentine Republic* (ICSID Case No. ARB/03/19, Award of 19 May 2005).

244 Pannatier and Ducrey, 'Water Concessions', 289; see also the discussion on a human right to water in Fitzmaurice, 'Human Right to Water'; see also the discussion in Ghoshray, 'Searching for Human Rights'.

as those involving water utilities. In fact, its sole focus on the protection of the investor renders such consideration a virtual impossibility.

4. *Methanex*

Methanex Corp. v. *United States* (*Methanex*) involved a challenge by a Canadian investor to health and environmental regulation enacted in the United States.[245] Methyl tertiary butyl ether (MTBE) is a fuel additive which increases the oxygen levels in unleaded petrol and operates as an octane enhancer for the fuel.[246] From 1996, however, the substance was found to be leaking from storage tanks and was detected in the drinking water systems in California.[247] California considered MTBE-contaminated water posed a significant threat to human health and safety and to the quality of the environment.[248] As a result, the Governor of California issued an Executive Order in 1999 declaring that use of the chemical would be phased out by 2002.[249]

Methanex Corporation was a Canadian manufacturer of methanol, one of the main ingredients in producing MTBE.[250] It was also the primary supplier of methanol to Californian manufacturers of MTBE.[251] The company argued that the Californian measures not only deprived it of a substantial portion of its customer base, goodwill, and market for methanol in California, but effectively transferred its market share to its competitor, the United States' ethanol industry.[252] Methanex filed a claim under NAFTA, seeking US$970 million in damages for alleged regulatory expropriation of its investment, breach of the fair and equitable treatment standard, and a violation of national treatment obligations.[253]

The final award in *Methanex* found in favour of the host state.[254] A key aspect of the decision was its treatment of the regulatory takings question.[255] Methanex had argued that the regulation was expropriatory because it interfered with its reasonably-to-be-expected economic benefit of its customer base, goodwill, and market share.[256] The tribunal rejected the company's arguments, stating:

245 *Methanex Corporation.* 246 Mann, *The Final Decision.*
247 Gaines, 'Methanex Corp.', 683. 248 *Methanex Corporation*, p. 1370.
249 Governor of California, Executive Order D-5-99, 25 March 1999.
250 *Methanex Corporation*, 1368. 251 Ibid. 252 Ibid., 1372.
253 Ibid., 1371–2; NAFTA, adopted 17 December 1992, 1992 32 ILM 612 (entered into force 1 January 1994).
254 *Methanex Corporation*, p. 1464. 255 Ibid., pp. 1456–7.
256 Dougherty, 'Methanex v. United States', 746–7.

As a matter of general international law, a non-discriminatory regulation for a public purpose, which is enacted in accordance with due process and which affects, inter alia, a foreign investor or investment is not deemed expropriatory and compensatory unless specific commitments had been given to the then putative foreign investor contemplating investment that the government would refrain from such regulation.[257]

This approach in the *Methanex* decision led a number of commentators to assert that concerns at the effects on domestic regulation of investor–state arbitration had not been realised.[258] This seems a little premature. Although clearly a step in the right direction towards limiting the scope for challenges to environmental regulation, a decision, albeit a high-profile one, in favour of the host state does not remedy systemic issues.[259] As Bernasconi-Osterwalder and Brown Weiss argue:

Proponents of the current framework will argue that the concerns are misplaced because in many of the disputes the host state prevailed, not the investor. This disregards the fact that expansive readings of investor guarantees - even if resulting in a rejection of the investor claims in individual cases - can have a chilling effect on legislators wishing to comply with NAFTA rules. Additionally, the costs of the dispute settlement procedures on host States are significant and must be considered for the evaluation of the status quo.[260]

In fact, the comment has also been made that the decision in *Methanex* was awarded under NAFTA, and a similar approach is rare in awards made under bilateral investment treaties.[261] The explanation proffered is that it is only under NAFTA that a major capital-exporting state has had to face an increasing flow of investor claims and that this has led to more measured interpretations of treaty provisions.[262] As such, the practice under bilateral investment treaties may be less affected by the *Methanex* approach.[263] It is possible then that there may be more awards in the vein of *Tecmed*[264] under the Acuerdo para la Promoción y Protección Reciproca de Inversiones entre el Reino de España y los

[257] *Methanex Corporation*, p. 1456.

[258] See, e.g., Gaines, 'Methanex Corp', 685, 689; Amirfar and Dreyer, 'Thirteen Years', 45–6, 56.

[259] Bernasconi-Osterwalder and Brown Weiss, 'International Investment Rules', 288; Lawrence, 'Chicken Little Revisited'.

[260] Bernasconi-Osterwalder and Brown Weiss, 'International Investment Rules', 288.

[261] Van Harten, *Investment Treaty Arbitration*, p. 146; NAFTA adopted 17 December 1992, 1992 32 ILM 612 (entered into force 1 January 1994).

[262] Van Harten, *Investment Treaty Arbitration*, p. 146.

[263] *Methanex Corporation*.

[264] *Tecnicas Medioambientales Tecmed S.A.*

Estados Unidos Mexicanos (Spain–Mexico Bilateral Investment Treaty), in which the tribunal stated:

> we find no principle stating that regulatory administrative actions are *per se* excluded from the scope of the Agreement, even if they are beneficial to society as a whole – such as environmental protection – particularly if the negative or economic impact of such actions on the financial position of the investor is sufficient to neutralize in full the value, or economic or commercial use of its investment without receiving any compensation whatsoever.[265]

Indeed, the *Azurix*[266] award discussed above was delivered almost a year after the *Methanex* decision.[267] Yet, it does not adopt the narrower view of *Methanex*,[268] but rather it follows the expansive *Tecmed* approach,[269] under which environmental regulation remains open to challenge as indirect expropriation.[270] It is unlikely that the *Methanex* decision[271] alone will stem the flow of potential claimants from challenging regulatory changes when their businesses are affected by new legislation. There is no binding system of precedent in investment treaty arbitration requiring the application of the *Methanex* reasoning.[272] And there is no appellate body to ensure that this approach is consistently adopted by arbitral tribunals.[273]

The *Methanex* claim is another illustration of the way in which misuse of investor protection mechanisms has become normalised. Legitimate environmental and human health regulation is being targeted as a violation of an investment treaty despite this not being the original intention of the Parties to NAFTA.[274] Although the ultimate decision

[265] Ibid., para. 164; *Acuerdo para la Promoció n y Protecció n Reciproca de Inversiones entre el Reino de España y los Estados Unidos Mexicanos*, signed 22 June 1995 (entered into force 18 December 1996).

[266] *Azurix Corp.* (Award of 2006).

[267] The award in *Azurix Corp.* was delivered on 14 July 2006; the award in *Methanex Corporation* was delivered on 7 August 2005.

[268] *Methanex Corporation.* [269] *Tecnicas Medioambientales Tecmed S.A.*

[270] *Azurix Corp.* (Award of 2006), paras 309–10. [271] *Methanex Corporation.*

[272] Mann, *The Final Decision*, p. 9; Lawrence, 'Chicken Little Revisited', 292–3.

[273] Reform of the dispute settlement system, advocating the establishment of a permanent appellate body for international investment disputes is discussed in detail in Chapter 6.

[274] Dougherty, 'Methanex v. United States', 735, 743. Dougherty states that the original intention was for Chapter 11 to be used as a protective mechanism against arbitrary and capricious discrimination, not as a 'sword' against legitimate environmental regulation; NAFTA, adopted 17 December 1992, 1992 32 ILM 612 (entered into force 1 January 1994).

found in favour of the position taken by California,[275] the very fact that the claim proceeded to a hearing at all points to a flaw in the system – regulation enacted for legitimate public welfare purposes should not be within the scope of scrutiny under international investment treaties.[276]

5. *Santa Elena*: calculation methodology

International rules of foreign investment protection and environmental norms also collided in the case of *Compañía del Desarrollo de Santa Elena S.A.* v. *Costa Rica* (*Santa Elena*).[277] The case involved a large area of coastline and rainforest brimming with unique biodiversity situated in the Guanacaste Province of Costa Rica.[278] The land was owned by a Costa Rican company that had been formed by an American syndicate and in which the majority of shareholders were American citizens, Compañía del Desarrollo de Santa Elena (CDSE).[279] The original aim of the company had been to develop the site as a tourist resort.[280] On the issuing of an expropriating decree for the site, there was no complaint as to the right of Costa Rica to expropriate the property. There was, however, a dispute as to the amount of compensation due to CDSE.[281]

Costa Rica referred to its international legal obligations to protect such a unique ecological site and sought to argue that the environmental purposes for which the taking was carried out should affect the methodology for valuing the property.[282] The tribunal held that the environmental objectives of the expropriation, and the fact that it was done in fulfilment of international environmental obligations, did not alter the application of international rules on foreign investment protection.[283] They were not relevant considerations in determining the valuation methodology for compensation assessment.[284] The tribunal stated that:

> While an expropriation or taking for environmental reasons may be classified as a taking for a public purpose, and thus may be legitimate, the fact that the Property was taken for this reason does not affect either the nature or the measure of the compensation to be paid for the taking. That is, the purpose of

[275] *Methanex Corporation.* [276] Lawrence, 'Chicken Little Revisited', 305–6.

[277] *Compania del Desarrollo de Santa Elena S.A.* v. *The Republic of Costa Rica*, (2000) 39 *International Legal Materials* 1317, ('*Compania del Desarrollo de Santa Elena, S.A.*').

[278] Ibid., 1320. [279] Ibid. [280] Ibid. [281] Ibid., 1320–1.

[282] Ibid., 1323; Sands, *Principles*, pp. 1070–1.

[283] *Compania del Desarrollo de Santa Elena S.A.*, p. 1329.

[284] Ibid.; Sands, 'Searching for Balance', 203–4.

protecting the environment for which the Property was taken does not alter the legal character of the taking for which adequate compensation must be paid. The international source of the obligation to protect the environment makes no difference.

Expropriatory environmental measures – no matter how laudable and beneficial to society as a whole – are, in this respect, similar to any other expropriatory measures that a state may take in order to implement its policies: where property is expropriated, even for environmental purposes, whether domestic or international, the state's obligation to pay compensation remains.[285]

Sands makes the comment that in *Santa Elena*, international investment rules took precedence over both national and international norms of environmental protection.[286] The award failed to make even the slightest concession to non-investment priorities of the international community, such as the preservation of the global environment, and to assisting developing states in their endeavours to comply with those priorities.[287] Sands points out that strict enforcement of foreign investment protection rules on compensation requirements may preclude developing states from complying with international environmental obligations as it is unlikely they will have the funds to pay full market value for expropriated property.[288] It is of continuing concern that international investment law can frustrate environmental objectives in this way and it is clear that investors will use this mechanism if it remains available. For example, a claim based on similar factual circumstances to *Santa Elena*, involving an area in Costa Rica set aside to protect endangered turtles, was recently resolved through the International Centre for the Settlement of Investment Disputes (ICSID) in favour of the claimant.[289] Sands suggests that balance is what is called for – a balancing of the relevant interests in international law at play in the particular circumstances without absolute exclusion of any of those interests – and that while security for foreign investors is necessary, it should not come at too high an environmental cost.[290]

[285] *Compania del Desarrollo de Santa Elena S.A.*, p. 1329.

[286] Sands, 'Searching for Balance', 204.

[287] See, e.g., the Millennium Development Goals, United Nations.

[288] Sands, 'Searching for Balance', 204

[289] *Marion Unglaube* (Notice of Intent of 2008), (Award, 16 May 2012); ICSID was established pursuant to the *Convention on the Settlement of Investment Disputes between States and Nationals of Other States*, signed 18 March 1965, (1966) 575 UNTS 159 (entered into force 14 October 1966).

[290] Sands, 'Searching for Balance', 204–5.

B. *Fair and equitable treatment*

Challenges to environmental regulation on the grounds of indirect expropriation also often include allegations of a breach of the fair and equitable treatment standard.[291] In the context of an alleged regulatory taking, the claim of unfair and inequitable treatment will implicate either administrative decision-making that has impacted on the investment in the form of a denial of permission to carry out an activity or a change in the law.[292] The key elements in the standard of fair and equitable treatment are the legitimate expectations of the investor regarding the regulatory framework and whether due process has been followed.[293]

1. Legitimate expectations and a stable legal and business framework

The way in which arbitral tribunals have assessed the legitimate expectations of the investor has been particularly significant for the development of the fair and equitable treatment standard. Tribunals have taken as their starting point an examination of the law at the time at which the investment was entered into and any specific representations made by the host state to the investor.[294] This has, almost organically, become closely linked with the idea of a stable legal and business environment, the implications of which are extensive. Indeed, it has recently been held that the 'stability of the legal and business framework is ... an essential element of fair and equitable treatment.'[295] Such an approach is an expansive reading of the minimum standards of treatment and is unquestionably favourable to investors.[296] And the reach of this standard continues to increase through further arbitral interpretation. For example, the *Tecmed* award elaborates on what is required by the fair and equitable treatment standard:

[291] See, e.g., *Methanex Corporation*; *S.D. Myers Inc.* (Partial Award of 2000); *Ethyl Corporation* (Award of 1998).

[292] McLachlan, Shore and Weiniger, *International Investment Arbitration*, pp. 226, 233–4; Dolzer and Schreuer, *International Investment Law*, pp. 133–5, 142.

[293] Newcombe and Paradell, *Law and Practice*, p. 279; McLachlan, Shore, and Weiniger, *International Investment Arbitration*, p. 234.

[294] McLachlan, Shore, and Weiniger, *International Investment Arbitration*, pp. 234–8; Dolzer and Schreuer, *Principles of International*, p. 134; Tudor, *Fair and Equitable Treatment*, pp. 163–72.

[295] *Occidental Exploration and Production Co* v. *Republic of Ecuador* (UNCITRAL, Case No. UN3467, Final Award of 1 July 2004) ('*Occidental Exploration and Production Co.*'), para. 183.

[296] Van Harten, *Investment Treaty Arbitration*, pp. 88–90.

The Arbitral Tribunal considers that this provision of the Agreement, in light of the good faith principle established by international law, requires the Contracting Parties to provide to international investments treatment that does not affect the basic expectations that were taken into account by the foreign investor to make the investment. The foreign investor expects the host State to act in a consistent manner, free from ambiguity and totally transparently in its relations with the foreign investor, so that it may know beforehand any and all rules and regulations that will govern its investments, as well as the goals of the relevant policies and administrative practices or directives, to be able to plan its investment and comply with such regulations.[297]

The broad scope of this interpretation can place a 'heavy burden' on host states.[298] Although the obligation to maintain a stable legal and business environment does not mean that regulation can never change, it does have the potential to constrain host state policy space. At its worst, the requirement to 'know beforehand any and all rules and regulations that will govern its investments'[299] could certainly preclude the accommodation of advances in scientific knowledge or shifts in social values through the enactment of more stringent forms of regulation. Furthermore, although the need to preserve the ability of host states to regulate on matters of public interest has been acknowledged,[300] recognition does not necessarily translate into application. The issue is again where arbitral tribunals draw the line between a valid exercise of regulatory power by the host state and compensable action.[301] And, as the objective of protecting foreign investment is given primacy in bilateral investment treaties, and often in their interpretation by arbitral tribunals, adequate consideration of public interest issues in investment disputes has not been a priority.[302]

297 *Tecnicas Medioambientales Tecmed S.A.*, 173. This approach has been adopted in a number of subsequent awards, such as, *MTD Equity Sdn. Bhd. & MTD Chile S.A.* v. *Chile* (ICSID Case No. ARB/01/7, ad hoc Committee's Decision on the Respondent's Request for a Continued Stay of Execution of 1 June 2005), 105–6; *CMS Gas Transmission Company* v. *Argentine Republic* (ICSID Case No. ARB/01/8, Award of 12 May 2005 ('*CMS Gas Transmission Company* (Award of 2005)'); *Azurix Corp.* (Award of 2006), paras 360–1, 372, 392, 408.

298 Marshall, *Fair and Equitable Treatment.*

299 *Tecnicas Medioambientales Tecmed S.A.*, 173.

300 See, e.g., *Saluka Investments B.V. (The Netherlands)* v. *The Czech Republic* (UNCITRAL, Partial Award of 17 March 2006).

301 Van Harten, *Investment Treaty Arbitration*, pp. 92–4.

302 Ibid., pp. 121, 136–8; see, e.g., the comments of the tribunal in *Azurix Corp.* (Award of 2006), para. 372:

A third element is the frustration of expectations that the investor may have legitimately taken into account when it made the investment. The standards of conduct agreed by the parties to a BIT presuppose a favorable disposition towards

The lack of weight that is given to the public welfare role of government by arbitral tribunals in investor–state disputes is troubling, as the resulting awards can have far-reaching implications for host states.[303] In assessing the application of the legitimate expectations requirement, Van Harten comments on the award of US$133 million in *CMS Gas Transmission Company* v. *Argentine Republic*:

> The arbitrators concluded among other things that, regardless of whether the government acted in good faith in adopting policies that harmed CMS Energy's business, Argentina bore an 'objective' responsibility under international law to ensure a stable and predictable business environment for foreign investors, even in the midst of financial meltdown. Further, the arbitrators decided that the investor's right to compensation was not extinguished or moderated by circumstances of public emergency.[304]

The concern is that even where states enact regulation in good faith, they can leave themselves open to investor claims of a violation of the stable legal and business framework component of the legitimate expectations requirement of fair and equitable treatment.[305] It is difficult to overestimate the potential repercussions of this development in interpretation. As discussed by Van Harten,[306] its reach has already been evidenced in the series of recent claims against Argentina following its regulatory response to a national emergency[307] – surely, if a social,

foreign investment, in fact, a pro-active behavior of the State to encourage and protect it. To encourage and protect investment is the purpose of the BIT. It would be incoherent with such a purpose and the expectation created by such a document to consider that a party to the BIT has breached the obligation of fair and equitable treatment only when it has acted in bad faith or its conduct can be qualified as outrageous or egregious.

303 Van Harten, *Investment Treaty Arbitration*, pp. 3, 123–4. Van Harten refers to the significant sums involved in damages awards and how exacting this can be on the public funds of developing states. He refers to the extensive costs involved in defending investor claims. And he also refers to the impact awards can have on the regulatory function of the host state and on the lives of its citizens.

304 *CMS Gas Transmission Company* (Award of 2005); Van Harten, *Investment Treaty Arbitration*, p. 230.

305 See the discussion in Van Harten, *Investment Treaty Arbitration*, pp. 93–4.

306 Ibid., p. 3.

307 Argentina enacted emergency legislation in 2001. The measure sought to avert a financial crisis that had spilled over into national social and political turmoil, including riots in which people had been killed. See for a discussion of this series of events, Van Harten, *Investment Treaty Arbitration*, pp. 1–3. Argentina has faced multiple claims arising out of these events, see e.g. *CMS Gas Transmission Company* (Award of 2005); *Enron Corp. & Ponderosa Assets LP* v. *Argentina* (ICSID Case No ARB/01/3, Award of 7 October 2007); *Sempra Energy International* v. *Argentina* (ICSID Case No

political, and financial national catastrophe of the kind that took place in Argentina in 2001–2 is not sufficient to override the expectations of the investor at the inception of the investment, it does not bode well for more routine regulatory changes. Indeed, Weiler and Wälde have commented that no matter how legitimate new environmental regulation might be, it must still also comply with the requirements of international investment law,[308] reflecting a viewpoint that was to form the central reasoning of *Tecmed*[309] and *Azurix*[310] years later. In other words, if a more stringent environmental regulatory regime is brought in to achieve a legitimate public purpose, such as the mitigation of climate change impacts, it will need to meet the stable legal and business environment test before a host state can legislate in this way without triggering a right of compensation. Without doubt, this is potentially a substantial restraint on the ability of governments to make policy decisions and legislate in the public interest.[311]

It is troubling that fair and equitable treatment should have been interpreted so as to correlate to providing the investor, at the time of entering into the investment, with all the rules and regulations that will govern the investment for the life of the investment. The development of such expansive interpretations, however, becomes less surprising when the extreme nature of the investment community's mistrust of environmental regulation is understood. In the views of Wälde and Kolo, the international economic expansionism of capital-exporting states needs to be shielded from the neo-socialist protectionism that is embodied in legitimate environmental regulation:

> the previously socialist/statist attitude to foreign investment popularly expressed through the New International Economic Order (NIEO) in the 1970s and its emphasis on national sovereignty – but which lost its appeal – has been reincarnated in the environmentalist movement, with the environmental cause being used as a Trojan horse by statist/bureaucrats, protectionists, environmentalists and others who oppose continuing trade and investment liberalisation and the role of global markets. Because of the moral high ground it occupies, concern over the environment provides a convenient platform for even the most unlikely bedfellows to challenge the emerging institutions of the global

ARB/02/16, Award of 28 September 2007); *LG&E Energy Corp.* v. *Argentina* (ICSID Case No. ARB/02/1, Award of 25 July 2007).

308 Weiler and Wälde, 'Investment Arbitration', 26–7.

309 *Tecnicas Medioambientales Tecmed S.A.*, 164.

310 *Azurix Corp.* (Award of 2006), para. 310.

311 Van Harten, *Investment Treaty Arbitration*, pp. 89–90.

economy under environmental, human rights, protectionist, nationalist and sovereignty-based, statist and communitarian headings.[312]

Views such as these leave little room for a balanced conceptualisation of the relationship between foreign investor and the host state or for a rational discussion of improvements that need to be made to the investment rules that govern that relationship. They also illustrate the way in which traditional investor approaches to the environment continue to inform the discourse and replicate traditional patterns – the investment sector continues to attempt to neutralise challenges to the prevailing investment regime through the use of legal doctrine, invocation of the need for depoliticisation, and resort to demonising stereotypes.

2. Fair and equitable treatment for the host state?

Indeed, Sornarajah has questioned the validity of the very emergence of the legitimate expectations requirement, arguing that it is a product of recent partial 'arbitral law-making' that is heavily weighted towards furthering the interests of foreign investors.[313] He has queried why the fair and equitable standard of treatment extends only to investors.[314] Is it not fair and equitable, he asks, to allow host states to hold multinational corporations accountable for their activities?[315] Is it not fair and equitable to create defences for host states where investors have engaged in conduct that detrimentally

[312] Wälde and Kolo, 'Environmental Regulation', 811–12; for further examples of similar views on host state activities, see Baker, 'Denial of Justice', pp. 187–191; see also the views of Todd Weiler in which critics of the award in *Metalclad* are cast in a particularly negative light as extremists, contrasted with the reasonableness of investment lawyers, the implication being, of course, that if one criticises international investment law in any way, then the critic is necessarily not an expert investment lawyer. Weiler goes on to approve of the position of the 'investment lawyer', declaring it to be the correct assessment of the case, in Weiler, 'Good Faith and Regulatory Transparency', 701, 701:

> The 'story' of *Metalclad* v. *Mexico* has become quite well known in different circles; it just so happens that it has been told in dramatically different ways, depending upon the circle. In circles inhabited by the opponents of trade and investment liberalization, as well as those who more generally profess an amorphous 'anti-globalization' ethos, *Metalclad* is a story about the rights of foreign corporations trumping the popular will of the citizens of a small, Mexican municipality. For trade and investment lawyers and associated policy analysts, it is just a familiar story – about international investment being held hostage to regulatory decision-making in a developing country.

[313] Sornarajah, 'The Fair and Equitable Standard', 165, 174, 176. [314] Ibid., 180.

[315] Ibid.

affects the environment of the host state, the health of its citizens, or violates human rights?[316]

In exploring these very issues, Muchlinski points to the potential for new defences to investor complaints as a result of objectionable conduct on the part of the investor.[317] He examines a number of cases in which tribunals have considered the unconscionable conduct or poor judgement of the investor to be relevant in determining the dispute.[318] For Muchlinski, this indicates the capacity of tribunals to balance investor and host state interests appropriately.[319] He also proffers, however, the idea that a more systematic jurisprudential approach may develop in which investor conduct could form an essential component of the fair and equitable treatment standard.[320] Whilst, arguably, tribunals already have a selection of tools available to balance public and private interests should they choose to use them, central issues still include the sufficiency of scope of those mechanisms, together with the irregularity and inconsistency with which tribunals opt to so engage. Presently, there is no requirement compelling arbitral panels to consider investor conduct in the context of fair and equitable treatment allegations. However, embedding within the fair and equitable treatment standard an investor condition of refraining from unconscionable conduct, as Muchlinski suggests, would significantly shift the imbalance that currently exists within this investor protection guarantee.

Although it may do so in the future, systematic inclusion of investor conduct has not yet found form within the fair and equitable treatment standard. While the evolution of such a condition would be a substantial reform of international investment law, it still leaves legitimate public welfare regulation vulnerable to challenge where there has been no reprehensible conduct or foolhardy business decisions on the part of the investor. Furthermore, the suggested operation of an investor conduct defence would appear to be limited to preventing investor claims from succeeding, rather than also forming the basis for the making of corresponding complaints by host states or their affected citizens against investors. Accordingly, along with the

[316] Ibid. [317] Muchlinksi, 'Caveat Investor'.

[318] See, e.g., *Methanex Corporation*; *Waste Management* v. *Mexico* (2004) 43 *International Legal Materials* 967; *Noble Ventures Inc* v. *Romania* (ICSID Case No. ARB/01/11, Award of 12 October 2005); *Azinian* v. *Mexico* (ICSID Case No. ARB(AF)/97/2, Award of 1 November 1999).

[319] Muchlinski, 'Caveat Investor', 556. [320] Ibid., 556–7.

emergence of defensive investor conduct requirements, it would also be useful to explore avenues through which a more proactive mechanism for host state protection could be developed.

C. *National treatment*

Like most principles of international investment law, the national treatment standard has a deceptively simple formulation. It tends to consist of a provision guaranteeing in one form or another that foreign investors and their investments are to be 'accorded treatment no less favourable than that which the host state accords to its own investors'.[321] It is in the fleshing out of the term that the issues have arisen. In particular, determining whether treatment is less favourable has involved the development of several analytical steps. The most significant of these being an assessment of whether or not the foreign investor and domestic operators are in 'like circumstances' and then whether or not the foreign investor has suffered less favourable treatment than those domestic investors.[322]

1. Like circumstances

It is not only the language of the national treatment standard that is very broad; it is the potential scope of 'like circumstances' as well. It is a relative measurement in that the base line is determined by how the host state treats domestic investors in similar circumstances to that of the foreign investor. For this reason, the range of regulation and governmental decision-making to which the standard could be applied is potentially limitless,[323] recognition of which, again, underscores the far-reaching implications of investor protections. In comparing the circumstances of foreign and domestic investors, the 'like circumstances' component necessarily entails the making of value judgements. And not only as to how similar they are in fact, but even also as to which criteria are to be considered in that assessment.[324]

Such value judgements play a significant role in national treatment violation claims as the arbitral panel's approach to interpretation is

[321] Dolzer and Schreuer, *Principles of International*, p. 178.

[322] Ibid., pp. 179–80; McLachlan, Shore, and Weiniger, *International Investment Arbitration*, p. 251.

[323] Van Harten, *Investment Treaty Arbitration*, pp. 84–5. [324] Ibid.

central to its findings – the more expansive the determination of likeness, the more probable it becomes that the regulation in question will be captured.[325] This, in turn, renders the ability of governments to develop sometimes controversial policies all the more circumscribed. Indeed, as illustrated in the analysis of investor–state disputes above, a distinct leaning towards expansive interpretations is apparent within the reasoning of many arbitral awards. In this way, those value judgements contribute to the incremental development of standards of protection that go well beyond shielding investors from arbitrary or bad faith conduct, and instead operate as a form of insurance against the impact of future legitimate public welfare regulation.[326]

The inevitability of such contestation becomes apparent when the realities of progressive policy-making and implementation are considered. For example, host states seeking to introduce new policies and regulation to support sustainable development or to raise environmental standards will necessarily differentiate between proposed projects, investments, and products on the basis of their capacity to fulfil the state's public policy goals.[327] Taking such initiatives potentially exposes host states to investor claims of discriminatory treatment if regulation is introduced prohibiting certain activities, excluding participation in commercially advantageous schemes, or where one project is selected over another, and a foreign investor is detrimentally affected to a significant degree – and the only basis for differentiating between otherwise identical circumstances is that the domestic investment meets sustainability, environmental, or other public policy criteria. Once more, the centrality of arbitrator interpretation to dispute outcomes emerges; in this context, in the importance of determinations of assessment criteria.

It is particularly significant, then, that the criteria by which 'like circumstances' are assessed have generally been limited to commercial considerations.[328] Tribunals have not tended to engage in in-depth

325 Ibid.

326 Ibid., pp. 84–91; in particular, Van Harten refers to *S.D. Myers, Inc.* v. *Canada* (UNCITRAL, Partial Award (Decision on the Merits) of November 2000); *Ethyl Corporation* (Award of 1998); *Metalclad Corporation* (Award of 2000); *Occidental Exploration and Production Co*; *Pope & Talbot* v. *Canada*, Award on the Merits of Phase II, 10 April 2001.

327 Von Moltke, *An International Investment Regime?*.

328 Werksman, Baumert, and Dubash, 'International Investment Rules', 75; Salgado, 'The Case Against', 1061; Center for International Environmental Law, *Foreign Investment and Sustainable Development*.

evaluations of all the investors' circumstances, preferring 'a relatively simple test of comparison with the most directly comparable local investor or investors in the same business sector.'[329] This traditional approach excludes such factors as the social or environmental impact of an activity from the criteria determining the comparability of the circumstances of investors.[330] Measured as against commercial criteria alone, any attempted differentiation based on environmental grounds would run the risk of violating national treatment obligations.

Such a conclusion as to the constraining operation of a key investor protection should give rise to a significant degree of disquiet. However, given the historical evolution of international investment law, it is, perhaps, instead, unremarkable that prevailing approaches place host states in such a position.

2. Fact of differentiation and justification

There are also additional significant factors involved in the assessment of the conduct or regulation in question. In particular, arbitral panels largely focus on the effect of the measure on the foreign investor, rather than on the purpose or motive behind the measure.[331] It follows from this line of reasoning, therefore, that actual intent to discriminate against the investor on the basis of nationality is not necessary.[332] It also means that the legitimate public welfare purpose of the measure will not be a factor in determining whether discrimination has occurred. The result of this particular focus can have far-reaching implications for host states – regulation of general application that affects a foreign investor to a greater extent than domestic investors can be captured within national treatment obligations.[333] My concern here is that this is, again, an interpretative approach that is overly favourable towards investors and runs the risk of inappropriately encroaching into areas of legitimate domestic law-making and policy development.

[329] McLachlan, Shore, and Weiniger, *International Investment Arbitration*, p. 253.

[330] See the discussion in Werksman, Baumert, and Dubash, 'Clean Development Mechanism', 74–5.

[331] See, e.g., *S.D. Myers Inc* (Partial Award of 2000); see also the discussion in McLachlan, Shore, and Weiniger, *International Investment Arbitration*, p. 251.

[332] Dolzer and Schreuer, *Principles of International*, p. 181.

[333] Van Harten, *Investment Treaty Arbitration*, pp. 85–6.

On occasion, tribunals also refer to whether there are any 'rational grounds' on which differentiation between the investors may be justified.[334] This consideration should allow for sufficient host state 'public policy space', and, in theory, it does.[335] However, the difficulty lies in the way in which arbitral tribunals apply this avenue of exception, and, as Dolzer and Schreuer comment, the precise nature of the grounds that might qualify remains uncertain.[336] The tendency of investors to seek ever-more extensive coverage and of arbitral panels to favour expansive interpretations of investor protections[337] suggest that this justification exception may not be as useful as it perhaps appears. For example, it did not prevent the arbitral panel in *S.D. Myers* finding a violation of national treatment obligations, even though the measure prohibiting the export of hazardous waste was enacted so as to comply with obligations under a multilateral environmental agreement.[338] Furthermore, additional qualifications have been applied, limiting the potential scope of this 'rational grounds' justification and re-emphasising investment protection. To this end, in *Pope & Talbot* v. *Canada*, the tribunal provided that differential treatment would violate national treatment obligations unless the measures had:

> a reasonable nexus to rational government policies that (1) do not distinguish, on their face or *de facto*, between foreign-owned and domestic companies, and (2) do not otherwise unduly undermine the investment liberalizing objectives of NAFTA.[339]

When contemplating this approach in a range of contemporary contexts, however, a key concern emerges that this type of investor claim may impact disproportionately upon progress towards sustainable

334 Dolzer and Schreuer, *Principles of International*, pp. 181–3; McLachlan, Shore, and Weiniger, *International Investment Arbitration*, p. 251; see also the comments in *S.D. Myers Inc* (Partial Award of 2000), para. 250.

335 For a discussion on the concept of reduction of 'policy space', see Cho and Dubash, *Investment Rules*.

336 Dolzer and Schreuer, *Principles of International*, pp. 181–3.

337 Van Harten, *Investment Treaty Arbitration*, pp. 85–9.

338 *S.D. Myers Inc.* (Partial Award of 2000). It was argued that the measure was made in compliance with the Convention on the Control of Transboundary Movement of Hazardous Wastes and their Disposal, opened for signature 22 March 1989, (1989) 28 ILM 657 (entered into force 1992) (Basel Convention). This case was discussed briefly above in section I.B.4 of this chapter. The arbitral panel's treatment of Canada's international environmental obligations under the Basel Convention is discussed in detail below in Chapter 5.

339 *Pope & Talbot* v. *Canada*, Award on the Merits of Phase II, 10 April 2001, para. 78.

development within developing states.[340] The pursuit of increased development trajectories will continue to be a primary focus for many developing host states, and, in order to give effect to sustainability programmes, new regulation and governmental decision-making favouring activities that promote sustainable development will be necessary. In considering this eventuality, Cordonier Segger argues that it will be difficult to implement such measures without affecting the interests of foreign investors already operating within the state – and this possibility points to the potential for 'regulatory chill'.[341]

D. *Regulatory chill*

The interaction between international investment liberalisation and environmental protection objectives has generated the discourse on pollution havens, capital flight, and regulatory chill.[342] These theories are based on the notion that the fear of decreased investment inflows, increased capital outflows, and investor–state arbitration leads host state governments to reduce or 'freeze' environmental standards.[343] Whether these outcomes have been realised in practice remains a matter of contention.[344] However, if borne out, this mode of interaction between the investor and the environment of the host state can be conceptualised as a further manifestation of the traditional relationship between capital-exporting nations and host states. If such a framing is adopted, it can be seen that the host state again remains in a reactive position, repeatedly responding to a foreign investment market that is shaped by capital-exporting states. In this scenario, the use of the environment of the host state and the exposing of its citizens to regulation of a less stringent standard occurs so as to comply with foreign investor requirements.

1. Pollution havens, capital flight, and regulatory chill

It is not in question that foreign investment inflows can potentially involve substantial benefits for host states.[345] Increased levels of capital

[340] See the discussion in Cordonier Segger, 'From Protest to Proposal', 146, 155.

[341] Ibid. [342] Zarsky, 'Havens, Halos and Spaghetti'; Neumayer, *Greening Trade*.

[343] Bernasconi-Osterwalder and Brown Weiss, 'International Investment Rules', 277, 288; Neumayer, *Greening Trade*, pp. 41–90; Zarsky, 'Havens, Halos and Spaghetti'.

[344] Neumayer, *Greening Trade*, pp. 41–90.

[345] Zarsky, 'Havens, Halos and Spaghetti', 49, 65–7; Hunter, Salzman and Zaelke, *International Environmental Law*, pp. 1268–4; Gallagher and Zarsky, 'No Miracle Drug', 13–15, 31–7.

in the economy, the initiation of new infrastructure projects, increased employment levels, increased economic growth rates, and the introduction of new, safer, more efficient technologies can, overall, generate wealth and increase standards of living in host states.[346] From the corporate perspective, there are also many reasons for a decision to engage in foreign direct investment. It is generally a move designed to lower costs or to generate further profits through expansion into new markets.[347] The reduction of costs might be achieved through low-cost production processes, cheaper labour, an abundance of inexpensive raw materials, tax incentives, or avoidance of import/export tariffs.[348]

A significant cause of consternation amongst commentators, however, is the means by which such costs-savings are made and the consequences of these activities for host states, and, in particular, for local communities. The concern surrounds whether these lower costs, and the consequential increased levels of foreign investment, are being achieved at the expense of the social fabric or the environmental conditions of the local community.[349] Are the production processes cheaper because the environmental standards are lower or because the true environmental costs are not reflected in the prices? Is the actual cost of repairing environmental damage from corporate activities an externality imposed on the local community? Is the cost of labour cheaper because there are no worker protection measures in place? In the midst of fierce competition to attract foreign investment, will states lower their domestic environmental and health standards, effectively engaging in what is called a regulatory 'race-to-the-bottom', so as to reduce further the costs of doing business and to become more attractive to potential foreign investors?[350] In summary, what are the environmental politico-legal consequences of inter-state competition for foreign investment?[351]

346 Hunter, Salzman, and Zaelke, *International Environmental Law*, pp. 1268–74; see the connections made between foreign investment and progress towards sustainable development in Mann et al., *IISD Model International Agreement*; de Waart, 'Sustainable Development'; Mabey and McNally, *Foreign Direct Investment*, p. 4; Zarsky, 'Havens, Halos and Spaghetti', 49, 65–7; *Agenda 21, Report of the UNCED*, UN Doc A/CONF.151/26/Rev.1 (vol.I) (1992), 31 ILM 874, chapter 2, para. 2.23.

347 Hunter, Salzman, and Zaelke, *International Environmental Law*, p. 1269.

348 Ibid.

349 Ibid.; Zarsky, 'Havens, Halos and Spaghetti'; Neumayer, *Greening Trade*, pp. 41–67.

350 Hunter, Salzman, and Zaelke, *International Environmental Law*, pp. 1269–74; Zarsky, 'Havens, Halos and Spaghetti'; Neumayer, *Greening Trade*, pp. 41–67.

351 Esty and Geradin, 'Environmental Protection', 15–21.

These questions raise the spectre of 'pollution havens' and 'regulatory chill'. The basic premise of the pollution haven theory is that in order to remain competitive in the market for foreign investment, states will set low environmental standards, or enact adequate standards but not enforce them, and then compete with each other in the continued unravelling of environmental restrictions – hence the description 'race-to-the-bottom'.[352] In this scenario, it is projected that multinational corporations, unable to continue environmentally damaging practices in developed states, will be able to export those practices to developing states with significantly lower environmental protection measures, producing so-called 'pollution havens'.[353]

What empirical evidence there is suggests that the pollution haven theory has not been borne out in practice.[354] Neumayer groups the studies that have been undertaken into three categories:[355]

a) those designed to assess whether differing environmental standards affect investment inflows;[356]
b) those designed to assess whether production processes within developing states have become more pollution-intensive;[357] and
c) those designed to assess whether there have been outflows of 'dirty' industries from developed states.[358]

Neumayer concludes that although there is scant evidence for the existence of pollution havens, this does not demonstrate their non-existence, citing insufficient data and painting it as a notoriously difficult

[352] Zarsky, 'Havens, Halos and Spaghetti'; Neumayer, *Greening Trade*, p. 41.
[353] Neumayer, *Greening Trade*.
[354] Ibid., p. 43; Esty and Geradin, 'Environmental Protection', 7, 15; Zarsky, 'Havens, Halos and Spaghetti', 57–9.
[355] Neumayer, *Greening Trade*, pp. 43, 50–4.
[356] Ibid.; see the studies cited by Neumayer, e.g., Y. Xing and C. D. Kolstad, *Do Lax Environmental Regulations Attract Foreign Investments?* (1998) Santa Barbara, University of California; G. S. Eskeland and A. E. Harrison, *Moving to Greener Pastures? Multinationals and the Pollution Haven Hypothesis* (1997) Washington DC, World Bank.
[357] See the studies cited by Neumayer, e.g., R. E. B. Lucas, D. Wheeler and H. Hettige, *Economic Development, Environmental Regulation, and the International Migration of Toxic Industrial Pollution 1960–88* (1992) Washington DC, World Bank; M. Mani and D. Wheeler, '*In Search of Pollution Havens? Dirty Industry in the World Economy, 1960–1995*, *OECD Conference on Foreign Direct Investment and the Environment*, The Hague, Netherlands, 28–9 January 1999.
[358] See the studies cited by Neumayer, e.g., H. J. Leonard, *Pollution and the Struggle for the World Product: Multinational Corporations, Environment, and International Comparative Advantage* (Cambridge University Press, 1988).

phenomenon to assess.[359] He does, however, suggest that there is evidence for a more subtle and troubling effect of the pollution haven theory – international environmental 'regulatory chill'.[360]

Proponents of the regulatory chill theory argue that merely a fear of capital flight and a loss of competitiveness in international markets can prevent policy-makers from raising environmental standards.[361] No actual movement of investment dollars to states offering pollution havens is required; only the existence of the fear that there might be capital flight.[362] Again, it is difficult to ascertain whether or not the theory has translated into reality as, in this case, the hypothesis is premised on the absence of activity.[363] However, several commentators have concluded that there is evidence for the existence of environmental regulatory chill due to the fear of a loss of foreign investment.[364] Specific examples in the European Union and United States have been identified where arguments proffered by industry lobbyists warning of capital flight and a loss of competitiveness had a chilling effect on ecological tax reform measures designed to bring about reductions in energy use and greenhouse gas emissions.[365]

2. Investor–state arbitration and regulatory chill

A version of the regulatory chill theory is tied into investor–state arbitration. The argument is that the threat of investor claims against the host state may preclude the strengthening of environmental regulation.[366] It has been suggested that the fear of facing investor claims not only encompasses the potential for large damages awards, but is also driven

[359] Neumayer, *Greening Trade*, pp. 55–7; see also Clapp, 'Pollution Haven Debate'.

[360] Neumayer, *Greening Trade*, pp. 68–71.

[361] Ibid.; Esty and Geradin, 'Environmental Protection', 19–21; Zarsky, 'Havens, Halos and Spaghetti', 65–67; Clapp, 'Pollution Haven Debate', 16–17; Wagner, 'Nature Beyond', 469–71.

[362] Clapp, 'Pollution Haven Debate', 17; Esty and Geradin, 'Environmental Protection', 16; Neumayer, *Greening Trade*, pp. 68–9.

[363] Neumayer, *Greening Trade*, p. 69; Clapp, 'Pollution Haven Debate', 17.

[364] Clapp, 'Pollution Haven Debate', 16–17; Neumayer, *Greening Trade*, pp. 69–71; Zarsky, 'Havens, Halos and Spaghetti', 65–7; Esty and Geradin, 'Environmental Protection', 19–21.

[365] Neumayer, *Greening Trade*, pp. 69–71; Esty and Geradin, 'Environmental Protection', 19–21.

[366] Bernasconi-Osterwalder and Brown Weiss, 'International Investment Rules', 277, 288; Tienhaara, 'What You Don't Know', 80, 85–7; Peterson, 'All Roads', 139; Clapp, 'Pollution Haven Debate', 17; Werksman, Baumert, and Dubash, 'Clean Development Mechanism'.

by the substantial costs involved in defending arbitral proceedings.[367] Given that the average costs to host states in defending investor claims are in the region of US$1.5–2.5 million, although it can be significantly higher,[368] host state apprehension is understandable. Furthermore, it is not unknown for damages awards to be in the hundreds of millions of dollars.[369] Compounding the costs issues, host states may also face multiple claims with alleged damages in this vicinity.[370] These are significant sums for developing states, particularly when they may well lack the technical capacity to defend these claims adequately.[371]

Of particular note on this issue, is that the threat of investor–state arbitration has been used informally by investors lobbying against the introduction of new regulation.[372] Peterson comments that '[p]racticing lawyers do admit that they hear rumours of investors applying informal pressure upon host states – while brandishing an investment treaty as a potential legal stick.'[373] It is, of course, a practice that is virtually impossible to monitor.[374] However, instances that have come to light suggest that there is substance to the regulatory chill theory. Specifically, scholars point to recent incidents such as that of the foreign-owned mining companies in Indonesia, a multinational tobacco company in Canada, and the *Ethyl Corp.* case.[375]

(a) Indonesia, forestry laws, and the foreign-owned mining companies

This incident involved the enactment of new forestry laws which prohibited open-cast mining in designated 'protection forests' on environmental grounds.[376] More than 150 mining companies were affected by

[367] Bernasconi-Osterwalder and Brown Weiss, 'International Investment Rules', 288; Tienhaara, 'What You Don't Know', 80.

[368] Tienhaara, 'What You Don't Know', 80; Van Harten, *Investment Treaty Arbitration*, pp. 123–4.

[369] See, e.g., the award of US$353 million in *CME Czech Republic BV* v. *Czech Republic* (Final Award of 14 March 2003); see also the award of US$133 million in *CMS Gas Transmission Company* (Award of 2005).

[370] Argentina is a case in point. The country is facing a myriad of multi-million dollar claims arising out of its enactment of emergency legislation in 2001; see for a discussion of this series of events, Van Harten, *Investment Treaty Arbitration*, pp. 1–3.

[371] Tienhaara, 'What You Don't Know', 80–1; Garcia, 'Dirty Little Secrets', 363–4.

[372] Peterson, 'All Roads', 139; Mann, *Private Rights*.

[373] Peterson, 'All Roads', 139.

[374] Ibid.

[375] Ibid.; Tienhaara, 'What You Don't Know', 87–96; Gross, 'Inordinate Chill'; *Ethyl Corporation* (Award of 1998).

[376] Tienhaara, 'What You Don't Know', 88; Gross, 'Inordinate Chill', 894; Tienhaara, *Expropriation*, pp. 217–27.

the prohibition.[377] The companies asserted that the regulation was in violation of their agreements with the government and threatened the state with international investment arbitration to ensure the inapplicability of the new legislation to their mining operations.[378] The Indonesian government subsequently enacted regulation that effectively exempted from the new forestry law the mining companies that already held licences.[379]

For Tienhaara, there are a number of factors that support a conclusion of regulatory chill in this instance.[380] First, the Indonesian government had become very wary of international arbitration following an award made against its state-owned oil and gas company, Pertamina, in which it had been required to pay US$261 million in compensation to an American-owned company in a dispute over the cancellation of a geothermal project.[381] The home states of the mining company investors were also applying informal diplomatic pressure on the Indonesian government to resolve the matter in a manner satisfactory to their investor nationals.[382] And, furthermore, the government had received advice that its exposure to foreign-owned mining companies would be in the realm of US$31 billion if the forestry laws remained effective against those companies – funds which the Indonesian government did not have available to spend on meeting successful arbitral awards.[383]

(b) Philip Morris and Canada's tobacco legislation

Peterson refers to another series of events that point to regulatory chill in operation.[384] He cites the example of the actions of Philip Morris following the announcement by the Canadian government that it intended to tighten its regulation of cigarette packaging.[385] Philip Morris engaged Carla Hills, a former United States trade representative, to lobby on its behalf and threatened Canada on a number of occasions

[377] Tienhaara, 'What You Don't Know', 89.

[378] Ibid., 89, 92; WALHI and JATAM (Mining Advocacy Network), (Press Release, 4 April 2002) 'Mining Industry Threatens Indonesia with International Arbitration', available at www.jatam.org/english/case/conservation/uploaded/press_release_4_April_2002.pdf (last accessed 12 March 2008).

[379] Tienhaara, 'What You Don't Know', 92. [380] Ibid., 94–6.

[381] Tienhaara, 'What You Don't Know', 94–5. *Final Award in an Arbitration Procedure under the UNCITRAL Arbitration Rules between Karaha Bodas Company and Perusahaan Pertambangan Minyak dan Gas Bumi Negara and Pt PLN*, 18 December 2000; see also the discussion of the Pertamina arbitration in Wells, 'Double Dipping'.

[382] Tienhaara, 'What You Don't Know', 94. [383] Ibid., 95.

[384] Peterson, 'All Roads', 139. [385] Ibid.

with investor–state arbitration under NAFTA if it went ahead with the proposed 'plain packaging' requirements and a prohibition on the use of the terms 'mild' and 'light' on cigarette labels.[386] Canada did not pursue the enactment of more stringent regulation of cigarette packaging.[387] Commentators have concluded that this reversal of policy was influenced by the threat of investor–state arbitration.[388]

In a further development on this issue, Philip Morris has recently moved against Uruguay, following its introduction of tobacco legislation that prohibits the use of the descriptions 'mild' and 'light' and requires pictorial public health warnings on the packaging of cigarettes.[389] The company filed a request for arbitration with ICSID in February 2010, alleging that the measures breach the Switzerland–Uruguay bilateral investment treaty,[390] specifically, in that they amount to uncompensated expropriation of the company's intellectual property, a breach of the fair and equitable treatment standard, and unreasonable impairment of the use of its investment.[391] Of particular note, is the aggressive framing of the company's request for relief, seeking not merely compensatory damages for losses on its investments, but also an order for suspension of Uruguay's regulatory measures.[392] In adopting such a stance, Philip Morris makes its intentions plain that this issue is not solely about receiving compensation;

[386] Ibid.; see the discussion on the potential 'chilling effect' of tobacco company threats of investor–state arbitration and violations of trade agreements, and specifically on the actions of Philip Morris in response to the proposed Canadian legislation, in Weismann, *International Trade Agreements*; see also the arguments put forward in Philip Morris, *Submission by Philip Morris International Inc in Response to the National Center for Standards and Certification Information Foreign Trade Notification No. G/TBT/N/CAN/22* (2002), available at www.takingontobacco.org/pmresponsetonoi.pdf (last accessed 11 December 2011).

[387] Peterson, 'All Roads', 139.

[388] Ibid., see also the discussion in Schneiderman, 'Taking Investments Too Far', pp. 218, 225.

[389] Peterson, 'Uruguay'.

[390] *Philip Morris Brand Sàrl (Switzerland), Philip Morris Products S.A. (Switzerland) and Abal Hermanos S.A. (Uruguay)* v. *Oriental Republic of Uruguay*, (ICSID Case No. ARB/10/7); *Accord entre la Confédération Suisse et la République Orientale de l'Uruguay Concernant la Promotion et la Protection Réciproques des Investissements* (entered into 7 October 1988), available at www.unctad.org/sections/dite/iia/docs/bits/switzerland_uruguay_fr.pdf (last accessed 14 March 2010).

[391] International Centre for Trade and Sustainable Development, 'Tobacco Company Files Claim'.

[392] Peterson, 'Uruguay'.

it is also very much concerned with influencing the substance of host state domestic policy and regulation. As of July 2012, the claim was continuing, addressing matters related to jurisdiction.

In 2011, Philip Morris also gave notice of its intention to bring an investor–state claim against Australia, the first such claim filed against the country, in response to its planned 'plain packaging' legislation for tobacco. The legislation has since been enacted[393] and Philip Morris Asia Ltd is pursuing a claim under the Hong Kong–Australia bilateral investment treaty.[394] The regulation in question provides that, although brand names are permitted on tobacco products, they are required to be packaged in plain material devoid of all logos or branding images. The grounds for Philip Morris' complaint are of the same ilk as that brought against Uruguay, that is, that the legislation prevents the full use of its intellectual property and, accordingly, expropriates its investment, violates the fair and equitable treatment standard guaranteed in the Hong Kong–Australia bilateral investment treaty, and fails to provide full protection and security to its investments as required under the treaty. Philip Morris also argues that the purported public health purpose of the regulation is, in fact, not served by the specific measures taken under the legislation, but will instead feed the black market trade in illegal cigarettes.[395] A decision on this matter is not expected for some years. However, as other countries are considering the introduction of 'plain packaging' tobacco legislation, the outcome of this investor–state dispute will have significant repercussions.[396] And, as an aside, it should also be noted that it is a multi-pronged response that has been generated by the introduction of Australia's new tobacco legislation. In addition to the claim under the bilateral investment treaty, Philip Morris also pursued a constitutional challenge

[393] Tobacco Plain Packaging Act (2011), Cth Act No. 148 of 2011.

[394] Agreement between the Government of Hong Kong and the Government of Australia for the Promotion and the Protection of Investments, 1748 UNTS 385 (signed 15 September 1993, entered into force 15 October 1993); *Philip Morris Asia Ltd* v. *The Commonwealth of Australia, In the Matter of Arbitration under the Arbitration Rules of the United Nations Commission on International Trade Law 2010, Notice of Arbitration*, 21 November 2011, available at www.ag.gov.au/Internationallaw/Documents/Philip+Morris+ Asia +Notice+of+Arbitration.pdf (last accessed 8 March 2012).

[395] *Philip Morris Asia Limited* v. *The Commonwealth of Australia.*

[396] The United Kingdom, New Zealand, France, Canada, Finland, and Turkey are considering proposals to introduce more restrictive tobacco regulations; ASH, *Plain Packaging*, (July 2012), available at http://ash.org.uk/files/documents/ASH_699.pdf (last accessed 24 August 2012).

to the legislation in the Australian domestic courts.[397] The Ukraine, Honduras, and the Dominican Republic have also requested consultations with Australia under the Dispute Settlement Understanding of the World Trade Organisation (WTO).[398]

(c) Ethyl Corp. *v.* Canada

As discussed above, this case involved Canada's decision to prohibit trade in MMT on the basis of health and environmental concerns.[399] In enacting the restrictive legislation, the Canadian government had adopted a precautionary approach in the face of inconclusive scientific evidence as to the impacts of MMT. Through the operation of investor–state arbitration, that public welfare decision would have been subject to a process of review according to rules that do not give adequate weight to public welfare interests.[400] In reversing its policy decisions and in repealing the legislation following the pursuit of investor–state arbitration by Ethyl Corp, the Canadian government signalled that it was not willing to risk that process. The implications of this case point to political conditions in which investor action taken to preserve an individual commercial position can constrain governments in their regulatory decision-making – in other words, regulatory chill via investor–state arbitration.[401] There is little doubt that governments should be able to make policy decisions on the health and environment of their citizens, such as the Canadian stance on MMT, without the threat of investor–state arbitration being a consideration in the decision-making process. This case does suggest, however, that investor–state arbitration can play a role in the chilling of more stringent environmental regulation.[402]

[397] *JT International S.A.* v. *Commonwealth of Australia; British American Tobacco Australasia Limited & Ors* v. *Commonwealth of Australia* [2012] HCA 30.

[398] *Australia – Certain Measures Concerning Trademarks and Other Plain Packaging Requirements Applicable to Tobacco Products and Packaging*, Request for Consultations, DS/434, 13 March 2012.

[399] *Ethyl Corporation* (Award of 1998); see the discussion of the facts in this case at section II.A.1 of this chapter; see also the discussion in Soloway, 'Environmental Regulation'.

[400] Soloway, 'Environmental Regulation', 119.

[401] Ibid.; Tienhaara, 'What You Don't Know'; Peterson, 'All Roads'; see also Tienhaara, 'Regulatory Chill', 606.

[402] Schneiderman, 'Taking Investments Too Far', 225; Tienhaara, 'What You Don't Know'; Peterson, 'All Roads'; Mann, *Private Rights*; see also the discussion of this case in Peterson and Gray, *International Human Rights*.

For all the concrete expressions of investor complaint embodied in filed claims under investment treaties, the regulatory chill theory also gives cause for disquiet. In operation, it is generally a subtle creature and is difficult to detect. And yet, it has the potential to frustrate initiatives designed to implement national and global environmental objectives. Whilst this capacity is concerning enough in the abstract, it takes on a particular potency in the face of imminent global environmental risks such as climate change. Accordingly, the next section examines the implications of investor–state arbitration for the implementation of climate change mitigation measures.

E. International investment law and climate change mitigation measures

Concern has been expressed that rules of international investment law may impede the domestic implementation of climate change mitigation measures.[403] It is clear from the discussion in the sections above that there is a potential for claims to be brought by investors alleging that environmental regulatory measures amount to indirect expropriation, discriminatory treatment, or a breach of the fair and equitable treatment standard. Given this propensity, it is also conceivable that regulatory measures designed to address climate change may be challenged by foreign investors affected by the change in the law. It is this prospect that points to a potential for regulatory chill to affect the strengthening of climate change mitigation measures in host states.[404]

1. European emissions trading

Indeed, climate-related claims of discriminatory treatment giving rise to a right of compensation have already occurred within the context of the European Union.[405] Allocated emissions rights under the European Emissions Trading Scheme[406] generated protest and court action in

[403] Werksman, Baumert, and Dubask, 'Clean Development Mechanism'; Brown, 'Settlement of Disputes', 380–1; Miles, 'International Investment Law'; Marshall and Murphy, *Climate Change*.

[404] Werksman, Baumert, and Dubask, 'Clean Development Mechanism', 77.

[405] *Arcelor S.A.* v. *European Parliament and Council* (2004) Case T-16/04 ('*Arcelor S.A.*'); Belgian Arbitration Court, Arrest No. 92/2006, 7 June 2007; French Council of State, Arrest No. 287110, 8 February 2007; see the discussion in Boute, 'Combating Climate Change', 231–3.

[406] Council Directive 2003/87/EC, Establishing a Scheme for Greenhouse Gas Emission Allowance Trading with the Community and Amending Council Directive 96/61/EC, [2003] OJ L275/32.

2004 by a major steel manufacturer, Arcelor.[407] Prior to the introduction of the scheme, the company had enjoyed an essentially unrestricted level of carbon emissions. For this reason, the constraints introduced under the Emissions Trading Scheme involved a significant change to the economic and legal conditions under which the investments in the company had originally been made.[408]

Arcelor objected to its inclusion within the scheme in circumstances where other comparable sectors, such as the aluminium, chemical, and plastics industries, were not subject to similar restrictions. The company challenged the validity of the regulation, including the European Emissions Trading Directive as well as the implementing legislation enacted in Belgium and France.[409] Arcelor alleged that:[410]

- the regulation amounted to a violation of its property rights and the freedom to pursue economic activity;
- the required purchase of emissions rights at an unpredictable market price breached the principle of legal certainty; and
- the regulation was discriminatory, in that it did not apply to comparable, competing sectors such as aluminium manufacturers, producers of plastic, or waste incineration facilities.

The Belgian Arbitration Court dismissed the claim.[411] The French Council of State dismissed the first two grounds for the claim, but referred the discrimination question to the European Court of Justice.[412] The question was framed in the following terms:

> Is Directive 2003/87/EC of 13 October 2003 valid in the light of the principle of equal treatment, in so far as that Directive makes the greenhouse gas emission allowance trading scheme applicable to installations in the steel sector without including in its scope the aluminium and plastic industries?[413]

[407] *Arcelor S.A.*; Belgian Arbitration Court, Arrest No. 92/2006, 7 June 2007; French Council of State, Arrest No. 287110, 8 February 2007.

[408] Boute, 'Combating Climate Change', 231.

[409] Ibid., 231–2; Posser and Altenschmidt, 'European Union Emissions Trading Directive', 67–70; Council Directive 2003/87/EC, Establishing a Scheme for Greenhouse Gas Emission Allowance Trading with the Community and Amending Council Directive 96/61/EC, [2003] OJ L275/32.

[410] *Arcelor S.A.*; [2004] OJ C71/36–C71/37; Boute, 'Combating Climate Change', 231–2.

[411] Boute, 'Combating Climate Change', 232. [412] Ibid.

[413] *Société Arcelor Atlantique et Lorraine and others* v. *Premier Ministre, Ministre de l'Économie, des Finances et de l'Industrie, Ministre de l'Écologie et du Développement Durable*, Case C-127/07; [2007] OJ C117/8 (*Société Arcelor Atlantique*).

The Court released its decision in December 2008, upholding the European Union Emissions Trading Scheme and supporting its incremental approach of including some sectors, but not others.[414] It is the reasoning adopted by the Court, however, that may be of interest for future investor–state disputes. The Court held that the various industrial sectors were comparable sources of carbon emissions on the grounds that all emissions contribute to dangerous interference with the global climate system and all economic sectors could potentially participate in an emissions trading scheme.[415] The Court then determined that the European Union Emissions Trading Scheme was subjecting comparable sectors to differential treatment through its application to the steel industry without the inclusion of the chemical and aluminium sectors.[416] The differential treatment was, however, justified because of the novelty and complexity of the scheme, which meant that a 'step-by-step' approach to its introduction was appropriate. The Court also held that the exclusion of the chemical sector was appropriate as the large number of installations would have made the scheme difficult to administer. The different levels of carbon emissions between the non-ferrous metal sector and the steel industry also meant that the differential treatment could be justified.[417]

It is particularly interesting that the Court did not refer to the underlying objectives of the climate change mitigation measures embodied within the emissions trading scheme in justifying the differential treatment. Rather, it was the functional requirements of the scheme that rendered the discrimination permissible. In the context of an investor–state dispute, a key aspect of the complaint is often not the government policy behind the regulation, but in the detail of its form, implementation, or effect. For this reason, it is unlikely that an investor will challenge the rationale behind climate-related measures, but their application in particular circumstances. Certainly, the Court's reasoning is helpful for investors in that it establishes a *prima facie* comparability between carbon emitters. And the justification that satisfied the European Court of Justice is unlikely to impress an investor–state arbitral tribunal, being, in essence, that discriminatory treatment is

414 *Société Arcelor Atlantique*; Judgment of the European Court of Justice (ECJ), 16 December 2008.

415 *Société Arcelor Atlantique*; Judgment of the ECJ, 16 December 2008.

416 Ibid., see also the discussion in van Zeben, 'European Emissions'.

417 *Société Arcelor Atlantique*; Judgment of the ECJ, 16 December 2008.

acceptable because the regulatory scheme is novel, complex, and still in its infancy.

Arcelor's claim was framed according to the particular approach to the protection of property rights within the European Convention on Human Rights,[418] and European jurisprudence on the principles of legal certainty and protection of investors' legitimate expectations.[419] However, it is not difficult to see their application in an investor–state dispute under a bilateral investment treaty. On the introduction of significant climate change mitigation measures that severely restrict the current operating practices of large-scale carbon emitters, challenges to those regulations from foreign-owned entities can be expected.[420] It is likely that the allegations would be framed as indirect expropriation, a breach of fair and equitable treatment, or a violation of the national treatment or most-favoured-nation treatment standards.[421] Whether or not such claims are successful will turn on questions of the method of application of new schemes, the effects of the measures on the investment, the legitimate expectations of the investor, and the interpretation of requirements to maintain a stable legal and business environment. The outcome will largely depend on the line of reasoning adopted by tribunals in the future. If the *Methanex*[422] approach is followed, climate-related regulation will most likely be beyond the reach of investment treaties. If, on the other hand, the *Azurix*[423] and *Tecmed*[424] reasoning is preferred, the outcome is less certain.

The possibility of an investor challenge to climate change mitigation regulation will continue to be of increasing concern to host states. It is likely that foreign investors facing severely restricted operating capacities, or indeed even phase-out requirements, will seek to recoup their losses through the avenues available under bilateral investment agreements. Indeed, foreign investors have recently threatened to invoke the Hong Kong–Australia bilateral investment treaty in the context of the

[418] Art. 1, First Additional Protocol to the Convention for the Protection of Human Rights and Fundamental Freedoms, opened for signature 20 March 1952; Convention for the Protection of Human Rights and Fundamental Freedoms, opened for signature 4 November 1950, 213 UNTS 222 (entered into force 3 September 1953).

[419] *Boute*, 'Combating Climate Change', 229–30.

[420] See, e.g., the discussion on the increasing wave of litigation within the European Union initiated by both states and companies following the introduction of more stringent carbon emissions restrictions, in Kanter and Castle, 'EU Wrangling'.

[421] Schill, 'Investment Treaties', 371.

[422] *Methanex Corporation.*

[423] *Azurix Corp.* (Award of 2006).

[424] *Tecnicas Medioambientales Tecmed S.A.*

introduction of an emissions trading scheme.[425] And it is not certain at all that arbitral tribunals determining such disputes would decline such claims. With respect to the *Arcelor* claim,[426] Boute asserted that it would have been politically difficult for the European Court of Justice to have ruled in any way other than supportive of the emissions trading scheme,[427] but such political constraints do not operate on ad hoc arbitral panels in investor–state disputes. Although the decision in *Methanex*[428] is encouraging, the approach to environmental regulation espoused in *Santa Elena*,[429] *Metalclad*,[430] *Tecmed*,[431] and *Azurix*[432] is also available to tribunals – and without a central appellate facility to settle the issue and bring consistency to the reasoning of awards in investor–state disputes, the uncertainty will remain.[433]

2. The international legal framework to address climate change

Continuing with the subject of climate change, further interrelated concerns have been raised that measures to promote the use of renewable energy and to implement obligations under the international legal framework established by the United Nations Framework Convention on Climate Change (UNFCCC),[434] the Kyoto Protocol,[435] and any post-2012 instruments, may conflict with international investment rules.[436] As is to be expected, the key issues include the operation of national

[425] Smith, 'Canberra Faces Legal Challenge Over Carbon Scheme', 24 November 2009, *Financial Times*, available at www.ft.com/cms/s/0/00cced94-d898-11de-b63a-00144feabdc0.html?catid=24 (last accessed 11 December 2011); Agreement between the Government of Hong Kong and the Government of Australia for the Promotion and Protection of Investments, signed on 15 September 1993, www.unctad.org/sections/dite/iia/docs/bits/hongkong_australia.pdf (last accessed 11 December 2011).

[426] *Arcelor S.A.v European Parliament and Council* (2004) Case T-16/04; *Société Arcelor Atlantique*.

[427] Boute, 'Combating Climate Change', 232.

[428] *Methanex Corporation*.

[429] *Compania del Desarrollo de Santa Elena S.A.*

[430] *Metalclad Corporation* (Award of 2000).

[431] *Tecnicas Medioambientales Tecmed S.A.*

[432] *Azurix Corp.* (Award of 2006).

[433] Reform of the dispute settlement system is addressed in Chapters 5 and 6.

[434] United Nations Framework Convention on Climate Change, opened for signature 9 May 1992, 31 ILM 849 (entered into force 24 March 1994).

[435] Kyoto Protocol to the United Nations Framework Convention on Climate Change, opened for signature 11 December 1997, (1998) 37 ILM 22 (entered into force 16 February 2005).

[436] Werksman, Baumert, and Dubash, 'Clean Development Mechanism'; Werksman and Santoro, 'Investing in Sustainable Development', 191; Gentry and Ronk, 'International Investment Agreements', 25, 65–70.

treatment requirements, as well as the fair and equitable treatment standard and guarantees to protect against uncompensated indirect expropriation on new climate-related regulation.[437]

(a) Key international mechanisms in carbon emission reductions

The Kyoto Protocol requires state parties listed in Annex I of the UNFCCC to reduce their carbon emissions to certain specified levels.[438] In addition to encouraging energy efficiency measures and the restructuring of industrial sectors, the Kyoto Protocol also provides a number of flexible mechanisms to assist with the process of carbon emission reductions.[439] These include the use of carbon emissions trading schemes, joint implementation projects, and the Clean Development Mechanism, now generally referred to as 'the Kyoto Mechanisms'.[440]

The Clean Development Mechanism allows Annex I states to finance emission reduction projects within non-Annex I parties and obtain credit for those reductions.[441] It was hoped that a mechanism of this kind would encourage investment flows from developed to developing states in low-carbon projects and renewable energy technology.[442] And it is Article 12(2) of the Protocol that expressly reflects this attempted alignment of environmental and economic interests:

> The purpose of the clean development mechanism shall be to assist Parties not included in Annex I in achieving sustainable development and in contributing to the ultimate objective of the Convention, and to assist Parties included in

[437] Werksman and Santoro, 'Investing in Sustainable Development', 198–205; Gentry and Ronk, 'International Investment Agreements', 67; Werksman, Baumert, Dubash, 'Clean Development Mechanism'.

[438] Kyoto Protocol to the United Nations Framework Convention on Climate Change, opened for signature 11 December 1997, (1998) 37 ILM 22, Art. 3 (entered into force 16 February 2005).

[439] Ibid., Arts 2, 6, 12, and 17.

[440] Ibid., Arts 6, 12 and 17. Joint implementation involves the collaboration of two Annex I parties. Art. 6 of the Protocol allows Annex I parties to transfer to, or acquire from, each other emission reduction credits produced by projects that are aimed at generating emission reductions. This enables developed states to invest in renewable energy and low-carbon projects in other developed states and apply the credits generated to their own emission reduction targets.

[441] Ibid., Art. 12. 'Annex I states' are Annex I parties to the UNFCCC, being the designated developing states. The Kyoto Protocol obligates Annex I parties to ensure that their carbon emissions do not exceed their assigned amounts. Annex B of the Protocol contains these negotiated individual targets for each developed state.

[442] Werksman and Santoro, 'Investing in Sustainable Development', 193; Kulovesi, 'The Private Sector', 147.

Annex I in achieving compliance with their quantified emission limitation and reduction commitments under Article 3.[443]

The incentive for Annex I parties is the opportunity to credit reductions they have financed at a reduced rate in other countries to their own emission reduction obligations.[444] The operation of the mechanism, however, was clearly not developed solely with the involvement of states in mind; it was also structured to include the private sector.[445]

Shifting to a low-carbon economy has opened up innumerable investment opportunities. And the Kyoto Mechanisms have played a role in that process, creating new markets and encouraging private sector interest in renewable energy sources and low-carbon technology.[446] This commercial involvement has now moved beyond direct forms such as the development of renewable energy facilities in electricity markets or the operation of Clean Development Mechanism or joint implementation projects. It has also extended into the creation of auxiliary markets such as the provision of supporting services such as carbon brokerage, carbon project consultancy or legal advice,

443 Kyoto Protocol to the United Nations Framework Convention on Climate Change, opened for signature 11 December 1997, (1998) 37 ILM 22, Art. 12(2) (entered into force 16 February 2005).

444 Freestone and Streck, 'Introduction', 49–50; Kulovesi, 'The Private Sector', 147.

445 Kyoto Protocol to the United Nations Framework Convention on Climate Change, opened for signature 11 December 1997, (1998) 37 ILM 22, Art. 12(9) (entered into force 16 February 2005); see also the discussion in Freestone and Streck, 49–50; Kulovesi, 'The Private Sector', 147.

446 Richardson, *Socially Responsible Investment Law*, p. 39; Werksman and Santoro, 'Investing in Sustainable Development', 193–5; Fershee, 'Changing Resources', 50; see the discussion in Ferrey, 'The New Power Generation'; see e.g. the discussion in United Nations Environment Programme (UNEP), 'Investors Flock to Renewable Energy and Efficiency Technologies: Climate Change Worries, High Oil Prices and Government Help Top Factors Fuelling Hot Renewable Energy Investment Climate' (Press Release, 20 June 2007), available at www.unep.org/Documents.Multilingual/Default.asp?DocumentID=512&ArticleID=5616&l=en (last accessed 20 January 2010) (UNEP Press Release 1); UNEP, 'Renewable Energy Accelerates Meteoric Rise: 2007 Global Status Report Shows Perceptions Lag Reality' (Press Release, 28 February 2008), available at www.unep.org/Documents.Multilingual/Default.asp?DocumentID=528&ArticleID=5754&l=en (last accessed 20 January 2010) (UNEP Press Release 2); UNEP, 'Environment Ministers Meet to Accelerate Transition to a Low Carbon Society: Huge Investment Opportunities in Energy Savings to Renewables and Reduced Deforestation to Climate Proofing if Markets can be Mobilized' (Press Release, February 2008), available at www.unep.org/Documents.Multilingual/Default.asp?DocumentID=528&ArticleID=5745&l=en (last accessed 23 January 2010) (UNEP Press Release 3).

financiers and financial analysts, carbon emissions verification services, and the manufacture of low-carbon products.[447]

More long-term certainty is still required regarding the form of a post-Kyoto regime, the international carbon market, its regulatory structures, and the emission reductions targets of individual states so as to stimulate further investment in low-carbon technology.[448] However, market indicators point to a sustained and substantial level of investment in this sector. In this regard, the international market for carbon emissions credits has experienced a marked increase in activity since the Kyoto Protocol entered into force in February 2005.[449] Although the Clean Development Mechanism is still in its infancy, already over 2,000 projects have been approved and registered.[450] Investment in wind, solar, and bio-fuel technology has rapidly grown.[451] Overall, the international carbon market and global levels of investment in renewables are now worth billions of dollars every year.[452] Given the emergence and progression of these markets, it is likely that there will also be an increase in the use of mechanisms to protect and further the promotion of investment in renewable energy at the domestic level. This could entail such measures as the regulation of access rights to major electricity grids, incentive tariffs, carbon taxes, renewable energy tax exemptions, mandatory renewable energy quotas, grants, and concessional financing.[453]

As foreshadowed by the earlier discussion on the *Arcelor* case,[454] however, the investment–climate change interface is not all about investment opportunity in renewables and low-carbon technology. It is also possible that low-carbon investment incentives may constitute

[447] Kulovesi, 'The Private Sector', 150–3; UNEP Press Release 3, 'Environment Ministers'.

[448] Freestone and Streck, 'Introduction', 55; Doelle, 'The Cat Came Back', 264.

[449] Freestone and Streck, 'Introduction', 51; Carr and Rosembuj, 'Flexible Mechanisms', 51; Kyoto Protocol to the United Nations Framework Convention on Climate Change, opened for signature 11 December 1997, (1998) 37 ILM 22, art. 12(9) (entered into force 16 February 2005).

[450] UNFCCC Secretariat, Clean Development Mechanism, *CDM Statistics* (February 2010), available at http://cdm.unfccc.int/Statistics/index.html (last accessed 11 December 2011).

[451] UNEP Press Releases 1, 2, and 3.

[452] Freestone and Streck, 'Introduction', 51; UNEP Press Releases 1, 2, and 3.

[453] Gentry and Ronk, 'International Investment Agreements'.

[454] *Arcelor S.A.; Société Arcelor Atlantique et Lorraine and others* v. *Premier Ministre, Ministre de l'Économie, des Finances et de l'Industrie, Ministre de l'Écologie et du Développement Durable*, Case C-127/07.

discrimination against investors in high carbon-emitting operations and, as such, violate investor protection guarantees in international investment agreements.[455] The concern is that regulatory measures to address climate change may be subject to challenges of the kind recently seen in other areas of environmental regulation.

(b) Discrimination

It is not overstating the issue to suggest that special incentives offered by a host state for renewable energy projects, new restrictions on carbon emissions, or the prohibition of particular activities altogether could discriminate against carbon-intensive investment projects.[456] Arguments based on discriminatory treatment of a foreign investor could involve an assessment of whether the carbon-intensive project was 'like' a less carbon-intensive project, or a renewable energy project.[457] Such an assessment would prove problematic on the criteria by which 'like circumstances' have generally been assessed in the past. As discussed above, on the whole, the chosen criteria have been limited to commercial considerations.[458] And, on this basis, differentiation between two otherwise similar projects solely on the grounds of carbon intensity may well not be permissible.

It has been suggested that, from the perspective of trade law, climate-related measures, including initiatives such as the European Union Emissions Trading Scheme,[459] are problematic and implicate WTO agreements.[460] In particular, there is concern surrounding the operation of non-discrimination requirements. In this regard, Green asserts that WTO non-discrimination obligations are potentially engaged by the domestic implementation of climate-related regulation such as mandatory emission caps, energy efficiency requirements, emissions

455 Ibid., 67.

456 Werksman, Baumert, and Dubash, 'Clean Development Mechanism', 70–7; Werksman and Santoro, 'Investing in Sustainable Development'; Gentry and Ronk, 'International Investment Agreements', 65–70.

457 Gentry and Ronk, 'International Investment Agreements', 67; Werksman, Baumert, and Dubash, 'Clean Development Mechanism', 74–5.

458 Werksman, Baumert, and Dubash, 'Clean Development Mechanism', 75; Salgado, 'The Case Against', 1061. 'Like circumstances' is discussed in detail in section II.C of this chapter.

459 Council Directive 2003/87/EC, Establishing a Scheme for Greenhouse Gas Emission Allowance Trading with the Community and Amending Council Directive 96/61/EC, [2003] OJ L275/32.

460 Green, 'Climate Change'; Martin, 'Trade Law Implications'; Bradnee Chambers, 'International Trade Law', 87.

trading schemes, and even eco-labelling and voluntary state-industry agreements.[461] Martin goes so far as to conclude that the exclusion of non-parties to the Kyoto Protocol from participation in the European Union Emissions Trading Scheme is a violation of the General Agreement on Tariffs and Trade[462] and the General Agreement on Trade in Services.[463] He focuses, in particular, on the exclusion of American emissions brokers from operating within the scheme.[464]

There is always a need for caution in seeking to make analogies as between trade and investment law. The rules and their application have their own nuances and it is an error to be too ready to draw conclusions about one field from the experiences of the other. However, concerns raised by Green and Martin at the potential breach of national treatment and most-favoured-nation standards in the WTO context are, in many respects, transferable to that of international investment. Regulation establishing commercially advantageous schemes excluding the participation of new and existing carbon-intensive operations or related services and increasingly restrictive climate-related measures may attract investor challenges on similar bases to that suggested by Green and Martin. Indeed, Werksman, Baumert, and Dubash have drawn attention to the interaction between trade and investment standards, expressing their concern at the application of the WTO 'like circumstances' approach to the categorisation of Clean Development Mechanism projects in future investor–state disputes.[465]

There are certainly differences in the interpretation of national treatment as between the trade and investment contexts. Furthermore, arbitral panels in investor–state disputes are inconsistent on whether or not it is even appropriate to draw on WTO jurisprudence at all. However, what is increasingly apparent is that these differences point to a more constraining effect on governments under investor protections rather than less. As DiMascio and Pauwelyn argue, national

[461] Green, 'Climate Change', 143–7.

[462] General Agreement on Tariffs and Trade, Annex 1A, Agreement Establishing the World Trade Organization, opened for signature 15 April 1994, (1994) 33 ILM 1125 (entered into force 1 January 1995).

[463] General Agreement on Trade in Services, Annex 1B, Agreement Establishing the World Trade Organization, opened for signature 15 April 1994, (1994) 33 ILM 1125 (entered into force 1 January 1995).

[464] Martin, 'Trade Law Implications'.

[465] Werksman, Baumert, and Dubash, 'Clean Development Mechanism', 74–5.

treatment requirements under international investment agreements may, in fact, be even more extensive than under WTO rules.[466] The reason being that in the trade context, national treatment obligations apply only to actual products, whereas its investor protection manifestation applies throughout the life of the investment and to any rules, regulations, or governmental decisions that affect any part of the operation of the investment.[467] With this in mind, it becomes clear that the expansive nature of national treatment requirements under investor protection rules is, indeed, a potential concern for the introduction of new climate-related measures.

There have, however, also been some encouraging developments on the issue of criteria for the consideration of the 'likeness' of projects. The award in *Parkerings-Compagniet AS* v. *Republic of Lithuania* (the *Parkerings Award*) made a break-through ruling in considering cultural heritage and environmental impacts as a component of the criteria for 'like circumstances'.[468] This dispute involved the tender process for the construction and operation of a major car parking development to control traffic and protect the integrity of the historic Old Town of the City of Vilnius, Lithuania.[469] In affirming the validity of the decision to approve one development project over another, the Tribunal stated that 'the situation of the two investors will not be in *like circumstances* if a justification of the different treatment is established.'[470] The Tribunal went on to say that 'The historical and archaeological preservation and environmental protection could be and in this case were a justification for the refusal of the project.'[471] In other words, it was the difference in the archaeological and environmental impacts that distinguished the otherwise very similar investment projects and rendered them not in 'like circumstances'.

This decision has important implications beyond its immediate fact situation. Key amongst those is that it points to the ecological impact of an investor's project as a determinative factor in the 'like circumstances' test. If this approach is followed in future investor–state disputes, then the potential for non-discrimination requirements in international investment agreements to frustrate climate change mitigation regulation

[466] DiMascio and Pauwelyn, 'Nondiscrimination', 59, 67–8; see also the discussion in Adlung and Molinuevo, 'Bilateralism in Services Trade', 384.

[467] DiMascio and Pauwelyn, 'Nondiscrimination', 67–8.

[468] *Parkerings-Compagniet AS* v. *Republic of Lithuania* (ICSID Arbitration Case No. ARB/05/8, Award of 11 September 2007), paras 375, 392.

[469] Ibid., paras 51–2. [470] Ibid., para. 375. [471] Ibid., para. 392.

would be significantly reduced. It would, of course, help to clarify the issue if international investment agreements expressly stated, or provided in an interpretative note, that ecological impact was a relevant criterion for consideration of 'like circumstances'. Indeed, Gentry and Ronk suggest that international investment agreements should be even more specific and state that energy from renewable and non-renewable sources are not in 'like circumstances'.[472] Such a move would greatly assist the alignment of international investment law with the objectives of the Kyoto Protocol and any post-Kyoto instrument.[473]

(c) *Indirect expropriation and fair and equitable treatment*

In addition to the suggestion of complaints grounded in discrimination, the potential for an investor climate-related claim on the basis of indirect expropriation has also been raised.[474] The envisaged context is one in which an investor in a non-renewable energy project takes issue with regulation introduced to encourage greater investment in renewable energy sources, measures taken to facilitate Clean Development Mechanism projects in developing states, and regulation that limits current carbon emission levels or prohibits carbon-intensive activity.[475] The predicted objection is that new regulation substantially reduces the value of existing investments in non-renewable energy projects.[476] Gentry and Ronk conclude that although measures taken to encourage renewable energy sources are unlikely to impact sufficiently to constitute expropriation, prohibitions on certain activities or products may amount to a regulatory taking.[477]

Furthermore, the question of whether the measures are a breach of the fair and equitable treatment standard remains a live issue. A claim based on a breach of this protection guarantee would also involve allegations that prohibitions on certain activities, phase-outs for the use of particular materials, or severe restrictions on emissions output

[472] Gentry and Ronk, 'International Investment Agreements', 27.

[473] Kyoto Protocol to the United Nations Framework Convention on Climate Change, opened for signature 11 December 1997, (1998) 37 ILM 22 (entered into force 16 February 2005).

[474] Gentry and Ronk, 'International Investment Agreements', 68–70; Werksman, Baumert, and Dubash, 'Clean Development Mechanism', 77.

[475] Werksman, Baumert, and Dubash, 'Clean Development Mechanism', 77; Gentry and Ronk, 'International Investment Agreements', 68–70.

[476] Gentry and Ronk, 'International Investment Agreements', 68–70; Werksman, Baumert, and Dubash, 'Clean Development Mechanism', 77.

[477] Gentry and Ronk, 'International Investment Agreements', 70.

had amounted to a substantial change in the legal and business environment for carbon-intensive operations. The legitimate expectations of the investor at the time of entering into the investment would be examined, as would the impact of any applicable stabilisation clauses.[478] While it may be difficult to argue that climate change mitigation measures were not foreseeable for investments entered into more recently, the 'basic expectations'[479] of investors when entering into much earlier carbon-intensive operations would certainly be affected by regulation seeking to shift economies to a low-carbon approach.

(d) Differing viewpoints

The potential interaction between investment rules and climate-related measures remains a contentious issue. For Schill, international investment agreements are unlikely to prevent the introduction of climate change mitigation measures.[480] In his exploration of the issue, he prefaces his conclusion with the comment that this will be the case 'provided these measures do not discriminate against foreign investors, impose proportionate burdens nor unreasonably change the regulatory framework.'[481] In other words, there will be no problem with new climate change mitigation regulation provided it complies with current international investment rules. This approach is problematic on two grounds.

(i) Necessarily discriminatory The first difficulty with Schill's approach is that climate-related measures are necessarily discriminatory as against carbon-intensive sectors and it is likely that as emissions reduction targets become more stringent, the burdens imposed on particular operations will increase substantially.[482] The proviso that Schill places on his conclusions comprises the very issues that have been the subject of challenges to environmental regulation – that they are discriminatory, impose substantial burdens, and constitute a breach of the requirement to provide a stable legal and business

[478] Stabilisation clauses are examined in this chapter at section II.E.3.

[479] See, e.g., the reasoning in *Tecnicas Medioambientales Tecmed S.A.*, 173.

[480] Schill, 'Investment Treaties', 470, 477. [481] Ibid., 477.

[482] See generally for a discussion of the costs of climate change mitigation measures being felt disproportionately by certain sectors, Stern, *The Stern Review*; Green, 'Climate Change', 144–5, also refers to the potential for particular industries to bear disproportionate costs of climate change mitigation.

environment.[483] Given the experience of the European Union with the *Arcelor* claim,[484] it is most unlikely that foreign investors affected by tightening restrictions on carbon emissions will not attempt to recoup their losses through means available under international investment agreements.

Indeed, the question of compensation for existing carbon-intensive operations in the energy sector is already being traversed.[485] In particular, the prospect of national emissions trading in a number of states has sparked lobbying for compensation in the form of free distribution of emissions allocations and less-restrictive legislation.[486] In a cap-and-trade system, allocations to one entity reduces the pool available to other operations, including competitors, and, as such, the decisions taken on permit distribution will impact substantially on business and industry costs and value.[487]

Within the Australian context, particular sectors and individual corporations have already engaged in substantial lobbying to frame their own positions as 'emissions-intensive' or 'trade-exposed' so as to receive higher emissions allocations in the distribution process.[488] The allocation process itself means that 'the Government will inevitably be forced to favour some companies and sectors over others.'[489] And the prospect of difficult governmental decisions points to the potential for foreign investor claims alleging less favourable treatment than their domestic competitors.[490] The Australian government has adopted a

[483] See, e.g., the cases discussed above, *Ethyl Corporation* (Award of 1998); *Azurix Corp.* (Award of 2006); *Metalclad Corporation* (Award of 2000); *Tecnicas Medioambientales Tecmed S.A.*

[484] *Arcelor S.A.*; *Société Arcelor Atlantique*. See also further reports of industry concerns at potential losses and potential for legal action, Kanter and Castle, 'EU Wrangling'; Gow, 'Mittal Says EU Emission Cap Will Limit Growth'; Kanter, 'As EU Goes Greener'; Shah, 'UK Launches Action'.

[485] Burtraw and Palmer, *Compensation Rules*.

[486] Ibid.; Murray, 'Companies Brace'; see also the discussion in Peeters, Weishaar, and de Cendra de Larragan, 'EU ETS'; WWF-Australia, 'No Compensation'.

[487] Burtraw and Palmer, *Compensation Rules*, pp. 1, 3; Murray, 'Companies Brace'.

[488] See, e.g., the position in Australia set out in Murray, 'Companies Brace'.

[489] Murray, 'Companies Brace'.

[490] Brown, 'The Settlement of Disputes', 372–3, 380–1; see also for a discussion of potential investor claims in respect of electricity restructuring in Canada, 'International Legal Expert says Ontario's Electricity Program Violates NAFTA', *Canada Newswire*, 14 February 2005, IATP, Trade Observatory, available at www.iatp.org/tradeobservatory/headlines.cfm?refID=48594 (last accessed 23 June 2008); see also the website of Appleton & Associates, describing the firm's areas of expertise as including investor–state arbitration, international investment law, and international

compensation-based approach to the problem, in both its initial draft legislation, Carbon Pollution Reduction Scheme, which did not pass into law, and in its Clean Energy Act, which was ultimately passed in 2011.[491] In so doing, the government effectively acknowledges the substantial additional costs its proposed energy reforms will place on carbon-intensive industries and has opted to provide compensation and free emission permits or units to those facilities qualifying as 'carbon-intensive', 'emissions-intensive', and 'trade-exposed'.[492] The scheme under the initial draft legislation did not create automatic rights to compensation and established a complex set of criteria in order to qualify for assistance under the programme. That draft legislation did send a signal, however, that compensable takings would be generated by the regulatory changes, stating that:

> The object of this Part is to contribute to the maintenance of investor confidence in electricity generation. It does so by providing limited transitional assistance in respect of generation assets, where:
> (a) money was invested in those assets before the Commonwealth Government announced its support for a scheme to reduce pollution caused by emissions of carbon dioxide and other greenhouse gases; and
> (b) those assets are likely to suffer a significant decline in value as a result of the introduction of such a scheme.[493]

That signal remained in the legislation that ultimately passed into law embodied within Part 8 of the 2011 Clean Energy Act, a division of the Act solely devoted to assistance for coal-fired electricity generators. The object of Part 8 is stated as being:

> to maintain energy security with the introduction of this Act and the associated provisions. It does so by providing transitional assistance in respect of highly emissions-intensive generation assets so as to:
> (a) help generators that face sizeable losses in the value of their assets; and
> (b) support investor confidence, and underpin the investment in generation assets that is required to ensure that Australia's future energy security needs are met.[494]

environmental agreements such as the Kyoto Protocol, and stating specifically that 'we provide advice on the unique challenges associated with the issuance and trading of Greenhouse Gas Emission credits', available at www.appletonlaw.com/index.htm (last accessed 23 June 2008).

491 Clean Energy Act 2011 (No. 131 of 2011, Cth, Australia).

492 Carbon Pollution Reduction Scheme (Cth, Australia); Clean Energy Act 2011, s.143.

493 Carbon Pollution Reduction Scheme (Cth, Australia), s. 174.

494 Clean Energy Act 2011, s. 159.

Even with the already extensive compensation measures under the draft scheme, industry continued to lobby the government for even further increases in compensation and to exclude whole sectors from emissions restrictions altogether.[495] Indeed, foreign investors in Australian coal-fired power generators threatened to invoke the Hong Kong–Australia bilateral investment treaty if the emissions trading scheme was enacted as initially proposed under the Carbon Pollution Reduction Scheme.[496] CLP Holdings Ltd asserted that the scheme and level of compensation risked breaching Australia's treaty obligations and that 'if laws to cut carbon emissions led to a fall in value of its Australian assets, it would seek to recover losses.'[497] The scheme was not enacted as proposed and the threat of arbitration dissipated.

The approach to compensation in the energy reforms attracted criticism from Ross Garnaut, the Australian government's former climate change advisor, for its potential to discriminate amongst operators. He argued that the payment of compensation and free permit allocations were protectionist, potentially breached international trade rules, and could lead Australia into a trade war.[498] Future investor–state disputes over climate-related measures are unlikely to be framed in such dramatic terms. However, it is entirely possible that these will instead take on a form more like the planning disputes already regularly filed in domestic courts and tribunals where the issues involve restrictions generated by the changing climate, such as permits for carbon emissions, water use restrictions, or coastal development prohibitions.[499] Indeed, it is likely that versions of the *Vattenfall AB* v.

[495] Macey, 'Investors Demand End'.

[496] Smith, 'Canberra'; Agreement between the Government of Hong Kong and the Government of Australia for the Promotion and Protection of Investments, signed on 15 September 1993, available at www.unctad.org/sections/dite/iia/docs/bits/hongkong_australia.pdf (last accessed 4 February 2010).

[497] Ibid. The Australian emissions trading scheme was not enacted in the form it was initially proposed in the Carbon Pollution Reduction Scheme due to the political events of November and December 2009 in Australia. The then-Opposition Leader, Malcolm Turnball, was removed as leader of the Liberal Party due to his support for a modified version of the Government's proposed emissions trading scheme and replaced with a self-confessed 'climate-sceptic', Tony Abbott. Following the change in leadership and Liberal Party climate change policy, the Bill did not receive the necessary support to pass into law.

[498] Arup, 'Coal Funding under Fire'.

[499] See, e.g., the following Australian cases: *Northcape Properties Pty Ltd* v. *District Council of Yorke Peninsula* [2008] SASC 57 ('*Northcape*'); *Gippsland Coastal Board* v. *South Gippsland Shire Council (No 2)* [2008] VCAT 1545 ('*Gippsland Coastal Board*'); *Gray* v. *Minister for Planning* (2006) 152 LGERA 258 ('*Gray*') regarding a coal mine proposal.

Federal Republic of Germany (*Vattenfall*) dispute over the failure to issue emissions and water use permits for the operation of a coal-fired power plant will occur in which climate change effects are expressly cited.[500] This very issue was recently raised in the European Parliament, questioning the implications of the *Vattenfall* dispute for climate protection measures implemented under European law.[501]

To date, investors have not yet pursued claims under bilateral investment treaties in relation to the imposition of new climate change mitigation measures. It appears that where new legislation has been enacted, it has not yet reached a level of impact on foreign-owned investments to provoke claims or that compensation is being paid on the introduction of new regulation. It is likely, however, that once compensation funds are not flowing so freely, permit allocations become more restrictive, and developing states begin to implement new climate-related measures, investor challenges will occur. In the long term, we can expect climate change to become a regular feature in investor–state disputes over development applications, activity prohibitions, and permit denials, in much the same way as it has already done so in domestic planning cases.[502]

(ii) Traditional investor viewpoints Schill's approach to the interface between climate change and investment rules is also problematic because it reflects the traditional stance of the foreign investor – there is no suggestion that international investment rules should be shifted to accommodate the social and environmental needs of the host state. Essentially, Schill is arguing that environmental regulation must comply with the requirements of international investment law rather than ensuring investment law adapts so as not to restrict the introduction of climate change mitigation measures. An alternative to Schill's approach, of course, would be to explore new techniques to reshape investment rules. For example, Werksman, Baumert, and Dubash propose that future international investment agreements should carve out exemptions for public welfare regulation, and, in particular, should not

500 *Vattenfall AB* v. *Federal Republic of Germany*, Request for Arbitration, 30 March 2009.

501 R. Harms (Verts/Hale) to the Commission, 'Written Question: Investment Protection Proceedings Brought by Vattenfall AB Against the Federal Republic of Germany', *Parliamentary Questions*, 17 September 2009, available at www.europarl.europa.eu/sides/getDoc.do?pubRef=-//EP//TEXT+WQ+E-2009-4343+0+DOC+XML+V0//EN (last accessed 9 November 2009).

502 See, e.g., *Northcape*; *Gippsland Coastal Board*; *Gray*.

inappropriately constrain host states in the implementation of their obligations under multilateral environmental agreements.[503]

Again, there have been some recent developments that are encouraging. Norway released a draft text of a model bilateral investment treaty in January 2008 (Norwegian Model BIT), which incorporated provisions designed to produce a more balanced investment treaty that protects not only investment, but also the regulatory function of host states.[504] The commentary attached to the Norwegian Model BIT declared that it would enable Norway:

> to lead the development from one-sided agreements that only safeguard the interests of the investor to comprehensive agreements that safeguard the regulative needs of both developed and developing countries, making investors accountable while ensuring them predictability and protection. Future investment agreements should address the totality of international legal agreements by referring to agreements of relevance to the regulatory authority of the states as regards, for example, sovereignty over resources and environmental regulations.[505]

The Norwegian Model BIT also included provisions to preserve environmental protection measures,[506] consider the developmental needs of the host state,[507] and introduce investor social responsibility obligations.[508] This is a model that would have moved international investment law forward, beginning the process of producing a more balanced, equitable legal framework for the twenty-first century. Unfortunately, in a less than encouraging move in June 2009, the Norwegian

503 Werksman, Baumert, and Dubash, 'Clean Development Mechanism', 59–60.

504 Ministry of Trade and Industry, Norway, Draft Model Bilateral Investment Agreement (December 2007), available at www.regjeringen.no/nb/dep/nhd/dok/Horinger/Horingsdokumenter/2008/horing—modell-for-investeringsavtaler/-4.html?id=496026 (last accessed 15 December 2011).

505 Ministry of Trade and Industry, *Comments on the Model for Future Investment Agreements* (2007) 10, available at www.regjeringen.no/upload/NHD/Vedlegg/hoeringer/2008/Forklarende%20vedlegg%20(engelsk)%20-%20final.doc (last accessed 14 December 2011).

506 Ministry of Trade and Industry, Norway, Draft Model Bilateral Investment Agreement, Arts 11, 12, and 24; see also commentary in Ministry of Trade and Industry, *Comments on the Model for Future Investment Agreements*, Art. 11.

507 Ministry of Trade and Industry, Norway, Draft Model Bilateral Investment Agreement, Preamble; see also commentary in Ministry of Trade and Industry, *Comments on the Model for Future Investment Agreements*, Art. 11.

508 Ministry of Trade and Industry, Norway, Draft Model Bilateral Investment Agreement, Art. 3; see also commentary in Ministry of Trade and Industry, *Comments on the Model for Future Investment Agreements*, Art. 12.

government announced that, after having received substantial feedback on the draft text, it would no longer be pursuing that particular form for its model bilateral investment treaty.[509]

3. Stabilisation clauses and climate change

Speculating somewhat further on the potential for investor protections to affect climate-related measures, there are also implications in the use of stabilisation clauses in contracts between host states and foreign investors. Stabilisation clauses are essentially a tool to preserve the legal and business environment in which the investment has been established.[510] They take different forms, but their purpose is uniform in seeking to protect foreign investment from political risk. One type of stabilisation clause seeks to prevent the application of changes in the law to the contract or the investment throughout the life of the project.[511] These provisions have a 'freezing' affect on host state regulation – they freeze the law applicable to the investment to that which was in force when the investor entered into the contract.[512] In this way, foreign investors are able to insulate their investments from the effect of more stringent environmental regulation or social law reform.[513]

Other key manifestations of stabilisation clause are the economic equilibrium clause, compensation clause, and the hybrid clause.[514] Economic equilibrium clauses require the state to restore the original economic equilibrium of the contract where a change in the law impacts detrimentally on the financial returns of the investment. This can be achieved through compensation, renegotiation of the terms of the contract, or the application of additional beneficial measures to redress the change generated by the new regulation.[515] Compensation clauses do not preclude the enactment of new regulation. Rather, any

[509] Vis-Dunbar, 'Norway Shelves its Draft Model'. The Norwegian Model BIT is examined in detail below in Chapter 6.

[510] Maniruzzaman, 'The Pursuit', 122.

[511] Tienhaara, 'What You Don't Know', 83; Sornarajah, *Foreign Investment*, p. 407; Verhoosel, 'Foreign Direct Investment', 455; Shemberg and Aizawa, *Stabilization Clauses*.

[512] Tienhaara, 'What You Don't Know', 83.

[513] Shemberg and Aizawa, *Stabilization Clauses*, pp. 4, 38–9; Tienhaara, 'What You Don't Know', 83–4.

[514] Maniruzzaman, 'The Pursuit', 127; Shemberg and Aizawa, *Stabilization Clauses*, pp. 24–31; Sheppard and Crockett, 'Stabilisation Clauses'.

[515] Shemberg and Aizawa, *Stabilization Clauses*, p. 6; Maniruzzaman, 'The Pursuit', 127; Sheppard and Crockett, 'Stabilisation Clauses'.

losses suffered as a result of the legislation will need to be recompensed by the host state.[516] Lastly, so-called 'hybrid' clauses combine elements of freezing, compensation, and economic equilibrium clauses.[517]

Stabilisation clauses in various forms are widely used in investor–state contracts and are regularly used in the extractive industries, water sector, transportation, infrastructure, and the electricity sector.[518] These contract provisions have the potential to impact on a state's ability to regulate in the public interest as they are innately directed at changes in legislation, are often of a very wide scope, and apply throughout the life of the investment.[519] Concerns have also been raised more generally at the nature of investor–state contracts, such as the lack of transparency or scope for public comment during negotiations, inequities reflected within the contract, the potential impact on environments, sustainable development needs, and human rights of local communities, and the fact that very few contracts are publicly available even after their conclusion.[520]

Renegotiation of contracts have occasionally occurred as a result of public outcry at agreements that have come to light,[521] and variations of stabilisation clauses have been developed in response to criticisms at the inflexibility of classic 'freezing' clauses and their constraining affect on host state policy space.[522] In particular, Sheppard and Crockett argue that the introduction of new public welfare regulation can be accommodated through appropriate drafting of stabilisation clauses.[523] Suggested mechanisms to limit the scope of stabilisation clauses include exemptions for public welfare regulation, precluding the application of the stabilisation clause to environmental regulation or human rights measures.[524] Such carve-outs could take the form of express exemptions or could operate through a 'compliance with international law' exception. This approach would allow the incorporation into the contract of new rules of customary international law or the provisions

516 Sheppard and Crockett, 'Stabilisation Clauses'.
517 Shemberg and Aizawa, *Stabilization Clauses*, pp. 6, 8. 518 Ibid., pp. 4, 17–18, 39.
519 Ibid., p. 39; Maniruzzaman, 'The Pursuit', 156–7.
520 See, e.g., Cotula, 'Foreign Investment Contracts'; Mann, *International Investment Agreements*; Ayine et al., 'Lifting the Lid'; Pacific Environment, *The Environmental*; Global Witness, *Heavy Mittal?*; Amnesty International, *Human Rights*.
521 See, e.g., the Baku-Tbilisi-Ceyhan Pipeline Company, *BTC Human Rights Undertaking*; see also Global Witness, *Update on the Renegotiation*.
522 Maniruzzaman, 'The Pursuit', 126; Sheppard and Crockett, 'Stabilisation Clauses'.
523 Sheppard and Crockett, 'Stabilisation Clauses'.
524 Ibid.; Cotula, 'Reconciling Regulatory Stability', 172.

of treaties concluded by the host state.[525] Cotula also argues for the adoption of an 'evolutionary approach' to the interpretation of stabilisation clauses.[526] This would entail the consideration of a wide range of factors in the application of the stabilisation clause, including any new international obligations of the host state.[527] In addition, there is also the potential for the use of additional instruments attaching to the contract, such as a 'Human Rights Undertaking'.[528] This was a technique that was used in the contracts arising out of the Baku–Tbilisi–Ceyhan pipeline project (the BTC Undertaking) following protest at, amongst other matters, the breadth of the stabilisation clause once the agreements became public.[529] The BTC Undertaking constituted a separate, but linked, document from the original contracts and it essentially provided that the investors would not assert claims under the contract in relation to new host state human rights measures. As such, it provides a useful model in the exploration of mechanisms to create more socially and environmental responsible relationships between foreign investors and host states.

The investor–host state contract is indeed a potential space in which more equitable environmental and social relationships could occur. In the highly sensitive area of energy contracts, consideration of these issues during contract negotiations, together with realistic expectations of contract performance and investment returns, could assist with avoidance of future problems between the facility operators, local residents, and state officials. And it is certainly encouraging to see the discourse turning to consider how such goals could be realised in practice.[530] Unfortunately, however, it also appears that carve-outs for new environmental regulation, human rights programmes, or social law reform are currently rare in investor–state contracts, and, instead,

525 Cotula, 'Reconciling Regulatory Stability', 174–5. 526 Ibid. 527 Ibid., 176–7.

528 Shemberg and Aizawa, 'Stabilisation Clauses', 39; Cotula, 'Reconciling Regulatory Stability', 173–4.

529 Cotula, 'Reconciling Regulatory Stability', 173–4; the Baku–Tbilisi–Ceyhan Pipeline Company, *BTC Human Rights Undertaking*. The Baku–Tbilsi–Ceyhan oil pipeline project was designed to transport oil from the Caspian Sea at Baku, Azerbaijan, across Azerbaijan, Georgia, and Turkey to emerge at Ceyhan on the Mediterranean coast of Turkey ready for transportation to Western markets. The project was controversial on a number of levels, including multiple human rights and environmental issues during construction and, once made public, the terms of the host state agreements for the operation of the pipeline. The Baku–Tbilisi–Ceyhan project is discussed in detail below in Chapter 4.

530 See, e.g., the discussion in Sheppard and Crockett, 'Stabilisation Clauses: A Threat'; Cotula, 'Reconciling Regulatory Stability'.

such agreements primarily adopt approaches that either ring-fence the investor from the effect of new regulation or require compensation for regulatory changes.[531] For this reason, again, it would seem that a significant hurdle to the realisation of more socially and environmentally balanced investor–state contracts is cultural.

On the whole, the underlying cultural approach within the investment community has tended to be one of hostility towards the enactment of new public welfare regulation. For example, Wälde and Ndi have drawn attention to the potential for new environmental measures to impact significantly upon investments and have argued that stabilisation clauses may be an appropriate way of ensuring they do not apply to an investor.[532] Of particular relevance to international efforts to address climate change are the comments that changes in environmental law can be prompted by new technologies, new perspectives, and new international standards, and that it is desirable to circumvent their operation and ensure their inapplicability to a foreign investor's operations:

> Perhaps most relevant at the moment is the imposition of new environmental obligations by subsequent regulation or by an administrative/judicial ruling reinterpreting existing law on which the investment decision may to some extent have been based. New environmental obligations – unpredicted and therefore not incorporated into the investment decision – can emerge from the application of existing law to newly emerging 'natural' situations and by the introduction, under existing law, of new techniques of environmental assessment and mitigation. Environmental law may therefore change through new interpretation, not untypical for the often very general and open-ended formulations in such laws, or by the introduction of completely new or amended environmental legislation. It can also change if hitherto not-applied environmental law is applied, perhaps in a discriminating manner only against 'deep-pocket' foreign investors. Such changes, unforeseen in content, scope, and impact by the company (and probably also by the government) at the time of the investment decision, may be prompted by the emergence of new technologies, by new perspectives on both the damages created by a project and the reasonableness of new ways to deal with them, by continuously emerging international standards, and by the emergence and increasing political

[531] Shemberg and Aizawa, 'Stabilisation Clauses', 39; see also the discussion in Maniruzzaman, 'The Pursuit', 156; see also Cotula, 'Reconciling Regulatory Stability', 168–71, 174.

[532] Wälde and Ndi, 'Stabilizing International Investment Commitments', 230–1; for a discussion emphasising respect for private property as a fundamental right, see Appleton, 'Regulatory Takings', 35–6, 39, 46–7.

influence of national or international environmental organizations. While environmental liability is seen as a major political risk in transition economies, unforeseen environmental opposition and restrictions constitute, at the moment, a major (and, in natural resources/energy projects, the prime) political risk facing developers of new industrial projects in Western countries. With this experience in mind, it is understandable that foreign investors will wish to protect their position at the moment of their most favorable bargaining power – i.e., when dealing with a weak (developing or transition) government anxious to attract investment before and during the negotiations for an attractive investment project.[533]

This approach suggests that it may be difficult to create more sustainability-oriented investor–state contracts. In their analysis, Wälde and Ndi frame environmental regulation as a negative to be frustrated – a political risk that requires neutralising. Stabilisation clauses are offered as a mechanism to implement that neutralisation, insulating investments from the application of new environmental regulation. For investors, the use of such clauses appears to have been an appealing option, their prevalence in current practice having been confirmed in the 2008 Shemberg and Aizawa report.[534] Given the purpose of stabilisation clauses, being to create less host state policy space and constrain options for new governmental action, their continued use in investor–state agreements is also likely to impact on the effectiveness of new climate-related measures. Accordingly, even though domestic regulation will be enacted to combat climate change, large segments of economic activity conducted by foreign investors may well remain exempt from its operation.

III. Conclusion

The questions explored in this chapter have arisen out of the multi-layered nature of the foreign investment-environmental protection discourse. In particular, the focus has been on the polarised positions that have largely characterised the interaction between international investment law and environmental issues. What emerges is, unsurprisingly, a picture of multiple sites of contestation and repetition of age-old patterns of engagement. In examining incidents and cases that have fuelled pressure to reshape international investment law, this chapter has

[533] Wälde and Ndi, 'Stabilizing', 230–1; see also the views expressed in Baker, 'Denial of Justice', 188–91.

[534] Shemberg and Aizawa, *Stabilization Clauses*.

argued that such tensions are symptomatic of the core character of modern international investment law, the fundamental tenets of which were forged during European political and commercial expansionism from the seventeenth to early twentieth centuries. Once such an historical account is adopted, the examples discussed reveal that, for all its appearance of neutrality, international investment law continues to reflect imperialist conceptualisations of the environment in two central ways – (i) the non-engagement of international investment law with the impact of investor activity on the local communities and the environment of the host state; and (ii) the framing of environmental regulation as a violation of investment treaties.

Illustrations of prevailing investor approaches to the use of the environment in host states were presented in this chapter's examination of the Ok Tedi Mine, Texaco in Ecuador, and Union Carbide in Bhopal, exemplifying the commodification of the environment for the use of foreign investors. The analysis in this chapter also demonstrated the manipulation of legal doctrine to legitimise that approach. I have argued here that this mode of interaction between investors, states, and affected communities, characterised by assertions, challenges, and responses to power, continues traditional patterns supporting the interests of the investor, excluding those of the host state, and seeking to neutralise threats to the dominant legal framework.

Reflecting on the historical context of investor–state arbitration, I have suggested in this chapter that the development of this dispute resolution mechanism also fits within this traditional framework of challenge and response. And through the categorisation of environmental regulation as indirect expropriation, a violation of national treatment requirements, and a breach of the fair and equitable treatment standard, that mechanism effectively operates as a tool with which to neutralise host state attempts to create space for environmental protection. Again, well-entrenched patterns of challenge and response find form.

I have argued that investor indifference to the condition of the environment of host states, and to the impact of their operations within them, can be seen as a part of a cultural approach to the host state that dominated the emergence of international investment law and has pervaded it ever since. The characterisation of environmental regulation as hostile to the interests of foreign investors and in need of neutralising is a modern manifestation of this investment culture of control and indifference grounded in imperialist frameworks. In being utilised to great effect to support the interests of foreign investors, international investment law has been a central tool in perpetuating that culture.

This book maintains that such a one-sided role for international investment law needs to change. And recently, there has been some movement to address the criticisms often directed at investor–state arbitration and investment treaties. In this regard, the consideration of environmental impact in the *Parkerings Award*[535] and the approach to environmental regulation in *Methanex*[536] are encouraging. Calls for an international legal framework to regulate the conduct of multinational corporations continue and the focus on infusing social and environmental responsibility practices throughout the foreign investment sector is sharpening. In particular, the corporate social responsibility movement and the emergence of the sustainable finance and responsible investment sectors point to new paths forward for international investment law. Accordingly, Chapter 4 examines these emerging 'hints at synergy' between the investment sector and environmental protection objectives and reflects upon the question: even with these shifts in approach, can such ingrained forms of interaction ever truly change?

535 *Parkerings-Compagniet AS* v. *Republic of Lithuania* (ICSID Arbitration Case No. ARB/05/8, Award of 11 September 2007).

536 *Methanex Corporation.*

4 Hints at synergy

The question with which I was faced at this point in my research was: is radical reform of international investment law realistic? And, if so, through what channels could such reshaping occur? Or, indeed, is it the case that the groundwork has, in one form or another, already begun? Reflecting on these issues, it seemed to me that new trends in corporate behaviour emerging over the last decade could, potentially, provide just such a catalyst for change and could, ultimately, influence the substantive development of international investment law.

The adoption of voluntary codes setting standards for environmental corporate conduct, the integration of corporate social responsibility (CSR) programmes, the establishment of 'ethical' investment funds, and the emergence of the 'sustainable finance' movement all reflect an increasing shift in emphasis in the business community towards accommodating public concerns at the role of multinational corporations in socially and environmentally harmful practices.[1] As attention has turned to the wider effects of corporate practices, companies have had to respond to pressure from consumers, non-governmental organisations, shareholders, and other stakeholders to improve their social and environmental performance.[2] For the corporate sector, the

[1] Assadourian, 'Transforming Corporations', 171–89; McBarnet, 'Corporate Social Responsibility', p. 9; OECD, *Corporate Responsibility*; Jeucken, *Sustainability in Finance*. 'Sustainable finance' is the term coined to describe the process of integrating environmental and social criteria into investment and financing decision-making. This concept is discussed in detail in section II of this chapter. Sustainable finance and CSR are closely interrelated and although this chapter considers them in separate sections for convenience of analysis, there are significant connections between the movements.

[2] OECD, *Foreign Direct Investment*, pp. 14–15; Gunningham and Sinclair, *Voluntary Approaches*; Cernea, 'The Ripple Effect', 65, 67–8.

development of codes of conduct and the embracing of the concept of CSR has been a strategic response to such pressures.[3] In this chapter, I examine those responses and explore their implications for international investment law.

In recent years, traditional conceptualisations of the environment developed within the foreign investment sector, and reinforced by international investment law, have been challenged by a complex range of factors. In particular, the drive to reshape the substance of international investment law has been given form and momentum within the wider context of the CSR and sustainable finance movements. As the concepts advocated by these movements become an increasingly accepted part of business practice, it seems that they also point to the future development of more socially and environmentally responsible principles of international investment law. They hint at possible future synergies between the foreign investment sector and environmental protection objectives and, indeed, they could provide the basis for a recharacterisation of the traditional foreign investor–host state relationship. Reflecting on these possibilities, I argue in this chapter that the CSR and sustainable finance movements could provide a key platform from which to bring about reform in the foreign investment sector. I also argue that when such initiatives are viewed through a constructivist prism,[4] they indicate pre-normative CSR activity already occurring within the investment field. Accordingly, it is projected that CSR programmes and voluntary code specifications will gradually become the expected minimum standard of conduct, will increasingly appear in soft law instruments, and may well, ultimately, manifest in the development of binding principles of international investment law.

In exploring this potential, section I of this chapter analyses key elements of CSR, the increasing role of law in the framing of expectations and requirements placed on companies via CSR, the emerging principles of sustainability and corporate social and environmental responsibility, and the implications of these developments for international investment law. Section II examines the possible role of the sustainable finance movement in the reform of international investment law. It considers the proliferation of voluntary codes of

[3] OECD, *Foreign Direct Investment*, pp. 14–15; Gunningham and Sinclair, *Voluntary Approaches*, p. 2.

[4] See the Introduction of this book for a discussion of constructivism and international law; see also Brunnée and Toope, 'International Law and Constructivism'.

environmental corporate conduct as an important manifestation of the sustainable finance and CSR movements. In addition, it also examines the emergence of socially responsible institutional investment as a generator of change in investment practice and law.

These new developments in multinational corporate conduct and foreign investment practices inevitably point to the question: why are they not yet reflected in international investment law? Chapter 3 argued that the reasons for this absence involve a complex interplay of the traditional foreign investor–host state relationship, the maintaining of entrenched links between the home state and their investors, and the use of legal mechanisms to reproduce economic imperialism. This chapter progresses that argument, proposing that new CSR and sustainability practices should be reflected in international investment law to assist with counteracting those traditional conceptualisations. Not that they are without their own problems, of course, and these are also explored. However, in arguing that the rules and principles of international investment law need to be adapted to reflect a more balanced, ecologically sustainable, and socially responsible approach to foreign investment, this chapter does propose that emerging CSR and sustainability principles are a potential channel through which that goal may be realised.

Although these new trends in corporate behaviour point to a more harmonious relationship for international investment law and environmental protection measures, the speed of any reconceptualisation process should not be overstated. At present, this CSR and sustainability activity is not reflected in prevailing approaches of foreign investors to the environment of the host state. Furthermore, the translation of CSR principles into the operations of multinational corporations abroad, and not merely within their home state, requires the overcoming of certain barriers. At the outset, there would appear to be difficulties posed by the status of corporations under international law. Although there has been some movement away from the restrictive approach, traditionally, multinational corporations are not considered subjects of international law, and, as such, it has been argued that international legal obligations cannot be imposed on them.[5] In many ways, however, a more challenging difficulty is cultural. Effective reform is not simply a matter of breaking down the conventional hostility of business to environmental issues, but also requires a conversion of the traditional

[5] See the discussion in Muchlinski, 'Corporate Social Responsibility', 431, 432–3; see also Zerk, *Multinationals*, pp. 72–6.

treatment of the host state within international investment law, the magnitude of such a task becoming apparent when its various manifestations are considered:

- The commodification of the environment of the host state for the use of the foreign investor.
- The non-engagement of international investment law with the effect of investor activity on the local communities and environment of the host state.
- The reproduction of imperialist patterns.
- The alignment of interests of private investors and home states.
- The present 'otherness' of the host state in international investment law.

As discussed in Chapter 3 of this book, attempted interference with the ability of the foreign investor to utilise the environment of the host state tends to be met with hostility.[6] To overcome this reflex reaction, the cultural shift required within the foreign investment sector will be significant and is likely to take some time, if it occurs at all. So it is with this in mind that I start exploring the idea of current CSR practices and the sustainable finance movement as representing an important place from which to begin transforming international investment law.

I. Corporate social and environmental responsibility

The underlying premise of CSR is not new. Questions surrounding the moral, social, and environmental responsibilities of commercial enterprise stretch back centuries.[7] However, a new energy has been injected into the concept over the last few decades – so much so, that it has attained a 'buzzword' status, if not yet a formal binding status, in international law and policy. Increasing concern at the magnitude of global social and environmental issues, and at the role of corporations in generating or exacerbating these problems, has fuelled this recent focus on CSR, driving attempts to reconcile financial requirements with a more broadly conceived set of corporate responsibilities.[8]

[6] See, e.g., Wälde and Kolo, 'Environmental Regulation'; Wälde and Ndi, 'Stabilizing International Investment', 230–1. For further examples of similar views see Baker, 'Denial of Justice', 187–91; see also the comments in Weiler, 'Good Faith', 701.

[7] Zerk, *Multinationals*, p. 15; Richardson, *Socially Responsible*, p. 108; Harwell Wells, 'Cycles of Corporate Social Responsibility', 77.

[8] Richardson, *Socially Responsible*, p. 108; McBarnet, 'Corporate Social Responsibility', 9; Zerk, *Multinationals*, pp. 16–23; see also Assadourian, 'The State of Corporate

This reframing of corporate obligation has been assisted by the introduction of the 'triple-bottom-line' approach, moving corporate responsibility beyond solely that of maximisation of profits for shareholders to encompass social and environmental accountability as well.[9] It has involved suggestions that fiduciary obligations of directors should be reconceived so as to encompass social and environmental responsibility to a wider set of stakeholders than shareholders.[10] The CSR discourse has also revolved around the motivation for voluntary corporate adoption of CSR policies, involving the consideration of the business case and ethical case rationales.[11] It seems, however, that legal obligation is increasingly associated with CSR, indicating pre-normative activity for this concept. Indeed, the debate has recently shifted to whether the adoption of CSR policies and practices is actually still voluntary or whether they have already attained a character that is inextricably entwined with legal obligation.[12] This has significant implications for the reshaping of international investment norms. As one aspect of the CSR movement has developed into a distinct category of 'socially responsible investment',[13] the evolution of more concrete legal principles in CSR also points to the potential for similar developments within the investment sector. For this reason, key issues in CSR and their implications for reform of international investment law are explored in the next sections of this chapter.

A. *Key elements of corporate social responsibility*

At the heart of the CSR discourse lies the question: what obligations do corporations owe to the communities within which they operate?[14] The different theories of obligation run the full spectrum of opinion. At one end, is the theory of shareholder primacy, under which the

Responsibility'; see also the discussion in Epstein, 'The Good Company'; Weissbrodt, 'International Standard-Setting', 374–5.

9 McBarnet, 'Corporate Social Responsibility', 9; Barnard, 'Corporate Boards', 302–3; Elkington, *Cannibals with Forks*.

10 Richardson, *Socially Responsible*, pp. 233–46; Worthington, 'Reforming Directors' Duties'; see the discussion in Williams and Conley, 'Triumph or Tragedy', 353–6.

11 Richardson, *Socially Responsible*, pp. 108–9; Gunningham, 'Corporate Environmental Responsibility', 476.

12 McBarnet, 'Corporate Social Responsibility', 11–13; Zerk, *Multinationals*, pp. 34–6.

13 See the discussion in Richardson, *Socially Responsible*, pp. 108–11; see also the discussion on socially responsible investment in Assadourian, 'The State', 581–3.

14 Zerk, *Multinationals*, p. 15; Harwell, 'The Cycles', 77; see also the discussion in Vives, 'Corporate Social Responsibility', 199; Kerr, 'The Creative Capitalism Spectrum', 852–6.

corporation's sole responsibility is, within the confines of the law, to maximise profit for its shareholders.[15] At the other end of the scale is the view that the corporate entity itself is a detriment to society.[16] The majority of CSR advocates take a view somewhere between these two extremes, generally arguing either that corporations' shareholder obligations do, in fact, require them to operate in a socially and environmentally responsible manner, or that corporations have responsibilities to a wider set of stakeholders than solely shareholders.[17]

1. Defining corporate social responsibility

The classical view of the corporation is as a private entity, the sole purpose of which is to generate profits for its shareholders. Within this theory, society benefits as a by-product of corporate economic activity with social benefits flowing indirectly from the economic prosperity of financially successful companies.[18] The notion of CSR challenges this traditional understanding of the role of the corporation.[19] Although there is no universal definition or agreement on the scope or extent of application of this concept, CSR explores the idea that social obligations do, may, or should attach to corporations.[20]

There are numerous positions within the CSR debate, each focusing on different factors, such as, for example:[21]

a) the corporation as a purely economic organisation versus a social construct;
b) the corporation as a private business or as an entity created by the state operating in the public sphere; and
c) the extent of a corporation's obligations to its shareholders relative to any obligations to stakeholders and the wider community.

[15] Zerk, *Multinationals*, p. 16; Vivas, 'Corporate Social Responsibility', 199; see, for an example of this view, Friedman, *Capitalism and Freedom*; see also the discussion of Friedman's views and other theories of corporate obligation in Brown, 'No Good Deed', 368–70.

[16] See, e.g., Bakan, *The Corporation*.

[17] Zerk, *Multinationals*, pp. 16–17; see the discussion in McBarnet, 'Corporate Social Responsibility', p. 9; see also the discussion in Budzynski, 'Can a Feminist Approach'.

[18] See the discussion of Friedman's views in Zerk, *Multinationals*, p. 16.

[19] Williams, 'Corporations Theory', 707.

[20] Ibid.; Ashford, 'What is the "New"', 1192; see also the discussion in Neal, 'Corporate Social Responsibility'.

[21] Williams, 'Corporations Theory'; see also the discussion on the role of business in society in Siegele and Ward, 'Corporate Social Responsibility', 136; see also the discussion in Branson, 'Corporate Governance'; see also the discussion in Choudhury, 'Serving Two Masters'.

There are also a variety of approaches to the notion of CSR itself, each with a slightly different nuance, examples of which are encapsulated in the following extracts:

a) ... corporate responsibility means that a corporation acts in an ecologically sustainable and socially beneficial manner – preventing ecological degradation, producing useful and healthy products, treating workers and host communities justly, and using its vast influence to improve the well-being of society and not just its bottom line.[22]

b) For ICC, corporate responsibility (CR) is the voluntary commitment by business to manage its activities in a responsible way. More broadly, CR includes the efforts by business to contribute to the society in which it operates.[23]

c) Corporate responsibility involves the search for an effective 'fit' between businesses and the societies in which they operate. The notion of 'fit' recognises the mutual dependence of business and society – a business sector cannot prosper if the society in which it operates is failing and a failing business sector inevitably detracts from general wellbeing. 'Corporate responsibility' refers to the actions taken by businesses to nurture and enhance this symbiotic relationship.[24]

d) CSR essentially involves a shift in the focus of corporate responsibility from profit maximisation for shareholders within the obligations of the law to responsibility to a broader range of *stake*holders, including communal concerns such as protection of the environment, and accountability on ethical as well as legal obligations. It is a shift from 'bottom line' to 'triple bottom line', as it is sometimes put, from 'profits; to 'people, planet and profits', or indeed to 'profits and principles'.[25]

e) Foreign direct investment benefits will also need to be more widely distributed and match in a more satisfactory manner the expectations of all stakeholders in civil society, governments, business, labour, environment and other non-governmental organisations. Increased direct investment, economic development and responsible corporate behaviour would now appear to be the critical components of the winning strategy.[26]

f) ... we campaign for the vision of a sustainable world in which corporations' drive for profit is balanced by the interest of society at large and respects human, social and environmental rights. To ensure such a vision, we are convinced that legally enforceable mechanisms based on internationally agreed standards and principles in the areas of human, social and

[22] Assadourian, 'Transforming Corporations', 172.

[23] International Chamber of Commerce, *The Role of the United Nations*.

[24] OECD, *Corporate Responsibility*, p. 7.

[25] McBarnet, 'Corporate Social Responsibility', 9. Emphasis in original.

[26] OECD, *Foreign Direct Investment*, p. 3.

environmental rights are necessary to reverse the unsustainable impacts of business activities.[27]

As illustrated above, agreement on the importance of the concept of CSR does not necessarily iron out the subtle differences in interpretation of the term and in the form it takes in practice. As noted by Zerk, the particular framing of the definition of CSR tends to reflect the position already held by the advocate.[28] For example, business lobby groups reiterate the voluntary nature of CSR, arguing that it entails taking action beyond legal requirements.[29] Non-governmental organisations (NGOs) often describe CSR in terms of obligations, ethical imperatives, or as a broad concept requiring positive action, not merely the avoidance of harm, such as, the production of environmentally friendly or socially beneficial goods, rather than only the employment of safe and non-damaging manufacturing processes.[30] This division is replicated in the discourse surrounding the motivation for corporate uptake of CSR policies – the business case and ethical case approaches.[31]

2. Corporate motivation: business case versus ethical case

The business case approach to CSR professes that operating as a 'good' global corporate citizen improves the financial performance of a company.[32] There is certainly a growing appreciation amongst business representatives that CSR can enhance the reputation of the corporation and avoid negative publicity.[33] A corporate culture of responsible

[27] Friends of the Earth Europe, *Corporate Campaign*.

[28] Zerk, *Multinationals*, pp. 29–30; see also the comments in Evans, 'New Collaborations', 314–15.

[29] Zerk, *Multinationals*, pp. 29–30; see, e.g., the comments of the ICC, *The Role of the United Nations*; see also the views of R. Kyte, Vice President for Business Advisory Services at the International Finance Corporation, in Kyte, 'Balancing Rights'; see also the discussion in Whitehouse, 'Corporate Social Responsibility'.

[30] Zerk, *Multinationals*, p. 30; see e.g. the description in Assadourian, 'Transforming Corporations', 172.

[31] Richardson, *Socially Responsible*, pp. 109–11; see also the discussion on this issue with specific reference to corporate environmental responsibility in Gunningham, 'Corporate Environmental Responsibility', 477–9.

[32] Assadourian, 'Transforming Corporations', 172–3; Richardson, *Socially Responsible*, p. 110; Gunningham, 'Corporate Environmental Responsibility', 477–80; Zerk, *Multinationals*, p. 33; Blackburn, 'Sustainability'; Guzy, 'Reconciling Environmentalist', 414; Forster, 'Environmental Responsibilities'; Di Leva, 'Sustainable Development', 17–18; Snierson, 'Green is Good'.

[33] Gunningham and Sinclair, *Voluntary Approaches*, pp. 2–7; Gunningham, 'Corporate Environmental Responsibility', 479–80; see also the discussion in Siegele and Ward; see also the discussion in Blackburn, 'Sustainability'; Newberg, 'Corporate Codes', 267–8.

environmental management is said to reduce commercial risks in foreign investment activities.[34] There is a sense that voluntary codes of environmental corporate conduct, initially developed to ensure environmental credibility and to maintain the so-called 'social licence to operate',[35] are increasingly going on to form the expected standards of environmental corporate behaviour generally.[36]

On the other hand, transformation underlies the ethical case for the adoption of CSR. Within this model, the corporation is framed as a socially and environmentally responsible entity that engages in commercial enterprise.[37] Its focus remains financial success and profits, but embedded within a CSR context, which requires social and environmental considerations to become an inherent part of the corporation's decision-making processes and operations.[38] This approach means that corporate decisions and activities can be justified solely on social and environmental grounds rather than relying on a business case justification.[39]

A controversial feature of the business case approach to CSR is that financial considerations still have a 'veto-like' primacy on social and environmental issues. In distinct contrast to the ethical model, the rationale behind the business-oriented approach means that where there are genuinely competing considerations, the financial factors can

[34] Forster, 'Environmental Responsibilities', 69–71, 73–4.

[35] The importance of maintaining environmental credibility and the 'social license to operate' is discussed in detail in Gunningham and Sinclair, *Voluntary Approaches*, pp. 2–7; Gunningham, 'Corporate Environmental Responsibility'.

[36] The Equator Principles, discussed below, is a recent example. See the discussion on the evolution of World Bank initiatives on socially and environmentally responsible codes of practice into expected standards or norms of corporate behaviour in Cernea, 'The Ripple Effect'; for a discussion of firm-based adoption by multinational corporations of global environmental standards, see Rock and Angel, *Industrial Transformation*, pp. 151, 170–6; as another example of the response in the private sector, see the advice given by Australian commercial law firm Allens Arthur Robinson to its clients:

> Having now been adopted by lenders who provide the bulk of project finance around the globe, the Equator Principles are close to becoming an industry standard so it is important that borrowers and lenders understand their potential impact on project financing transactions.

Allens Arthur Robinson, 'The Equator Principles – Guidelines for Responsible Project Financing', *Focus Project Finance*, August 2005, 1, available at http://www.aar.com.au (last accessed 15 December 2011).

[37] Richardson, *Socially Responsible*, pp. 109–10. [38] Ibid.

[39] Gunningham, 'Corporate Environmental Responsibility'; see also Gunningham, Kagan, and Thornton, *Shades of Green*, pp. 100–2.

still have an overwhelming influence in corporate decision-making.[40] In this way, the business case approach renders the adoption of CSR-related policies dependent on their acceptability to economic criteria, which rather begs the question of whether CSR is capable of inducing substantial change away from the 'business as usual' model.[41] This aspect, in particular, adds fuel to the 'voluntary versus mandatory' debate regarding CSR regulatory options. It highlights the contested viewpoints surrounding reliance on voluntary codes of conduct and other forms of 'reflexive' regulation to achieve uniformly effective CSR.[42] Given the predominance of the business case approach to CSR, this would also seem to provide weight to the argument that what is required to change corporate behaviour is legally enforceable CSR regulation.[43]

Perhaps causing these distinctions over the legal status of CSR to become less important, however, are the recent shifts within the discourse, now examining the often subtle interplay between forms of governance and legal tools.[44] A number of scholars argue that the lines between public and private CSR regulation are increasingly blurred, rendering the insistence on voluntarism by business groups less and less relevant.[45] For example, McBarnet points to the indirect means by which CSR is being progressively transformed from voluntary practice

[40] Richardson, *Socially Responsible*, p. 110; see also for a discussion on the limits of the business case approach to CSR, Davidsson, 'Legal Enforcement', 532; for arguments that corporate social responsibility constitutes an appropriation of morality to fit the rationality of the market, see Shamir, 'Corporate Social Responsibility'; see also the criticisms in Macleod, 'Corporate Social Responsibility', 545–6, 551–2.

[41] Richardson, *Socially Responsible*, p. 110; Blowfield and Frynas, 'Setting New Agendas', 512; see also the discussion in Fishman, 'Binding Corporations', 1447–50.

[42] 'Reflexive' regulation entails the use of mechanisms other than traditional 'command and control' legislation to induce certain behavioural outcomes, such as policy tools, incentive-based schemes, reporting initiatives, or taxing public 'bads'. See further on reflexive regulation, Richardson, *Socially Responsible*, p. 28; Teubner, 'Substantive and Reflexive Elements'; Ayres and Braithwaite, *Responsive Regulation*; Orts, 'Reflexive Environmental Law'.

[43] See the discussion in Richardson, *Socially Responsible*, pp. 109–11; see also Davidsson, 'Legal Enforcement', 547–53; see Deva, 'Sustainable Good Governance', 745–7; see, e.g., NGO commentary, Corporate Responsibility Coalition, *A Big Deal?*; see also World Wildlife Fund, *Comments on the Green Paper*.

[44] See, e.g., McBarnet, 'Corporate Social Responsibility', pp. 12–13, 31–44; see also Richardson, *Socially Responsible*, pp. 194–5, 380–2; see also the discussion in Gill, 'Corporate Governance'; see further the doctrinal discussion in Testy, '"New" Corporate Social Responsibility'.

[45] McBarnet, 'Corporate Social Responsibility', 12–13, 31–44; Wood, 'Green Revolution'; see also Picciotto, 'Rights, Responsibilities', 144–50.

into legal requirement.[46] She argues that states, civil society, and corporations are indirectly compelling CSR practices through new corporate disclosure regulation,[47] shareholder activism,[48] private law remedies under the United States' Alien Tort Claims Act,[49] false advertising legislation,[50] and contractual obligations imposed on corporate suppliers.[51] McBarnet does not suggest that indirect mechanisms are the sole answer to inducing more socially responsible corporate behaviour. Indeed, she discusses the role of an international regulatory framework, the multi-layered forms of CSR political and legal interaction, and the need for a cultural shift in the dismissive approach of multinational corporations to both national and international regulation as instruments of control of global business.[52] Her key points, however, are that it is no longer accurate to depict CSR policies and practices purely as voluntary, that the role of law in CSR is manifesting in a variety of ways, and that these trends are likely to continue in the future to cement the legal character of CSR.[53]

In a slightly different vein to McBarnet, Wood also addresses the shifting emphasis of law in CSR. However, rather than taking a broad approach encompassing numerous mechanisms, Wood adopts a very specific focus. He examines the development, implementation, and monitoring of voluntary corporate environmental management systems.[54]

[46] McBarnet, 'Corporate Social Responsibility', 31–44.

[47] Ibid., 32–7; see, e.g., Companies Act (UK) 2006; Occupational Pension Schemes (Investment, and Assignment, Forfeiture, Bankruptcy) (Amendment) Regulations 1999 (UK), SI 1999/1849; European Accounts Modernisation Directive 2003/51/EC No. 2003 L178/2; Investment Company Act (United States) 2003; see also the discussion on disclosure, voluntary codes, and the law in Monsma and Buckley, 'Non-Financial Corporate Performance'.

[48] McBarnet, 'Corporate Social Responsibility', 37–8.

[49] Alien Tort Claims Act (United States) 1789, 28 USC §1350.

[50] McBarnet, 'Corporate Social Responsibility', pp. 38–42; see e.g. *Kasky* v. *Nike, Inc.*, 45 P 3d 243 (Cal. 2002) in which it was argued that Nike had breached Californian regulations by stating that its suppliers were in compliance with its code of conduct when, in fact, sweatshop conditions were operated by suppliers; see also the discussion in Lu, 'Corporate Codes of Conduct'.

[51] McBarnet, 'Corporate Social Responsibility', 42–3. [52] Ibid., 44–56.

[53] Ibid., 54–6.

[54] Wood, 'Green Revolution', 123; Wood defines an environmental management system as 'a system of policies, procedures, structures, and practices that enables an organization to anticipate, identify, and manage the environmental impacts of its activities.' ISO 14000 is an example of an attempt to standardise such systems, setting out the requirements for an ISO-compliant environmental management system. For a different approach again to assessing environmental management performance, see Johnson, 'Do the Good Guys Always Wear Green?'.

He argues that the roles of private standardisation bodies, public authorities, and the law are entwining in the design and application of these systems, transcending traditional categories of governmental and private sector regulation.[55] Wood points to the political nature of industry-initiated schemes, to the increasing adoption by public authorities of corporate environmental management systems for use in governmental policy instruments, to the incorporation of the standards in these systems into legislation, and to the influence of public authorities on the substance of the standards.[56] Again, the idea is that the law, government, private authority, and power inequalities are deeply involved in the operation of voluntary corporate environmental management systems – to a much greater extent than is acknowledged by portraying CSR initiatives as voluntary.

Echoing these CSR-related regulatory developments, recent trends emerging in corporate practice reflect the view that corporations do have obligations to operate in a socially and environmentally responsible manner.[57] Increasingly, multinational corporations are behaving as if they have responsibilities to entities beyond their shareholders.[58] Corporate cooperation with governments, NGOs, and local stakeholders is now widely regarded as a key component in achieving the Millennium Development Goals and global sustainable development,[59] the implications of which for multinational corporations include the need to modify, or change entirely, the way in which they conduct their foreign investment activities. The globalised environment also means that foreign investor operations in developing countries are already being assessed by civil society according to socially and environmentally responsible standards of conduct, and this, in turn, functions as an

[55] Wood, 'Green Revolution', 125–6.

[56] Ibid., 124–6; see also the discussion in Neal, 'Corporate Social Responsibility', 469–73; see more generally on the issue of private authority within public regulation, Freeman, 'The Private Role in Public Governance'.

[57] Richardson and Wood, 'Environmental Law', pp. 1, 11–12; Moore Dickerson, 'How Do Norms'.

[58] Moore Dickerson, 'How Do Norms', 1436–47. In particular, Moore Dickerson discusses corporate engagement with the working conditions of their employees and those of their subsidiaries and suppliers, with the anti-corruption movement, and with collectively held human rights. See also the discussion on a paradigm shift in corporate management towards environmentally sustainable practices in Barnard, 'Corporate Boards', 291–2, 301.

[59] Richardson and Wood, 'Environmental Law', 11–12; see United Nations, *United Nations Millennium Development Goals*.

informal enforcement mechanism of CSR expectations.[60] This market pressure for improved corporate conduct, greater transparency, and more expansive forms of corporate accountability is continuing to grow – and corporations are responding to that informal demand for behavioural change.[61] Not only are CSR expectations shifting the culture in which multinational corporations operate, they are driving change in the behaviour of corporate actors, and, in so doing, are contributing to the future crystallisation of what Moore Dickerson terms a 'norm of corporate social responsibility'.[62]

B. Emerging principles of sustainability and corporate social and environmental responsibility

At a fundamental level, these issues of corporate conduct and norm-creation also engage more philosophical questions as to which sets of values should be reflected within CSR requirements – what assumptions, ideologies, and outcomes are involved in seeking to infuse corporate activity with ethics-based approaches grounded in a global framework, and, indeed, also in continued corporate resistance to such pressure?[63] These are questions for which there are no straightforward answers and which have potentially confronting implications for claims to universality of a CSR value system. It is unsurprising, therefore, that the discourse has, in many ways, side-stepped these issues and turned already to principles and standards from international labour instruments, international environmental law, and human rights law to explore potential content for emerging principles of CSR.[64]

This process of identifying the substantive elements of CSR norms is examined in the sections below, as are their potential impacts on the character of international investment law. A combination of principles emerging out of international environmental law, sustainable development law, CSR standards, and the sustainable finance movement could clearly influence international investment law and foreign investment practices in numerous ways. Their incorporation into investment

60 McBarnet, 'Corporate Social Responsibility', 14–17; see also the discussion in Bunn, 'Global Advocacy'; see also the discussion on reputational risk as a driver of corporate compliance with human rights norms, in Keenan, 'Financial Globalization'.

61 Bunn, 'Global Advocacy'; McBarnet, 'Corporate Social Responsibility', 14–17; Moore Dickerson, 'How Do Norms'.

62 Moore Dickerson, 'How Do Norms'.

63 See the discussion in Muchlinski, 'International Business Regulation', 81.

64 Ibid.; Zerk, *Multinationals*, pp. 263–76.

decision-making and dispute resolution could reorient the sole focus on investor protection that currently dominates international investment law, requiring the consideration of a broader set of issues, rules, and stakeholders. In particular, principles of corporate social and environmental responsibility and of ecologically sustainable development would assist with addressing the traditional relationship between foreign investor and the environment of the host state, the non-engagement of international investment law with the impact of investor activity on the local communities and environment of the host state, investor accountability issues, and the cultural framework within which transnational investment activity occurs.

1. The process of norm-creation and corporate social responsibility

The emergence of norms is an interactive process involving the assertion of principles, identification of behaviour reflecting their content, and a belief in the legal character of the new principles.[65] It is a gradual, continuous process of evolution and reinforcement of concepts, expected conduct, dialogue amongst actors on the international plane, and assimilation of international principles into domestic law, policy, and practices.[66] Traditionally, of course, norm-creation has been solely the realm of states.[67] A rule of customary international law crystallises as such when there is consistent state practice accompanied by *opinio juris*, being the belief that states are legally obligated to so act.[68] Although it remains the case that states ultimately confer legal status on a concept either through its acceptance as a rule of customary international law or its inclusion in treaties, recent transformations in international law-making have seen non-state actors impacting on the evolution of principles of international law.[69] Complex processes have become

[65] Moore Dickerson, 'How Do Norms', 1433–4; Brownlie, *Principles*, pp. 6–10; for a constructivist account of the emergence of norms in international law, see Arend, 'Do Legal Rules', 128–40.

[66] Brownlie, *Principles*, pp. 6–10; Arend, 'Do Legal Rules', 128–40; Braithwaite and Drahos, *Global Business Regulation*, p. 32; Koh, 'Review Essay', 2603; Riedel, 'Standards and Sources'; Chayes and Handler Chayes, *The New Sovereignty*, pp. 112–34.

[67] Brierly, *The Law*, p. 1; Sands, 'Turtles and Torturers'; Triggs, *International Law*, pp. 11–12, 23; Danilenko, *Law-Making*, pp. 75–87.

[68] Brierly, *The Law*, pp. 59–62; Brownlie, *Principles*, pp. 6–10; Zerk, *Multinationals*, p. 262; Meron, 'The Continuing Role', 239.

[69] Sands, 'Turtles and Torturers'; Crawford, *International Law*, pp. 19–22; Sands, 'The Environment'; Spiro, 'Globalization'; Gunning, 'Modernizing', 221; Mertus,

engaged, in which the activities of international organisations, NGOs, multinational corporations, and international financial institutions are contributing significantly to the development of emerging principles of corporate social and environmental responsibility for the financing and investment sectors.[70]

From a constructivist perspective, 'soft law' instruments and other CSR initiatives, whether originating from states, NGOs, industry, or international organisations, are creating pre-normative 'noise'.[71] The multitude of instruments, codes, concepts, standards, and policies related to CSR specifications have not only firmly placed the issue on the international agenda, but are also part of the process of exploring the most effective mechanisms to bring about more socially and environmentally responsible corporate conduct. At the same time, this interplay of actors, instruments, and differing forms of CSR implementation is also leading to the internalisation of a CSR rationale within the business community – in other words, the normalisation or mainstreaming of CSR within the private sector.[72] It also constitutes a mutually reinforcing mode of interaction between emerging norms and corporate conduct.[73] Of course, the significance of this trend should not be overstated. CSR has not yet crystallised into a rule of customary international law. The conduct of states does not consistently reflect the existence of such a rule.[74] On a number of levels, however, it does appear that state behaviour is being influenced by the pre-normative CSR activities of non-state actors – and this points to the future emergence of international customary rules on CSR.[75] What can be said is that CSR principles are in the process of emerging; they are shaping the discourse; they are creating expectations

'Considering Nonstate Actors', 537, 562; Koh, 'Transnational Legal Process', 203–4; Mertus, 'Doing Democracy Differently'. The transformations in international law are discussed in detail below in Chapter 5.

70 Moore Dickerson, 'How Do Norms', 1433–4; Picciotto, 'Rights'; Hunter, 'Civil Society', 437–8, 467–9.

71 See the discussion in Zerk, *Multinationals*, 101–2; see also Brunnée and Toope, 'International Law'; for a discussion on the role of soft law, states and non-state actors in the process of international legalisation, see Abbott and Snidal, 'Hard and Soft Law', 421–3.

72 Gill, 'Corporate Governance', 461–2; Abbott and Snidal, 'Strengthening International Regulation'.

73 Moore Dickerson, 'How Do Norms', 1433; Shaffer, 'How Business Shapes Law'; Steinhardt, 'Soft Law', 934–6.

74 Zerk, *Multinationals*, pp. 276, 299–300.

75 Ibid., pp. 243, 262–3; Moore Dickerson, 'How Do Norms', 1433, 1460.

of state and corporate conduct; and they are underpinning calls for a multilateral treaty on CSR.[76]

(a) CSR-related norms

For many scholars, the CSR discourse has now advanced to a point where it is appropriate to speculate on which concepts or standards could be considered emerging principles of international law on corporate social and environmental responsibility and accountability.[77] In essence, such newly proffered norms are mostly drawn from international environmental law, national environmental regulatory mechanisms, international human rights law, international labour standards, international law on sustainable development, corporate practice, standards developed by international organisations, administrative principles on public participation, and NGO commentary.[78] In particular, Zerk identifies the following as concepts that may well be used to found a treaty-based CSR regime or that have the potential to evolve into rules of customary international law on CSR: minimum international health, safety, and environmental standards; supply-chain responsibility; sustainable development; obligations to warn of dangers; obligations to consult; the precautionary principle; environmental impact assessment; procedural requirements for openness and transparency; and external monitoring.[79]

Indeed, Muchlinski refers to the 'General Policies' of the Organisation for Economic Cooperation and Development (OECD) Guidelines on Multinational Enterprises (the OECD Guidelines)[80] as reflecting 'an emerging consensus on the social obligations of MNEs [multinational

[76] Zerk, *Multinationals*, pp. 243–4, 262–3; see the discussion in Bunn, 'Global Advocacy', pp. 1304–6; McCorquodale, 'Human Rights and Global Business', 89, 111–14; for an example of a CSR treaty proposal, see Friends of the Earth, *Towards Binding Corporate Accountability*.

[77] See, e.g., Zerk, *Multinationals*, pp. 262–77; see also the discussion in Hunter, 'Civil Society Networks', 437–8, 477; see also Williams and Conley, 'Corporate Social Responsibility', 102–4; for a discussion on emerging CSR norms of international sustainable mineral development law, see Seck, 'Home State Responsibility'.

[78] See, e.g., Zerk, *Multinationals*, pp. 262–77; see also the discussion in Hunter, 'Civil Society Networks', 437–8, 477; Williams and Conley, 'Corporate Social Responsibility'.

[79] Zerk, *Multinationals*, pp. 263–76; for a discussion on the contentious nature of establishing the scope for corporate responsibilities, see Mares, 'Transnational Corporate Responsibility'.

[80] OECD, *OECD Guidelines*.

enterprises]'.[81] This particular use of terminology indicates an important shift in the language surrounding corporate responsibility. In describing a general acceptance of the existence of corporate 'social obligations', Muchlinksi exemplifies an increasing trend in identifying, as well as in fact contributing to, the constructivist pre-normative process of internalisation of concepts and the current cementing of expected standards of corporate behaviour into legal principles. The General Policies of the OECD Guidelines are wide-ranging in scope, and illustrate the expansive direction of these solidifying expectations:

Enterprises should take fully into account established policies in the countries in which they operate, and consider the views of other stakeholders. In this regard, enterprises should:

1. Contribute to economic, social and environmental progress with a view to achieving sustainable development.
2. Respect the human rights of those affected by their activities consistent with the host government's international obligations and commitments.
3. Encourage local capacity building through close co-operation with the local community, including business interests, as well as developing the enterprise's activities in domestic and foreign markets, consistent with the need for sound commercial practice.
4. Encourage human capital formation, in particular by creating employment opportunities and facilitating training opportunities for employees.
5. Refrain from seeking or accepting exemptions not contemplated in the statutory or regulatory framework related to environmental, health, safety, labour, taxation, financial incentives, or other issues.
6. Support and uphold good corporate governance principles and develop and apply good corporate governance practices.
7. Develop and apply effective self-regulatory practices and management systems that foster a relationship of confidence and mutual trust between enterprises and the societies in which they operate.
8. Promote employee awareness of, and compliance with, company policies through appropriate dissemination of these policies, including through training programmes.
9. Refrain from discriminatory or disciplinary action against employees who make *bona fide* reports to management or, as appropriate, to the competent public authorities, on practices that contravene the law, the *Guidelines* or the enterprise's policies.

[81] Muchlinksi, 'Corporate Social Responsibility', 637, 643–4.

10. Encourage, where practicable, business partners, including suppliers and subcontractors, to apply principles of corporate conduct compatible with the *Guidelines*.
11. Abstain from any improper involvement in local political activities.[82]

The United Nations Norms on the Responsibilities of Transnational Corporations and Other Business Enterprises with Regard to Human Rights (the UN Norms)[83] is another important example of the trend towards specifying CSR expectations and establishing the substance of emerging CSR principles. The UN Norms focus on the direct application of international human rights obligations to multinational corporations. This departure from traditional state-centred doctrine is introduced on the basis that such companies are 'organs of society' and therefore 'are also responsible for promoting and securing the human rights set forth in the Universal Declaration of Human Rights'.[84] It was this attempt at direct application that proved to be the most controversial aspect of the UN Norms, generating a visceral response from some quarters.[85] Although the UN Norms embodied a novel approach to giving effect to international corporate responsibility, imposing international obligations on non-state actors is not without precedent.[86] As such, conceptually, the mechanism is not as problematic as it is, at times, portrayed.[87] Reflecting the controversy that surrounded its attempted reshaping

[82] OECD, *OECD Guidelines*. The OECD Guidelines also contain specific sections on, amongst others, environmental protection, labour standards, disclosure procedures, and corruption.

[83] United Nations Economic and Social Council, *Norms on the Responsibilities of Transnational Corporations and Other Business Enterprises with Regard to Human Rights*, UN ESCOR, 55th session, Agenda item 4, UN Doc E/CN.4/Sub.2/2003/12/Rev.2 (2003).

[84] Ibid., Preamble; see for further information on the UN Norms, Weissbrodt and Kruger, 'Norms on the Responsibilities'.

[85] See, e.g., International Chamber of Commerce and the International Organisation of Employers, *Joint Views of the IOE and ICC on the Draft "Norms on the Responsibilities of Transnational Corporations and Other Business Enterprises with Regard to Human Rights"* (March 2004), available at www.reports-and-materials.org/IOE-ICC-views-UN-norms-March-2004.doc (last accessed 15 December 2011); see the discussion on responses to the UN Norms in Kinley and Chambers, 'The UN Human Rights', 447–9; see also the discussion in Corporate Europe Observatory, 'Shell Leads'.

[86] Zerk, *Multinationals*, pp. 76–83; Kinley and Chambers, 'The UN Human Rights', 479–80; Kinley and Tadaki, 'From Talk to Walk', 993–4; Clapham, *Human Rights Obligations*, pp. 59–83; Stephens, 'The Amorality of Profit'; Nolan, 'With Power', 584–6, 600; Deva, 'Human Rights Violations', 48–56.

[87] Nolan, 'With Power', 584–6, 600; Kinley and Chambers, 'The UN Human Rights', 447–9; see also Ruggie, *Interim Report* [60]–[65].

of corporate obligations, the UN Norms have remained a non-binding instrument. That does not mean, however, that it is without legal significance. Indeed, the structuring of the norms as directly applicable to multinational corporations can, in fact, be viewed as part of a gradual process of normalising the idea that entities other than states owe obligations at the international level. Furthermore, the instrument also illustrates what Braithwaite and Drahos describe as 'modelling' in the developmental stages of law-making.[88] In this respect, not only do the UN Norms contribute to the emergence of CSR principles on human rights, but they also provide a template on which to base any future initiatives, or, perhaps, even a binding multilateral agreement on corporate conduct.[89]

Explorations into the evolution of CSR principles and into developing an international regulatory framework to govern the conduct of multinational corporations are still at an early stage.[90] However, they do point to a new direction in both business practices and in the conceptualisation of approaches to international regulation of multinational corporations.[91] In much the same way, they also foreshadow future directions in international investment law, including the possible development of socially and environmentally responsible investment principles and the balancing of investor protection with investor responsibilities.

2. CSR-related norms and international investment law

Earlier chapters of this book have illustrated that the core objectives of international investment law are concerned solely with investor protection. Despite the small steps discussed below, there remains, on the whole, very little movement from within governmental and arbitral investment circles to redress this imbalance by introducing investor responsibility principles into international investment agreements or

88 Braithwaite and Drahos, *Global Business Regulation*, pp. 539–43; Muchlinski, 'Corporate Social', 658.

89 Muchlinski, 'Corporate Social', 658; Picciotto, 'Rights'; see also the discussion on 'international standard-setting' in Weissbrodt, 'International Standard-Setting'; Kinley, Nolan and Zerial, 'The Norms', 459, 460; Backer, 'Multinational Corporations'.

90 Zerk, *Multinationals*, p. 277 Kinley, Nolan, and Zerial, 'The Norms', 460; Weissbrodt, 'Corporate Social Responsibility'.

91 McBarnet, 'Corporate Social Responsibility'; Zerk, *Multinationals*; Weissbrodt, 'Corporate Social Responsibility'; see the critique of voluntary approaches in McInerney, 'Putting Regulation Before Responsibility'; see also the discussion on CSR regulation through international transparency and disclosure requirements in Backer, 'From Moral Obligation'.

investor–state arbitration.[92] Lack of political will on the part of capital-exporting states has been identified as a significant reason for this inactivity.[93] I would also suggest that the dominance of the traditional foreign investor conceptualisation of the host state and its embodiment within international investment law is a further reason for the state of inertia on this issue.

Pressure to reform this elemental nature of international investment law, however, continues to increase from NGOs, media, affected communities, scholars, and host states, and remains a potent source of tension surrounding this field of law.[94] Somewhat ironically, pressure is also being generated by the shifting practices of corporations.[95] In this regard, it can be seen that the continuous interaction between business response and the modern CSR movement is gradually altering the cultural environment in which transnational business is conducted. Arguably, it is driving change towards more socially responsible corporate conduct and is advancing the development of CSR principles. And, in so doing, it is also contributing to the pressure to reshape international investment law and balance investor rights with responsibilities.[96]

(a) Encouraging signs

Although capital-exporting states largely remain reluctant to include substantive investor responsibilities within international investment agreements,[97] there are now encouraging indications that the legal side of the investment sector is beginning to respond to shifting business cultures and external pressures to reform.[98] Labelled as a 'new generation'

[92] Muchlinski, 'Corporate Social', 681. Problems with the current system of investor–state arbitration are discussed in Chapters 3, 6, and 7.

[93] Muchlinski, 'Corporate Social', 681; van Harten, *Investment Treaty Arbitration*, p. 179; Cosbey et al., *Investment and Sustainable Development*.

[94] The withdrawal of Bolivia from the Convention on the Settlement of Investment Disputes between States and Nationals of Other States (ICSID Convention) is an example of host state protest at the effect of investor protections under bilateral investment treaties. Bolivia gave notification of its withdrawal to ICSID on 2 May 2007. See the commentary from IISD, 'Bolivia Notifies World Bank of Withdrawal from ICSID, pursues BIT Revisions', *Investment Treaty News*, 9 May 2007, available at www.bilaterals.org/article.php3?id_article=8221 (last accessed 15 December 2011); see also the critique in Soloway, 'Environmental Regulation'; Bernasconi-Osterwalder and Brown Weiss, 'International Investment Rules', p. 263.

[95] Keenan, 'Financial Globalization', 513, 522–3, 560–2.

[96] Muchlinski, 'Corporate Social', 682–4; Picciotto, 'Rights', 132–3.

[97] Muchlinski, 'Corporate Social', 681.

[98] Subedi, *International Investment Law*, pp. 157–9.

of bilateral investment treaties,[99] several recent international investment agreements have introduced express references to sustainable development, protection of the environment, and the health and safety of the public.[100]

(i) New Model BITs for Canada and the United States Appreciation amongst developed states of the potential policy constraints posed by international investment law has increased significantly as a result of the Canadian and American experience under the North American Free Trade Agreement (NAFTA).[101] Both Canada and the United States have had investor claims filed against them, challenging regulatory measures aimed at protection of public health and the environment.[102] Experiencing investor–state arbitration from the perspective of a host state has forced these traditionally strong advocates of high-level investor protection to reassess the impact of those rules.[103] This shift in perception was given a concrete manifestation in the development of the new United States' and Canadian model bilateral investment treaties in 2004, the United States having then conducted a further review that resulted in the issuing of its latest model in 2012 (respectively, the

[99] The term 'new generation BITs' has been widely adopted to refer to recent bilateral investment treaties that include references to sustainable development, labour laws, or protection of the environment in an attempt to address host state interests, see further the discussion in Shan, 'From "North–South Divide"', 652, 656.

[100] Ibid.; Newcombe, 'Sustainable Development', 399; see e.g. the United States–Uruguay Bilateral Investment Treaty, Treaty between the United States of America and the Oriental Republic of Uruguay Concerning the Encouragement and Reciprocal Protection of Investment (2005), available at www.unctad.org/sections/dite/iia/docs/bits/US_Uruguay.pdf (last accessed 15 March 2009); see also the Canada–Peru BIT, Agreement between Canada and the Republic of Peru for the Promotion and Protection of Investments (2006), available at www.international.gc.ca/trade-agreements-accords-commerciaux/assets/pdfs/Canada-Peru10nov06-en.pdf (last accessed 4 April 2009).

[101] North American Free Trade Agreement (NAFTA), adopted 17 December 1992, 1992 32 ILM 612 (entered into force 1 January 1994); Van Harten, *Investment Treaty Arbitration*, p. 146; Sands, *Lawless World*, pp. 121–2, 139–41.

[102] Notable examples include *Methanex Corporation* v. *United States of America* (2005) 44 *International Legal Materials* 1345; *S.D. Myers, Inc* v. *Canada*, Partial Award (Decision on the Merits), November 2000; *Ethyl Corporation* v. *Canada*, Jurisdiction Phase (1999) 38 *International Legal Materials* 708.

[103] Shan, 'From "North–South Divide"', 650–3; Sands, *Lawless World*, pp. 121–2, 139–41; McIlroy, 'Canada's New Foreign Investment Protection', 646; Newcombe and Paradell, *Law and Practice of Investment Treaties*, p. 61.

United States Model BIT and the Canadian Model BIT).[104] It should be noted that although there are some new aspects to the 2012 Model, it does not, in fact, differ greatly from the 2004 Model and no changes were made to the substantive investment protections. In this respect, it was disappointing that the opportunity was not taken to build significantly on the reformist indicators of the 2004 Model.

a. Beginning to incorporate sustainability

Engaging with a range of non-investment issues, these model BITs have introduced several elements that may begin to reorient the one-sided emphasis of international investment agreements. For example, the Canadian Model BIT specifically incorporates sustainable development into its preamble in the following way:

> Recognizing that the promotion and the protection of investments of investors of one Party in the territory of the other Party will be conducive to the stimulation of mutually beneficial business activity, to the development of economic cooperation between them and to the promotion of sustainable development.[105]

This provision stops short of requiring the encouragement of sustainable development. However, the express reference to the promotion of sustainable development sends a new signal concerning emphasis and context, and, potentially, could be used as an interpretive aid in resolving disputes to allow for more sustainability-oriented interpretations of the agreement's substantive obligations. Manifesting in a different form, but with an essentially similar purpose, the United States Model BIT expressly introduces into the preamble of the bilateral investment treaty consideration of the interaction between investor activities and the wider concerns of the host state:

[104] United States State Department, Treaty between the Government of the United States of America and the Government of [Country] Concerning the Encouragement and Reciprocal Protection of Investments (2004) (United States' 2004 Model BIT), available at www.state.gov/documents/organization/117601.pdf (last accessed 21 March 2010); United States State Department, Treaty between the Government of the United States of America and the Government of [Country] Concerning the Encouragement and Reciprocal Protection of Investments (2012) (United States' 2012 Model BIT), available at www.ustr.gov/sites/default/files/BIT%20text%20for%20ACIEP%20Meeting.pdf (last accessed 25 August 2012); Canada, Model Foreign Investment Protection Agreement (2004) (Canadian Model BIT), available at www.international.gc.ca/assets/trade-agreements-accords-commerciaux/pdfs/2004-FIPA-model-en.pdf (last accessed 29 April 2009).

[105] Canadian Model BIT, Preamble.

> Desiring to achieve these objectives in a manner consistent with the protection of health, safety, and the environment, and the promotion of internationally recognized labor rights.[106]

In a progressive move, the United States Model BIT also seeks to address the issue of investor challenges to public welfare regulation through a tightening of the provisions on expropriation:

> Except in rare circumstances, non-discriminatory regulatory actions by a Party that are designed and applied to protect legitimate public welfare objectives, such as public health, safety, and the environment, do not constitute indirect expropriation.[107]

This is a particularly significant step, as it is directed towards the actual scope of the guaranteed protection. The carve-out is, of course, limited to allegations of expropriation and does not remove public welfare regulation from the ambit of challenge as violations of the fair and equitable treatment standard or national treatment requirements. Accordingly, these other investor protection guarantees still remain potent constraints on governmental decision-making and regulation in the public interest.[108] Attempting to clarify the application of the fair and equitable treatment standard in the United States Model BIT, Article 5 provides that the host state 'shall accord to covered investments treatment in accordance with customary international law, including fair and equitable treatment and full protection and security.'[109] The difficulty is that substantial controversy still surrounds both the content of the fair and equitable treatment standard at customary international law and the way in which the customary rule interacts with the form it takes within bilateral investment treaties.[110] For all the apparent progress in this modification, therefore, it may have minimal practical effect on the way in which the fair and equitable standard is invoked.

[106] United States' Model BIT, Preamble. [107] Ibid., Art. 4(b), Annex B.

[108] See, e.g., awards finding violations of fair and equitable treatment in *Azurix Corp.* v. *Republic of Argentina* (ICSID Case No. ARB/01/12, Award of July 14 2006); *Tecnicas Medioambientales Tecmed, SA* v. *United Mexican States* (2004) 43 *International Legal Materials* 133; see also the discussion in Sornarajah, 'The Fair and Equitable Standard', p. 165; see also the discussion on national treatment requirements in DiMascio and Pauwelyn, 'Nondiscrimination in Trade', 59, 67–8.

[109] United States' Model BIT, Art. 5; see the discussion in Newcombe, 'Sustainable Development', 401–2; see also the discussion in Ryan, 'Meeting Expectations', 756–760.

[110] See the discussion in Newcombe, 'Sustainable Development', 402; Ryan, 'Meeting Expectations', 756–60.

The United States Model BIT also includes specific references to the need for environmental sensitivity, stating that:

> Nothing in this Treaty shall be construed to prevent a Party from adopting, maintaining, or enforcing any measure otherwise consistent with this Treaty that it considers appropriate to ensure that investment activity in its territory is undertaken in a manner sensitive to environmental concerns.[111]

Again, there is somewhat of an internally counterproductive effect with this provision. In one sense, its inclusion indicates that consideration is to be given to environmental protection objectives when assessing investor claims of treaty violation via environmental measures. However, at the same time, it can be little more than an interpretive aid as the words 'otherwise consistent with this Treaty' ensure that it does not curb or override substantive investor protections guranteed in the bilateral investment treaty.[112]

Borrowing from trade law, the Canadian Model BIT introduces a 'General Exceptions' provision comparable to that seen in World Trade Organisation (WTO) instruments.[113] Once more, this arguably provides a further tool to delineate the scope of investor protections and limit their application to regulatory measures. It is questionable, however, whether this exception improves on the current host state position, as measures must still meet stringent requirements relating to their application.[114] For the section to be invoked successfully, the challenged regulation must not have been applied in a manner that would arbitrarily or unjustifiably discriminate between investments or have constituted a disguised restriction on investment.[115] As these very allegations are often at the heart of investor complaints aimed at the operation of new regulatory measures, even under the new approach of the Canadian Model BIT, public welfare regulation remains exposed.

b. *Using the Model BITs*

It has been argued that the United States' and Canadian model BITs have narrowed the reach of investor protections and reduced the level of

[111] United States' Model BIT, Art. 12.
[112] Newcombe, 'Sustainable Development', 400.
[113] Canadian Model BIT, Art. 10; see, e.g., General Agreement on Tariffs and Trade, Annex 1A, Agreement Establishing the World Trade Organization, opened for signature 15 April 1994, (1994) 33 ILM 28, Art. XX (entered into force 1 January 1995).
[114] Newcombe, 'Sustainable Development', 401.
[115] Canadian Model BIT, Art. 10.

protection available to North American investors.[116] There have certainly been refinements. However, other than a more nuanced approach to indirect expropriation, the substantive host state obligations have largely been left intact, sustainability requirements have not been incorporated into the substantive provisions, and corresponding investor responsibilities have not been introduced. But what these model BITs have done is to include new elements that indicate a shift in perspective and suggest a slightly different emphasis. This, in turn, points to the need for investors to revise their expectations on the way in which sustainability issues may be considered in future disputes.

The innovations of these model BITs are now in use, having been employed as templates for recent United States' and Canadian BITs, such as the 2005 United States–Uruguay Bilateral Investment Treaty[117] and the 2006 Canada–Peru Bilateral Investment Treaty.[118] It appears that this new approach is also influencing the negotiation of investment treaties as between other states as well, giving rise to the label 'new generation BITs'.[119] As mentioned above, this description has been given to agreements that have narrowed the definition of 'investment', refined provisions on indirect expropriation, and referred to the protection of health, safety, the environment, and labour rights.[120] Although there has been little attempt to incorporate sustainability principles into the substantive protections guaranteed under these bilateral investment treaties, the reframing of the context in which the obligations sit and the more nuanced reading of expropriation do point to an increasing trend towards modification of the traditional approach to investor protection.[121] These developments create a sense that further evolutionary movement is possible; that they foreshadow

[116] Ryan, 'Meeting Expectations', 757–61.

[117] United States–Uruguay BIT, Treaty between the United States of America and the Oriental Republic of Uruguay Concerning the Encouragement and Reciprocal Protection of Investment (2005), available at www.unctad.org/sections/dite/iia/docs/bits/US_Uruguay.pdf (last accessed at 15 March 2009).

[118] Canada–Peru BIT, Agreement between Canada and the Republic of Peru for the Promotion and Protection of Investments (2006), available at www.international.gc.ca/trade-agreements-accords-commerciaux/assets/pdfs/Canada-Peru10nov06-en.pdf (last accessed 4 April 2009).

[119] Shan, 'From "North–South Divide"', 651–2; United Nations Conference on Trade and Development (UNCTAD), *Recent Developments* (2005).

[120] UNCTAD, *Recent Developments* (2005), pp. 4–5; Shan, 'From "North–South Divide"', 652.

[121] See the discussion on increasing trends in renegotiating bilateral investment treaties and the impact of model BITs reflecting environmental and social issues in UNCTAD, *Recent Developments (2007–2008)*.

the eventual realisation of socially and environmentally responsible principles in the investment field; and that they, perhaps, even indicate a future successful reassertion of the host state as a visible and 'protected' entity within international investment law, able to call upon its principles for recourse in the face of damage from investor activity.

(ii) Hints at synergy in the case law Potential for a future reorientation of international investment law can also be found in a small number of progressive statements made in recent investor–state disputes. For example, the approach to environmental regulation in *Methanex Corp.* v. *United States of America*,[122] excluding non-discriminatory regulation for a public purpose from consideration as expropriation, illustrated an appreciation of the wider public interest issues involved in the dispute.[123] Taking an unconventional approach, the reasoning of the award in *Glamis Gold Ltd* v. *United States of America*,[124] which concerned mining on lands of indigenous cultural significance, explored fair and equitable treatment in the context of the customary international law minimum standard, equating its requirements with a modern-day version of the *Neer Claim* standard.[125] And, in a further break-through ruling, the tribunal in *Parkerings-Compagniet AS* v. *Republic of Lithuania* (the *Parkerings Award*) considered cultural heritage and environmental impacts as a component of the criteria for 'like circumstances' in a claim for alleged breach of national treatment obligations.[126]

Each of these three awards addressed contentious, yet very different, subject matter, and each, through diverse mechanisms, found space for the needs of local communities in determining investor complaints. At

[122] *Methanex Corp.* v. *United States of America* (2005) 44 *International Legal Materials* 1345.

[123] See the discussion in Bernasconi-Osterwalder and Brown Weiss, 'International Investment Rules', p. 288; Lawrence, 'Chicken Little Revisited'; Dougherty, 'Methanex v. United States'.

[124] *Glamis Gold Ltd* v. *United States of America*, Award, 8 June 2009, available at http://ita.law.uvic.ca/documents/Glamis_Award.pdf (last accessed 15 December 2011).

[125] *Neer Claim (United States* v. *Mexico)* (1926) 4 *Reports of International Arbitral Awards* 60. This case established that outrageous, egregious, or bad faith conduct was necessary on the part of the host state before international minimum standards of investor protection would be breached. See also the discussion in Kahn, 'Striking NAFTA Gold'. The North American Free Trade Agreement expressly refers to the customary international law standard for fair and equitable treatment NAFTA, adopted 17 December 1992, 1992 32 ILM 612 (entered into force 1 January 1994).

[126] *Parkerings-Compagniet AS* v. *Republic of Lithuania*, (ICSID Arbitration Case No. ARB/05/8, Award of 11 September 2007), paras 375, 392, available at http://ita.law.uvic.ca/documents/Pakerings.pdf (last accessed 2 October 2009).

a broader level, of course, it would be preferable for CSR norms, human rights standards, and ecological sustainability principles to be expressly incorporated into international investment agreements and remove the need for reliance on indirect application by arbitral tribunals. This is particularly so, as investor–state arbitral panels do not tend to avail themselves of the opportunity to refer to relevant principles from international human rights law, environmental law, or international labour standards, preferring to maintain that consideration of such principles would require straying into areas of social and economic policy.[127] However, as Muchlinksi argues, the very decision not to engage with the interaction of these principles and adopt a 'creative interpretation' of the provisions in bilateral investment treaties is in itself a political decision.[128]

(b) The centrality of CSR for responsible investment

In fact, CSR norms will be integral to the development of more socially and environmentally responsible principles of international investment law. In particular, emerging principles of CSR on labour conditions, human rights, environmental protection, and corrupt practices would be the most obvious areas for inclusion in a reconceptualised model of international investment law, whether as references in investment treaties or as interpretation tools in the resolution of investor–state disputes.[129] Indeed, Muchlinski argues that a more balanced approach to investor rights and responsibility that takes account of CSR norms may well be necessary if international investment agreements and the system of investor–state arbitration are to maintain a sense of legitimacy at all.[130]

The current lack of any reflection of CSR norms in investment treaties and in investor–state dispute resolution highlights the disconnect between recent CSR-related corporate practice and international investment law. It is also out of step with transformations occurring in international law more generally, such as the integration of principles from other areas of law, the development of global public law, the increasing role of non-state actors on the international plane, and moves to address the international accountability of private actors.[131] Indications are that

[127] Muchlinski, 'Corporate Social', 683; see also the discussion in Sornarajah, 'The Clash of Globalizations', 13–17.

[128] Muchlinski, 'Corporate Social', 683. [129] Ibid., 682.

[130] Ibid., 682–4; see also the discussion in Kelley, 'Multilateral Investment Treaties'.

[131] These trends, and their implications for transforming international investment law, are explored in detail below in Chapter 6. For a discussion of these issues, see

international law is headed towards greater exploration and cementing of these trends and that, without a substantial reorientation, international investment law will be very much at odds with this new character. As a consequence, incorporation of emerging CSR norms into international investment law could not only assist with redressing the traditional foreign investor conceptualisation of the host state, but it could also contribute to ensuring the legitimacy within the international legal order of investor protection treaties in the twenty-first century.

As section I of this chapter has discussed, there are now hints of synergy between transnational corporate activity and environmental protection measures. Although international investment law remains deeply entrenched within a traditional framework, some areas of investor corporate practice are moving towards a more CSR-related approach. The consideration of socially and environmentally responsible standards in foreign investment and financing practices is being driven by the CSR movement, NGOs, market forces, and consumer choice, but it is also now being directed through the conscious choices of those within the finance sector. Leading private investment banks, public financial institutions, and corporations are now not only adopting internal policies that reflect the objectives of CSR programmes, but are also integrating environmental and social criteria into their investment and financing decision-making.[132] This new approach to the provision of financial services is now commonly referred to as 'sustainable finance'.[133] And together with emerging CSR norms and practices, the sustainable finance movement also provides a potential channel through which to influence the direction of international investment law.

II. Sustainable finance

The impetus for the sustainable finance movement grew out of the perceived failure of traditional environmental regulatory techniques together with a more sophisticated NGO identification of the causes

Crawford, *International Law*, pp. 17–22; see also Sands, 'Turtles and Torturers'; Krisch and Kingsbury, 'Introduction'; Slaughter, *A New World Order*; Garcia, 'Globalization'; Sands, 'Searching for Balance'; Sands, 'Treaty, Custom'.

132 Assadourian, 'Transforming Corporations'; Richardson, *Socially Responsible*, pp. 1–2; Barnard, 'Corporate Boards'.

133 See, e.g., United Kingdom Department for Environment, Food and Rural Affairs, 'The London Principles'; see also WWF and BankTrack, *Shaping the Future*; see also International Finance Corporation, 'What is Sustainable Investing?'.

of corporate environmental degradation – the focus widened to encompass not only those operations that carried out environmentally harmful activities, but also to those who financed them.[134] Although there is no comprehensive definition, the concept of sustainable finance encompasses the lending and investment activities of private equity financiers and institutional investors, as well as entities from the public sector such as the World Bank and multilateral development banks.[135] At its broadest, sustainable finance refers to the 'mainstreaming of environmental and socio-economic criteria into lending, investment and other financial services.'[136] The NGO community tends to interpret it as requiring more innate changes in approach, such as a deep-rooted commitment to social and environmental responsibility, transparency, accountability, and precaution.[137]

As with most fields in international law and policy, sustainable finance also interacts with a varied range of disciplines. In particular, sustainable finance has a significant role in the wider context of sustainable development. Indeed, it is increasingly recognised that the adoption of socially and environmentally responsible financing is a key component in the promotion of sustainable development.[138] As the availability of funding tends to determine whether or not a major infrastructure or transnational project proceeds, the financing of environmentally unsound projects has come to be seen as a source of unsustainable development in itself, even though, traditionally, financiers and investors have not been held accountable for their decisions to provide capital on socially or environmentally harmful projects.[139] The sustainable finance movement, however, has sought to reorient this approach, firmly placing the spotlight on the activities of financiers and investors. And by 2000, financial institutions had become targets in NGO campaigns to reform

[134] Richardson, 'Sustainable Finance', 309.

[135] Richardson, *Socially Responsible*, pp. 2–6; Richardson, 'Sustainable Finance', 309–10.

[136] IFC, 'What is Sustainable Investing?'.

[137] See, e.g., BankTrack, the Collevecchio Declaration on Financial Institutions and Sustainability.

[138] Richardson, *Socially Responsible*, pp. 2–3, 9–12; Thomas, 'The Green Nexus'; Social Investment Organization, 'Sustainable Development'; for a discussion on the need for regulation to direct foreign investment into sustainable development, see also Gallagher and Zarsky, 'No Miracle Drug', 13; for the connection between sustainable development and the need for socially and environmentally responsible foreign investment, see also Zarsky, 'Havens, Halos and Spaghetti'; Mabey and McNally, *Foreign Direct Investment*.

[139] Richardson, *Socially Responsible*, pp. 3–7.

their lending criteria and to direct their financing decisions towards supporting, rather than impeding, sustainable development.[140]

It was within this context that a number of high-profile voluntary codes of corporate conduct emerged as a response to the increased scrutiny of the financial and investment sectors.[141] Questions remain as to whether these voluntary codes have gone far enough and whether they, in fact, induce significantly improved corporate conduct. Indeed, Richardson argues that a 'chasm' exists in the aims of socially responsible financing and investment and the practices of financiers.[142] He argues that 'the time has come for regulation to address this lacuna and target the financial sector.'[143]

In exploring the recent emergence of the sustainable finance movement, this section examines the implications of its parallel dynamics for foreign investment practices and the development of international investment law. It argues that sustainable finance and the calls for greater regulation of this sector are creating an atmosphere of accountability that is fuelling pressure to reform international investment law. In the course of this analysis, it also suggests that the voluntary codes themselves could provide useful building blocks from which to design more socially and environmentally responsible principles of international investment law.

A. *Voluntary codes of environmental corporate conduct*

There is a vast array of voluntary codes in operation at local, national, regional, and international levels.[144] These instruments adopt a variety of approaches, ranging from industry or government initiatives, industry-third party collaboration, and company–NGO partnerships, through to sustainability directives aimed at multiple sectors and private agreements between multiple stakeholders.[145] However, voluntary environmental codes do share common elements and can be defined as follows:

140 Richardson, 'Sustainable Finance', 309; Monahan, 'Principles in Question'; Sohn, 'NGO Spotlight'; Wright, 'For Citigroup'.

141 See, e.g., the Equator Principles (Washington, DC, 4 June 2003), available at www.equator-principles.com (last accessed 24 August 2008); Monahan, 'Principles in Question'; Sohn, 'NGO Spotlight'; Wright, 'For Citigroup'.

142 Richardson, *Socially Responsible*, pp. 3–4.

143 Ibid., p. 4.

144 Gunningham and Sinclair, *Voluntary Approaches*; Wood, 'Voluntary Environmental Codes', 229, 232–3; Baram, 'Multinational Corporations', 33; Jackson, 'Global Corporate Governance', 70–2.

145 Jackson, 'Global Corporate Governance', 75–85; see also Besmer, 'The Legal Character', 289–91.

Commitments undertaken by one or more polluters or resource users, in the absence of an express legal requirement to do so, prescribing norms to regulate their behavior in relation to their interaction with the environment.[146]

Within this field, some of the most significant recent initiatives at the international level have involved the financing and investment sectors, including the launch of the Equator Principles in 2003[147] and the United Nations Principles for Responsible Investment in 2006.[148] These regimes and a selection of other relevant voluntary codes are examined in this section to indicate possible paths through which a more harmonious relationship between foreign investors and environmental protection objectives could be pursued.[149]

1. General corporate codes

(a) *The CERES Principles*

An initiative developed in the United States following the *Exxon-Valdez* oil spill in Alaska in 1989, the Coalition for Environmentally Responsible Economies (CERES) has sought to bring about changes in corporate culture and practice through a two-fold approach:

- The development of a series of guiding principles to which companies commit and then implement throughout their operations on a continuing basis; and
- The promotion of environmentally, socially, and financially responsible investment policies.[150]

CERES is a framework organisation which 85 financial and investment organisations, pension fund managers, environmental organisations, and other public interest groups have joined as members.[151] Over 70 companies, many of which have transnational operations, have adopted the CERES Principles. These companies include General Motors, the

146 Wood, *Environmental Law*, p. 230. 147 Equator Principles, above n. 141.

148 United Nations, *United Nations Principles for Responsible Investment* (2006), available at www.unpri.org/principles/ (last accessed 24 April 2010).

149 Other CSR-related initiatives directed at the financing and investment sector include the United Nations Environment Programme Finance Initiative, available at www.unepfi.org/ (last accessed 15 December 2011); the London Principles of Sustainable Finance, available at www.cityoflondon.gov.uk/Corporation/living_environment/sustainability/sustainable_finance.htm (last accessed 12 April 2007); Global Sullivan Principles of Social Responsibility, available at www.thesullivanfoundation.org/gsp/default.asp (last accessed 12 January 2010).

150 Forster, 'Environmental Responsibilities', 74–5; see CERES, *Investors*.

151 CERES, *Investors*.

Body Shop International, American Airlines, Aveda, Coca-Cola, Nike, and Time Warner.[152] The Principles begin with an overarching pledge on the role and responsibilities of corporations regarding their environmental conduct. Setting out their own commitments, signatory companies are required to prepare a version of the following declaration:

> By adopting these principles, we publicly affirm our belief that corporations and their shareholders have a direct responsibility for the environment. We believe that corporations must conduct their business as responsible stewards of the environment and seek profits only in a manner that leaves the Earth healthy and safe. We believe that corporations must not compromise the ability of future generations to sustain their needs.
>
> We recognise this to be a long-term commitment to update our practices continually in light of advances in technology and new understandings in health and environmental science. We intend to make consistent, measurable progress in implementing these Principles and to apply them wherever we operate throughout the world.[153]

Substantively, the CERES Principles consist of specific commitments regarding:

1) The protection of the biosphere;
2) The sustainable use of natural resources;
3) The reduction and safe disposal of waste;
4) The use of sustainable energy sources and improved energy efficiency within their own operations and in the products they manufacture;
5) The reduction of environmental health and safety risks to their employees and to the communities in the vicinity of their operations;
6) The sale of products and services that minimise adverse environmental impacts and the provision of information regarding any such impacts;
7) The restoration of environments and compensation to persons harmed by the company's operations;
8) The disclosure of incidents that may endanger health or the environment;
9) The establishment of internal management structures with the capability and responsibility for addressing environmental issues and for informing the Board of Directors and Chief Executive Officer of all environmental matters relating to the company's operations;

[152] See list of CERES companies, available at www.ceres.org/coalitionandcompanies/company_list.php (last accessed 28 August 2008).

[153] IISD, *Business and Sustainable Development*. As an example in practice, see the statement made by General Motors, available at www.gm.com/company/gmability/sustainability/reports/00/links/ceres_principles.html (last accessed 25 August 2008).

10) The conducting of an annual self-evaluation of the company's environmental performance and implementation of the Principles. The company must complete an annual review, known as a 'CERES Report', and provide this Report to the public.[154]

The collaborative origins of the CERES Principles are regarded as instrumental in the relative success of this code.[155] In this respect, the input from both the NGO community and business sector is said to have imbued the regime with a combination of both legitimacy and practicability, the ensuing effect of which is that the adoption of the CERES Principles is regarded as a considerable commitment.[156] This is particularly so as companies are expected to change their internal procedures as well as their external activities so as to reflect the substance of the code.[157] Clearly, they are not legally enforceable commitments. However, the public reporting procedures and monitoring systems by both CERES and other NGOs provide a certain level of external pressure on companies to operate in keeping with the spirit of the regime and to make substantive progress towards implementing the commitments.[158] And recently, CERES has been influential in emphasising climate change risk as an issue for corporate governance, investment fiduciaries, and shareholder value.[159]

(b) The ICC: Business Charter for Sustainable Development

The International Chamber of Commerce (ICC) Business Charter for Sustainable Development (the Charter) is an example of an industry-driven initiative.[160] It was a direct response to the 1987 Report of the Brundtland Commission, *Our Common Future*,[161] and its call for a global

[154] CERES Principles available at www.ceres.org/coalitionandcompanies/principles.php (last accessed 28 August 2008); see also the discussion in Pink, 'The Valdez Principles', 180–6; see also the discussion in Zondorak, 'A New Face', 471–3.

[155] Richardson, *Socially Responsible*, pp. 404–5; see also the discussion on 'consensus-building' in Smith, 'The CERES Principles', 312.

[156] Richardson *Socially Responsible*, pp. 404–5 ; Forster, 'Environmental Responsibilities', 77; see also the discussion in Nash and Ehrenfeld, 'Code Green', 19–20.

[157] Forster, 'Environmental Responsibilities', 77; Pink, 'The Valdez Principles', 190–1.

[158] Nash and Ehrenfeld, 'Code Green'; Richardson, *Socially Responsible*, pp. 404–5; Smith, 'The CERES Principles', 313; Nash and Ehrenfeld, 'Codes of Environmental Management', 512–16.

[159] Barnard, 'Corporate Boards', 292–3, 296, 298; CERES Sustainable Governance Project, *Value at Risk*; Investor Network on Climate Risk, *INCR Overview*.

[160] Business and Sustainable Development, *ICC Business*; International Chamber of Commerce (ICC), *What is ICC*.

[161] World Commission on Environment and Development, *Our Common Future*.

shift in corporate practices.[162] The Charter was designed to provide a tool for companies worldwide to improve their environmental performance and to participate in the move to sustainable development.[163] Its stated objective is to encourage the widest possible range of corporations, across all sectors, to commit to responsible environmental corporate governance systems and practices, to improve corporate environmental performance overall, to change management structures and practices so as to assist with achieving that improvement, to assess progress towards these environmental goals, and to report publicly, as well as internally, on any such progress.[164]

Essentially, the Charter is a mechanism through which an internal corporate cultural shift can be implemented. Through raising the profile of environmental issues and infusing a particular approach to corporate governance and practice throughout all operations, it is intended that environmental considerations will become as much an expected factor in corporate decision-making as financial matters. The focus for the ICC initiative is the promotion of sustainable development through sixteen principles of corporate environmental management. Covering matters such as shifting corporate priorities, employee education, increased energy efficiency, the provision of products and services that have no undue environmental impacts, the adoption of a precautionary approach to corporate activities, and compliance and monitoring issues, the Charter is designed to be a framework document on which to build individual programmes of action for each corporation.[165]

With over 2,300 companies and business associations as signatories, the Charter has been widely endorsed by the business sector.[166] There is a sense, however, that this code suffers from the legitimacy issues endemic in industry-only initiatives – the claim that superficial changes are made to company operations, but an approach of 'business as usual'

[162] Business and Sustainable Development, *ICC Business*; see also the discussion of the Charter in Christmann and Taylor, 'Globalization and the Environment', 124; for a discussion on the blurring of private and public international law in private sector voluntary codes and the Business Charter for Sustainable Development as an example of this 'new global commerce law', see Brown Weiss, 'The Rise or Fall of International Law', 354.

[163] ICC, *The Business Charter*. [164] Ibid.

[165] Ibid., pp. 2–3; see also the discussion in Forster, 'Environmental Responsibilities', 77–8; see also Baram, 'Multinational Corporations', 50–4; Eden, 'Using Sustainable Development', 163; Pesapane Lally, 'ISO 14000', 521–2.

[166] ICC, *The Business Charter*; Besmer, 'The Legal Character', 286; Rondinelli and Berry, 'Environmental Citizenship', 74–5.

essentially remains.[167] As a motivating factor in the development of the Charter was to deflect attempts to introduce international regulation of corporate environmental conduct at the United Nations Conference on Environment and Development (UNCED),[168] the unease surrounding this code has some basis. The ICC actively lobbied for business-friendly policies at UNCED, seeking to 'ensure that their voice was heard'.[169] Concern at the purpose of the Charter was fuelled by the ICC position taken at the 2002 World Summit on Sustainable Development,[170] at which it argued that legally binding measures to regulate transnational corporate conduct were unnecessary because voluntary codes were sufficient to induce the desired changes in corporate behaviour.[171] It is, therefore, unsurprising that, as a lobby group, the ICC continues to resist the integration of social and environmental responsibility principles into international agreements on trade, investment, and finance.[172]

For many scholars, concerns remain at the impact of business lobby groups on the CSR debate and at their robust promotion of voluntary codes of corporate conduct.[173] The increasing engagement between environmental NGOs, multinational corporations, and industry groups has led to a significantly greater level of business participation in shaping the CSR discourse.[174] This has generated some apprehension at the

167 Richardson, *Socially Responsible*, pp. 388–9; Eden, 'Using Sustainable Development', 163; Hsia, 'Foreign Direct Investment', 679–81; see for an example of NGO concerns at the 'business-as-usual' model, Greenpeace, 'Climatewash'.

168 Nash and Ehrenfeld, 'Code Green', 503–4; Eden, 'Using Sustainable Development', 163–4; *Report of the United Nations Conference on Environment and Development (UNCED)*, UN Doc A/CONF.151/6/Rev.1 (1992), 31 ILM 874 (1992).

169 Nash and Ehrenfeld, 'Code Green', 503; Eden, 'Using Sustainable Development', 163–4.

170 *Report of the World Summit on Sustainable Development*, UN Doc A/CONF.199/20 (2002).

171 Bennett and Burley, 'Corporate Accountability', pp. 372, 381–2. This complaint at the motivation of the ICC is also reflected more generally in the concern that business groups lobby for voluntary codes to preclude the introduction of legislation; on this point, see the discussion in Zerk, *Multinationals*, pp. 100–1; see further on this more general point, Williams, 'Civil Society Initiatives', 465–6.

172 See, e.g., ICC, *World Business Message*; see also the discussion in Richardson, *Socially Responsible*, 395, 475; Eden, 'Using Sustainable Development', 166–7.

173 See, e.g., the discussion in Zerk, *Multinationals*, p. 100; Williams, 'Civil Society Initiatives'; Richardson, *Socially Responsible*, pp. 393–4; Shamir, 'Corporate Social Responsibility'; see also the discussion in Christmann and Taylor, 'Globalization and the Environment', 126; Neal, 'Corporate Social Responsibility', 469–73.

174 Neal, 'Corporate Social Responsibility', 469–73; Zerk, *Multinationals*, pp. 100–2; Najam, 'World Business Council', 69.

corresponding level of business influence this engagement brings to the development of international policy and law regarding CSR – and concern that outcomes will be weighted towards facilitating the objectives of multinational corporations.[175] There is, indeed, some need for caution in this regard. As was explored in Chapters 1, 2, and 3 of this book, the use of legal mechanisms to entrench the positions of foreign investors and capital-exporting states has a long history, and imperialism has continued to find avenues for reproduction in the twentieth and twenty-first centuries.[176] As such, the way in which corporate involvement manifests in the process of developing CSR-related standards, principles, or international instruments may result in manipulation of the regulatory outcomes. Certainly, the level of corporate resistance to a binding multilateral agreement on CSR, and the continued reiteration of the success of voluntary codes, can be framed as a further manifestation of economic imperialism within international investment law and policy.

(c) United Nations Global Compact

The United Nations Global Compact (UN Global Compact) is a voluntary initiative designed to promote the notion of 'partnership' between the private sector, governments, the United Nations, NGOs, and other civil society stakeholders.[177] It consists of ten principles addressing four key areas: human rights, environmental protection, labour standards, and anti-corruption measures.[178] Signatories to the UN Global Compact are expected to endorse the principles, bring their own corporate practices into alignment with the principles, and submit annual sustainability reports on their operations.[179] To maintain a level of credibility, the UN

175 Richardson, *Socially Responsible*, pp. 393–4 discusses the power relations involved in voluntary regimes; see also Bennett and Burley, 'Corporate Accountability'; Najam, 'World Business Council', 69; see Wood, 'Green Revolution', for a discussion on the implications of the intertwining of public and private spheres in voluntary codes, the necessarily political nature of corporate promotion of these voluntary initiatives, and the specific endorsement of private sector regimes by public authorities; see also Shamir, 'De-Radicalisation'.

176 Anghie, '"The Heart of My Home"', 505–6; Anghie, 'Finding the Peripheries'.

177 United Nations Global Compact, *UN Global Compact*; see the discussion in Richardson, *Socially Responsible*, pp. 408–10; see also Deva, 'Global Compact', 115; Kuper, 'Harnessing Corporate Power', 11.

178 United Nations Global Compact, *UN Global Compact*.

179 Ibid.; see also the discussion in Deva, 'Global Compact', 115; S. D. Murphy, 'Taking Multinational Corporate Codes', 411–13.

Global Compact has instigated a complaints procedure through which allegations of non-compliance can be made.[180] It has also established a 'de-registering' process if a company fails to file its implementation report for two consecutive years, attracting a listing as an 'inactive' participant.[181] The initiative emphasises, however, that the United Nations does not have a policing or enforcement role in ensuring compliance with the principles, but rather that dialogue with industry and individual corporations is its preferred approach.[182]

Just as there are many of the polarised positions on the politico-legal interaction surrounding foreign investment, corporate conduct, and environmental protection objectives, so too are there differing viewpoints on the implications of the UN Global Compact. It has been suggested that the instrument serves to further the interests of corporations in maintaining the focus on voluntary initiatives and in shifting perceptions of the role of the United Nations from one of 'regulator' to 'partner'.[183] The non-binding character of the instrument and the generality of the principles have also caused concern as their scope allows companies to be in compliance with only minimal change in their practices.[184] However, an alternative reading is also possible. As corporate signatories agree to conduct themselves in accordance with a series of principles based on international human rights, international environmental law, and international labour standards, the UN Global Compact can be understood as advancing the goal of direct application of international CSR norms to multinational corporations.[185] Or, at the very least, it can be seen as contributing to the shaping of the CSR

[180] United Nations Global Compact, *Integrity Measures*; Richardson, *Socially Responsible*, p. 409; see the discussion in Deva, 'Global Compact', 119–120.

[181] For a listing of 'inactive' companies, see United Nations Global Compact, *Inactive Participants*.

[182] See the discussion in Deva, 'Global Compact', 146–7; Cetindamar and Husoy, 'Corporate Social Responsibility Practices', 166–7.

[183] See the discussion in Richardson, *Socially Responsible*, p. 409; Deva, 'Global Compact'; Raghavan, 'TNCs, Global Compact'; Utting, 'The Global Compact'; Taylor, 'The UN and the Global Compact', 975–7, 980–1; Bruno and Karliner, 'The UN's Global Compact'; Nolan, 'The United Nations', 445–6.

[184] Deva, 'Global Compact', 128–33; Richardson, *Socially Responsible*, p. 409; Kuper, 'Harnessing Corporate Power', 10–11; Murphy, 'Taking Multinational', 413; see the discussion in Kell, 'The Global Compact'; Narula, 'The Right to Food', 753; Whitehouse, 'Corporate Social Responsibility', 309–11; see also the criticisms in Shaughnessy, 'Human Rights'.

[185] Richardson, *Socially Responsible*, p. 409; Whitehouse, 'Corporate Social', 313; Meyer and Stefanova, 'Human Rights', 514–15.

discourse, global governance methodology, and cultural expectations of socially and environmentally responsible corporate conduct.[186]

2. Voluntary codes in the financing and investment sector

In recent times, voluntary codes of corporate conduct explicitly addressing the financing and investment sectors have become increasingly common and have served as focal points around which the sustainable finance movement has developed. In essence, they espouse socially and environmentally responsible principles for the activities associated with the international provision of capital and expressly extend the concept of CSR to investors and financiers. In doing so, they continue to embed CSR as the expected standard of corporate conduct, generate evidence of emerging CSR principles in international law, and serve as pre-normative indicators specifically for future principles in international investment law.

(a) *United Nations Principles for Responsible Investment*

The United Nations Principles for Responsible Investment (UNPRI) is a further important normative code for corporate conduct.[187] However, in this instance, the intended sphere of influence moves beyond the codes of general application discussed earlier and specifically targets institutional investors. Established in April 2006 under the auspices of the UN Global Compact and UNEP Finance Initiative,[188] the UNPRI had an impressive opening. On their launch in New York, the UNPRI were signed by major financial institutions responsible for US$2 trillion in assets. Five days later, at the European launch in Paris, the investment funds had doubled – a further 18 key institutional investors had signed the UNPRI, bringing the level of investment funds under the control of 'Responsible Investment' houses to US$4 trillion.[189] By 2012, more than

[186] See the discussion in Richardson, *Socially Responsible*, p. 409; Narula, 'The Right to Food', 755; see the general comments on the emergence of expected standards of conduct in Waddock, Bodwell, and Graves, 'Responsibility', 138; Thérien and Pouliot, 'The Global Compact', 55–7; see Barnett and Duvall, 'Power in International Politics', 60–1; Bigge, 'Bring on the Bluewash', 9–12.

[187] Normative codes are described by Richardson as those providing 'substantive principles and guidance toward desirable performance.' They 'set goals or benchmarks to move financiers from perpetuating or mere tinkering of existing unsustainable practices.' Richardson, *Socially Responsible*, pp. 381–2.

[188] United Nations Global Compact, 'United Nations Secretary-General'.

[189] United Nations Press Release, 'International Funds Worth $4 Trillion Now Endorse UN Principles for Responsible Investment' (May 2006), available at www.unpri.org/files/20060501_press/un-unepfi-gc_press_20060501.pdf (last accessed 12 February 2009).

1,000 investment entities, controlling over US$30 trillion in assets, had signed the UNPRI.[190] The rapid expansion of the UNPRI and its operational requirements led to the establishment in 2010 of the PRI Association in the United Kingdom to manage the financial and legal affairs of the UNPRI.[191]

The UNPRI consist of six principles and thirty-five 'possible actions' through which investors can integrate environmental, social, and corporate governance matters into their operations.[192] These directives address internal investment analysis and decision-making policies, a function that should, simultaneously, also promote cultural change within signatory institutions. Additionally, the principles and actions encourage active ownership activities, such as filing shareholder resolutions to promote long-term environmentally and socially responsible corporate conduct. UNPRI signatories also pledge to request appropriate disclosure from the companies in which they invest. Furthermore, the UNPRI point to education initiatives, reporting requirements, and the need to infuse a culture of acceptance of the Principles throughout the investment industry.[193]

Queries remain over the capacity of the UNPRI to effect change in the practices of target companies. It is very much embedded within a business case approach to responsible investment, does not require its signatories to provide formal, public reporting of their implementation progress, does not require CSR and ecological sustainability factors to be determinative of any ultimate investment decisions, and does not require specific quotas of socially and environmentally responsible companies within their investment portfolios.[194] Again, however, like the CSR movement as a whole and initiatives such as the UN Global Compact, the UNPRI is impacting in a cultural sense, normalising the consideration of social and environmental factors in corporate

[190] United Nations Principles for Responsible Investment (UNPRI), available at www.unpri.org/principles/ (last accessed 12 August 2012); see also the discussion in Richardson, *Socially Responsible*, pp. 399–402; see also comments in Siebecker, 'Trust & Transparency', 123–4.

[191] UNPRI, above n. 190.

[192] Ibid. See also the discussion on the UNPRI in Kerr, 'A New Era', 359.

[193] UNPRI, above n. 190.

[194] Richardson, *Socially Responsible*, pp. 400–1; Deva, 'Sustainable Good Governance', 127–8; Richardson, 'Keeping Ethical', 559; see the discussion on the variance in approach of UNPRI signatories in Sandberg et al., 'The Heterogeneity'; see a general critique of the UNPRI in Howell, 'Globalization', 246–7; see the criticisms in Global Compact Critics, *Seriousness of Firms' Commitment*.

decision-making in the investment sector – and, in this sense, it is contributing to the establishment of international CSR norms for financiers and investors.[195]

(b) Collevecchio Declaration

The Collevecchio Declaration on Financial Institutions and Sustainability[196] was developed by a coalition of NGOs in 2003 as an alternative to more insipid, industry-led initiatives.[197] Its six principles were designed to encompass the multi-faceted nature of the concept of sustainable finance and they paint a significantly more stringent picture of what sustainable finance requires than do business sector initiatives. For example, Principle 1 of the Collevecchio Declaration sets out the depth of commitment to sustainability required by the NGO perspective on sustainable finance – it also illustrates the gulf that still exists between industry and NGO approaches:

Commitment to sustainability

Financial institutions (FIs) must expand their missions from ones that prioritise profit maximisation to a vision of social and environmental sustainability. A commitment to sustainability would require FIs to fully integrate the consideration of ecological limits, social equity, and economic justice into corporate strategies and core business areas (including credit, investing, underwriting, advising), so that sustainability objectives are placed on an equal footing with shareholder maximisation and client satisfaction; and to strive to finance transactions that promote sustainability.[198]

The Declaration also contains principles addressing transparency, accountability, responsibility, the application of the precautionary principle, and a commitment to fostering and supporting sustainability in markets, governmental policy, and regulation.[199] Its essential approach is to establish a comprehensive framework for change, providing umbrella-like normative principles together with concrete steps towards implementing sustainable financing policies and practices.

[195] See the discussion on the UNPRI becoming a key 'benchmark' for socially responsible investment, in Richardson, *Socially Responsible*, pp. 401–2, 448.

[196] BankTrack, *Collevecchio Declaration on Financial Institutions and Sustainability*.

[197] Key actors were Friends of the Earth, Rainforest Action Network and WWF. See the discussion in Richardson, *Socially Responsible*, pp. 402–4; see also the discussion of the Collevecchio Declaration in Missbach, 'The Equator Principles', 81–2.

[198] BankTrack, *Collevecchio Declaration on Financial Institutions and Sustainability*, Principle 1.

[199] Ibid., Principles 2–6.

As an NGO initiative, this code does not suffer from the legitimacy issues of business-developed programmes such as the ICC Charter.[200] At the same time, however, it has not gained the support of financiers, a somewhat problematic result for a code directed at financiers. Although over 100 organisations have committed to the Declaration, only one of these is from the finance industry – the remainder are mostly NGOs.[201] Despite the lack of endorsement from the business sector, the Declaration is an impressive ethical framework by which to gauge the conduct of financiers and the adequacy of other voluntary codes.[202] It also illustrates the limitations of voluntary codes and the reluctance of financiers and investors to sign on to commitments that may require fundamental changes to business practices. This strengthens the arguments of those, such as Richardson, calling for closer regulation of transnational financing and investment:

> When governments fail to regulate international financial markets, the advantages of the current array of instruments become even more apparent, as they help to overcome the shortcomings of global politics where agreement on intergovernmental policies and regulations can take many years to happen. Over the long term, nonetheless, current SRI [socially responsible investment] governance beyond the state is very likely to be insufficient to regulate the unseen polluters.[203]

(c) The Equator Principles

A key voluntary code directed at the private equity sector is the Equator Principles.[204] It has a different format, focus, and audience from the UNPRI, and, as it sets out the specific procedures to be followed in financing proposed projects, it is an example of what Richardson has termed 'process standards'.[205] The Equator Principles were developed by the World Bank's International Finance Corporation (IFC) and a number of key private investment banking houses as a response to increasing pressure from NGOs and the public to refrain from funding socially and

200 Richardson, *Socially Responsible*, pp. 402; Richardson, 'Financing Sustainability', 87–8.

201 BankTrack, *Collevecchio Declaration: The Role and Responsibility of Financial Institutions*; Richardson, *Socially Responsible*, p. 402. The large pension fund, CalPERS, has adopted the Declaration.

202 Richardson, *Socially Responsible*, p. 404; Missbach, 'The Equator Principles', 81–8; see also the discussion on the Collevecchio Declaration in Waygood, *Capital Market Campaigning*, p. 168.

203 Richardson, *Socially Responsible*, p. 452.

204 Equator Principles, above n. 141.

205 Richardson, *Socially Responsible*, p. 411; Richardson, 'Financing Sustainability', 89.

environmentally harmful projects.[206] The resulting initiative is a voluntary code setting out criteria by which loan applications are to be assessed and ongoing management of projects is to be conducted.

(i) Key elements of the Equator Principles The underlying spirit of the Equator Principles is contained in the Preamble:

> The Equator Principles Financial Institutions (EPFIs) have consequently adopted these Principles in order to ensure that the projects we finance are developed in a manner that is socially responsible and reflect sound environmental management practices. By doing so, negative impacts on project-affected ecosystems and communities should be avoided where possible, and if these impacts are unavoidable, they should be reduced, mitigated and/or compensated for appropriately ... We therefore recognise that our role as financiers affords us opportunities to promote responsible environmental stewardship and socially responsible development ...
>
> These Principles are intended to serve as a common baseline and framework for the implementation by each EPFI of its own internal social and environmental policies, procedures and standards related to its project financing activities. We will not provide loans to projects where the borrower will not or is unable to comply with our respective social and environmental policies and procedures that implement the Equator Principles.[207]

The core function of the Equator Principles is to give effect to these stated objectives through a series of criteria, standards, and processes by which the environmental and social impacts of any proposed project can be assessed. Banks adopting these principles undertake not to provide loans on projects where the borrower is unable to comply with the requisite environmental and social standards.[208] After three years in operation, the Equator Principles Financial Institutions (EPFIs) conducted a review of the provisions and, in July 2006, released the Revised Equator Principles or Equator II.[209] A further review is currently

[206] Monahan 'Principles in Question'; Richardson, *Socially Responsible*, p. 411; Sohn, 'NGO Spotlight'; Wright, 'For Citigroup'; Richardson, 'The Equator Principles', 285; Wright and Rwabizambuga, 'Institutional Pressures', 97–9; O'Sullivan and O'Dwyer, 'Stakeholder Perspectives'.

[207] Equator Principles, Preamble, available at www.equator-principles.com/documents/Equator_ Principles.pdf (last accessed 24 August 2008).

[208] Ibid. See Richardson, *Socially Responsible*, pp. 411–12; see further Richardson, 'The Equator Principles'; see also the discussion in Wright and Rwabizambuga, 'Institutional Pressures', 99.

[209] Equator Principles, available at www.equator-principles.com/documents/Equator_Principles.pdf (last accessed 28 August 2008); see also the discussion in

underway, manifesting in the release for comment in August 2012 of the draft Equator Principles III, or 'EPIII' as it is commonly known.

Amongst other changes to the current regime, EPIII proposes an important expansion of its application, seeking to include project-related corporate loans where all five of the following criteria are met:

i. the loan is related to a single Project,
ii. the total aggregate loan amount is at least US$100 million,
iii. the EPFI's individual Initial Exposure is at least US$50 million,
iv. the loan tenor is at least two years, and
v. the borrower has Effective Operational Control (either direct or indirect) over the Project.[210]

Other aspects of the current framework remain the same in substance. For example, Equator II applies to projects with a capital cost of US$10 million or more and this remains the case in EPIII. The initial threshold in 2003 had been US$50 million, but this was lowered to US$10 million in recognition that projects of a lesser capital cost could also have significant social and environmental impacts.[211] On receipt of an application for a loan, an EPFI begins the assessment process with an initial categorisation of the proposed project into one of three groups based on its potential environmental and social risks:

- Projects fall within Category A if they are:

  Projects with potential significant adverse environmental and social risks and/or impacts that are diverse, irreversible or unprecedented.[212]

- Projects fall within Category B if they constitute a lesser threat to the environment or social fabric of communities, the criteria being:

  Projects with potential limited adverse environmental and social risks and/or impacts that are few in number, generally site-specific, largely reversible and readily addressed through mitigation measures.[213]

Hunter, 'Civil Society Networks', 450–1; see the discussion in Richardson, *Socially Responsible*, p. 412.

210 Draft EPIII, available at www.equator-principles.com/resources/EPIII_PACKAGE.pdf (last accessed 28 August 2012).

211 Richardson, *Socially Responsible*, p. 412.

212 Equator Principles, Principle 1, Review and Categorisation, Exhibit I: Categorisation of Projects, Category A, available at www.equator-principles.com/documents/Equator_Principles.pdf (last accessed 24 August 2012); EPIII, Principle 1, available at www.equator-principles.com/resources/EPIII_PACKAGE.pdf (last accessed 28 August 2012).

213 Equator Principles, Principle 1, Category B; EPIII, Principle 1, available at www.equator-principles.com/resources/EPIII_PACKAGE.pdf (last accessed 28 August 2012).

- Proposed projects with minimal or no social or environmental risks and/or impacts are placed within Category C.[214]

The loan applicant for a Category A or B project must provide to the financier an Environmental and Social Assessment (ESA) which addresses the environmental and social risk factors raised in the initial categorisation assessment.[215] Amongst other considerations, the ESA must satisfactorily address issues such as:

- Sustainable management and the use of renewable natural resources;
- Protection of human health, cultural properties and biodiversity, including endangered species and sensitive ecosystems;
- The use of dangerous substances;
- Socio-economic impacts;
- Involuntary resettlement;
- Impacts on indigenous peoples and communities; and
- Pollution prevention and waste minimization.[216]

In addition to such risk factors, EPIII has also inserted extensive provisions specifically addressing climate change-related matters such as the viability of the project in changing weather conditions. The original standards were associated with the World Bank and the IFC Pollution Prevention and Abatement Guidelines and IFC Safeguard Policies. The IFC conducted a review of these policies in 2006, the result of which is the new IFC Performance Standards.[217] Equator II is linked with these new IFC standards,[218] and so, where applicable, the ESA provided by the prospective borrower must also have attested to the project's compliance with these standards.[219] In an ongoing process of self-assessment, the IFC launched a review of its implementation progress of the new standards in September 2009, with an updated version of its Performance Standards released in January 2012.[220]

214 Equator Principles, Principle 1, Category C; EPIII, Principle 1, available at www.equator-principles.com/resources/EPIII_PACKAGE.pdf (last accessed 28 August 2012).

215 Equator Principles, Principle 2, Social and Environmental Assessment.

216 Equator Principles, Principle 2, Exhibit II.

217 IFC Performance Standards on Social and Environmental Sustainability, available at www.ifc.org/enviro (last accessed 15 December 2011); see Richardson, *Socially Responsible*, pp. 411–12; see the discussion in Hunter, 'Civil Society Networks', 450–1; see the discussion on the impact of the IFC Standards on corporate conduct in Morgera, 'Significant Trends'.

218 Equator Principles, Principle 3, Applicable Social and Environmental Standards.

219 Ibid.

220 IFC, *IFC Policy and Performance Standards on Social and Environmental Responsibility and Policy on Disclosure of Information: Review and Update, 'Progress Report on Phase I of Consultation'*

Under Principle 5, public consultation and effective stakeholder engagement is required for all Category A projects and may be required where appropriate for Category B. Consultation with the affected communities must be carried out 'in a structured and culturally appropriate manner'.[221] Equator II states that this consultation process will ensure free, prior, and informed consultation with the affected communities and will facilitate their informed participation as a means to establish, to the satisfaction of the financier, whether a project has adequately incorporated the affected communities' concerns.[222] Principle 7 is linked to these consultation requirements, stipulating that an independent environmental and social consultant, who is not directly associated with the borrower, must review the ESA documentation and the consultation process documents to assess the proposed project's compliance with the Principles.[223] Equator II also inserted provisions to ensure ongoing monitoring of the project over the life of the loan. In this respect, under Principle 9, EPFIs must appoint an independent environmental and social expert, or require the borrower to retain qualified and experienced external experts, to verify the monitoring information that the borrower is providing to the EPFI.[224]

Of particular note on the subject of monitoring and review, is that Equator II also made provision for a complaints procedure. A grievance mechanism must be established for Category A projects, and again for Category B if it is appropriate, as part of the project management system.[225] The aim is to ensure consultation and community engagement throughout the construction and operation of the project and to facilitate resolution of any concerns and grievances raised by anyone from the affected communities. It does not, however, constitute a formal dispute resolution system and the EPFIs emphasise that signing the Principles does not attach additional legal obligations or liabilities

(11 January 2010), available at www.ifc.org/ifcext/policyreview.nsf/AttachmentsByTitle/PhaseI_Progress_Report1-11-10.pdf/$FILE/PhaseI_Progress_Report1-11-10.pdf (last accessed 24 March 2010); IFC, *Performance Standards on Environmental and Social Sustainability* (1 January 2012), available at www1.ifc.org/wps/wcm/connect/115482804a0255db96fbffd1a5d13d27/PS_English_2012_Full-Document.pdf?MOD=AJPERES (last accessed 28 August 2012).

221 Equator Principles, Principle 5, Consultation and Disclosure; EPIII, Principle 5, Stakeholder Engagement.

222 Ibid. 223 Equator Principles, Principle 7, Independent Review.

224 Equator Principles, Principle 9, Independent Monitoring and Reporting.

225 Equator Principles, Principle 6, Grievance Mechanism.

capable of forming the basis of an action against an EPFI.[226] The acceptance of a loan offer from an EPFI does have ongoing implications for the project developers, the most significant of which is that failure to comply with the environmental and socially related conditions of the loan may amount to a default, resulting in the calling-in of the loan.[227]

(ii) The Equator Principles in operation The Equator Principles were launched with the goal of becoming the industry standard for project financing assessment processes. As seventy-four financial institutions have adopted the Equator Principles to date, being banks which account for over 85 per cent of global project financing, the Principles are close to fulfilling that intention.[228] In many respects, however, the Equator Principles have remained controversial. In particular, NGOs have expressed concern that the mode of implementation of the Principles will be the determinative factor in their success and they have queried the implementation record of EPFIs.[229]

In addition to the implementation issue, there has also been disagreement as to what precisely the Principles require of EPFIs. NGOs have expressed the view that EPFIs should provide loans to initiatives that are actively positive for the environment.[230] The adoption of such an approach would, for example, entail financing renewable energy projects, but require the rejection of applications outright for environmentally harmful activities, such as fossil fuel projects.[231] It is fairly clear that EPFIs take a different view. For EPFIs, the Principles provide a mechanism to achieve two specific goals, rather than requiring the exclusion of whole industry sectors from their pool of potential borrowers, those goals being:

226 Equator Principles, Disclaimer.

227 Richardson, *Socially Responsible*, pp. 413–14; Allens Arthur Robinson, above n. 36; Monahan, 'Principles in Question'; Hardenbrook, 'The Equator Principles', 199.

228 The Equator Principles, available at www.equator-principles.com/join.shtml (last accessed 28 August 2012); Allens Arthur Robinson, above n. 36, 1; Sohn, 'NGO Spotlight', 2; see the discussion in Richardson, *Socially Responsible*, pp. 413–14.

229 Richardson, 'The Equator Principles', 287; Missbach, 'The Equator Principles'; O'Sullivan and O'Dwyer, 'Stakeholder Perspectives'; Richardson, 'Financing Sustainability', 92–3; see, e.g., the discussion in Sohn, 'NGO Spotlight'; Shamir, 'Corporate Social Responsibility', 387–8; BankTrack, *Going Round in Circles*; see also the critique in Herz et al., *The International Finance Corporation's Performance Standards*.

230 Monahan, 'Principles in Question'; see also the ideas expressed in O'Riordan, 'Converting the Equator Principles'.

231 Monahan, 'Principles in Question'.

- To manage social, environmental and reputation risk arising from individual projects; and
- To promote more socially and environmentally responsible corporate practices amongst their borrowers.[232]

Effective implementation of the Principles and the nature of projects receiving finance are emerging as highly contentious issues in the operation of the Equator Principles. What is also becoming apparent, is that, without satisfactory resolution, these issues have implications for the future success of the Principles as a tool to achieve more socially and environmentally responsible financing and investment.

a. Positive developments

There have certainly been promising developments in the implementation of the Equator Principles. There has been anecdotal evidence of the rejection of finance applications due to non-compliance with the Equator Principles,[233] the modification of proposed projects, and the raising of awareness of social and environmental issues throughout the industry.[234] With particular reference to reshaping the culture of the financial sector, a 2005 review of the Principles conducted by the international law firm Freshfields Bruckhaus Deringer went so far as to say that their 'impact on the financial market generally and their success in redefining market considerations has been far greater than anyone could have predicted'.[235]

This 'impact' to which Freshfields refers is the type of cultural shift that fuels pressure to reorient foreign investment practices and principles of international investment law towards a more socially and

[232] Ibid., 1–2; see generally for a discussion of the importance of protection of reputation in the adoption of the Equator Principles in Wright and Rwabizambuga, 'Institutional Pressures'.

[233] Although this is unlikely to have been the sole reason for non-acceptance: see, e.g., the comments of S. Odendahl, Royal Bank of Canada, reported in Bulleid, 'Putting Principles into Practice'.

[234] See, e.g., Allens Arthur Robinson, 'The Equator Principles', reporting on the rejection of projects that are unable to comply with the Equator Principles standards and reporting on the heightened awareness of the potential social and environmental factors involved in proposed projects.

[235] Freshfields Bruckhaus Deringer, *Banking on Responsibility: Equator Principles Survey 2005, The Banks* (July 2005) 1, available at www.freshfields.com/publications/pdfs/practices/12057.pdf (last accessed 15 December 2011); see also the comments of Wright and Rwabizambuga, 'Institutional Pressures', 100–1; see also the discussion on the improvement in CSR-related conduct in EPFIs compared to non-EPFIs in Scholtens and Dam, 'Banking on the Equator'; see also Kamijyo, 'The "Equator Principles"', 38.

environmentally responsible sector. It also points to why these developments in sustainable finance have such significance for the evolution of principles of responsible conduct in international investment law – cultural shifts in the acceptability of modes of conduct tend to precede law reform reflecting those changes in values and practices.[236] In this regard, it is significant that the mode of global standard-setting embodied within the Equator Principles is also reflected within other international financing institutions, and, because of the interrelated process between the World Bank, the IFC, and the private sector in creating the Equator Principles, similar approaches have encompassed both the public sphere and private equity financiers.[237] Interestingly, there are also indications that the Principles are already being applied in areas outside of project finance, such as export finance and corporate loans.[238] And such extensions in practice have then gone on to find reflection in the formal Equator Principles via the inclusion of corporate loans within the scope of EPIII.[239] In this context, further sectoral cross-over seems likely, and, as social and environmental responsibility becomes standard practice within global project financing, it also becomes increasingly unjustifiable for the foreign investment sector to maintain the inapplicability of similar considerations to its activities. In the long-term, this period, marked by the proliferation of voluntary codes and standard-setting for the finance and investment sectors, may well come to be seen as the pre-normative phase in the emergence of more balanced principles of international investment law.

In the meantime, however, the Equator Principles are beginning to introduce more transparent processes into project financing. Although EPFIs have been reluctant to provide specific details of their implementation measures, limited data are beginning to be released through annual Corporate Responsibility Reports and the introduction of reporting requirements under Equator II.[240] Barclays, for instance, discusses its application of the Equator Principles in 2005, disclosing that of the six high-risk projects that were considered, two were rejected. Of the

236 Zerk, *Multinationals*, pp. 101–2; Braithwaite and Drahos, *Global Business Regulation*, p. 32.

237 Morgera, 'Significant Trends', 151, 186–8; see also the discussion in Wright, 'Setting Standards', p. 51.

238 Bergius, 'Environmental Standards'; Watchman, 'Banks, Business', 46, 48.

239 EPIII, Scope, available at www.equator-principles.com/resources/EPIII_PACKAGE.pdf (last accessed 28 August 2012).

240 Richardson, *Socially Responsible*, pp. 415–16; Balch, 'Building a Better World'.

sixty-eight projects in total that were reviewed in 2005 (including medium- and low-risk projects), Barclays declined to provide finance on twenty-five.[241] Barclays revealed that, in 2006, it rejected six projects of the thirty-six loan applications considered.[242] Barclays further stated that it required the borrowers on the thirty approved loans to change aspects of the project to take better account of social and environmental impacts.[243] In 2007, the Equator Principles were applied to fifty-four project finance deals considered by Barclays, nine of which were not financed, and modifications in light of social and environmental considerations were required in the remaining approved forty-five projects.[244] Continuing its approach of limited data disclosure, Barclays reported that it considered the environmental and social risks of 260 projects in 2008, thirty-one of which it assessed against the Equator Principles. Twenty-nine of these projects were financed, ten of which required changes; two were not funded.[245] Its 2011 *Citizenship Report* reveals very little regarding its application of the Equator Principles, stating simply that 219 transactions were referred to its Environmental and Social Risk Management Team, twenty-six of which were project finance transactions. The distribution of those projects was as follows: five in Category A, nineteen in Category B, and two in Category C.[246]

As another example, the Royal Bank of Canada disclosed in 2004 that it had applied the Equator Principles in three instances: on an oil-sands project in Canada and on two oil and gas projects in developing states.[247] The bank's *Corporate Responsibility Report* for 2005 attests to the application of the Principles on two international projects in the energy sector.[248] Its 2009 report shows that the bank acted as an advisor on five Category B projects in the energy and chemical sectors and financed one Category C infrastructure deal in 2008.[249] In 2010, its report reveals that it assessed seven transactions under the Equator Principles. The bank participated as an advisor on three projects and financed four that were subject to the Equator Principles. Of these, one was Category A, four were Category B,

[241] Barclays PLC, *Corporate Responsibility Report 2005*; see the discussion in Richardson, *Socially Responsible*, p. 416.

[242] Barclays PLC, *Corporate Responsibility Report 2006*.

[243] Ibid., see also the discussion in Richardson, *Socially Responsible*, p. 416.

[244] Barclays PLC, *Sustainability Review 2007*.

[245] Barclays PLC, *Sustainability Review 2008*.

[246] Barclays PLC, *Citizenship Report 2011*, 44.

[247] Bulleid, 'Putting Principles'.

[248] Royal Bank of Canada, *Corporate Responsibility Report 2005*, 25; see also Richardson, *Multinationals*, p. 416.

[249] Royal Bank of Canada, *2009 Corporate Responsibility Report*.

and two were Category C. The report also states that one transaction was an oil and gas project, one was in renewable energy, three were in the power generation sector, and two were infrastructure projects.[250]

In a further illustration of this type of reporting, HSBC revealed that, in 2004, twelve projects were rejected 'where non-compliance with the Equator Principles was a contributory factor.'[251] In 2005, sixty-seven projects were approved and categorised as Equator Principles-compliant; seven projects were declined.[252] And, for 2006, HSBC disclosed that it considered eighty projects for compliance with the Equator Principles, four of which were declined and seventy-six approved. Of these financed projects, forty-two fell into either Category A or B of the Principles' classifications.[253]

The provision of this form of data is, of course, an advance on the paucity of information that has traditionally been publically available on the consideration of social and environmental factors in financing decisions. However, it also remains of limited use without the qualitative details of the way in which the Equator Principles were applied both at the decision-making stage and throughout the monitoring of projects. A very few EPFIs are seeking to address this deficiency, although, even then, the approach remains one of presenting carefully selected case studies.[254]

In a parallel development to these disclosure initiatives, implementation methodology is also starting to take a more detailed and advanced form. Adopting a targeted approach, a number of individual EPFIs are translating the Equator Principles into sector-specific environmental policies and guidelines. This approach identifies sectors which necessarily involve social and environmental risk, seeks to assist with the practical application of the Principles to these sectors, and aims to ensure consistent treatment of high-risk projects.[255] HSBC, for example, has adopted a range of sector-specific guidelines for lending on

[250] Royal Bank of Canada, *2010 Corporate Responsibility Report*.

[251] HSBC, *Corporate Social Responsibility Report 2004*, pp. 10–11.

[252] HSBC, *Corporate Social Responsibility Report 2005*, p. 12.

[253] HSBC, *Corporate Social Responsibility Report 2006*, p. 19; see also the discussion in Richardson, *Socially Responsible*, p. 416.

[254] See, e.g., Barclays PLC, *Sustainability Review 2008*; see also the report submitted to the Equator Principles Secretariat by Citigroup, *Managing Our Environmental Performance*.

[255] See, e.g., HSBC, *Equator Principles, Sector Guidelines*, available at www.hsbc.com/hsbc/csr/our-sustainable-approach-to-banking/products-and-services (last accessed 15 December 2011).

projects involving the energy sector, chemicals industry, forestry sector, and freshwater infrastructure.[256]

With respect to the forestry industry, HSBC emphasises sustainable forestry management. It will not support projects involving commercial logging in Primary Tropical Moist Forests and High Conservation Value Forests and gives preference to those projects where Forest Stewardship Council certification has been obtained.[257] The bank's policy in the energy sector is to support 'a transition to a lower carbon economy.'[258] It seeks to do this through lending on projects which meet its sustainability requirements, promote energy efficiency, and develop low-carbon technologies. HSBC does point out, however, that it will also finance fossil fuel projects where the environmental and social risks are addressed.[259] With respect to freshwater infrastructure, HSBC has based its guidelines on international standards, stating that it will follow the World Commission on Dams Framework for Decision-Making. HSBC will not finance any dam projects located in or substantially impacting on critical natural habitats, sites on the Register of Wetlands of International Importance of the Ramsar Convention, or World Heritage sites.[260]

Overall, the Equator Principles are certainly a step in the right direction towards the realisation of more socially and environmentally responsible financing and investment practices.[261] Furthermore, when looking at the Principles in the wider context of norm-creation within the field, this code is also a significant component in the pre-normative 'noise' described by Braithwaite and Drahos as part of the process of creating regimes.[262] However, in this instance, significant problems with implementation still remain. Whilst this raises issues

256 Ibid.

257 HSBC, *Equator Principles, Sector Guidelines*, 'Forest Land and Forest Products Sector Guideline', available at www.hsbc.com/hsbc/csr/our-sustainable-approach-to-banking/products-and-services (last accessed 15 December 2011).

258 HSBC, *Equator Principles, Sector Guidelines*, 'Energy Sector Risk Policy', available at www.hsbc.com/hsbc/csr/our-sustainable-approach-to-banking/products-and-services (last accessed 15 December 2011).

259 Ibid.

260 HSBC, *Equator Principles, Sector Guidelines*, 'Freshwater Infrastructure Sector Guideline', available at www.hsbc.com/hsbc/csr/our-sustainable-approach-to-banking/products-and-services (last accessed 15 December 2011).

261 Richardson, 'The Equator Principles', 289; Hardenbrook, 'The Equator Principles', 226; Wright, 'Setting Standards'; Watchman, Delfino and Addison, *EP2: The Revised Equator Principles*; Schaper, 'Leveraging Green Power'.

262 Braithwaite and Drahos, *Global Business Regulation*, p. 32; see also the discussion on the exhibiting of 'law-like' characteristics in Wright, 'Setting Standards', 52.

regarding the norm-creating character of the Equator Principles, it also points to the need for more state-driven international regulation of financiers and investors.

b. Concerns and controversy

Despite the positive implications of the Equator Principles in creating expectations of social and environmental corporate conduct, it is becoming increasingly apparent that there are legitimate concerns surrounding their implementation. Many EPFIs have not developed comprehensive sector-specific lending guidelines and even those that have are still not releasing the details of their actual implementation record.[263] As a result of this EPFI reluctance to provide specific qualitative information on their transactions, it is difficult for the public to gauge how well the Equator Principles are working. Indeed, without more detailed information, it is also virtually impossible to assess whether the sector is transforming into a more socially and environmentally responsible field. For this reason, NGOs have called for greater transparency in the details of project approvals and rejections to address this information deficit.[264]

There have also been concerns at 'free-rider' banks – those financial institutions that have signed the Principles to obtain the reputational benefits, but have no actual intention of changing their lending practices. The concern is that this practice will devalue the Equator Principles. In response, NGOs suggested that a monitoring and accountability system ought to be developed by the EPFIs, together with strict timeframes by which to demonstrate compliance with their commitments.[265] To address this issue, Equator II introduced a new reporting requirement, Principle 10, according to which EPFIs must report annually on their Principles-related transactions.[266] Given, however, that even setting out the sectors from which projects were drawn is expressly stated as going beyond the minimum requirements of Principle 10,[267] the obligations are not exacting. To comply with this provision, the minimum

[263] Durbin et al., WWF, *Shaping the Future*.

[264] Ibid.; see the discussion in Richardson, *Socially Responsible*, pp. 414–15; see also in Shamir, 'Corporate Social Responsibility', 387–8; see also Baue, 'Revised Equator Principles'; BankTrack, *The Outside Job: Turning the Equator Principles towards People and Planet* (October 2011), available at www.banktrack.org/download/the_outside_job/111021_the_outside_job_final.pdf (last accessed 29 August 2012).

[265] BankTrack, *Equator Principles II*, p. 12; Wright and Rwabizambuga, 'Institutional Pressures', 91.

[266] Equator Principles, *Guidance to EPFIs*. [267] Ibid.

requirement is merely to quantify the number of project financing applications in which the Equator Principles were considered, and, of those, to differentiate the number that were Category A, B, or C projects.[268] From the reports available on the Equator Principles website, it appears that many EPFIs choose to provide minimal additional transactional details.[269] Responding to concerns at the scant information provided, EPIII has sought to increase the transparency in reporting by EPFIs. The new Principle 10 proposed in EPIII requires the following:

For all Category A and, as appropriate, Category B Projects located in non-OECD countries and OECD countries not designated as High-Income, the EPFI will require the borrower to disclose the Assessment documentation and the ESMP [Environmental and Social Management Plan] online. The borrower will take account of and document the process and results of the stakeholder consultation, including any actions agreed resulting from the consultation process. For Projects with adverse environmental or social impacts, disclosure should occur early in the Assessment process, and in any event before the Project construction commences, and on an ongoing basis.

For all Category A and, as appropriate Category B Projects, in all countries, the EPFI will require the borrower to publicly report greenhouse gas emission levels during the operational phase for Projects emitting over 100,000 tonnes of CO_2 equivalent annually. Refer to Annex A for detailed requirements on greenhouse gas emissions reporting.

EPFI Reporting Requirements

The EPFI will report publicly at least annually on transactions screened and closed, and about its Equator Principles implementation processes and experience, taking into account appropriate confidentiality considerations. The EPFI will report according to the minimum reporting requirements detailed in Annex B.[270]

In addition to providing a general breakdown of data regarding the categorisation, sector, and region of projects screened under the EPIII, EPFIs are also required under Annex B to provide certain project-specific information. Annex B states:

Project-Specific Data reporting is:

- applicable only to Project Finance transactions that have reached Financial Close,
- subject to obtaining client consent,

[268] Ibid.

[269] Equator Principles, *Reporting Status*, 10 March 2010, available at www.equator-principles.com/reporting.shtml (last accessed 26 March 2010); see also the discussion in Wright, 'Setting Standards', 66–8.

[270] EPIII, Principle 10, available at www.equator-principles.com/resources/EPIII_PACKAGE.pdf (last accessed 29 August 2012).

- subject to applicable local laws and regulations, and
- subject to any reduction in the rights, or increase in the liability, of the EPFI.

The EPFI will seek client consent at a time during the loan documentation process deemed appropriate by the EPFI or at Financial Close.

The EPFI will submit data (or a link to the data on their website) to the Equator Principles Secretariat for publication on the Equator Principles website. The data will include:

- Project name (as per the loan agreement);
- Sector: Mining, Infrastructure, Oil and Gas, Power, Others;
- Region: Americas, Europe Middle East and Africa, Asia Pacific;
- The calendar year in which the loan reached Financial Close.[271]

Despite the fact that more substantive or qualitative details are rarely provided under the current framework, what appears to be emerging as one of most contentious areas in assessing the implementation and effectiveness of the Equator Principles is the nature of some projects that have been financed or are under consideration for financing by EPFIs. As one NGO puts it: 'The proof is in the portfolio.'[272] The following two highly controversial projects illustrate the character of this debate.

i. Baku-Tbilisi-Ceyhan pipeline

The Baku-Tbilisi-Ceyhan oil pipeline project was designed to transport oil from the Caspian Sea at Baku, Azerbaijan, across Azerbaijan, Georgia, and Turkey to emerge at Ceyhan on the Mediterranean coast of Turkey ready for transportation to Western markets.[273] For many NGOs, the financing of this project by EPFIs[274] demonstrates that the Principles are not being implemented, as a range of socially and environmentally detrimental aspects to the project should have precluded its financing by EPFIs.[275] These factors included human rights issues

[271] EPIII, Annex B, available at www.equator-principles.com/resources/EPIII_PACKAGE.pdf (last accessed 29 August 2012).

[272] BankTrack, *Improvements Made*; see also the critique in the Corporate Responsibility Coalition, *A Big Deal?*.

[273] BankTrack, *Principles, Profits*.

[274] The Equator Banks involved in this project were: ABN AMRO, Citigroup, Mizuho, Société Générale, Banca Intesa, Dexia, HVB, ING, KBC, Royal Bank of Scotland, and West LB.

[275] See, e.g., BankTrack, *Principles, Profits*, pp. 13–17; see also the discussion in Richardson, 'Equator Principles', 287–8; Richardson, *Socially Responsible*, p. 416; Missbach, 'The Equator Principles', 80–8; see also the discussion on the Baku-Tbilisi-Ceyhan pipeline in Lee, 'Enforcing the Equator Principles', 370.

involving repressive policies and practices towards Kurdish communities. Environmental concerns centred on the fact that the pipeline was being placed through important and ecologically sensitive wetlands and through the Borjomi National Park, threatening the habitat of a number of species of endangered birds and sources of mineral water. In addition, problems were also identified with the use of inappropriate material as a coating on the pipeline, risking ruptures and major oil leaks into the wetlands and National Park.[276]

Nine EPFIs contributed to the financing of this project, the rationale being that the social and environmental issues had been adequately addressed by the borrower. Suellen Lazarus, from the International Finance Corporation, defended the financing, stating that the Baku-Tbilisi–Ceyhan pipeline:

> was really the poster child for the Equator Principles ... We think it was a real success for Equator because the banks were able to make themselves comfortable with the issues and deal with them.[277]

In other words, the Equator Principles require banks to point out to the borrower the social and environmental issues raised by a proposed project and to address these factors to the satisfaction of the EPFI. There is little resolution, however, on the extent of the appropriate approach, that is, whether EPFIs should act in accordance with the spirit of the Principles as well as fulfilling their strict procedural requirements. The Baku-Tbilisi-Ceyhan pipeline exemplified this distinction. In this instance, NGOs claimed that even after finance approval, the project still violated the Equator Principles in over 100 ways.[278] In contrast, the International Finance Corporation considered the project was compliant with its standards, maintaining that environmental risks had been minimised, emphasising the EPFIs' adherence to the procedural requirements of the Principles, and focusing on the Principles' success as a framework for consultation between the EPFIs, the borrowers, and stakeholders.[279] This response, in itself, lends weight to arguments that the consultative

[276] BankTrack, *Principles, Profits*; Amnesty International, *Human Rights on the Line*; see also the discussion in Waters, 'Who Should Regulate the Baku-Tbilisi-Ceyhan Pipeline?'.
[277] Bulleid, 'Putting Principles'.
[278] Ibid.; Friends of the Earth, 'Friends of the Earth Blasts World Bank'; see also the discussion in Richardson, *Socially Responsible*, p. 416; see Affolder, 'Cachet Not Cash', 155–7.
[279] See, in particular, the comments of S. Lazarus reported in Bulleid, 'Putting Principles'; see see also Affolder, 'Cachet Not Cash', 157; see comments in IFC, *BTC Pipeline*.

processes and participatory approaches employed in the Baku-Tbilisi-Ceyhan pipeline were not designed to ensure substantive input from new actors, but to preclude disruption of the project – and that the role of the Equator Principles, in general, is primarily that of a tool to legitimise the activities of the financial sector rather than to engender substantial change.[280] The response of the International Finance Corporation also suggests that, while improvements will certainly be made to operating practices in large-scale projects, expectations of fundamental reform for the sector should not rest solely on the Equator Principles.

The Baku-Tbilisi-Ceyhan pipeline is also noteworthy in a different sense. The contracts involved in this project take on a further layer of significance when considered in the wider context of international investment law and historical patterns of legal doctrine manipulation. The construction and operation of the pipeline were facilitated through a series of interlinked agreements including a treaty between Azerbaijan, Georgia, and Turkey (the Azerbaijan-Georgia-Turkey Agreement)[281] and host government agreements between the states and the oil company consortium (Host Government Agreements).[282] It is interesting to see that features within these agreements are reminiscent of the methodology behind Grotius' treatises, *De Iure Praede* (the law of prize and booty) and *De Mare Liberum* (freedom of the high seas) – that is, the creation of new international law to justify the state's protection of private commercial interests.[283] In much the same way as Grotius constructed a legal basis for the activities of the Dutch East India Company, so too did the lawyers representing the oil company consortium in drafting

280 O'Sullivan and O'Dwyer, 'Stakeholder Perspectives'; see arguments on the problematic nature of casting EPFIs as 'guardians of socio-moral sensibilities' in Shamir, 'Corporate Social Responsibility', 388–9; see, in particular, Carroll, *New Approaches*.

281 Agreement Among the Azerbaijan Republic, Georgia and the Republic of Turkey, 18 November 1999, available at http://subsites.bp.com/caspian/BTC/Eng/agmt4/agmt4.PDF (last accessed 15 December 2011).

282 Host Government Agreement between and among the Government of the Azerbaijan Republic and the Main Export Pipeline Participants, 17 October 2000, available at http://subsites.bp.com/caspian/BTC/Eng/agmt1/agmt1.PDF (last accessed 20 January 2009); Host Government Agreement between and among the Government of Georgia and the Main Export Pipeline Participants, 28 April 2000, available at http://subsites.bp.com/caspian/BTC/Eng/agmt2/agmt2.PDF (last accessed 15 December 2011); Host Government Agreement between and among the Government of the Republic of Turkey and the Main Export Pipeline Participants, undated, available at http://subsites.bp.com/caspian/BTC/Eng/agmt3/agmt3.PDF (last accessed 15 December 2011).

283 Porras, 'Constructing International Law', 744–7, 802–4; van Ittersum, 'Hugo Grotius'; Borschberg, 'The Seizure of the *Sta. Catarina*', 32, 57.

the Azerbaijan–Georgia–Turkey Agreement and the Host Government Agreements.[284] The stated purpose of the Azerbaijan–Georgia–Turkey Agreement is 'to give the Project's legal and commercial terms the support and framework of international law [in order to] ensure principles of freedom of transit of Petroleum'.[285] Indeed, that well-known principle of 'freedom of transit of Petroleum'. The lawyers for the oil company consortium literally invented a new principle, elevating protection of oil into a rule of public international law and invoking a rights-based discourse to legitimise this approach.[286] Viewed from an historical perspective, this attempt to construct new principles in support of the commercial interests of the foreign investor clearly replicates the approach to manipulation of legal doctrine that was adopted at the inception of international investment law.

ii. Sakhalin II

Sakhalin II, based offshore and across Sakhalin Island, Russia, proved to be another controversial oil and gas project in which EPFIs were linked to the provision of finance. This large-scale project involved an international consortium of energy companies, which, in 1994, together established the project's operating company, Sakhalin Energy Investment Company (SEIC). Governing the development, operation, and revenue streams of Sakhalin II is a production-sharing agreement that was entered into between SIEC and the Russian Federation.[287] During the 2000s, NGOs drew attention to the potentially disastrous impacts on the environment and local community of the planned development.[288] The damaging effects of the project stem from the positioning of the platforms and pipelines through the feeding grounds of the endangered Western Pacific gray whale, threatening the species with extinction,

[284] See the discussion on the creation of new principles of international law by the oil consortium's lawyers that were responsible for drafting the legal instruments governing the project, in Reyes, 'Protecting'.

[285] Agreement Among the Azerbaijan Republic, Georgia and the Republic of Turkey, Preamble, para. 4, 18 November 1999, available at http://subsites.bp.com/caspian/BTC/Eng/agmt4/agmt4.PDF (last accessed 15 December 2011).

[286] Reyes, 'Protecting', 867–9.

[287] Sakhalin Energy, *What is a 'Production Sharing Agreement?'*; Sakhalin Energy, *Our Partners*.

[288] See, e.g., Platform, *Principal Objections*; WWF, *Sakhalin II*; BankTrack, Correspondence to Royal Bank of Scotland, 15 September 2006, available at www.banktrack.org (last accessed 15 December 2011); see also the discussion in Richardson, 'Equator Principles', 288; see also Richardson, *Socially Responsible*, p. 417.

and through highly sensitive wild salmon runs across the island. The project proposed to dump waste into the Gulf of Aniva, an important fisheries area for the local communities. There is also concern at the high seismic activity in the area and the risk this poses for a catastrophic pipeline rupture leaching vast amounts of oil into the marine and terrestrial ecosystems.[289] BankTrack, an NGO that monitors the activities of financial institutions, alleges that by 2008, damage had already occurred to salmon-spawning rivers and whales had been exposed to excessive noise levels, further endangering the species.[290] As EPFIs participated in financing the project, the assertion has been that the Equator Principles are not fundamentally shifting practices within the finance and investment sector towards a more socially and environmentally responsible approach.[291]

A spokesperson for ABN AMRO, an EPFI that was, at the time, seeking to provide finance for the project, and ultimately did so, stated that the concerns of NGOs were misplaced. According to the bank, the Equator Principles have provided a framework against which to fully assess the non-financial risks posed by the project and have facilitated discussions between the bank and the project developers regarding the problematic aspects of the project.[292] Ultimately, following modifications to the project, several EPFIs participated in financing the project, with Credit Suisse also taking a leading role as financial advisor on the development.[293]

The financing of the project was by no means the only controversial aspect of Sakhalin II. In 2006, the Russian Federation alleged that the consortium had not complied with state environmental regulations, and, under threat of prosecution and licence withdrawal, the majority shareholding in SIEC was eventually transferred to Gazprom, the Russian state-owned energy company.[294] These actions gave rise to allegations of expropriation of the interests of the international oil companies and

[289] Platform, *Principal Objections*; WWF, *Sakhalin II*; see also the discussion in Norlen and Gordon, 'Eschrichtus (Whale)'; see also the description of oil company practices on Sakhalin Island and Northern Siberia, Houck, 'Light from the Trees', 369.

[290] BankTrack, *Sakhalin II Oil*.

[291] Hardenbrrok, 'The Equator Principles', 215–17; also Lee, 'Enforcing', 370.

[292] Balch, 'Building'.

[293] BankTrack, *Sakhalin II Oil*; see also Richardson, *Socially Responsible*, p. 417. The EPFIs involved in financing Sakhalin II included Credit Suisse Group, Royal Bank of Scotland, ABN AMRO, Sumitomo Mitsui Banking Corporation, Mizuho Corporate Bank, Société Générale, BNP Paribas, Bank of Tokyo-Mitsubishi, and Standard Chartered Bank.

[294] Bradshaw, 'The Greening', 272–5.

that the environmental measures had been a pretext to force a renegotiation of the project agreements.[295] The circumstances were considered particularly irregular as, once effective control of SIEC had been transferred to Gazprom, there was no further suggestion from the Russian authorities of non-compliance with environmental conditions.[296]

3. The importance but insufficiency of voluntary codes

For all the sense of activity surrounding the sustainable finance movement, a central question remains for this chapter: what is the significance for international investment law of the proliferation of voluntary environmental codes of corporate conduct? The implications for the investment field are, perhaps, both direct and indirect. At the very least, the emergence of these codes is an indication of a general socio-political shift in the public's expectations of corporate behaviour. In other words, it is no longer acceptable to be merely profitable. That financial success must now also be achieved without damaging the people, communities, and environments with which corporations come into contact. The increasing corporate uptake of voluntary codes can also be regarded as an indication of a change in the attitude of a growing section of the business community itself – human rights and environmental NGOs should no longer necessarily be approached with hostility, but rather as a source of potential collaborative partners.[297]

However, what is also clear is that voluntary codes will not achieve widespread improved CSR-related corporate conduct on their own.[298] They are but one element in a complex mix of governance tools used to regulate the conduct of corporations, which includes direct governmental regulation, voluntary initiatives, self-regulation, monitoring by NGOs, public pressure, market forces, incentive-based reflexive regulation, shareholder activism, litigation, private contracts, the requirements of 'ethical investment funds', and the loan conditions of financiers such as

[295] Ibid.; Mosolova, 'Russia Hits Shell'; Webb, 'Russia Threatens Shell'; Blomfield, 'Kremlin "Bullying"'; Macalister and Parfitt, '$20bn Gas Project'.

[296] Bradshaw, 'The Greening', 272–5.

[297] Gill, 'Corporate Governance', 461–2; Forster, 'Environmental Responsibilities'.

[298] Zerk, *Multinationals*, pp. 243–4, 262–3; Bunn, 'Global Advocacy', 1304–6; Hsia, 'Foreign Direct', 681; Howell, 'Globalization', 248–9; Gunningham and Sinclair, *Voluntary Approaches*, pp. 2, 21–7; Whitehouse, 'Corporate Social', 309–11; for a discussion on the need for global regulation of financiers and investors see Richardson, *Socially Responsible*, pp. 3–4.

the EPFIs.[299] And yet, not even this combination of measures is adequate to ensure the universal application of a more socially and environmentally responsible approach to transnational corporate conduct. Accordingly, the search for appropriate regulatory mechanisms needs to look with more urgency to an international framework comprising binding CSR norms.[300]

Of particular significance for those seeking to reform international investment law is the realisation that the emergence of voluntary codes is indicative of a regulatory gap in the governance of multinational corporations and it constitutes one manifestation of attempts to fill that space.[301] There is also a parallel trend in the establishment of ad hoc complaints' procedures regarding the conduct of multinational corporations, both within these voluntary codes and other international institutions.[302] Again, this is part of the exploration of corporate accountability mechanisms and is testament to the need for appropriate dispute settlement systems arising out of the transnational projects of financiers and investors.[303] Scholars have, however, pointed to the inadequacy of current complaints' mechanisms, highlighting the narrow scope of mandates, credibility issues, the lack of meaningful remedies, and the pressing need for an independent and centralised body to hear matters involving investor conduct on transnational projects.[304] It is increasingly apparent that the limited regulatory functions of voluntary initiatives and ad hoc complaints' procedures are insufficient to realise widespread global-level CSR and significant reform of foreign investment law, policy, and practices. These instruments are certainly not a substitute for a treaty on CSR or for the insertion of more CSR-related provisions into international investment agreements.

299 McBarnet, 'Corporate Social Responsibility', 12–13, 31–44; Richardson, *Socially Responsible*, pp. 568–70; Miles, 'Targeting Financiers', 947.

300 Zerk, *Multinationals*, pp. 243–4, 262–3; McCorquodale, 'Human Rights and Global Business', 111–14; Bunn, 'Global Advocacy', 1304–6; Clapp, 'Global Environmental Governance'.

301 Bridgeman and Hunter, 'Narrowing', 188–90; Chesterman, 'The Turn to Ethics', 603.

302 See, e.g., the World Bank Inspection Panel and the complaints' mechanism required for individual projects under the Equator Principles; see the discussion in Bridgeman and Hunter, 'Narrowing'; see further for a discussion on the World Bank Inspection Panel, Hunter, 'Using the World Bank'; see also for an alternative structure for the World Bank Inspection Panel, Carrasco and Guernsey, 'The World Bank'.

303 Bridgeman and Hunter, 'Narrowing', 188–91, 207, 218–23.

304 Carrasco and Guernsey, 'The World Bank'.

Indeed, the continued corporate resistance to a binding international regulatory framework on CSR and the strong emphasis from business lobby groups on the success of voluntary codes can be framed as a further manifestation of economic imperialism within international investment law and policy. It can be read as another attempt to maintain the persistent disengagement of international investment law from the effect of investor activity on the local communities and environments of host states. And it can be conceptualised as a continuation of the history of manipulation of legal mechanisms to entrench the interests of foreign investors under international law. The question, of course, then becomes one of whether or not it is possible to break from this past of misuse of legal doctrine and mechanisms. If so, an important first step might be to treat voluntary initiatives as generators of change, as purveyors of a cultural shift, and as stepping stones to more concrete forms of international regulation, rather than as a replacement for binding CSR-related norms in international investment law.

B. *Sustainability standards at the World Bank*

Alongside voluntary codes for the private sector, a parallel process of pressure to reform has also been underway in multilateral public sector financing. Social and environmental criteria have been established for assessing project finance applications at international financial institutions, such as the World Bank, the IFC, and other multilateral development banks.[305] The World Bank's 'safeguard policies' on social and environmental issues, in particular, have been influential in establishing programmes at other multilateral development banks, including the Asian Development Bank and the African Development Bank.[306] Through cross-referencing or direct replication of the World Bank's policies, these standards are gradually harmonising into a set of social and environmental standards for public financing of large-scale development projects.[307] The adoption of these sustainability standards points to shifting cultural approaches within international financial institutions, but they may well also themselves constitute emerging

[305] Hunter, 'Civil Society Networks', 437–8; Shihata, 'The World Bank'.

[306] Hunter, 'Civil Society Networks', 442–3; see also the discussion on responsible financing by multilateral development banks in Richardson, *Socially Responsible*, p. 202; Cordonier Segger and Khalan, *Sustainable Development Law*, p. 180; see, e.g., World Bank, *Operational Policies: Environmental Assessment*.

[307] Cernea, 'The "Ripple Effect"'; Hunter, 'Civil Society Networks', 437–8, 442–3; see also the discussion in Wright, 'Setting Standards', 52, 65–6.

principles in international law.[308] They certainly support the development of international sustainability standards in the finance sector.[309] And they also contribute to the increasing pressure on the global finance and investment sectors for a more developed culture of accountability.[310]

1. The World Bank's safeguard policies and accountability measures

Public concern at the harmful effects of projects funded by the World Bank drew critical attention to its financing policies.[311] In particular, the criticism identified a disregard for the impacts of projects on local communities, breaches of human rights, and environmental degradation linked to developments such as the Polonoroeste road construction through the Amazon in Brazil and the Sardar Sarovar dam project in India.[312] The negative publicity generated by these controversial projects triggered the development of a set of policies addressing human rights, environmental issues, and community concerns in the 1980s and 1990s for incorporation into lending decision-making.[313] As a consequence, there are now requirements for environmental impact assessments to be conducted for proposed projects.[314] A further illustration of those new policies can be found in the limitations on financing for forestry operations, such as the avoidance of projects that would involve significant degradation of critical forests and support

308 Hunter, 'Civil Society Networks', 437; see the discussion on shifting identities and cultures in Park, 'Transnational Environmental Advocacy'.

309 See the discussion in Hunter, 'Civil Society Networks', 466–8; see also the discussion in Park, 'Norm Diffusion'; Handl, 'The Legal Mandate'.

310 Hunter, 'Civil Society Networks', 477; see the discussion on the wider impact of the World Bank's policies in Jägers, 'Bringing Corporate Social Responsibility', 177, 194; see for a discussion on the need for accountability in the finance sector, Richardson, *Socially Responsible*; see for an example of NGO commentary on accountability in the finance sector, Mineral Policy Institute, *The Buck's Gotta Stop Somewhere*; see also the discussion in Handl, 'The Legal Mandate'.

311 Hunter, 'Civil Society Networks', 438–9; Fox and Brown , *The Struggle for Accountability*, pp. 1–9; see the discussion on the impact of grassroots environmental activism in both developing and developed states on World Bank policy in Rajagopal, 'From Resistance'.

312 Hunter, 'Civil Society Networks', 438–9; Rajagopal, 'From Resistance', 562–7; Clark, 'Boundaries in the Field', 216–17.

313 Clark, 'Boundaries', 216; Hunter, 'Civil Society Networks', 438–9; Hunter, 'Using the World Bank', 204; see for a discussion on the interaction between grass-roots activism in developing states and shifts in World Bank policy, Rajagopal, 'From Resistance'.

314 World Bank, *Operational Policies: Environmental Assessment*; Cordonier Segger and Khalfan, *Sustainable Development Law*, p. 180; Hunter, 'Civil Society Networks', 440.

for projects using sustainable logging techniques.[315] In order to obtain World Bank financing, projects must avoid or mitigate adverse impacts on indigenous peoples and avoid or minimise involuntary resettlement.[316] The standards also address issues of cultural property, the safety of dams, and appropriate procedures for projects on international watercourses.[317] In a move to arrest additional criticisms at the opaque nature of the activities of the World Bank, concerns that the standards were implemented inconsistently, and reports that the policies were often violated, reform measures on transparency and accountability were also initiated.[318] In particular, the World Bank Inspection Panel was established to provide an avenue for project-affected communities to request a review of compliance with the Bank's social and environmental standards.[319]

In what Cernea describes as 'the ripple effect',[320] these measures have been instrumental in generating a shift in culture in financing and investment activities beyond the sphere of the World Bank.[321] Following on from the drafting of the safeguard policies at the World Bank, other multilateral development banks began designing programmes for the consideration of social and environmental issues in lending decisions.[322] Under NGO pressure, the focus on accountability then stretched to the IFC, extending its reach into the private sector.[323] This has, in turn, been

315 World Bank, *Operational Policies: Forests*; Hunter, 'Civil Society Networks', 440.

316 World Bank, *Operational Policies: Indigenous Peoples*; World Bank, *Operational Policies: Involuntary Resettlement*; Hunter, 'Civil Society Networks', 441.

317 World Bank, *Operational Policies: Cultural Property*; World Bank, *Operational Policies: Projects on International Waterways*; Hunter, 'Civil Society Networks', 441.

318 Clark, 'Boundaries', 205–6; Hunter, 'Using the World Bank', 204–5; Hunter, 'Civil Society Networks', 442; see also Roessler, 'The World Bank's Lending', 106–7, 128–9, 132–3.

319 Bridgeman and Hunter, 'Narrowing', 208–9; Hunter, 'Civil Society Networks', 442; Hunter, 'Using the World Bank', 205; Clark, 'Boundaries', 216–18; Carrasco and Guernsey, 'The World Bank'; Roessler, 'The World Bank's Lending', 119.

320 Cernea, 'The Ripple Effect'.

321 Ibid.; Hunter, 'Civil Society Networks', 437–8, 469, 477; Park, 'Transnational Environmental Advocacy'; Genoveva Hernandez Uriz, 'The Application', 77–8, 80–1, 119; see also the discussion in Halina Ward, *Public Sector*.

322 Hunter, 'Civil Society Networks', 442–3; Richardson, *Socially Responsible*, p. 202; see the discussion on the influence of the World Bank's environmental impact assessment requirements in Cordonier Segger and Khaflan, *Sustainable Development Law*, p. 180.

323 Hunter, 'Civil Society Networks', 443–5; Hunter, 'Using the World Bank', 210–11; Likosky, *Law, Infrastructure*, pp. 118–22; see also the discussion on the establishment of a Compliance Advisor/Ombudsman at the IFC in Bridgeman and Hunter, 'Narrowing', 210–13.

reinforced by the introduction of the Equator Principles, applying similar and interlinked standards to private equity banks.[324] From a constructivist perspective, which focuses on the shared understandings amongst actors and the socially constructed processes of norm-creation,[325] all these developments contribute to the cementing of international standards on socially and environmentally responsible lending and investment decision-making. Significantly for the arguments put forward in this book, they also point to the eventual emergence of such principles in international finance and investment law.

2. The World Bank and imperialism

A note of caution is, however, required in this discussion of new approaches within the programmes of the World Bank. The introduction of social and environmental criteria into project funding at the World Bank and IFC certainly advances the crystallisation of international sustainability standards for the finance sector. It also points to the likelihood of increased pressure to extend sustainability requirements to the operations of investors protected under international investment agreements. However, a problematic aspect of the World Bank's lending criteria is that they suffer from allegations of modern-day imperialism themselves.[326]

The World Bank and the International Monetary Fund (IMF) often require fundamental restructuring of the borrowing state's social and economic policies to promote privatisation and liberalisation of trade and investment.[327] The rationale for this approach is the furtherance of reform, development, and economic progress – it also has the effect of furthering the neo-liberal interests of Western capital-exporting states and of extending the reach of the World Bank and the IMF into managing almost all spheres of domestic policy within developing states.[328] Such restructuring can operate to the social detriment of recipient states as the required reform programmes are not generally tailored

[324] Likosky, *Law Infrastructure*, pp. 118–22; Hunter, 'Civil Society Networks', 445.

[325] See also Brunnée and Toope, 'International Law'; see Park, 'How Transnational'; see also Park, 'The World Bank Group'.

[326] See, e.g., the discussion in Anghie, *Imperialism*, pp. 256–63; Gathii, 'The Limits', 207, 226–30.

[327] Anghie, *Imperialism*, pp. 258–263; Likosky, *Law, Infrastructure*, p. 39.

[328] Rajagopal, 'From Resistance', 546; Anghie, *Imperialism*, pp. 258–63; Gathii, 'The Limits', 220–30; Anghie, 'Time Present', 244, 247–54; see also the discussion in Chimni, 'Alternative Visions', 391–3, 401–2.

to the particular needs of each state.[329] There have been instances of immense social and economic upheaval following on from the introduction of World Bank and IMF programmes – for example, in the disruption of health services, increased unemployment rates, escalation in food prices, and even riots.[330] Scholars suggest that, in particular, the position of women in developing states has been detrimentally affected by IMF and World Bank reforms.[331] Anghie argues that through its specific approach to 'development' and the concept of 'good governance', the World Bank is able to justify the imposition of these control mechanisms, which ultimately direct the social and economic conditions of borrowing states in a way that actually disadvantages them in the global economy.[332] Furthermore, the World Bank and IMF approach to poverty alleviation and development ensures that attention remains fixed on the domestic conditions within recipient states, rather than on reform of the international economic system.[333] Reflecting on these circumstances in an historical context, it would appear that past patterns of reframing international mechanisms, concepts, and law for application to developing states, are again being reproduced in the operations of the World Bank and the IMF.[334]

In light of this assessment of World Bank activities, the proposal in this book to reorient international investment law also needs to be alive to such a critique. It is likely that a different structure to the current network of bilateral investment treaties would be necessary to achieve the suggested reorientation – one that is the product of genuine engagement between capital-exporting states, capital-importing states, local community groups, representatives of indigenous peoples, NGOs, and other stakeholders. It is, however, unlikely that new structures of this kind will be developed in the immediate future. Accordingly, it is

[329] Anghie, *Imperialism*, p. 259; see the discussion in Skogly, 'Structural Adjustment'; Rampersad, 'Coping with Globalization'; see also Ngugi, 'Forgetting Lochner'.

[330] Skogly, 'Structural Adjustment', 763; Anghie, *Imperialism*, pp. 259–60; Chossudovsky, *The Globalization of Poverty*; Oloka-Onyango, 'Beyond the Rhetoric', 21–9.

[331] Anghie, *Imperialism*, p. 259; Rittich, *Recharacterizing Restructuring*, pp. 235–62; Elson, 'Gender Awareness'; Sadasivan, 'The Impact of Structural Adjustment'.

[332] Anghie, *Imperialism*, pp. 258–68; Anghie, 'Time Present', 254–63, 270; Anghie, 'Civilization and Commerce'; see also Gathii, 'Good Governance'; see also the discussion in Harvey, 'Neoliberalism'.

[333] Anghie, *Imperialism*, p. 268; Anghie, 'Time Present', 254–63; see also the discussion in Gathii, 'Neoliberalism, Colonialism', 2054–5.

[334] Anghie, *Imperialism*, pp. 258–68; Rajagopal, 'From Resistance'; Anghie, 'Time Present', 286–9; Pahuja, 'The Postcoloniality', 465; Rajagopal, 'International Law', 20–2; see also the discussion in Fidler, 'A Kinder, Gentler System'.

suggested that interim steps be taken through the inclusion of investor social and environmental responsibility provisions into international investment agreements and through their use in interpreting obligations in investor–state disputes.

For a number of reasons, such proposals should escape criticism as imposition of Western values. As they are indeed seeking to break the hold of the foreign investor over the host state, the requirements of responsibility are directed at the private investor, not at the regulatory structures of the host state. There is, therefore, no attempt to impose sustainability conditionality on developing states. Rather, it is a mechanism to empower host states to regulate on public welfare matters should they wish to do so, without the threat of investor–state arbitration. The proposal in this book is focused on bringing the host state into the equation as an active participant in international investment agreements. Realising this aim requires investors under international law to conduct themselves in a way that is conducive to the health and well-being of the local communities and environments in which their operations are based. Perhaps one of the most effective ways in which to direct improved corporate conduct would be the development of an international investor accountability tribunal to adjudicate on the complaints of affected communities. However, in the meantime, a relatively simple reform would be the insertion of requirements into investment treaties that home states allow their legal systems to hear civil actions from those affected by the international investment activities of their nationals.[335] Such a mechanism should assist the most vulnerable communities within host states through directly accessing investor accountability, independent of the position their government takes on these issues.

The residual sense of unease that I have at my own proposal, however, is that imperialism may find a manifestation in even this attempt to remove it. For as historical patterns have shown, international instruments and legal doctrine are repeatedly given new shape or application so as to entrench the interests of capital-exporting states and political and private elites. As Anghie argues, the concepts and ideals of good governance are not innately objectionable. It is, however, their manifestation when applied to developing states that gives these legal mechanisms

[335] See, e.g., this suggestion in Mann et al., *IISD Model International Agreement*; McCorquodale and Simons, 'Responsibility beyond Borders'; Sornarajah, *The International Law*, pp. 155–70.

their imperialist character.[336] Indeed, Shamir argues that the terms 'sustainability' and 'no rights without responsibility' have, in fact, already been appropriated by the neo-liberal project, gradually shifting their meaning within the CSR discourse.[337] As such, it is entirely conceivable that the insertion of socially and environmentally responsible provisions into international investment agreements may at some point in the future be used by developed states or interpreted by arbitral panels so as to require host states to take action detrimental to their own interests. Acknowledging that possibility is perhaps the first step in reducing the likelihood of it occurring and in enabling the exploration of paths to the realisation of a reconceptualised international investment law free from the replication of historical patterns of imperialism.

C. Socially responsible institutional investment and international investment law

In addition to the development of voluntary codes and standards in multilateral financial institutions, sustainable finance also manifests in the investment decisions of pension funds, mutual funds, managed funds at financial institutions, and insurance company funds.[338] The emergence of this type of socially responsible institutional investment (SRII) in the form of private sector 'ethical investment funds' is a further area adding to the pre-normative noise surrounding CSR and generating pressure to reshape international investment law.

1. Facilitating socially responsible institutional investment

Although there is no universal definition for SRII, it has been described as:

> an investment process that considers the social and environmental consequences of investments, both positive and negative, within the context of rigorous financial analysis.[339]

The SRII movement is directed towards a number of objectives. Reflecting the conceptual approach of other areas of sustainable finance, SRII seeks to influence the conduct of financiers and fund managers so

336 Anghie, *Imperialism*, pp. 271–2. 337 Shamir, 'Time Present', 381–2.

338 Richardson, 'Sustainable Finance', 318; Richardson, *Socially Responsible*, pp. 1–7, 62–9; Hardenbrook, 'The Equator Principles', 214–15; Fairfax, 'Making the Corporation Safe', 84–5.

339 Social Investment Forum, *2005 Report*; Hardenbrook, 'The Equator Principles', 214–15; Richardson, 'Do the Fiduciary Duties', 147. Richardson includes 'ethical consequences' in the definition as well as social and environmental consequences.

that social, environmental, and ethical considerations are infused into their decision-making.[340] Its particular focus provides an avenue for investors to support corporations that reflect their own social and environmental values.[341] And it seeks to induce change in the social and environmental practices of corporations in general through the promise of capital investment – the premise being that CSR and sustainable corporate environmental management will be rewarded with greater investment; irresponsible social and environmental practices will repel socially responsible investors.[342] Just as with voluntary codes and CSR programmes, however, the role of SRII should not be viewed in isolation. Rather, the mechanism's transformative potential should be seen as a contributory one, as a component of a complex web of governance tools steering the financial sector, and corporations generally, towards more socially and environmentally responsible practices.[343]

(a) SRII screening

In its broadest sense, SRII tends to involve a process of screening companies according to environmental and social criteria to determine whether or not to invest in them.[344] Screening can take a positive or negative approach to categorising companies. As a result, the social and environmental criteria on which investment decisions are based vary between funds, although the essential methodology tends to be similar. By way of illustration, positive screening can entail versions of the following:[345]

340 Richardson, *Socially Responsible*, p. 8; Guay et al., 'Non-governmental Organizations'; Adams and Knutsen, 'A Charitable Corporate'.

341 Guay, 'Non-governmental'; Sparkes, *Socially Responsible Investment*, pp. 17–19; Kelley, 'Law and Choice', 358–9.

342 Assadourian, 'Transforming Corporations', 180–1; Richardson, *Socially Responsible*, p. 8; Sparkes, *Socially Responsible Investment*, pp. 13–14, 17–19, 42; Chesterman, 'The Turn to Ethics'; Sparkes and Cowton, 'The Maturing'.

343 See generally Richardson, *Socially Responsible*; Sparkes, *Socially Responsible Investment*, pp. 13–14, 42.

344 Jeucken, *Sustainability in Finance*, pp. 188–90; Richardson, 'Sustainable Finance', 311–12; Richardson, 'Do the Fiduciary', 147–8; Sparkes and Cowton, 'The Maturing', 47–8; Kelley, 'Law and Choice', 358; Heinkel, Kraus, and Zechner, 'The Effect of Green Investment', 431–2; Knoll, 'Ethical Screening'; O'Brien Hylton, '"Socially Responsible" Investing', 7–10; Fairfax, 'Easier Said Than Done?', 789–90.

345 Forster, 'Environmental Responsibilities', 71–2; Jeucken, *Sustainability in Finance*, pp. 188–90; Richardson, 'Do the Fiduciary, 147–8; Sparkes and Cowton, 'The Maturing', 48; Kelley, 'Law and Choice', 358; Adams and Knutsen, 'A Charitable Corporate', 215; Glass Geltman and Skvoback, 'Environmental Law', 473–5.

- investing in companies that actively engage in environmentally positive activities, such as research and development into renewable energy sources; and
- investing in companies that pursue policies that are beneficial for the environment, such as those that adopt energy efficiency programmes, obtain energy from renewable sources and implement comprehensive recycling and waste reduction programmes.

In contrast, the approach adopted by funds in negative screening can involve:[346]

- excluding companies from share portfolios that engage in environmentally harmful activities, such as those employing unsustainable logging practices; and
- excluding whole sectors from share portfolios, so that investments are not made in any company belonging to sectors of industry considered by the fund to be environmentally or socially harmful, such as the fossil fuel, pesticide, tobacco or mining industries.

(b) Disclosure and fiduciary duties

Unlike SRII, conventional financing practices have not systematically taken social, environmental, or ethical factors into account in investment decision-making. Furthermore, as financiers and institutional investors have not traditionally been held accountable for the detrimental social and environmental effects of the projects in which they invest, the governance frameworks have not been conducive to SRII.[347] In recent times, however, SRII has gained more traction within the financial community as the business case for CSR has become more widely appreciated, and, for example, as poor corporate environmental management becomes an indicator of general levels of financial risk.[348] Non-financial disclosure, therefore, has become an important tool in the operation of SRII.[349]

[346] Richardson, 'Do the Fiduciary', 147–8; Forster, 'Environmental Responsibilities', 71–2; Jeucken, *Sustainability in Finance*, pp. 188–90; Sparkes and Cowton, 'The Maturing', 47–8; Kelley, 'Law and Choice', 358; Glass Kelley, 'Law and Choice', 473–5; Adams and Knutsen, 'A Charitable Corporate', 214–15; see also the discussion in Hummels and Timmer, 'Investors in Need'.

[347] Richardson, *Socially Responsible*, pp. 3–7, 14.

[348] Ibid., p. 110; Richardson, 'Do the Fiduciary', 147; Forster, 'Environmental Responsibilities', 69–71, 73–4; Smith, 'The CERES Principles', 308; Monsma and Olsen, 'Muddling Through', 156–61; Hockets and Moir, 'Communicating Corporate Responsibility'; see also the discussion in Scholtens, 'Finance as a Driver'.

[349] Richardson, *Socially Responsible*, p. 319; Guay et al., 'Non-governmental Organizations'; Monsma and Olson, 'Muddling Through', 156–61; see also the discussion in Snyder,

Socially responsible investment decision-making is based on available non-financial information on corporate operations – and voluntary reporting regimes and national disclosure requirements have emerged as particularly significant means through which this type of information can be disseminated and assessed.[350] For example, voluntary reporting programmes include the Global Reporting Initiative, which facilitates the exchange of reporting information and provides a framework for the drafting of corporate sustainability reports.[351] National regulatory mechanisms reinforcing sustainability objectives have also been developed, such as the United Kingdom's Companies Act, which requires directors to report:

> to the extent necessary for an understanding of the development, performance or position of the company' business … information about environmental matters (including the impact of the company's business on the environment); [and] social and community issues, including information about any policies of the company regarding these matters and the effectiveness of the policies.[352]

The Act further supports the concept of CSR and facilitates the objectives of SRII through its reframing of the fiduciary duties of company directors. The Act requires directors to promote the success of the company and includes non-financial factors in the list of matters for consideration:

> s.172 Duty to Promote the Success of the Company
>
> (1) A director of a company must act in the way he considers, in good faith, would be most likely to promote the success of the company for the benefit of its members as a whole, and in doing so have regard (amongst other matters) to—

'Holding Multinational Corporations Accountable', 566–7; Kysar, 'Sustainable Development', 2156–60.

350 Snyder, 'Holding Multinational', 570–6; Richardson, 'Sustainable Finance', 337–9; Richardson, *Socially Responsible*, pp. 303, 319; Siebecker, 'Trust and Transparency'; Monsma and Olsen, 'Muddling Through', 156–76; see see also the discussion on disclosure of risk regulation in Williams and Conley, 'Triumph or Tragedy', 322–35; see also Hummels and Timmer, 'Investors in Need'; see also Lin, 'Corporate Social and Environmental Disclosure'; Williams, 'Corporate Law', 1641–2, 1645.

351 Global Reporting Initiative, *What is GRI?*; see the discussion in Richardson, *Socially Responsible*, 420–2; see also the discussion on the Global Reporting Initiative in Simaika, 'The Value of Information', 360–2; see more generally the discussion on corporate social reporting in Hess, 'Social Reporting'; see also Gioseffi, 'Corporate Accountability'.

352 Companies Act 2006, s. 417(5); see the discussion in Richardson, *Socially Responsible*, pp. 323–4; see also Clark and Knight, 'Implications of the UK Companies Act'; see also the discussion on mandatory disclosure requirements and voluntary initiatives in Lin, 'Corporate Social'.

(a) the likely consequences of any decision in the long term,
(b) the interests of the company's employees,
(c) the need to foster the company's business relationships with suppliers, customers and others,
(d) the impact of the company's operations on the community and the environment,
(e) the desirability of the company maintaining a reputation for high standards of business conduct, and
(f) the need to act fairly as between members of the company.[353]

This characterisation of directors' duties moves away from the notion that duties are owed exclusively to shareholders.[354] Together with the reporting requirements under the Companies Act, this approach can assist with greater access to material information for SRII. However, as Richardson argues, it is likely that express reform of the fiduciary duties owed by fund managers to investors will also be required before a fundamental shift in mainstream institutional investment practices can be induced.[355] This is largely due to widely held assumptions about fiduciary duties on trustees of pension funds that require such trustees 'to act prudently and loyally in the best interests of their beneficiaries' – and that this precludes SRII.[356] Richardson argues that fiduciary duties do not necessarily conflict with SRII, but that measures taken to clarify that position, to expressly allow the consideration of sustainability factors, or, indeed, to require such consideration, would assist with greater mainstreaming of SRII.[357] Recently, there have been

[353] Companies Act 2006, s. 172; see Richardson, *Socially Responsible*, p. 236; see also the discussion in Williams and Conley, 'Triumph or Tragedy', 354–6; see also the discussion of directors' duties in Worthington, 'Reforming Directors'; Clark and Knight, 'Implications'; Lowry, 'The Duty of Loyalty', 615–22; see further the discussion on these issues in the Australian context in McConvill and Joy, 'The Interaction of Directors' Duties'.

[354] Richardson, *Socially Responsible*, pp. 236–8; Williams and Conley, 'Triumph or Tragedy', 354–6; see also the discussion in Hummels and Timmer, 'Investors in Need', 73; see the arguments that corporate law does not conflict with unprofitable CSR-related decision-making in Elhauge, 'Sacrificing Corporate Profits'; Williams and Conley, 'An Emerging Third Way?', 499–500.

[355] Richardson, *Socially Responsible*, pp. 569–70; see also the discussion on reforming fiduciary duties in Richardson, 'Sustainable Finance', 185–201.

[356] Richardson, 'Sustainable Finance', 147; see the discussion in Richardson, *Socially Responsible*, pp. 221–34; see also the views expressed in Whitehouse, 'Corporate Social Responsibility'.

[357] See the discussion in Richardson, *Socially Responsible*, pp. 221–34, 550–9, 567–70; Richardson, 'Sustainable Finance', 147–9.

encouraging moves in that direction. For example, regulations under the Pensions Act (UK) require pension fund trustees to disclose in their statement of investment principles:

(i) The extent (if at all) to which social, environmental or ethical considerations are taken into account in the selection, retention, and realisation of investments; and
(ii) The policy (if any) directing the exercise of the rights (including voting rights) attaching to investments.[358]

This particular approach to disclosure was intended both to counteract the view that trustee fiduciary duties are in conflict with SRII and to promote greater transparency in the institutional investment sector.[359] Engagement with this mode of facilitating SRII has continued to increase as other states have also introduced legislation requiring greater disclosure of the way in which social, environmental, and ethical criteria are factored into pension fund investment activities.[360] However, although cultural changes are gradually occurring within the institutional investment community, and there has been a growth in specialist ethical investment funds, the actual implementation of socially responsible investment decision-making in the mainstream sector remains questionable, with certain pension funds still expressly professing that social, environmental, and ethical considerations are not specifically taken into account in investment decisions.[361] Richardson provides a number of examples, including that of a product disclosure statement from Colonial First State's Managed Investment Fund:

[358] Occupational Pension Schemes (Investment) Regulations (2005) cll. 2(3)(b)(vi)–(3)(c); Pensions Act 1995 (UK); see the discussion in Richardson, *Socially Responsible*, p. 304; see also Sparkes, *Socially Responsible Investment*, pp. 6–7; see also Sparkes and Cowton, 'The Maturing', 49; Gifford, 'Measuring', 142; see also the discussion on pension reform in Richardson, 'Financing Environmental Change', 175–9; see further Mathieu, *Response of UK Pension Funds*.

[359] Richardson, *Socially Responsible*, p. 304.

[360] See, e.g., the following regulation cited in Richardson, *Socially Responsible*, pp. 304–6, *Versicherungsaufsichtsgesetz*, s. 10a Abs. 1, Appendix D, Chapter III, 2 (CC); *Altersvorsorgevertraege-Zertifizierungsgesetz*, s. 7 Abs.4; *Gesetzesentwurf Alterseinkuenftegesetz*, art.5 (Germany); *Loi Pensions Complémentaires* – LPC, (April 28, 2003) Art. 42(3), *Moniteur Belge* (2nd ed.) (May 15, 2003) 26,407 (Belgium); *Decreto Legislativo* (December 5, 2005) Art. 6(14) (Italy); Financial Services Reform Act (2001) (Australia).

[361] Richardson, *Socially Responsible*, pp. 309–13; see also the comments in Berger, Australian Conservation Foundation, *Disclosure*; see also Wheeler et al., *Comparative Study*, pp. 18–19; see the discussion on specialist ethical investment funds in Richardson, 'Sustainable Finance', 312.

We do not specifically take into account environmental, social or ethical considerations when making an investment decision for the fund, as unitholders have differing views about such issues. As the responsible entity for the fund, we therefore cannot take into account individual unitholders' particular interests if doing so may have a financial impact on the returns for other investors.[362]

The launch of the UNPRI in 2006 certainly raised the profile of the market for SRII.[363] And although ethical investment funds still possess only a small slice of the investment market, it is regarded as a dynamic and growing sector, evidenced by the emergence of ethical investment 'tracking' instruments, such as the Dow Jones Sustainability Group Index and the British Financial Times Stock Exchange ethical index.[364] Despite the growth in activity and interest, however, scholars question whether SRI funds can actually achieve their stated desired outcomes in modifying corporate behaviour.[365] As Richardson argues, it will be difficult for SRII to transform the investment sector on its own without the introduction of regulatory changes at the domestic and international levels.[366] This not only lends general support to the calls for an international regulatory framework governing corporate conduct, but also more specifically to the calls for closer regulation of financiers and investors that have been generated by the global financial crisis of 2008–10.[367] In considering international mechanisms to ensure greater accountability in the financial sector, it is an opportune moment to extend that exploration beyond corporate governance and liquidity regulation to include other factors as well, such as social and environmental accountability of financiers and investors.

362 Richardson, *Socially Responsible*, p. 312; Berger, *Disclosure*, p. 2.

363 UNPRI; see also the discussion in Richardson, *Socially Responsible*, pp. 399–402.

364 Dow Jones Sustainability Group Index, available at www.sustainability-indexes.com (last accessed 15 December 2011); Financial Times Stock Exchange Ethical Index, available at www.ftse.com/Indices/FTSE4Good_Index_Series (available at 15 December 2011); see the discussion in Richardson, 'Sustainable Finance', 312; see also Richardson, 'Financing Sustainability', 101–3.

365 See, e.g., Branson, 'Corporate Governance', 632–5; Haigh and Hazelton, 'Financial Markets'; Schepers and Prakash Sethi. 'Do Socially Responsible Funds'.

366 Richardson, *Socially Responsible*, pp. 523–40, 569–70; see also the discussion on reforming fiduciary duties in Richardson, 'Sustainable Finance', 185–201; see also the examination of ways to design regulation so as to support socially responsible institutional investment in Richardson, 'Enlisting Institutional Investors'.

367 See, e.g., the discussion in Crotty, 'Structural Causes'; Wade, 'From Global Imbalances'; see also the discussion on disclosure regulation following the global credit crisis and social and environmental corporate disclosure in Clark and Knight, 'Implications'.

2. Implications for international investment law

This discussion on SRII leads to a consideration of what implications these developments may have for international investment law. Much like the proliferation of voluntary codes of corporate conduct, SRII is indicative of a socio-political shift in the public's expectations of corporate behaviour and of changes in the business dynamic for the financing and investment sector. The rationale behind sustainable finance, that social, environmental, and financial factors should be taken into account in decision-making, is an increasingly normalised part of doing business in project lending and investment – and SRII is contributing to this culture. Arguably, this combination of factors is shifting perceptions of the appropriate role of financiers and investors and of their accountability for social and environmental consequences of transnational activities. In cultivating the linking of investment with social and environmental responsibility, SRII is part of the pre-normative noise providing a backdrop to the discourse surrounding the engagement of international investment law with non-investment issues.

Indeed, the practices in SRII and the potential harmonising of standards under the UNPRI[368] will intensify pressure on international investment law to reflect the social and environmental considerations that increasingly impact on decision-making within the sector. As SRII fosters the view that investors are implicated in the activities of the companies in which they invest, it highlights the lack of a corresponding principle in international investment law. When viewed against the SRII approach, the non-engagement of international investment law with the effect of investor activity on local communities and environment of the host state is thrown into stark relief. For this reason, not only could SRII provide a basis from which to begin a recharacterisation of the traditional foreign investor–host state relationship, it could also contribute to the crystallisation of emerging principles of sustainability within the financing and investment sectors. Again, much like the voluntary codes, however, SRII is also only one tool in a complex mix of governance mechanisms directing financing and investment towards more socially and environmentally responsible practices. There is no suggestion that it is sufficient in itself to bring about the necessary transformation of these sectors – and it is certainly not a replacement

[368] UNPRI, above n. 190.

for an international regulatory framework governing the conduct of transnational financiers and investors.

III. Conclusion

From the foregoing analysis, it can be seen that there is potential for future synergies between the foreign investment sector and sustainability objectives – but also that this is not yet reflected in international investment law. With this in mind, I have explored the shifts in corporate behaviour, the advent of voluntary codes of corporate conduct, the development of social and environmental standards in project lending, the growth in SRII, and the emergence of a global culture in which it is increasingly difficult to engage in socially and environmentally damaging practices without repercussions for the corporation. I have argued that these parallel trends are contributing to a process of infusing sustainability approaches in financing and investment practices, with which international investment law is now out of step. In so doing, these movements are challenging the traditional conceptualisation of the foreign investor–host state relationship. And, for this reason, they may perhaps present an avenue for defusing the imperialist origins that remain alive in modern international investment law.

In its account of ongoing CSR and sustainable finance processes, this chapter has argued that CSR norms will be integral to the development of socially and environmentally responsible principles of international investment law. In particular, they will be essential if the host state is to access protective principles under international investment agreements, to regulate in the public interest without the spectre of investor–state claims, and to hold foreign investors accountable on the international plane for their conduct. Emerging international CSR principles on environmental protection, human rights, and labour conditions are clearly relevant to this process of reorienting international investment law. Their continuing infusion through business practices is cementing their status as expected standards of corporate conduct.

What has also emerged is that this process of normalising CSR in transnational capital movement is also fuelling pressure to reshape international investment law. As the disconnect between corporate practice, socio-political expectations of appropriate corporate conduct, and the substantive requirements of the law becomes ever more apparent, it also becomes increasingly difficult to justify the maintenance of international investment rules that take no account of corporate social and environmental practice. Indeed, voluntary codes of corporate conduct provide a useful preliminary framework from which to develop concrete provisions for insertion into international investment agreements. At the very least, they are pointing to the future direction of international corporate regulation and are readying the investment sector for compliance with future legal obligation.

Setting a new path in international investment law requires substantive reorientation of its current principles, new approaches within international investment agreements, genuine dialogue between stakeholders, procedural reform in investor–state dispute resolution, and, ultimately, a treaty governing the conduct of transnational financiers and investors. This chapter has examined the CSR and sustainable finance movements as possible generators of change directed towards the realisation of such transformative conditions. Chapters 5 and 6 take the next step and explore the ways in which international law might be used to translate these hints at synergy into concrete measures of reform for international investment law.

PART III

Foreign investment law, practices, and policy: future trends

5 Transformation in international law: applying developments to foreign investment

In considering recent transformations in international law, it appeared to me that several new developments could contribute significantly to the reorientation of international investment law. In particular, the advent of non-state actors and transnational networks, the increasing focus on global public law and justice, and the transfer of concepts and principles across separate areas of international law and between domestic and international legal systems, have all led to shifts in emphasis in the international legal order.[1] There remains, however, a reluctance within the investment community to reflect these developments to their fullest extent. Certainly, a disinclination is manifest amongst capital-exporting states to engage with transnational civil society, to acknowledge the public interest in investment disputes, and to integrate principles from non-investment areas of international law.[2] In this way, the field of international investment law is out of step with current trends in public international law – and this disconnect becomes ever more stark as the investment community continues to resist calls for change.

This chapter examines these new developments on the international stage and argues that they are contributing to current pressure to reform international investment law. At the same time, however, it also contends that they simultaneously provide channels through which international investment law can be reformed. In this regard, I argue that the influence of epistemic communities and transnational

[1] See, e.g., the discussion in Sands, 'Turtles and Torturers'; Slaughter, *A New World Order*; Krisch and Kingsbury, 'Introduction'.

[2] See the discussion in Muchlinksi, 'Corporate Social Responsibility', 637; see also Hirsch, 'Interactions', 154.

networks could effect a cultural change within the investment arbitral community, state advisors, and treaty-negotiators. The consistent application of global public law principles of transparency and public participation in investor–state arbitration could redress the legitimacy concerns surrounding this system of dispute resolution.[3] Embracing the more fluid approach of recent international jurisprudence towards the transfer of concepts and principles between fields of international law could see the remoulding of investment law through the consideration of environmental and human rights principles.[4] With such a potential in mind, I wanted to explore the role these recent transformative developments in international law-making could play in the reshaping of international investment law.

For this reason, section I of this chapter initially sets out the changing nature of the international legal system. It examines, in particular, the trend towards the integration of principles and cross-sectoral application of rules amongst areas of international law. It considers recent cases and international instruments in which this approach has been applied and subject areas that are likely to be particularly influential in the future direction of international investment law. Section II examines emerging frameworks of global public law and argues that this approach is directly relevant for the current system of investor–state dispute resolution. Section III analyses theories reflecting on the increasing influence of transnational networks and epistemic communities in international law and politics and considers the implications of these developments for reform in international investment law. Overall, this chapter explores ways in which the 'hints at synergy' identified in Chapter 4 may crystallise within international investment law through the adoption of new approaches manifesting in international law.

Central to the generation of such change will be an appreciation of the field's historical patterns and the way in which these emerge even as the discipline engages with shifts in international law. Shedding light on this tendency, Chapter 5 argues that an array of key structural

[3] See generally the discussion on legitimacy issues in investor–state arbitration in Van Harten, *Investment Treaty Arbitration*; see also Brower, Brower, and Sharpe, 'The Coming Crisis'; see also Sornarajah, 'The Clash', 13–17; Tienhaara, 'Third Party Participation', 230–1.

[4] See, e.g., *United States-Import Prohibition of Certain Shrimp and Shrimp Products, Report of the Appellate Body*, 38 ILM 118 (1999); see the discussion on the transfer of concepts and principles in Sands, 'Treaty, Custom'.

changes have been occurring in the international legal system over several decades, but that international investment law has engaged with only those elements that promote investor protection. For example, the increasing role of the individual on the international plane has manifested in the development of investor–state arbitration, but not in a system for those affected by investor activity to bring actions under international law. This selectivity to the application of advances in international law reflects traditional investor approaches to the evolution of international investment law. And it reproduces an imperialist use of international law as a mechanism to support solely investor protection and the interests of capital-exporting states. Such ingrained approaches are not easy to shift; indeed, even identifying them can attract hostility. However, I argue in this chapter that embracing a broader range of recent developments in international law would certainly result in a more representative and balanced model of international investment law, but it would also constitute an opportunity to break from those imperialist patterns within the investment framework and would re-engage investment regulation with public international law to the fullest extent. Whether the investment community ultimately avails itself of that opportunity, however, is another question altogether.

I. Shifts in the system: accelerated law-making and interacting principles

A. *The changing nature of the international legal system*

International law is an organic system, evolving continuously both in its content and in its structures – and this capacity for change has become increasingly apparent over the last fifty years.[5] As Crawford observes, international law is presently in 'a period of comparative openness and re-formation',[6] and that there is a 'sense of fluidity, opportunity and uncertainty'.[7] Key frameworks and mechanisms remain in place, such as the state and the use of treaty-making and customary rules, but a reconceptualisation of many facets of the international legal system is in progress.[8] This is a far cry from the classical model of international

[5] Sands, 'Turtles and Torturers'; Crawford, *International Law*; Triggs, *International Law*, pp. 17–20; Spiro, 'Globalization'; see also the discussion in Shelton, 'Protecting Human Rights'; Higgins, 'International Law'.

[6] Crawford, *International Law*, p. 17. [7] Ibid. [8] Ibid.; Sands, 'Turtles and Torturers'.

law, which is of a system concerned solely with the governing of relations between states.[9] As it developed throughout the eighteenth and nineteenth centuries, the focus for international law was very much on the preservation of sovereign rights and its central tenet was non-interference in the internal affairs of other states.[10] Furthermore, there was a presumption that states were entitled to act as they wished, unless there was an express restriction on their conduct. As the primary objective of the system was the avoidance of military conflict between states, the range of subject matter regulated by international law was limited.[11]

International law, as a system, has been moving away from this classical model for some time.[12] And it is clear that a gradual shift in perspective towards globalism has been instrumental in this reappraisal.[13] Recognising that global issues are complex, interrelated, and require a correspondingly sophisticated approach to their resolution has operated as a significant catalyst in the remoulding of international law and its mechanisms.[14] It has led to the increasing use of 'soft law' instruments in the search for more dynamic and responsive tools to address global issues.[15] It has also seen the emergence of new substantive areas in international law and new actors within the international legal order.[16] The rate of international law-making has accelerated, the number of international rules has multiplied, and the fora in which to hear international disputes have proliferated.[17] Indeed, the 'globalisation' of international law has made significant encroachments on the

[9] Brierly, *The Law of Nations*, p. 1; Triggs, *International Law*, pp. 11–12, 23.

[10] Sands, 'Turtles and Torturers', 529–30. [11] Ibid.; Higgins, 'International Law', 84.

[12] Higgins, 'International Law', 82–5; Crawford, *International Law*, p. 17; Sands, 'Turtles and Torturers', 527; Sterio, 'The Evolution', 213–16.

[13] Sands, 'Turtles and Torturers', 537–8; Garcia, 'Globalization and the Theory', 9–10; Higgins, 'International Law', 82–5; Berman, 'From International Law'.

[14] See the discussion in Abbott and Snidal, 'Strengthening International Regulation'; see in the context of international environmental law, Boer, 'The Globalisation of Environmental Law'.

[15] Dupuy, 'Soft Law'; Jackson, 'Global Corporate Governance', 44–7; Dupuy, 'Customary International Law', p. 458.

[16] Spiro, 'Globalization, International', 570; Sands, 'Turtles and Torturers', 548–9; Higgins, 'International Law', 82–5; Sterio, 'The Evolution', 215–18; Raustiala, 'Participatory Revolution'; Mertus, 'Considering Nonstate Actors'; Gunning, 'Modernizing Customary International Law', 221; Koh, 'Transnational Legal Process', 203–4.

[17] Sands, 'Turtles and Torturers', 548–9; Higgins, 'International Law', 82–3; Sterio, 'The Evolution', 218–20; see also the discussion in Romano, 'The Proliferation'; Treves, 'Conflicts'.

traditional impregnability of state sovereignty, rendering what occurs within state borders now of considerable legitimate legal interest to the international community.[18]

This era has not only seen the emergence of new substantive principles and rules of customary international law, but also new categories of international rules, introducing structural changes to the regulatory system. With the acceleration of international law-making, it has now become commonplace to talk of 'emerging' principles of international law and 'emerging' rules of international customary law.[19] These emerging norms do not yet have full legal status, yet they do represent a new class of embryonic or potential obligation – in this sense, they evidence modes of current state practice, set out the way in which states are expected to conduct themselves, and indicate the principles that are most likely to form rules of customary international law in the future.[20] In an interactive process of engagement amongst the many global actors and their activities, 'soft law' instruments have become increasingly important in the development of new concepts and principles within international law. In particular, such instruments alter the discourse and frame the 'political thinking' on the issues in new ways.[21] In themselves, they influence state decision-making and are often chosen as the most appropriate mechanism to achieve specific global outcomes. But soft law can also constitute the preliminary stages in the formation of 'hard law', either as a precursor to the conclusion of a treaty or as a contribution to the crystallisation of customary rules.[22] Indeed, soft law instruments are even contributing to the development of new branches of law, as evidenced by the burgeoning area of international law on sustainable development since the Rio Declaration on Environment and Development and Agenda 21.[23] While the precise

[18] Sands, 'Turtles and Torturers', 535–8; Gunning, 'Modernizing Customary', 220–1; Boer, 'The Globalisation'; Sterio, 'The Evolution'; see also the discussion in Percival, 'The Globalization'; for a discussion on globalisation, international law, and jurisdictional issues, see Berman, 'The Globalization'.

[19] Sands, *Principles*, pp. 231–2; see also Weeramantry, *Universalising*, 456–63 for a discussion on the evolution of the concept of sustainable development into a part of international law, and for a discussion on 'Some Emerging Principles of International Law'.

[20] Sands, *Principles*, pp. 124, 231–2; see also the discussion in Gunning, 'Modernizing Customary', 220–34; Boyle and Chinkin, *The Making of International Law*, pp. 222–6.

[21] Berman, 'From International Law', 492–507; Palmer, 'New Ways', 269–70; Slaughter, Tulumello, and Wood, 'International Law', 370–1.

[22] Palmer, 'New Ways', 269–70; Abbott and Snidal, 'Hard and Soft Law', 421–3.

[23] Dupuy, 'Formation'; Jackson, 'Global Corporate Governance'; Boer, 'Sustainability Law'; see also the discussion on 'Emergent Legal Principles', sustainable development,

character of the normativity of soft law remains a contested subject, what can be said is that the evolution, proliferation, and deepening influence of soft law instruments reflects both the changing nature of the international legal system and the range of factors that now shape state behaviour.[24]

The transfer of concepts and principles between substantively discrete areas of law and between domestic, regional, and international legal systems has also been a central factor in the progressive development of international law.[25] As Sands states:

> International law is traditionally presented as an agglomeration of more or less distinct and free standing subject areas: the law of the sea, air law, human rights, economic development, free trade, environment, intellectual property, and other subjects tend to be treated as self-contained areas. We now know that this is not the case.[26]

In line with this modern conceptualisation, recent models have adopted more integrated approaches to the substantive development of international law, seeking to balance interests, to allow for the interchange of principles between fields of international law, and to encourage vertical interaction between domestic, regional, and international legal systems.[27] More expansive methodologies are being utilised in which treaties are considered in light of rules of international customary law.[28] There is a sense that where proceedings in international courts and tribunals impact significantly on public interest issues, voices in addition to those of states should be present.[29] In reflecting on the

and 'soft law' in Brownlie, *Principles*, pp. 278–80; Rio Declaration on Environment and Development, Report of the United Nations Conference on Environment and Development (UNCED), UN Doc. A/CONF.151/6/Rev.1 (1992), 31 ILM 874 (1992); Agenda 21, Report of the UNCED, UN Doc. A/CONF.151/26/Rev.1 (vol.1) (1992), 31 ILM 874 (1992).

24 Palmer, 'New Ways', 269–70; Guzman, 'A Compliance-Based Theory', 1879–81; Chayes and Handler Chayes, *The New Sovereignty*, p. 2; see for a fundamental critique of delineating a category of international instrument as soft law in Raustiala, 'Form and Substance'.

25 Sands, 'Treaty', 88–91; Sands, 'Searching for Balance'; see also the discussion in McLachlan, 'The Principle of Systemic Integration'.

26 Sands, 'Turtles and Torturers', 549.

27 Berman, 'From International Law', 488–507; Sands, 'Searching for Balance', 200–2; Sands, 'Treaty', 88–91.

28 Sands, 'Turtles and Torturers', 549–50; Birnie, Boyle, and Redgwell, *International Law*, pp. 109–10; see, e.g., the analysis in *United States-Import Prohibition of Certain Shrimp and Shrimp Products, Report of the Appellate Body*, 38 ILM 118 (1999); *Gabčikovo-Nagymaros* (Hungary/Slovakia) (1997) ICJ Reports 7, para 112, 140.

29 Sands, 'Turtles and Torturers', 546.

cumulative effects of these developments, scholars maintain that they indicate a transformation of the international legal system towards one which has public law at its base and has a fluid approach, interrelating national, regional, and international law.[30]

Examining international investment law against a background of these shifts in approach, it becomes apparent that key developments have been absorbed into the investment field on only a very selective basis, incorporating those elements that support the position of capital-exporting states and their investor nationals.[31] At a fundamental level, although international investment law is located within public international law, it is a sector that remains culturally aligned with the interests of private business.[32] This has left it at direct odds with generalised transformations in international law that seek to increase public participation and the involvement of non-governmental organisations (NGOs), to give effect to ethics-based legal concepts, to increase the accountability of private actors within international law, and to transfer appropriate principles within discrete fields of international law. It can certainly be seen that integrated interpretative methodology is not being adopted in the resolution of international investment disputes or in the development of principles of international investment law.[33] Quite clearly, emerging principles of global public law such as transparency and accountability are not fully implemented in investor–state arbitration and the public interest is not given equal consideration alongside investor protection.[34] The desirability of incorporating non-investment principles or considering environmental or human rights issues within international investment law is, of course, a contested

[30] Ibid., 530, 556–7; Krisch and Kingsbury, 'Introduction: Global'; Garcia, 'Globalization and the Theory'; Sterio, 'The Evolution'.

[31] The manifestation of these preferences is discussed in detail in section I.2(b), II, and III of this chapter.

[32] Sornarajah, 'The Clash of Globalizations'; see the discussion on the private and public dimensions of investor–state arbitration in Van Harten, *Investment Treaty Arbitration*, pp. 3–6, 58–62, 123–5, 153–64; see the discussion in Tienhaara, *The Expropriation*, pp. 54–7, 143–7, 276; Odumosu, 'The Law and Politics'; see, e.g., the views expressed in Baker, 'Denial of Justice', 187, 187–91; see also, e.g., the opinions expressed in Wälde and Ndi, 'Stabilizing International Investment'; this issue is explored in depth below in section III of this chapter.

[33] See the discussion in Sands, 'Searching for Balance'.

[34] Van Harten, *Investment Treaty Arbitration*, pp. 3–6, 58–62, 123–5, 153–64; Tienhaara, 'Third Party Participation'; Sornarajah, 'The Clash of Globalizations'; Soloway, 'Environmental Regulation'; Cosbey et al., *Investment and Sustainable*; Mann et al., *IISD Model International Agreement*.

subject. Indeed, Sands characterises this issue as essentially polarising participants in the discourse into two conceptually opposed camps, and, upon which, there still appears to be little concurrence.[35]

In approaching this field with a reformist eye, I suggest that the development of international investment law would be greatly enhanced if a wider selection of systemic advances in international law-making were also embraced by the investment community and their states. In particular, this would encourage a more progressive, balanced, and accessible system of investment dispute resolution and it would create a more dynamic framework in which the development of socially and environmentally responsible principles of international investment law could be cultivated. Fully adopting these new developments in the international legal system would also address legitimacy concerns that currently surround investor–state arbitration as a dispute settlement system.[36] Furthermore, it could contribute to the reorientation of international investment law, framing the host state as an active participant with rights rather than as solely a passive entity with obligations.

B. *Transferring principles and integrating issues*

In light of the fact that international investment law interacts with a wide range of policy areas and public interest issues, this book argues that consideration of non-investment issues within investment instruments and investor–state disputes is appropriate. Given this position, then, the question becomes one of how an integrated approach might manifest in international investment instruments and dispute resolution. As a starting point, turning to contemporary cross-sectoral practice outside the investment field provides a useful precedent for consideration of this issue.

Recent international jurisprudence addressing varied subject matter illustrates cross-sectoral referencing of principles in the determination of disputes. And with the proliferation of dispute resolution fora and the articulation of emerging principles of integration and of sustainable development, there is also a greater readiness within international courts and tribunals to engage with social, environmental, and economic factors at issue in an integrated fashion.[37] Furthermore,

[35] Sands, 'Searching for Balance', 202.

[36] Van Harten, *Investment Treaty Arbitration*; Cosbey et al., *Investment and Sustainable*; Mann et al., *IISD Model International Agreement*.

[37] Sands, *Principles*, pp. 131–3; Sands, 'Treaty'; Stephens, 'Multiple International Courts', 234, 242–64; for a discussion on the use of sustainable development as a 'modifying'

examining the current use of cross-sectoral approaches within international law also serves to highlight the way in which the investment sector's generally isolated consideration of applicable law is out of step with the more progressive developments in international law.

1. Cross-sectoral instruments

The cross-sectoral reach of areas such as international environmental and human rights law is exemplified in the focus of recent instruments and initiatives that address these issues embedded within different contexts. In particular, such integrated methodology has become a mainstream approach since the United Nations Conference on Environment and Development (UNCED) in 1992, which expressly linked environmental and developmental law and policy.[38] Indeed, central characterisations of the current evolutionary phase of international environmental law were embodied within UNCED, crystallising around the interdependence of global problems, integration, effective implementation of environmental regulation, clarification of emerging principles, and the concept of sustainable development.[39] Giving effect to these themes has necessarily involved the consideration of issues, interests, and principles from diverse fields. This, in turn, has incidentally normalised integrated methodologies within a broader context and resulted in the corresponding consideration of environmental issues within diverse areas of international law and policy, such as trade, development, health, human rights, security, and armed conflict.[40] So much so, that it is now widely acknowledged that this integrated model is the most appropriate way in which to respond to global challenges.[41]

(a) Integration within soft law instruments

International law-making now draws on a rich array of sources of law, moving beyond treaties and custom to utilise soft law instruments.[42] In

norm in the application of conflicting primary norms, see Lowe, 'Sustainable Development', 19, 33–7.

38 United Nations, *Earth Summit*; see also the discussion in Sands, 'Treaty', 90–1; Stephens, 'Multiple International Courts', 235–6.

39 Sands, *Principles*, p. 51; for earlier phases in the development of international environmental as a distinct field, see Sands, *Principles*, pp. 25–50.

40 Ibid., pp. 69, 294–7, 308–16; Birnie, Boyle and Redgwell, *International Law and the Environment*, pp. 205–8, 271–98, 753–6; Boer, 'The Globalisation'.

41 Sands, *Principles*, pp. 3–5, 11–12; Triggs, *International Law: Contemporary*, pp. 11–12, 23.

42 Guzman, 'A Compliance-Based Theory', 1879–81; Berman, 'From International Law', 488–507; Sterio, 'The Evolution', 218–19; Chayes and Chayes, *The New Sovereignty*, p. 2;

part because of its non-binding character, soft law is being used to perform a number of central functions in international relations and law-making. In contrast to the lengthy processes entailed in the conclusion of treaties and the crystallisation of rules of customary international law, the relative ease with which soft law instruments can be negotiated and altered renders them ideal mechanisms when a rapid response to global issues is required.[43] At times considered as evidence of state practice or *opinio juris*, or even as an intermediary signal of future 'hard law', the norms contained within soft law instruments interact closely with treaty obligations and custom.[44] And, as a reflection of these dynamic processes, fluidity in the exchange of concepts amongst disciplines is also common in the substance of soft law instruments.[45]

The field of international development law and policy, for example, is illustrative of this integrated approach within both soft law instruments and other programmes. A range of different types of international instruments exemplify the contextual consideration of development issues, such as the Rio Declaration on Environment and Development,[46] Agenda 21,[47] the World Bank's 'safeguard policies' on social and environmental issues in project finance for developing states,[48] the United Nations Millennium Development Goals,[49] the Monterrey Consensus on Financing for Development,[50] the Johannesburg Declaration on

Shelton, 'Normative Hierarchy', 319; Gruchalla-Wesierski, 'A Framework'; Chinkin, 'The Challenge'.

43 Palmer, 'New Ways', 269–70; Abbott and Snidal, 'Hard and Soft Law', 421–3; Guzman, 'A Compliance-Based Theory', 1879–81; Shelton, 'Normative Hierarchy', 319–20; Slaughter, Tulumello, and Wood, 'International Law', 370–1.

44 Shelton, 'Normative Hierarchy', 319–20; Palmer, 'New Ways', 269–70; see also the discussion in Weissbrodt and Kruger, 'Norms on the Responsibilities', 914–15.

45 Sands, 'Treaty', 88–91; see generally the discussion in Sterio, 'The Evolution', 215–20; see also the discussion specifically on sustainable development and soft law instruments in Marong, 'From Rio to Johannesburg', 30–2.

46 Rio Declaration on Environment and Development, Report of the UNCED, UN Doc. A/CONF.151/6/Rev.1 (1992), 31 ILM 874 (1992).

47 Agenda 21, Report of the UNCED, UN Doc. A/CONF.151/26/Rev.1 (vol.I) (1992), 31 ILM 874.

48 The World Bank, *Operational Manual: Operational Policies: Environmental Assessment*, World Bank OP 4.01 (January 1999).

49 United Nations Millennium Declaration, UNGA Res. A/55/2 (2000); United Nations Development Goals, available at www.un.org/millenniumgoals/ (last accessed 16 December 2011).

50 Monterrey Consensus of the International Conference on Financing for Development, UN Doc. A/AC.257/32 (2002), available at www.un.org/esa/ffd/monterrey/MonterreyConsensus.pdf (last accessed 16 December 2011).

Sustainable Development,[51] the Doha Ministerial Declaration linking trade and environmental protection,[52] the Conference on the World Financial and Economic Crisis and its Impact on Development,[53] and the United Nations Global Compact (UN Global Compact).[54] In practice, this approach means that while the focus of these instruments is on development, the issues are not considered in artificial isolation from other relevant factors.

(b) Institutional developments and non-state actors

Cross-sectoral framing of issues has also evolved in parallel with the exploration of new governance options and the emergence of new actors operating within the international sphere.[55] The activities of non-state actors, and new methods of engagement between states and non-state actors, have been instrumental in the cross-sectoral infusion of concepts, principles, and issues. In particular, there has been an emphasis on the fostering of 'partnerships' and new collaborations.[56] For example, a significant feature of the 2002 World Summit on Sustainable Development was the focus on partnerships to promote sustainable development.[57] Illustrative of this approach to global governance, the Johannesburg Plan of Implementation provides that:

> the implementation [of the outcomes of the Summit] should involve all relevant actors through partnerships, especially between Governments of the North and South, on the one hand, and between Governments and major groups, on the other, to achieve the widely shared goals of sustainable development. As reflected in the Monterrey Consensus, such partnerships are key to pursuing sustainable development in a globalizing world.[58]

[51] Johannesburg Declaration on Sustainable Development, Report of the United Nations World Summit on Sustainable Development, UN Doc. A/CONF. 199/20 (2002), available at www.un.org/esa/sustdev/documents/WSSD_POI_PD/English/POI_PD.htm (last accessed 17 July 2009).

[52] Declaration of the Fourth Ministerial Conference, Doha, Qatar, WT/MIN(01)/DEC/1, 20 November 2001, paras 31–3.

[53] Conference on the World Financial and Economic Crisis, Report of the Secretary-General, UN Doc. A/CONF.214/4 (2009), available at www.un.org/ga/search/view_doc.asp?symbol=A/CONF.214/4&Lang=E (last accessed 16 December 2011).

[54] United Nations Global Compact (2000), available at www.unglobalcompact.org/ (last accessed 16 December 2011).

[55] Sands, *Principles*, pp. 112–22; Scherr and Gregg, 'Johannesburg'.

[56] Sands, *Principles*, pp. 112–22; Scherr and Gregg, 'Johannesburg'.

[57] Scherr and Gregg, 'Johannesburg', 439–40.

[58] *Johannesburg Plan of Implementation, Report of the World Summit on Sustainable Development*, UN Doc A/CONF.199/20 (2002) para.3, available at www.un.org/esa/sustdev/documents/WSSD_POI_PD/English/WSSD_PlanImpl.pdf (last accessed 25 July 2010).

The UN Global Compact provides another example of this emphasis on collaborative engagement, combining new institutional techniques with a cross-sectoral approach. As discussed earlier in Chapter 4, it promotes voluntary partnerships between governments, corporations, NGOs, and United Nations' agencies to address issues related to human rights, the environment, economic activity, developing markets, labour rights, and anti-corruption measures.[59]

A number of NGOs and research organisations have specifically focused on integrating issues and facilitating the cross-fertilisation of principles between fields of international law.[60] For example, the Washington-based Center for International Environmental Law has a specific programme dedicated to the intersection of human rights law and international environmental law.[61] The IUCN (International Union for Conservation of Nature), as a hybrid organisation of governmental and non-governmental members, has several cross-cutting programmes, including 'Business and Biodiversity',[62] 'Social Policy' in Conservation,[63] and 'Species Trade and Use'.[64] The IUCN has also issued a statement on armed conflict and principles of environmental protection and included provisions on military activities and the environment in its Draft Covenant on Environment and Development.[65] The London-based NGO Foundation for International Environmental Law and Development (FIELD) has three work streams, one of which is devoted to 'Trade, Investment and Sustainable Development'.[66] The rationale for the International Institute for Sustainable Development (IISD) is necessarily the integration of social, economic, and environmental issues, with key research themes encompassing 'Climate Change and Energy', 'Governance', 'Foreign Investment for Sustainable Development',

59 United Nations Global Compact, *Corporate Citizenship*; see the discussion in Richardson, *Socially Responsible*, pp. 409–10; Barnett and Duvall, 'Power'; see also the discussion in Cetindamar and Husoy, 'Corporate Social Responsibility'; Whitehouse, 'Corporate Social Responsibility'.

60 The use of the term 'cross-fertilisation' for the transfer of principles within international law was coined by Sands, 'Treaty'; for his discussion on the role of non-state actors in new trends in international law, see also Sands, 'Turtles and Torturers', 527, 530, 556–7.

61 Center for International Environmental Law, *Human Rights*.

62 IUCN, *Business and Biodiversity*. 63 IUCN, *Social Policy*.

64 IUCN, *Our Work Programmes*.

65 IUCN, *Statement: Armed Conflict*; IUCN, *Draft Covenant*.

66 Foundation for International Environmental Law and Development, *Trade, Investment and Sustainable Development*.

'Networks and Partnerships', and 'Sustainable Markets'.[67] And the Centre for International Sustainable Development Law (CISDL) further exemplifies an integrated approach with its multi-pronged international legal research agenda designed to 'promote sustainable societies and the protection of ecosystems'[68] through diverse programmes, such as 'Trade, Investment and Financial Law for Sustainable Development', 'Biodiversity and Biosafety', 'Health and Hazards', 'Climate Change', 'Natural Resources', and 'Human Rights and Poverty Eradication in Sustainable Development Law'.[69]

From an interactive and process-oriented perspective on international law and international relations, it can be seen that this type of engagement from NGOs has contributed to the framing of international issues in an integrated fashion.[70] It has also normalised the idea of transferring principles as amongst previously isolated fields of international law, and, in particular, has extended the reach of the concept of sustainable development well beyond international environmental law. With respect to the investment sector, the work of organisations such as FIELD, IISD, and CISDL has specifically directed attention to the wider implications of foreign investment practices and has advocated the application of an integrated approach to international investment law.[71] In locating foreign investment law and policy within a framework of sustainability, these organisations have not only placed pressure on the investment sector to incorporate principles from other areas of international law, but, at the same time, they also provide channels through which reshaping of the law could occur. For example, their work points to the areas most in need of reform, illustrates the way in which socially and environmentally responsible investment principles could manifest, and

[67] IISD, *Our Knowledge: Themes*.

[68] Centre for International Sustainable Development Law, *About the CISDL*.

[69] Centre for International Sustainable Development Law, *CISDL Legal Programmes*.

[70] See further the discussion above in Chapter 2 on the role of environmental NGOs in global politico-legal issues and the development of international law and policy. In particular, see the discussion on the influence of NGOs in international law and politics in Sands, 'Turtles and Torturers', 527, 530, 556–7; Raustiala, 'The "Participatory Revolution"', 571–3; Hobb, 'Global Challenges'; see generally Princen and Finger, *Environmental NGOs*; Betsill and Corell, 'Introduction', pp. 2–3.

[71] See, e.g., Mann and von Moltke, *NAFTA's Chapter 11*; von Moltke, *An International Investment Regime?*; Cordonier-Segger, Gehring and Newcombe, *Sustainable Development*; Foundation for International Environmental Law and Development and International Institute for Environment and Development, *Governance of Oil and Gas Contracts in Kazakhstan*.

provides templates for the adoption of an integrated approach in international investment instruments.[72] In this way, the discourse has moved on from solely identifying the problematic aspects of bilateral investment agreements to exemplifying how change might be given effect.

Although capital-exporting states largely remain averse to the adoption of an integrated approach within international investment instruments,[73] there has been an emerging level of engagement with non-investment issues from within the sustainable finance movement.[74] This has seen institutional investors, such as pension funds, work with the United Nations to launch the United Nations Principles for Responsible Investment (UNPRI)[75] and private equity banks work with NGOs to establish the Equator Principles for transnational project finance.[76] Whilst these are encouraging steps, such developments have not yet triggered a substantial cultural shift within the broader legal investment community of private practitioners, corporate counsel, investment treaty-negotiators, and arbitrators in which engagement with NGOs and non-investment issues would become standard practice. As a consequence, initiatives such as the UNPRI have not translated into a wider acceptance of the need for an integrated approach to the development of international investment law.

(c) Treaties and incorporation of non-investment principles

Integrated methodologies having largely been disregarded, how, then, are non-investment issues addressed, if at all, within investment treaties? Possible approaches could include the direct incorporation of

[72] See, e.g., Cordonier-Segger, Gehring, and Newcombe, *Sustainable Development*; Foundation for International Environmental Law and Development and International Institute for Environment and Development, *Governance of Oil*; Mann et al., *IISD Model International Agreement*; Cosbey et al., *Investment and Sustainable Development*; International Institute for Sustainable Development, *Revising the UNCITRAL Arbitration Rules*.

[73] Muchlinksi, 'Corporate Social Responsibility', in Muchlinksi, Ortino and Schreuer, *The Oxford Handbook*, pp. 637, 681.

[74] As discussed in detail above in Chapter 4. See generally, Richardson, *Socially Responsible*; see also Richardson, 'Sustainable Finance', p. 309.

[75] United Nations, *Principles for Responsible Investment*; United Nations Global Compact, 'United Nations Secretary-General Launches "Principles for Responsible Investment"'.

[76] Equator Principles, the Equator Principles (Washington, DC, 4 June 2003), available at www.equator-principles.com (last accessed 16 December 2011); see Chapter 4 for a discussion on the Equator Principles; see further Richardson, 'The Equator Principles', 285; Wright and Rwabizambuga, 'Institutional Pressures'.

non-investment principles into the text of the treaty, indirect incorporation as an interpretative tool in disputes, or the inclusion of references to non-investment issues within the preamble of treaties.[77]

(i) Express incorporation Traditionally, bilateral investment treaties have solely been concerned with matters of investor protection, omitting any substantial form of engagement with extraneous issues. Such treaties have not integrated principles from other areas of international law nor, indeed, even referred to non-investment issues.[78] There has certainly been no attempt to create anything as far-reaching as binding investor responsibility requirements,[79] nor any exploration of international mechanisms through which detrimental investor impacts on the environment and local communities of host states could be addressed.[80] There has also been a notable failure to incorporate sustainability considerations into interpretations given to investor protections in arbitral awards.[81]

In an acknowledgement of the host state perspective, however, there have recently been developments in investment treaties designed to introduce a level of engagement with non-investment issues.[82] Although still limited in scope, these may point to the possibility of more substantial reforms in the future. Moving away from the traditional approach, 'new generation BITs'[83] have included express references to sustainable development, protection of the environment, and the health and safety of the public.[84] As discussed in Chapter 4 above, these developments have been driven by the experiences of Canada and

[77] See the discussion on incorporation of principles into treaties generally in French, 'Treaty Interpretation', 284, 292–307.

[78] Newcombe, 'Sustainable Development'.

[79] Cosbey et al., *Investment and Sustainable Development*; Mann et al., *IISD Model International Agreement*.

[80] Mann et al., *IISD Model International Agreement*; Bridgeman and Hunter, 'Narrowing the Accountability Gap'; see also the discussion in Zerk, *Multinationals*, pp. 262–77; Deva, 'Sustainable Good Governance', 745–7; for an example of a treaty proposal for corporate social responsibility, see Friends of the Earth, *Towards Binding Corporate Accountability*.

[81] See the discussion on the treatment of public interest issues in Choudhury, 'Recapturing Public Power', 788, 831–2.

[82] These developments are discussed above in detail in Chapter 4; see also the discussion in Newcombe, 'Sustainable Development'.

[83] As mentioned in Chapter 4, the term 'new generation BITs' has been adopted to refer to recent bilateral investment treaties that refer to non-investment issues; see, in particular, the discussion in Shan, 'From "North-South Divide"', 652, 656.

[84] Ibid.; Newcombe, 'Sustainable Development', 399; see e.g. the United States–Uruguay BIT, Treaty between the United States of America and the Oriental Republic of Uruguay

the United States as respondents under the North American Free Trade Agreement (NAFTA).[85] Both states have had investor claims filed against them, challenging public welfare regulation,[86] and this experience has led them to revisit their approach to bilateral investment treaties.[87] Amongst other modifications, the new United States' and Canadian model bilateral investment treaties inserted references to non-investment issues (United States Model BIT; Canadian Model BIT).[88]

These references to non-investment issues signal the adoption of a different approach by the United States and Canada and also indicate a greater appreciation from these states, having experienced investor–state arbitration as a host state, of the wider context in which investor protection occurs. That said, however, the substantive host state obligations still largely reflect those of traditional bilateral investment treaties. Although there are references to sustainable development, environmental protection, or labour rights in the preambles and in clauses stating that environmental or labour measures 'otherwise consistent' with the treaty may be adopted by state parties, requirements to consider non-investment issues

Concerning the Encouragement and Reciprocal Protection of Investment (2005), available at www.unctad.org/sections/dite/iia/docs/bits/US_Uruguay.pdf (last accessed 15 March 2009); see also the Canada–Peru BIT, Agreement between Canada and the Republic of Peru for the Promotion and Protection of Investments (2006), available at www.international.gc.ca/trade-agreements-accords-commerciaux/assets/pdfs/Canada-Peru10nov06-en.pdf (last accessed 4 April 2009).

85 North American Free Trade Agreement (NAFTA), adopted 17 December 1992, 1992 32 ILM 612 (entered into force 1 January 1994); Van Harten, *Investment Treaty Arbitration*, p. 146; Sands, *Lawless World*, pp. 121–2, 139–41.

86 Notable examples include *Methanex Corporation* v. *United States of America* (NAFTA, Arbitral Tribunal, Final Award on Jurisdiction and Merits of 3 August 2005); *S.D. Myers Inc* v. *Canada* (UNCITRAL, Partial Award of 13 November 2000) ('*S.D. Myers Inc* (Partial Award of 2000)'); *Ethyl Corporation* v. *Canada* (UNCITRAL, Award on Jurisdiction of 24 June 1998).

87 Shan, 'From "North–South Divide"', 650–3; McIlroy, 'Canada's New Foreign Investment', 646; Newcombe and Paradell, *Law and Practice*, p. 61.

88 United States State Department, Treaty between the Government of the United States of America and the Government of [Country] Concerning the Encouragement and Reciprocal Protection of Investments (2004); (United States' 2004 Model BIT), available at www.state.gov/documents/organization/38710.pdf (last accessed 29 July 2009); United States State Department, Treaty between the Government of the United States of America and the Government of [Country] Concerning the Encouragement and Reciprocal Protection of Investments (2012) (United States' 2012 Model BIT), available at www.ustr.gov/sites/default/files/BIT%20text%20for%20ACIEP%20Meeting.pdf (last accessed 25 August 2012) (United States' Model BIT); Canada, Model Foreign Investment Protection Agreement (2004) (Canadian Model BIT), available at www.international.gc.ca/assets/trade-agreements-accords-commerciaux/pdfs/2004-FIPA-model-en.pdf (last accessed 29 April 2009).

and enforceable positive obligations from other areas of international law have not been incorporated into the operational provisions of the treaty texts.[89] As such, although the impression is one of substantial reform, in terms of actual outcomes, investor protections have not been significantly modified.[90] The most that can be expected is a shift in emphasis in interpretation of treaty obligations in arbitral awards.

It will be interesting to see whether the 'new generation BITs' make any significant difference at all to the way in which non-investment issues are considered in investment treaty disputes. This is largely because change consequential on interpretation will be dependent on the approach of arbitrators to such issues, pointing to the question – to what extent will arbitral tribunals apply domestic policy considerations or non-investment principles to dilute the collateral impact of investor protections even under the 'new generation BITs'? A certain degree of scepticism as to the likelihood of a significant change in direction arises from the fact that the capacity to consider principles from other areas of international law already currently exists via Article 31(3)(c) of the Vienna Convention on the Law of Treaties (the Vienna Convention),[91] and yet it is not readily used in investor–state arbitration to assist with justifications for host state action.[92] Indeed, at times, tribunals have shown a distinct disinclination to give any weight to relevant obligations from other areas of international law.[93] Culturally, it is a dispute resolution system that appears more comfortable with the traditions of international commercial arbitration than public international law.[94] And, as a result, there has been very little engagement with the idea of

[89] See the discussion in Newcombe, 'Sustainable Development', 400–2.

[90] Other than a more nuanced approach to indirect expropriation as discussed above in Chapter 4. The potency of other key investor protections regularly invoked to challenge public welfare regulation, however, remains, such as the fair and equitable treatment standard, national treatment standard, and prohibition on discriminatory treatment.

[91] Vienna Convention on the Law of Treaties, opened for signature 23 May 1969, 1155 UNTS 331, Art. 31(3)(c) (entered into force 27 January 1980). The potential for using this mechanism in investment disputes is examined in detail in section (c)(ii) below.

[92] Hirsch, 'Interactions'; see the discussion of *Pope & Talbot* in McLachlan, 'The Principle', 298.

[93] See, e.g., the award in *Compañía del Desarrollo de Santa Elena S.A.* v. *Costa Rica, Rectification of Award* (ICSID Case No. ARB/96/1, Award of 8 June 2000) ('*Compañía del Desarrollo de Santa Elena S.A.* (Award of 2000)').

[94] Van Harten, *Investment Treaty Arbitration*, pp. 122–31, 152–75; Sornarajah, 'The Clash of Globalizations', 13–17; Tienhaara, 'Third Party Participation', 230–1; Reinisch, 'The Broader Picture', 201.

incorporating principles from areas of international law such as human rights law or environmental law to support the policy needs of host states.[95] However, several awards have, in fact, referred to rules of general international law.[96] Accordingly, sections below examine the circumstances in which such references were made, the reasoning adopted in these awards, and the potential for incorporation of environmental and human rights principles into investment treaty disputes. First, however, this section's examination continues of cross-sectoral references in treaties and jurisprudence within public international law more generally.

(ii) 'Applicable rules of international law' A number of treaties invite the application of rules from further areas of international law through references to the law contained in other treaties, customary international law, or general principles.[97] Examples include the WTO Dispute Settlement Understanding, which seeks to clarify the meaning of provisions 'in accordance with customary rules of interpretation of public international law'.[98] The United Nations Convention on the Law of the Sea (UNCLOS) contains numerous references to general international law,[99] such as Article 2(3) which states that 'sovereignty over the territorial sea is exercised subject to this Convention and to other rules of

[95] Reinisch, 'The Broader Picture', pp. 201–2; Hirsch, 'Interactions', 154; McLachlan, 'Investment Treaties', 376.

[96] See, e.g., *Marvin Roy Feldman Karpa* v. *United Mexican States* (2001) 40 *International Legal Materials* 615 ('*Marvin Roy Feldman Karpa*'); *Pope & Talbot Inc* v. *Canada* (UNCITRAL, Award in Respect of Damages of 31 May 2002 ('*Pope & Talbot Inc* (Award in Damages of 2002)'); *MTD Equity Sdn. Bhd. & MTD Chile S.A.* v. *Chile* (ICSID Case No. ARB/01/7, Award of 25 May 2004) ('*MTD Equity Sdn. Bhd. & MTD Chile S.A.* (Award of 2004)'); *Compañía del Desarrollo de Santa Elena S.A.* (Award of 2000); *CMS Gas Transmission Company* v. *Argentine Republic* (ICSID Case No. ARB/01/8, Award of 12 May 2005 ('*CMS Gas Transmission Company* (Award of 2005)'); *LG&E Energy Corp.* v. *Argentina* (ICSID Case No. ARB/02/1, Award of 25 July 2007) ('*LG&E Energy Corp.* (Award of 2007)'); *CMS Gas Transmission Company* v. *Argentine Republic* (ICSID Case No. ARB/01/8 (Decision on Application for Annulment of 25 September 2007) ('*CMS Gas Transmission Company* (Decision on Annulment of 2007)').

[97] French, 'Treaty Interpretation', 293–4.

[98] Understanding on Rules and Procedures Governing the Settlement of Disputes, Art. 3.2, Annex 2, Agreement Establishing the World Trade Organization, opened for signature 15 April 1994, (1994) 33 ILM 28 (entered into force 1 January 1995).

[99] United Nations Convention on the Law of the Sea, opened for signature 10 December 1982, (1982) 21 ILM 1261 (entered into force 16 November 1994); see the discussion in French, 'Treaty Interpretation', 294; see also Wood, 'The International Tribunal', 359–60.

international law'.[100] The Rome Statute Establishing the International Criminal Court permits the Court to apply not only the provisions of the Statute itself, but also:

(b) ... applicable treaties and the principles and rules of international law, including the established principles of the international law of armed conflict

(c) ... general principles of law ... provided that those principles are not inconsistent with this Statute and with international law and internationally recognized norms and standards.[101]

This approach has also been adopted in international investment agreements. For example, the Treaty between the United States of America and the Republic of Argentina Concerning the Reciprocal Encouragement and Protection of Investment provides that:

Any dispute between the Parties concerning the interpretation or application of the Treaty ... shall be submitted, upon the request of either Party, to an arbitral tribunal for binding decision *in accordance with the applicable rules of international law.*[102]

NAFTA and the Energy Charter Treaty also include references to the potential application of extraneous rules of international law, providing that 'a Tribunal established under this Section shall decide the issues in dispute in accordance with this Agreement and applicable rules of international law.'[103] The United States Model BIT also sets out that 'the tribunal shall decide the issues in dispute in accordance with this Treaty and applicable rules of international law'.[104]

There are also two specific treaty interpretation mechanisms of particular relevance for the application of non-investment principles in investment treaty arbitration – Article 31(3)(c) of the Vienna

[100] United Nations Convention on the Law of the Sea, opened for signature 10 December 1982, (1982) 21 ILM 1261, Art. 2(3) (entered into force 16 November 1994). See also Arts 22, 58, 74, 83, 87, and 235 for references to rules of international law.

[101] Rome Statute Establishing the International Criminal Court (1998) 37 ILM 999, Art. 21.1.

[102] Treaty between the United States of America and the Republic of Argentina Concerning the Reciprocal Encouragement and Protection of Investment, signed 14 November 1991, Art. VIII (entered into force 20 October 1994), available at www.unctad.org/sections/dite/iia/docs/bits/argentina_us.pdf (last accessed 16 December 2011). Emphasis added.

[103] NAFTA, adopted 17 December 1992, 1992 32 ILM 612, Art. 1131(1) (entered into force 1 January 1994); see also Energy Charter Treaty, Art. 26(6), Annex I, Final Act of the European Energy Charter Conference, 17 December 1994, 34 ILM 373.

[104] United States' Model BIT, Art. 30(1).

Convention[105] and Article 42(1) of the Convention on the Settlement of Investment Disputes between States and Nationals of other States (the ICSID Convention).[106] Article 42(1) of the ICSID Convention sets out that, where the investment treaty is silent on choice of law in a dispute, the tribunal is required to apply host state law 'and such rules of international law as may be applicable'.[107] The generic provision in Article 31(3)(c) of the Vienna Convention applies to all treaties and permits the consideration of rules of international law sourced from outside the treaty in question to assist with the interpretation of that treaty:

> There shall be taken into account, together with the context:
>
> ...
>
> (c) any relevant rules of international law applicable in the relations between the parties.[108]

These treaty interpretation mechanisms have the potential to operate as channels through which non-investment principles could play a greater role in the resolution of investment disputes. Indeed, in a number of arbitral awards, there has already been limited exploration of the interaction between investment treaties and public international law in general.[109] However, the resultant decisions have not been responsive to the environmental or human rights concerns raised by host states.[110] It is this failure on the part of arbitral panels to use mechanisms already available to engage adequately with environmental and human rights concerns that illustrates the importance of the adjudicative process for jurisprudential development in this area. In fact, it will be central to the

[105] Vienna Convention on the Law of Treaties, opened for signature 23 May 1969, 1155 UNTS 331, Art. 31(3)(c) (entered into force 27 January 1980).

[106] Convention on the Settlement of Investment Disputes between States and Nationals of Other States, signed 18 March 1965, (1966) 575 UNTS 159 (entered into force 14 October 1966).

[107] Ibid., Art. 42(1).

[108] Vienna Convention on the Law of Treaties, opened for signature 23 May 1969, 1155 UNTS 331, Art. 31(3)(c) (entered into force 27 January 1980); see also the discussion in Pauwelyn, *Conflict of Norms*, pp. 253–74.

[109] See, e.g., *Marvin Roy Feldman Karpa*; *Pope & Talbot Inc* v. *Canada* (Award on Damages of 2002); *MTD Equity Sdn. Bhd.* v. *Chile* (ICSID Case No. ARB/01/7, Decision on Annulment of 21 March 2007) (*MTD Equity Sdn. Bhd. & MTD Chile S.A.* (Decision on Annultment of 2007)'); *Compañía del Desarrollo de Santa Elena S.A.* (Award of 2000); *CMS Gas Transmission Company* (Award of 2005); *LG&E Energy Corp.* (Award of 2007); *CMS Gas Transmission Company* (Decision on Annulment of 2007).

[110] Reinisch, 'The Broader Picture', 201–2; McLachlan, 'Investment Treaties', 376; Hirsch, 'Interactions', 154.

future emergence of an international investment law that is responsive to non-investment issues. Accordingly, this next section examines the way in which cross-sectoral issues have been addressed in international jurisprudence and then, specifically, within investment disputes.

2. Cross-sectoral jurisprudence

(a) *General precedents*

An increasing number of cases heard in international courts and tribunals are cross-referencing principles as amongst traditionally distinct areas of international law and discussing rules of customary international law in the context of treaty interpretation.[111] Such an approach embodies a greater fluidity in the application of international law, and it could also potentially lead to a more cohesive treatment of complex disputes that involve more than one area of international law.[112] The following selection of cases illustrates this trend towards cross-sectoral consideration of principles and customary rules.

(i) Case Concerning the Gabčikovo-Nagymaros Dam Project The *Case Concerning the Gabčikovo-Nagymaros Project* involved the implementation of a treaty between Hungary and Czechoslovakia to build and operate a system of dams, locks and power stations on the Danube River (the 1977 Treaty).[113] However, at a broader level, the dispute between the two states ultimately also concerned the interaction between competing norms of international law - state responsibility and treaty law on the one hand; and, on the other, principles of international environmental law.[114]

The dispute arose in 1989, as the Czechoslovakian component of the project was nearing completion, but before the Hungarian section had moved beyond preliminary stages. By this time, there was significant opposition to the project within Hungary.[115] As a result of such strong

111 Sands, 'Treaty', 91–100; French, 'Treaty Interpretation'; Birnie, Boyle, and Redgwell, *International Law*, pp. 109–10.

112 French, 'Treaty Interpretation', 285; see also the discussion in Sands, 'Environmental Protection', pp. 369, 403–9.

113 *Case Concerning the Gabčikovo-Nagymaros Project (Hungary/Slovakia)* (1997) ICJ Rep 7; *Hungary–Czechoslovakia Treaty Providing for the Construction and Joint Operation of the Gabčikovo-Nagymaros Barrage System* done on 16 September 1977, 1109 UNTS 236. It should be noted that the dispute in 1997 was between Hungary and Slovakia.

114 Sands, 'Treaty', 100–1; Stephens, *International Courts*, p. 1734; Higgins, 'Natural Resources', 87, 105–6.

115 *Case Concerning the Gabčikovo-Nagymaros Project (Hungary/Slovakia)* (1997) ICJ Rep 7, paras 31, 34.

domestic sentiment, an assessment of the ecological impact of the operation of the dams on the Danube and its surrounding river systems was conducted, following which, in 1989, Hungary suspended construction works.[116] Hungary attempted to terminate the 1977 Treaty and sought to justify its actions through the alleged existence of a 'state of ecological necessity', arguing that the purported termination should be viewed in the context of modern international environmental law.[117]

In ascertaining the legal status of the attempted termination, as well as other acts of both states, the International Court of Justice (ICJ) looked outside the 1977 Treaty and considered it appropriate to draw on principles of international environmental law. The Court noted that 'newly developed norms of environmental law are relevant for the implementation of the Treaty',[118] and expressly invoked the concept of sustainable development, stating:

Throughout the ages, mankind has, for economic and other reasons, constantly interfered with nature. In the past, this was often done without consideration of the effects upon the environment. Owing to new scientific insights and to a growing awareness of the risks for mankind – for present and future generations – of pursuit of such interventions at an unconsidered and unabated pace, new norms and standards have been developed, set forth in a great number of instruments during the last two decades. *Such new norms have to be taken into consideration, and such new standards given proper weight, not only when States contemplate new activities but also when continuing with activities begun in the past.* This need to reconcile economic development with protection of the environment is aptly expressed in the concept of sustainable development.[119]

Continuing in this vein, the majority judgment of the ICJ applied the concept of sustainable development to the *Gabčikovo–Nagymaros* dispute, and determined that:

For the purposes of the present case, this means that the Parties together should look afresh at the effects on the environment of the operation of the Gabčikovo power plant. In particular they must find a satisfactory solution for the volume

[116] *Case Concerning the Gabčikovo-Nagymaros Project (Hungary/Slovakia)* (1997) ICJ Rep 7, Memorial of the Republic of Hungary, 2 May 1994, paras 3.74–3.75; see also the discussion on the environmental objections to the project in Schwabach, 'Diverting the Danube', 296–8; see also on this point, Bostian, 'Flushing the Danube', 407–9.

[117] *Case Concerning the Gabčikovo-Nagymaros Project (Hungary/Slovakia)* (1997) ICJ Rep 7, Memorial of the Republic of Hungary, 2 May 1994, paras 10.06–10.40.

[118] *Case Concerning the Gabčikovo-Nagymaros Project (Hungary/Slovakia)* (1997) ICJ Rep 7, para. 112.

[119] Ibid., para. 140. Emphasis added.

of water to be released into the old bed of the Danube and into the side-arms on both sides of the river.

It is not for the Court to determine what shall be the final result of these negotiations to be conducted by the Parties. It is for the Parties themselves to find an agreed solution that takes account of the objectives of the Treaty, which must be pursued in a joint and integrated way, as well as the norms of international environmental law and the principles of the law of international watercourses.[120]

In this case, the ICJ considered it appropriate to interpret the 1977 Treaty in light of general principles of international environmental law, and, accordingly, adopted an integrated approach to the interpretation of international instruments. The Court read into the 1977 Treaty requirements to take account of environmental considerations and norms from international environmental law in its application. Furthermore, the Court also gave effect to the concept of sustainable development within a treaty that did not address environmental issues, and, in so doing, pointed to the normative utility of the principle in dispute resolution outside of the environmental context.[121]

(ii) Shrimp-Turtle In many respects, the WTO Appellate Body constitutes the archetypal issue-specific dispute settlement body. Designed to resolve disputes between states regarding alleged violations of international trade rules, it is unsurprising that its primary focus has been on the application of its regime-specific regulatory framework.[122] However, on occasion, an integrated approach to interpretation has been adopted by the Appellate Body, pronouncing most notably in *US–Standards for Reformulated and Conventional Gasoline* that the rules of the WTO are not to be interpreted in 'clinical isolation from public international law'.[123] There are, of course, trade disputes in which

120 Ibid., paras 140–1.

121 Sands, *Principles*, p. 255; see also the discussion in Sec, 'Do Two Wrongs Make a Right?'; it should also be noted that although 'sustainable development' constituted a concept for the majority of the ICJ, for Vice-President Weeramantry, it had already attained the status of a principle to be applied in balancing the competing interests of environmental protection and development needs; see the *Case Concerning the Gabčikovo-Nagymaros Project (Hungary/Slovakia)* (1997), *Separate Opinion of Vice-President Weeramantry*, available at www.icj-cij.org/docket/files/92/7383.pdf (last accessed 16 December 2011).

122 See the discussion on international issue-specific dispute resolution fora in Stephens, 'Multiple International Courts', 227–30.

123 *US–Standards for Reformulated and Conventional Gasoline*, Report of the Appellate Body, WT/DS52/AB/R (20 May 1996); see the discussion in Sands, 'Turtles and Torturers', 550;

adjudicators have chosen not to incorporate rules from other areas of international law.[124] However, a significantly more sensitive jurisprudential approach towards other regimes is also apparent, as illustrated in the reasoning of *US-Import Prohibition of Certain Shrimp and Shrimp Products* (the *Shrimp–Turtle Dispute*), a dispute involving the consideration of environmental principles within the international trade context.[125]

The *Shrimp–Turtle Dispute* arose out of legislation enacted by the United States prohibiting the importation of shrimp from 'uncertified' states.[126] The rationale for the measure was that shrimp from certain states was being harvested with commercial fishing technology that resulted in high incidental mortality rates for endangered species of sea turtle.[127] Under the domestic regulatory regime in the United States, certification could be obtained by states attesting to the use of turtle excluder devices or other comparable methods of turtle exclusion in shrimp-harvesting practices. However, India, Malaysia, Pakistan and Thailand were amongst those countries unable to obtain the necessary certification, and, accordingly, the import prohibition applied to their shrimp. As a result of the prohibition, these four states launched a challenge to the United States' legislation, on the grounds that it was in violation of the General Agreement on Tariffs and Trade 1994 (GATT 1994).[128]

At first instance, the WTO Panel found the United States' restriction to be inconsistent with Article XI:1 of GATT 1994 and that it was not justified under the environment-related exception contained in Article XX(g).[129] Ultimately, the Appellate Body determined that although the legislation

Stephens, 'Multiple International Courts', 254; see also the discussion in Kelly, 'Power', 86–90.

124 See, e.g., the Panel Report in *European Communities-Measures Affecting the Approval and Marketing of Biotech Products*, WT/DS291, WT/DS292, WT/DS293 (29 September 2006).

125 *US–Import Prohibition of Certain Shrimp and Shrimp Products*, Report of the Appellate Body, WT/DS58/AB/R, 1998, (1999) 38 *International Legal Materials* 118; see Sands, 'Turtles and Torturers'; see the discussion on sensitivity within the WTO to the values embodied within other regimes in Kelly, 'Power', 86–90; Stephens, 'Multiple International Courts', 256–60; Ala'i, 'Free Trade'; see also Chang, 'Environmental Trade Measures'.

126 Sea Turtle Conservation Amendments to the Endangered Species Act 1973 (US), Public Law 101–62, sec. 609, 103 Stat. 998, 1037 (1989).

127 *US-Import Prohibition of Certain Shrimp and Shrimp Products*, Report of the Appellate Body, WT/DS58/AB/R, para. 1–2, 12 October 1998, (1999) 38 *International Legal Materials* 118.

128 General Agreement on Tariffs and Trade, Annex 1A, Agreement Establishing the World Trade Organization, opened for signature 15 April 1994, (1994) 33 ILM 28 (entered into force 1 January 1995); *US–Import Prohibition of Certain Shrimp and Shrimp Products*, Report of the Panel, WT/DS58/R, 15 May 1998.

129 *US-Import Prohibition of Certain Shrimp and Shrimp Products*, Report of the Panel, WT/DS58/R, 15 May 1998. Article XX(g) states:

was justified under Article XX(g), it failed to meet the requirements of the *chapeau* of Article XX, as the manner in which the measure had been applied by the United States had amounted to arbitrary and unjustifiable discrimination against shrimp exporters from the complainant states.[130]

Despite the outcome on the facts, the reasoning of the Appellate Body was nothing short of transformative in two central ways.[131] First, finding that a state had a legal interest in the activities of other states with respect to a migratory species recognised linkages and legal interests that had not previously been thought to exist.[132] Secondly, in finding that the import prohibition was provisionally justified under Article XX(g), the Appellate Body employed an integrated approach to the interpretation of a WTO treaty, drawing on general principles of international environmental law to inform the application of GATT 1994.[133] Specifically, the Appellate Body called for a reading of Article XX(g) 'in the light of contemporary concerns of the community of nations about the protection and conservation of the environment', and linked this in with the principle of sustainable development.[134] The term 'sustainable development' is not expressly used in the operative provisions of the GATT 1994. However, the Appellate Body noted that 'The preamble of the WTO Agreement – which informs not only the GATT 1994, but also the other covered agreements – explicitly acknowledges "the objective of sustainable development"',[135] and further stated that 'This concept has been generally accepted as integrating economic and social development and environmental protection.'[136] The Appellate Body also

> Subject to the requirement that such measures are not applied in a manner which would constitute a means of arbitrary or unjustifiable discrimination between countries where the same conditions prevail, or a disguised restriction on international trade, nothing in this Agreement shall be construed to prevent the adoption or enforcement by any contracting party of measures:
>
> ...
>
> (g) relating to the conservation of exhaustible natural resources if such measures are made effective in conjunction with restrictions on domestic production or consumption.

130 *US-Import Prohibition of Certain Shrimp and Shrimp Products*, Report of the Appellate Body, WT/DS58/AB/R, 12 October 1998, (1999) 38 *International Legal Materials* 118.

131 Sands, 'Turtles and Torturers', 533–5.

132 Ibid.; see also the discussion in Ala'i, 'Free Trade', 1166–9; see also the discussion in Howse, 'The Appellate Body Rulings', 499–516.

133 *US-Import Prohibition of Certain Shrimp and Shrimp Products*, Report of the Appellate Body, WT/DS58/AB/R, 12 October 1998, (1999) 38 *International Legal Materials* 118, paras 125–45.

134 Ibid., para. 129. 135 Ibid. 136 Ibid., para. 129, fn. 107.

referred to a wide range of international environmental instruments to assist with its application of Article XX of GATT 1994. In particular, it referred to other treaties, such as UNCLOS,[137] the Convention on International Trade in Endangered Species of Wild Fauna and Flora (CITES),[138] and the United Nations Convention on Biological Diversity (Convention on Biodiversity).[139] Significantly, the Appellate Body also made use of soft law, such as Agenda 21,[140] the Rio Declaration,[141] and the Decision of Ministers at Marrakesh to establish a permanent Committee on Trade and Environment,[142] to reshape its understanding of Article XX and give the provision that 'contemporary' reading it was seeking.[143]

(iii) Al-Adsani Exploration into the relationship between treaties and international customary law has also found form in the context of human rights and principles of state immunity.[144] Specifically, *Al-Adsani* v. *United Kingdom*[145] addressed the interaction between general principles of international law on state immunity, the Vienna Convention,[146] and Article 6 of the European Convention, which provides for a right of access to the courts.[147] On the facts, this case involved a claim brought in the United Kingdom against Kuwait for civil damages for torture suffered within Kuwait. The law on state

[137] United Nations Convention on the Law of the Sea, opened for signature 10 December 1982, (1982) 21 ILM 1261 (entered into force 16 November 1994).

[138] Convention on International Trade in Endangered Species of Wild Fauna and Flora, opened for signature 3 March 1973, 993 UNTS 243 (entered into force 1 July 1975).

[139] United Nations Convention on Biological Diversity, opened for signature 5 June 1992, (1992) 31 ILM 822 (entered into force 29 December 1993).

[140] *Agenda 21, Report of the UNCED*, UN Doc A/CONF.151/26/Rev.1 (vol.I) (1992), (1992) 31 ILM 874.

[141] *Rio Declaration on Environment and Development, Report of the UNCED*, UN Doc A/CONF.151/6/Rev.1 (1992), (1992) 31 ILM 874 .

[142] Uruguay Round Ministerial Decision, *Decision on Trade and Environment*, Marrakesh, Preamble, 14 April 1994, World Trade Organization, available at www.wto.org/english/docs_e/legal_e/56-dtenv_e.htm (last accessed 16 December 2011).

[143] Ibid., paras 130–4, 154; see also the discussion in Stephens, 'Multiple International Courts', 257–259.

[144] See, e.g., *Al-Adsani* v. *United Kingdom* (2002) 34 EHRR 11 (ECHR) ('*Al-Adsani* (EHRR, 2002)'); *Fogarty* v. *United Kingdom* (2001) 123 ILR 54; *McElhinney* v. *Ireland* (2001) 123 ILR 73.

[145] *Al-Adsani* (EHRR 2002).

[146] Vienna Convention on the Law of Treaties, opened for signature 23 May 1969, 1155 UNTS 331, Art. 31(3)(c) (entered into force 27 January 1980).

[147] European Convention for the Protection of Human Rights and Fundamental Freedoms, 4 November 1950, 213 UNTS 222, Art. 6(1); see the discussion in Caplan, 'State Immunity'.

immunity was raised as a bar to the continuation of proceedings. In taking the matter to the European Court of Human Rights, the Applicant argued that Article 6 of the European Convention for the Protection of Human Rights and Fundamental Freedoms (European Convention) guaranteed a right of access to the courts and that the law on state immunity did not constitute a legitimate and proportionate restriction on this right.[148] The Court disagreed, emphasising that the right of access to the courts was not absolute[149] and that it had to be interpreted against a background of other rules of international law:

> the Convention has to be interpreted in the light of the rules set out in the Vienna Convention on the Law of Treaties of 23 May 1969, and that Article 31 § 3 (c) of that treaty indicates that account is to be taken of 'any relevant rules of international law applicable in the relations between the parties'. The Convention, including Article 6, cannot be interpreted in a vacuum. The Court must be mindful of the Convention's special character as a human rights treaty, and it must also take the relevant rules of international law into account . . . The Convention should so far as possible be interpreted in harmony with other rules of international law of which it forms part, including those relating to the grant of State immunity.
>
> It follows that measures taken by a High Contracting Party which reflect generally recognised rules of public international law on State immunity cannot in principle be regarded as imposing a disproportionate restriction on the right of access to a court as embodied in Article 6 § 1. Just as the right of access to a court is an inherent part of the fair trial guarantee in that Article, so some restrictions on access must likewise be regarded as inherent, an example being those limitations generally accepted by the community of nations as part of the doctrine of State immunity.[150]

In this instance, the Court's use of rules of international law extraneous to the European Convention is particularly interesting for the potential incorporation of non-investment principles into bilateral investment treaties. The reason for this is that, as McLachlan points out, the Court does not appear to draw on rules outside the treaty in question to illuminate that treaty text so much as to address directly competing rules of international law.[151] And ultimately, it resolved the issue by applying those extraneous rules to modify the application of the treaty.

[148] *Al-Adsani* (EHRR, 2002), para. 51; see also the discussion in McLachlan, 'The Principle', 305–6.

[149] *Al-Adsani* (EHRR, 2002), paras 53–4.

[150] Ibid., paras 55–6.

[151] McLachlan, 'The Principle', 305–6.

(iv) Oil Platforms The interaction between treaty provisions, customary international law, and the use of Article 31(3)(c) of the Vienna Convention[152] was also expressly addressed in the *Case Concerning Oil Platforms (Iran* v. *United States of America)* (*Oil Platforms*).[153] This dispute involved the operation of a treaty between Iran and the United States, the Treaty of Amity, Economic Relations and Consular Rights (the 1955 Treaty).[154] The question for determination was whether or not the destruction by the United States of Iranian oil platforms was a breach of the 1955 Treaty or was instead justified by self-defence.[155] A key issue on this point revolved around the extent of the role of customary international law on the use of force and self-defence in resolving the matter.

Article XX 1(d) of the 1955 Treaty stated:

> The present Treaty shall not preclude the application of measures:
>
> ...
>
> (d) necessary to fulfil the obligations of a High Contracting Party for the maintenance or restoration of international peace and security, or necessary to protect its essential security interests.[156]

In order to determine what measures could fall within the term 'necessary' within this provision, the ICJ then examined the international rules on the use of armed force, including the circumstances in which a justification of self-defence would apply.[157] It also used Article 31(3)(c) as a means to consider these extraneous rules in the operation of the 1955 Treaty, stating:

> under the general rules of treaty interpretation, as reflected in the 1969 Vienna Convention on the Law of Treaties, interpretation must take into account 'any relevant rules of international law applicable in the relations between the parties' (Article 31, paragraph 3(c)). The Court cannot accept that Article XX, paragraph 1(d), of the 1955 Treaty was intended to operate wholly

152 Vienna Convention on the Law of Treaties, opened for signature 23 May 1969, 1155 UNTS 331, Art. 31(3)(c) (entered into force 27 January 1980).

153 *Case Concerning Oil Platforms (Iran* v. *United States of America)* (2003) 42 *International Legal Materials* 1334 ('*Oil Platforms* (2003)').

154 Treaty of Amity, Economic Relations and Consular Rights between Iran and the United States of America (1955) signed on 15 August 1955 (entered into force 16 June 1957).

155 *Oil Platforms* (2003), para. 26.

156 Treaty of Amity, Economic Relations and Consular Rights between Iran and the United States of America (1955) signed on 15 August 1955, Art. XX(1)(d) (entered into force 16 June 1957).

157 Ibid., para. 40.

independently of the relevant rules of international law on the use of force, so as to be capable of being successfully invoked, even in the limited context of a claim for breach of the Treaty, in relation to an unlawful use of force. The application of the relevant rules of international law relating to this question thus forms an integral part of the task of interpretation entrusted to the Court by . . . the 1955 Treaty.[158]

Ultimately, the ICJ did incorporate rules on the use of force into the interpretation of the obligations contained within the Treaty.[159] However, this approach was controversial, even amongst the judges presiding over the case.[160] In particular, Judge Buergenthal maintained that the Court's jurisdiction was limited to only those matters placed before it by the parties and that this excluded the consideration of rules going beyond those matters.[161] Judge Higgins also disagreed with the approach of the Court, encapsulating her concerns in the following statement:

The Court has, however, not interpreted Article XX, 1(d), by reference to the rules on treaty interpretation. It has rather invoked the concept of treaty interpretation to displace the applicable law.[162]

Despite the controversy and unease at the implications of using Article 31(3)(c) of the Vienna Convention,[163] it is clear that international courts and tribunals do refer to rules outside of the treaty in question when considered relevant. Consequently, there is a growing body of recent jurisprudence, in which adjudicators have engaged in cross-sectoral analysis, using concepts and principles from various areas of international law to inform the interpretation and application of treaties. Within the context of investor–state arbitration, however, there has been a distinct disinclination to engage with principles from international environmental law, human rights law, or sustainable development law so as to contextualise host state obligations under bilateral

158 Ibid., para. 41; see also the discussion in McLachlan 'The Principle', 307; see also French, 'Treaty Interpretation', 287–91.

159 *Oil Platforms* (2003), paras 40–1.

160 French, 'Treaty Interpretation', 287–90; McLachlan, 'The Principle', 307–9.

161 *Oil Platforms* (2003), Separate Opinion of Judge Buergenthal, paras 22–3; see also the discussion in McLachlan, 'The Principle', 307; see also French, 'Treaty Interpretation', 287–91; see also the critique of the ICJ's reasoning in Berman, 'Reflections'.

162 *Oil Platforms* (2003), Separate Opinion of Judge Higgins, para. 49.

163 For a discussion on the general reluctance to use Art. 31(3)(c), see Sands, 'Treaty', 95–7, 101; Vienna Convention on the Law of Treaties, opened for signature 23 May 1969, 1155 UNTS 331, Art. 31(3)(c) (entered into force 27 January 1980).

investment treaties.[164] There have, of course, been recent instances in which customary international rules or principles from other areas of international law have been referred to in arbitral awards – not so much to allow consideration of non-investment issues, but to bolster investor claims.

(b) Investor–state awards: engaging general public international law

Several investor–state awards have made reference to aspects of public international law beyond the investment treaty in question.[165] Although some tribunals have expressly emphasised that investment treaties fall within the wider international law framework,[166] they have also, on the whole, been very selective in the particular rules that have been considered, effectively 'cherry-picking' some rules and discounting others.[167] McLachlan has argued that a strict application of Articles 31 and 32 of the Vienna Convention should preclude this type of 'rule selection'.[168] He explains that the Vienna Convention interpretative process still requires a central focus on the treaty text first and foremost, but that this can then be followed by an application of general international law so as to illuminate that text.[169] However, this is not necessarily the way that arbitral tribunals have approached the incorporation of non-investment rules of international law. Accordingly, this

[164] Reinisch, 'The Broader Picture', 201–2; see also the discussion in Muchlinski, 'Corporate Social Responsibility', 681–3; McLachlan, 'Investment Treaties', 376.

[165] See, e.g., *Marvin Roy Feldman Karpa*; *Pope & Talbot Inc* v. *Canada* (Award on Damages of 2002); *MTD Equity Sdn. Bhd. & MTD Chile S.A.* (Decision on Annultment of 2007); *Compañía del Desarrollo de Santa Elena S.A.* (Award of 2000); *CMS Gas Transmission Company* (Award of 2005); *LG&E Energy Corp.* (Award of 2007); *CMS Gas Transmission Company* (Decision on Annulment of 2007).

[166] See, e.g., *Asian Agricultural Products Ltd* v. *Republic of Sri Lanka* (1990) 4 ICSID Rep 245, 257:

> A bilateral investment treaty is not a self-contained closed legal system limited to provide for substantive material rules of direct applicability, but it has to be envisaged within a wider juridical context in which rules from other sources are integrated through implied incorporation methods, or by direct reference to certain supplementary rules, whether of international law character or of domestic law nature.

See also *MTD Equity Sdn. Bhd. & MTD Chile S.A.* (Decision on Annultment of 2007):

> the Tribunal had to apply international law as a whole to the claim, and not the provisions of the BIT in isolation.

[167] See, e.g., the treatment given to international environmental principles in *Compañía del Desarrollo de Santa Elena S.A.* (Award of 2000) and in *S.D. Myers Inc.* v. *Canada*, Jurisdiction Phase (1999) 38 *International Legal Materials* 708.

[168] McLachlan, 'Investment Treaties', 390. [169] Ibid.

section explores the treatment given to these issues in recent investment arbitration.

(i) Fair and equitable treatment: treaties and customary international law Controversy has surrounded the emergence of an expansive jurisprudential meaning of the 'fair and equitable treatment' standard under investment treaties and its interrelationship with customary international law. The award in *Pope & Talbot Inc.* v. *Canada* opened the way for wide interpretations of the fair and equitable treatment standard, holding that the treaty standard was not limited to minimum standards of treatment under customary international law.[170] Such a reading greatly extended the scope of investor protection guarantees.[171] As a result, following the award, the NAFTA Free Trade Commission issued an interpretative note to the effect that the concept of fair and equitable treatment did not require treatment beyond that required by the customary international law minimum standard.[172]

In fact, however, tribunals have continued to afford expansive readings into the treaty standard. Indeed, the damages phase of *Pope & Talbot* v. *Canada* was held after the issuing of the NAFTA Free Trade Commission interpretative note, and, accordingly, the tribunal chose to address the content of the customary international law standard. It determined that as the customary international law standard was not static, it had already evolved so as to encompass the treaty-sourced concept of fair and equitable treatment.[173] It also held that the modern understanding of the customary international law rule had shifted to such an extent that the traditional minimum standard criteria of the *Neer Claim*,[174] 'egregious' conduct, was not required – lesser degrees of conduct would trigger a breach of both the modern minimum standard and the fair and equitable treatment standard.[175] In so doing, the tribunal effectively maintained the scope of its initial decision on the merits.

Although one of the exciting qualities of international customary law is its capacity to evolve in an organic fashion, the response of the

170 *Pope & Talbot* v. *Canada*, Award on the Merits of Phase II, 10 April 2001 ('*Pope & Talbot* (Award of Phase II of 2001)').

171 Van Harten, *Investment Treaty Arbitration*, pp. 88–90.

172 NAFTA Free Trade Commission, Interpretation of NAFTA Chapter 11 (31 July 2001) 6 ICSID Rep 567, 568; see also the discussion in McLachlan, 'Investment Treaties', 380–1.

173 *Pope & Talbot Inc* v. *Canada* (Award on Damages of 2002), paras 46, 52–67.

174 *Neer* v. *United Mexican States* (1926) IV RIAA 60.

175 *Pope & Talbot Inc.* v. *Canada* (Award on Damages of 2002), paras 46, 52–67.

damages *Pope & Talbot* v. *Canada* tribunal[176] to the Commission's Interpretative Note was a particularly pro-investor form of manipulation of the customary international law rule. Such an approach to the fair and equitable standard has been taken even further by arbitral panels, introducing the investor's 'legitimate expectations' component and the requirement for maintenance of a stable legal and business environment.[177] Again, this extends well beyond the traditional scope of the customary international minimum standard of treatment of investors.[178] It does, however, accord with historical patterns of doctrine manipulation to support foreign investors' activities, reproducing legal techniques seen throughout the seventeenth to twentieth centuries to develop investor protections and legitimise investor operations.

(ii) US–Argentina BIT and the doctrine of necessity cases Several investor–state arbitral tribunals have addressed the question of whether or not the defence of necessity was available to Argentina under both its bilateral investment treaty with the United States and customary international law for claims arising out of the 2001–2 financial crisis.[179] And they have come to different conclusions – *CMS Gas Transmission Co* v. *Argentina (CMS)*,[180] *Enron Corp & Ponderosa Assets LP* v. *Argentina (Enron)*,[181] and *Sempra Energy International* v. *Argentina (Sempra)*[182] determined that it was not open to Argentina to rely on the defence of necessity; *LG&E*

176 Ibid.

177 See *Tecnicas Medioambientales Tecmed S.A.* v. *United Mexican States* (2004) 43 *International Legal Materials* 133, 173 ('*Tecnicas Medioambientales Tecmed S.A.*'); *Occidental Exploration and Production Co.* v. *Republic of Ecuador* (UNCITRAL, Case No. UN3467, Final Award of 1 July 2004), para. 183; see the discussion in Van Harten, *Investment Treaty Arbitration*, pp. 88–90; Marshall, *Fair and Equitable Treatment*.

178 Van Harten, *Investment Treaty Arbitration*, pp. 88–90; Marshall, *Fair and Equitable*, p. 10.

179 As discussed above in Chapter 3, Argentina enacted emergency legislation in 2001 in response to a financial crisis that had spilled over into national social and political turmoil, including riots in which people had been killed. See for a discussion of this series of events, Van Harten, *Investment Treaty Arbitration*, pp. 1–3. Argentina has faced multiple claims arising out of these events, see e.g. *CMS Gas Transmission Company* (Award of 2005); *Enron Corp Ponderosa Assets L.P.* (Award of 2007); *Sempra Energy International* v. *Argentina* (ICSID Case No. ARB/02/16, Award of 28 September 2007) ('*Sempra Entergy International* (Award of 2007)'); *LG&E Energy Corp.* (Award of 2007). See also the Treaty Concerning the Reciprocal Encouragement and Protection of Investment between the United States of America and the Argentine Republic, signed 14 November 1991 (entered into force 20 October 1994).

180 *CMS Gas Transmission Company* (Award of 2005).

181 *Enron Corp. Ponderosa Assets L.P.* (Award of 2007).

182 *Sempra Entergy International* (Award of 2007).

Energy Corp. v. *Argentina* (*LG&E*)[183] and *Continental Casualty Company* v. *Argentine Republic*,[184] on the other hand, held that the defence was available.

In the *CMS* case,[185] the tribunal approached the issue of availability of a necessity defence by first looking at customary international law, rather than the terms of the treaty.[186] As explained by the *CMS* Annulment Committee, this methodology led to errors of law.[187] Instead, the starting point should have been Article XI of the Treaty Concerning the Reciprocal Encouragement and Protection of Investment between the United States of America and the Argentine Republic (US–Argentina BIT), which states:

> This treaty shall not preclude the application by either Party of measures necessary for the maintenance of public order, the fulfilment of its obligations with respect to the maintenance of restoration of international peace or security, or the protection of its own essential security interests.[188]

The *CMS* tribunal, however, appeared to conflate this provision into the customary international law defence of necessity. In so doing, it only gave consideration to whether the factual circumstances in the case met the requirements under the customary defence embodied within Article 25 of the International Law Commission Articles on State Responsibility.[189] The tribunal held that those requirements were not met and did not consider the application of Article XI of the US–Argentina BIT in any substantive way.[190]

Essentially adopting the approach of the tribunal in *LG&E*, the *CMS* Annulment Committee strongly criticised the reasoning and

183 *LG&E Energy Corp.* (Award of 2007).

184 *Continental Casualty Company* v. *Argentine Republic* (ICSID Case No. ARB/03/9, Award of 5 September 2008).

185 *CMS Gas Transmission Company* (Award of 2005).

186 McLachlan, 'Investment Treaties', 387.

187 *CMS Gas Transmission Company* (Decision on Annulment of 2007), paras 129–35.

188 Treaty Concerning the Reciprocal Encouragement and Protection of Investment between the United States of America and the Argentine Republic, Art. XI, signed 14 November 1991 (entered into force 20 October 1994).

189 *CMS Gas Transmission Company* (Decision on Annulment of 2007), para. 123; see also the discussion in McLachlan, 'Investment Treaties', 387, 390; International Law Commission, Articles on Responsibility of States for Internationally Wrongful Acts, UNGAOR, 56th Sess., Supp. No. 10, UN Doc. A/56/10.

190 *CMS Gas Transmission Company* (Decision on Annulment of 2007), para. 123; McLachlan, 'Investment Treaties', 387; *Enron* and *Sempra* adopted a similar approach.

methodology of the *CMS* tribunal.[191] In contrast to the *CMS* tribunal, the *LG&E* tribunal had considered the specific wording of the same treaty, the US–Argentina BIT, and had determined that, on the facts, the conditions necessary to trigger the operation of the provision had been met by the financial crisis. The tribunal also looked to customary international law, but referred to it as a mechanism to illuminate the text of the treaty.[192]

The *CMS* Annulment Committee distinguished the roles of Article XI of the US–Argentina BIT and the customary law defence of necessity, pointing out that the treaty provision provided 'a threshold requirement' which meant that if its conditions were met, the treaty obligations did not apply to Argentina.[193] The converse position is embodied in the operation of the customary law defence of necessity – there has already been a breach of international obligations and the question is then whether a defence is available to excuse that breach.[194] The *CMS* award, however, was not annulled, despite the errors of law. Article 52 of the ICSID Convention sets out the limited grounds on which an award can be annulled,[195] including where the tribunal has manifestly exceeded its powers and where the award has failed to state the reasons on which it was based.[196] The *CMS* Annulment Committee determined that the errors in the *CMS* award did not fall within these strict categories of Article 52, and, accordingly, it was not within with its mandate to annul the award.[197]

The *CMS*, *Enron*, and *Sempra* cases[198] exemplify an inaccurate use of non-investment principles in the interpretation of investment treaties. Clearly, the use of principles from customary international law and

[191] McLachlan, 'Investment Treaties', 388; *CMS Gas Transmission Company* (Decision on Annulment of 2007), paras 129–35; *LG&E Energy Corp.* (Award of 2007), paras 206, 245–58.

[192] *LG&E Energy Corp.* (Award of 2007), para. 245–58; McLachlan, 'Investment Treaties', 388.

[193] *CMS Gas Transmission Company* (Decision on Annulment of 2007), para. 129.

[194] Ibid.

[195] Convention on the Settlement of Investment Disputes between States and Nationals of Other States, signed 18 March 1965, (1966) 575 UNTS 159, Art. 52 (entered into force 14 October 1966).

[196] Ibid., Art. 52(1)(b) and (e).

[197] *CMS Gas Transmission Company* (Decision on Annulment of 2007); McLachlan, 'Investment Treaties', 386.

[198] *CMS Gas Transmission Company* (Award of 2005); *Enron Corp. Ponderosa Assets L.P.* v. *Republic of Argentina* (ICSID Case ARB 01/3, Award of 22 May 2007) ('*Enron Corp. Ponderosa Assets L. P.* (Award of 2007)'); *Sempra Entergy International* (Award of 2007).

other areas of international law in investor–state arbitration needs to be given a more structured and systematic framework. Perhaps, as McLachlan argues, a considered application of Article 31(3)(c) would provide that structure.[199] However, the conclusions of the *CMS* Annulment Committee also point to a more fundamental need in the investor–state arbitration system – an effective, authoritative appellate facility. On appeal, a panel such as that constituted in the *CMS* Annulment Committee would not have been constrained by the narrow mandate for annulment and could have corrected the error of reasoning in the *CMS* award. At a broader level, an appellate body would also provide much-needed guidance on the way in which arbitral tribunals should use customary international law in the interpretation of investment treaties. And this could lead to a sophisticated and consistent form of interaction between international investment law and non-investment rules and principles.

(iii) Host state international environmental obligations Generally speaking, conflicting host state obligations under non-investment treaties do not fare well in their treatment by arbitrators in investor–state disputes. Despite the lack of a formal hierarchy as amongst treaties to which a state has consented, the obligations under international investment agreements are effectively given priority by arbitral tribunals in investment disputes. Two cases, in particular, illustrate this approach in the context of obligations under international environmental agreements, *Compañia del Desarrollo de Santa Elena S.A.* v. *The Republic of Costa Rica* (*Santa Elena*)[200] and *S.D. Myers, Inc.* v. *Canada* (*S.D. Myers*).[201]

a. Santa Elena

In *Santa Elena*, Costa Rica raised the argument that its international environmental obligations ought to have a bearing on the methodology used for calculating the compensation due to the investor following an expropriation of property.[202] Costa Rica argued[203] that as the property

[199] McLachlan, 'Investment Treaties', 390.

[200] *Compañia del Desarrollo de Santa Elena S.A.* v. *The Republic of Costa Rica* (2000) 39 *International Legal Materials* 1317 ('*Compañia del Desarrollo de Santa Elena S.A.*').

[201] *S.D. Myers Inc* (Partial Award of 2000).

[202] *Compañia del Desarrollo de Santa Elena S.A.* This case is discussed in further detail above in Chapter 3.

[203] In its Counter Memorial (not publicly available on ICSID's website), an account of which is set out in Todd Weiler, *International Investment Law*, 763–4.

constituted a unique ecological site, it was under an obligation to preserve the area pursuant to several international environmental agreements, including the Convention Concerning the Protection of the World Natural and Cultural Heritage,[204] the Ramsar Convention on Wetlands of International Importance especially as Waterfowl Habitat,[205] the Convention on Biological Diversity,[206] and the Central American Regional Convention for the Management and Conservation of Natural Forest Ecosystems and the Development of Forest Plantations.[207] Costa Rica reasoned that, in light of its international obligations, the methodology for determining compensation should take the environmental objective of the expropriation into account and adopt an 'appropriate' valuation as opposed to the 'full compensation' at a 'market' valuation sought by the investor.[208] The Tribunal, however, stated that:

> While an expropriation or taking for environmental reasons may be classified as a taking for a public purpose, and thus may be legitimate, the fact that the Property was taken for this reason does not affect either the nature or the measure of the compensation to be paid for the taking. That is, the purpose of protecting the environment for which the Property was taken does not alter the legal character of the taking for which adequate compensation must be paid. The international source of the obligation to protect the environment makes no difference.
>
> Expropriatory environmental measures – no matter how laudable and beneficial to society as a whole – are, in this respect, similar to any other expropriatory measures that a state may take in order to implement its policies: where property is expropriated, even for environmental purposes, whether domestic or international, the state's obligation to pay compensation remains.[209]

In ascertaining the amount of compensation due to the investor, the tribunal did not give any weight to Costa Rica's competing international environmental obligations, did not modify the application of the

[204] Convention for the Protection of the World Cultural and Natural Heritage, opened for signature 16 November 1972, (1972) 11 ILM 1358 (entered into force 17 December 1975).

[205] Ramsar Convention on Wetlands of International Importance especially as Waterfowl Habitat, opened for signature 2 February 1971, 996 UNTS 245 (entered into force 21 December 1975).

[206] United Nations Convention on Biological Diversity, opened for signature 5 June 1992, 31 ILM 822 (entered into force 29 December 1993).

[207] Regional Convention for the Management and Conservation of Natural Forest Ecosystems and the Development of Forest Plantations, signed 29 October 1993.

[208] *Compañia del Desarrollo de Santa Elena S.A.*, 1322–3.

[209] *Compañia del Desarrollo de Santa Elena S.A.*, 1329.

investment obligations, nor contextualise the investment principles. In prioritising investment rules in this way, the tribunal deprived those non-investment obligations of meaningful effect.[210]

b. S.D. Myers

In *S.D. Myers*, Canada also pointed to its international environmental obligations in seeking to justify the introduction of a new measure prohibiting the export of a hazardous chemical product, polychlorinated biphenyl (PCBs).[211] Canada argued that the measure was made in compliance with the Convention on the Control of Transboundary Movement of Hazardous Wastes and their Disposal (Basel Convention).[212] Despite Canada being a party to the Basel Convention, however, the tribunal found that there was 'no legitimate environmental reason for introducing the ban'.[213] The tribunal went on to state that even where there are genuine environmental protection concerns, if there is a variety of methods through which those environmental objectives can be achieved, host states must implement those measures in a manner that is 'most consistent with open trade'[214] – and in adopting a blanket prohibition on the export of PCB waste products, Canada had not met this requirement.[215]

Again, although the host state's international obligations under a multilateral environmental agreement were briefly acknowledged by the investment arbitral tribunal, they were also then treated dismissively. The tribunals in both *Santa Elena* and *S.D. Myers* refer to the existence of environmental obligations but then render those obligations ineffectual through the unmodified prioritising of investment protection guarantees. This approach reflects the general reluctance of arbitral tribunals in investor–state disputes to contextualise investor rights, interpret them against a background of non-investment obligations, or integrate principles from international environmental law into investment treaties.[216]

[210] See the discussion in Sands, 'Searching for Balance', 204.

[211] *S.D. Myers Inc.* (Partial Award of 2000); *Interim Order Respecting the PCB Waste Export Production Regulations* (Canada, 20 November 1995). This Interim Order was converted into a Final Order on 26 February 1996.

[212] Convention on the Control of Transboundary Movement of Hazardous Wastes and their Disposal, opened for signature 22 March 1989, (1989) 28 ILM 657 (entered into force 5 May 1992).

[213] *S.D. Myers Inc.* (Partial Award of 2000). [214] Ibid., 1431. [215] Ibid., 1437.

[216] McLachlan, 'Investment Treaties', 376; Reinisch, 'The Broader Picture', 201–2; see also the discussion on cross-regime fertilisation in investor–state disputes in Ratner, 'Regulatory Takings', 525–8.

(iv) Human rights jurisprudence It should, of course, be pointed out that awards in investor–state arbitration have certainly referred to human rights jurisprudence.[217] However, the interesting aspect is the way in which investor–state arbitral tribunals have utilised principles from international human rights law – not, as might be expected, to alleviate the impacts of investor activities on affected local communities within host states, but to bolster investor claims.[218] In particular, tribunals have looked to the extensive body of jurisprudence generated in the European Court of Human Rights and the Inter-American Court of Human Rights regarding an individual's right to private property and the right to peaceful enjoyment of possessions to frame investors' claims as violations of human rights.[219]

Engagement of this kind with human rights principles is illustrated by, for example, the tribunals in *Ronald S Lauder* v. *the Czech Republic*[220] and *Tecnicas Medioambientales Tecmed, SA* v. *United Mexican States* (*Tecmed*).[221] Case law from both the Inter-American Court of Human Rights and the European Court of Human Rights was used in these cases to determine the scope of obligations owed under bilateral investment treaties regarding expropriation.[222] Framing investor claims as human rights claims was also given extensive treatment in the separate opinion of Wälde in *International Thunderbird Gaming Corp.* v. *United*

217 See, e.g., *In the Matter of a UNCITRAL Arbitration between Ronald S Lauder* v. *The Czech Republic*, Final Award, 3 September 2001; *Tecnicas Medioambientales Tecmed S.A.*; *Azurix Corp.* v. *Republic of Argentina* (ICSID Case No. ARB/01/12, Award of 14 July 2006) ('*Azurix Corp.* (Award of 2006)'); *In the Matter of a NAFTA Arbitration under UNCITRAL Arbitration Rules between International Thunderbird Gaming Corp.* v. *United Mexican States* (UNCITRAL, Award of 26 January 2006) ('*Thunderbird Gaming Corp.*').

218 Peterson, *Human Rights*.

219 See, e.g., *In the Matter of a UNCITRAL Arbitration between Ronald S Lauder* v. *the Czech Republic* (UNCITRAL, Final Award of 3 September 2001); *Tecnicas Medioambientales Tecmed S.A.*; *Azurix Corp.* (Award of 2006). E.g., these awards have referred to, amongst others, *Mellacher* v. *Austria* (1989) 169 European Court of Human Rights (ser. A); *Matos e Silva, Lda* v. *Portugal* 1996–IV European Court of Human Rights; *Baruch Ivcher Bronstein* v. *Peru* (2001) Inter-American Court of Human Rights (ser. C) No. 74; *James* v. *United Kingdom* (1986) 98 European Court of Human Rights (ser. A).

220 *In the Matter of a UNCITRAL Arbitration between Ronald S. Lauder* v. *The Czech Republic*, Final Award, 3 September 2001.

221 *Tecnicas Medioambientales Tecmed S.A.*

222 *In the Matter of a UNCITRAL Arbitration between Ronald S. Lauder* v. *The Czech Republic*, Final Award, 3 September 2001; *Tecnicas Medioambientales Tecmed S.A.* These awards referred to *Mellacher* v. *Austria* (1989) 169 European Court of Human Rights (ser. A); *Baruch Ivcher Bronstein* v. *Peru* (2001) Inter-American Court of Human Rights (ser. C) No. 74; *James* v. *United Kingdom* (1986) 98 European Court of Human Rights (ser. A); see also the discussion in Peterson, *Human Rights*, p. 23.

Mexican States.[223] Wälde gives the impression that the investor–state relationship is akin to 'David and Goliath', characterising it as one of innate inequality. And, as such, he argues, the rationale for investor–state arbitration is analogous to that of judicial review functions seen in the European Court of Human Rights, the European Court of Justice, or the Inter-American Human Rights Court – to protect the rights of the individual:

> International commercial arbitration assumes roughly equal parties engaging in sophisticated transnational commercial transactions. Investment arbitration is fundamentally different from international commercial arbitration. It governs the situation of a foreign investor exposed to the sovereignty, the regulatory, administrative and other governmental powers of a state. The investor is frequently, if not mostly, in a position of structural weakness, exacerbated often by inexperience (in particular in the case of smaller, entrepreneurial investors). Investment arbitration does not therefore set up a system of resolving disputes between presumed equals as in commercial arbitration, but a system of protection of foreign investors that are, by exposure to political risk, lack of familiarity with and integration into, an alien political, social, cultural, commercial, institutional and legal system, at a disadvantage.
>
> ... more appropriate for investor–state arbitration are analogies with judicial review relating to governmental conduct – be it international judicial review (as carried out by WTO dispute panels and Appellate Body, by the European- or Inter-American Human Rights Courts, or European Court of Justice) or national administrative courts judging the disputes of individual citizens over alleged abuse by public bodies of their governmental powers.[224]

On this basis, Wälde draws on human rights principles, importing jurisprudence from the European Court of Justice and the European Court of Human Rights into the investment treaty standard of fair and equitable treatment.[225] Adopting an explicitly pro-investor analysis, he argues that within the human rights context, 'legitimate expectation' is a fundamental principle governing relations between the individual and the state, and that, as such, it is appropriate to incorporate this concept into the investment treaty standard of fair and equitable

223 *In the Matter of a NAFTA Arbitration under UNCITRAL Arbitration Rules between International Thunderbird Gaming Corp.*

224 Ibid., paras 12–13; for a similar characterisation of the investor–state relationship, see also Baker, 'Denial of Justice', 188–91.

225 *In the Matter of a NAFTA Arbitration under UNCITRAL Arbitration Rules between International Thunderbird Gaming Corp.*

treatment.[226] In this way, through the appropriation of the language and principles of human rights, Wälde elevates the commercial grievance of an investor to a fundamental human right.

In the course of his enquiry, Wälde also traverses a wide array of non-investment sources of law to bolster his claim to the existence of a general principle of legitimate expectation, conflating 'legitimate expectation' with the substantive international law principle of 'good faith' and the treaty interpretation principle set out in Article 31 of the Vienna Convention.[227] In addition to human rights jurisprudence, he also refers to comparative contract law, a variety of domestic administrative law systems, and jurisprudence from the WTO.[228] Wälde clearly approaches investment treaties as embedded within general international law and was comfortable using non-investment principles to construct a particular reading of guaranteed investor protections. However, this was for the purpose of supporting foreign investment protection. It is troubling, although perhaps not surprising, that the same willingness to import principles from other areas of international law has not been prevalent in arbitral awards when the issue is the constraining of investor activity in accordance with international environmental or human rights law. This selectivity in the methodology of interpretation in investor–state arbitration again reflects a predilection for expansive constructions of treaty obligations, and, indeed, also the lengthy historical pattern of manipulation of legal doctrine to legitimise investor activities and entrenchment of the 'otherness' of the host state under international investment law.

3. Embracing recent transformative developments

International law is clearly an ever-evolving set of processes, a complex 'normative system' of which all treaties form a part – and this character requires treaties to be read against that wider backdrop of public

[226] Ibid., see also the discussion in Fry, 'International Human Rights Law', 83–9. Fry makes the error of answering the critique that investment awards do not adequately address human rights concerns by discussing awards that frame investor claims in terms of human rights violations, and, in so doing, fails to differentiate the human rights of investors from those of local communities within host states.

[227] *In the Matter of a NAFTA Arbitration under UNCITRAL Arbitration Rules between International Thunderbird Gaming Corp.*

[228] Ibid., paras 27–30.

international law.[229] The approach recently taken by international courts and tribunals emphasises that relevant norms crystallising into rules of customary international law should be taken into account in interpreting treaties.[230] And this overarching premise of public international law also encompasses investment treaties. There needs, therefore, to be a greater degree of openness to the inclusion of non-investment principles in arbitral awards determining investment disputes. As discussed, there has recently been a certain level of engagement with non-investment jurisprudence in the use of human rights principles to strengthen investor claims.[231] However, the adoption of transformative developments within the international legal system needs to be expanded beyond solely those that support the activities of the investor. It can be seen that the response from the investment community to the increasing transfer of principles amongst discrete areas of international law has been to appropriate the language of human rights to support investor claims. There now also needs to be a reflection of those developments in international law that compel greater engagement with environmental concerns, the human rights of local communities affected by investor activity, and public participation mechanisms. In other words, investor–state tribunals need to allow in the influence of human rights law or environmental principles to temper investor rights.

II. Global administrative law and investor–state arbitration

'Global administrative law' is a term that has recently been coined by scholars to describe patterns of modern global governance.[232] The term itself embodies an investigation into the nature and connections between forms of transnational regulation, international institutions, private industry standards, international review mechanisms, transnational networks, new actors on the international plane – and the

[229] Crawford, *International Law*, p. 17; McLachlan, 'The Principle', 282; Sands, 'Turtles and Torturers'; for a description of international law as a normative process, see Higgins, *Problems and Process*, p. 1.

[230] See, e.g., *Case Concerning the Gabčikovo–Nagymaros Project (Hungary/Slovakia)* (1997) ICJ Rep 7; see the discussion in Stephens, 182, 186–7; Boyle, 'The *Gabcikovo–Nagymaros Case*'.

[231] *In the Matter of a NAFTA Arbitration under UNCITRAL Arbitration Rules between International Thunderbird Gaming Corp.*

[232] Marks, 'Naming Global', 995. In particular, New York University, School of Law, has established a Global Administrative Law Research Project, from which the term 'Global Administrative Law' has emerged. See the project website, available at http://iilj.org/GAL/ (last accessed 16 December 2011).

emergence of shared administrative law principles within these forms of governance.[233] Its particular focus is on the legal mechanisms, principles, and practices that address issues of transparency, public participation, accountability, and review within national administrative law systems and at the global level.[234] It is concerned with issues of legitimacy, power, good governance, and democracy.[235]

A. Conceptualisations, politics, and the application of public law principles

Investor–state arbitration is also a part of this web of international administrative functions and entities.[236] It is, as Van Harten and Loughlin point out, an international dispute resolution mechanism unique in its structure and function.[237] Individuals may bring a claim to an international adjudicatory body directly against a state; individuals may compel a state to respond to claims at the international level without first exhausting local remedies; these claims involve a review of public state actions; a public law remedy of damages is sought by investor claimants; and enforcement of damages awards can be implemented against state assets through the courts of other states.[238]

However, there remains a central question regarding this manifestation of global administrative law: if investor–state arbitration is a component of global administrative law, which is in turn concerned with issues of transparency, public participation, and due process, for whom do these 'rule of law' principles operate? Are they solely for the benefit of the investor in their interaction with the host state? This question arises because host state conduct is reviewed in investor claims to assess whether it has displayed such characteristics. And yet, the procedural framework for investor–state arbitration does not allow for full transparency, public participation, or review of awards.[239] Oral hearings are

[233] Kingsbury, Krisch, Stewart, and Wiener, 'Global Governance', 2. For examples, Kingsbury, Krisch, Stewart, and Weiner refer to the WTO, the World Bank, the OECD, the Clean Development Mechanism under the Kyoto Protocol, the Basle Committee of central bankers, and the standards and review mechanisms associated with these institutions.

[234] Ibid., 3–5.

[235] Ibid.; see also the discussion in de Burca, 'Developing Democracy'; see further the discussion in Kingsbury, Krisch, and Stewart, 'The Emergence', 47–51.

[236] Van Harten and Loughlin, 'Investment Treaty Arbitration'.

[237] Ibid., 122–3, 149–50. [238] Ibid.

[239] Tienhaara, 'Third Party Participation', 230–1; Van Harten, *Investment Treaty Arbitration*, p. 159; Cosbey et al., *Investment and Sustainable*; Sornarajah, 'A Coming Crisis', 39; see also the discussion in Franck, 'Integrating Investment'.

generally conducted behind closed doors. Public participation, if permitted at all, is limited to the filing of *amicus curiae* briefs.[240] Court documentation is not readily available to the public. Full awards tend to be published only if the parties consent.[241] There is no appeals mechanism.[242] There are issues of due process surrounding the appointment of arbitrators who are also simultaneously acting as counsel in other investor–state disputes.[243] And there is no security of tenure for arbitrators.[244] Despite its subject matter in assessing state conduct, the procedural model of dispute settlement in investor–state arbitration remains based on private commercial dispute resolution, which emphasises confidentiality, enforcement of contractual obligations, and the importance of commercial considerations.[245]

In other words, only certain aspects of the 'global administrative project' appear to be applicable to investor–state arbitration. The investor–state arbitral system is presented as providing a neutral forum in which the regulatory actions of the host state are reviewed and due process for the investor can be assured.[246] The 'fair and equitable treatment' standard is regaled as a mechanism to assess the transparency and legitimacy of host state conduct and to determine whether due process was followed in host state administrative decision-making and proceedings.[247] However, there seems to be little application of such principles to investor–state arbitration itself. In the current system,

240 Sornarajah, 'The Clash of Globalizations'; Tienhaara, 'Third Party Participation'; see also the discussion in Choudhury, 'Recapturing Public Power'; Franck, 'The Legitimacy Crisis'.

241 See the discussion in Tienhaara, 'Third Party Participation'.

242 Van Harten, *Investment Treaty Arbitration*, pp. 180–2; Crawford, 'Is There a Need'; see also the discussion in Tams, 'An Appealing Option?', 31–3; see also Sammartano, 'The Fall of a Taboo'.

243 Van Harten, *Investment Treaty Arbitration*, pp. 172–3; Cosbey et al., *Investment and Sustainable*, 6; see also the comments in Buergenthal, 'Proliferation of Disputes', 498; Slaoui, 'The Rising Issue'; Dezalay and Garth, *Dealing in Virtue*, pp. 49–51. Dezalay and Garth include investor–state arbitration as falling within their study of international commercial arbitration. Accordingly, their comments on arbitrators are applicable to both solely private-party arbitration and investor–state disputes.

244 Van Harten, *Investment Treaty Arbitration*, pp. 168–72; Cosbey et al., *Investment and Sustainable*, p. 6; Sornarajah, 'The Clash of Globalizations', 17.

245 Sornarajah, 'The Clash of Globalizations', 13–17; Tienharra, 'Third Party Participation', 230–1.

246 See, e.g., Weiler and Wälde, 'Investment Arbitration'; see also the Separate Opinion of Wälde in *In the Matter of a NAFTA Arbitration under UNCITRAL Arbitration Rules between International Thunderbird Gaming Corp.*

247 See, e.g., the discussion in Schill, 'Fair and Equitable'.

there is insufficient transparency and public participation in the conduct of proceedings that implicate the public interest. Most certainly, it is deficient in the lack of an appeals facility to ensure the accuracy and consistency of treaty interpretation in arbitral awards.

Reflecting on these latest trends and their rhetoric, it seems that the historical dynamics of empire are again finding avenues for reproduction in the discourse surrounding investor–state arbitration as a form of global administrative law. It seems to me that the framing of investor–state arbitration as the embodiment of the rule of law, good governance, and neutrality is,[248] quite clearly, a perpetuation of the rationale for the assertion of an international minimum standard in the nineteenth century and the creation of ICSID in the twentieth – removal of the dispute from the 'politicised' environment of the host state to the neutrality of international adjudication. Indeed, there have been express references to such an association, with Weiler and Wälde adopting a particularly patronising stance, regarding the conclusion of investment treaties as a positive indicator of state 'maturity':

> The state that refuses to contract effectively (by means of specific arbitral agreements or general investment treaties) may be regarded as the equivalent of the light-headed juvenile who needs protection from its own foolhardy actions, rather than as a serious player on the world stage. Joining the club of multilateral economic treaties therefore implies some degree of maturity, self- and externally anchored discipline. A 21st century version of the 19th century club of 'civilised nations' may well have emerged, though under different labels related to contemporary notions of proper governance.[249]

Against a background of statements such as this, it is unsurprising that a degree of scepticism remains amongst developing states as to the political agenda for investment liberalisation and the 'good governance' drive of institutions such as the World Bank and International Monetary Fund.[250] Attention has, of course, also been drawn to the limited conceptualisation of global administrative law generally adopted by scholars.[251] Chimni, for example, argues that it should not be conceived of as solely procedural, but should also encompass substantive rules so as to preclude the emergence of international

248 Ibid., see also Weiler and Wälde, 'Investment Arbitration'.

249 Weiler and Wälde, 'Investment Arbitration', 4.

250 See the discussion in Anghie, *Imperialism, Sovereignty*, pp. 256–68; Gathii, 'The Limits', 207, 220–30. The relationship between the good governance policies of the World Bank and the IMF and imperialism is discussed above in Chapters 2 and 4.

251 See, e.g., the critique in Chimni, 'Co-option'.

administrative agencies disconnected from the human rights, environmental, and economic needs of developing states.[252] He argues that the global administrative project is 'today being shaped by a transnational capitalist class that seeks to legitimize unequal laws and institutions and deploy it to its advantage.'[253] Certainly, the current framing of investor–state arbitration as the embodiment of good governance and the rule of law is representative solely of the perspective of political and private elites. And it will remain so without the incorporation of substantive principles from other areas of international law to inform the interpretation of treaties so as to support host state needs and without the application of administrative principles of transparency and public participation to investor–state arbitration itself.

B. *Individuals on the international plane*

The emerging recognition of the individual on the international stage is a potent feature of global administrative law. In a system that has traditionally been solely 'state-centred', the increasingly visible role of the individual in international law is transformative.[254] This evolving presence has largely occurred through the development of human rights law, a field that has itself emerged over the last sixty years, and via the establishment of procedural mechanisms to hear allegations of human rights violations.[255]

Substantive human rights principles have been encapsulated within a number of key instruments, such as the United Nations Universal Declaration on Human Rights,[256] the International Covenant on Civil

[252] Ibid., 817, 826–7. Chimni specifically refers to the definition of Kingsbury, Krisch and Stewart, 'The Emergence', 29, which defines global administrative law as:

> the operation of existing or possible principles, procedural rules and reviewing and other mechanisms relating to the accountability, participation, and assurance of legality in global governance.

See also the discussion in Garcia, 'Globalization and the Theory', 22–6, emphasising the necessity for the development of a normative component to global public law so as to ensure a system of international administrative law grounded in 'the ethics of justice'.

[253] Chimni, 'Co-option', 806.

[254] See the discussion of the role of non-state actors in Sands, 'Turtles and Torturers', 532; Brand, 'External Sovereignty', 1692–3, 1695–6; see also Maogoto and Kindiki, 'A People', 108–10, 112, 119.

[255] Steiner, Alston, and Goodman, *International Human Rights*, pp. 17, 160–1; Buergenthal, 'The Evolving International'; Ratner and Abrams, *Accountability*, pp. 5–9.

[256] Universal Declaration on Human Rights, GA Resolution 217A (III), UNGAOR, 3rd Sess., 183rd plen mtg, UN Doc A/RES/217A.

and Political Rights,[257] the International Covenant on Economic, Social and Cultural Rights,[258] the European Convention on Human Rights,[259] the American Convention on Human Rights,[260] and the African Charter on Human and Peoples' Rights.[261] Human rights principles are also sourced from customary international law, the practices of numerous international institutions, and the jurisprudence of domestic and international courts and tribunals.[262] However, it was the creation of procedural mechanisms permitting individuals to petition United Nations human rights committees and courts, such as the European Court of Human Rights and the Inter-American Court of Human Rights, that assured the 'individual' such a prominent place within the international sphere.[263]

Indeed, the establishment of procedural mechanisms enabling individuals to bring a complaint against a state for alleged violations of human rights law has not only accelerated the rate of jurisprudential developments in this area, but it has also incrementally increased the scope of legal personality for individuals.[264] Individuals clearly do not possess the full international legal personality of states.[265] However, there is a measure of recognition in international law, not only of individual rights, but also of responsibilities.[266] An increasing focus on holding individuals to account for human rights violations under international law is also linked with the progressive development of

257 International Covenant on Civil and Political Rights, opened for signature 16 December 1966, 999 UNTS 171 (entered into force 23 March 1976).

258 International Covenant on Economic, Social and Cultural Rights, opened for signature 16 December 1966, 993 UNTS 3 (entered into force 3 January 1976).

259 European Convention for the Protection of Human Rights and Fundamental Freedoms, opened for signature 4 November 1950, 213 UNTS 221 (entered into force 3 September 1953).

260 American Convention on Human Rights, opened for signature 22 November 1969, 9 ILM 673 (entered into force 18 July 1978).

261 African Charter on Human and Peoples' Rights, opened for signature 21 June 1981, 21 ILM 58 (entered into force 21 October 1986).

262 Steiner, Alston, and Goodman, *International Human Rights*, pp. 16–17, 160–1; Triggs, *International Law: Contemporary*, pp. 881–3.

263 Triggs, *International Law: Contemporary*, pp. 951–3; see the discussion in Buergenthal, 'The Evolving International'.

264 Triggs, *International Law: Contemporary*, pp. 951–3; see the discussion on the international responsibility of individuals in Shelton, 'Globalization', 311–12.

265 Brownlie, *Principles*, pp. 65–7, 553–8; see also the discussion in Hollis, 'Private Actors', 243.

266 Shelton, 'Globalization and the Erosion', 311–14; Ratner and Abrams, 'Regulatory Takings', 5–9, 167–76.

international criminal law and the creation of an institutional framework for prosecuting those individuals,[267] such as the International Criminal Tribunal for the Former Yugoslavia,[268] the International Criminal Tribunal for Rwanda,[269] and the International Criminal Court.[270] The cumulative effect of these developments has been to shift the place of the individual within the international legal system to that of a more active, visible presence.[271]

The question that then immediately springs to mind is how this modern emergence of the individual within international law has impacted on international investment law. In essence, it has been another exercise in 'cherry-picking'.[272] Mechanisms have not developed within international investment law for aggrieved individuals harmed by investor activities to make formal claims against foreign investors within an international setting. Mechanisms have, however, been established to ensure the individual investor a hearing on the international stage. Again, a selective approach in the development of international investment law and dispute resolution has co-opted certain transformative elements of international law, but ignored others.

In this fashion, the modern visibility of the individual on the international plane has manifested in investor–state arbitration, through which an individual foreign investor is able to claim directly against the host state in front of an international tribunal. It has not evolved so as to permit individuals harmed by investor activities to have recourse to international investment law. This selectivity replicates patterns seen throughout the emergence and development of international investment law in reproducing the dynamic of empire – the establishment of principles and mechanisms to support the activities of capital-exporting states and their investors. Anghie has set out the many ways

267 See the discussion in Shelton, 'Globalization and the Erosion', 311–14; Buergenthal, 'The Evolving International', 801–3; Triggs, *International Law*, pp. 968–9; Chesterman, 'An International Rule of Law?', 345.

268 Statute of the International Criminal Tribunal for the Former Yugoslavia, UN Doc. S/RES/827, (1993) 32 ILM 1203.

269 Statute of the International Criminal Tribunal for Rwanda UN Doc. SC Res 955 (1994) 33 ILM 1600.

270 Rome Statute for the International Criminal Court, opened for signature 17 July 1998, UN Doc. A/CONF.183/9, 37 ILM 999 (entered into force 1 July 2002).

271 Sands, 'Turtles and Torturers', 532; Crawford, *International Law*, pp. 19–21; Brand, 'External Sovereignty', 1692–3, 1695–6; Maogoto and Kindiki, 'A People Betrayed', 108–10, 112, 119.

272 'Cherry-picking' also characterised the use of rules discussed earlier in section B.2(b) of this chapter.

in which colonialism continues to find subtle and pervasive manifestations into the twenty-first century.[273] As I have reiterated throughout this book, imperialism has also repeatedly found form in the historical evolution of international investment law and remains imbued within its modern framework. The establishment of investor–state arbitration without corresponding mechanisms under international investment law for the hearing of complaints by individuals affected by investor activity contributes to the maintenance of that tradition.

Conversely, there perhaps also exists a more positive path to be taken in the future development of the interaction between investor–state arbitration and global administrative law. Indeed, a question for consideration is whether aspects of global administrative law could, in fact, play a role in unravelling the repetition of particular historical patterns. For example, adoption of public law principles of transparency and public participation would certainly address key legitimacy concerns surrounding the system of investment dispute resolution.[274] The creation of international mechanisms through which investor activity could be reviewed at the instigation of those allegedly harmed by investor operations would also ensure a more balanced engagement with the individual within investment law frameworks. Evidently, such steps taken in isolation would not redress the 'otherness' of the host state within international investment law. However, combined with significant shifts in the substantive law, they could contribute to a reorienting of the core underlying approaches that inform investment law, practices, and dispute resolution. In this way, requiring investment arbitration to adhere to global public law principles could contribute to the infusion of a culture in which it is natural to consider the social, environmental, and developmental needs of the host state in investment disputes.

III. Networks, epistemic communities, and the investment sector

Shifts in international governance, structures, actors, and law-making over the last fifty years have transformed the modern international legal and political landscape on a number of levels.[275] These processes

[273] Anghie, 'The Heart of My Home', 505–6.

[274] Van Harten, *Investment Treaty Arbitration*, pp. 153–64; Cosbey et al., *Investment and Sustainable*; Sornarajah, 'The Clash of Globalizations', 13–17.

[275] Crawford, *International Law*, p. 17; Sands, 'Turtles and Torturers'; Abbott and Snidal, 'Hard and Soft Law'.

have included the emergence of transnational networks, epistemic communities, and non-state actors that exert informal, but influential, modes of governance and knowledge-creation in international law and politics.[276] And, increasingly, significant ideas, international policies, modes of governance, and pre-normative behaviour are emerging from the interaction of 'sub-state' officials and non-state actors.[277] Constructivist theorists have long recognised the role of activities of this kind in the development of the international legal and political order.[278] They have drawn attention to the transformative role of a variety of actors on the emergence of international norms, on state behaviour and cooperation, and on shaping state beliefs, identities and understandings.[279] For example, as discussed above in the Introduction, and in Chapter 4 in the context of emerging norms of corporate social responsibility, Brunnée and Toope point to the invaluable nature of non-state activity in norm-creation:

> Pre-legal normativity is valuable in itself, and is not purely a set of instruments on the road to law. But looking back from the perspective of a legal norm or system, one can see that the actors involved in pre-legal norm creation and elaboration serve also as builders of the legal system ... NGOs, corporations, informal intergovernmental expert networks, and a variety of other groups are actively engaged in the creation of shared understandings and the promotion of learning amongst states.[280]

In particular, epistemic communities, NGOs, and transgovernmental networks operate so as to develop transformative ideas, establish discourses, and reiterate shared beliefs. They frame issues, lobby governments, and inject viewpoints into new contexts. These knowledge-creating entities can even function in a quasi-administrative role through coordinated procedures, collaborative programmes, information exchange, critical analysis, socialisation, and peer pressure.[281]

276 Slaughter, *A New World*; Krisch and Kingsbury, 'Introduction: Global'; Spiro, 'Non-Governmental Organizations', 770.

277 Slaughter, *A New World*; Danish, 'International Relations Theory', 205, 214.

278 See, e.g., Danish, 'International Relations', 216–18; Brunnée and Toope, 'International Law and Constructivism'.

279 Danish, 'International Relations', 216–18; Brunnée and Toope, 'International Law and Constructivism'.

280 Brunnée and Toope, 'International Law and Constructivism', 70; see also Brunnée and Toope, *Legitimacy and Legality*.

281 Slaughter, *A New World*; Sands, *Principles*, pp. 112–17; Raustiala, 'The "Participatory Revolution"', 538; Haas, 'Epistemic Communities', 791; Kingsbury, 'Global Environmental', 63, 79–80; Hobb, 'Global Challenges', 193.

Indeed, these channels are central to the effective spread of new ideas and the creation of new perspectives.[282] This type of informal transnational engagement and knowledge-generation could have a profound effect on international investment law. If the shared understandings and values of those operating within the foreign investment sector can be shifted to a more socially and environmentally responsible position, then the legal principles may start to follow suit.

A. *Networks, transnational business, and inter-systemic conflict*

Multinational corporations, institutional investors, transnational financiers, and international arbitrators – these are groups around which informal networks are already in place and through which it may be possible to effect a cultural change in the investment community. NGOs have already been able to use such networks to infuse a more ecological and human rights-based outlook into the discourse on the role of multinational corporations in the international community.[283] And this, in turn, has led to the potential hints at synergy between the foreign investment sector and environmental protections objectives explored above in Chapter 4 – an emergent influence on transnational business practices of concepts such as corporate social responsibility, the sustainable finance movement, initiatives such as the United Nations Global Compact,[284] and socially and environmentally responsible institutional investment.[285] Interestingly, within a constructivist framing of this activity, these developments are simultaneously products and purveyors of change in the discourse on the appropriate role and function of business in the global community. However, the law on foreign investment protection does not yet reflect this increasing openness towards notions of socially and environmentally responsible transnational business practice. The question, therefore, remains as to how to

[282] See the discussion in Haas, 'Epistemic Communities'; Dryzek, 'Paradigms and Discourses', 44.

[283] Haas, 'Epistemic Communities'; Spiro, 'Non-Governmental Organizations'; Sands, 'Turtles and Torturers'.

[284] United Nations Global Compact, available at www.unglobalcompact.org/ (last accessed 16 December 2011).

[285] McBarnet, 'Corporate Social Responsibility', p. 9; Bunn, 'Global Advocacy'; see also the discussion on reputational risk as a driver of corporate compliance with human rights norms, in Keenan, 'Financial Globalization; see above at Chapter 5 for a detailed treatment of the business community response to corporate social responsibility expectations.

generate a corresponding shift in the law and integrate non-investment principles into international investment law.

Theories on inter-systemic conflicts of law between global sectors point to the futility of seeking resolution to the clash of international environmental and investment norms without addressing the underlying vision of the actors.[286] Fischer-Lascano and Teubner argue that the fragmentation of global law, and the resultant collision of international norms between separate regimes, represents 'deep contradictions between colliding sectors of a global society'.[287] As the root cause is not so much the colliding norms as the colliding social sectors, the law in itself cannot reconcile conflicting systems in international law.[288] Fischer-Lascano and Teubner assert that the most that can be hoped for is 'a weak normative compatibility of the fragments'.[289]

The question then is: if the complexities of contemporary international society are acknowledged, can those multiplicities of perspective find reflection in the law? Where space is made for multiple viewpoints, can the divisions within the social sectors be lessened, commonalities emphasised, and alignments created? And can this lead to circumstances in which shared understandings and normative integration can more easily occur? Although still contentious and problematic, it has been argued that this is occurring to a degree in certain sectors. For example, for some scholars, international human rights norms and economic globalisation are not necessarily diametrically opposed in all circumstances.[290] As perspectives within business cultures have shifted and discourses altered, so new convergences emerged, namely principles of corporate social responsibility, sustainable development, and the proliferation of the public-private partnership.[291] A process of this nature needs to occur within international arbitration circles and amongst those responsible for investment treaty negotiation so as to address the fundamental 'colliding' of the various 'social sectors' engaged in this field. The challenge is to induce further change, and at

[286] See, e.g., Fischer-Lescano and Teubner, 'Diversity or Cacophony?', 1004; see also the discussion on the complexities of private/public interaction in Teubner, 'Values'.

[287] Fischer-Lascano and Teubner, 'Diversity or Cacophony?', 1045.

[288] Ibid.; see also the work of the International Law Commission, *Fragmentation of International Law*; see also the discussion on avoidance of norm conflict in international disputes through approaches to interpretation in Milanovic, 'Norm Conflict'.

[289] Fischer-Lascano and Teubner, 'Diversity or Cacophony?', 1004.

[290] Kinley, 'Human Rights', 257–8.

[291] Ibid.; see also the discussion in McBarnet, 'Corporate Social Responsibility'; see also Kinley, *Civilising Globalisation*; Moore Dickerson, 'How Do Norms and Empathy'.

an accelerated pace, within the foreign investment sector and to reach legal decision-makers in the field of international investment law. It is, perhaps, with this in mind that Brunnée and Toope's theories on an interactional account of international law and 'communities of practice' can come into play.[292]

B. *Arbitrators as an epistemic community*

International commercial arbitrators and counsel have been characterised as an 'epistemic community or issue network', the members of which share a belief in the primacy of an international system of private dispute resolution and possess shared understandings of the importance of international business values.[293] Certainly, the same can be said for the select group of arbitrators presiding over investor–state disputes. Indeed, investment arbitrators were expressly included within Dezalay and Garth's assessment of international commercial arbitrators.[294] As a key epistemic community within the investment sector, arbitrators are central to knowledge-creation in the field of international investment law. In presiding over investor–state disputes, they interpret the treaty texts, determine the direction of international investment law, and legitimise selected legal arguments submitted to them. These arbitrators shape the way in which the law emerges from the contested approaches of the parties to disputes. The reasoning in their awards influences the political choices of both investors and host states alike. And they effectively operate as the 'gate-keepers' for the stimulation of new understandings within the law.

This community of international arbitrators is a small one.[295] The inner circle has been described as the 'mafia' or the 'club', a community into which it is difficult to gain entrance.[296] Divided along generational lines, the community is characterised as comprising two groups, that of the 'grand old men of arbitration', the pioneers of international arbitration, and the younger 'technocrats', who emphasise their technical

[292] Brunnée and Toope, 'International Law'; see also Brunnée and Toope, *Legitimacy and Legality*.

[293] Dezalay and Garth, *Dealing in Virtue*, p. 16.

[294] Ibid., pp. 5–24, see for the inclusion of discussion on ICSID, oil nationalisations, the *Iran–United States Claims Tribunal*, and the arbitral careers of leading figures in ICSID, UNCITRAL, and ICC arbitrations.

[295] Ibid., pp. 10, 46. [296] Ibid., pp. 10, 28–9, 46, 50–1.

skill, business know-how, and specialisation in arbitration.[297] The overall mode of organisation, however, is one of:

> an epistemic community or issue network organised around certain beliefs in an ideal of international private justice, but it is also an extremely competitive market involving big business and megalawyering. To understand it requires an understanding of both the ideals *and* the competition for business.[298]

1. The cultural approach underlying investor–state arbitration

This characterisation has significant implications in examining the resistance of arbitrators to incorporating environmental and human rights considerations into their decision-making in investor–state disputes. Dezalay and Garth contend that arbitrators and counsel are engaged in a dual process of creating a legitimate transnational legal order for private dispute resolution while simultaneously needing to court the continued purchase of their services from business entities.[299] At the very least, this reliance on the business community for its survival creates a slant in the system towards accommodating the needs and values of the business community. However, the authors also point to the fiercely competitive nature of the market for securing large and prestigious arbitral instructions and how this competitiveness shapes the field of international arbitration in fundamental ways:

> Both the processes and the outcomes of particular cases and arbitration in general depend on the characteristics of the arbitrators. ... the selection is a key decision in winning or losing. The attorneys for the parties well understand that the 'authority' and 'expertise' of arbitrators determine their clout within the tribunal. The operation of the market in the selection of arbitrators therefore provides a key to understanding the justice that emerges from the decisions of arbitrators.[300]

In other words, in order to succeed in the international market, arbitrators and potential arbitrators note the factors that are valued in the market place and that lead to reappointments. They adjust their own

[297] Ibid., pp. 34–7. E.g., in 1996, Dezalay and Garth categorised Professor Pierre Lalive and Judge Gunner Lagergren as members of the pioneering group of 'grand old men of arbitration', and Jan Paulsson and Yves Derains as members of the new generation of 'technocrats'.

[298] Ibid., p. 16. Emphasis in original.

[299] Ibid., pp. 8, 16, 70; see the discussion on the lessening of space for the public interest within the creation of international trade and investment regimes and transnational dispute resolution fora in David Trubek et al., 'Symposium'.

[300] Dezalay and Garth, *Dealing in Virtue*, pp. 8–9, 16, 29.

conduct to display those characteristics and align themselves with 'successful' arbitrators.[301] To a certain degree, this inevitably involves demonstrating an affinity with the objectives of international commerce.[302] This cultural dynamic within arbitral circles is, in turn, also reflected in the knowledge-creation processes within international investment law – the public declaration of an arbitrator's knowledge, expertise, and cultural approach that is embodied in his or her awards. Through repetition of interpretations of the law, the informal pressures to emulate high-profile arbitrators, and the subtle reiteration of ideological structures, it is a system that reinforces the prevailing conceptualisations that operate within international investment law.

The concern to which these processes give rise is encapsulated in Sornarajah's expression of disquiet at a system which encourages its decision-makers to have one eye on 'the securing of their next appointment to a tribunal on the basis of their display of commercial probity and their loyalty to the values of multinational business.'[303] Systemically, there are strong disincentives for arbitrators to give weight to non-commercial considerations in the matters before them or to engage with the wider context of investment activity, such as the application of principles of sustainable development to the dispute. Indeed, there is very little place in the current system for an arbitrator who acts boldly and incorporates applicable principles from other areas of international law.

The implications of this are significant. Arbitrators in investor–state disputes comprise an epistemic community responsible for knowledge-creation within international investment law. If the underlying culture of that community requires a conservative adherence to private sector commercial values, investor protection will remain at the forefront of arbitrators' concerns. This is not to say that host states do not ever prevail in investor–state arbitration – they do.[304] It is also not an issue that is directed at the personal integrity of individual arbitrators.[305] It is

[301] Ibid., p. 29; Borgen, 'Transnational Tribunals', 724–8; see also the tendency of members of a discipline to reiterate and replicate the regime's normative bases in Kennedy, 'Disciplines of International Law', 12–13.

[302] Dezalay and Garth, *Dealing in Virtue*, p. 70; see, e.g., the polarising way in which those advocating more space for regulatory autonomy within international investment law are characterised as opposed to the rationality of 'investment lawyers', in Weiler, 'Good Faith', 701.

[303] Sornarajah, 'The Clash of Globalizations', 17.

[304] Franck, 'Development and Outcomes'.

[305] Cosbey et al., *Investment and Sustainable*.

more a commentary on the wider systemic framework in which these decisions are made and the cultural base from which arbitrators begin their analysis into the issues in dispute. With which core understandings do arbitrators approach their task? And, fundamentally, which concerns of the parties are subconsciously most valued by the arbitrators?

2. Reorienting the cultural approach?

The traditional lack of engagement with non-investment issues witnessed in international investment law has been cultivated within the epistemic communities of those arbitrators involved in international commercial and investor–state arbitration. These circles exert a powerful influence over the culture underlying decision-making in investment disputes.[306] As such, shifting the understandings that shape the dominant cultures within these transnational networks and epistemic communities is central to the emergence of a more balanced manifestation of international investment law. In this way, the same mechanisms that have assisted in the maintenance of the current system could also be utilised to transform it.

The infusion of a culture that is not dismissive of public interest issues and antagonistic to the integration of principles from other areas of public international law is likely to result in decision-makers for whom it is the norm to consider the social, environmental, and developmental needs of the host state in investment disputes. The question to which this proposition gives rise is, of course: what will generate a cognitive transformational shift of this kind?

There is no definitive answer. But were the following conditions ever to materialise, they would certainly contribute to just such a cognitive realignment. First, an appreciation of the importance of host state policy space and public interest factors needs to be enhanced amongst arbitrators. The validity of an integrated approach to the application of principles of international law needs to be embraced by investment solicitors, counsel, and arbitrators. And greater engagement on these issues is essential between professional organisations, practitioners, and academics. To this end, there needs to be further dispersion and reiteration of ideas on socially and environmentally responsible

306 Sornarajah, 'The Clash of Globalizations'; Dezelay and Garth, *Dealing in Virtue*, pp. 8–9, 16, 29, 70; see also the discussion on the central role of ideas and ideology in the creation of law and policy in international trade regulation in Lang, 'Reflecting'.

investment in publications and at international conferences. Pressure for reform exerted through issue networks of organisations, such as the International Institute for Sustainable Development, can normalise the idea of a more balanced model for international investment law.[307] Furthermore, wider recognition that modern international investment law continues to be informed by nineteenth-century conceptualisations would be a significant first step in redressing those influences. Continued interaction with a variety of perspectives will broaden the understandings of those responsible for decision-making in investment disputes and for negotiating investment treaties. And this could ultimately lead to a different type of knowledge emerging for the investment sector. However, as this kind of cultural shift is likely to be a gradual process, it may require further generational change within this community before it becomes standard practice for the social and environmental needs of the host state to be considered on a par with the rights of the investor.

IV. Conclusion

Recent transformations in modern international law have led to a more fluid, dynamic, and responsive international legal system.[308] We can see that the role of non-state actors, the emergence of transnational networks, the acceleration of law-making, the cross-pollination of concepts and principles, and the increasing focus on global public law and justice have all challenged the traditional model of international law.[309] These developments have also challenged the outmoded frameworks of international investment law. The contrast in approach has thrown into relief the reluctance of investor–state arbitral tribunals to inform their interpretations of treaty texts with principles from non-investment areas of international law to support host state activity, as well as the significance of underlying cultures within transnational networks of international arbitrators in maintaining that approach. The trends in modern international law have drawn attention to the lack of engagement with non-investment issues within investment treaties and have

[307] Mann et al., *IISD Model International Agreement*.

[308] Crawford, *International Law*, p. 17; Sands, 'Turtles and Torturers'; Spiro, 'Globalization, International'; Higgins, 'International Law'.

[309] Sands, 'Turtles and Torturers'; Crawford, *International Law*; Raustiala, 'The "Participatory Revolution"'; Hobb, 'Global Challenges'; Slaughter, *A New World*; Garcia, 'Globalization and the Theory'; Peel, 'Giving the Public a Voice'.

also highlighted the lack of adherence in investor–state arbitration to emerging public law principles of transparency and public participation.

These new developments within the international legal system have contributed to pressure to reform international investment law. This chapter has argued, however, that in response to these recent shifts within international law, the investment sector has been inappropriately selective in adopting solely those developments that promote investment protection. In this regard, the investor–state mechanism was constructed to permit individual investors to engage with host states directly on the international stage.[310] In furtherance of this approach, human rights principles have begun to appear in the reasoning of arbitral awards to justify investors' claims.[311] And, in a particularly insidious manifestation of historical patterns, investor–state arbitration is being framed as an ideal form of global administrative law and the embodiment of the rule of law.[312]

In reflecting on these issues, I have argued that such a one-sided adoption of developments in the international legal system perpetuates the patterns of imperialist origin that have become entrenched within international investment law. Embracing the full array of transformative influences, however, would entail the introduction of environmental and human rights considerations into the substantive text of investment treaties, the establishment of a mechanism through which individuals affected by investor activity could bring a complaint at the international level, and the use of non-investment principles in the reasoning of arbitral tribunals to support the social, economic, and environmental needs of host states. Opening up to the full effect of recent developments in international law in this way would result in a more balanced model for international investment law, a potential means through which to break imperialist patterns within investment frameworks, and a comprehensive engagement with the current direction of international law. Such conclusions, of course, inevitably lead to further questions, the most significant of which is how such a 'transformed' international investment law would manifest in practice.

[310] Newcombe and Paradell, *Law and Practice*, p. 27; Dolzer and Schreuer, *Principles*, p. 20.

[311] See, e.g., the Separate Opinion of T. Wälde, *In the Matter of a NAFTA Arbitration under UNCITRAL Arbitration Rules between International Thunderbird Gaming Corp.*

[312] Schill, 'Fair and Equitable Treatment'; Weiler and Wälde, 'Investment Arbitration'.

6 Paths towards a reconceptualised international law on foreign investment

The questions with which this book has engaged seem to point inexorably towards the need for significant reform in the international governance of the foreign investment sector. Advocating such a position, of course, also necessarily leads to the consideration of a series of further questions: what would a reconceptualised international investment law look like? What concrete steps need to be taken to bring about a transformation in international investment law and policy? What new norms on investment might emerge out of the recently heightened focus on the social and environmental responsibilities of multinational corporations and on the role of foreign investment in the promotion of sustainable development? This chapter addresses these questions, analysing several substantive and procedural options for reform.

In reflecting on the necessary substantive changes to international investment law, section I examines treaty-based options, including the calls for a balanced multilateral agreement on investment[1] and for a binding international agreement to regulate the conduct of multinational corporations.[2] This section proposes the form in which specific provisions in a socially and environmentally responsible investment agreement could be drafted. Section I also examines substantive change grounded in customary international law. It analyses the way in which norms of international investment law are likely to be affected by international environmental law, corporate social responsibility standards, and the sustainable finance movement.

In section II, I consider procedural reform of the dispute settlement system for international investment disputes. I argue for increased

[1] Mann et al., *IISD Model International Agreement*.

[2] Friends of the Earth, 'Towards Binding Corporate Accountability'.

transparency and public participation measures to be incorporated within the largely opaque system of investor–state arbitration. To this end, this chapter examines recent initiatives designed to improve these aspects and to address concerns at the legitimacy of investor–state arbitration.[3] It also argues for the establishment of an appellate body to address the consistency issues inherent in the current decentralised system of investment arbitration.[4] In the course of this enquiry, it examines possible reform to the system under the International Centre for the Settlement of Investment Disputes (ICSID),[5] the calls for an international investment court,[6] and the inclusion of an appellate body structure within an entirely new multilateral agreement to regulate international investment.[7]

Speculating on the significance of an appeals facility, I argue that the provision of one centralised appellate body for investment disputes would not only address the jurisprudential problems of inconsistency within the current system, but would likely remedy a number of substantive issues in need of reform as well. In this vein, I would suggest that an appellate body has the potential to produce a more sophisticated reading of international investment law, utilising an integrated approach in much the same way as the Appellate Body of the World Trade Organisation (WTO) has done in the context of international trade disputes.[8] With the consideration of principles from other areas of international law, it is more likely that the broader social and environmental issues involved in investor–state arbitration would have a more receptive hearing than is currently the case. In the course of the discussion on the need for an appellate body, this chapter also draws attention to the attributes of arbitrators in the current system, the selection process for their appointment to tribunals, and the implications of a systemic 'investor bias' within investment dispute

[3] Newcombe, 'Sustainable Development'; see Brower, Brower and Sharpe, 'The Coming Crisis'; Tienhaara, 'Third Party Participation'.

[4] See generally the discussion on legitimacy issues in investor–state arbitration as well as on the need for an appellate body in Van Harten, *Investment Treaty Arbitration*; see generally Sauvant, *Appeals Mechanism*; Franck, 'The Legitimacy Crisis'.

[5] Convention on the Settlement of Investment Disputes between States and Nationals of Other States, opened for signature 18 March 1965, 575 UNTS 159 (entered into force 14 October 1966);

[6] Van Harten, *Investment Treaty Arbitration*, pp. 180–4.

[7] Mann et al., *IISD Model International Agreement*.

[8] See, e.g., *US-Import Prohibition of Certain Shrimp and Shrimp Products*, Report of the Appellate Body, WT/DS58/AB/R, 12 October 1998, 38 ILM 118 (1999).

resolution.[9] Indeed, the establishment of a permanent appellate body would also have the potential to address many of these concerns in addition to those focused on inconsistency in decision-making.

Implementation of the measures suggested in this chapter will need to overcome significant obstacles before effective reform can be realised in the short term. A key stumbling block is political will on the part of developed states – a general reluctance to loosen the high-level investment protection obtained under international investment agreements is quite apparent.[10] There are also vested interests amongst a range of actors in investor–state arbitration in maintaining its current decentralised structure and its focus on investor protection.[11] Furthermore, it would seem that the design of this system also, in fact, flows into the interpretation and application of investment treaties, precluding development of principles that would challenge prevailing doctrines of high-level investor protection. In addition, as I have argued throughout this book, there are entrenched patterns of assertion, challenge, and reassertion of investor-supportive dynamics within international investment law that must also be overcome.

Although this chapter explores the way in which a reconceptualised investment framework might manifest, it is also realistic as to the timeframe for achieving that transformation. For this reason, it proposes an incremental approach as the immediate path forward. Initial steps would involve the inclusion of socially and environmentally responsible provisions within future bilateral investment treaties and more contextualised interpretations of current investment agreements. It also advocates the introduction of substantial reform measures in the area of transparency and public participation. And it emphasises the importance of stimulating a cultural shift within the investment arbitral community. If adopted together as constituent parts of a more comprehensive reform programme, it is possible that taking these steps

[9] See the discussion in Tams, 'An Appealing Option?'; Cosbey et al., *Investment and Sustainable Development*.

[10] Cosbey et al., *Investment and Sustainable Development*, p. 27; Van Harten, *Investment Treaty Arbitration*, p. 179.

[11] Sornarajah, 'The Clash'; see also Dezalay and Garth, *Dealing in Virtue*, pp. 8–9. As mentioned in Chapter 5, Dezalay and Garth include investor–state arbitration as falling within their study of international commercial arbitration. As such, their comments on the structure of the dispute settlement system and the role of arbitrators are applicable to both private-party arbitration and investor–state disputes.

would set international investment law on a path that could ultimately break the cycles of re-emergence of imperialism.

I. Socially and environmentally responsible foreign investment

It will have become apparent throughout the foregoing chapters of this book that I locate a key problem with modern international investment law in its focus on the protection of investors' rights and on the promotion of foreign investment to the exclusion of other relevant interests. What, then, are the concrete ways in which substantive reform might manifest?

A. Treaty-based reform

One proposal to induce more socially and environmentally responsible investment practices is via a multilateral agreement such as the Model International Agreement on Investment for Sustainable Development drafted by the International Institute for Sustainable Development (IISD Model Agreement).[12] Another is the now-shelved draft text for a Norwegian model bilateral investment treaty (Norwegian Model BIT).[13] And the final model examined arises out of the corporate social responsibility movement – Friends of the Earth have put forward a proposal for a multilateral convention on corporate accountability (the FOE Proposal).[14]

1. IISD Agreement on Investment for Sustainable Development

Although attempts to negotiate the Multilateral Agreement on Investment (MAI) failed in 1998,[15] interest amongst states remains in developing a

[12] Mann et al., *IISD Model International Agreement*.

[13] Ministry of Trade and Industry, Norway, Draft Model Bilateral Investment Agreement (December 2007), available at www.regjeringen.no/nb/dep/nhd/dok/Horinger/Horingsdokumenter/2008/horing—modell-for-investeringsavtaler/-4.html?id=496026 (last accessed 17 December 2011).

[14] Friends of the Earth, 'Towards Binding Corporate Accountability'.

[15] See the text of the draft Multilateral Agreement on Investment at OECD Negotiating Group on the Multilateral Agreement on Investment, Draft Consolidated Text, 22 April 1998, available at www1.oecd.org/daf/mai/pdf/ng/ng987r1e.pdf (last accessed 17 December 2011); see also Geiger, 'Regulatory Expropriations', 96–7; Tieleman, *The Failure of the Multilateral Agreement*.

global regulatory framework for international investment.[16] Furthermore, there are also indications that the emphasis is shifting within the political discourse to the possible accommodation of investor responsibilities within such a framework.[17] Against this backdrop, a number of approaches have been explored by NGOs,[18] the most developed of which is that proposed by the IISD using sustainable development as its platform.[19]

The connection between encouraging an influx of foreign investment and the promotion of sustainable development is well-established.[20] Therefore, it is unsurprising that the desirability of a regime to regulate international investment in accordance with sustainable development objectives has been emphasised by various commentators.[21] To realise this ideal regime, IISD has produced a highly developed and comprehensive model agreement.[22] It is the product of extensive consultation that began in 2003 under two interlinked programmes, the Southern Agenda on Investment and the Model Agreement initiative, with discussions ranging across developing and developed states and across legal and political sectors.[23]

The IISD recognises that foreign investment is a crucial element in the promotion of sustainable development, and, accordingly, does not argue that investor protection should be revoked or investment discouraged.[24] It does assert, however, that the prevailing model for bilateral investment treaties was developed over fifty years ago and, as a creature of its own political context, focused solely on protection for foreign investors.[25] It argues that this one-sided approach is untenable in the twenty-first century and that international investor protection needs to be remodelled so as to cater for current global political and economic conditions.[26] Essentially, the proposed substantive reform entails addressing this imbalance in rights and obligations of the investor, host state, and home state. The IISD Agreement seeks to maintain high

[16] Zerk, *Multinationals*, p. 280; Werksman, Baumert, and Dubash, 'Will International Investment', 79.

[17] Zerk, *Multinationals*, p. 280. [18] Ibid.

[19] Mann et al., *IISD Model International Agreement*.

[20] *Agenda 21*, *Report of the UNCED*, UN Doc A/CONF.151/26/Rev.1 (vol.I) (1992), 31 ILM 874, Chapter 2, para. 2.23; Subedi, 'Foreign Investment', p. 413; Muchlinski, 'Towards a Multilateral', p. 429; de Waart, 'Sustainable Development', p. 273; Nieuwenhuys, 'Global Development', p. 295.

[21] See in particular, Muchlinski, 'Towards a Multilateral', pp. 437–49; Nieuwenhuys, 'Global Development'; Cosbey et al., *Investment and Sustainable*.

[22] Mann et al., *IISD Model International Agreement*. [23] Ibid., p. iii. [24] Ibid., pp. x–xi.

[25] Ibid. [26] Ibid., pp. x–xi.

levels of investor protection,[27] but also to prescribe social and environmental obligations to the investor[28] and to ensure that foreign investment contributes to sustainable development in the host country.[29] In order to achieve this, IISD substantially redrafted standard provisions common in bilateral investment treaties, key elements of which are now examined.

(a) Preamble and Objective articles

In many bilateral investment treaties, the Preamble and Objective provisions focus solely on the aim of increasing levels of foreign investment and of ensuring high protection of investments.[30] Although seemingly innocuous, the importance of these articles has recently become apparent. In the course of arbitral proceedings, tribunals have referred to the Preamble or objectives of a bilateral investment treaty to assist with their interpretation of the rights and obligations of the parties to the agreement.[31] Inevitably, this has meant that an interpretation consistent with the objectives of the treaty has been adopted, that is, one that enhances investor protection.[32] To address this issue, the IISD Agreement proposes the following more balanced Preamble and Objective provisions:

Preamble:

The Parties,

Seeking to promote sustainable development at the national, regional and global levels;

Understanding sustainable development as being development that meets the needs of the present without compromising the ability of future generations

[27] Ibid., pp. 12–20, Arts 5–10. [28] Ibid., pp. 22–30, Arts 12–18. [29] Ibid., p. 4, Art. 1.

[30] Ibid., pp. 2–3; Newcombe, 'Sustainable Development'; see, e.g., Treaty between the United States of America and the Republic of Argentina Concerning the Reciprocal Encouragement and Protection of Investment, signed 14 November 1991, Art. VIII (entered into force 20 October 1994), available at www.unctad.org/sections/dite/iia/docs/bits/argentina_us.pdf (last accessed 25 July 2009).

[31] Van Harten, *Investment Treaty Arbitration*, pp. 121, 136–8; see, e.g., the comments in *Azurix Corp.* v. *Argentine Republic* (ICSID Case No. ARB/01/12, Award of July 14 2006), para. 372:

> The standards of conduct agreed by the parties to a BIT presuppose a favorable disposition towards foreign investment, in fact, a pro-active behavior of the State to encourage and protect it. To encourage and protect investment is the purpose of the BIT. It would be incoherent with such a purpose and the expectation created by such a document to consider that a party to the BIT has breached the obligation of fair and equitable treatment only when it has acted in bad faith or its conduct can be qualified as outrageous or egregious.

[32] Van Harten, *Investment Treaty Arbitration*, pp. 121, 136–8.

to meet their own needs, and recognizing the contribution of the 1992 Rio Declaration on Environment and Development, the 2002 World Summit on Sustainable Development and the Millennium Goals to our understanding of sustainable development;

Recognizing that the promotion of sustainable investments is critical for the further development of national and global economies, as well as for the pursuit of national and global objectives for sustainable development;

Understanding further that the promotion of such investments requires cooperative efforts of investors, host governments and home governments;

Recognizing the development of protections for foreign investors in international law to date;

Affirming the progressive development of international law and policy on the relationships between multinational enterprises and host governments as seen in such international instruments as the ILO Tripartite Declaration on Multinational Enterprises and Social Policy; the OECD Guidelines for Multinational Enterprises; and the United Nations' *Norms and Responsibilities of Transnational Corporations and Other Business Enterprises with Regards to Human Rights*;

Seeking an overall balance of rights and obligations in international investment between investors, host countries and home countries; and

Recognizing that an international investment agreement should reflect the basic principles of transparency, accountability and legitimacy for all participants in foreign investment processes,

Have agreed as follows:

Article 1: Objective

The objective of this Agreement is to promote foreign investment that supports sustainable development, in particular in developing and least-developed countries.[33]

In establishing the overarching objectives of the agreement, these provisions strike a balance between the interests of the investor and the host state. They recognise substantive investor protections currently provided by international law, but link this in with the goal of promoting sustainable development. They acknowledge the importance of foreign investment to the economic development of developing states, but seek to bring in methods of reviewing the conduct of multinational corporations through references to documents such as the United Nations' Norms and Responsibilities of Transnational Corporations and Other Business Enterprises with Regards to Human Rights.[34]

The IISD Model Agreement Preamble and Objective provisions constitute a step in the right direction, moving away from the current

[33] Mann et al., *IISD Model International Agreement*, Preamble, Art. 1.

[34] United Nations Economic and Social Council, *Norms on the Responsibilities*.

preoccupation with investor protection to a more balanced approach. However, for a full reorientation of international investment law, there will need to be a more explicit setting of investment within the context of ecological sustainability. While there are references to the Rio Declaration,[35] the World Summit on Sustainable Development,[36] and the Millennium Goals,[37] there also needs to be an express acknowledgement that investment activity is subject to the ecological limitations of the environment at both a local and global level. The Preamble would also benefit from express ethical references as guiding principles so as to bring international investment law closer to the 'just world order' and global public law framework grounded in justice envisaged by scholars such as Chimni, Garcia, and Slaughter.[38]

(b) Investor rights

Part II of the IISD Model Agreement sets out the protection measures for foreign investors. It includes the standard references in bilateral investment treaties to national treatment,[39] most-favoured-nation treatment,[40] minimum international standards of treatment such as fair and equitable treatment and full protection and security,[41] and expropriation provisions.[42] The IISD Model Agreement, however, modifies these standard provisions with a series of measures designed to alleviate the one-sided nature of these traditional protections.

(i) National treatment and most-favoured-nation Similar to most bilateral investment treaties, the IISD Model Agreement accords to foreign investors treatment no less favourable than is accorded to domestic investors or investors of any other Party to the Agreement 'in like circumstances'.[43] Traditionally, the criteria by which 'like circumstances' are assessed have

[35] *Rio Declaration on Environment and Development, Report of the UNCED*, UN Doc. A/CONF.151/6/Rev.1 (1992), 31 ILM 874 (1992).

[36] See the *Johannesburg Declaration on Sustainable Development, Report of the United Nations World Summit on Sustainable Development*, UN Doc. A/CONF. 199/20 (2002), available at www.un.org/esa/sustdev/documents/WSSD_POI_PD/English/POI_PD.htm (last accessed 17 July 2009).

[37] *United Nations Millennium Declaration*, UNGA Res. A/55/2 (2000); *United Nations Development Goals*, available at www.un.org/millenniumgoals/ (last accessed 17 December 2011).

[38] As discussed above in Chapter 5, see Garcia, 'Globalization'; Slaughter, *New World Order*; see also the discussion in Chimni, 'Co-option'.

[39] Mann et al., *IISD Model International Agreement*, Art. 5. [40] Ibid., Art. 6.

[41] Ibid., Art. 7. [42] Ibid., Art. 8. [43] Ibid., Arts 5–6.

been limited to commercial considerations.[44] Problematically, such an approach excludes the environmental impact of an activity from the assessment criteria.[45] As discussed above in Chapter 3, on the basis of a set of commercially oriented criteria, investors with otherwise similar projects will inevitably be categorised as being 'in like circumstances', and discrimination on environmental grounds will be in breach of national treatment or most-favoured-nation provisions.

Directed precisely at this issue of limited assessment criteria, the IISD Agreement removes the need for interpretation by arbitral panels and ensures that the like circumstances test is not restricted to commercial considerations. To address the complex nature of investment and its effects, Article 5 expressly expands the criteria to 'an overall examination' of the particular circumstances of the investment, including:[46]

a) its effects on third persons and the local community;
b) its effects upon the local, regional or national environment, or the global commons;
c) the sector the investment is in;
d) the aim of the measure concerned;
e) the regulatory process generally applied in relation to the measure concerned; and
f) other factors directly related to the investment or investor in relation to the measure concerned.

With this relatively simple step, a more expansive approach to assessment criteria could be introduced to preclude determinations of like circumstances based solely on commercial considerations. This would assist with ensuring, for example, that the development of more environmentally responsible technologies and the pursuit of more ecologically sustainable investment projects would not be hindered by national treatment or most-favoured-nation provisions. As mentioned above in Chapters 3 and 4, environmental factors were at issue in the consideration of alleged national treatment violations in *Parkerings-Compagniet AS* v. *Republic of Lithuania* (the *Parkerings Award*), an award which set out the broad approach to assessing criteria for like circumstances in investment arbitration:

[44] Werksman, Baumert, and Dubash, 'Will International Investment', 75; see also Salgado, 'The Case Against', 1061; Center for International Environmental Law, *Foreign Investment*.

[45] Weksman, Baumert, and Dubash, 'Will International Investment', 74–5.

[46] Mann et al., *IISD Model International Agreement*, Art. 5(E).

- the two investors must be in the same economic or business sector;
- they must have been treated differently as a result of a host state governmental measure; and
- no policy or legitimate objective behind the measure justifies the differential treatment.[47]

The break-through element in the *Parkerings Award* was its consideration of cultural heritage and environmental impacts as a component of those criteria. The tribunal found that the difference in the archaeological and environmental impacts distinguished the otherwise very similar investment projects, rendering them not in like circumstances.[48] This decision also has a wider significance. Indeed, the analysis in the *Parkerings Award* has, in fact, taken a step towards that envisaged in Article 5 of the IISD Agreement.[49] Not only does it indicate a new level of responsiveness within investment arbitration to environmental concerns, but it has opened the way for the ecological impact of an investor's project, business, or activities to operate as a determinative factor in the like circumstances test. Furthermore, this new-found consideration of ecological concerns has the potential to spread beyond the application of the like circumstances test and influence other substantive areas of international investment law. When considered in this context, the *Parkerings Award* clearly points to the possibility of a less hostile approach to non-investment issues within investor–state arbitration and to more substantial reforms in the future. From a constructivist perspective,[50] this decision may also constitute an indicator of the early stages of a fundamental transformation within international investment law – or, conversely, it may become part of the historical pattern of assertion and response to high-level investor protection and provoke responses that lead to a reversion to the traditional position.

(ii) Expropriation The IISD Model Agreement prohibits the direct or indirect expropriation of investments unless the following criteria are met:

- the expropriation is carried out for a public purpose;
- it is non-discriminatory;

[47] *Parkerings-Compagniet AS* v. *Republic of Lithuania*, (ICSID Arbitration Case No. ARB/05/8, Award of 11 September 2007), para. 371.

[48] Ibid., paras 375, 392.

[49] Mann et al., *IISD Model International Agreement*, Art. 5.

[50] See Brunnée and Toope, 'International Law'; for a constructivist account of the emergence of norms in international law, see Arend, 'Do Legal Rules Matter?', 128–40; for a constructivist viewpoint on the impact of impact of decisions of international courts and tribunals, see Abbott, 'International Relations Theory', 362–77.

- it is carried out in accordance with due process of law; and
- prompt, effective and appropriate compensation is paid.[51]

The provision directs that 'appropriate compensation' is usually to be assessed as the fair market value of the investment immediately prior to the expropriation, but it also allows for consideration of the conduct of the investor in determining the final level of damages.[52] The provision addresses current concerns at investor targeting of domestic regulation through the inclusion of the following sub-paragraph:

> Consistent with the right of states to regulate and the customary international law principles on police powers, *bona fide*, non-discriminatory regulatory measures taken by a Party that are designed and applied to protect or enhance legitimate public welfare objectives, such as the public health, safety and the environment, do not constitute an indirect expropriation under this Article.[53]

The IISD argues that this formulation makes it clear that regulation enacted for public welfare purposes will not constitute an expropriation of an investment, but still preserves investor protection through the *bona fide* and non-discriminatory requirements.[54] However, as an investor can still have the regulation examined by an arbitral tribunal to assess its compliance with the *bona fide* and non-discriminatory conditions, as well as under other investor protections such as the fair and equitable treatment standard, public welfare regulation remains open to challenge despite this provision. Although this means that the 'Investor Rights' section of the IISD Model Agreement still retains the strong traditional investor protection measures that currently exist under bilateral investment treaties, there are also significant measures throughout the whole instrument to signal a more balanced approach to investment protection. In particular, this is represented in the introduction of investor obligations.

(c) Investor obligations

As bilateral investment treaties are between states, and investors are not party to those agreements, the ability to impose obligations on investors has been questioned.[55] Conceptually, however, it is not as difficult to construct a legal pathway to obligation as is sometimes portrayed. Zerk

[51] Mann et al., *IISD Model International Agreement*, Art. 8.

[52] Ibid., Art. 8(B); for a discussion on the issue of investor conduct conditionality, see Muchlinksi, 'Caveat Investor'.

[53] Mann et al., *IISD Model International Agreement*, Art. 8(I).

[54] Ibid.

[55] See the discussion in Zerk, *Multinationals*, pp. 280–1.

points out that states are now no longer the only subjects of international law and that, accordingly, states can assign responsibilities in international law to other actors.[56] Furthermore, investors are able to claim the benefit of investor protection measures under international investment agreements even although they are not party to the agreement. It is not unreasonable to assume that where investors have been granted rights under an international agreement between states, and are increasingly operating as individual non-state actors in the operation of international law through the investor–state dispute resolution mechanism, they can also be burdened with responsibilities under that same agreement.[57] To give effect to the notion of 'with privilege comes responsibility', the IISD Model Agreement counter-balances the rights granted to investors with the imposition of obligations.[58]

(i) Aspirational provisions Along with more concrete measures discussed below, the IISD Model Agreement introduces new aspirational duties for investors. In an attempt to shift prevailing emphases within the foreign investment sector, investors are to strive to contribute to the development objectives of the host state.[59] Furthermore, they are to 'strive to make the maximum feasible contributions to the sustainable development of the host state and local community through high levels of socially responsible practices',[60] and '[w]here standards of corporate social responsibility increase, investors should strive to apply and achieve the higher level standards.'[61]

(ii) Pre-establishment phase The IISD Model Agreement also includes new prescriptive obligations. Key elements include the requirement to comply with environmental and social impact assessment procedures

[56] Ibid., pp. 72–6, 262; see also the discussion in Muchlinski, 'Corporate Social Responsibility', 431, 432–3; see further the discussion in Kinley and Chambers, 'The UN Human Rights Norms'; Kinley and Tadaki, 'From Talk to Walk', 993–4; Clapham, *Human Rights Obligations*, pp. 59–83.

[57] See Chapter 5 above for a discussion on the increasing visibility of the individual on the international stage and the imposition of individual responsibility through the development of human rights law and international criminal law; see also Shelton, 'Globalization', 311–12; Buergenthal, 'The Evolving'.

[58] Mann et al., *IISD Model International Agreement*, Arts 11, 12, 14, and 16; see the discussion on rights and responsibilities in Kinley and Tadaki, 'From Talk to Walk'; see also Nolan, 'With Power', 584–605.

[59] Mann et al., *IISD Model International Agreement*, Art. 11.

[60] Ibid., Art. 16(A).

[61] Ibid., Art. 16(C).

and criteria in the pre-establishment phase of the investment,[62] public access to the impact assessments,[63] and the application of the precautionary principle to investor decision-making on receipt of the environmental impact assessment.[64] It is encouraging to see fundamental principles of international environmental law expressly included in the substantive text of the IISD Model Agreement. However, this should not be limited solely to the pre-establishment stage of the investment. Ongoing environmental monitoring and application of international environmental principles will be required to ensure the continued ecological sustainability of investment projects. Furthermore, a central component in the reconceptualisation of international investment law is reorienting its emphasis so that investment activity sits within the broader context of the environment. This entails working within the ecological limitations of the local and global environment and the application of principles such as the precautionary principle to decision-making throughout the life of the investment. At times, this will require corporations to decline to take a particular course of action or to modify their proposed operations.

(iii) Post-establishment obligations The IISD Model Agreement takes an integrated approach and draws on international standards from outside investment law to design its post-establishment obligations.[65] Article 14 sets out requirements for environmental management systems that accord with good practice requirements and ISO 14001 standards.[66] There must be compliance with the International Labour Organisation's Declaration on Fundamental Principles and Rights of Work.[67] Investors must not carry out, cause to be carried out, or be complicit in, human rights' violations.[68] Furthermore, investors are required to ensure that they do not 'manage or operate the investments in a manner that circumvents international environmental, labour and human rights obligations' of either the host or home state.[69] These

[62] Ibid., Art. 12(A) and (B). [63] Ibid., Art. 12(C). [64] Ibid., Art. 12(D).

[65] Ibid., pp. 25–6; for a discussion on an integrated approach to international law see Sands, 'Treaty, Custom'; see the discussion on incorporation of principles into treaties generally in French, 'Treaty Interpretation', 284, 292–307.

[66] Mann et al., *IISD Model International Agreement*, Art. 14(A); ISO 14001 *Environmental Management Systems*.

[67] Mann et al., *IISD Model International Agreement*, Art. 14(C); *International Law Organisation Declaration on Fundamental Principles and Rights at Work*, 86th Session of the General Conference of the International Labour Organisation, Geneva, 18 June 1998, available at www.ilo.org/declaration/thedeclaration/textdeclaration/lang-en/index.htm (last accessed 17 December 2011).

[68] Mann et al., *IISD Model International Agreement*, Art. 14(B). [69] Ibid., Art. 14(D).

provisions are a welcome advance in the introduction of more socially and environmentally responsible standards into international investment law. With respect to the environmental measures, however, it would be preferable to include express references to specific principles of international environmental law in addition to good practice standards. Positive obligations, directly applicable to the investor, to adhere to specific international environmental principles should also be included, rather than solely the negative obligation not to circumvent obligations held by the host or home state. Serving an additional and more subtle function, this requirement would also be directed at long-term behavioural change, assisting in redressing the prevailing approach of the investment sector towards the environment, traditionally one grounded in the acceptability of unfettered resource exploitation.

Cognisant of the likely objections to this provision, the IISD pre-emptively asserts that Article 14 does not contain new principles.[70] Whilst this statement is strictly correct, it does not reflect the controversy that will be generated by their application to a new context, particularly as the international investment community has traditionally resisted challenges to high-level investor protection, and, in particular, attempts to apply an integrated approach to international investment law. Resistance to any attempt to incorporate these substantive provisions into future bilateral investment treaties should, therefore, be expected.

Even in the face of such hostility, however, the development of model agreements such as the IISD Model Agreement, demonstrating how an integrated approach to international investment law could operate, will continue to pressure the investment community to accommodate international environmental principles, human rights, and health and safety standards. Progressively, this type of pressure should see the traditional position of the international investment community become increasingly untenable and should ultimately lead to a more socially and environmentally responsible approach to foreign investment. As discussed above in Chapter 4, there are already signs that this process is under way. For example, the calls for greater transparency and for the involvement of NGOs in investor–state arbitration are beginning to make an impact, having recently led to the acceptance of *amicus curiae* briefs in a number of recent environment-related investment

[70] Ibid., p. 25.

arbitral proceedings.[71] They have also contributed to the inclusion of specific provisions in the United States' and Canadian model bilateral investment treaties allowing for the acceptance of *amicus* briefs and public access to the proceedings, documents, and awards.[72] Developments such as these indicate an increasing level of engagement with non-investment issues and an acknowledgement of the need to respond to the wider concerns generated by the operation of international investment law.[73]

(iv) Investor liability In a move that will prove controversial within the business sector, Article 17 of the IISD Model Agreement also addresses a central concern surrounding the way in which multinational corporations operate – the lack of legal accountability within international law and, in a practical sense, within both host and home states for investor activities in the host state.[74] The effects of this gap in the international regulatory framework have been illustrated by high-profile examples of corporate environmental misconduct within host states, such as those discussed above in Chapter 3, in which obtaining compensation for the damage caused was exceedingly difficult and the sums that were recovered were inadequate.[75] Article 17 seeks to overcome this legal lacuna by enabling the use of home state courts for civil actions for significant damage, personal injury, or loss of life in the host state as a

[71] See *Methanex Corporation* (Award of 2005); *Biwater Gauff Ltd* v. *United Republic of Tanzania* (ICSID Case No. ARB/05/22, Procedural Order No. 5 of 2 February 2007) ('*Biwater Gauff Ltd* (Procedural Order of 2007)'); see also the discussion in Tienhaara, 'Third Party Participation'.

[72] United States State Department, Treaty between the Government of the United States of America and the Government of [Country] Concerning the Encouragement and Reciprocal Protection of Investments (2004) (United States' Model BIT), available at www.ustr.gov/assets/Trade_Sectors/Investment/Model_BIT/asset_upload_file847_6897.pdf (last accessed 29 April 2009); United States State Department, Treaty between the Government of the United States of America and the Government of [Country] Concerning the Encouragement and Reciprocal Protection of Investments (2012) (United States' 2012 Model BIT), available at www.ustr.gov/sites/default/files/BIT%20text%20for%20ACIEP%20Meeting.pdf (last accessed 25 August 2012); Canada, Model Foreign Investment Protection Agreement (2004) (Canadian Model BIT), available at www.international.gc.ca/assets/trade-agreements-accords-commerciaux/pdfs/2004-FIPA-model-en.pdf (last accessed 29 April 2009).

[73] Newcombe, 'Sustainable Development', 399; Reinisch, 'Investment and . . .', 201.

[74] Mann et al., *IISD Model International Agreement*, p. 28, Art. 17; see further for suggested multilateral frameworks to regulate the conduct of multinational corporations in Zerk, *Multinationals*, pp. 243–4, 262–3; McCorquodale and Simons, 'Responsibility Beyond Borders'; Bunn, 'Global Advocacy', 1304–6.

[75] See the discussion in Cassels, 'Outlaws'; Chopra, 'Multinational Corporations'; Rogge, 'Towards Transnational'; Chesterman, 'Oil and Water'.

result of acts or decisions of the investor.[76] Via a relatively simple mechanism, this initiative would redress the lack of responsiveness of international investment law to the impact of investor activity on the local communities and environment of the host state, providing home and host state forum options for the hearing of claims. In so doing, it would also be a significant step in breaking historical patterns within international investment law, allowing those affected by investor operations to choose how they would wish to pursue compensation for any damage suffered.

(d) *Host state obligations*

Seeking to ensure a balanced approach towards the interests of both investors and the host state, Part 4 of the IISD Model Agreement elaborates on the minimum treatment standards to which Article 7 refers. For example, Article 19 expressly requires host states to ensure that their administrative, legislative, and judicial processes do not operate in a manner that is arbitrary or denies procedural fairness to investors.[77] This section does not, however, include an 'umbrella clause'. The so-called umbrella clause generally constitutes a broad provision to the effect that a host state must comply with all obligations it has assumed with respect to an investor.[78] In omitting such a provision, the IISD is seeking to preclude the extension of investor protection measures to any type of breach of contract, licence, or permit.[79] The IISD asserts that an umbrella clause is unnecessary, as host state obligations to foreign investors are set out in the IISD Model Agreement in a specific and clear manner and its omission will prevent the bringing of inappropriate claims for breach of contract through the operation of expansive, 'catch-all' provisions.[80]

Part 4 also introduces a number of other measures designed to redress the imbalance in the focus of bilateral investment treaties. So as to counter the potential for the 'race to the bottom' syndrome,[81] Article 20 expressly places an obligation on host states not to waive or derogate from domestic labour, public health and safety, and environmental standards

[76] Mann et al., *IISD Model International Agreement*, Art. 17. [77] Ibid., Art. 19(A).

[78] Dolzer and Schreuer, *Principles*, p. 153; Newcombe and Paradell, *Law and Practice*, pp. 437–8; McLachlan, Shore, Weiniger, *International Investment Arbitration*, pp. 92–3.

[79] Mann et al., *IISD Model International Agreement*, p. 33. [80] Ibid.

[81] See above in Chapter 3 for a discussion of the 'race-to-the-bottom' and pollution haven theories; see also Neumayer, *Greening Trade*, pp. 41–3; see also Zarsky, 'Havens, Halos and Spaghetti'; see also Clapp, 'Pollution Haven Debate'.

in seeking to encourage foreign investment.[82] Article 21 is drawn from the side agreements on labour and the environment to the North American Free Trade Agreement (NAFTA),[83] the North American Agreement on Environmental Cooperation[84] and the North American Agreement on Labor Cooperation,[85] and requires states to ensure that high domestic levels of environmental, labour, and human rights protection are maintained.[86] However, even IISD acknowledges that these requirements will be difficult to police.[87]

(e) Host state rights

(i) Inherent rights of states The IISD introduces a provision entitled 'Inherent Rights of States' to ensure that international investment agreements will be interpreted with objectives beyond solely that of protecting investor rights.[88] Article 25 provides that host states have the right to pursue their own development objectives,[89] to take regulatory measures to ensure that development is consistent with the goals and objectives of sustainable development and with other social and economic policy objectives,[90] and that the rights of host states are to 'be understood as embedded within a balance of the rights and obligations of investors and investments and host states'.[91] Again, a full reconceptualisation of international investment law will need a stronger emphasis on development and investment occurring within an ecologically sustainable framework. It would also benefit from express references to core ethical principles that underpin the 'inherent rights of states' and their interaction with the activities of investors throughout the life of the investment. However, the significance of expressly setting out the rights of host states to pursue their own needs within an investment law framework cannot be underestimated. Not only does this provide host states with concrete provisions to point to in asserting the need for domestic policy space, but it also introduces the presence of the host state into international investment law as an active participant. In other words,

[82] Mann et al., *IISD Model International Agreement*, Art. 20.

[83] Ibid., p. 34; North American Free Trade Agreement (NAFTA), adopted 17 December 1992, 1992 32 ILM 612 (entered into force 1 January 1994).

[84] North American Agreement on Environmental Cooperation, signed 14 September 1993 (entered into force 1 January 1994).

[85] North American Agreement on Labor Cooperation, signed 14 September 1993 (entered into force 1 January 1994).

[86] Mann et al., *IISD Model International Agreement*, Art. 21. [87] Ibid., p. 33.

[88] Ibid., p. 38. [89] Ibid., Art. 25(A). [90] Ibid., Art. 25(B). [91] Ibid., Art. 25(C).

it addresses the 'otherness' that has remained innately within the core nature of international investment law.

(ii) Performance requirements The IISD Model Agreement also strikes a balance between the interests of investors and the host state on the contentious issue of performance requirements. It allows the host state to set performance requirements at the pre-establishment stage of the investment, deeming them in compliance with the national treatment and most-favoured-nation provisions of the IISD Model Agreement, ensuring that the investor is aware of all such conditions prior to taking the decision to invest.[92] However, after the investment has been established, the imposition of performance requirements is subject to the investor protection provisions contained within the Agreement.[93] This differentiation allows host states to realise key benefits of foreign investment, but in a manner that is transparent for the investor.

(f) Home state rights and obligations

In keeping with its innovative approach, the IISD Model Agreement also includes a number of proposed measures regarding the home state, the most significant of which is Article 31. Under this provision, home states ensure that their legal systems must allow civil claims relating to the international investment activities of their nationals to be brought in their courts.[94]

(g) Assessment of the IISD Model Agreement

The IISD Model Agreement is an excellent template with which to move forward the debate on socially and environmentally investment law and to bring about cultural changes in the investment sector. Commentators are already urging its use as a model in specific bilateral and regional negotiations.[95] Kible and Schutz have noted that even if the IISD Model Agreement is not adopted as a whole new instrument, it could be useful for interpreting or amending existing treaties so as to address concerns at the effects of the current system on the domestic policy space of host states.[96]

Of particular significance is the progress the IISD Model Agreement makes towards the development of more socially and environmentally

[92] Ibid., pp. 39–40, Art. 26. [93] Ibid., Art. 26(B). [94] Ibid., Art. 31.

[95] See, e.g., Salgado, 'The Case Against', 1066; Kibel and Schutz, 'Rio Grande Designs', 250.

[96] Kibel and Schutz, 'Rio Grande Designs', 250.

responsible international investment norms. Its careful articulation of rights and obligations, the balancing of investor protection with investor responsibilities, and the framing of the Agreement within the concept of sustainable development demonstrate that a balanced approach to international investment law is possible. It provides a concrete manifestation of a reconceived international investment law – one that redresses the traditional sole focus on investors' rights. However, it is also possible to take the reconceptualisation of international investment law even further to ensure that ecological sustainability is reflected in its norms and that a cultural shift ultimately occurs within the foreign investment sector. In addition to the provisions of the IISD Model Agreement, an ecologically sustainable investment law should also contain:

(i) An express acknowledgement that investment activity is subject to the ecological limitations of the environment at both a local and global level and that these limitations must be factored into investment decision-making.
(ii) A stronger emphasis on the legal principles embodied within the concept of sustainable development and on what is required of both states and investors in achieving sustainable investment. To this end, there should be an express delineation of the principles of intergenerational and intragenerational equity, sustainable use requirements, and the principle of integration of environmental, economic, and development considerations, together with the expectation that these principles will be applied by both states and investors in their investment decision-making.
(iii) Express references to core ethical principles underpinning the IISD Model Agreement, such as the integration of equality, social equity, ecological sustainability, economic justice, and good governance into investment decision-making.
(iv) Positive obligations, directly applicable to the investor, to adhere to specific international environmental principles throughout the life of the investment, such as the precautionary principle, the principle of sustainable use of natural resources, and the preventative approach.

With its detailed and comprehensive approach, it is likely that the IISD Model Agreement will influence any future negotiations for investment agreements that seek to balance the interests of investors and host states. Another recent instrument that has also sought to progress this discourse is the Norwegian Model BIT.[97] This initiative is of particular

[97] Ministry of Trade and Industry, Norway.

significance as it was proposed by a capital-exporting state, and, as such, constitutes the actual drafting practice of a state rather than an ideal model put forward by an NGO.

2. The Norwegian Model BIT

In January 2008 Norway released a draft text of the Norwegian Model BIT, seeking feedback and comment from interested parties and stakeholders.[98] Its express purpose was to take international investment agreements in a new direction, towards a balancing of investor and host state interests.[99] To achieve this goal, the Norwegian Model BIT contains a number of revolutionary aspects. For example, it extends carve-outs for public welfare regulation beyond indirect expropriation to national treatment and most-favoured-nation treatment standards.[100] It imports a WTO-style set of general exceptions relating to, amongst others, measures necessary 'to protect human, animal or plant life or health' or 'for the protection of the environment'.[101] And it also introduces the concept of corporate social responsibility into the substantive provisions of bilateral investment treaties. Article 32, entitled 'Corporate Social Responsibility', is framed in terms of an obligation on states 'to encourage investors to conduct their investment activities in compliance with the OECD Guidelines for Multinational Enterprises and to participate in the United Nations Global Compact'.[102] It does not impose corporate social responsibility obligations directly on investors, but it does send a clear signal that there has been a shift in expectations of investor conduct. The preamble reinforces this impression with its express references to mutually supportive interpretations of investment treaty provisions and international environmental agreements, the promotion of sustainable investments, a commitment to human rights, and the importance of corporate social responsibility.[103]

[98] Ministry of Trade and Industry, *Comments*. [99] Ibid.

[100] Ministry of Trade and Industry, Norway, Arts 3 and 4.

[101] Ibid., Art. 24. This provision is similar to that seen in the General Agreement on Tariffs and Trade, Annex 1A, Agreement Establishing the World Trade Organization, opened for signature 15 April 1994, (1994) 33 ILM 28, Art. XX (entered into force 1 January 1995). General Exceptions provisions have appeared in several 'new generation BITs'.

[102] Ministry of Trade and Industry, Norway, Art. 32.

[103] Ibid., Preamble; for the suggestion that contextual standards also ought to be adopted in BITs to take account of the relative development stages of states and in this way shape a more attainable standard of treatment for developing states to meet, see Alexander, 'Taking Account of Reality'.

Certainly, at this stage, what can be said is that the development of instruments such as the IISD Model Agreement and the Norwegian Model BIT indicates a key shift in the discourse. The focus has moved on from solely identifying the problematic aspects of investment treaties to exemplifying how change might be given effect and providing templates for more balanced, socially responsible, and sustainable international investment agreements. Significantly, as a number of recent bilateral investment treaties have adopted a less averse stance towards sustainable development issues,[104] future agreements may well even begin to reflect some of the more controversial provisions in the IISD Model Agreement and the Norwegian Model BIT. On the other hand, this progression may instead prove to be more 'episodic' than a permanent state of advancing towards more socially and environmentally responsible investment agreements.[105] The withdrawal of the Norwegian Model BIT in June 2009, due to the inability to find common ground amongst the polarised positions of interested parties, exemplifies just such a process of transformational measures followed by reversion.

3. A multilateral convention on corporate accountability

A further treaty-based option for reform in the investment sector has come from the corporate social responsibility movement. Moving beyond the raft of voluntary initiatives that have emerged over the last few decades, Friends of the Earth has proposed the creation of a binding international framework to regulate the conduct of multinational corporations.[106] The authors argue that corporations need to be accountable to stakeholders other than company shareholders and, to implement this agenda, a binding set of comprehensive international rules on corporate accountability needs to be developed.[107]

[104] Treaty between the United States of America and the Oriental Republic of Uruguay Concerning the Encouragement and Reciprocal Protection of Investment (2005), available at www.unctad.org/sections/dite/iia/docs/bits/US_Uruguay.pdf (last accessed 17 December 2011); see also Agreement between Canada and the Republic of Peru for the Promotion and Protection of Investments (2006), available at www.international.gc.ca/trade-agreements-accords-commerciaux/assets/pdfs/Canada-Peru10nov06-en.pdf (last accessed 17 December 2011).

[105] Newcombe, 'Sustainable Development', 406. Newcombe refers to a suggestion made by Howard Mann to Newcombe that the process of reform may be episodic and not necessarily a lineal one in which progress continues to move forward.

[106] Friends of the Earth, 'Towards Binding Corporate'.

[107] Ibid., 1–4; see also further suggestions in Zerk, *Multinationals*, pp. 243–4, 262–3; see also McCorquodale and Simons, 'Responsibility Beyond Borders'; Bunn, 'Global Advocacy';

Just as with the IISD Model Agreement, the FOE proposal also requires signatory states to implement a series of measures at the national level.[108] Although a number of these correlate to the IISD approach,[109] the FOE proposal also has valuable additional elements. In particular, it suggests the imposition of duties on directors of publicly listed companies to take full account in corporate decision-making of any negative environmental and social effects of company activities and to report on the environmental and social impacts of company operations.[110] This requirement is designed to establish a procedural principle of reporting on issues beyond those related to the financial interest of shareholders.[111] In focusing the company's attention on its own environmental impacts, and in upgrading the importance of the issue by making it a reportable matter, such a measure would assist with the infusion of a more environmentally aware approach in the foreign investment sector.

The FOE proposal argues for the establishment of high minimum environmental, social, labour, and human rights standards based on existing international agreements,[112] and for the direct application of those standards to corporations.[113] It also raises the issue of 'ecological debt', which entails the idea that developed states are indebted to the developing world because of the exploitation of 'Southern' resources and the environmental degradation caused in pursuit of 'Northern' development.[114] With reference to the accumulation of further ecological debt, the FOE proposal includes ecosystem degradation and restoration as liability issues for multinational corporations.[115]

In similar fashion to the IISD Model Agreement,[116] the FOE proposal allows for affected communities to seek redress in the home state of a company for injuries resulting from the activities of the corporation in

see also Ward, 'Securing Transnational', 472–4; Clapp, 'Global Environmental Governance'.

108 Friends of the Earth, 'Towards Binding Corporate', 6.

109 Ibid., 6, 9; such as the obligation on states to establish high minimum environmental, labour and human rights standards and the use of existing international agreements to give guidance on the substance of those standards: Measure 5, and the obligation to carry out environmental impact assessments: Measure 1.

110 Ibid., Measures 1, 6.

111 Ibid., Measure 6.

112 Ibid., Measure 5.

113 Ibid., Measures 2, 7–8.

114 Mickelson, 'Critical Approaches', 262, 274–5; Martinez-Alier, *The Environmentalism of the Poor*; see also Guha and Martinez-Alier, *Varieties of Environmentalism*.

115 Friends of the Earth, 'Towards Binding Corporate', 8.

116 Mann et al., *IISD Model International Agreement*, Art. 17.

the host state.[117] However, the FOE proposal also includes a provision enabling decisions of directors and corporate representatives to be challenged by 'interested parties'.[118] As a corollary of imposing duties regarding the environmental and social impacts of corporate activities, it provides a mechanism for reviewing the discharging of those duties.[119] These measures could be particularly useful in bringing an ecological outlook to the foreign investment community as they would oblige directors and officers of multinational corporations to give consideration to the environmental and social impact of corporate activities and to be accountable for their decision-making in this regard. Introducing a public reporting system for the social and environmental impacts of corporate decision-making and operations would normalise the process, ultimately embedding it within the cultures of companies operating at a transnational level.

B. Emerging principles of sustainability and corporate social and environmental responsibility

A treaty-based option is not the only mechanism through which a transformation of foreign investment law and practices can be effected; it is likely that customary international rules will also play a role. If an integrated approach to the interpretation of investment treaties is adopted, principles emerging out of international environmental law, sustainable development law, corporate social responsibility standards, and the sustainable finance movement may affect the future evolution of norms in international investment law.

As discussed above in Chapter 4, key emerging sustainability and corporate social responsibility principles include sustainable development, the precautionary principle, transparency requirements, and supply chain responsibility.[120] It is no exaggeration to suggest that such principles have the potential to transform international investment law in fundamental ways. This transformative quality is largely

[117] Friends of the Earth, 'Towards Binding Corporate', Measures 3, 8. [118] Ibid.
[119] Ibid.
[120] Other principles include the principle of integration, socially and environmentally responsible lending practices for financiers, requirements to conduct environmental impact assessments, minimum international environmental, social justice, human rights and health and safety standards,consultation with local and indigenous communities, obligations to warn of risks posed by corporate activities or products, access to information and public participation, and carbon disclosure. See Zerk, *Multinationals*, pp. 16, 262–76.

due to their recognition that corporate operations do not occur in a vacuum, but have flow-on effects at local and global levels. In contemplating their infusion throughout the foreign investment sector, then, a question emerges as to what form such principles might take.

The most likely immediate effect would be the development of mandatory procedural norms. This would see the introduction of compulsory social and environmental impact assessment at the pre-establishment stage, public reporting on localised impacts throughout the life of the investment, carbon disclosure requirements for investment projects, sustainability reporting for corporations, and required procedures for consultation with local and indigenous communities. Such procedural norms would reflect the interactive quality of investor activity with its social and natural environment, beginning to place investor operations within their wider context. This approach could be furthered through the integration of principles from other areas of international law into substantive investment norms. In a socially and ecologically sustainable form of international investment law, the principle of sustainable development would be fundamental, framing foreign investment decision-making, international investment agreements, and the resolution of investor–state disputes. Tribunals could no longer exclude the consideration of sustainable development in assessing investor claims and it would be less likely that host state measures taken in pursuit of sustainability would be found in breach of treaty provisions. It would not be permissible to disregard host state obligations under multilateral environmental agreements, international human rights conventions, or international labour standards. Indeed, the fact that the disputed state action was taken pursuant to these obligations would be relevant in determining whether a treaty violation had occurred.

An ecological outlook infused through the foreign investment sector would require investor activity to be guided by the ecological limitations of the earth's resources. Fully implemented, such an approach would see the shelving of transnational projects with too great a detrimental social and environmental impact. Ideally, as a matter of course, multinational corporations would adopt the most environmentally sustainable mode of operation. The application of the precautionary principle would require investors to consider the environmental effects of their activities and to take action to avert the risk of environmental damage, even where no scientific certainty of an adverse outcome existed. The substantive nature of many large-scale investment projects would shift away from the extractive industries, such as mining and oil and gas, to renewable energy projects, and a boom in eco-technology development would emerge. In an interactive process of normalising responsible investment practices, it would become second nature for actors in the investment sector to consider the social and environmental impacts of their activities and to act on them – and it could lead to the emergence of socially and environmentally responsible international investment norms.

II. Reform of the dispute settlement system

Treaty-based reform and the application of principles of sustainability and corporate social and environmental responsibility to the investment sector would certainly reshape the substance of international investment law. The resolution of disputes, however, also plays a central role in the development of international investment law, and, as such, reform of the dispute settlement system is a crucial link in creating paths to a more socially and environmentally responsible international investment law. In both direct and more subtle fashion, structural and procedural elements of investor–state arbitration impact on the way in which public interest issues are addressed in investment disputes. Most significantly, at a core level, they perpetuate a system that is culturally antagonistic to the adequate consideration of public policy in investment disputes.[121] It is clear that, ultimately, such approaches can affect the ability of states to implement public welfare regulation and pursue domestic policy needs.[122]

A. *Transparency, legitimacy, and public participation*

Key procedural issues stem from the decentralised system of non-permanent arbitral tribunals, its commercial emphasis, and the confidentiality surrounding proceedings. The lack of any governing framework leads to inconsistent decisions on the same issues, even on essentially the same dispute.[123] The lack of transparency, whereby proceedings are

[121] See the discussion on the views of members of the investment sector 'that an arbitrator is not the guardian of public policy, that his duties are towards the parties only, and that he must confine himself to the determination of disputes involving private interests' in Mayer, 'Reflections', 246–7.

[122] Mann et al., *IISD Model International Agreement*; Cosbey et al., *Investment and Sustainable*; see also Delaney and Barstow Magraw, 'Procedural Transparency', 721.

[123] See, e.g., the *Lauder Cases: In the Matter of a UNCITRAL Arbitration between Ronald S. Lauder and the Czech Republic*, Final Award, 3 September 2001; *CME Czech Republic B.V. (the*

largely held behind closed doors and awards are only published if the parties consent, is in contravention of basic public law principles.[124] For these reasons, the legitimacy of the system of investor–state arbitration is increasingly questioned.[125]

1. New transparency and public participation initiatives

The way in which treaty obligations are interpreted under bilateral investment treaties is central to the goal of creating policy space for host state needs within international investment law. However, it is not only the substantive obligations that are instrumental in this regard – procedural rules in investor–state arbitration also have a significant cultural impact on the character of this dispute settlement mechanism. As international commercial arbitration has provided the dominant model for the conduct of arbitral proceedings in investment disputes, confidentiality has been a primary feature of investor–state arbitration.[126] Whilst those features can be appropriate in commercial disputes, in applying that model to investment, however, the differences become apparent. By far the most significant of these is that investor–state disputes are not solely commercial – they innately involve matters of public interest.[127] And, accordingly, these disputes can implicate the ability of the host state to pursue public welfare policies and

Netherlands) v. *Czech Republic* (UNCITRAL, Partial Award of 13 September 2001; Final Award of 14 March 2003); see also the discussion in Yannaca-Small, 'Parallel Proceedings', pp. 1008, 1009–10; see also Joubin-Bret, 'The Growing Diversity', p. 137.

124 Van Harten, *Investment Treaty Arbitration*, p. 159.

125 Tienhaara, 'Third Party Participation'; Van Harten, *Investment Treaty Arbitration*; Brower, Brower, and Sharpe, 'The Coming Crisis'; Tienhaara, 'What You Don't Know'; von Moltke, *An International Investment Regime?*.

126 Tienhaara, 'Third Party Participation', 230–1; Van Harten, *Investment Treaty Arbitration*, p. 159; Sornarajah, 'The Clash', 13–17.

127 There is public interest in investor–state arbitration and not international commercial arbitration because:

a) investor–state arbitration often involves public service sectors;
b) government regulation enacted for public welfare purposes may be the subject of the dispute;
c) the presence of a state in the arbitration triggers good governance obligations;
d) the costs of defending claims and financing compensation awards will draw on public funds;
e) the threat of arbitration from an investor can have a 'chilling' effect on government policy and prevent the raising of environmental standards, health and safety standards, and labour conditions.

See Tienhaara, 'Third Party Participation', 230; International Institute for Sustainable Development, *Revising the UNCITRAL Arbitration*.

sustainable development objectives. Without sufficient access to information on the claims and proceedings, public participation, a full consideration of relevant issues, and progress towards sustainable development can be impeded. As such, there is a pressing need for greater transparency in the conduct of investment disputes.

(a) ICSID Rules

Recently, there have been a number of initiatives directed towards transparency and public participation issues in investor–state arbitration. For example, ICSID implemented a series of reforms in 2006 that included new rules relating to non-disputing party access to the proceedings and the acceptance of *amicus curiae* briefs.[128] ICSID Rule 37(2) embodies a significant step towards creating space for the consideration of sustainability issues within investment arbitration as it allows the tribunal to receive *amicus* briefs even without the consent of the parties. The tribunal is still required to consult with the parties, but it can override their wishes. There has been an attempt to balance the parties' need for a fair resolution to the dispute uncomplicated by irrelevant or prejudicial submissions and the public interest in ensuring all relevant issues are addressed via a number of safeguards that must be in place before the arbitrators can accept the written submissions of a non-disputing party. These measures include the need for non-disputing parties to establish a sufficient interest in the subject matter of the dispute, the consideration of the extent to which the non-disputing party would assist the tribunal by contributing a perspective, knowledge, or insight that is in some way different from the parties to the dispute, and whether or not the submission would address a matter within the scope of the dispute.[129] This particular procedural reform marks a significant shift in approach to investment arbitration.

However, even following the 2006 amendments, the ICSID Rules on access to the oral hearings do not go far enough in ensuring adequate levels of transparency in investment disputes. ICSID Rule 32(2) only allows non-disputing party access if the parties agree. If one party

[128] The amended ICSID Rules are available at www.worldbank.org/icsid/highlights/03-04-06.htm (last accessed 17 December 2011); see also the discussion in Tienhaara, 'Third Party Participation'; see Newcombe, 'Sustainable Development', 388; see also McLachlan, Shore, and Weiniger, *International Investment Arbitration*, pp. 57–60.

[129] ICSID Rule 37(2); see the discussion in Tienhaara, 'Third Party Participation'; see also Newcombe, 'Sustainable Development', 388; McLachlan, Shore and Weiniger, *International Investment Arbitration*, pp. 57–8.

objects, therefore, the non-disputing party will be excluded from the oral hearings.[130] The differing approach between the two ICSID Rules was reflected in the procedural decision in *Biwater Gauff (Tanzania)* v. *United Republic of Tanzania*, in which *amicus* submissions were permitted, but access to documents and the hearings was denied.[131] This can leave NGOs with an ineffective right of intervention. Without access to the pleadings in the dispute, the ability of NGOs to file meaningful and informed *amicus* submissions is severely curtailed. And without access to the oral hearings, transparency conditions in investor–state arbitration remain at their current opaque level.

(b) Transparency measures within bilateral investment treaties

There have been attempts to address transparency issues in more recent bilateral investment treaties. Precipitated by the United States' and Canadian Model BITs' provision for open proceedings and the submission of *amicus curiae* briefs,[132] so-called 'new generation BITs' have adopted a more transparent approach to the conduct of hearings.[133] For example, the Treaty between the United States of America and the Oriental Republic of Uruguay Concerning the Encouragement and Reciprocal Protection of Investment,[134] and the Agreement between Canada and the Republic of Peru for the Promotion and Protection of Investments, both provide for public access to the hearings, non-disputing party access to the pleadings, and the acceptance of non-disputing party submissions.[135]

Again, these developments are particularly encouraging as they address key concerns surrounding the confidentiality and lack of public participation in investor–state arbitration. Most notably, they also point

[130] ICSID Rule 32(2); Newcombe, 'Sustainable Development', 391; see also Tienhaara, 'Third Party Participation'.

[131] *Biwater Gauff Ltd* (Procedural Order of 2007); see also the discussion in Tienhaara, 'Third Party Participation'; see also UNCTAD, 'Latest Developments'.

[132] United States' Model BIT, Arts 28 and 29; Canadian Model BIT, Arts 34, 35, 38 and 39.

[133] Newcombe, 'Sustainable Development'; see also Shan, 'From "North–South Divide"', 652, 656.

[134] Treaty between the United States of America and the Oriental Republic of Uruguay Concerning the Encouragement and Reciprocal Protection of Investment (2005) Arts 28 and 29, available at www.unctad.org/sections/dite/iia/docs/bits/US_Uruguay.pdf (last accessed 15 March 2009).

[135] Agreement between Canada and the Republic of Peru for the Promotion and Protection of Investments (2006) Arts 34, 35, 38 and 39, available at www.international.gc.ca/trade-agreements-accords-commerciaux/assets/pdfs/Canada-Peru10nov06-en.pdf (last accessed 4 April 2009).

to future trends towards more openness in the conduct of proceedings. However, it may take some time before this model becomes the norm in practice, as, at present, the majority of bilateral investment treaties do not contain these enhanced transparency and public participation measures. As a result, the conditions of confidentiality and lack of capacity for *amicus* submissions still remain the predominant practice for investor–state arbitration. And this will continue to hinder the assessment of current investor impact on public welfare policies and sustainability issues.

2. Arbitrators, institutional architecture, and conflicts of interest

In conjunction with the more specific criticisms on transparency and *amicus* briefs, there are also allegations of a more general nature, regarding the existence of systemic 'investor bias' in the determination of investment disputes.[136] In particular, it is most problematic that the very structure of the dispute settlement model is based on private commercial dispute resolution, which is predominantly concerned with enforcement of contractual obligations, commercial considerations, and confidentiality.[137] It is not currently a system designed to accommodate adequate consideration of the social, environmental, ethical, and human rights issues that arise in investor–state disputes.[138] This predisposition towards the primacy of commercial interests is compounded by the method of selecting an arbitral tribunal, in which there is no security of tenure for arbitrators, and the parties, or the arbitral facility, choose the arbitrators.[139]

As discussed above in Chapter 5, the choice of arbitrator is a crucial component of the arbitral process.[140] Dezalay and Garth point to the market for obtaining arbitral appointments and describe a process that values the display of an affinity with international commerce.[141] As the dynamics within the tribunal can be determinative of the outcome, that is, the most weight is given to the view of the arbitrator with

136 Tams, 'An Appealing Option?', 31–3; Sornarajah, 'The Clash of Globalizations'.

137 Tienhaara, 'Third Party Participation', 230–1; Sornarajah, 'The Clash of Globalizations', 13–17.

138 Sornarajah, 'The Clash of Globalizations', 17.

139 Cosbey et al., *Investment and Sustainable*, p. 6; Sornarajah, 'The Clash of Globalizations', 17; Van Harten, *Investment Treaty Arbitration*, pp. 168–72.

140 Dezalay and Garth, *Dealing in Virtue*, pp. 8–9.

141 Ibid., pp. 8–9, 70.

the greatest 'authority' and 'expertise',[142] the overarching system in which arbitrators in investor–state disputes operate is central to their reluctance to address non-investment issues and engage in bold decision-making.

There are further concerns at the lack of independence of arbitrators. Compounding the issues involved in panel dynamics is the fact that the current system actually allows for arbitrators to appear as counsel in separate cases.[143] This means that counsel in one investment dispute, arguing for a particular interpretation of a provision, can also act as arbitrator on other investment disputes involving similar issues, leading to the unsettling possibility that decisions made in their capacity as arbitrator may later be used to influence the interpretation of the law applicable to their own clients.[144] An undesirable practice of repeat appointments has also developed where 'counsel selecting an arbitrator who, next time around when the arbitrator is counsel, selects the previous counsel as arbitrator'.[145] The issue is not so much directed at the conduct of individual arbitrators, as at a system that allows those lines to be blurred.[146] It is of particular concern that a system so heavily weighted towards the preservation of commercial interests is determining questions that affect significant matters of public policy, the interests of multiple stakeholders, and the ability of states to regulate the environment, human rights, and health and safety of their citizens.

It will be evident from the analysis carried out in this book that I am of the view that the current investment dispute settlement framework is unsatisfactory. It is not, however, irredeemable, or, indeed, wholly defective. The establishment of a centralised and permanent appellate body for investment arbitration, together with the appropriate rules on transparency and receipt of *amicus* briefs, would address many of the concerns set out above. In addition, it would also bring international investment law into line with principles of an emerging global public law framework.[147] Furthermore, it is likely that an appeals facility

[142] Ibid., pp. 8–9, 16, 29, 70

[143] Ibid., pp. 49–51; Cosbey et al., *Investment and Sustainable*, p. 6; Van Harten, *Investment Treaty Arbitration*, pp. 172–3.

[144] Cosbey et al., *Investment and Sustainable*, p. 6; Van Harten, *Investment Treaty Arbitration*, pp. 172–3; Buergenthal, 'The Proliferation of Disputes', 498; see also the comments of Philippe Sands reported in Balkiss Salamain, 'London Barrister'.

[145] Buergenthal, 'The Proliferation of Disputes', 498.

[146] Cosbey et al., *Investment and Sustainable*, p. 6.

[147] See, e.g., Garcia, 'Globalization and the Theory'; Krisch and Kingsbury, 'Introduction'.

would bring a more progressive approach to the development of international investment law. An analogous precedent for this can be found in decisions of the WTO Appellate Body, such as US–Import Prohibition of Certain Shrimp and Shrimp Products,[148] which integrated the consideration of principles of international environmental law into the interpretation of trade rules.[149] It is likely that opening up the analysis of international investment norms to the influence of principles from other areas of international law would provide a more receptive hearing to the social and environmental issues involved in investor–state arbitration. Accordingly, the next section examines several options for creating an appeals facility that may assist in driving the reconceptualisation of international investment law.

B. *An appellate facility for investor–state arbitration*

1. Appellate body within ICSID

The discourse has recently focused on the issue of whether an appellate body could help restore legitimacy to investor–state arbitration.[150] As the dominant dispute resolution mechanism in investor–state arbitration,[151] it is, therefore, not surprising that ICSID has also turned its attention to the need for an appeals facility. In particular, ICSID has acknowledged the potential for inconsistent awards in investment arbitration and has identified this potential as a systemic problem.[152] In exploring the need for an appeals facility, ICSID noted the increasing number of investment cases, the interest expressed by member states in such a mechanism, and the beneficial effects it would have in enhancing the perception of investor–state arbitration outside the arbitration community.[153] The initial fervour has, however, slowed somewhat as several states took a negative view of the proposal.[154] These views were expressed despite the conclusion of several free trade agreements and

[148] See, e.g., *US-Import Prohibition of Certain Shrimp and Shrimp Products*, Report of the Appellate Body, WT/DS58/AB/R, 12 October 1998, 38 ILM 118 (1999).

[149] Sands, 'Turtles and Torturers'; see the discussion in Stephens, 'Multiple International Courts', 263, 265.

[150] For views supportive of an appellate facility, see, e.g., the discussion in Van Harten, *Investment Treaty Arbitration*, pp. 153–75, 180; Franck, 'The Legitimacy Crisis'; see also Bower, 'Structure, Legitimacy'; Gal-Or, 'The Concept of Appeal'; Gantz, 'An Appellate Mechanism'.

[151] Van Harten, *Investment Treaty Arbitration*, p. 27.

[152] ICSID, 'Possible Improvements'. [153] Ibid.

[154] Tams, 'An Appealing Option?', 6; Investment Treaty News, 'ICSID Member-Governments'; see the discussion in Walsh, 'Substantive Review', 444–5.

bilateral investment treaties that anticipate the future creation of an appeals facility for investor–state disputes.[155]

There are conflicting viewpoints on the desirability of an appellate body established within ICSID for a variety of reasons. Opponents at one end of the spectrum argue that there are no fundamental problems with the investor–state arbitration system to justify such a significant structural change, that there are no realistic options currently 'on the table' for consideration, and that an appeals facility goes against the *raison d'être* of international arbitration as a relatively quick and less expensive alternative to domestic litigation.[156] Advocates of this final point argue that allowing appeals would remove the finality of the award, drag out the dispute, extend the period of uncertainty, and increase costs.[157] Conversely, Sammartano suggests that these objections could be met fairly easily through a range of tight procedural regulations and prescribed timeframes for the hearing of appeals.[158] He also characterises the notion that parties prefer a final, unreviewable award even if it reflects an inaccurate application of the law as a myth, and that this should not be used as an argument against an appeals facility.[159]

Others oppose the establishing of an appellate body within ICSID for entirely different reasons.[160] The concerns here are that the private nature of the system remains intact, along with the preservation of a value system that places private commercial interests above public policy measures.[161] Creating an appellate body within the ICSID framework would certainly assist in alleviating the problem of inconsistent arbitral awards. However, leaving international investment disputes at first instance within the current fragmented and decentralised system of arbitration does not address the other equally important public law issues of transparency, accountability, and investor bias. These

155 Tams, 'An Appealing Option?', 5; see e.g. Treaty between the United States of America and the Oriental Republic of Uruguay Concerning the Encouragement and Reciprocal Protection of Investment (2005) Art. 28.10, available at www.unctad.org/sections/dite/iia/docs/bits/US_Uruguay.pdf (last accessed 17 December 2011).

156 See the discussion in Tams, 'An Appealing Option?', 34; see also the discussion on the origins of commercial arbitration as an alternative to litigation in Van Harten, *Investment Treaty Arbitration*, pp. 59–61; see the critiques in Legum, 'Options to Establish an Appellate Mechanism', p. 231; see also Paulsson, 'Avoiding Unintended Consequences', p. 241.

157 See the discussion in Tams, 'An Appealing Option?', 34; see also the discussion in Sammartano, 'The Fall of a Taboo', pp. 388–91.

158 Ibid., 388–9. 159 Ibid., 387.

160 See, e.g., Van Harten, *Investment Treaty Arbitration*, p. 167. 161 Ibid.

broader issues have led to proposals for the establishment of a permanent international investment court.[162]

2. A permanent international investment court or tribunal

Proponents of the creation of an international investment court argue that this institutional option would address many of the concerns surrounding the current ad hoc system of investor–state arbitration, but would also build on the existing framework of bilateral investment treaties rather than discarding it altogether.[163] Van Harten, for example, puts forward a proposal for an international court that has jurisdiction to hear investor–state disputes both at first instance and as an appeals facility.[164] This would be a mechanism that sat above the current investment treaty network, adjudicating on disputes arising under bilateral or regional investment treaties. He argues that judges should be long-term appointments to the court and should be selected by states so as to ensure their independence and accountability.[165]

Van Harten argues that this institutional response to problems with investor–state arbitration is the most realistic reform option precisely because it is a procedural response and does not address substantive concerns.[166] He argues that with so many bilateral investment treaties in existence and a multitude of failed attempts to garner a multilateral investment treaty, radical reform of the system is unlikely to secure the necessary level of state support.[167] Van Harten's proposal would certainly restore public law principles to investor–state dispute resolution. It would make a fundamental difference to a range of problems derived from the decentralised ad hoc system of investor–state arbitration and the method of selection of arbitrators. However, while such

[162] Ibid., pp. 180–4; Sammartano, 'The Fall of a Taboo', 391–2.

[163] See, e.g., Van Harten, *Investment Treaty Arbitration*. See also the proposals by Sammartano, 'The Fall of a Taboo', 391–2; Schwebel, 'The Creation and Operation', p. 115; Holtzmann, 'A Task for the 21st Century', 109.

[164] Van Harten, *Investment Treaty Arbitration*, p. 180.

[165] Ibid., pp. 180–3. Van Harten argues that state-based appointments to an appellate facility are necessary to ensure accountability. He counters the argument that such a system would produce a bias towards host states by arguing that appointments would come from both capital-exporting and capital-importing states. Van Harten suggests that we will have to trust that states would appoint appropriate experts. He argues that as states represent the interests of a wide range of stakeholders, are accountable to their citizens, and could hold judges accountable for their decisions, democratic principles demand that states, rather than the investment community, appoint the judges to any future international investment court.

[166] Ibid., p. 180. [167] Ibid.

institutional change is necessary, it is not sufficient to achieve reform. What is also needed is an express transformation of substantive norms of international investment law to a more socially and environmentally acceptable set of rules and principles. Only with this type of reform will balance be achieved between the need for regulatory autonomy of the host state and adequate protection for investors. As such, a dispute settlement body, incorporating an appeals facility, within a new multilateral agreement on sustainable finance, investment, and corporate social and environmental responsibility is the most appropriate procedural option for the resolution of investment disputes.

3. Appellate body within a new responsible investment convention

A fundamental part of any new socially and environmentally responsible multilateral agreement on investment will be reform of the current international investment dispute resolution system. Clearly, I am of the view that a new centralised approach needs to be adopted, embodied in the creation of one decision-making facility, which has jurisdiction to hear investor–state disputes at both first instance and at appeals level. As Van Harten suggests, the adjudicators would need to be appointed for a fixed term of some years, preferably in the region of seven to ten, and should be selected by a committee of capital-exporting and capital-importing states to ensure judicial independence and accountability.[168] There needs to be public access to the documents filed by the parties, to the oral proceedings, and to the final awards. There also needs to be a mechanism by which *amicus curiae* briefs are accepted. In this way, the transparency, consistency, and accuracy problems in investor–state arbitration could be addressed, the inappropriate emphasis on preservation of commercial interests could be removed, and more room could be made in the system for host state regulatory autonomy.

The IISD Model Agreement recognises the need to marry procedural reform with substantive progress. It provides for a two-level dispute settlement body embedded within a convention containing investor responsibilities as well as rights.[169] I would suggest that this approach is the most appropriate model to bring about a transformation of foreign investment practices and international investment law. In particular, its combining of procedural reform with more balanced substantive principles better reflects the needs of all states and their

[168] Ibid., p. 182. [169] Mann et al., *IISD Model International Agreement.*

citizens in the twenty-first century. The most effective way to advance this goal would be to pursue the conclusion of a multilateral treaty following the template of the IISD Model Agreement but with further expansion on sustainable finance, ecologically sustainable investment, and corporate social and environmental responsibility.

This is unlikely to occur, however, without a cultural transformation in the foreign investment sector. As discussed above in Chapter 5, a cultural shift needs to take place within international arbitration circles and amongst investment treaty negotiators so that it becomes natural to consider the environmental, social, and developmental needs of the host state and their affected citizens on a par with the rights of the investor. Without such a transformation in perspective, significant reform of international investment law and its dispute settlement system is improbable – and the modern framework for international investment regulation will remain one imbued with nineteenth-century conceptualisations.

III. Conclusion

There are a number of parallel paths to the realisation of a reconceptualised ecologically sustainable international investment law. This chapter has argued that a multilayered approach combining these various strategies would be the most effective way to transform foreign investment law, policy, and practices. From a constructivist perspective, the current activity surrounding the development of a balanced socially and environmentally responsible international investment legal framework suggests that this process is already at a pre-normative stage and should ultimately lead to a new type of investment law. There are, however, several concrete steps that can be taken in the immediate future to accelerate that development and to ensure that traditional patterns of challenge and response do not re-emerge to counteract current momentum towards reform.

First, a significant tangible step would be the incorporation of provisions into new bilateral investment treaties to reflect more responsible investment. This would be an important incremental development, pursued with a view to negotiating a multilateral agreement in the image of the IISD Model Agreement. A multilateral agreement of this kind would also need to go further, however, and include emerging principles of corporate social responsibility and sustainable finance, a stronger emphasis on ecological sustainability, express references to core ethical principles, and the direct application of principles of international environmental law to investors. In this regard, it is also crucial that multinational corporations are brought within an international regulatory framework. As discussed in Chapter 4, voluntary initiatives and market mechanisms are important in transforming the landscape in which business operates, but it is now also time to bring a strong element of global obligation to the way in which corporations and investors conduct themselves.[170] A multilateral agreement directed at corporate social and environmental responsibility and sustainable investment is essential to achieving that global reach.

As has emerged from the discussions in this and previous chapters, reform of the dispute settlement system will be a key factor in bringing about a transformation in international investment law. It is imperative that the current decentralised structure comprising non-accountable and temporary tribunals is replaced with a permanent two-tier forum with an appeals facility. Ideally, this would occur within the framework of a new responsible investment agreement rather than as a standalone procedural reform. However, prospective paths to reform will not be realised without a substantial cultural shift amongst key actors in the investment sector. In this regard, such cultural transformation could be effected through the less formal channels of transnational networks.[171] Although the process of reorienting perspectives is by no means complete, the groundwork has been done on shifting the culture in business circles through raising the awareness of corporations and the public as to the necessity of socially and environmentally responsible corporate conduct.[172] This same process needs to occur for those involved in the development of international investment law, the drafting of investment treaties, and the determination of investor–state disputes. It is unlikely that fundamental change will occur in international investment law until the perspectives of those in these select communities are altered and they perceive it as entirely natural that foreign investment should promote socially and ecologically sustainable

[170] Zerk, *Multinationals*, pp. 243–4, 262–3; see also McCorquodale and Simons, 'Responsibility Beyond Borders'; Bunn, 'Global Advocacy'; Friends of the Earth, 'Towards Binding Corporate'; Mann et al., *IISD Model International Agreement*.

[171] See the discussion in, Slaughter, *A New World Order*; see also Dryzek, 'Paradigms and Discourses', 44; Krisch and Kingsbury, 'Introduction'; Danish, 'International Relations Theory', 205.

[172] Kinley, 'Human Rights', 257–8.

development. Concerted effort is therefore required to utilise informal channels to shift perspectives in international investment legal circles.

There are, of course, significant obstacles to reform and to the realisation of a socially and environmentally responsible international investment sector. Clearly, these include the current dispute settlement system and the prevailing approach of arbitrators to public interest issues and to the application of general principles of international law in investor–state disputes. A further problem is the political will of capital-exporting states to negotiate balanced bilateral investment treaties or to engage in multilateral negotiations for a balanced global agreement on investment. There is certainly a reluctance to loosen the international investor protection regime that has been carefully constructed and controlled by capital-exporting states for the last 200 years.[173] It can be seen that this reluctance is a continuation of the historical patterns of assertion, challenge, and response that have characterised the development of international investment law. On the other hand, again largely driven by self-interest, there is a glimmer of realisation of the need for a balanced global investment regime as developed states begin to find themselves on the receiving end of investor–state complaints.[174] This is an encouraging development. It should eventually lead to a re-evaluation of the system of investor–state arbitration and to a reorientation of substantive international investment norms so as to equip the twenty-first century with international law that reflects its values and needs. There remains a sense of apprehension, however, in that such optimism has been expressed before,[175] only later to prove unfounded as the undulating patterns of challenge and response have seen the traditional position of the investor repeatedly reasserted.

Ultimately, it is hoped that a new phase for foreign investment protection law and practices is emerging. Although a fully developed socially and environmentally responsible international investment law may not crystallise in the immediate future, processes of engagement to remould foreign investment law and practices to fit within a framework

[173] Cosbey et al., *Investment and Sustainable*, p. 27; Van Harten, *Investment Treaty Arbitration*, p. 179; Vandevelde, 'A Brief History', 190.

[174] Sands, *Lawless World*, pp. 121–2, 139–41.

[175] See the discussion above in Chapter 2 on the optimism experienced by postcolonial states and the attempts of the New International Economic Order to reshape international investment law. See further the discussion in Mickelson, 'Rhetoric and Rage', 362; Richardson, 'Environmental Law', 2.

of sustainable development have started. Procedural inroads have been made, allowing greater access to investor–state proceedings and provision for the filing of *amicus curiae* briefs.[176] Substantively, cultural heritage and environmental impacts have been considered as criteria for determining whether investment projects were in 'like circumstances'.[177] These steps are indicators of a broader direction in which investor–state arbitration and investment treaty negotiation should continue to develop and produce new norms of responsible investment law. Progressively, the traditional position of the international investment sector and capital-exporting states should become increasingly untenable and give way to a more socially and environmentally responsible approach to foreign investment, leading to reconceptualised bilateral investment treaties and, ultimately, to a new global regulatory framework for international investment law. In this way, cycles of reproducing imperialism within international investment law could be broken.

176 See *Methanex Corporation* (Award of 2005); *Biwater Gauff Ltd* (Procedural Order of 2007); see also e.g. Treaty between the United States of America and the Oriental Republic of Uruguay Concerning the Encouragement and Reciprocal Protection of Investment (2005) Art. 28.10, available at www.unctad.org/sections/dite/iia/docs/bits/US_Uruguay.pdf (last accessed 15 March 2009); see further the discussion in Tienhaara, 'Third Party Participation'; see also Newcombe, 'Sustainable Development'.

177 *Parkerings-Compagniet AS* v. *Republic of Lithuania*, (ICSID Arbitration Case No. ARB/05/8, Award of 11 September 2007), para. 371.

7 Conclusion: patterns of power in international investment law

There is a detectable ebb and flow to the entwining of politics, commerce, and law in the history of international investment law. The primary concerns of this book have been to reflect on those processes and to bring an historical perspective to the consideration of contemporary understandings and controversies within this field. Throughout the foregoing chapters, therefore, I have sought to shed light on the historical, political, and commercial dynamics involved in the evolution of international investment law and the way in which these interests continue to inform its modern context. What has emerged from these investigations is a story of 'assertion of power and responses to power'[1] in the creation and sustaining of the international rules on protection of foreign investment.

In analysing the origins of international investment law, rather than taking the starting point as the late 1950s and 1960s, I have been able to accentuate the repetition of the original dynamics of imperialism throughout the development of its principles, treaties, and dispute resolution structures. Most importantly, perhaps, adopting such an approach places the investment law controversies of the twenty-first century into an historical context, locating current tensions as a part of this ongoing mode of interaction. It seemed to me that without knowledge of the historical framework, individual incidents, awards, arguments, principles, objections, and developments can only ever be understood in isolation and, therefore, only with a shallow and incomplete perspective.

[1] The power relations involved in processes of emergence of legal rules and regimes is explored in Benton, *Law and Colonial Cultures*; see also the theories of Byers, *Custom, Power*, pp. 35–40.

We have seen that, from its inception to the current time, the construction of principles and rules of international investment law has been characterised by a contest of interests between capital-exporting states and host states, investors, and local communities. The outcome of these contests has manifested within the law, largely legitimising the position asserted by investors and capital-exporting states and shaping it into an instrument that protected solely investors. Furthermore, the repetition of that dynamic of assertion, challenge, and reassertion of high-level investor protection has also meant that its original conceptualisations embedded in imperialism have remained imbued within modern international investment law. In adopting an historical analysis of this field, I came to the view that current controversies surrounding the sector are not fundamentally new, but rather are manifestations of unresolved power dynamics that have dominated the development of international investment law since its emergence in the nineteenth century. For this reason, I have argued that transforming its modern framework will require the breaking of ingrained patterns and the shifting of entrenched positions. And that, of course, is something that may well not eventuate.

The theories in this book, then, emerged from an examination of the origins of international investment law, the challenges raised to prevailing doctrines, and the responses from capital-exporting states and their legal communities throughout the nineteenth and twentieth centuries. Pursuing that story entailed engagement with interdisciplinary approaches, histories of imperialism, discourses on international law-making, and specific principles, doctrines, and instruments from international investment law. Through this process, the connections between the socio-political circumstances involved in the emergence of international rules on foreign investment protection, the substance of the rules in the nineteenth century, and their current content and structure became increasingly apparent. For me, a picture crystallised of international investment law having been shaped in fundamental ways through the operation of imperialism – and of those dynamics continuing to find form throughout the last century, repeating imperialist modes of interaction into the present day. In other words, those same nineteenth-century approaches continue to inform the current substance and structure of international investment law.

The implications of such conclusions are, perhaps, confronting, particularly given current trends in presenting investor–state arbitration as the epitome of the 'rule of law', neutrality, and objectivity in international dispute resolution.[2] Indeed, the position at which I arrived during this research is that a fundamental rearticulation of the present system of foreign investment protection is required. For this reason, I then explored possible avenues through which such reform could be conducted and turned to examine the recent emergence of corporate social responsibility, the sustainable finance movement, and transformations in international law-making. We have seen that these elements are contributing to current pressure to reform international investment law, while also simultaneously providing channels through which reorientation of this field could occur. The concern, however, is that historical patterns of assertion, challenge, and reassertion will be reproduced in response to these attempts to reshape international investment law. Given the history of this field, it would be unsurprising if new doctrine or mechanisms were to emerge to neutralise the effect of these developments and maintain the one-sided focus on investor protection within investment treaty regimes – and, in this way, stymied the potential hints at synergy between investment law and non-investment fields that are currently beginning to take shape. It is this appreciation of the historical context of international investment law that has left me at the conclusion of my research somewhat more equivocal as to the likelihood of fundamental change than at the outset of this enquiry.

In this regard, the centrality of cultural shift within both political and arbitral circles to the realisation of any substantial transformation within international investment law has been emphasised throughout this book. Without doubt, the infusion of a culture among legal decision-makers in the investment field that is more appreciative of host state policy space, the public international law character and context of investment law, and notions of investor responsibility will be essential if any such transformation is to occur. And, even then, as enduring conceptualisations continue to inform the modern reluctance to accommodate visions of the law other than that of high-level investor protection, it is, in any case, likely to be an ongoing project. This book has identified possible ways in which to bring about just such a transformation. Building on the momentum created by the corporate social responsibility and sustainable finance movements, reorienting the investment sector is certainly feasible if the key reforms set out in earlier chapters are adopted. It is hoped that the more comprehensive cognitive and cultural

[2] See, e.g., Schill, 'Fair and Equitable'; see also Weiler and Wälde, 'Investment Arbitration'.

shift required of the legal community of advisors, arbitrators, and treaty-negotiators to bring about a reconceptualised international investment law will gradually emerge in the near future. In questioning prevailing doctrines, in shedding light on the pervasive nature of historical dynamics within international investment law, and in pointing to progressive paths for transformation, it is also hoped that this book will contribute to that process.

Bibliography

BOOKS AND JOURNAL ARTICLES

Abbott, K. W., 'International Relations Theory, International Law, and the Regime Governing Atrocities in Internal Conflicts' (1999) 93 *The American Journal of International Law* 361.

Abbott, K. W. and Snidal, D., 'Hard and Soft Law in International Governance' (2000) 54 *International Organization* 421.

'Strengthening International Regulation Through Transnational New Governance: Overcoming the Orchestration Deficit' (2009) 42 *Vanderbilt Journal of Transnational Law* 501.

Abelowitz, D., 'Discrimination and Cultural Genocide in the Oil Fields of Ecuador: The U.S. as a Forum for International Dispute' (2001) 7 *New England International and Comparative Law Annual* 145.

Abraham, C. M. and Abraham, S., 'The Bhopal Case and the Development of Environmental Law in India' (1991) 40:2 *The International and Comparative Law Quarterly* 334.

Abs, H. and Shawcross, H., 'The Proposed Convention to Protect Private Foreign Investment' (1960) 9 *Journal of Public Law* 115.

Adam, B. D., 'Post-Marxism and the New Social Movements' (1993) 30 *The Canadian Review of Sociology and Anthropology* 316.

Adams, E. S. and Knutsen, K. D., 'A Charitable Corporate Giving Justification for the Socially Responsible Investment of Pension Funds: A Populist Argument for the Public Use of Private Wealth' (1995) 80 *Iowa Law Review* 211.

Adams, J., 'Principals and Agents, Colonists and Company Men: The Decay of Colonial Control in the Dutch East Indies' (1996) 61 *American Sociological Review* 12.

Adlung, R. and Molinuevo, M., 'Bilateralism in Services Trade: Is There Fire Behind the (BIT-) Smoke?' (2008) 11:2 *Journal of International Economic Law* 365.

Affolder, N., 'Cachet Not Cash: Another Sort of World Bank Group Borrowing' (2006) 14 *Michigan State Journal of International Law* 141.

Akita, Shigeru (ed.), *Gentlemanly Capitalism, Imperialism and Global History* (Basingstoke: Palgrave, 2002).

Ala'i, P., 'Free Trade or Sustainable Development? An Analysis of the WTO Appellate Body's Shift to a More Balanced Approach to Trade Liberalization' (1999) 14 *American University International Law Review* 1129.

Alexander, E. A., 'Taking Account of Reality: Adopting Contextual Standards for Developing Countries in International Investment Law' (2008) 48 *Virginia Journal of International Law* 817.

Alexandrowicz, C. H., *An Introduction to the History of the Law of Nations in the East Indies: 16th, 17th and 18th Centuries* (Oxford: Clarendon Press, 1967).

Alvarez, J. E., 'Contemporary Foreign Investment Law: An "Empire of Law" or the "Law of Empire"?' (2009) 60 *Alabama Law Review* 943.

Amerasinghe, C. F,. *State Responsibility for Injuries to Aliens* (Oxford: Clarendon Press, 1967).

Amirfar, C. M. and Dreyer, E. M., 'Thirteen Years of NAFTA's Chapter 11: The Criticisms, The United States' Responses, and Lessons Learned' (2007) 20 *New York International Law Review* 39.

Anand, R., *New States and International Law* (Delhi: Vikas Publishing, 1972).

Anderson, M., 'Transnational Corporations and Environmental Damage: Is Tort Law the Answer?' (2002) 41 *Washburn Law Journal* 399.

Andrade, T., 'Pirates, Pelts, and Promises: The Sino-Dutch Colony of Seventeenth Century Taiwan and the Aboriginal Village of Favorolong' (2005) 64 *The Journal of Asian Studies* 295.

Anghie, A., '"The Heart of My Home": Colonialism, Environmental Damage, and the Nauru Case' (1993) 34 *Harvard International Law Journal* 445.

'Finding the Peripheries: Sovereignty and Colonialism in Nineteenth-Century International Law' (1999) 40 *Harvard International Law Journal* 1.

'Civilization and Commerce: The Concept of Governance in Historical Perspective' (2000) 45 *Villanova Law Review* 887.

'Time Present and Time Past: Globalization, International Financial Institutions, and the Third World' (2000) 32 *New York University Journal of International Law and Politics* 243.

Imperialism, Sovereignty and the Making of International Law (Cambridge University Press, 2004).

Appleton, B., 'Regulatory Takings: The International Law Perspective' (2002) 11 *New York University Environmental Law Journal* 35.

Arasaratnam, S., 'Monopoly and Free Trade in Dutch–Asian Commercial Policy: Debate and Controversy within the VOC' (1973) 4 *Journal of Southeast Asian Studies* 1.

Arend, A. C., 'Do Legal Rules Matter? International Law and International Politics' (1998) 38 *Virginia Journal of International Law* 107.

Ashford, R., 'What is the "New" Corporate Social Responsibility?: The Socio-Economic Foundation of Corporate Law and Corporate Social Responsibility' (2002) 76 *Tulane Law Review* 1187.

Assadourian, E., 'The State of Corporate Responsibility and the Environment' (2006) 18 *Georgetown International Environmental Law Review* 571.

'Transforming Corporations' in The Worldwatch Institute, *State of the World 2006* (London: Earthscan, 2006).

Ayres, I. and Braithwaite, J., *Responsive Regulation: Transcending the Deregulation Debate* (Oxford University Press, 1992).

Backer, L. C., 'Multinational Corporations, Transnational Law: The United Nations' Norms on the Responsibilities of Transnational Corporations as a Harbinger of Corporate Social Responsibility in International Law' (2006) 37 *Columbia Human Rights Law Review* 55.

'From Moral Obligation to International Law: Disclosure Systems, Markets and the Regulation of Multinational Corporations' (2008) 39 *Georgetown Journal of International Law* 591.

Bakan, J., *The Corporation: The Pathological Pursuit of Profit and Power* (New York: Simon and Schuster, 2004).

Baker, M., 'Denial of Justice in Local Courts' in Ortino, F., Sheppard, A. and Warner, H. (eds.), *Investment Treaty Law: Current Issues* (London: British Institute of International and Comparative Law, 2006).

Ball, J., *Indonesian Legal History: 1602–1848* (Chatswood: Oughtershaw Press, 1982).

Baram, M. S., 'Multinational Corporations, Private Codes, and Technology Transfer for Sustainable Development' (1994) 24 *Environmental Law* 33.

Barnard, J. W., 'Corporate Boards and the New Environmentalism' (2007) 31 *William and Mary Environmental Law and Policy Review* 291.

Barnett, M. and Duvall, R., 'Power in International Politics' (2005) 59 *International Organization* 39.

Barton, G., *Empire Forestry and the Origins of Environmentalism* (Cambridge University Press, 2002).

Bauer, J., 'Introduction' in Bauer, J. (ed.), *Forging Environmentalism: Justice, Livelihood, and Contested Environments* (New York: M.E. Sharpe, 2006).

Baxi, U., *Inconvenient Forum and Convenient Catastrophe: The Bhopal Case* (Bombay: N.M. Tripathi, 1986).

Beekman, E. M., *Troubled Pleasures: Dutch Colonial Literature from the East* (Oxford University Press, 1996).

Been, V. and Beauvais, J. C., 'The Global Fifth Amendment? NAFTA's Investment Protections and the Misguided Quest for an International "Regulatory Takings" Doctrine' (2003) 78 *New York University Law Review* 30

Beinart, W. and Hughes, L., *Environment and Empire* (Oxford University Press, 2007).

Benford, R. D. and Snow, D. A., 'Framing Processes and Social Movements: An Overview and Assessment' (2000) 26 *Annual Review of Sociology* 611.

Bennett, C. and Burley, H., 'Corporate Accountability: An NGO Perspective' in Stephen Tully (ed.) *Research Handbook on Corporate Legal Responsibility* (Cheltenham: Edward Elgar, 2005) 372.

Benton, L., *Law and Colonial Cultures: Legal Regimes in World History, 1400–1900* (Cambridge University Press, 2002).

A Search for Sovereignty: Law and Geography in European Empires, 1400–1900 (Cambridge University Press, 2010).

Bergman, M. S., 'Bilateral Investment Protection Treaties: An Examination of the Evolution and Significance of the U.S. Prototype Treaty' (1983) 16 *New York University Journal of International Law & Politics* 1.

Berman, F., 'Reflections on the ICJ's Oil Platforms Decision: Treaty "Interpretation" in a Judicial Context' (2004) 29 *Yale Journal of International Law* 315.

Berman, P. S., 'The Globalization of Jurisdiction' (2002) 151 *University of Pennsylvania Law Review* 311.

'From International Law to Law and Globalization' (2005) 43 *Columbia Journal of Transnational Law* 485.

Bernasconi-Osterwalder, N. and Brown Weiss, E., 'International Investment Rules and Water: Learning from the NAFTA Experience' in Brown Weiss, E., Boisson de Chazournes, L. and Bernasconi-Osterwalder, N. (eds.), *Fresh Water and International Economic Law* (Oxford University Press, 2005).

Besmer, V., 'The Legal Character of Private Codes of Conduct: More Than Just a Pseudo-Formal Gloss on Corporate Social Responsibility' (2006) 2 *Hastings Business Law Journal* 279.

Betsill, M. M., 'Transnational Actors in International Environmental Politics' in Betsill, M., Hochstetler, K. and Stevis, D. (eds.), *International Environmental Politics* (Hampshire: Palgrave Macmillan, 2006).

Betsill, M. M. and Corell, E., 'Introduction to NGO Diplomacy' in Betsill, M. M. and Corell, E. (eds.), *NGO Diplomacy: The Influence of Nongovernmental Organizations in International Environmental Negotiations* (MIT Press, 2008).

Bhagwati, J. N., 'Introduction' in Bagwati, J. N. (ed.), *The New International Economic Order* (MIT Press, 1977).

Bigge, D. M., 'Bring on the Bluewash: A Social Constructivist Argument Against Using *Nike* v. *Kasky* to Attack the U.N. Global Compact' (2004) 14 *International Legal Perspectives* 6.

Birnie, P., Boyle, A. and Redgwell, C., *International Law and the Environment*, 3rd edn, (Oxford University Press, 2009).

Blackburn, W. R., 'Sustainability as a Business Operating System' (2004) 19 *Natural Resources & Environment* 27.

Blowfield, M. and Jedrzej, G. F., 'Setting New Agendas: Critical Perspectives on Corporate Social Responsibility in the Developing World' (2005) 81 *International Affairs* 499.

Blumberg, P. I., 'Asserting Human Rights against Multinational Corporations under United States Law: Conceptual and Procedural Problems' (2002) 50 *The American Journal of Comparative Law* 493.

Blumenwitz, D., 'Treaties of Friendship, Commerce and Navigation' in Bernhardt, R. (ed.), *Encyclopedia of Public International Law* (1992–2002).

Blussé, L., 'No Boat to China: The Dutch East India Company and the Changing Pattern of the China Sea Trade, 1635–1690' (1996) 30 *Modern Asian Studies* 51.

Boer, B., 'The Globalisation of Environmental Law: The Role of the United Nations' (1995) 20 *Melbourne University Law Review* 101.

'Sustainability Law for the New Millennium and the Role of Environmental Legal Education' (2000) 123 *Water, Air, and Soil Pollution* 447.

Boggs, C., *Social Movements and Political Power: Emerging Forms of Radicalism in the West* (Philadelphia: Temple University Press, 1986).

Borchard, E. M., 'Contractual Claims in International Law' (1913) 13 *Columbia Law Review* 457.

The Diplomatic Protection of Citizens Abroad (New York: The Banks Law Publishing Company, 1919).

'The "Minimum Standard" of the Treatment of Aliens' (1940) 38 *Michigan Law Review* 445.

Borgen, C. J., 'Transnational Tribunals and the Transmission of Norms: The Hegemony of Process' (2007) 39 *George Washington International Law Review* 685.

Borschberg, P., 'The Seizure of the *Sta. Catarina* Revisited: The Portuguese Empire in Asia, VOC Politics and the Origins of the Dutch-Johor Alliance (1602–c.1616) (2002) 33(1) *Journal of Southeast Asian Studies* 31.

Bosselmann, K., *When Two Worlds Collide: Society and Ecology* (Auckland: RSVP Publishing Company, 1995).

Bostian, I. L., 'Flushing the Danube: The World Court's Decision Concerning the Gabčikovo Dam' (1998) 9 *Colorado Journal of International Environmental Law and Policy* 401.

Boute, A., 'Combating Climate Change and Securing Electricity Supply: The Role of Investment Protection Law' (2007) 16 *European Environmental Law Review* 227.

Bowen, H. V., 'Investment and Empire in the Later Eighteenth Century: East India Stockholding 1756–1791' (1989) 42 *The Economic History Review* 186.

Bowett, D., 'State Contracts With Aliens: Contemporary Developments on Compensation for Termination or Breach' (1988) 59 *The British Year Book of International Law* 49.

Boyle, A. E., 'The *Gabcikovo-Nagymaros Case*: New Law in Old Bottles' (1997) 8 *Yearbook of International Environmental Law* 17.

Boyle, A. E. and Chinkin, C. M., *The Making of International Law* (Oxford University Press, 2007).

Bradshaw, M., 'The 'Greening' of Global Project Financing: The Case of the Sakhalin-II Offshore Oil and Gas Project' (2007) 51 *Canadian Geographer* 255.

Braithwaite, J. and Drahos, P., *Global Business Regulation* (Cambridge University Press, 2000).

Brand, R. A., 'External Sovereignty and International Law' (1995) 18 *Fordham International Law Journal* 1685.

Branson, D. M., 'Corporate Governance "Reform" and the New Corporate Social Responsibility' (2001) 62 *University of Pittsburgh Law Review* 605.

Braudel, F., *The Wheels of Commerce: Civilization & Capitalism 15th–18th Century*, 4th edn, (New York: Harper & Row, 1986).

Brenton, T., *The Greening of Machiavelli: The Evolution of International Environmental Politics* (London: Earthscan, 1994).

Brewer, T. L. and Young, S., *The Multilateral Investment System and Multinational Enterprises* (Oxford University Press, 1998, reprinted 2001).
Bridgeman, N. L. and Hunter, D. B., 'Narrowing the Accountability Gap: Toward a New Foreign Investor Accountability Mechanism' (2008) 20 *Georgetown International Environmental Law Review* 187.
Brierly, J. L., *The Law of Nations: An Introduction to the International Law of Peace*, 6th edn, (Oxford: Clarendon Press, 1963).
Brookens, B. O., 'Diplomatic Protection of Foreign Economic Interests: The Changing Structure of International Law in the New International Economic Order' (1978) 20 *Journal of Interamerican Studies and World Affairs* 37.
Broughton, E., 'The Bhopal Disaster and its Aftermath: A Review' (2005) 4:6 *Environmental Health: A Global Access Science Source* 1.
Brower, C. N., Brower II, C. H. and Sharpe, J. K., 'The Coming Crisis in the Global Adjudication System' (2003) 19:4 *Arbitration International* 415.
Brown, C., 'The Settlement of Disputes Arising in Flexibility Mechanism Transactions under the Kyoto Protocol' (2005) 21: 3 *Arbitration International* 361.
Brown, E. F., 'No Good Deed Goes Unpunished: Is There a Need for a Safe Harbor for Aspirational Corporate Codes of Conduct?' (2008) 26 *Yale Law & Policy Review* 367.
Brown Weiss, E., 'The Rise or Fall of International Law' (2000) 69 *Fordham Law Review* 345.
Brownlie, I., *Principles of Public International Law*, 7th edn, (Oxford University Press, 2008).
Brunnée, J. and Toope, S. J., 'International Law and Constructivism: Elements of an Interactional Theory of International Law' (2000) 39 *Columbia Journal of Transnational Law* 19.
Legitimacy and Legality in International Law: An Interactional Account (Cambridge University Press, 2010).
Bruno, K. and Karliner, J., 'The UN's Global Compact: Corporate Accountability and the Johannesburg Earth Summit' (2002) 45 *Development* 33.
Budzynski, C. A., 'Can a Feminist Approach to Corporate Social Responsibility Break Down the Barriers of the Shareholder Primacy Doctrine?' (2006) 38 *University of Toledo Law Review* 435.
Buergenthal, T., 'The Evolving International Human Rights System' (2006) 100 *American Journal of International Law* 783.
'The Proliferation of Disputes, Dispute Settlement Procedures and Respect for the Rule of Law (2006) 22:4 *Arbitration International* 495.
Bunn, I. D., 'The Right to Development: Implications for International Economic Law' (2000) 15 *American University International Law Review* 1425.
'Global Advocacy for Corporate Accountability: Transatlantic Perspectives from the NGO Community' (2004) 19 *American University International Law Review* 1265.
Byers, M., *Custom, Power and the Power of Rules: International Relations and Customary International Law* (Cambridge University Press, 1999).

Cain, P. J. and Hopkins, A., *British Imperialism: 1688–2000* (New York: Longman, 2002).

Caplan, L. M., 'State Immunity, Human Rights, and Jus Cogens: A Critique of the Normative Hierarchy Theory' (2003) 97 *American Journal Of International Law* 741.

Carlston, K. S., 'Concession Agreements and Nationalization' (1958) 52:2 *The American Journal of International Law* 260.

Carr, C. and Rosembuj, F., 'Flexible Mechanisms for Climate Change Compliance: Emission Offset Purchases under the Clean Development Mechanism' (2008) 16 *New York University Environmental Law Journal* 44.

Carrasco, E. R. and Kose, M. A., 'Income Distribution and the Bretton Woods Institutions: Promoting an Enabling Environment for Social Development' (1996) 6 *Transnational Law & Contemporary Problems* 1.

Carruthers, D. and Rodriguez, P., 'Mapuche Protest, Environmental Conflict and Social Movement Linkage in Chile' (2009) 30 *Third World Quarterly* 743.

Carson, R., *Silent Spring* (Boston: Houghton Mifflin, 1962).

Cassels, J., 'Outlaws: Multinational Corporations and Catastrophic Law', (2000) 31 *Cumberland Law Review* 311.

Cernea, M. M., 'The "Ripple Effect" in Social Policy and its Political Content: A Debate on Social Standards in Public and Private Development Projects' in Likosky, M. B. (ed.), *Privatising Development: Transnational Law, Infrastructure and Human Rights* (Bedfordshire: Brill Academic Publishers, 2005).

Cetindamar, D. and Husoy, K., 'Corporate Social Responsibility Practices and Environmentally Responsible Behavior: The Case of the United Nations Global Compact' (2007) 76 *Journal of Business Ethics* 163.

Chambers, W. B., 'International Trade Law and the Kyoto Protocol: Potential Incompatibilities' in Chambers, W. B. (ed.) *Inter-Linkages: The Kyoto Protocol and the International Trade and Investment Regimes* (New York: United Nations University Press, 2001).

Chang, H. F., 'Environmental Trade Measures, the Shrimp-Turtle Rulings and the Ordinary Meaning of the Text of the GATT' (2005) 8 *Chapman Law Review* 25.

Chasek, P. S., Downie, D, L., Porter, G., and Welsh Brown, J., *Global Environmental Politics* (Boulder: Westview Press, 2006).

Chattergee, S. K., 'The Charter of Economic Rights and Duties of States: An Evaluation After 15 Years' (1991) 40 *International and Comparative Law Quarterly* 66.

Chaturvedi, V. (ed.), *Mapping Subaltern Studies and the Postcolonial* (London: Verso, 2000).

Chayes, A. and Handler Chayes, A., *The New Sovereignty: Compliance with International Regulatory Agreements* (Harvard University Press, 1995).

Chen, L., 'Law, Empire, and Historiography of Modern Sino–Western Relations: A Case Study of the Lady Hughes Controversy in 1784' (2009) 27 *Law and History Review* 1.

Cheng, B., *General Principles of Law as Applied by International Courts and Tribunals* (London: Steven & Sons, 1987).

Chesterman, S., 'Oil and Water: Regulating the Behaviour of Multinational Corporations Through Law' (2004) 36 *New York University Journal of International Law and Politics* 307.

'An International Rule of Law?' (2008) 56 *The American Journal of Comparative Law* 331.

'The Turn to Ethics: Disinvestment from Multinational Corporations for Human Rights Violations – The Case of Norway's Sovereign Wealth Fund' (2008) 23 *American University International Law Review* 577.

Chimni, B. S., 'Alternative Visions of Just World Order: Six Tales from India' (2005) 46 *Harvard International Law Journal* 389.

'Co-option and Resistance: Two Faces of Global Administrative Law' (2005) 37 *New York University Journal of International Law and Politics* 799.

Chinkin, C. M., 'The Challenge of Soft Law: Development and Change in International Law' (1989) 38 *International and Comparative Law Quarterly* 850.

Chopra, S. K, 'Multinational Corporations in the Aftermath of Bhopal: The Need for a New Comprehensive Global Regime for Transnational Corporate Activity' (1994) 29 *Valparaiso University Law Review* 235.

Chossudovsky, M., *The Globalization of Poverty: Impacts of IMF and World Bank Reforms* (London: Zed Books, 1997).

Choudhury, B., 'Recapturing Public Power: Is Investment Arbitration's Engagement of the Public Interest Contributing to the Democratic Deficit?' (2008) 41 *Vanderbilt Journal of Transnational Law* 775.

'Serving Two Masters: Incorporating Social Responsibility into the Corporate Paradigm' (2009) 11 *University of Pennsylvania Journal of Business Law* 631.

Christie, G. C., 'What Constitutes a Taking of Property under International Law?' (1964) 38 *British Yearbook of International Law* 307.

Christmann, P. and Taylor, G., 'Globalization and the Environment: Strategies for International Voluntary Environmental Initiatives' (2002) 16 *The Academy of Management Executive* 121.

Clagett, B., '*Forum Non Conveniens* in International Environmental Tort Suits: Closing the Doors of U.S. Courts to Foreign Plaintiffs' (1996) 9 *Tulane Environmental Law Journal* 513.

Clapham, A., *Human Rights Obligations of Non-State Actors* (Oxford University Press, 2006).

Clapp, J., 'What the Pollution Haven Debate Overlooks' (2002) 2 *Global Environmental Politics* 11.

'Global Environmental Governance for Corporate Responsibility and Accountability' (2005) 5(3) *Global Environmental Politics* 23.

Clark, D. L., 'Boundaries in the Field of Human Rights: The World Bank and Human Rights: The Need for Greater Accountability' (2002) 15 *Harvard Human Rights Journal* 205.

Clark, G. L. and Knight, E. R. W., 'Implications of the UK Companies Act 2006 for Institutional Investors and the Market for Corporate Social Responsibility' (2009) 11 *University of Pennsylvania Journal of Business Law* 259.

Clarke, R. F., 'A Permanent Tribunal of International Arbitration: Its Necessity and Value' (1907) 1 *The American Journal of International Law* 342.

Coglianese, C., 'Social Movements, Law, and Society: The Institutionalization of the Environmental Movement' (2001) 150 *University of Pennsylvania Law Review* 85.

Cordonier Segger, M. and Khalan, A., *Sustainable Development Law: Principles, Practices and Prospects* (Oxford University Press, 2004).

Cotula, L., 'Reconciling Regulatory Stability and Evolution of Environmental Standards in Investment Contracts: Towards a Rethink of Stabilization Clauses' (2008) 1 *Journal of World Energy Law & Business* 158.

Commoner, B., *The Closing Circle: Nature, Man and Technology* (New York: Knopf, 1972).

Coolsaet, R., 'Trade and Diplomacy' (2004) 5 *International Studies Perspectives* 61.

Cone II, S. M., 'The Environment and the Law: The Environment and the World Trade Organization' (2002) 46 *New York Law School Law Review* 615.

Connell, J., 'Trans-National Environmental Disputes: Are Civil Remedies More Effective for Victims of Environmental Harm?' (2007) 10 *Asia Pacific Journal of Environmental Law* 39.

Corea, G., 'UNCTAD and the New International Economic Order' (1977) 53 *International Affairs* 177.

Crane, W., 'Corporations Swallowing Nations: The OECD and the Multilateral Agreement on Investment' (1998) 9 *Colorado Journal of International Environmental Law and Policy* 429.

Craven, M., *The Decolonization of International Law: State Succession and the Law of Treaties* (Oxford University Press, 2007).

Crawford, J., *International Law as an Open System: Selected Essays* (London: Cameron and May, 2002).

'Is There a Need for an Appellate System?' (2005) 2 *Transnational Dispute Management* 8.

Crotty, J., 'Structural Causes of the Global Financial Crisis: A Critical Assessment of the 'New Financial Architecture' (2009) 33 *Cambridge Journal of Economics* 563.

Cutler, A. C., 'Critical Reflections on the Westphalian Assumptions of International Law and Organization: A Crisis of Legitimacy' (2001) 27 *Review of International Studies* 133.

Cutler, A. C., Haufler, V. and Porter, T., *Private Authority and International Affairs* (State University of New York Press, 1999).

Daly, H. E., 'Sustainable Growth? No Thank You' in Mander, J. and Goldsmith, E., *The Case Against the Global Economy: and for a Turn Towards the Local* (San Francisco: Sierra Club Books, 1996).

Danaghare, D. N., 'Subaltern Consciousness and Populism: Two Approaches in the Study of Social Movements in India' (1988) 16 *Social Scientist* 18.

Danilenko, G. M., *Law-Making in the International Community* (Dordrecht: Martinus Nijhoff Publishers, 1993).

Danish, K. W., 'International Relations Theory' in Bodansky, D. Jutta Brunnée and Ellen Hey (eds.), *The Oxford Handbook of International Environmental Law* (Oxford University Press, 2007).

Davidsson, P. A., 'Legal Enforcement of Corporate Social Responsibility within the EU' (2002) 8 *Columbia Journal of European Law* 529.

Davis, L. E. and Huttenback, R. A., *Mammon and the Pursuit of Empire: the Economics of British Imperialism* (Cambridge University Press, 1988).

Dawson, F. G. and Head, I. L., *International Law, National Tribunals, and the Rights of Aliens* (Syracuse University Press, 1971).

De Burca, G., 'Developing Democracy Beyond the State' (2008) 46 *Columbia Journal of Transnational Law* 221.

Delaney, J. and Barstow Magraw, D., 'Procedural Transparency' in Muchlinski, P., Ortino, F. and Schreuer, C. (eds.), *The Oxford Handbook of International Investment Law* (Oxford University Press, 2008).

DeSombre, E. R., *The Global Environment and World Politics*, 2nd edn (New York: Continuum, 2007).

Detter, I., 'The Problem of Unequal Treaties' (1966) 15 *International and Comparative Law Quarterly* 1069.

Deva, S., 'Human Rights Violations by Multinational Corporations and International Law: Where from Here?' (2003) 19 *Connecticut Journal of International Law* 1.

'Sustainable Good Governance and Corporations: An Analysis of Asymmetries' (2006) 18 *Georgetown International Environmental Law Review* 707.

'Global Compact: A Critique of the U.N.'s "Public-Private" Partnership for Promoting Corporate Citizenship' (2006) 34 *Syracuse Journal of International Law and Commerce* 107.

De Vattel, E., *The Law of Nations*, Book II, ch.VI (1758) (translation).

De Vries, J. and Van der Woude, A., *The First Modern Economy: Success, Failure, and Perseverance of the Dutch Economy, 1500–1815* (Cambridge University Press, 1997).

De Waart, P., 'Sustainable Development through a Socially Responsible Trade and Investment Regime' in Schrijver, N. and Weiss, F. (eds.), *International Law and Sustainable Development: Principles and Practice* (Leiden: Martinus Nijhoff, 2004).

Dezalay, Y. and Garth, B. G., *Dealing in Virtue: International Commercial Arbitration and the Construction of a Transnational Legal Order* (University of Chicago Press, 1996).

Diani, M., 'The Concept of Social Movement' (1992) 40 *Sociological Review* 1.

'The Concept of Social Movement' in Nash, K. (ed.), *Readings in Contemporary Political Sociology* (Oxford: Blackwell Publishers, 2000).

Di Leva, C. E., 'Sustainable Development and the World Bank's Millennium Development Goals' (2004) 19 *Natural Resources & Environment* 13.

DiMascio, N. and Pauwelyn, J., 'Nondiscrimination in Trade and Investment Treaties: Worlds Apart or Two Sides of the Same Coin?' (2008) 102 *American Journal of International Law* 48.

Dobson, A., *Green Political Thought*, 2nd edn, (London: Routledge, 1995).
Doelle, M., 'The Cat Came Back, or the Nine Lives of the Kyoto Protocol' (2006) 16 *Journal of Environmental Law and Practice* 261.
Dolzer, R., 'New Foundations of the Law of Expropriation of Alien Property' (1981) 75 *The American Journal of International Law* 553.
Dolzer, R. and Schreuer, C., *Principles of International Investment Law* (Oxford University Press, 2008).
Doman, N. R., 'Postwar Nationalization of Foreign Property in Europe' (1948) 48 *Columbia Law Review* 1125.
Dougherty, K., 'Methanex v. United States: The Realignment of NAFTA Chapter 11 with Environmental Regulation' (2007) 27 *Northwestern Journal of International Law and Business* 735.
Doyle, M. W., *Empires* (Ithaca: Cornell University Press, 1986).
Dryzek, J. S., 'Paradigms and Discourses' in Bodansky, D., Brunnée, J. and Hey, E. (eds.), *The Oxford Handbook of International Environmental Law* (Oxford University Press, 2007).
Dryzek, J. S., Downes, D., Hunnold, C., et al. *Green States and Social Movements: Environmentalism in the United States, United Kingdom, Germany, and Norway* (Oxford University Press, 2003).
Dudden, A., *Japan's Colonization of Korea: Discourse and Power* (University of Hawaii Press, 2005).
Dunlap, T. R., 'Ecology and Environmentalism in the Anglo Settler Colonies' in Griffiths, T. and Robin, L. (eds.), *Ecology and Empire: Environmental History of Settler Societies* (Edinburgh: Keele University Press, 1997).
Dupuy, P., 'Soft Law and the International Law of the Environment' (1991) 12 *Michigan Journal of International Law* 420.
'Formation of Customary International Law and General Principles' in Bodansky, Brunnée and Hey (eds.) in Bodansky, D., Brunnée, J. and Hey, E. (eds.), *The Oxford Handbook of International Environmental Law* (Oxford University Press, 2007).
Eagleton, C., *The Responsibility of States in International Law* (New York: Banks Law Publishing Co., 1928).
Eckersley, R., *Environmentalism and Political Theory: Toward an Ecocentric Approach* (State University of New York Press, 1992).
Edelman, M., 'Social Movements: Changing Paradigms and Forms of Politics' (2001) 30 *Annual Review of Anthropology* 285.
Eden, S. E., 'Using Sustainable Development: The Business Case' (1994) 4 *Global Environmental Change* 160.
Ehrlich, P., *The Population Bomb* (New York: Ballantine Books, 1968).
Eichengreen, B., 'Historical Research on International Lending and Debt' (1991) 5 *The Journal of Economic Perspectives* 149.
Elhauge, E., 'Sacrificing Corporate Profits in the Public Interest' (2005) 80 *New York University Law Review* 733.
Elkington, J., *Cannibals with Forks: The Triple Bottom Line of 21st Century Business*, 2nd edn, (Gabriola Island: New Society Publishers, 2002).

Elkins, Z., Guzman, A. T. and Simmons, B. A., 'Competing for Capital: The Diffusion of Bilateral Investment Treaties 1960–2000' (2006) 60 *International Organization* 811.

Elson, D., 'Gender Awareness in Modeling Structural Adjustment' (1995) 23(11) *World Development* 1851.

Engel, S. and Martin, B., 'Union Carbide and James Hardie: Lessons in Politics and Power' (2006) 20:4 *Global Society* 475.

Epstein, E. M., 'The Good Company: Rhetoric or Reality? Corporate Social Responsibility and Business Ethics Redux' (2007) 44 *American Business Law Journal* 207.

Esty, D. C. and Geradin, D., 'Environmental Protection and International Competitiveness' (1998) 32 *Journal of World Trade* 5.

Evans, M. D., 'New Collaborations for International Development: Corporate Social Responsibility and Beyond' (2007) 62 *International Journal* 311.

Eyreman, R. and Jamison, A., *Social Movements: A Cognitive Approach* (Pennsylvania State University Press, 1991).

Fachiri, A. P., 'Expropriation and International Law' (1925) 6 *British Year Book of International Law* 159.

Fairfax, L. M., 'Easier Said Than Done? A Corporate Law Theory for Actualizing Social Responsibility Rhetoric' (2007) 59 *Florida Law Review* 771.

'Making the Corporation Safe for Shareholder Democracy' (2008) 69 *Ohio State Law Journal* 53.

Farer, T. J., 'The United States and the Third World: A Basis for Accommodation' (1975) 54 *Foreign Affairs* 83.

Fatouros, A. A., 'International Law and the Third World' (1964) 50 *Virginia Law Review* 783.

'International Law and the Internationalized Contract' (1980) 74 *The American Journal of International Law* 134.

Feller, A. H., 'Some Observations on the Calvo Clause' (1933) 27 *The American Journal of International Law* 461.

Ferguson Jr., C. C., 'The Politics of the New International Economic Order' (1977) 32 *Proceedings of the Academy of Political Science* 142.

Ferrey, S., 'The New Power Generation: Environmental Law and Electricity Innovation: Why Electricity Matters, Developing States Matter, and Asia Matters Most of All' (2007) 15 *New York University Environmental Law Journal* 113.

Fershee, J. P., 'Changing Resources, Changing Market: The Impact of a National Renewable Portfolio Standard on the U.S. Energy Industry' (2008) 29 *Energy Law Journal* 49.

Fidler, D. P., 'A Kinder, Gentler System of Capitulations? International Law, Structural Adjustment Policies, and the Standard of Liberal, Globalized Civilization' (2000) 35 *Texas International Law Journal* 387.

'International Human Rights Law in Practice: The Return of the Standard of Civilization' (2001) 2 *Chicago Journal of International Law* 137.

Fieldhouse, D. K., *The Colonial Empires: A Comparative Survey from the Eighteenth Century* (London: Weidenfeld and Nicolson, 1966).

Finnemore, M. and Sikkink, K., 'International Norm Dynamics and Political Change' (1998) 52 *International Organization* 887.

Fischer, P., 'Historic Aspects of Concession Agreements' in Alexandrowicz, C. H., *Studies in the History of Nations* (The Hague: Martinus Nijhoff, 1972).

Fischer-Lescano, A. and Teubner, G., 'Diversity or Cacophony? New Sources of Norms in International Law Symposium: Regime-Collisions: The Vain Search for Legal Unity in the Fragmentation of Global Law' (2004) 25 *Michigan Journal of International Law* 999.

Fischer Williams, J., 'International Law and the Property of Aliens' (1928) 9 *British Year Book of International Law* 1.

Fishlow, A., 'Lessons from the Past: Capital Markets During the 19th Century and the Interwar Period' (1985) 39 *International Organization* 383.

Fishman, B. C., 'Binding Corporations to Human Rights norms through Public Law Settlement' (2006) 81 *New York University Law Review* 1433.

Fitzmaurice, M., 'The Human Right to Water' 18 *Fordham Environmental Law Review* 537.

Fitzpatrick, P., 'Terminal Legality: Imperialism and the (De)composition of Law' in Kirkby, D. and Colebourne, C. (eds.), *Law, History, Colonialism: The Reach of Empire* (Manchester University Press, 2001).

Flannery, T. F., 'The Fate of Empire in Low- and High-Energy Ecosystems' in Griffiths, T. and Robin, L. (eds.), *Ecology and Empire: Environmental History of Settler Societies* (Edinburgh: Keele University Press, 1997).

Fletcher, I. C., Ono, T. and Roy, A., 'Justice for Bhopal' (2005) 91 *Radical History Review* 7.

Flickema, T. O., 'The Settlement of the Paraguayan–American Controversy of 1859: A Reappraisal' (1968) 25(1) *The Americas* 49.

'Sam Ward's Bargain: A Tentative Reconsideration' (1970) 50 *The Hispanic American Historical Review* 538.

Flory, M., 'Adapting International Law to the Development of the Third World' (1982) 26 *Journal of African Law* 12.

Foighel, I., *Nationalization: A Study in the Protection of Alien Property in International Law* (London: Stevens & Sons Limited, 1957, reprinted 1982).

Nationalization and Compensation (London: Steven and Sons, 1964).

Forster, M., 'Environmental Responsibilities of Transnational Companies' in Heng, L. L., et al. (eds.), *Current Legal Issues in the Internationalization of Business Enterprises* (Singapore: Butterworths, 1996).

Fox, J. A. and Brown, L. D. (eds.), *The Struggle for Accountability: The World Bank, NGOs, and Grassroots Movements* (MIT Press, 1998).

Francioni, F., 'Compensation for Nationalisation and Foreign Property: The Borderland Between Law and Equity' (1975) 24 *International and Comparative Law Quarterly* 255.

Franck, S. D., 'The Legitimacy Crisis in Investment Law and Arbitration: Privatising Public International Law through Inconsistent Decisions' (2005) 73 *Fordham Law Review* 1521.

'Foreign Direct Investment, Investment Treaty Arbitration and the Rule of Law' (2006) 19 *Pacific McGeorge Global Business and Development Law Journal* 337.

'Integrating Investment Treaty Conflict and Dispute System Design' (2007) 92 *Minnesota Law Review* 161.

'Development and Outcomes of Investment Treaty Arbitration' (2009) 50(2) *Harvard International Law Journal* 435.

Freeman, A. V., 'Recent Aspects of the Calvo Doctrine and the Challenge of International Law' (1946) 40 *The American Journal of International Law* 121.

Freeman, J., 'The Private Role in Public Governance' (2000) 75 *New York University Law Review* 543.

Freestone, D. and Streck, C., 'Introduction - The Challenges of Implementing the Kyoto Mechanisms' (2007) 2 *Environmental Liability* 47.

French, D., 'Treaty Interpretation and the Incorporation of Extraneous Legal Rules' (2006) 55 *International and Comparative Law Quarterly* 281.

Frieden, J. A., 'International Investment and Colonial Control: A New Interpretation' (1994) 48(4) *International Organization* 559.

Friedman, M., *Capitalism and Freedom* (University of Chicago Press, 1962).

Friedmann, W., 'The Changing Dimensions of International Law' (1962) 62 *Columbia Law Review* 1147.

Fry, E., *The Politics of International Investment* (New York: McGraw-Hill, 1983).

Fry, J. D., 'International Human Rights Law in Investment Arbitration: Evidence of International Law's Unity' (2007) 17 *Duke Journal of Comparative & International Law* 77.

Gaastra, F. S., 'Competition or Collaboration? Relations between the Dutch East India Company and Indian Merchants around 1680' in Chaudhury, S. and Morineau, M. (eds.), *Merchants, Companies and Trade: Europe and Asia in the Early Modern Era* (Cambridge University Press, 1999).

Gaines, S. E., 'Methanex Corp. v. United States' (2006) 100 *The American Journal of International Law* 683.

Gall, H., 'An Introduction to Indonesian Legal History' (1996) *Journal of South African Law* 116.

Gallagher, J. and Robinson, R., 'The Imperialism of Free Trade' (1953) 6 *Economic History Review* 1.

Gallagher, K. P. and Zarsky, L., 'No Miracle Drug: Foreign Direct Investment and Sustainable Development' in Zarsky, L. (ed.) *International Investment for Sustainable Development: Balancing Rights and Rewards* (London: Earthscan, 2005).

Gal-Or, N., 'The Concept of Appeal in International Dispute Settlement' (2008) 19(1) *European Journal of International Law* 43.

Gantz, D. A., 'An Appellate Mechanism for Review of Arbitral Decisions in Investor–state Disputes: Prospects and Challenges' (2006) 39 *Vanderbilt Journal of Transnational Law* 39.

Garcia, C. G., 'All the Other Dirty Little Secrets: Investment Treaties, Latin America, and the Necessary Evil of Investor–state Arbitration' (2004) 16 *Florida Journal of International Law* 301.

Garcia, F., 'Globalization and the Theory of International Law' (2005) 11 *International Legal Theory* 9.

Gathii, J. T., 'The Limits of the New International Rule of Law on Good Governance', in Quashigah, E. F. and Okafor, O. C. (eds.), *Legitimate Governance in Africa: International and Domestic Legal Perspectives* (The Hague: Kluwer Law International, 1999).

'Good Governance as a Counter Insurgency Agenda to Oppositional and Transformative Social Projects in International Law' (1999) 5 *Buffalo Human Rights Law Review* 107.

'Neoliberalism, Colonialism and International Governance: Decentering the International Law of Governmental Legitimacy' (2000) 98 *Michigan Law Review* 1996.

'Imperialism, Colonialism, and International Law' (2007) 54 *Buffalo Law Review* 1013.

'Third World Approaches to International Economic Governance' in Falk, R., Rajagopal, B. and Stevens, J. (eds.), *International Law and the Third World: Reshaping Justice* (New York: Routledge-Cavendish, 2008).

Geiger, R., 'Regulatory Expropriations in International Law: Lessons from the Multilateral Agreement on Investment' (2002) 11 *New York University Environmental Law Journal* 94.

Gentry, B., 'Foreign Direct Investment and the Environment: Boon or Bane?' in OECD, *Foreign Direct Investment and the Environment* (Paris: OECD Publishing, 1999).

Gentry, B. S. and Ronk, J., 'International Investment Agreements and Investments in Renewable Energy' in Parker, L., Ronk, J., Gentry, B., *From Barriers to Opportunities: Renewable Energy Issues in Law and Policy* (New Haven: Yale School of Forestry and Environmental Studies, 2007).

Gess, K. N., 'Permanent Sovereignty Over Natural Resources: An Analytical Review of the United Nations Declaration and its Genesis' (1964) 13 *International and Comparative Law Quarterly* 398.

Ghoshray, S., 'Searching for Human Rights to Water Amidst Corporate Privatisation in India: Hindustan Coca-Cola Pvt Ltd v. Perumatty Grama Panchayat' 19 *Georgetown International Environmental Law Review* 643.

Gifford, J., 'Measuring the Social, Environmental and Ethical Performance of Pension Funds' (2004) 53 *Journal of Australian Political Economy* 139.

Gill, A., 'Corporate Governance as Social Responsibility: A Research Agenda' (2008) 26 *Berkeley Journal of International Law* 452.

Gioseffi, S., 'Corporate Accountability: Achieving Internal Self-Governance Through Sustainability Reports' (2004) 13 *Cornell Journal of Law and Public Policy* 503.

Glass Geltman, E. and Skvoback, A. E., 'Environmental Law and Business in the 21st Century: Environmental Activism and the Ethical Investor' (1997) 22 *Iowa Journal of Corporation Law* 465.

Gledhill, J., 'Agrarian Social Movements and Forms of Consciousness' (1988) 7 *Bulletin of Latin American Research* 257.

Goodin, R. E., *Green Political Theory* (Oxford: Polity Press, 1992).

Green, A., 'Climate Change, Regulatory Policy and the WTO: How Constraining Are Trade Rules?' (2005) 8 *Journal of International Economic Law* 143.

Gross, S. G., 'Inordinate Chill: BITs, Non-NAFTA MITs, and Host-State Regulatory Freedom: An Indonesian Case Study' (2003) 24:3 *Michigan Journal of International Law* 893.

Grove, R., 'Conserving Eden: The (European) East India Companies and their Environmental Policies on St Helena and in Western India, 1660 to 1854' (1993) 35:2 *Comparative Studies in Society and History* 318.

Green Imperialism: Colonial Expansion, Tropical Island Edens and the Origins of Environmentalism, 1600–1860 (Cambridge University Press, 1995).

'Scotland in South Africa: John Croumbie Brown and the Roots of Settler Environmentalism' in Griffiths, T. and Robin, L. (eds.), *Ecology and Empire: Environmental History of Settler Societies* (Edinburgh: Keele University Press, 1997).

Gruchalla-Wesierski, T., 'A Framework for Understanding Soft Law' (1984) 30 *McGill Law Journal* 37.

Guay T., et al., 'Non-governmental Organizations, Shareholder Activism, and Socially Responsible Investments: Ethical, Strategic and Governance Implications' (2004) 52 *Journal of Business Ethics* 125.

Guha, R., *The Unquiet Woods: Ecological Change and Peasant Resistance in the Himalaya* (Oxford University Press, 1989).

Guha, R. and Martinez-Alier, J., *Varieties of Environmentalism: Essays North and South* (London: Earthscan, 1997).

Gunning, I. R., 'Modernizing Customary International Law: The Challenge of Human Rights' (1991) 31 *Virginia Journal of International Law* 211.

Gunningham, N., 'Corporate Environmental Responsibility: Law and the Limits of Voluntarism' in McBarnet, D., Voiculescu, A. and Campbell, T. (eds.), *The New Corporate Accountability: Corporate Social Responsibility and the Law* (Cambridge University Press, 2007).

Gunningham, N., Kagan, R. A. and Thornton, D., *Shades of Green: Business, Regulation and Environment* (Stanford University Press, 2003).

Guzman, A. T., 'Why LDCs Sign Treaties That Hurt Them: Explaining the Popularity of Bilateral Investment Treaties' (1998) 38 *Virginia Journal of International Law* 639.

'A Compliance-Based Theory of International Law' (2002) 90 *California Law Review* 1823.

Guzy, G. S., 'Reconciling Environmentalist and Industry Differences: The New Corporate Citizenship "Race to the Top"?' (2002) 17 *Journal of Land Use and Environmental Law* 409.

Haas, P., 'Epistemic Communities' in Bodansky, D., Brunnée, J. and Hey, E. (eds.), *The Oxford Handbook of International Environmental Law* (Oxford University Press, 2007).

Habermas, J., 'New Social Movements' (1981) 49 *Telos* 33.

Hackworth, G., *Digest of International Law* (Washington: Government Printing Office).

Haigh, M. and Hazelton, J., 'Financial Markets: A Tool for Social Responsibility?' (2004) 52 *Journal of Business Ethics* 59.

Hammond, R. J., 'Economic Imperialism: Sidelights on a Stereotype' (1961) 21 *The Journal of Economic History* 582.

Handl, G., 'The Legal Mandate of Multilateral Development Banks as Agents for Change Toward Sustainable Development' (1998) 92 *American Journal of International Law* 642.

Hardenbrook, A., 'The Equator Principles: The Private Financial Sector's Attempt at Environmental Responsibility' (2007) 40 *Vanderbilt Journal of Transnational Law* 197.

Harvey, D., 'Neoliberalism as Creative Destruction' (2007) 610 *The Annals of the American Academy of Political and Social Science* 22.

Headick, D. R., *The Tools of Empire: Technology and European Imperialism in the Nineteenth Century* (Oxford University Press, 1981).

Heinkel, R., Kraus, A. and Zechner, J., 'The Effect of Green Investment on Corporate Behavior' (2001) 36 *The Journal of Financial and Quantitative Analysis* 431.

Henley, D., 'Conflict, Justice, and the Stranger–King Indigenous Roots of Colonial Rule in Indonesia and Elsewhere' (2004) 38 *Modern Asian Studies* 85.

Henshaw, P., 'The "Key to South Africa" in the 1890s: Delagoa Bay and the Origins of the South African War' (1998) 24:3 *Journal of Southern African Studies* 527.

Herrick, K., 'The Merger of Two Systems: Chinese Adoption and Western Adaptation in the Formation of Modern International Law' (2004) 33 *Georgia Journal of International and Comparative Law* 685.

Hershey, A. S., 'The Venezuelan Affair in Light of International Law' (1903) 51 *The American Law Register, University of Pennsylvania Law Review* 249.

'The Calvo and Drago Doctrines' (1907) 1 *The American Journal of International Law* 26.

Herz, J. H., 'Expropriation of Foreign Property' (1941) 2 *The American Journal of International Law* 243.

Herz, R. L., 'Litigating Environmental Abuses Under the Alien Tort Act: A Practical Assessment', (2000) 40 *Virginia Journal of International Law* 545.

Hess, D., 'Social Reporting: A Reflexive Law Approach to Corporate Social Responsiveness' (1999) 25 *Iowa Journal of Corporation Law* 41.

Heyman, M. C. E., 'International Law and the Settlement of Investment Disputes Relating to China' (2008) 11(3) *Journal of International Economic Law* 507.

Higgins, R., 'International Law in a Changing International System' (1999) 58:1 *Cambridge Law Journal* 78.

'Natural Resources in the Case Law of the International Court' in Boyle, A. E. and Freestone, D. (eds.), *International Law and Sustainable Development: Past Achievements and Future Challenges* (Oxford University Press, 1999).

Hilson, G., 'An Overview of Land Use Conflicts in Mining Communities' (2002) 19 *Land Use Policy* 65.

Hirsch, M., '*Interactions between Investment and Non-Investment Obligations in International Investment Law*' in Muchlinski, P., Ortino, F. and Schreuer, C. (eds.), (Oxford University Press, 2008).

Hobb, S., 'Global Challenges to Statehood: The Increasingly Important Role of Nongovernmental Organizations' (1997) 5 *Indiana Journal of Global Legal Studies* 191.

Hockets, K. and Moir, L., 'Communicating Corporate Responsibility to Investors: The Changing Role of the Investor Relations Function' (2004) 52 *Journal of Business Ethics* 85.

Hollis, D. B., 'Private Actors in Public International Law: Amicus Curiae and the Case for Retention of State Sovereignty' (2002) 25 *Boston College International and Comparative Law Review* 235.

Holtzmann, H. H., 'A Task for the 21st Century: Creating a New International Court for Resolving Disputes on the Enforceability of Arbitral Awards' in Hunter, M., Marriott, A. L. and Veeder, V. V. (eds.), *Internationalization of International Arbitration: The LCIA Centenary* (London: Martinus Nijhoff Publishers, 1995).

Holwick, S., 'Transnational Corporate Behaviour and its Disparate and Unjust Effects on the Indigenous Cultures and the Environment of Developing Nations: *Jota* v. *Texaco*, a Case Study' (2000) 11 *Colorado Journal of International Environmental Law and Policy* 183.

Hood, M., *Gunboat Diplomacy 1895–1905: Great Power Pressure in Venezuela* (London: Allen & Unwin, 1975).

Hopkins, A. G., 'Informal Empire in Argentina: An Alternative View' (1994) 26 *Journal of Latin American Studies* 469.

Hornsey, G., 'Foreign Investment and International Law' (1950) 3 *The International Law Quarterly* 552.

Houck, O. A., 'Light from the Trees: The Stories of Minors Oposa and the Russian Forest Cases' (2007) 19 *Georgetown International Environmental Law Review* 321.

Howell, R., 'Globalization and the Good Corporation: Whither Socially Responsible Investment?' (2008) 27 *Human Systems Management* 243.

Howse, R., 'The Appellate Body Rulings in the Shrimp/Turtle Case: A New Legal Baseline for the Trade and Environment Debate' (2002) 27 *Columbia Journal of Environmental Law* 491.

Hsia, S., 'Foreign Direct Investment and the Environment: Are Voluntary Codes of Conduct and Self-Imposed Standards Enough?' (2003) 9 *Environmental Law* 673.

Huang, T. F. T., 'Some International and Legal Aspects of the Suez Canal Question' (1957) 51 *The American Journal of International Law* 277.

Hummels, H. and Timmer, D., 'Investors in Need of Social, Ethical, and Environmental Information' (2004) 52 *Journal of Business Ethics* 73.

Hunter, D., 'Using the World Bank Inspection Panel to Defend the Interests of Project-Affected People' (2003) 4 *Chicago Journal of International Law* 201.

'Civil Society Networks and the Development of Environmental Standards at International Financial Institutions' (2008) 8 *Chicago Journal of International Law* 437.

Hunter, D., Salzman, J. and Zaelke, D., *International Environmental Law and Policy*, 2nd edn, (New York: Foundation Press, 2002).

Hurrell, A. and Kingsbury, B., 'The International Politics of the Environment: An Introduction' in Hurrell, A. and Kingsbury, B. (eds.), *The International Politics of the Environment: Actors, Interests and Institutions* (Oxford University Press, 1992).

Hyndman, D., 'Academic Responsibilities and Representation of the Ok Tedi Crisis in Postcolonial Papua New Guinea' (2001) 13:1 *The Contemporary Pacific* 33.

Ignatow, G., *Transnational Identity Politics and the Environment* (Lanham, MA: Lexington Books, 2007).

Inter-American Bar Association, 'Report of the Third Conference of the Inter-American Bar Association, August 1944' (1944) 26 *Journal of Comparative Legislation and International Law* 55.

Irwin, D., 'Mercantilism as Strategic Trade Policy: The Anglo-Dutch Rivalry for the East India Trade' (1991) 99:6 *The Journal of Political Economy*, 1296.

Jackson, K. T., 'Global Corporate Governance: Soft Law and Reputational Accountability' (2010) 35 *Brooklyn Journal of International Law* 41.

Jacobs, M., 'Sustainable Development as a Contested Concept' in Dobson, A. (ed.), *Fairness and Futurity: Essays on Environmental Sustainability and Social Justice* (Oxford University Press, 1999).

Jägers, N., 'Bringing Corporate Social Responsibility to the World Trade Organisation' in McBarnet, D. Voiculescu, A. and Campbell, T., *The New Corporate Accountability: Corporate Social Responsibility and the Law* (Cambridge University Press, 2007).

Jamieson, D., 'Justice: The Heart of Environmentalism' in Sandler, R. and Pezzullo, P. C. (eds.), *Environmental Justice and Environmentalism: The Social Justice Challenge to the Environmental Movement* (MIT Press, 2007).

Jamison, A., *The Making of Green Knowledge: Environmental Politics and Cultural Transformation* (Cambridge University Press, 2001).

Jasanoff, S., 'Bhopal's Trials of Knowledge and Ignorance' (2007) 98 *Isis* 344.

Jessup, P. C., 'Non-Universal International Law' (1973) 12 *Columbia Journal of Transnational Law* 415.

Jeucken, M., *Sustainability in Finance: Banking on the Planet* (Delft: Eburon Publishers, 2004).

Johnson, L., 'Do the Good Guys Always Wear Green? An Analytical Framework to Evaluate Businesses' Relationships to the Natural Environment' (2008) 10 *Journal of Law & Social Challenges* 55.

Joubin-Bret, A., 'The Growing Diversity and Inconsistency in the IIA System' in Sauvant, K. P. (ed.), *Appeals Mechanism in International Investment Disputes* (2008).

Kahn, J. C., 'Striking NAFTA Gold: Glamis Advances Investor–State Arbitration' (2009) 33 *Fordham International Law Journal* 101.
Kameri-Mbote, A. P. and Cullet, P., 'Law, Colonialism and Environmental Management in Africa' (1997) 6(1) *Review of European Community and International Environmental Law* 23.
Kamijyo, M., 'The "Equator Principles": Improved Social Responsibility in the Private Finance Sector' (2004) 4 *Sustainable Development Law & Policy* 35.
Kaye, R., 'Transnational Environmental Litigation' (2007) 24 *Environmental Planning Law Journal* 35.
Keay, J., *The Honourable Company: A History of the English East India Company* (London: Harper Collins, 1991).
Keck, M. E. and Sikkink, K., *Activists Beyond Borders: Advocacy Networks in International Politics* (Ithaca: Cornell University Press, 1998).
Keenan, P. J., 'Financial Globalization and Human Rights' (2008) 46 *Columbia Journal of Transnational Law* 509.
Kell, G., 'The Global Compact: Selected Experiences and Reflections' (2005) 59:1 *Journal of Business Ethics* 69.
Kelley, G., 'Multilateral Investment Treaties: A Balanced Approach to Multinational Corporations' (2001) 39 *Columbia Journal of Transnational Law* 483.
Kelley, T., 'Law and Choice of Entity on the Social Enterprise Frontier' (2009) 84 *Tulane Law Review* 337.
Kelly, C. R., 'Power, Linkage and Accommodation: The WTO as an International Actor and its Influence on Other Actors and Regimes' (2006) 24 *Berkeley Journal of International Law* 79.
Kennedy, D., 'International Law and the Nineteenth Century: History of an Illusion' (1997) 17 *Quinnipiac Law Review* 99.
'The Disciplines of International Law and Policy' (1999) 12 *Leiden Journal of International Law* 9.
Kerr, J. E., 'The Creative Capitalism Spectrum: Evaluating Corporate Social Responsibility Through a Legal Lens' (2008) 81 *Temple Law Review* 831.
'A New Era of Responsibility: A Modern American Mandate for Corporate Social Responsibility' (2009) 78 *UMKC Law Review* 327.
Kibel, P. S. and Schutz, J. R., 'Rio Grande Designs: Texans' NAFTA Water Claim Against Mexico' (2007) 25 *Berkeley Journal of International Law* 228.
Kimerling, J., 'The Environmental Audit of Texaco's Amazon Oil Fields: Environmental Justice or Business as Usual?' (1994) 7 *Harvard Human Rights Journal* 199.
'Indigenous Peoples and the Oil Frontier in Amazonia: The Case of Ecuador, ChevronTexaco, and Aguinda v. Texco (2006) 38 *New York University Journal of International Law and Politics* 413.
'Transnational Operations, Bi-National Injustice: CheveronTexaco and Indigenous Huarani and Kichwa in the Amazon Rainforest in Ecuador' (2007) 31 *American Indian Law Review* 445.

Kingsbury, B., 'Global Environmental Governance as Administration: Implications for International Law' in Bodansky, D., Brunnée, J. and Hey, E. (eds.), *The Oxford Handbook of International Environmental Law* (Oxford University Press, 2007).

Kingsbury, B., Krisch, N. and Stewart, R. B., 'The Emergence of Global Administrative Law' (2005) 68 *Law & Contemporary Problems* 15.

Kingsbury, B., Krisch, N., Stewart, R. B. and Wiener, J. B., 'Global Governance as Administration – National and Transnational Approaches to Global Administrative Law' (2005) 68 *Law & Contemporary Problems* 1.

Kinley, D., 'Human Rights, Globalization and the Rule of Law: Friends, Foes or Family?' (2002) 7 *UCLA Journal of International Law and Foreign Affairs* 239.

Civilising Globalisation: Human Rights and the Global Economy (Cambridge University Press, 2009).

Kinley, D. and Chambers, R., 'The UN Human Rights Norms for Corporations: The Private Implications of Public International Law' (2006) 6(3) *Human Rights Law Review* 447.

Kinley, D. and Tadaki, J., 'From Talk to Walk: The Emergence of Human Rights Responsibilities for Corporations at International Law' (2004) 44 *Virginia Journal of International Law* 931.

Kinley, D., Nolan, J. and Zerial, N., '"The Norms are Dead! Long Live the Norms!" The Politics Behind the UN Human Rights Norms for Corporations' in McBarnet, D., Voiculescu, A. and Campbell, T. (eds.), *The New Corporate Accountability: Corporate Social Responsibility and the Law* (Cambridge University Press, 2007).

Kirkby, D. and Coleborne, C., 'Introduction' in Kirkby, D. and Colebourne, C. (eds.), *Law, History, Colonialism: The Reach of Empire* (Manchester University Press, 2001).

Knaap, G. J., 'A City of Migrants: Kota Ambon at the End of the Seventeenth Century' (1991) 51 *Indonesia* 105.

Knoll, M. S., 'Ethical Screening in Modern Financial Markets: The Conflicting Claims Underlying Socially Responsible Investment' (2002) 57 *The Business Lawyer* 681.

Koh, H. H., 'Review Essay: Why Do Nations Obey Law?' (1997) 106 *Yale Law Journal* 2599.

Koskenniemi, M., *The Gentle Civilizer of Nations: The Rise and Fall of International Law 1870–1960* (Cambridge University Press, 2002).

Krisch, N. and Kingsbury, B., 'Introduction: Global Governance and Global Administrative Law in the International Legal Order' 17(1) (2006) *The European Journal of International Law* 1.

Kronfol, Z., *Protection of Foreign Investment: A Study on International Law* (Leyden: A.W. Sijthoff, 1972).

Kulovesi, K., 'The Private Sector and the Implementation of the Kyoto Protocol: Experiences, Challenges and Prospects' (2007) 16:2 *Review of European Community and International Environmental Law* 145.

Kunz, J. L., 'The Mexican Expropriations' (1940) 5(1) *NYU School of Law Contemporary Pamphlets Series.*

Kuper, A., 'Harnessing Corporate Power: Lessons from the UN Global Compact' (2004) 47 *Development* 9.

Kysar, D. A., 'Sustainable Development and Private Global Governance' (2005) 83 *Texas Law Review* 2109.

Kyte, R., 'Balancing Rights with Responsibilities: Looking for the Global Drivers of Materiality in Corporate Social Responsibility and the Voluntary Initiatives that Develop and Support Them' (2008) *American University International Law Review* 559.

Lally, A. P., 'ISO 14000 and Environmental Cost Accounting: The Gateway to the Global Market' (1998) 29 *Law & Policy in International Business* 501.

Lang, A. T. F., 'Reflecting on "Linkage": Cognitive and Institutional Change in the International Trading System' (2007) 70 *The Modern Law Review* 523.

Langman, L., 'From Virtual Public Spheres to Global Justice: A Critical Theory of Internetworked Social Movements' (2005) 23 *Sociological Theory* 42.

Lapres, D. A., 'Principles of Compensation for Nationalised Property' (1977) 26 *International and Comparative Law Quarterly* 97.

Lawrence, J. C., 'Chicken Little Revisited: NAFTA Regulatory Expropriations After Methanex' (2006) 41 *Georgia Law Review* 261.

League of Nations, Committee of Experts for the Progressive Codification of International Law, 'Responsibility of States for Damage Done in their Territories to the Person or Property of Foreigners' (1926) 20(2) *The American Journal of International Law* 176.

Lee, D., 'The Growing Influence of Business in U.K. Diplomacy' (2004) 5 *International Studies Perspective* 50.

'Empire Rising: International Law and Imperial Japan' (2006) 23 *UCLA Pacific Basin Law Journal* 195.

Lee, V., 'Enforcing the Equator Principles: An NGO's Principled Effort to Stop the Financing of a Paper Pulp Mill in Uruguay' (2007) 6 *Northwestern University Journal of Human Rights* 354.

Legum, B., 'Options to Establish an Appellate Mechanism for Investment Disputes' in Sauvant, K. P. (ed.), *Appeals Mechanism in International Investment Disputes* (Oxford University Press, 2008).

Leopold, A., *A Sand County Almanac* (Oxford University Press, 1949).

Lev, D. S., 'Colonial Law and the Genesis of the Indonesian State' (1985) 40 *Indonesia* 57.

Likosky, M. B., *Law, Infrastructure, and Human Rights* (Cambridge University Press, 2006).

Lillich, R. B., 'The Diplomatic Protection of Nationals Abroad: An Elementary Principle of International Law Under Attack' (1975) 69 *The American Journal of International Law* 359.

'The Current Status of the Law of State Responsibility for Injuries to Aliens' in Lillich, R. B. (ed.), *International Law of State Responsibility for Injuries to Aliens* (Charlottesville: University Press of Virginia, 1983).

Lin, L., 'Corporate Social and Environmental Disclosure in Emerging Securities Markets' (2009) 35 *North Carolina Journal of International Law and Commercial Regulation* 1.

Lindley, M. F., *Acquisition and Government of Backward Territory in International Law* (London: Longmans, Green and Co., 1926).

Lipson, C., *Standing Guard: Protecting Foreign Capital in the Nineteenth and Twentieth Centuries* (University of California Press, 1985).

Lomborg, B., *The Skeptical Environmentalist: Measuring the Real State of the World* (Cambridge University Press, 2001).

Loth, V. C., 'Armed Incidents and Unpaid Bills: Anglo-Dutch Rivalry in the Banda Islands in the Seventeenth Century' (1995) 29 *Modern Asian Studies* 705.

Lowe, V., 'Sustainable Development and Unsustainable Arguments' in Boyle, A. and Freestone, D. (eds.), *International Law and Sustainable Development: Past Achievements and Future Challenges* (Oxford University Press, 1999).

Lowenthal, D., 'Empires and Ecologies: Reflections on Environmental History' in Griffiths, T. and Robin, L. (eds.), *Ecology and Empire: Environmental History of Settler Societies* (Edinburgh: Keele University Press, 1997).

Lowry, J., 'The Duty of Loyalty of Company Directors: Bridging the Accountability Gap Through Efficient Disclosure' (2009) 68 *Cambridge Law Journal* 607.

Lu, S., 'Corporate Codes of Conduct and the FTC: Advancing Human Rights through Deceptive Advertising Law' (2000) 38 *Columbia Journal of Transnational Law* 603.

Lyons, M. 'A Case Study in Multinational Corporate Accountability: Ecuador's Indigenous Peoples' Struggle for Redress' (2004) 32 *Denver Journal of International Law and Policy* 701.

MacKenzie, J. M., 'Empire and the Ecological Apocalypse: the Historiography of the Imperial Environment' in Griffiths, T. and Robin, L. (eds.), *Ecology and Empire: Environmental History of Settler Societies* (Edinburgh: Keele University Press, 1997).

Macleod, S., 'Corporate Social Responsibility within the European Union Framework' (2005) 23 *Wisconsin International Law Journal* 541.

Malanczuk, P., *Akehurst's Modern International Law*, 7th edn, (New York: Routledge, 1997).

Maniruzzaman, A. F. M., 'The Pursuit of Stability in International Energy Investment Contracts: A Critical Appraisal of the Emerging Trends' (2008) 1 *Journal of World Energy Law & Business* 121.

Maogoto, J. N. and Kindiki, K., 'A People Betrayed – The Darfur Crisis and International Law: Rethinking Westphalian Sovereignty in the 21st Century' (2007) 19 *Bond Law Review* 102.

Mares, R., 'Transnational Corporate Responsibility for the 21st Century: Defining the Limits of Corporate Responsibilities Against the Concept of Legal Positive Obligations' (2009) 40 *George Washington International Law Review* 1157.

Marks, S., 'Naming Global Administrative Law' (2005) 37 *New York University Journal of International Law and Politics* 995.

Marong, A. B., 'From Rio to Johannesburg: Reflections on the Role of International Legal Norms in Sustainable Development' (2003) 16 *Georgetown International Environmental Law Review* 21.

Martin, M., 'Trade Law Implications of Restricting Participation in the European Union Emissions Trading Scheme' (2007) 19 *Georgetown International Environmental Law Review* 437.

Martinez-Alier, J., *The Environmentalism of the Poor: A Study of Ecological Conflicts and Valuation* (Northampton: Edward Elgar, 2002).

Mathew, W. M., 'The Imperialism of Free Trade: Peru, 1820–1870' (1968) 21 *The Economic History Review* 562.

Mathur, C. and Morehouse, W., 'Twice Poisoned Bhopal: Notes on the Continuing Aftermath of the World's Worst Industrial Disaster' (2002) 62 *International Labour and Working-Class History* 69.

Mayer, P., 'Reflections on the International Arbitrator's Duty to Apply the Law: The 2000 Freshfields Lecture' (2001) 17(3) *Arbitration International* 235.

McBarnet, D., 'Corporate Social Responsibility Beyond Law, Through Law, For Law: The New Corporate Accountability' in McBarnet, D., Voiculescu, A. and Campbell, T. (eds.), *The New Corporate Accountability: Corporate Social Responsibility and the Law* (Cambridge University Press, 2007).

McConvill, J. and Joy, M., 'The Interaction of Directors' Duties and Sustainable Development in Australia: Setting Off on the Uncharted Road' (2003) 27 *Melbourne University Law Review* 116.

McCormick, J., *The Global Environmental Movement: Reclaiming Paradise* (London: Belhaven, 1989).

McCormick, J., 'The Role of Environmental NGOs in International Regimes' in Axelrod, R. S., Leonard Downie, D. and Vig, N. J. (eds.), *The Global Environment: Institutions, Law, and Policy*, 2nd edn (Washington, CQ Press, 2005).

McCorquodale, R., 'Human Rights and Global Business' in Bottomley, S. and Kinley, D. (eds.), *Commercial Law and Human Rights* (Aldershot: Ashgate-Dartmouth, 2002).

McCorquodale, R. and Simons, P., 'Responsibility Beyond Borders: State Responsibility for Extraterritorial Violations by Corporations of International Human Rights Law' (2007) 70 *Modern Law Review* 598.

McDonald, J., 'The Multilateral Agreement on Investment: Heyday or Mai-Day for Ecologically Sustainable Development?' (1998) 22 *Melbourne University Law Review* 617.

McFarland Sanchez-Moreno, M. and Higgins, T., 'No Recourse: Transnational Corporations and the Protection of Economic, Social, and Cultural Rights in Bolivia' (2004) 27 *Fordham International Law Journal* 1663.

McGowan, P. J. and Kordan, B., 'Imperialism in World-System Perspective: Britain 1870–1914' (1981) 25 *International Studies Quarterly* 43.

McIlroy, J., 'Canada's New Foreign Investment Protection and Promotion Agreement: Two Steps Forward, One Step back?' (2004) 5 *The Journal of World Investment & Trade* 621.

McInerney, T., 'Putting Regulation Before Responsibility: Towards Binding Norms of Corporate Social Responsibility' (2007) 40 *Cornell International Law Journal* 171.

McLachlan, C., 'The Principle of Systemic Integration and Article 31(3)(c) of the Vienna Convention' (2005) 54 *International and Comparative Law Quarterly* 279.

'Investment Treaties and General International Law' (2008) 57 *International and Comparative Law Quarterly* 361.

McLachlan, C., Shore, L. and Weiniger, M., *International Investment Arbitration: Substantive Principles* (Oxford University Press, 2007).

McLean, J., 'The Transnational Corporation in History: Lessons for Today?' (2004) 79 *Indiana Law Journal* 363.

McNair, Lord A., 'The General Principles of Law Recognized by Civilised Nations' (1957) 33 *British Yearbook of International Law* 1.

Meadows, D., et al., *Limits to Growth* (New York: Universe Books, 1972).

Melville, E. G. K., 'Global Developments and Latin American Environments' in Griffiths, T. and Robin, L. (eds.), *Ecology and Empire: Environmental History of Settler Societies* (Edinburgh: Keele University Press, 1997).

Mercier, A., 'Commercial Diplomacy in Advanced Industrial States: Canada, the UK, and the US' (2007) No. 108 *Discussion Papers in Diplomacy*, The Hague, The Netherlands Institute of International Relations 'Clingendael'.

Meron, T., 'The Continuing Role of Custom in the Formation of International Humanitarian Law' (1996) 90 *American Journal of International Law* 238.

Mertus, J., 'Doing Democracy Differently: The Transformative Potential of Human Rights NGOs in Transnational Civil Society' (1998) *Third World Legal Studies* 205.

'Considering Nonstate Actors in the New Millennium: Toward Expanded Participation in Norm Generation and Norm Application' (2000) 32 *New York University Journal of International Law and Politics* 537.

Meyer, W. H. and Stefanova, B., 'Human Rights, the UN Global Compact, and Global Governance' (2001) 34 *Cornell International Law Journal* 501.

Mickelson, K., 'Rhetoric and Rage: Third World Voices in International Legal Discourse' (1998) 16 *Wisconsin International Law Journal* 353.

'Critical Approaches' in Bodansky, D., Brunnée, J. and Hey, E. (eds.), *The Oxford Handbook of International Environmental Law* (Oxford University Press, 2007).

Milanovic, M., 'Norm Conflict in International Law: Whither Human Rights?' (2009) 20 *Duke Journal of Comparative & International Law* 69.

Miles, K., 'Targeting Financiers: Can Voluntary Codes of Conduct for the Investment and Financing Sectors Achieve Environmental and Sustainability Objectives?' in Deketelaere, K., et al. (eds.), *Critical Issues in Environmental Taxation*, vol. 5 (Oxford University Press, 2008).

'Sustainable Development, National Treatment and Like Circumstances in Investment Law' in Cordonier Segger, M., Gehring, M. and Newcombe, A.

(eds.), *Sustainable Development in International Investment Law* (Dordrecht: Kluwer Law International, 2010).
Miller, W., 'The Finlay Papers' (1924) 39 *The English Historical Review* 386.
Mittelman, J. H., 'Globalisation and Environmental Resistance Politics' (1998) 19 *Third World Quarterly* 847.
Missbach, A., 'The Equator Principles: Drawing the Line for Socially Responsible Banks? An Interim Review from an NGO Perspective' (2004) 47 *Development* 78.
Monsma, D. and Buckley, J., 'Non-Financial Corporate Performance: The Material Edges of Social and Environmental Disclosure' (2004) 11 *University of Baltimore Journal of Environmental Law* 151.
Monsma, D. and Olsen, T., 'Muddling Through Counterfactual Materiality and Divergent Disclosure: The Necessary Search for a Duty to Disclose Material Non-Financial Information' (2007) 26 *Stanford Environmental Law Journal* 137.
Moore, J. B., A History and Digest of the International Arbitrations to which the United States has been a Party (Washington: Government Printing Office, 1898).
A Digest of International Law: as embodied in diplomatic discussions, treaties and other international agreements, international awards, the decisions of municipal courts, and the writings of jurists (1906).
Moore Dickerson, C., 'How Do Norms and Empathy Affect Corporation Law and Corporate Behavior? Human Rights: The Emerging Norm of Corporate Social Responsibility' (2002) 76 *Tulane Law Review* 1431.
Morgera, E., 'The UN and Corporate Environmental Responsibility: Between International Regulation and Partnerships' (2006) 15(1) *Review of European Community and International Environmental Law* 93.
'Significant Trends in Corporate Environmental Accountability: The New Performance Standards of the International Finance Corporation' (2007) 18 *Colorado Journal of International Environmental Law* 151.
Morvay, W., 'Unequal Treaties' in Bernhardt, R. *Encyclopedia of Public International Law* (1992–2002).
Muchlinski, P. T., 'The Bhopal Case: Controlling Ultrahazardous Industrial Activities Undertaken by Foreign Investors' (1987) 50(5) *The Modern Law Review* 545.
'Towards a Multilateral Investment Agreement (MAI): The OECD and WTO Models and Sustainable Development' in Weiss, F., Dentes, E. and De Waart, P. (eds.), *International Economic Law with a Human Face* (The Hague: Kluwer Law International, 1998).
'International Business Regulation: An Ethical Discourse in the Making?' in Campbell, T. and Miller, S. (eds.), *Human Rights and the Moral Responsibilities of Corporate and Public Sector Organisations* (The Hague: Kluwer Law International, 2004).
'"Caveat Investor"? The Relevance of the Conduct of the Investor under the Fair and Equitable Treatment Standard' (2006) 55 *International and Comparative Law Quarterly* 527.
Multinational Enterprises and the Law, 2nd edn (Oxford University Press, 2007).

'Corporate Social Responsibility and International Law: The Case of Human Rights and Multinational Enterprises' in McBarnet, D., Voiculescu, A. and Campbell, T. (eds.), *The New Corporate Accountability: Corporate Social Responsibility and the Law* (Cambridge University Press, 2007).

'Corporate Social Responsibility' in Muchlinksi, P., Ortino, F. and Schreuer, C. (eds.), *The Oxford Handbook of International Investment Law* (Oxford University Press, 2008).

Murali, A., 'Whose Trees? Forest Practices and Local Communities in Andhra, 1600–1922' in Arnold, D. and Guha, R. (eds.), *Nature, Culture, Imperialism: Essays on the Environmental History of South Asia* (Oxford University Press, 1995).

Murphy, S. D., 'Taking Multinational Corporate Codes of Conduct to the Next Level' (2005) 43 *Columbia Journal of Transnational Law* 389.

Najam, A., 'World Business Council for Sustainable Development: The Greening of Business or a Greenwash?' (1999–2000) *Yearbook of International Co-operation on Environment and Development* 65.

Narula, S., 'The Right to Food: Holding Global Actors Accountable Under International Law' (2006) 44 *Columbia Journal of Transnational Law* 691.

Nash, J., 'Interpreting Social Movements: Bolivian Resistance to Economic Conditions Imposed by the International Monetary Fund' (1992) 19 *American Ethnologist* 275.

Nash, J. and Ehrenfeld, J., 'Code Green: Business Adopts Voluntary Environmental Standards' (1996) 38 *Environment* 16.

'Codes of Environmental Management Practice: Assessing Their Potential as a Tool for Change' (1997) 22 *Annual Review of Energy and the Environment* 487.

Neal, A. C., 'Corporate Social Responsibility: Governance Gain or Laissez-Faire Fig Leaf?' (2008) 29 *Comparative Labor Law & Policy Journal* 459.

Neal, L., 'The Dutch and English East India Companies Compared: Evidence from the Stock and Foreign Exchange Markets' in Tracey, J. D. (ed.), *The Rise of Merchant Empires: Long-Distance Trade in the Early Modern World 1350–1750* (Cambridge University Press, 1990).

Neufeld, H., *The International Protection of Private Creditors from the Treaties of Westphalia to the Congress of Vienna (1648–1815)* (Leyden: A. W. Sijthoff, 1971).

Neumayer, E., *Greening Trade and Investment: Environmental Protection without Protectionism* (London: Earthscan, 2001).

Neumayer, E. and Spess, L., 'Do Bilateral Investment Treaties Increase Foreign Direct Investment to Developing Countries?' (2005) 33(10) *World Development* 1567.

Newberg, J. A., 'Corporate Codes of Ethics, Mandatory Disclosure, and the Market for Ethical Conduct' (2005) 29 *Vermont Law Review* 253.

Newcombe, A., 'Sustainable Development and Investment Treaty Law' (2007) 8 *The Journal of World Investment & Trade* 357.

Newcombe, A. and Paradell, L., *Law and Practice of Investment Treaties: Standards of Treatment* (The Hague: Kluwer Law International, 2009).

Ngugi, J., 'The Decolonization-Modernization Interface and the Plight of Indigenous Peoples in Post-Colonial Development Discourse in Africa' (2002) 20 *Wisconsin International Law Journal* 297.

'Forgetting Lochner in the Journey from Plan to Market: The Framing Effect of the Market Rhetoric in Market-Oriented Reforms' (2008) 56 *Buffalo Law Review* 1.

Nieuwenhuys, E., 'Global Development through International Investment Law: Lessons Learned for the MAI' in Schrijver, N. and Weiss, F. (eds.), *International Law and Sustainable Development: Principles and Practice* (Leiden: Martinus Nijhoff Publishers, 2004).

Nolan, J., 'The United Nations' Compact with Business: Hindering or Helping the Protection of Human Rights?' (2005) 24 *University of Queensland Law Journal* 445.

'With Power Comes Responsibility: Human Rights and Corporate Accountability' (2005) 28(3) *University of New South Wales Law Journal* 581.

Norlen, D. and Gordon, D., 'Eschrichtus (Whale) and Hucho (Salmon): Multilateral Development Banks' EIA Process and the Costs to Biodiversity' (2007) 22 *Natural Resources & Environment* 30.

Northrop, S. A., 'Exporting Environmental Justice by Importing Claimants: The Suitability and Feasibility of the Globalization of Mass Tort Actions' (2006) 18 *Georgetown International Environmental Law Review* 779.

Norton, P. M., 'A Law of the Future or a Law of the Past? Modern Tribunals and the International Law of Expropriation' (1991) 85 *American Journal of International Law* 474.

O'Brien Hylton, M., '"Socially Responsible" Investing: Doing Good Versus Doing Well in an Inefficient Market' (1992) 42 *American University Law Review* 1.

Odum, H., *Environment, Power and Society* (New York: Wiley-Interscience, 1971).

Odumosu, I. T., 'The Law and Politics of Engaging Resistance in Investment Dispute Settlement' (2007) 26 *Penn State International Law Review* 251.

OECD, *Foreign Direct Investment, Development and Corporate Responsibility* (Paris: OECD Publishing, 2000).

OECD, *Corporate Responsibility: Private Initiatives and Public Goals* (Paris: OECD Publishing, 2001).

Ofodile, U. E., 'Trade, Empires and Subjects – China–Africa Trade: A New Fair Trade Arrangement, or the Third Scramble for Africa' (2008) 41 *Vanderbilt Journal of Transnational Law* 505.

Okafor, O. C., 'Poverty, Agency and Resistance in the Future of International Law: An African Perspective' in Falk, R., Rajagopal, B. and Stevens, J. (eds.), *International Law and the Third World: Reshaping Justice* (New York: Routledge-Cavendish, 2008).

Oloka-Onyango, J., 'Beyond the Rhetoric: Reinvigorating the Struggle for Economic and Social Rights in Africa' (1995) 26 *California Western International Law Journal* 1.

Omvedt, G., *Reinventing Revolution: New Social Movements and the Socialist Tradition in India* (New York, M. E. Sharpe, 1993).

Oppenheim, L., *International Law: A Treatise* (1905–1906).
International Law, 3rd edn, (1920).
O'Riordan, T., *Environmentalism*, 2nd edn, (London: Pion Press, 1981).
'Converting the Equator Principles to Equator Stewardship' (2005) 47 *Environment* 1.
Ormrod, D., *The Rise of Commercial Empires: England and the Netherlands in the Age of Mercantilism, 1650–1770* (Cambridge University Press, 2003).
Orrega Vicuña, F., 'Carlos Calvo, Honorary NAFTA Citizen' (2002) 11 *New York University Environmental Law Journal* 19.
Orts, E. W., 'Reflexive Environmental Law' (1995) 89 *Northwestern University Law Review* 1227.
O'Sullivan, N. and O'Dwyer, B., 'Stakeholder Perspectives on a Financial Sector Legitimation Process: The Case of NGOs and the Equator Principles' (2009) 22 *Accounting, Auditing and Accountability Journal* 553.
Ott, D. H., 'Bhopal and the Law: The Shape of a New International Legal Regime' (1987) 7(3) *Third World Quarterly* 648.
Otto, D., 'Subalternity and International Law: The Problems of Global Community and the Incommensurability of Difference' (1996) 5 *Social and Legal Studies* 337.
Pauwelyn, J., *Conflict of Norms in Public International Law: How WTO Law Relates to Other Rules of International Law* (Cambridge University Press, 2003).
Pahuja, S., 'Comparative Visions of Global Order (Part 1): The Postcoloniality of International Law' (2005) 46 *Harvard International Law Journal* 459.
Decolonising International Law: Development, Economic Growth and the Politics of Universality (Cambridge University Press, 2011).
Palmer, G., 'New Ways to Make International Environmental Law' (1992) 86 *American Journal of International Law* 259.
Pannatier, S. and Ducrey, O., 'Water Concessions and Protection of Foreign Investments under International Law' in Brown Weiss, E., Boisson de Chazournes, L. and Bernasconi-Osterwalder, N. (eds.), *Fresh Water and International Economic Law* (Oxford University Press, 2005).
Park, S., 'How Transnational Environmental Advocacy Networks Socialize International Financial Institutions: A Case Study of the International Finance Corporation' (2005) 5 *Global Environmental Politics* 95.
'Norm Diffusion within International Organizations: A Case Study of the World Bank' (2005) 8 *Journal of International Relations and Development* 111.
'The World Bank Group: Championing Sustainable Development Norms?' (2007) 13 *Global Governance* 535.
Paul, J. R., 'Comity in International Law' (1991) 32 *Harvard International Law Journal* 1.
Paulsson, J., 'Arbitration Without Privity' (1995) 10 *ICSID Review–Foreign Investment Law Journal* 232.
'Avoiding Unintended Consequences' in Sauvant, K. P. (ed.), *Appeals Mechanism in International Investment Disputes* (Oxford University Press, 2008).

Peel, J., 'Giving the Public a Voice in the Protection of the Global Environment: Avenues for Participation by NGOs in Dispute Resolution at the European Court of Justice and World Trade Organization' (2001) 12 *Colorado Journal of International Environmental Law and Policy* 47.

Peers, D. M., 'Mars and Mammon: The East India Company and Efforts to Reform its Army 1796–1832' (1990) 33 *The Historical Journal* 385.

Peet, R. and Watts, M. (eds.), *Liberation Ecologies: Environment, Development, Social Movements* (London: Routledge, 1996).

Peeters, M., Weishaar, S. and De Cendra de Larragan, J., 'EU ETS: A Governance Perspective on the Choice between "Cap and Trade" and "Credit and Trade" for an Emissions Trading Regime' (2007) 16:7 *European Environmental Law Review* 191.

Penner, C. D., 'Germany and the Transvaal Before 1896' (1940) 12 *The Journal of Modern History* 31.

Pepper, D., *Roots of Modern Environmentalism* (London: Croom Helm, 1984).

Modern Environmentalism: An Introduction (London: Routledge, 1996).

Percival, R. V., 'The Globalization of Environmental Law: Fifteenth Annual Lloyd K Garrison Lecture on Environmental Law' (2009) 26 *Pace Environmental Law Review* 451.

Peterson, H. F., 'Edward A. Hopkins: A Pioneer Promoter in Paraguay' (1942) 22(2) *The Hispanic American Historical Review* 245.

Peterson, J. and Green Cowles, M., 'Clinton, Europe and Economic Diplomacy: What Makes the EU Different?' (1998) 11(3) *Governance: An International Journal of Policy and Administration* 251.

Peterson, L. E., 'All Roads Lead Out of Rome: Divergent Paths of Dispute Settlement in Bilateral Investment Treaties' in Zarsky, L. (ed.) *International Investment for Sustainable Development: Balancing Rights and Rewards* (London: Earthscan, 2005).

Pezzullo, P. C. and Sandler, R., 'Revisiting the Environmental Justice Challenge to Environmentalism' in Sandler, R. and Pezzullo, P. C. (eds.), *Environmental Justice and Environmentalism: The Social Justice Challenge to the Environmental Movement* (University of Alabama Press, 2007).

Philips, C. H., *The East India Company: 1784–1834* (Manchester University Press, 1961).

Picciotto, S., 'Rights, Responsibilities and Regulation of International Business' (2003) 42 *Columbia Journal of Transnational Law* 131.

Pillay, S., 'Absence of Justice: Lessons from the Bhopal Union Carbide Disaster for Latin America' (2006) 14 *Michigan State Journal of International Law* 479.

Pink, D. H., 'The Valdez Principles: Is What's Good for America Good for General Motors?' (1990) 8 *Yale Law & Policy Review* 180.

Pitruzzello, S., 'Trade Globalization, Economic Performance, and Social Protection: Nineteenth Century British Laissez-Faire and Post-World War II US-Embedded Liberalism' (2004) 58 *International Organization* 705.

Platt, D. C. M., *Finance, Trade, and Politics in British Foreign Policy: 1815–1914* (Oxford: Clarendon Press, 1968).

'Economic Factors in British Policy During the "New Imperialism"' (1968) 39 *Past and Present Society* 120.

Polletta, F. and Jasper, J. M., 'Collective Identity and Social Movements' (2001) 27 *Annual Review of Sociology* 283.

Porras, I. M., 'Constructing International Law in the East Indian Seas: Property, Sovereignty, Commerce and War in Hugo Grotius' De Iure Praede – The Law of Prize and Booty, or "On How to Distinguish Merchants from Pirates"' (2006) 31 *Brooklyn Journal of International Law* 741.

Posser, H. and Altenschmidt, S., 'European Union Emissions Trading Directive' (2005) 23 *Journal of Energy and Natural Resources* 60.

Prakash, O., 'Trade in a Culturally Hostile Environment: Europeans in the Japan Trade, 1500–1700' in Prakash, O. (ed.), *European Commercial Expansion in Early Modern Asia* (Aldershot: Ashgate, 1997) 117.

European Commercial Enterprise in Pre-Colonial India (Cambridge University Press, 1998)

Price, R., *Making Empire: Colonial Encounters and the Creation of Imperial Rule in Nineteenth-Century Africa* (Cambridge University Press, 2008).

Prince, P., 'Bhopal, Bougainville and Ok Tedi: Why Australia's *Forum Non Conveniens* Approach is Better' (1998) 47 *International and Comparative Law Quarterly* 573.

Princen, T. and Finger, M., *Environmental NGOs in World Politics: Linking the Local and the Global*, 2nd edn (London: Routledge, 2003).

Rahusen de Bruyn Kops, H., 'Not Such an 'Unpromising Beginning': The First Dutch Trade Embassy to India, 1655–1657' (2002) 36 *Modern Asian Studies* 535.

Rajagopal, B., 'International Law and the Development Encounter: Violence and Resistance at the Margins' (1999) 93 *American Society of International Law Proceedings* 16.

'From Resistance to Renewal: The Third World, Social Movements, and the Expansion of International Institutions' (2000) 41 *Harvard International Law Journal* 529.

International Law from Below: Development, Social Movements and Third World Resistance (Cambridge University Press, 2003).

'International Law and Social Movements: Challenges of Theorizing Resistance' (2003) 41 *Columbia Journal of Transnational Law* 397.

Ralston, J. H., *Venezuelan Arbitrations of 1903* (Washington: Government Printing Office, 1904).

Rampersad, F. B., 'Coping with Globalization: A Suggested Policy Package for Small Countries' (2000) 570 *The Annals of the American Academy of Political and Social Science* 115.

Ratner, S. R., 'Regulatory Takings in Institutional Context: Beyond the Fear of Fragmented International Law' (2008) 102 *American Journal of International Law* 475.

Ratner, S. R. and Abrams, J. S., *Accountability for Human Rights Atrocities in International Law: Beyond the Nuremburg Legacy*, 3rd edn (Oxford University Press, 2009).

Raustiala, K., 'The "Participatory Revolution" in International Environmental Law' (1997) 21 *Harvard Environmental Law Review* 537.

'Form and Substance in International Agreements' (2005) 99 *American Journal of International Law* 581.

Reid, C. L., *Commerce and Conquest: The Story of the Honourable East India Company* (1947).

Reinisch, A., '"Investment and . . ." – The Broader Picture of Investment Law' in Reinisch, A. and Knahr, C. (eds.), *International Investment Law in Context* (The Netherlands: Eleven International Publishing, 2008).

Reyes, A. S., 'Protecting the "Freedom of Transit of Petroleum": Transnational Lawyers Making (Up) International Law in the Caspian' (2006) 24 *Berkeley Journal of International Law* 842.

Richardson, B. J., 'Environmental Law in Postcolonial Societies: Straddling the Local–Global Institutional Spectrum' (2000) 11 *Colorado Journal of International Environmental Law & Policy* 1.

'Enlisting Institutional Investors in Environmental Regulation: Some Comparative and Theoretical Perspectives' (2002) 28 *North Carolina Journal of International Law & Commercial Regulation* 247.

'Financing Environmental Change: A New Role for Canadian Environmental Law' (2004) 49 *McGill Law Journal* 145.

'The Equator Principles: The Voluntary Approach to Environmentally Sustainable Finance' (2005) *European Environmental Law Review* 280.

'Sustainable Finance: Environmental Law and Financial Institutions' in Richardson, B. J. and Wood, S. (eds.), *Environmental Law for Sustainability* (Oxford: Hart Publishing, 2006).

'Do the Fiduciary Duties of Pension Funds Hinder Socially Responsible Investment?' (2007) 22 *Banking & Finance Law Review* 145.

'Financing Sustainability: The New Transnational Governance of Socially Responsible Investment' (2007) 17 *Yearbook of International Environmental Law* 73.

Socially Responsible Investment Law: Regulating the Unseen Polluters (Oxford University Press, 2008).

'Keeping Ethical Investment Ethical: Regulatory Issues for Investing for Sustainability' (2009) 87 *Journal of Business Ethics* 555.

Richardson, B. J. and Wood, S., 'Environmental Law for Sustainability' in Richardson, B. J. and Wood, S. (eds.), *Environmental Law for Sustainability* (Oxford: Hart Publishing, 2006).

Richardson, B. J., Imai, S. and McNeil, K., 'Indigenous Peoples and the Law – Historical, Comparative and Contextual Issues' in Richardson, B. J. Imai, S. and McNeil, K. (eds.), *Indigenous Peoples and the Law: Comparative and Critical Perspectives* (Oxford: Hart Publishing, 2009).

Richardson, B. J., Mgbeoji, I. and Botchway, F., 'Environmental Law in Post-Colonial Societies: Aspirations, Achievements and Limitations' in Richardson, B. J. and Wood, S. (eds.), *Environmental Law for Sustainability* (Oxford: Hart Publishing, 2006).

Riedel, E., 'Standards and Sources: Farewell to the Exclusivity of the Sources Triad in International Law?' (1991) 2(2) *European Journal of International Law* 58.

Rittich, K., *Recharacterizing Restructuring: Law, Distribution and Gender in Market Reform* (London: Kluwer Law International, 2002).

Timmons, R. J., 'Globalizing Environmental Justice' in Sandler, R. and Pezzullo, P. C. (eds.), *Environmental Justice and Environmentalism: The Social Justice Challenge to the Environmental Movement* (University of Alabama Press, 2007).

Rock, M. T. and Angel, D. P., *Industrial Transformation in the Developing World* (Oxford University Press, 2005).

Rodgers Kalas, P., 'The Implications of *Jota* v. *Texaco* and the Accountability of Transnational Corporations' (2000) 12 *Pace International Law Review* 47.

Rodrigues, Moog, M. G., *Global Environmentalism and Local Politics: Transnational Advocacy Networks in Brazil, Ecuador, and India* (State University of New York Press, 2004).

Roelofsen, C. G., 'Grotius and the Development of International Relations Theory: "The Long Seventeenth Century" and the Elaboration of a European States System' (1997) 17 *Quinnipiac Law Review* 35.

Roessler, T., 'The World Bank's Lending Policy and Environmental Standards' (2000) 26 *North Carolina Journal of International Law & Commercial Regulation* 105.

Rogge, M. J., 'Towards Transnational Corporate Accountability in the Global Economy: Challenging the Doctrine of Forum Non Conveniens in In Re: Union Carbide, Alfaro, Sequihua, and Aguinda' (2001) 36 *Texas International Law Journal* 299.

Romano, C. P. R., 'The Proliferation of International Judicial Bodies: The Pieces of the Puzzle', *New York University Journal of International Law and Politics*, 31 (1999) 709.

Rondinelli, D. A. and Berry, M. A., 'Environmental Citizenship in Multinational Corporations: Social responsibility and Sustainable Development' (2000) 18 *European Management Journal* 70.

Ruangsilp, B., *Dutch East Indian Merchants at the Court of Ayutthaya: Dutch Perceptions of the Thai Kingdom 1604–1765* (Leiden and Boston: Brill, 2007).

Rubin, S. J., 'Nationalization and Private Foreign Investment: The Role of Government' (1950) 2 *World Politics* 482.

Ryan, C. M., 'Meeting Expectations: Assessing the Long-Term Legitimacy and Stability of International Investment Law' (2008) 29 *University of Pennsylvania Journal of International Law* 725.

Sadasivan, B., 'The Impact of Structural Adjustment on Women: A Governance and Human Rights Agenda' (1997) 19 *Human Rights Quarterly* 630.

Said, E., *Culture and Imperialism* (New York: Alfred A. Knopf, 1993).

Salacuse, J. W., 'BIT by BIT: The Growth of Bilateral Investment Treaties and their Impact on Foreign Investment in Developing Countries' (1990) 24 *International Lawyer* 655.

Salgado, V. R., 'The Case Against Adopting BIT Law in the FTAA Framework' (2006) *Wisconsin Law Review* 1025.

Sammartano, M. R., 'The Fall of a Taboo: Review of the Merits of an Award by an Appellate Arbitration Panel and a Proposal for an International Appellate Court' (2003) 20:4 *Journal of International Arbitration* 387.

Sandberg, J., et al., 'The Heterogeneity of Socially Responsible Investment' (2009) 87 *Journal of Business Ethics* 519.

Sandrino, G. L., 'The NAFTA Investment Chapter and Foreign Investment in Mexico: A Third World Perspective' (1994) 27 *Vanderbilt Journal of Transnational Law* 259.

Sands, P., 'Treaty, Custom and the Cross-Fertilization of International Law' (1998) 1 *Yale Human Rights and Development Law Journal* 85.

'Environmental Protection in the Twenty-First Century: Sustainable Development and International Law' in Revesz, R. L., Sands, P. and Stewart, R. B. (eds.), *Environmental Law, the Economy and Sustainable Development* (Cambridge University Press, 2000).

'Turtles and Torturers: The Transformation of International Law' (2001) 33 *New York University Journal of International Law and Politics* 527.

'Searching for Balance: Concluding Remarks; Colloquium on Regulatory Expropriations in International Law' (2002) 11 *New York University Environmental Law Journal* 198.

Principles of International Environmental Law, 2nd edn (Cambridge University Press, 2003)

Lawless World: America and the Making and Breaking of Global Rules (New York: Viking Penguin, 2003).

Schaper, M., 'Leveraging Green Power: Environmental Rules for Project Finance' (2007) 9 *Business and Politics* 1.

Schepers, D. H. and Sethi. S. P., 'Do Socially Responsible Funds Actually Deliver What They Promise? Bridging the Gap Between the Promise and Performance of Socially Responsible Funds' (2003) 108(1) *Business and Society Review* 11.

Scherr, S. J. and Juge Gregg, R., 'Johannesburg and Beyond: The 2002 World Summit on Sustainable Development and the Rise of Partnerships' (2006) 18 *Georgetown International Environmental Law Review* 425.

Schill, S. W., 'Do Investment Treaties Chill Unilateral State Regulation to Mitigate Climate Change?' (2007) 24(5) *Journal of International Arbitration* 469.

Schneiderman, D., 'Taking Investments Too Far: Expropriations in the Semi-Periphery' in Griffith Cohen, M. and Clarkson, S. (eds.), *Governing Under Stress: Middle Powers and the Challenge of Globalization* (London: ZED Books, 2004).

Constitutionalizing Economic Globalization: Investment Rules and Democracy's Promise (Cambridge University Press, 2008).

Schnurmann, C., '"Wherever Profit Leads Us, to Every Sea and Shore . . .": the VOC, the WIC, and Dutch Methods of Globalization in the Seventeenth Century' (2003) 17: 3 *Renaissance Studies* 474.

Scholte, J., 'Global Capitalism and the State' (1997) 73: 3 *International Affairs* 427.

Scholtens, B. and Dam, L., 'Banking on the Equator: Are Banks that Adopted the Equator Principles Different from Non-Adopters?' (2007) 35 *World Development* 1307.

Schreuer, C., *The ICSID Convention: A Commentary* (Cambridge University Press, 2001).

Schrijver, N., *Sovereignty Over Natural Resources: Balancing Rights and Duties* (Cambridge University Press, 1997).

Schwabach, A., 'Diverting the Danube: The Gabčikovo-Nagymaros Dispute and International Freshwater Law' (1996) 14 *Berkeley Journal of International Law* 290.

Schwebel, S. M., 'The Creation and Operation of an International Court of Arbitral Awards' in Hunter, M., Marriott, A. L. and Veeder, V. V. (eds.), *Internationalisation of International Arbitration: The LCIA Centenary* (London: Graham & Trotman, 1995).

Scott, G. W., 'Some of the Causes of Conflict between Europe and Latin America' (1903) 22 *Annals of the America Academy of Political and Social Science* 71.

Sec, S., 'Do Two Wrongs Make a Right? Adjudicating Sustainable Development in the Danube Dam Case' (1999) 29 *Golden Gate University Law Review* 317.

Seck, S. L., 'Home State Responsibility and Local Communities: The Case of Global Mining' (2008) 11 *Yale Human Rights & Development Law Journal* 177.

Sethi, H., 'Survival and Democracy: Ecological Struggles in India' in Wignaraja, P. (ed.), *New Social Movements in the South: Empowering the People* (New Delhi: Vistar Publications, 1993).

Shaffer, G. C., 'How Business Shapes Law: A Socio-Legal Framework' (2009) 42 *Connecticut Law Review* 147.

Shalakany, A. A., 'Arbitration and the Third World: A Plea for Reassessing Bias Under the Specter of Neoliberalism' (2000) 41 *Harvard International Law Journal* 419.

Shamir, R., 'The De-Radicalisation of Corporate Social Responsibility' (2004) 30 *Critical Sociology* 669.

'Corporate Social Responsibility: Towards New Market-Embedded Morality?' (2008) 9 *Theoretical Inquiries in Law* 371.

Shan, W., 'From "North–South Divide" to "Private–Public Debate": Revival of the Calvo Doctrine and the Changing Landscape in International Investment Law' (2007) 27 *Northwestern Journal of International Law & Business* 631.

Shaughnessy, M., 'Human Rights and the Environment: The United Nations Global Compact and the Continuing Debate About the Effectiveness of Corporate Voluntary Codes of Conduct' (2000) Yearbook *Colorado Journal of International Environmental Law and Policy* 159.

Shea, D., *The Calvo Clause: A Problem of Inter-American and International Law and Diplomacy* (University of Minnesota Press, 1955).

Shelton, D., 'Globalization and the Erosion of Sovereignty in Honor of Professor Lichtenstein: Protecting Human Rights in a Globalized World' (2002) 25 *Boston College International and Comparative Law Review* 273.

'Normative Hierarchy in International Law' (2006) 100 *American Journal of International Law* 291

Sheppard, A. and Crockett, A., 'Stabilisation Clauses: A Threat to Sustainable Development?' in Cordonier Segger, M., Gehring, M. and Newcombe, A. (eds.), Sustainable Development in International Investment Law (The Hague, Kluwer Law International, 2010).

Sherman, R. and Eliasson, J., 'Trade Disputes and Non-State Actors: New Institutional Arrangements and the Privatisation of Commercial Diplomacy' (2006) 29:4 *The World Economy* 473.

Shihata, I. F. I., 'The Settlement of Disputes Regarding Foreign Investments: The Role of the World Bank with Particular Reference to ICSID and MIGA' (1986) 1 *Arab Law Quarterly* 265.

'The World Bank and the Environment: A Legal Perspective' (1992) 16 *Maryland Journal of International Law and Trade* 1.

Towards a Greater Depoliticization of Investment Disputes: The Roles of ICSID and MIGA (Washington: ICSID, 1993).

Siebecker, M. R., 'Trust & Transparency: Promoting Efficient Corporate Disclosure Through Fiduciary-Based Disclosure' (2009) 87 *Washington University Law Review* 115.

Siegele, L. and Ward, H., 'Corporate Social Responsibility: A Step Towards Stronger Involvement of Business in MEA Implementation?' (2007) 16(2) *Review of European Community and International Environmental Law* 135.

Simaika, A., 'The Value of Information: Alternatives to Liability in Influencing Corporate Behavior Overseas' (2005) 38 *Columbia Journal of Law and Social Problems* 321.

Simmons, P. J., 'Globalization at Work: Learning to Live with NGOs' (1998) Fall *Foreign Policy* 82.

Skogly, S. I., 'Structural Adjustment and Development: Human Rights - An Agenda for Change' (1993) 15(4) *Human Rights Quarterly* 751.

Slaoui, F., 'The Rising Issue of "Repeat Arbitrators": A Call for Clarification' (2009) 25 *Arbitration International* 103.

Slaughter, A., *A New World Order* (Princeton University Press, 2004).

Slaughter, A. M., Tulumello, A. S. and Wood, S., 'International Law and International Relations Theory: A New Generation of Interdisciplinary Scholarship' (1998) 92 *American Journal of International Law* 367.

Smith III, J. A., 'The CERES Principles: A Voluntary Code for Corporate Environmental Responsibility' (1993) 18 *Yale Journal of International Law* 307.

Snierson, J. F., 'Green is Good: Sustainability, Profitability, and a New Paradigm for Corporate Governance' (2009) 94 *Iowa Law Review* 987.

Snyder, A. M., 'Holding Multinational Corporations Accountable: Is Non-Financial Disclosure the Answer?' (2007) *Columbia Business Law Review* 565.

Sohn, L. and Baxter, R., Draft Convention on the International Responsibility of States for Injuries to Aliens (1961) 55 *American Journal of International Law* 545.

Soloway, J., 'Environmental Regulation as Expropriation: The Case of NAFTA's Chapter 11' (2000) 33 *Canadian Business Law Journal* 92.

Sornarajah, M., 'The Climate of International Arbitration' (1991) 8 *Journal of International Arbitration* 47.

'The Clash of Globalizations and the International Law on Foreign Investment: The Simon Reisman Lecture in International Trade Policy' (2003) 10:2 *Canadian Foreign Policy* 1.

'The Fair and Equitable Standard of Treatment: Whose Fairness? Whose Equity?' in Ortino, F., Liberti, L., Sheppard, A. and Warner, H. (eds.) *Investment Treaty Law, Current Issues II: Nationality and Investment Treaty Claims; Fair and Equitable Treatment in Investment Treaty Law* (London: British Institute of International and Comparative Law, 2007).

'A Coming Crisis: Expansionary Trends in Investment Treaty Arbitration' in Sauvant, K. P. (ed.) *Appeals Mechanism in International Investment Disputes* (Oxford University Press, 2008).

The International Law on Foreign Investment, 3rd edn, (Cambridge University Press, 2010).

Sparkes, R., *Socially Responsible Investment: A Global Revolution* (London: John Wiley and Sons, 2002).

Sparkes, R. and Cowton, C. J., 'The Maturing of Socially Responsible Investment: A Review of the Developing Link with Corporate Social Responsibility' (2004) 52 *Journal of Business Ethics* 45.

Spiro, P. J., 'Globalization, International Law and the Academy' (2000) 32 *New York University Journal of International Law and Politics* 567.

Spivak, G. C., 'Can the Subaltern Speak?' in Nelson, C. and Grossberg, L. (eds.), *Marxism and the Interpretation of Culture* (University of Illinois Press, 1988).

Stairs, K. and Taylor, P., 'Non-Governmental Organizations and the Legal Protection of the Oceans: A Case Study' in Hurrell, A. and Kingsbury, B. (eds.), *The International Politics of the Environment: Actors, Interests and Institutions* (Oxford University Press, 1992).

Steensgaard, N., 'The Dutch East India Company as an Institutional Innovation' in Aymard, M. (ed.), *Dutch Capitalism and World Capitalism* (Cambridge University Press, 1982).

Steiner, H. J., Alston, P. and Goodman, R., *International Human Rights Law in Context: Law, Morals, Politics*, 3rd edn, (Oxford University Press, 2008).

Steinhardt, R. G., 'Soft Law, Hard Norms: Competitive Self-Interest and the Emergence of Human Rights Responsibilities for Multinational Corporations' (2008) 33 *Brooklyn Journal of International Law* 933.

Stephens, B., 'The Amorality of Profit: Transnational Corporations and Human Rights' (2002) 20 *Berkeley Journal of International Law* 45.

Stephens, T., 'Multiple International Courts and the "Fragmentation" of International Environmental Law' (2006) 25 *Australian Yearbook of International Law* 227.

International Courts and Environmental Protection (Cambridge University Press, 2009).

Sterio, M., 'The Evolution of International Law' (2008) 31 *Boston College International and Comparative Law Review* 213.

Stern, N., *The Economics of Climate Change: The Stern Review* (Cambridge University Press, 2007).

Stiglitz, J., *Making Globalization Work: The Next Steps to Global Justice* (New York: W.W. Norton and Company, 2006).

Strange, S., 'Debts, Defaulters and Development' (1967) 43 *International Affairs* 516.

The Retreat of the State: The Diffusion of Power in the World Economy (Cambridge University Press, 1996).

Subedi, S. P., 'Foreign Investment and Sustainable Development' in Weiss, F., Dentes, E. and De Waart, P. (eds.), *International Economic Law with a Human Face* (1998).

International Investment Law: Reconciling Policy and Principle (Oxford: Hart Publishing, 2008).

Suter, C. and Stamm, H., 'Coping with Global Debt Crises: Debt Settlements 1820–1986' (1992) 34 *Comparative Studies in Society and History* 645.

Sutherland, L., *The East India Company in 18th Century Politics* (Oxford University Press, 1952).

Tarlock, D., 'Environmental Law: The Role of Non-Governmental Organizations in the Development of International Environmental Law' (1992) 68 *Chicago-Kent Law Review* 61.

Tarrow, S. G., *Power in Movement: Social Movements, Collective Action and Politics* (Cambridge University Press, 1994).

Power in Movement: Social Movements and Contentious Politics, 2nd edn, (Cambridge University Press, 1998).

Taylor, A. M., 'The UN and the Global Compact' (2000) 17 *New York Law School Journal of Human Rights* 975.

Testy, K. Y., 'What is the "New" Corporate Social Responsibility?: Linking Progressive Corporate Law with Progressive Social Movements' (2002) 76 *Tulane Law Review* 1227.

Teubner, G., 'Substantive and Reflexive Elements in Modern Law' (1983) 17 *Law and Society Review* 239.

'Values: State Policies in Private Law? A Comment on Hanoch Dagan' (2008) 56 *The American Journal of Comparative Law* 835.

Thérien, J. P. and Pouliot, V., 'The Global Compact: Shifting Politics of International Development' (2006) 12 *Global Governance* 55.

Thomas, C., 'Causes of Inequality in the International Economic Order: Critical Race Theory and Postcolonial Development' (1999) 9 *Transnational Law & Contemporary Problems* 1.

Thomas, W. L., 'The Green Nexus: Financiers and Sustainable Development' (2001) 13 *Georgetown International Environmental Law Review* 899.

Thompson, C. R., 'A Multifaceted Approach to the Regulation of Cyanide in Gold Mining Operations' (2005) 29 *Suffolk Transnational Law Review* 79.

Tienhaara, K., 'What You Don't Know Can Hurt You: Investor–State Disputes and the Protection of the Environment in Developing Countries' (2006) 6 *Global Environmental Politics* 73.

'Third Party Participation in Investment-Environment Disputes: Recent Developments' (2007) 16(2) *Review of European Community and International Environmental Law* 230.

The Expropriation of Environmental Governance: Protecting Foreign Investors at the Expense of Public Policy (Cambridge University Press, 2009).

Treves, T., 'Conflicts Between the International Tribunal for the Law of the Sea and the International Court of Justice' (1999) 31 *New York University Journal of International Law and Politics* 809.

Triggs, G. D., *International Law: Contemporary Principles and Practices* (Sydney: LexisNexis Butterworths Australia, 2006).

Trotter, R. C., Day, S. G. and Love, A. E., 'Bhopal, India and Union Carbide: The Second Tragedy' (1989) 8 *Journal of Business Ethics* 439.

Trubek, D., et al., 'Symposium: The Legal Profession: Global Restructuring and the Law: Studies of the Internationalization of Legal Fields and the Creation of Transnational Arenas' (1994) 44 *Case Western Reserve Law Review* 407.

Tsutsui, K., 'Global Civil Society and Ethnic Social Movements in the Contemporary World' (2004) 19 *Sociological Forum* 63.

Tudor, I., *The Fair and Equitable Treatment Standard in the International Law of Foreign Investment* (Oxford University Press, 2008).

Tung, K. and Cox-Alomar, R., 'Arbitral and Judicial Decision: The New Generation of China BITs in Light of *Tza Yap Shum* v. *Republic of Peru*' (2006) 17 *American Review of International Arbitration* 461.

Udobong, E. E., 'Multinational Corporations Facing the Long Arm of American Jurisdiction for Human Rights and Environmental Abuses: The Case of *Wiwa* v. *Royal Dutch Petroleum, Co.*' (2005) 14 *Southeastern Environmental Law Journal* 89.

United States Secretary of State to Mexican Ambassador (1 September 1938), reproduced in 'Mexico–United States: Expropriation by Mexico of Agrarian Properties Owned by American Citizens' (1938) 33 *American Journal of International Law Supplement* 181.

Uriz, G. H., 'The Application of the World Bank Standards to the Oil Industry: Can the World Bank Group Promote Corporate Responsibility?' (2002) 28 *Brooklyn Journal of International Law* 77.

Utting, P., 'The Global Compact and Civil Society: Averting a Collision Course' (2002) 12 *Development in Practice* 644.

Van Der Kroef, J. M., 'Indonesia and the Origins of Dutch Colonial Sovereignty' (1951) 10 *Far Eastern Quarterly* 151.

Van Harten, G., *Investment Treaty Arbitration and Public Law* (Oxford University Press, 2007).
Van Harten, G. and Loughlin, M., 'Investment Treaty Arbitration as a Species of Global Administrative Law' (2006) 17 *European Journal of International Law* 121.
Van Ittersum, M. J., 'Hugo Grotius in Context: Van Heemskerck's Capture of the *Santa Catarina* and its Justification in *De Jure Praedae* (1604–1606)' (2003) 31(3) *Asian Journal of Social Science* 511.
Vandevelde, K. J., 'A Brief History of International Investment Agreements' (2005) 12 *UC Davis Journal of International Law & Policy* 157.
Bilateral Investment Treaties: History, Policy, and Interpretation (Oxford University Press, 2010).
Verhoosel, G., 'Foreign Direct Investment and Legal Constraints on Domestic Environmental Policies: Striking a "Reasonable Balance between Stability and Change"' (1998) 29 *Law and Policy in International Business* 451.
Vertovec, S., 'Introduction to Globalization, Globalism, Environments and Environmentalism' in Vertovec, S. and Posey, D. A. (eds.), *Globalization, Globalism, Environments, and Environmentalism: Consciousness of Connections, The Linacre Lectures* (Oxford University Press, 2003).
Vives, A., 'Corporate Social Responsibility: The Role of Law and Markets and the Case of Developing Countries' (2008) 83 *Chicago-Kent Law Review* 199.
Vos, R., *Gentle Janus, Merchant Prince: The VOC and the Tightrope of Diplomacy in the Malay World, 1740–1800* (Leiden: KITVL Press, 1993).
Waddock, S. A., Bodwell, C. and Graves, S. B., 'Responsibility: The New Business Imperative' (2002) 16 *The Academy of Management Executive* 132.
Wade, R., 'From Global Imbalances to Global Reorganisations' (2009) 33 *Cambridge Journal of Economics* 539.
Wagner, M., 'Nature Beyond the Nation State Symposium: International Investment, Expropriation and Environmental Protection' (1999) 29 *Golden Gate University Law Review* 465.
Waibel, M., *Sovereign Defaults before International Courts and Tribunals* (Cambridge University Press, 2011).
Wälde, T. and Kolo, A., 'Environmental Regulation, Investment Protection and 'Regulatory Taking' in International Law' (2001) 50 *International and Comparative Law Quarterly* 811.
Wälde, T. W. and Ndi, G., 'Stabilizing International Investment Commitments: International Law Versus Contract Interpretation' (1996) 31 *Texas International Law Journal* 215.
Walker Jr., H., 'Modern Treaties of Friendship, Commerce and Navigation' (1957) 42 *Minnesota Law Review* 805.
Walsh, T. W., 'Substantive Review of ICSID Awards: Is the Desire for Accuracy Sufficient to Compromise Finality?' (2006) 24 *Berkely Journal of International Law* 444.
Wapner, P., *Environmental Activism and World Civic Politics* (State University of New York Press, 1996).

'The Democratic Accountability of Non-Governmental Organizations: Defining Accountability in NGOs' (2002) 3 *Chicago Journal of International Law* 197.

Ward, H., 'Securing Transnational Corporate Accountability Through National Courts: Implications and Policy Options' (2001) 24 *Hastings International and Comparative Law Review* 451.

Watchman, P., 'Banks, Business and Human Rights', *Butterworths Journal of International Banking and Financial Law*, February 2006.

Waters, C. P. M., 'Who Should Regulate the Baku-Tbilisi-Ceyhan Pipeline?' (2004) 16 *Georgetown International Environmental Law Review* 403.

Waygood, S., *Capital Market Campaigning: The Impact of NGOs on Companies, Shareholder Value and Reputational Risk* (London: Risk Books, 2006).

Weaver, J. C., 'The Construction of Property Rights on Imperial Frontiers: The Case of the New Zealand Purchase Ordinance of 1846' in Kirkby, D. and Coleborne, C. (eds.), *Law, History, Colonialism: The Reach of Empire* (Manchester University Press, 2001).

Weeramantry, C. G., *Nauru: Environmental Damage Under International Trusteeship* (Oxford University Press, 1992).

Universalising International Law (Leiden: Martinus Nijhoff Publishers 2004).

Weeramantry, C. and Berman, N., 'The Grotius Lecture Series' (1999) 14 *American University International Law Review* 1515.

Weiler, T. (ed.), *International Investment Law and Arbitration: Leading Cases from the ICSID, NAFTA, Bilateral Treaties and Customary International Law* (London: Cameron May, 2005).

'Good Faith and Regulatory Transparency: The Story of Metalclad v. Mexico' in Weiler, T. (ed.), *International Investment Law and Arbitration: Leading Cases from the ICSID, NAFTA, Bilateral Treaties and Customary International Law* (London: Cameron May, 2005).

Weiler, T. and Wälde, T. W., 'Investment Arbitration under the Energy Charter Treaty in the Light of New NAFTA Precedents: Towards a Global Code of Conduct for Economic Regulation (2004) 1 *Transnational Dispute Management* 1.

Weissbrodt, D., 'Corporate Social Responsibility in the International Context: Business and Human Rights' (2005) 74 *University of Cincinnati Law Review* 55.

'International Standard-Setting on the Human Rights Responsibilities of Businesses' (2008) 26 *Berkeley Journal of International Law* 373.

Weissbrodt, D. and Kruger, M., 'Norms on the Responsibilities of Transnational Corporations and Other Business Enterprises with Regard to Human Rights' (2003) 97 *American Journal of International Law* 901.

Wells, C. A. H., 'The Cycles of Corporate Social Responsibility: An Historical Retrospective for the Twenty-First Century' (2002) 51 *University of Kansas Law Review* 77.

Wells, L. T., 'Double Dipping in Arbitration Awards? An Economist Questions Damages Awarded Karaha Bodas Company in Indonesia' (2003) 19 *Arbitration International* 471.

Werksman, J. and Santoro, C., 'Investing in Sustainable Development: The Potential Interaction between the Kyoto Protocol and the Multilateral Agreement on Investment' in Bradnee Chambers, W., *Inter-Linkages: The Kyoto Protocol and the International Trade and Investment Regimes* (New York: United Nations University Press, 2001).

Werksman, J., Baumert, K. A. and Dubash, N. K., 'Will International Investment Rules Obstruct Climate Protection Policies? An Examination of the Clean Development Mechanism' (2003) 3 *International Environmental Agreements: Politics, Law and Economics* 59.

Weston, B. H., 'International Law and the Deprivation of Foreign Wealth: A Framework for Future Inquiry' (1968) 54 *Virginia Law Review* 1069.

'The Charter of Economic Rights and Duties of States and the Deprivation of Foreign-Owned Wealth' (1981) 75 *The American Journal of International Law* 437.

Westra, L., Bosselmann, K. and Westra, R. (eds.), *Reconciling Human Existence and Ecological Integrity* (London: Earthscan, 2008).

White, G., *Nationalization of Foreign Property* (London: Stevens and Sons, 1961).

White, H. G., 'Including Local Communities in the Negotiation of Mining Agreements: The Ok Tedi Example' (1995) 8 *The Transnational Lawyer* 303.

White, R. C. A., 'A New International Economic Order' (1975) 24 *International and Comparative Law Quarterly* 542.

'Expropriation of the Libyan Oil Concessions: Two Conflicting International Arbitrations' (1981) 30 *International and Comparative Law Quarterly* 1.

Whitehouse, L., 'Corporate Social Responsibility, Corporate Citizenship and the Global Compact: A New Approach to Regulating Corporate Social Power?' (2003) 3(3) *Global Social Policy* 299.

'Corporate Social Responsibility: Views from the Frontline' (2006) 63 *Journal of Business Ethics* 279.

Whiteman, M., *Damages in International Law* (Washington DC: US Government Printing Office, 1937).

Williams, C., 'Corporations Theory and Corporate Governance Law: Corporate Social Responsibility in an Era of Economic Globalization' (2002) 35 *University of California Davis Law Review* 705.

'Civil Society Initiatives and "Soft Law" in the Oil and Gas Industry' (2004) 36 *New York University Journal of International Law & Policy* 457.

'Corporate Law and the Internal Point of View in Legal Theory: A Tale of Two Trajectories' (2006) 75 *Fordham Law Review* 1629.

Williams, C. A. and Conley, J. M., 'Corporate Social Responsibility in the International Context: Is There an Emerging Fiduciary Duty to Consider Human Rights?' (2005) 74 *University of Cincinnati Law Review* 75.

'An Emerging Third Way? The Erosion of the Anglo-American Shareholder Value Construct' (2005) 38 *Cornell International Law Journal* 493.

'Triumph or Tragedy: The Curious Path of Corporate Disclosure Reform in the UK' (2007) 31 *William and Mary Environmental Law and Policy Review* 317.

Williams, M., 'Ecology, Imperialism and Deforestation' in Griffiths, T. and Robin, L. (eds.), *Ecology and Empire: Environmental History of Settler Societies* (Edinburgh: Keele University Press, 1997).

'The Role of Deforestation in Earth and World-System Integration' in Hornborg, A., McNiell, J. R. and Martinez-Alier, J. (eds.), *Rethinking Environmental History: World-System History and Global Environmental Change* (AltaMira Press, 2007).

Wilson, R. R., 'Property-Protection Provisions in United States Commercial Treaties' (1951) 45 *The American Journal of International Law* 83.

Winchester, S., *Krakatoa: The Day the World Exploded* (New York: HarperCollins, 2003)

Wood, M., 'The International Tribunal for the Law of the Sea and General International Law' (2007) 22(3) *The International Journal of Marine and Coastal Law* 351.

Wood, S., 'Green Revolution or Greenwash? Voluntary Environmental Standards, Public Law, and Private Authority in Canada' in Law Commission of Canada, *New Perspectives on the Public–Private Divide* (Vancouver: UBC Press, 2003).

'Voluntary Environmental Codes and Sustainability' in Richardson, B. J. and Wood, S. (eds.), *Environmental Law for Sustainability* (Oxford: Hart Publishing, 2006).

Woodhouse, E. J., 'The "Guerra del Agua" and the Cochabamba Concession: Social Risk and Foreign Direct Investment in Public Infrastructure' (2003) 39 *Stanford Journal of International Law* 295.

World Commission on Environment and Development, *Our Common Future: The Report of the World Commission on Environment and Development* (Oxford University Press, 1987).

Worster, Donald, *Nature's Economy: A History of Ecological Ideas*, 2nd edn (Cambridge University Press, 1994).

Worthington, S., 'Reforming Directors' Duties' (2001) 64 *Modern Law Review* 439.

Wortley, B. A., 'The Mexican Oil Dispute: 1938–1946' (1957) 43 *Problems of Public and Private International Law* 15.

Expropriation in Public International Law (Cambridge University Press, 1959).

Wright, C., 'Setting Standards for Responsible Banking: Examining the Role of the International Finance Corporation in the Emergence of the Equator Principles' in Biermann, F., Siebenhüner, B. and Schreyrogg, A. (eds.), *International Organizations in Global Environmental Governance* (London: Routledge, 2009).

Wright, C. and Rwabizambuga, A., 'Institutional Pressures, Corporate Reputation, and Voluntary Codes of Conduct: An Examination of the Equator Principles' (2006) 111 *Business and Society Review* 89.

Yackee, J. W., 'Pacta Sunt Servanda and State Promises to Foreign Investors Before Bilateral Investment Treaties: Myth and Reality' (2009) 32 *Fordham International Law Journal* 1550.

Yannaca-Small, K., 'Parallel Proceedings' in Muchlinski, P., Ortino, F. and Schreuer, C. (eds.), *The Oxford Handbook of International Investment Law* (Oxford University Press, 2008).

Yashar, D. J., *Contesting Citizenship in Latin America: The Rise of Indigenous Movements and the Postliberal Challenge* (Cambridge University Press, 2005).

'Resistance and Identity Politics in an Age of Globalization' (2007) 610 *The Annals of the American Academy of Political and Social Science* 160.

Yearley, S., 'Social Movements as Problematic Agents of Global Environmental Change' in Vertovec, S. and Posey, D. A. (eds.), *Globalization, Globalism, Environments, and Environmentalism: Consciousness of Connections, The Linacre Lectures* (Oxford University Press, 2003).

Cultures of Environmentalism: Empirical Studies in Environmental Sociology (New York: Palgrave Macmillan, 2005).

Ynsfran, P. M., 'Sam Ward's Bargain with President Lopez of Paraguay' (1954) 34(3) *The Hispanic American Historical Review* 313.

Zamora, S., 'Voting in International Economic Organizations' (1980) 74 *American Journal of International Law* 566.

Zarsky, L., 'Havens, Halos and Spaghetti: Untangling the Evidence about Foreign Direct Investment and the Environment' in OECD, *Foreign Direct Investment and the Environment* (Paris: OECD Publishing, 1999).

(ed.), *International Investment for Sustainable Development: Balancing Rights and Rewards* (London: Earthscan, 2005).

Zerk, J. A., *Multinationals and Corporate Social Responsibility: Limitations and Opportunities in International Law* (Cambridge University Press, 2006).

Zimmerman, M., 'From Animal Rights to Radical Ecology' in Zimmerman, M. (ed.), *Environmental Philosophy: From Animal Rights to Radical Ecology* (Englewood Cliffs: Prentice Hall, 1993).

Zondorak, V. A., 'A New Face in Corporate Environmental Responsibility: The Valdez Principles' (1991) 18 *Boston College Environmental Affairs Law Review* 457.

REPORTS, DIPLOMATIC CORRESPONDENCE, UNITED NATIONS DOCUMENTS, AND OTHER MISCELLANEOUS INTERNATIONAL MATERIALS

(1839–1840) 28 *British and Foreign State Papers* 1165, 1173.

(1840–1841) 29 *British and Foreign State Papers* 1225.

(1841–1842) 30 *British and Foreign State Papers* 111–120.

Agenda 21, Report of the UNCED, UN Doc. A/CONF.151/26/Rev.1 (vol.I), (1992) 31 ILM 874.

Agreement Among the Azerbaijan Republic, Georgia and the Republic of Turkey, 18 November 1999, available at http://subsites.bp.com/caspian/BTC/Eng/agmt4/agmt4.PDF (last accessed 15 December 2011).

Bedjaoui, M., *First Report on Succession of States in Respect of Rights and Duties Resulting From Sources Other Than Treaties* (1968) UN Doc. A/CN.4/204, in *Yearbook of the*

International Law Commission, II, 1968, UN Doc. A/CN.4/SER.A./1968 Add 1, 115.

Canada, Model Foreign Investment Protection Agreement (2004) (Canadian Model BIT), available at www.int%20ernational.gc.ca/assets/trade-agreements-accords-commerciaux/pdfs/2004-FIPA-model-en.pdf (last accessed 29 April 2009).

Charter of Economic Rights and Duties of States, GA Res 3281 (XXIX), UN Doc A/RES/3281 (XXIX) (1974).

Collevecchio Declaration on Financial Institutions and Sustainability (2003) BankTrack, available at www.banktrack.org/doc/File/banktrack%20publications/Collevecchio%20Declaration/030401%20Collevecchio%20Declaration.pdf (last accessed 12 April 2007).

Conference on the World Financial and Economic Crisis, *Report of the Secretary-General*, UN Doc. A/CONF.214/4 (2009), available at www.un.org/ga/search/view_doc.asp?symbol=A/CONF.214/4&Lang=E (last accessed 16 December 2011).

Council Directive 2003/87/EC, *Establishing a Scheme for Greenhouse Gas Emission Allowance Trading with the Community and Amending Council Directive* 96/61/EC, 2003 O.J. (L 275) 32.

Declaration on Permanent Sovereignty Over Natural Resources, GA Res 1803 (XVII), 17 GAOR, Supp. 17, UN Doc A/5217, 15 (1962).

Declaration on the Establishment of a New International Economic Order, GA Res 3201 (S-VI), UN Doc A/Res/S-6/3201 (1974).

Declaration of the Fourth Ministerial Conference, Doha, Qatar, WT/MIN(01)/DEC/1, 20 November 2001.

Equator Principles (Washington, DC, 4 June 2003), available at www.equator-principles.com (last accessed 24 August 2008).

Havana Charter for an International Trade Organization (1948) UN Conference on Trade and Employment, UN Doc. E/CONF.2/78, Sales no. 1948.II.D.4.

Host Government Agreement between and among the Government of the Azerbaijan Republic and the Main Export Pipeline Participants, 17 October 2000, available at http://subsites.bp.com/caspian/BTC/Eng/agmt1/agmt1.PDF (last accessed 20 January 2009).

Host Government Agreement between and among the Government of Georgia and the Main Export Pipeline Participants, 28 April 2000, available at http://subsites.bp.com/caspian/BTC/Eng/agmt2/agmt2.PDF (last accessed 15 December 2011).

Host Government Agreement between and among the Government of the Republic of Turkey and the Main Export Pipeline Participants, undated, available at http://subsites.bp.com/caspian/BTC/Eng/agmt3/agmt3.PDF (last accessed 15 December 2011).

International Chamber of Commerce, *International Code of Fair Treatment of Foreign Investment* (1948) reprinted in United Nations Conference on Trade and Development (UNCTAD), *International Investment Instruments: A Compendium* (New York: United Nations, 1996), vol. 3.

International Law Association, *Draft Statute of the Arbitral Tribunal for Foreign Investment and the Foreign Investment Court* (1948) reprinted in UNCTAD, *International Code*.

International Law Commission, *Articles on Responsibility of States for Internationally Wrongful Acts*, UNGAOR, 56th Sess., Supp. No. 10, UN Doc. A/56/10.

Fragmentation of International Law: Difficulties Arising from the Diversification and Expansion of International Law, Report of the Study Group of the International Law Commission, finalised by Koskenniemi, M., UN Doc. A/CN.4/L.682 (13 April 2006).

International Law Organisation, *Declaration on Fundamental Principles and Rights at Work*, 86th Session of the General Conference of the International Labour Organisation, Geneva, 18 June 1998, available at www.ilo.org/declaration/thedeclaration/textdeclaration/lang–en/index.htm (last accessed 17 December 2011).

Johannesburg Declaration on Sustainable Development, Report of the United Nations World Summit on Sustainable Development, UN Doc. A/CONF. 199/20 (2002).

Johannesburg Plan of Implementation, Report of the World Summit on Sustainable Development, UN Doc A/CONF.199/20 (2002).

Monterrey Consensus of the International Conference on Financing for Development, UN Doc. A/AC.257/32 (2002), available at www.un.org/esa/ffd/monterrey/MonterreyConsensus.pdf (last accessed 16 December 2011).

NAFTA Free Trade Commission, Interpretation of NAFTA Chapter 11 (31 July 2001) 6 ICSID Rep 567.

OECD, Multilateral Agreement on Investment, Draft Consolidated Text, 22 April 1998.

OECD Guidelines for Multinational Enterprises, General Policies, Article II, 19 (revised, 2000), available at www.oecd.org/dataoecd/56/36/1922428.pdf (last accessed 17 December 2008).

Permanent Sovereignty Over Natural Resources, GA Res. 1720 (XVI), 19 December 1961.

Permanent Sovereignty Over Natural Resources, GA Res. 2158 (XXI), 25 November 1966.

Report of the Ad Hoc Committee of the Sixth Special Session, UN GAOR, 6th Spec. Sess. (2229th plen. mtg.), UN Doc A/PV.2229 (1 May 1974).

Report of the United Nations Conference on Environment and Development (UNCED), UN Doc A/CONF.151/6/Rev.1 (1992), 31 ILM 874.

Report of the World Summit on Sustainable Development, UN Doc A/CONF.199/20 (2002).

Rio Declaration on Environment and Development, Report of the UNCED, UN Doc. A/CONF.151/6/Rev.1 (1992), (1992) 31 ILM 874.

Ruggie, J., *Interim Report of the Special Representative of the Secretary-General on the Issue of Human Rights and Transnational Corporations and Other Business Enterprises*, UN Doc. E/CN.4/2006/97 (2006).

UNCTAD, *Environment: UNCTAD Series on Issues in International Investment Agreements*, United Nations (2001) UNCTAD/ITE/IIT/23, 7, available at www.unctad.org/en/docs/psiteiitd23.en.pdf (last accessed 10 December 2011).

Foreign Direct Investment, Investment, Technology and Enterprise Development Programme, available at www.unctad.org/Templates/StartPage.asp?intItemID=2527&lang=1 (last accessed 10 December 2011).

Foreign Direct Investment: Statistics, available at www.unctad.org/Templates/WebFlyer.asp?intItemID=2190&lang=1 (last accessed 10 December 2011).

Foreign Portfolio Investment (FPI) and Foreign Direct Investment (FDI): Characteristics, Similarities, Complementarities and Differences, Policy Implications and Development Impact, Commission on Investment, Technology and Related Financial Issues: Expert Meeting on Portfolio Investment Flows and Foreign Direct Investment, Geneva, June 1999, 4, available at www.unctad.org/en/docs/c2em6d2&c1.en.pdf (last accessed 10 December 2011).

International Investment Rule-Making (2007) TD/B/COM.2/EM.21/2.

Recent Developments in International Investment Agreements, IIA Monitor No. 2, UNCTAD/WEB/ITE/IIT/2005/1 (30 August 2005) 4–5, available at www.unctad.org/en/docs/webiteiit20051_en.pdf (last accessed 15 December 2011).

Recent Developments in International Investment Agreements (2007–June 2008), IIA Monitor No. 2, UNCTAD/WEB/DIAE/IA/2008/1 (2008) 5, available at www.unctad.org/en/docs/webdiaeia20081_en.pdf (last accessed 15 December 2011).

World Investment Report 2007: Transnational Corporations, Extractive Industries and Development (2007) xv, available at www.unctad.org/en/docs/wir2007_en.pdf (last accessed 10 December 2011).

World Investment Report 2009: Transnational Corporations, Agricultural Production and Development (2009) iii, xvii, available at www.unctad.org/en/docs/wir2009_en.pdf (last accessed 10 December 2011).

UNFCCC Secretariat, Clean Development Mechanism, *CDM Statistics* (February 2010), available at http://cdm.unfccc.int/Statistics/index.html (last accessed 11 December 2011).

United Nations, *Arrangements for Consultation with Non-Governmental Organizations*, ESC res. 1296, UN ESCOR, 44th Sess., Supp. No.1, at 21, UN Doc. E/4548 (1968).

United Nations Millennium Declaration, UNGA Res. A/55/2 (2000); *United Nations Development Goals*, available at www.un.org/millenniumgoals/ (last accessed 17 July 2009).

United Nations Principles for Responsible Investment (2006), available at www.unpri.org/principles/ (last accessed 24 April 2010).

United Nations Economic and Social Council, *Norms on the Responsibilities of Transnational Corporations and Other Business Enterprises with Regard to Human Rights*, UN ESCOR, 55th sess, Agenda item 4, UN Doc. E/CN.4/Sub.2/2003/12/Rev.2 (2003).

United States State Department, Treaty between the Government of the United States of America and the Government of [Country] Concerning the Encouragement and Reciprocal Protection of Investments (2004) (United

States' Model BIT), available at www.state.gov/documents/organization/117601.pdf (last accessed 21 March 2010).

Universal Declaration on Human Rights, GA Resolution 217A (III), UNGAOR, 3rd Sess., 183rd plen mtg, UN Doc. A/RES/217A.

Uruguay Round Ministerial Decision, *Decision on Trade and Environment*, Marrakesh, Preamble, 14 April 1994, World Trade Organization, available at www.wto.org/english/docs_e/legal_e/56-dtenv_e.htm (last accessed 16 December 2011).

WEB-BASED MATERIAL, PRESS RELEASES, AND NEWSPAPER ARTICLES

Allens Arthur Robinson, 'The Equator Principles - Guidelines for Responsible Project Financing', *Focus On Project Finance* 1 (2005), available at www.aar.com.au/pubs/pdf/baf/fobafaug05.pdf (last accessed 7 January 2012).

Amazon Defense Coalition, 'ChevronToxico: The International Campaign to hold ChevronTexaco Accountable for its Toxic Contamination of the Ecuadorian Amazon', March 2005, available at http://cheverontoxico.com/article.php?id=110 (last accessed 10 December 2011).

'Historic Trial: Summary of Legal Case in Ecuador against ChevronTexaco', available at www.chevrontoxico.com/article.php?id=55 (last accessed 5 February 2008).

Amnesty International, 'Human Rights on the Line: the Baku–Tbilisi–Ceyhan Pipeline Project' (2003), available at www.amnestyusa.org/business/humanrightsontheline.pdf (last accessed 14 September 2009).

Arup, T., 'Coal Funding Under Fire', *Sydney Morning Herald*, 15 September 2009, available at www.smh.com.au/environment/coal-funding-under-fire-20090914-fny0.html (last accessed 9 November 2009).

Ayine, D. et al., 'Lifting the Lid on Foreign Investment Contracts: The Real Deal for Sustainable Development', *International Institute for Environment and Development Briefing Paper* (2005), available at www.iied.org/pubs/pdfs/16007IIED.pdf (last accessed 14 December 2011).

Baku–Tbilisi–Ceyhan Pipeline Company, BTC Human Rights Undertaking (22 September 2003), available at http://subsites.bp.com/caspian/Human%20Rights%20Undertaking.pdf (last accessed 11 December 2011).

Balch, O., 'Building a Better World (for Investors and Whales)', *The Banker* (July 2006), available at www.equator-principles.com/bbw.shtml (last accessed 28 August 2008).

BankTrack, Collevecchio Declaration: The Role and Responsibility of Financial Institutions (undated), available at www.banktrack.org/download/collevechio_declaration/030401_collevecchio_declaration_with_signatories.pdf (last accessed 15 December 2011).

Correspondence to Royal Bank of Scotland (15 September 2006), available at www.banktrack.org (last accessed 26 March 2010).

Equator Principles II: NGO Comments on the Proposed Revision of the Equator Principles (2006) 5, 12, available at www.banktrack.org (last accessed 15 December 2011).

'Improvements Made, But Principles Fail to Live Up to Their Potential' (July 2006), available at www.irn.org/programs/finance/index.php?id=060711halfloaf.html (last accessed 15 December 2011).

'Principles, Profits or Just PR? Triple P Investments under the Equator Principles: An Anniversary Assessment' (2004) 14, available at www.banktrack.org/download/principles_profits_or_just_pr_/040604_principles_profits_or_just_pr.pdf (last accessed 15 December 2011).

'Sakhalin II Oil and Gas Project', 18 July 2008, available at www.banktrack.org/show/dodgydeals/sakhalin_ii_oil_and_gas_project (last accessed 15 December 2011).

'Going Round in Circles: An Overview of BankTrack–EPFI Engagement on the Equator Principles, 2003–2010' (February 2010), available at www.banktrack.org/download/going_around_in_circles/100210_going_around_in_circles_post_mtg_version.pdf (last accessed 24 March 2010).

Barclays PLC, Corporate Responsibility Report 2005 (2006), available at www.barclays.com/corporateresponsibility/doclib/0697-133154-barclays_crr_2005.pdf (last accessed 28 August 2008).

Corporate Responsibility Report 2006 (2007) 23, available at http://group.barclays.com/Sustainability/Reporting?tab=1231781135055 (last accessed 25 March 2010).

Sustainability Review 2007 (2008), available at http://group.barclays.com/Sustainability/Reporting?tab=1231781135029 (last accessed 25 March 2010).

Sustainability Review 2008 (2009), available at http://group.barclays.com/Sustainability/Reporting/Sustainability-Report-2008 (last accessed 25 March 2010).

Baue, B., 'Revised Equator Principles Fall Short of International Best Practice for Project Finance', *SRI-Advisor*, 12 July 2006, available at www.sriadviser.com/article.mpl?sfArticleId=2055 (last accessed 15 December 2011).

Berger, C., Australian Conservation Foundation, 'Disclosure of Ethical Considerations in Investment Product Disclosure Statements: A Review of Current Practice in Australia' (August 2004), available at www.acfonline.org.au/uploads/res/res_investment_product_disclosure.pdf (last accessed 27 March 2010).

Bergius, S., 'Environmental Standards Loom Ever Larger in Banks' Lending Decisions', *ENDS Agenda!, Environmental Data Services* (December 2008), available at www.equator-principles.com/documents/ENDSReport12-08English.pdf (last accessed 23 March 2010).

Bhopal Medical Appeal and Sambhavna Trust, 'What Happened in Bhopal?', undated, available at www.bhopal.org/whathappened.html (last accessed 23 February 2008).

Bhopal.net, International Campaign for Justice in Bhopal, available at http://www.bhopal.net/index1.html (last accessed 16 January 2008).

Blomfield, A., 'Kremlin "Bullying" Leaves Western Energy Companies Furious', *The Telegraph*, United Kingdom, 23 September 2006, available at www.telegraph.co.uk/news/worldnews/1529634/Kremlin-bullying-leaves-western-energy-companies-furious.html (last accessed 15 December 2011).

British Institute of International and Comparative Law, Open Roundtable of the Investment Treaty Forum, 'Global Financial Crisis: Implications for Investment Arbitration', 18 February 2009, www.biicl.org/events/view/-/id/365/ (last accessed 29 March 2009).

Bulleid, R., 'Putting Principles into Practice', *Environmental Finance*, June 2004, available at www.equator-principles.com/ef2.shtml (last accessed 14 August 2008).

Burtraw, D. and Palmer, K., Compensation Rules for Climate Policy in the Electricity Sector, Resources for the Future (2007) SSRN, available at http://ssrn.com/abstract=1005680 (last accessed 4 April 2008).

Business and Industry Advisory Committee to the OECD, 'The Voice of OECD Business, About BIAC', available at www.biac.org/aboutus.htm (last accessed 10 January 2009).

Business and Sustainable Development, ICC Business Charter for Sustainable Development, available at www.bsdglobal.com/tools/principles_icc.asp (last accessed 11 August 2008).

Carroll, T., 'New Approaches to Opening Markets: The Baku–Tbilisi–Ceyhan Pipeline and the Deployment of Social and Environmental Risk Mitigation' (2010) 8–11, available at www.psa.ac.uk/2010/UploadedPaperPDFs/1157_1007.pdf (last accessed 11 December 2011).

Center for International Environmental Law, 'Human Rights and the Environment' (2005), available at www.ciel.org/Hre/programhre.html (last accessed 18 July 2009).

'Foreign Investment and Sustainable Development: Brief for the World Summit on Sustainable Development' (2002), available at www.ciel.org/Publications/investment.pdf (last accessed 11 December 2011).

Centre for International Sustainable Development Law, 'About the CISDL', available at www.cisdl.org/about.html (last accessed 16 December 2011).

'CISDL Legal Programmes', available at www.cisdl.org/programmes.html (last accessed 16 December 2011).

CERES, 'CERES: Investors and Environmentalists for Sustainable Prosperity', available at www.ceres.org (last accessed 15 December 2011).

CERES Sustainable Governance Project, 'Value at Risk: Climate Change and the Future of Governance' (2002), available at www.ceres.org/pub/publication.php?pid=37 (last accessed 15 December 2011).

Cho, A. H. and Dubash, N. Z., 'Will Investment Rules Shrink Policy Space for Sustainable Development? Evidence from the Electricity Sector', World Resources Institute Working Paper (2003), available at www.iisd.org/pdf/2003/trade_investment_rules.pdf (last accessed 5 April 2009).

Choudhury, B., 'More Politics Please: Reorienting the Depoliticized Nature of International Investment Agreements', conference paper presented at the American Society of International Law, Biennial Conference, International Economic Law Interest Group, *The Politics of International Economic Law: The Next Four Years* (November 2008) available at www.asil.org/files/ielconferencepapers/choudhury.pdf (last accessed 6 December 2011).

Citigroup, 'Managing Our Environmental Performance' (2009) 42, available at www.citigroup.com/citi/citizen/data/cr08_ch10.pdf (last accessed 25 March 2010).

Corporate Europe Observatory, 'Shell Leads International Business Campaign Against UN Human Rights Norms', *CEO Info Brief* (2004), available at http://archive.corporateeurope.org/norms.pdf (last accessed 15 December 2011).

Corporate Responsibility Coalition, 'A Big Deal? Corporate Social Responsibility and the Finance Sector in Europe' (2005), available at www.foe.co.uk/resource/reports/big_deal.pdf (last accessed 15 December 2011).

Cosbey, A., et al., 'Investment and Sustainable Development: A Guide to the Use and Potential of International Investment Agreements' (2004) International Institute for Sustainable Development, available at www.iisd.org/pdf/2004/investment_invest_and_sd.pdf (last accessed 5 January 2012).

Cotula, L., 'Foreign Investment Contracts', International Institute for Environment and Development Briefing Paper (2007), available at www.iied.org/pubs/pdfs/17015IIED.pdf (last accessed 14 December 2011).

DePalma, A., 'Nafta's Powerful Little Secret; Obscure Tribunals Settle Disputes, but Go Too Far, Critics Say', *New York Times*, 11 March 2001, available at www.feinstein.org/nytimes/naftaslittlesecret.html (last accessed 18 April 2008).

Dow Jones Sustainability Group Index, available at www.sustainability-indexes.com (last accessed 15 December 2011).

Durbin, W. W. F., et al., 'Shaping the Future of Sustainable Finance: Moving From Paper Promises to Performance' (2006) www.wwf.org.uk/filelibrary/pdf/sustainablefinancereport.pdf (last accessed 10 September 2008).

Epstein, J., 'Fit Me For a Gas Mask', *Latin Trade*, December 2000, available at http://findarticles.com/p/articles/mi_m0BEK/is_12_8/ai_67881260/pg_1 (last accessed 10 December 2011).

Equator Principles, 'Guidance to EPFIs on Equator Principles Implementation Reporting' (undated), available at www.equator-principles.com/documents/EPReporting_2007-06-12.pdf (last accessed 26 March 2010).

Financial Times Stock Exchange Ethical Index, available at www.ftse.com/Indices/FTSE4Good_Index_Series (available at 15 December 2011).

Foundation for International Environmental Law and Development, 'Trade, Investment and Sustainable Development,' available at www.field.org.uk/

workarea/trade%2C+investment+and+sustainable+development (last accessed 16 December 2011).

Foundation for International Environmental Law and Development and International Institute for Environment and Development, 'Governance of Oil and Gas Contracts in Kazakhstan' (2008), available at www.field.org.uk/work-areas/trade-investment-and-sustainable-development/investment/governance-oil-and-gas-contracts-kazakhstan (last accessed 19 July 2009).

Freshfields Bruckhaus Deringer, 'Banking on Responsibility: Equator Principles Survey 2005, The Banks' (July 2005) 1, available at www.freshfields.com/publications/pdfs/practices/12057.pdf (last accessed 15 December 2011).

Friends of the Earth, 'Friends of the Earth Blasts World Bank Group's Approval of the Controversial Baku–Ceyhan Oil Pipeline', November 2003, available at www.foe.org/new/releases/1103btc.html (last accessed 26 March 2008).

'Towards Binding Corporate Accountability' (2002), available at www.foei.org/en/publications/corporates/accountability.html (last accessed 12 December 2008).

Friends of the Earth Europe, 'Corporate Campaign: Big Business and its Impacts on Society', available at www.foeeurope.org/corporates/news/eu_debate.htm#caseformandatory (last accessed 15 December 2011).

General Motors, available at www.gm.com/company/gmability/sustainability/reports/00/links/ceres_principles.html (last accessed 25 August 2008).

Ghazi, P., 'Unearthing Controversy at the Ok Tedi Mine', July 2003, World Resources Institute, available at newsroom.wri.org/wrifeatures_text.cfm?ContentID=1895 (last accessed 10 December 2011).

Global Compact Critics, 'Seriousness of Firms' Commitment to the UN Principles for Responsible Investment Questioned', 10 February 2010, available at http://globalcompactcritics.blogspot.com/2010/02/seriousness-of-firms-commitment-to-un.html (last accessed 15 December 2011).

Global Sullivan Principles of Social Responsibility, available at www.thesullivanfoundation.org/gsp/default.asp (last accessed 12 January 2010).

Global Reporting Initiative, 'What is GRI?', undated, available at www.globalreporting.org/AboutGRI/WhatIsGRI/ (last accessed 27 March 2010).

Global Witness, 'Heavy Mittal? A State within a State: The Inequitable Mineral Development Agreement between the Government of Liberia and Mittal Steel Holdings NV' (2006), available at www.globalwitness.org/media_library_detail.php/156/en/heavy_mittal (last accessed 2 September 2009).

'Update on the Renegotiation of the Mineral Development Agreement between Mittal Steel and the Government of Liberia' (2007), available at www.globalwitness.org/.get./mittal_steel_update_en_aug_07.pdf (last accessed 2 September 2009).

Gow, D., 'Mittal Says EU Emission Cap Will Limit Growth', *The Guardian*, 30 July 2007, available at www.guardian.co.uk/business/2007/jul/30/europeanunion.environment/print (last accessed 4 April 2008).

Greenpeace, 'Climatewash – It's the All New Greenwash', *Greenpeace News* (27 July 2007), available at www.greenpeace.org/international/news/climatewash-greenwash-270707 (last accessed 15 August 2008).

Gunningham, N. and Sinclair, D., 'Voluntary Approaches to Environmental Protection: Lessons from the Mining and Forestry Sectors', OECD Global Forum on International Investment, OECD Conference on Foreign Direct Investment and the Environment: Lessons to be Learned from the Mining Sector (Paris, February 2002) 2, available at www.oecd.org/dataoecd/46/1/1819792.pdf (last accessed 15 December 2011).

Hallward-Driemeier, M., 'Do Bilateral Investment Treaties Attract FDI? Only a Bit . . . and They Could Bite' (2003) World Bank Policy Research Working Paper 3121, available at www-wds.worldbank.org/external/default/WDSContentServer/IW3P/IB/2003/09/23/000094946_03091104060047/additional/105505322_20041117160010.pdf (last accessed 23 February 2008).

Harms, R., (Verts/Hale) to the Commission, 'Written Question: Investment Protection Proceedings Brought by Vattenfall AB Against the Federal Republic of Germany', *Parliamentary Questions*, 17 September 2009, available at www.europarl.europa.eu/sides/getDoc.do?pubRef=-//EP//TEXT+WQ+E-2009-4343+0+DOC+XML+V0//EN (last accessed 9 November 2009).

Herz, S., et al., 'The International Finance Corporation's Performance Standards and the Equator Principles: Respecting Human Rights and Remedying Violations?' (2008), available at www.banktrack.org/download/the_international_finance_corporation_s_performance_standards_and_the_equator_principles_respecting_human_rights_and_remedying_violations_/0_final_ruggie_submission_august_6_.pdf (last accessed 28 March 2010).

Hirsch, A., 'Do Hedge Funds have Human Rights? Companies Using the Human Rights Act to Mitigate Loss of Profits are Turning it into a "Villains' Charter"', *Guardian*, 28 January 2009, available at www.guardian.co.uk/commentisfree/libertycentral/2009/jan/28/hedge-fund-human-rights (last accessed 6 December 2011).

HSBC, 'Corporate Social Responsibility Report 2004' (2005) 10–11, available at www.investis.com/reports/hsbc_csrr_2004_en/pdf/hsbc_csrr_2004_en.pdf (last accessed 15 December 2011).

'Corporate Social Responsibility Report 2005' (2006) 12, available at www.investis.com/reports/hsbc_csr_2005_en/report.php?type=1&page=14 (last accessed 15 December 2011).

'Corporate Social Responsibility Report 2006' (2007) 19, available at http://commercial.hsbc.com/1/PA_1_1_S5/content/assets/csr/2006_hsbc_cr_report.pdf (last accessed 15 December 2011).

'Equator Principles, Sector Guidelines', available at www.hsbc.com/hsbc/csr/our-sustainable-approach-to-banking/products-and-services (last accessed 15 December 2011).

'Equator Principles, Sector Guidelines', 'Energy Sector Risk Policy', available at www.hsbc.com/hsbc/csr/our-sustainable-approach-to-banking/products-and-services (last accessed 15 December 2011).

'Equator Principles, Sector Guidelines', 'Freshwater Infrastructure Sector Guideline', available at www.hsbc.com/hsbc/csr/our-sustainable-approach-to-banking/products-and-services (last accessed 15 December 2011).

IATP, Trade Observatory 'International Legal Expert says Ontario's Electricity Program Violates NAFTA', *Canada Newswire*, 14 February 2005, IATP, Trade Observatory, available at www.iatp.org/tradeobservatory/headlines.cfm?refID=48594 (last accessed 23 June 2008).

Illustrated London News, 25 January 1890, 'The Dispute with Portugal: Seizure of the Delagoa Bay Railway by the Portuguese June 26 1889'.

International Ban Asbestos Secretariat, 'UK Victory for African Asbestos Victims', June 2000, available at www.btinternet.com/~ibas/lords_cape.htm (last accessed 10 December 2011).

International Campaign for Justice in Bhopal, available at www.bhopal.org/aziza.html (last accessed 10 December 2011).

International Centre for the Settlement of Disputes, 'About ICSID', available at http://icsid.worldbank.org/ICSID/FrontServlet?requestType=CasesRH&actionVal=ShowHome&pageName=AboutICSID_Home (last accessed 6 December 2011).

International Centre for Trade and Sustainable Development, 'Tobacco Company Files Claim Against Uruguay Over Labelling Laws', *Bridges Weekly Trade News Digest*, 10 March 2010, available at http://ictsd.org/i/news/bridgesweekly/71988/ (last accessed 11 December 2011).

International Chamber of Commerce, 'What is ICC?', available at www.iccwbo.org/home/menu_what_%20is_icc.asp (last accessed 11 August 2008).

'The Business Charter for Sustainable Development', 1, available at www.iccwbo.org/home/environment/charter.asp (last accessed 30 August 2008).

'World Business Message for the UN Millennium Assembly on the Role of the UN in the 21st Century' (2003), available at www.iccwbo.org/id455/index.html (last accessed 15 December 2011).

'The Role of the United Nations in Promoting Corporate Responsibility' (Policy Statement, 21 June 2007) 1, available at www.iccwbo.org/uploadedFiles/ICC/policy/business_in_society/Statements/141-86%20rev2%20final.pdf (last accessed 12 January 2009).

International Chamber of Commerce and the International Organisation of Employers, Joint Views of the IOE and ICC on the Draft 'Norms on the Responsibilities of Transnational Corporations and Other Business Enterprises with Regard to Human Rights' (March 2004), available at www.reports-and-materials.org/IOE-ICC-views-UN-norms-March-2004.doc (last accessed 15 December 2011).

International Finance Corporation, 'BTC Pipeline and ACG Phase 1 Projects Environmental and Social Documentation: IFC Response to Submissions Received During the 120-Day Public Comment Period' (27 October 2003), available at www.ifc.org/ifcext/btc.nsf/AttachmentsByTitle/ESIAPublicCommentsResponse/$FILE/BTC+-+IFC+Reply+to+comments.pdf (last accessed 29 March 2010).

'Performance Standards on Social and Environmental Sustainability', available at www.ifc.org/enviro (last accessed 15 December 2011).

'IFC Policy and Performance Standards on Social and Environmental Responsibility and Policy on Disclosure of Information: Review and Update, Progress Report on Phase I of Consultation' (11 January 2010), available at www.ifc.org/ifcext/policyreview.nsf/AttachmentsByTitle/PhaseI_Progress_Report1-11-10.pdf/$FILE/PhaseI_Progress_Report1-11-10.pdf (last accessed 24 March 2010).

'What is Sustainable Investing?', www.ifc.org at 15 February 2007, (formerly 'What is Sustainable Finance?', at 26 September 2006).

International Institute for Sustainable Development (IISD), 'Bolivia Notifies World Bank of Withdrawal from ICSID, pursues BIT Revisions', *Investment Treaty News*, 9 May 2007, available at www.bilaterals.org/article.php3?id_article=8221 (last accessed 15 December 2011).

'Business and Sustainable Development: A Global Guide', available at www.bsdglobal.com/tools/principles_ceres.asp (last accessed 25 August 2008).

'Foreign Investment For Sustainable Development', available at www.iisd.org/investment/ (last accessed 6 December 2011).

'Our Knowledge: Themes', available at www.iisd.org/ (last accessed 16 December 2011).

'Revising the UNCITRAL Arbitration Rules to Address Investor–State Arbitrations' (2007), available at www.iisd.org/pdf/2007/investment_revising_uncitral_%20arbitration_september.pdf (last accessed 15 July 2009).

Investment Treaty News, 'ICSID Member-Governments OK Watered-Down Changes to Arbitration Process' (29 March 2006), available at www.iisd.org/pdf/2006/itn_mar29_2006.pdf (last accessed 17 December 2011).

Investor Network on Climate Risk, 'INCR Overview', available at www.incr.com/index.php?page=2 (last accessed 29 January 2009).

ISO 14001, 'Environmental Management Systems' (2004), available at www.iso.org/iso/iso_14000_essentials (last accessed 17 December 2011).

IUCN, 'Business and Biodiversity,' available at www.iucn.org/about/work/programmes/business/ (last accessed 16 December 2011).

Draft Covenant on Environment and Development (3rd edn, 2004) art. 32, Commentary 101–6, available at www.i-c-e-l.org/english/EPLP31EN_rev2.pdf (last accessed 16 December 2011).

'Our Work Programmes: Species Trade and Use Programme', available at www.iucn.org/about/work/programmes/species/our_work/species_trade_use/ (last accessed 18 July 2009).

'Social Policy', available at www.iucn.org/about/work/programmes/social_policy/ (last accessed 16 December 2011).

'Statement: Armed Conflict and the Environment', (2003), available at www.iucn.org/en/news/archive/2001_2005/press/iraqstatement210303.pdf (last accessed 26 July 2007).

Joint NGO Statement on the Multilateral Agreement on Investment, 'NGO/OECD Consultation on the MAI', 27 October 1997, available at www.protglob.hss.uts.edu.au/archive/issue1/lib7mai.htm (last accessed 6 December 2011).

Kanter, J., 'As EU Goes Greener, Industry Fears Cost', *The International Herald Tribune*, 7 January 2007 www.iht.com/bin/print.php?id=4128544 (last accessed 4 April 2008).

Kanter, J. and Castle, S., 'EU Wrangling on Carbon Emissions Moves into Courts', *The International Herald Tribune*, 31 July 2007, available at www.iht.com/articles/2007/07/31/business/emit.php (last accessed 11 December 2011).

Klein, N., 'Fighting Free Trade Laws' *The Guardian*, 1 March 2001, available at www.guardian.co.uk/print/0,,4144152-99819,00.html (last accessed 18 April 2008).

Knight, D., 'Mexico Ordered to Pay US Company 17 Million Dollars' *Inter Press Service*, 31 August 2000, Global Policy Forum, available at www.globalpolicy.org/socecon/envronmt/nafta.htm (last accessed 10 December 2011).

Labunska, I., et al., 'The Bhopal Legacy: Toxic Contaminants at the Former Union Carbide Factory Site, Bhopal, India', Greenpeace, 1999, pp. 2–3, 23–4, available at http://archive.greenpeace.org/toxics/toxfreeasia/bhopal.pdf (last accessed 10 December 2011).

London Principles of Sustainable Finance, available at www.cityoflondon.gov.uk/Corporation/living_%20environment/sustainability/sustainable_finance.htm (last accessed 12 April 2007).

Mabey, N. and McNally, R., 'Foreign Direct Investment and the Environment: From Pollution Havens to Sustainable Development', WWF, (August 1999), available at www.wwf.org.uk/filelibrary/pdf/fdi.pdf (last accessed 15 December 2011).

Macalister, T. and Parfitt, T., '$20bn Gas Project Seized by Russia', *The Guardian*, United Kingdom, 12 December 2006, available at www.guardian.co.uk/world/2006/dec/12/business.oil (last accessed 15 December 2011).

Macey, J., 'Investors Demand End to Emissions Trading Handouts', *Australian Broadcasting Corporation News*, 22 October 2009, available at www.abc.net.au/news/stories/2009/10/22/2720964.htm (last accessed 11 December 2011).

Mahnaz, M., 'Recent Developments in Regional and Bilateral Investment Treaties', International Institute for Sustainable Development (2008) 5 available at www.iisd.org/pdf/2008/dci_recent_dev_bits.pdf (last accessed 6 December 2011).

Mann, H., 'Private Rights, Public Problems', (2001) International Institute for Sustainable Development, available at www.iisd.org/trade/pubs.htm (last accessed 11 December 2011).

'The Final Decision in Methanex v. United States: Some New Wine in Some New Bottles' (2005) http://www.iisd.org/pdf/2005/commentary_methanex.pdf at 12 April 2008.

'International Investment Agreements, Business and Human Rights: Key Issues and Opportunities', International Institute for Sustainable Development (2008), available at www.iisd.org/pdf/2008/iia_business_human_rights.pdf (last accessed 24 October 2009).

Mann, H. and Von Moltke, K., 'NAFTA's Chapter 11 and the Environment: Addressing the Impacts of the Investor State Process on the Environment', International Institute for Sustainable Development, 6, (1999), available at www.iisd.org/pdf/nafta.pdf (last accessed 16 December 2011).

Mann, H., et al., IISD Model International Agreement on Investment for Sustainable Development (2006), pp. x–xi, International Institute for Sustainable Development, available at www.iisd.org/pdf/2005/investment_model_int_handbook.pdf (last accessed 14 December 2011).

Marshall, F., 'Fair and Equitable Treatment in International Investment Agreements', International Institute for Sustainable Development (2007), available at www.iisd.org/pdf/2007/inv_fair_treatment.pdf (last accessed 25 March 2009).

Marshall, F. and Murphy, D., 'Climate Change and International Investment Agreements: Obstacles or Opportunities?' (2009) International Institute for Sustainable Development, 21–34, available at www.iisd.org/pdf/2009/bali_2_copenhagen_iias.pdf (last accessed 11 December 2011).

Mathieu, E., 'Response of UK Pension Funds to the SRI Disclosure Regulation, UK Social Responsible Investment Forum' (October 2000), available at www.uksif.org/cmsfiles/uksif/ukpfsurv.pdf (last accessed 30 March 2010).

Miles, K., 'International Investment Law and Climate Change: Issues in the Transition to a Low Carbon World' (July 2008) Society of International Economic Law, Inaugural Conference, available at http://papers.ssrn.com/sol3/papers.cfm?abstract_id=1154588 (last accessed 11 December 2011).

Mineral Policy Institute, 'The Buck's Gotta Stop Somewhere: Social and Environmental Accountability in the Financing of Mining' (1998), available at http://users.nlc.net.au/mpi/reports/buck.html (last accessed 26 April 2010).

Ministry of Trade and Industry, Comments on the Model for Future Investment Agreements (2007) 10, available at www.regjeringen.no/upload/NHD/Vedlegg/hoeringer/2008/Forklarende%20vedlegg%20(engelsk)%20-%20final.doc (last accessed 14 December 2011).

Ministry of Trade and Industry, Norway, Draft Model Bilateral Investment Agreement (December 2007), available at www.regjeringen.no/nb/dep/nhd/dok/Horinger/Horings%20dokumenter/2008/horing—modell-for-investeringsavtaler/-4.html?id=496026 (last accessed 3 April 2008).

Monahan, J., 'Principles in Question', *The Banker* (March, 2005) 3, available at www.equator-principles.com/documents/Principles_in_question.pdf (last accessed 20 August 2008).

Mosolova, T., 'Russia Hits Shell with Sakhalin Licence Suspension', *Reuters*, 7 December 2006, available at www.alertnet.org/thenews/newsdesk/L07795173.htm (last accessed 15 December 2011).

Murray, L., 'Companies Brace for the Low-Carb Economy', *The Sydney Morning Herald*, 21 June 2008.

New York Times, 27 June 1889, 'Portugal Gives Offense: Delagoa Bay Railroad Cancelled. England Much Affronted and Claiming that Germany is Backing the Lisbon Authorities', New York Times Archives, available at http://query.nytimes.com/mem/archive-free/pdf?res=9B0%207E6DB133AE033A2575 4C2A9609C94689FD7CF (last accessed 22 January 2008).

1 July 1889, 'Going to Delagoa Bay: British Gunboats Ordered There to Protect British Interests', New York Times Archives, available at http://query.nytimes.com/mem/archive-free/pdf?res=9A0CE0DF143AEF33A25751 C0A9619C94689FD7CF (last accessed 22 September 2009).

29 July 1889, 'Disorder at Delagoa Bay', New York Times Archives, available at http://query.nytimes.com/mem/archive-free/pdf?_r=1&res= 9803E3DB133AE033A25753C3A9609 C94689FD7CF (last accessed 22 September 2009).

21 July 1900, 'Delagoa Bay Award Paid', New York Times Archives, http://query.nytimes.com/mem/archive-free/pdf?res=9803E4D9113BEE33 A25751C2A96%2019C946197D6CF at 22 January 2008.

Nova, S. and Sforza-Roderick, M., '"Worse than NAFTA": A Commentary on the Multilateral Agreement on Investment', Preamble Center for Public Policy, undated, available at www.globalpolicy.org/socecon/bwi-wto/mai2.htm (last accessed 6 December 2011).

Organization for Economic Co-operation and Development (OECD), Draft Convention on the Protection of Foreign Property (1967), available at www.oecd.org/dataoecd/35/4/39286571.pdf (last accessed 26 September 2009).

Pacific Environment, 'The Environmental, Social and Human Rights Impacts of Foreign Investment Contracts' (2006), available at https://pacificenvironment.rdsecure.org/downloads/The%20Environmental%20Social%20and%20%20Human%20Rights%20Impacts%20of%20Foreign%20Investment%20Contracts_4_.pdf (last accessed 12 October 2009).

Perlez, J. and Johnson, K., 'Behind Gold's Glitter: Torn Lands and Pointed Questions', *New York Times*, 24 October 2005, available at www.globalpolicy.org/socecon/tncs/2005/1024ring.htm (last accessed 18 January 2008).

Peterson, L. E., 'Analysis: Tribunal finds Several Treaty Breaches in Argentine Treatment of Water Firm', *Investment Treaty News*, 26 July 2006, available at www.iisd.org/pdf/2006/itn_july26_2006.pdf (last accessed 11 December 2011).

'Human Rights and Bilateral Investment Treaties: Mapping the Role of Human Rights Law within Investor–State Arbitration', International Centre for Human Rights and Democratic Development (2009), available at www.dd-rd.ca/site/_PDF/publications/globalization/HIRA-volume3-ENG.pdf (last accessed 2 March 2009).

'Uruguay: Philip Morris Files First-Known Investment Treaty Claim Against Tobacco Regulations', *Investment Arbitration Reporter*, 3 March 2010, available at www.bilaterals.org/spip.php?page=print&id_article=16921 (last accessed 11 December 2011).

Philip Morris, 'Submission by Philip Morris International Inc in Response to the National Center for Standards and Certification Information Foreign Trade Notification No. G/TBT/N/CAN/22' (2002), available at www.takingontobacco.org/pmresponsetonoi.pdf (last accessed 11 December 2011).

Platform, 'Principal Objections: Analysis of the Sakhalin II Oil and Gas Project's Compliance with the Equator Principles' (2004), available at www.platformlondon.org/carbonweb/documents/Sakh-EP-analysis.pdf (last accessed 15 December 2011).

Poulsen, L. S., 'Are South–South BITs Any Different? A Logistic Regression Analysis of Two Substantive BIT Provisions', conference paper presented at the American Society of International Law, Biennial Conference, International Economic Law Interest Group, 'The Politics of International Economic Law: The Next Four Years' (November 2008) 1, available at www.asil.org/files/ielconferencepapers/poulsen.pdf (last accessed 16 February 2009).

Raghavan, C., 'TNCs, Global Compact and Davos Face Critical NGOs', *South–North Development Monitor* (25 January 2001), available at www.twnside.org.sg/title/davos.htm (last accessed 15 December 2011).

Report by the Committee on International Investment and Multinational Enterprises (CIME) and the Committee on Capital Movements and Invisible Transactions (CMIT) to the Ministerial Council of the OECD, 5 May 1995, DAFFE/CMIT/CMIE(95)13FINAL, available at www1.oecd.org/daf/mai/htm/cmitcime95.htm (last accessed 18 March 2008).

Rose-Ackerman, S. and Tobin, J., 'When BITS Have Some Bite: The Political-Economic Environment for Bilateral Investment Treaties' (2006), available at www.law.yale.edu/documents/pdf/When_BITS_Have_Some_Bite.doc (last accessed 10 February 2009).

Royal Bank of Canada, 'Corporate Responsibility Report 2005' (2006) 25, available at www.rbc.com/responsibility/reports/2005report/pdf/CRR_ENG_GLOBAL_2005.pdf (last accessed 14 August 2008).

'2009 Corporate Responsibility Report and Public Accountability Statement' (2010) 49, available at www.rbc.com/responsibility/pdf/RBC-CRR-Report-2009-e.pdf (last accessed 15 December 2011).

2010 Corporate Responsibility Report and Public Accountability Statement (2011) 74, available at www.rbc.com/responsibility/pdf/RBC-CRR-Report-2010-e.pdf (last accessed 28 August 2012).

Sakhalin Energy, 'What is a "Production Sharing Agreement"?', undated, available at www.sakhalinenergy.com/en/ataglance.asp?p=aag_main&s=5 (last accessed 26 March 2010).

'Our Partners', undated, available at www.sakhalinenergy.com/en/aboutus.asp?p=our_partners (last accessed 15 December 2011).

Salamain, U. B., 'London Barrister Opposes Arbitrators Acting as Counsel', Global Arbitration Review, 7 October 2009, www.globalarbitrationreview.com/news/article/18979/london-barrister-opposes-arbitrators-acting-counsel/ (last accessed 14 October 2009).

Schill, S., 'Fair and Equitable Treatment under Investment Treaties as an Embodiment of the Rule of Law' (2006) IILJ Working Paper 2006/6, Global Administrative Law Series, available at http://iilj.org/publications/documents/2006-6-GAL-Schill-web.pdf (last accessed 21 August 2009).

Shah, S., 'UK Launches Action to Overturn EU Limit on Carbon Emissions', *Independent*, 19 October 2005, available at www.independent.co.uk/news/business/news/uk-launches-action-to-overturn-eu-limit-on-carbon-emissions-511581.html (last accessed 4 April 2008).

Shemberg, A. and Aizawa, M., 'Stabilization Clauses and Human Rights', *International Finance Corporation*, 4 (2008), available at www.ifc.org/ifcext/enviro.nsf/AttachmentsByTitle/p_StabilizationClausesandHumanRights/$FILE/Stabilization+Paper.pdf (last accessed 14 December 2011).

Smith, P., 'Canberra Faces Legal Challenge Over Carbon Scheme', 24 November 2009, *Financial Times*, available at www.ft.com/cms/s/0/00cced94-d898-11de-b63a-00144feabdc0.html?catid=24 (last accessed 11 December 2011).

Social Investment Forum, '2005 Report on Socially Responsible Investing Trends in the United States: 10-Year Review' 2 (2006) 2, available at www.socialinvest.org/pdf/research/Trends/2005%20Trends%20Report.pdf (last accessed 15 December 2011).

Social Investment Organization, 'Sustainable Development Depends on SRI: Dr. Gro Harlem Brundtland' (undated), available at www.socialinvestment.ca/News&Archives/news-0607-Brundtland.htm (last accessed 24 January 2009).

Sohn, J., 'NGO Spotlight Shifts to Private Sector', *Environmental Finance Magazine* (February, 2004), available at www.foe.org/new/news18.html (last accessed 15 December 2011).

Tams, C. J., 'An Appealing Option? The Debate about an ICSID Appellate Structure' (2006) 57 *Essays in Transnational Economic Law*, 31–3, Institut für Wirtschaftsrecht, available at www.wirtschaftsrecht.uni-halle.de/Heft57.pdf (last accessed 7 January 2012).

Tieleman, K., 'The Failure of the Multilateral Agreement on Investment and the Absence of a Global Public Policy Network: A Case Study for the UN Vision Project on Global Public Policy Networks' (2000), available at www.gppi.net/fileadmin/gppi/Tieleman_MAI_GPP_Network.pdf (last accessed 8 January 2008).

UNCTAD, 'Data Show Foreign Direct Investment Climbed Sharply in 2005' (Press Release, January 2006) UNCTAD/PRESS/PR/2006/002, available at www.unctad.org/press (last accessed 10 December 2011).

'Sharp Rise in FDI Driven by M&As in 2005', *UNCTAD Investment Brief* 1:2006 (2006), available at www.unctad.org/en/docs/webiteiia20061_en.pdf (last accessed 10 December 2011).

'Latest Developments in Investor–State Dispute Settlement', *IIA Monitor* No. 1 (2008) UNCTAD/WEB/ITE/IIA/2008/3, 11, available at www.unctad.org/en/docs/iteiia20083_en.pdf (last accessed 17 December 2011).

United Kingdom Department for Environment, Food and Rural Affairs, 'Financing the Future: The London Principles; The Role of UK Financial Services in Sustainable Development (The London Principles of Sustainable Finance)' (2002), available at www.cityoflondon.gov.uk/Corporation/living_environment/sustainability/sustainable_finance.htm (last accessed 15 December 2011).

United Nations, Press Release, 'International Funds Worth $4 Trillion Now Endorse UN Principles for Responsible Investment' (May, 2006), available at www.unpri.org/files/20060501_press/un-unepfi-gc_press_20060501.pdf (last accessed 12 February 2009).

'United Nations Principles for Responsible Investment' (2006), available at www.unpri.org/principles/ (last accessed 24 April 2010).

United Nations Environment Programme (UNEP), 'Waste from Consumption and Production: The Ok Tedi Case – A Pot of Gold', (2002), available at www.vitalgraphics.net/waste/html_file/18-19_consumption_oktedi.html (last accessed 22 January 2008).

'Investors Flock to Renewable Energy and Efficiency Technologies: Climate Change Worries, High Oil Prices and Government Help Top Factors Fuelling Hot Renewable Energy Investment Climate' (Press Release, 20 June 2007), available at www.unep.org/Documents.Multilingual/Default.asp?DocumentID=512&ArticleID=5616&l=en (last accessed 20 January 2010).

'Environment Ministers Meet to Accelerate Transition to a Low Carbon Society: Huge Investment Opportunities in Energy Savings to Renewables and Reduced Deforestation to Climate Proofing if Markets can be Mobilized' (Press Release, February 2008), available at www.unep.org/Documents.Multilingual/Default.asp?DocumentID=528&ArticleID=5745&l=en (last accessed 23 January 2010).

'Renewable Energy Accelerates Meteoric Rise: 2007 Global Status Report Shows Perceptions Lag Reality' (Press Release, 28 February 2008), available at www.unep.org/Documents.Multilingual/Default.asp?DocumentID=528&ArticleID=5754&l=en (last accessed 20 January 2010).

United Nations Environment Programme Finance Initiative (UNEPFI), http://www.unepfi.org/ at 14 April 2010.

United Nations Global Compact, 'UN Global Compact', available at www.unglobalcompact.org (last accessed 15 December 2011).

'Inactive Participants', available at www.unglobalcompact.org/CommunicatingProgress/inactive_participants.html (last accessed 18 February 2009).

'Integrity Measures', available at www.unglobalcompact.org/AboutTheGC/integrity.html (last accessed 18 February 2009).

'United Nations Secretary-General Launches "Principles for Responsible Investment"' (April, 2006), available at www.unglobalcompact.org/

NewsAndEvents/news_archives/2006_04_27.html (last accessed 16 August 2008).

'Corporate Citizenship in the World Economy' (2008), available at www.unglobalcompact.org/docs/news_events/8.1/GC_brochure_FINAL.pdf (last accessed 16 December 2011).

Van Zeben, J. A. W., 'The European Emissions Trading Scheme Case Law' (2009) Amsterdam Center for Law & Economics Working Paper No. 2009–12, available at http://ssrn.com/abstract=1462651 (last accessed 11 December 2011).

Vis-Dunbar, D., 'Norway Shelves its Draft Model Bilateral Investment Treaty', *Investment Treaty News* (8 June 2009), available at www.investmenttreatynews.org/cms/news/archive/2009/06/08/norway-shelves-its-proposed-model-bilateral-investment-treaty.aspx (last accessed 3 October 2009).

WALHI-Indonesian Forum for Environment, 'Conflict and Militarism', December 2004, www.eng.walhi.or.id/kampanye/psda/konflikmil/conflict_info/ (last accessed 12 February 2008).

Ward, H., 'Public Sector Roles in Strengthening Corporate Social Responsibility: Taking Stock' (2004), available at www.iied.org/pubs/pdfs/16014IIED.pdf (last accessed 23 April 2010).

Watchman, P. Q., Delfino, A. and Addison, J., 'EP2: The Revised Equator Principles: Why Hard-Nosed Bankers are Embracing Soft Law Principles' (2006), available at www.equator-principles.com/documents/ClientBriefing%20forEquatorPrinciples_2007-02-07.pdf (last accessed 28 March 2010).

Webb, T., 'Russia Threatens Shell with "Unlimited Fines" in New Sakhalin Deal', *The Independent*, 10 December 2006, available at www.independent.co.uk/news/business/news/russia-threatens-shell-with-unlimited-fines-in-new-sakhalin-deal-427769.html (last accessed 15 December 2011).

Weismann, R., 'International Trade Agreements and Tobacco Control: Threats to Public Health and the Case for Excluding Tobacco from Trade Agreements' (2003), available at www.takingontobacco.org/trade/tobacco.trade.v02.backgrd.pdf (last accessed 3 October 2009).

Wheeler, D., et al., 'Comparative Study of UK and Canadian Pension Fund Transparency Practices' (2004), available at www.pensionsatwork.ca/english/pdfs/thomson_march2005.pdf (last accessed 30 March 2010).

World Bank, 'Operational Policies: Environmental Assessment', World Bank OP 4.01 (January 1999), available at http://siteresources.worldbank.org/INTFORESTS/Resources/OP401.pdf (last accessed 26 March 2010).

'Operational Policies: Forests', World Bank OP 4.36 (November 2002), available at http://web.worldbank.org/WBSITE/EXTERNAL/PROJECTS/EXTPOLICIES/EXTOPMANUAL/0,,contentMDK:20064668~menuPK:4564185~pagePK:64709096~piPK:64709108~theSitePK:502184~isCURL:Y,00.html (last accessed 29 August 2012).

'Operational Policies: Cultural Property', World Bank OP 4.11 (August 1999), available at http://siteresources.worldbank.org/INTFORESTS/Resources/OP411.pdf (last accessed 11 December 2011).

'Operational Policies: Projects on International Waterways', World Bank OP 7.50 (June 2001), available at http://web.worldbank.org/WBSITE/EXTERNAL/PROJECTS/EXTPOLICIES/EXTOPMANUAL/0,,contentMDK:20064667~menuPK:64701637~pagePK:64709096~piPK:64709108~theSitePK:502184,00.html (last accessed 11 December 2011).

'Operational Policies: Involuntary Resettlement', World Bank OP 4.12 (December 2001), available at http://siteresources.worldbank.org/INTFORESTS/Resources/OP412.pdf (last accessed 11 December 2011).

'Operational Policies: Indigenous Peoples', World Bank OP 4.10 (July 2005), available at http://web.worldbank.org/WBSITE/EXTERNAL/PROJECTS/EXTPOLICIES/EXTOPMANUAL/0,,contentMDK:20553653~pagePK:64141683~piPK:64141620~theSitePK:502184,00.html (last accessed 11 December 2011).

World Wildlife Fund, 'Comments on the Green Paper', available at http://europa.eu.int/comm/employment_social/soc-dial/csr/csr_responses.htm (last accessed 14 January 2009).

Wright, C., 'For Citigroup, Greening Starts with Listening', *The Ecosystem Marketplace* (April, 2006), available at www.equator-principles.com/City.shtml (last accessed 20 August 2008).

WWF, 'Sakhalin II: The Truth Uncovered' (2006), available at www.assets.panda.org/downloads/sakhalinii_truth%20uncovered.pdf (last accessed 26 March 2010).

WWF and BankTrack, 'Shaping the Future of Sustainable Finance: Moving the Banking Sector from Promises to Performance' (2006), available at www.banktrack.org/doc/File/banktrack%20publications/Other%20BankTrack%20publications/0_060126%20Sustainable%20finance%20full%20report.pdf (last accessed 12 April 2007).

WWF-Australia, 'No Compensation for Electricity Generators under ETS', *WWF-Australia*, 2 July 2008, available at www.wwf.org.au/news/no-compensation-for-electricity-generators-under-ets/ (last accessed 8 November 2009).

Index

CAMBRIDGE STUDIES IN INTERNATIONAL AND COMPARATIVE LAW.

Books in the series

State Responsibility: The General Part
James Crawford

The Origins of International Investment Law
Kate Miles

The Crime of Aggression under the Rome Statute of the International Criminal Court
Carrie McDougall

Crimes against Peace and International Law
Kirsten Sellars

The Non-Legal in International Law
Fleur Johns

Armed Conflict and Displacement: The Protection of Refugees and Displaced Persons under International Humanitarian Law
Mélanie Jacques

Foreign Investment and the Environment in International Law
Jorge Viñuales

The Human Rights Treaty Obligations of Peacekeepers
Kjetil Larsen

Cyberwarfare and the Laws of War
Heather Harrison Dinniss

The Right to Reparation in International Law for Victims of Armed Conflict
Christine Evans

Global Public Interest in International Investment Law
Andreas Kulick

State Immunity in International Law
Xiaodong Yang

Reparations and Victim Support in the International Criminal Court
Conor McCarthy

Reducing Genocide to Law: Definition, Meaning, and the Ultimate Crime
Payam Akhavan

Decolonizing International Law: Development, Economic Growth and the Politics of Universality
Sundhya Pahuja

Complicity and the Law of State Responsibility
Helmut Philipp Aust

State Control over Private Military and Security Companies in Armed Conflict
Hannah Tonkin

'Fair and Equitable Treatment' in International Investment Law
Roland Kläger

The UN and Human Rights: Who Guards the Guardians?
Guglielmo Verdirame

Sovereign Defaults before International Courts and Tribunals
Michael Waibel

Making the Law of the Sea: A Study in the Development of International Law
James Harrison

Science and the Precautionary Principle in International Courts and Tribunals: Expert Evidence, Burden of Proof and Finality
Caroline E. Foster

Transition from Illegal Regimes in International Law
Yaël Ronen

Access to Asylum: International Refugee Law and the Globalisation of Migration Control
Thomas Gammeltoft-Hansen

Trading Fish, Saving Fish: The Interaction between Regimes in International Law
Margaret Young

The Individual in the International Legal System: Continuity and Change in International Law
Kate Parlett

The Participation of States in International Organisations: The Role of Human Rights and Democracy
Alison Duxbury

'Armed Attack' and Article 51 of the UN Charter: Evolutions in Customary Law and Practice
Tom Ruys

Science and Risk Regulation in International Law
Jacqueline Peel

Theatre of the Rule of Law: Transnational Legal Intervention in Theory and Practice
Stephen Humphreys

The Public International Law Theory of Hans Kelsen: Believing in Universal Law
Jochen von Bernstorff

Vicarious Liability in Tort: A Comparative Perspective
Paula Giliker

Legal Personality in International Law
Roland Portmann

Legitimacy and Legality in International Law: An Interactional Account
Jutta Brunnée and Stephen J. Toope

The Concept of Non-International Armed Conflict in International Humanitarian Law
Anthony Cullen

The Challenge of Child Labour in International Law
Franziska Humbert

Shipping Interdiction and the Law of the Sea
Douglas Guilfoyle

International Courts and Environmental Protection
Tim Stephens

Legal Principles in WTO Disputes
Andrew D. Mitchell

War Crimes in Internal Armed Conflicts
Eve La Haye

Humanitarian Occupation
Gregory H. Fox

The International Law of Environmental Impact Assessment: Process, Substance and Integration
Neil Craik

The Law and Practice of International Territorial Administration: Versailles to Iraq and Beyond
Carsten Stahn

Cultural Products and the World Trade Organization
Tania Voon

United Nations Sanctions and the Rule of Law
Jeremy Farrall

National Law in WTO Law: Effectiveness and Good Governance in the World Trading System
Sharif Bhuiyan

The Threat of Force in International Law
Nikolas Stürchler

Indigenous Rights and United Nations Standards
Alexandra Xanthaki

International Refugee Law and Socio-Economic Rights
Michelle Foster

The Protection of Cultural Property in Armed Conflict
Roger O'Keefe

Interpretation and Revision of International Boundary Decisions
Kaiyan Homi Kaikobad

Multinationals and Corporate Social Responsibility: Limitations and Opportunities in International Law
Jennifer A. Zerk

Judiciaries within Europe: A Comparative Review
John Bell

Law in Times of Crisis: Emergency Powers in Theory and Practice
Oren Gross and Fionnuala Ní Aoláin

Vessel-Source Marine Pollution:The Law and Politics of International Regulation
Alan Tan

Enforcing Obligations Erga Omnes *in International Law*
Christian J. Tams

Non-Governmental Organisations in International Law
Anna-Karin Lindblom

Democracy, Minorities and International Law
Steven Wheatley

Prosecuting International Crimes: Selectivity and the International Law Regime
Robert Cryer

Compensation for Personal Injury in English, German and Italian Law: A Comparative Outline
Basil Markesinis, Michael Coester, Guido Alpa and Augustus Ullstein

Dispute Settlement in the UN Convention on the Law of the Sea
Natalie Klein

The International Protection of Internally Displaced Persons
Catherine Phuong

Imperialism, Sovereignty and the Making of International Law
Antony Anghie

Necessity, Proportionality and the Use of Force by States
Judith Gardam

International Legal Argument in the Permanent Court of International Justice: The Rise of the International Judiciary
Ole Spiermann

Great Powers and Outlaw States: Unequal Sovereigns in the International Legal Order
Gerry Simpson

Local Remedies in International Law
C. F. Amerasinghe

Reading Humanitarian Intervention: Human Rights and the Use of Force in International Law
Anne Orford

Conflict of Norms in Public International Law: How WTO Law Relates to Other Rules of International Law
Joost Pauwelyn

Transboundary Damage in International Law
Hanqin Xue

European Criminal Procedures
Edited by. Mireille Delmas-Marty and John Spencer

The Accountability of Armed Opposition Groups in International Law
Liesbeth Zegveld

Sharing Transboundary Resources: International Law and Optimal Resource Use
Eyal Benvenisti

International Human Rights and Humanitarian Law
René Provost

Remedies against International Organisations
Karel Wellens

Diversity and Self-Determination in International Law
Karen Knop

The Law of Internal Armed Conflict
Lindsay Moir

International Commercial Arbitration and African States: Practice, Participation and Institutional Development
Amazu A. Asouzu

The Enforceability of Promises in European Contract Law
James Gordley

International Law in Antiquity
David J. Bederman

Money Laundering: A New International Law Enforcement Model
Guy Stessens

Good Faith in European Contract Law
Reinhard Zimmermann and Simon Whittaker

On Civil Procedure
J. A. Jolowicz

Trusts: A Comparative Study
Maurizio Lupoi

The Right to Property in Commonwealth Constitutions
Tom Allen

International Organizations before National Courts
August Reinisch

The Changing International Law of High Seas Fisheries
Francisco Orrego Vicuña

Trade and the Environment: A Comparative Study of EC and US Law
Damien Geradin

Unjust Enrichment: A Study of Private Law and Public Values
Hanoch Dagan

Religious Liberty and International Law in Europe
Malcolm D. Evans

Ethics and Authority in International Law
Alfred P. Rubin

Sovereignty over Natural Resources: Balancing Rights and Duties
Nico Schrijver

The Polar Regions and the Development of International Law
Donald R. Rothwell

Fragmentation and the International Relations of Micro-States: Self-Determination and Statehood
Jorri Duursma

Principles of the Institutional Law of International Organizations
C. F. Amerasinghe